W9-DJG-923

Literacy & Learning

IN THE CONTENT AREAS

Sharon Kane

STATE UNIVERSITY OF NEW YORK AT OSWEGO

Holcomb Hathaway, Publishers

Scottsdale, Arizona 85250

EDUCATION RESOURCE CENTER
University of Delaware
Newark, DE 19716-2940

T 79486

LA-P
K 134
2003

Library of Congress Cataloging-in-Publication Data

Kane, Sharon
    Literacy and learning in the content areas / Sharon Kane.
       p. cm.
    Includes bibliographical references and index.
    ISBN 1-890871-37-0
    1. Content area reading.   2. Language arts—Correlation with content subjects.   3.
Interdisciplinary approach in education.   I. Title.

LB1050.455 .K36 2003
372.6—dc21   2002027300

I dedicate this book to my sisters, Janie Trey and Ann Mazza.

Copyright © 2003 by Holcomb Hathaway, Publishers, Inc.

Holcomb Hathaway, Publishers, Inc.
6207 North Cattletrack Road
Scottsdale, Arizona 85250
(480) 991-7881
www.hh-pub.com

ISBN 1-890871-37-0

10 9 8 7 6 5 4 3 2 1

All rights reserved. No part of this publication may be reproduced,
stored in a retrieval system, or transmitted in any form or by any means,
electronic, photocopy, recording, or otherwise, without the prior written
permission of Holcomb Hathaway, Inc.

Printed in the United States of America.

Contents

Chapter 5

VOCABULARY DEVELOPMENT AND LANGUAGE STUDY   121

Chapter 6

COMPREHENSION AND CRITICAL THINKING   163

Chapter 7

WRITING IN THE CONTENT AREAS   199

Chapter 8

SPEAKING AND LISTENING: VITAL COMPONENTS OF LITERACY   237

Chapter 9

MULTILITERACIES: VISUAL, MEDIA, AND DIGITAL   267

Preface

Literacy and learning are essential and interconnected goals for students in the disciplines we teach. *Literacy and Learning in the Content Areas* shares ways in which content area teachers can enhance student learning of subject matter and skills while also fostering their growth in the many facets of literacy.

Future middle and high school teachers often enter the field expecting to teach the topics they love to students already proficient in reading and writing, and they may feel that literacy is a "requirement" that has been foisted upon them. Rather, literacy is key to learning in the content areas and to appreciating the rich treasure of knowledge in the various disciplines. Integrating literacy doesn't have to take a teacher's time or energy away from the study of math, art, history, science or any other subject. We can teach our students every day how to use writing, reading, viewing, speaking, and listening to become proficient in the subjects they study and to independently pursue curricular topics of interest.

This book will help provide readers with the knowledge, motivation, tools, and confidence for integrating literacy in their content area classrooms. It offers a unique approach to teaching content area literacy that gets readers actively engaged in reading and writing and the very activities that they will use to teach literacy to their own students.

Research indicates a major problem with aliteracy in our society. Even young people who can read well often choose not to read independently. Future as well as experienced teachers are not immune to this. Each semester, I begin my content area literacy class by asking students to answer the question, "Are you a reader and writer?" The answer is far too often a regretful "No" or "I used to be but now I'm too busy." I believe that content area literacy courses will not have a lasting impact unless these future and practicing teachers become readers and writers. *Literacy and Learning* works toward this goal through its interactive approach so that its readers will know how to reach this same goal with *their* students. Rather than passively learning about strategies for incorporating content area literacy activities, readers will get hands-on experience in such techniques as mapping/webbing, anticipation guides, K-W-L charts, and journal writing and reflection. By encouraging future and practicing teachers to become active readers and writers, this book will help equip them with the motivation and skills to encourage their own students to engage in reading, writing, speaking, listening, and visual learning across the curriculum to improve their learning in content area subjects.

Literacy and Learning also incorporates as a major theme the use of many different types of texts to teach literacy skills and strategies as well as to motivate interest in a subject area and enhance knowledge and understanding of content. Readers will learn not only how to effectively evaluate and use textbooks, but also how to integrate children's and young adult literature, primary sources, biographies, essays, and poetry in their teaching. Each chapter of this book includes lists of resources that make it a valuable tool for content area teachers. In fact, readers who flip through the text will find comprehensive book lists unparalleled by other content area books.

The book includes numerous concrete examples and teaching/learning situations for math, science, and social studies as well as others relating to music, health, art, and physical education. At the same time, it emphasizes interdisciplinary thinking, and readers are encouraged to make connections within and among fields.

Throughout the book, attention is given to the important issues of diversity, students with special needs, and teaching for social justice. Literacy is very much connected with the goals of positive change within our society. In this context, readers are offered opportunities to ponder how they can serve as change agents who can improve the scholastic lives of their students and, in the long term, help implement systemic change in schools and society.

Information on using technology for instruction is integrated throughout the book. Websites, software resources, and strategies for incorporating technology with literacy in content area lessons are also included.

Finally, *Literacy and Learning* demonstrates how wide and varied opportunities for reading, writing, listening, speaking, and viewing can help students meet national content knowledge standards and benchmarks, showing that a standards-based curriculum can use literacy strategies not as add-ons, but as integral to content teaching itself.

THE BOOK'S SPECIAL FEATURES

Embedded in each chapter are features that will help readers actively engage with issues, ideas, and suggestions. Throughout the chapters, you'll find the following tools:

- **BookTalks** introduce relevant books in many genres and subjects, encouraging readers to read the books for themselves and providing a model for booktalks in their own classrooms.

- **Activating Prior Knowledge** activities build on past experiences and stimulate critical thinking to prepare readers to learn complex theoretical and conceptual material about teaching, learning, and literacy. These activities also prepare readers to activate prior knowledge in their classrooms.

- **Action Research** activities encourage readers to improve the quality of their teaching through research, collaboration with peers, and observation and experimentation in the classroom.

- End-of-chapter **Getting Ready to Teach** activities help readers apply what they've learned to their particular content area in concrete ways.

As they modify the activities to fit their philosophy and the needs of their students, readers will be creating useful materials and strategies for their own content area courses.

THE VOICES AND STORIES IN OUR TEACHING

Esteemed scientist E. O. Wilson (2002) says that science consists of millions of stories, which become science when they are tested and woven into cause-and-effect explanations. These stories can be "the key to helping the non-scientist understand the great ideas of science" (p. 10). What teacher wouldn't want to make such stories available to her students? Wilson explains that stories—both those that are stored in our memories and those that we generate while interacting with the world—are essential to learning and remembering. Luckily for us teachers, there are stories for every discipline.

This textbook makes use of stories to teach in-service and preservice content area teachers about the learners in their midst (including themselves), and about strategies for integrating literacy into their discipline-specific teaching. It employs stories of and by students; it includes stories of successful practices by caring teachers; it invites readers to construct stories of vital and stimulating classrooms full of literacy and learning.

The students in your classes have stories to tell. There are stories of struggling to learn, to comprehend, to read. There are stories of intense interest in and love for certain curricular topics, or authors, or genres of literature; stories of searching for ways to fit in socially and interact with peers and adults; stories about faraway homelands, other languages, different cultures, the search for social justice; stories told through pictures, projects, and performances. One of the reasons teaching is so rewarding is that the stories are ever changing, ever being renewed. As we and our students grow more literate throughout the school year, a story of promise and potential is created. This book is meant to be a tool you can use to bring the story to fruition.

ACKNOWLEDGMENTS

There are many people to thank as I complete this book. My editors at Holcomb Hathaway, Colette Kelly and Gay Pauley, believed in the project from the start and saw me through the publication process. My students believed in me even before the book's inception, requesting a textbook that would reflect what went on in our course. And my students since its inception have been just as inspiring and helpful. Three of these students worked on the book: Jennifer Mahan when not a word had yet been written, Michele Boorum in the midst of revisions, and Branden Wood when the manuscript was nearly complete. Others contributed materials included in these pages as examples.

I respectfully thank the reviewers, all of whose work made this a better book. My thanks to Jane Partenen, University of Pittsburgh, whose thoroughness and generosity are unbounded; to Jay Button, SUNY Oswego, who was once my professor for Content Area Reading and has been my colleague, mentor, and friend ever since; Nancy L. Hadaway, University of Texas at Arlington; Richard Mezeske, Hope College; and Jesse Turner, Central Connecticut State University.

A sabbatical granted by the State University of New York at Oswego and a grant from United University Professions helped my progress immensely.

I am grateful to all the teachers who have allowed me to see their dedication in action and have shared strategies, ideas, success stories, and struggles. I especially thank Sharon Morley, who in my mind is peerless when it comes to managing a process classroom and bringing out the best in students; and team teachers Chris Leahey and Auddie Mastroleo, who took what they learned in my classes and ran with it, theorizing and constructing a collaborative content area project (described in Chapter 11) beyond what I could have foreseen. I also thank Juliana Bütz for allowing me to use a few of the scientific drawings she did in high school that show such talent and passion.

I thank my writing group, including Bonita Hampton, Mary Harrell, Tania Ramalho, and Bobbi Schnorr; and especially Chris Walsh and Jean Ann for their challenging but kind responses to multiple drafts.

I appreciate the daily joy of working with my awesome colleagues in the Curriculum and Instruction Department at Oswego State University. In particular, I thank Claire Putala, whom I consider the newest sister to join my family, and Pam Michel, kindred spirit, who always reminds me that life is a joyful adventure.

I am grateful for the moral and spiritual support provided by my friends, including Dorothy Albert, Rosemary Brown, Ellen Bütz, Liz DePartout, Ellen Laird, Kathy Olson, Patricia Spencer, Lyn Spies, Alexis Stowe, Michael Williams, and especially Father Vincent Kilpatrick.

My sons, Christopher and Patrick, taught me much about literacy throughout their childhoods; their experiences in school confirmed for me how much impact teachers have on children's motivation, learning, and love for knowledge. I thank them for constantly broadening my horizons and enriching my world. Finally, I honor the memory of my parents, Marijane and James Goughary, who filled my childhood with many books and much love.

Thanks to all who saw me through.

Introduction

Dear Readers,
Welcome to an exploration of how you can make literacy and learning come alive for the students in your content area courses. Because the teacher is the primary learner in any classroom, I hope that this book will add to your enthusiasm for reading, writing, and engaging in conversations about the topics you teach.

My voice will be present throughout the text, and I encourage you to grapple with what's here—to question, to argue, to rejoice, and to respond with exciting ideas of your own. Later, you will encourage your own students to do the same as they explore and learn.

Textbooks are philosophy-based, whether this is explicitly stated or not, and mine is no exception. The following are aspects of this text I'd like to note right away:

This text was designed as an interactive one. The book doesn't just *tell* and it doesn't just *show;* rather, it leads you to discover, construct, and reflect on knowledge. Passive reading won't work here; you are needed to make this text come alive. I've provided cues, questions, suggestions, and stimuli for experiences and activities throughout to guide you to this more active kind of reading. Once you've become an active reader, you'll be better equipped to teach your own students, no matter what your subject, no matter what their grade level or reading ability or interests, to engage with text in a way that makes it their own. This will be exemplified by the way your instructor uses this textbook; there will probably be times when she modifies, ignores, or critiques the book's suggestions. Follow her instructions, of course, but also reflect on her

I would make education a pleasant thing, both to the teacher and to the scholar. This discipline, which we allow to be the end of life, should not be one thing in the schoolroom, and another in the street. We should seek to be fellow students with the pupil, and should learn of, as well as with him [her], if we would be most helpful to him [her].

THOREAU, 1837

1

rationale for making the changes; this, too, will teach you about decisions teachers make based on context, student population, instructional philosophy, and practical constraints.

You'll try things out for yourselves, get a feel for the concepts and principles, create various types of reading guides, and leave with practical examples of strategies you can use in your discipline-based classes. By the time you finish your active reading of this book, you will know *yourselves* well as readers and writers, thereby gaining confidence as you seek to understand and enhance your students' literacy. I encourage you to keep a learning log, either a notebook or computer file, where you record your responses to what you're reading, as well as the answers to the questions posed in the Activating Prior Knowledge, Action Research, and Getting Ready to Teach features. You can think of and write about ways that you can apply strategies and make connections to the content you'll be teaching.

There is much focus on *listening to* adolescents and preadolescents. This book calls for a student-centered philosophy, allowing young people to help us define adolescent literacy. Quotes from real middle and high school students help you understand, respect, and appreciate their perspective. I use young adult (YA) literature to help you understand teens. The voices of all kinds of readers shine through the chapters of this text.

I also quote from those who, next to the kids themselves, understand adolescents best—YA authors, researchers, and teachers. You'll encounter the real words of experts in the fields of literacy instruction and literature.

This book is literature-based throughout. We'll reconsider how textbooks are used and might be better used, and we'll explore and perhaps reprioritize the use of the wide variety of materials available. Non-textbook sources are not considered merely supplementary; rather they are vital and integral to teaching and to students' reading. By the time you finish this book, you will likely know a lot more about primary sources and genres of literature than you did at the beginning, and this book can serve as a resource that will lead you to many others. I hope you'll visit bookstores and public libraries in addition to your college library to look for the *trade books* I refer to that might have the potential to enrich your own understanding of the subject you will teach. Now is a good time to begin a content area classroom library or at least a wish list for future reference. This text provides bibliographies and BookTalks to aid you in your quest for relevant materials for the curriculum in your discipline.

I have tried to attend to my students' wish for a reader-friendly textbook. Therefore, mixed in with the theories, strategies, and research results are anecdotes, literary tidbits, and personal musings. Each story is meant to demonstrate a point or make a connection or awaken some inquisitiveness on your part. I hope that I have created a textbook that is engaging and ultimately useful to your "composing a teaching life" (Vinz, 1996).

Many of the reading guides provided as models have been constructed by preservice teachers using discipline-specific texts they have selected. Thus, you will be learning from your peers; you can evaluate their examples and perhaps think of modifications and improvements, just as you may be doing with your own drafts and your classmates' work in progress. There is an emphasis on interdisciplinary guides, and readers are encouraged throughout to make connections within and among fields of study.

Throughout the book there is attention to issues relating to diversity and teaching for social justice. Literacy growth is a goal you must have for *every one* of your students, and literacy is very much connected with the goals of larger change within our society. It is our responsibility as teachers to serve as change agents; you'll be offered opportunities to ponder how you can be part of grassroots change that can improve the scholastic lives of your students and may eventually help implement systemic change in schools and society.

HANDS-ON AND MINDS-ON! AN INTRODUCTORY LITERACY EXPERIENCE

This section affords you the opportunity to experience first-hand many of the concepts and aspects of literacy that are developed throughout this book. I created the following activities and guides for you based on Lois Lowry's novel *The Giver* (1993). Your instructor may substitute comparable activities relating to a different text, but the principles are the same. Even if you don't read *The Giver* right now as part of a course, the activities below will serve as examples to help you see how teacher-constructed guiding activities help readers as they comprehend texts and think about content and ideas. But I encourage you to read this popular, thought-provoking masterpiece for your own enjoyment and knowledge.

PRE-READING AND READING ACTIVITIES

Teachers can help students get ready, both cognitively and emotionally, to read a text by providing an *anticipation guide* constructed to activate their thinking on the topics that are dealt with in that text. Please complete the anticipation guide on the following page, created to be used in conjunction with Lois Lowry's young adult novel, *The Giver* (1993).

When you've finished filling in the anticipation guide, if you're in class, select a partner or join a small group of your peers and compare answers. Add others' examples of utopian literature to your own. I'll help out, too. My students have provided *Utopia* (More, 1965), *Anthem* (Rand, 1995), *The Handmaid's Tale* (Atwood, 1986), *1984* (Orwell, 1949), *Animal Farm* (Orwell, 1954), *Watership Down* (Adams, 1974), *Lord of the Flies* (Golding, 1955), *Brave New World* (Huxley, 1932), *A Clockwork Orange* (Burgess, 1986), *Fahrenheit 451* (Bradbury, 1953), *Walden* (Thoreau, 1854), as well as the movie *The Matrix* (Warner Home Video, 1999) and the songs "Imagine" (Lennon, 1971), "Somewhere" (Sondheim & Bernstein, 1957), "The Impossible Dream," (Darion & Leigh, 1966), and "If We Only Have Love" (Brel, 1968). Inevitably, whenever I use this guide in a class, a discussion ensues about the fact that most of the works mentioned are really about societies that *fail* or turn out to be horrible places rather than the ideal places represented by the words and phrases that the students supplied in Question One. This is a perfect time for me to introduce the term *dystopia*, for some a new word to add to their vocabulary. I also show my students the resource *Encyclopedia of Utopian Literature* (Snodgrass, 1995), which gives many more examples, as well as a wealth of information about utopian authors, concepts, and historical background.

If you're reading this chapter outside class, please try to find another person with whom to discuss your responses to the exercise's statements. It's likely that you won't find total agreement, and discussion about the differences will be productive.

The next thing a teacher might do is to give a *booktalk*, a brief introduction that aims to entice the reader. The following BookTalk is my introduction.

Now read *The Giver*. Keep the anticipation guide you completed handy to see whether any of your answers change as a result of reading the book. Also, respond in a journal or learning log. Jot down things you think of as you read, then your reaction at the end of the story. What questions do you have for others? For the author? For your teacher? Read as actively as you can; instead of just absorbing information and plot, talk back, interact with this novel. Even talk to the characters if you wish.

BookTalk 1.1

"Memories
may be beautiful, and yet,
what's too painful to remember,
we simply choose to forget."

The Way We Were by Bergman & Hamlisch, 1973. Used with permission.

The anticipation guide you just completed caused you to think about whether you would erase painful memories if you could. You're about to read about a society that figured out a way to do just that. Its citizens also made other changes to eliminate many of the problems we experience today. Imagine a world where you'd *never* have to worry about losing a lover, deciding on risky career changes, being involved in a car accident, or going home to parents who fought. Welcome to Jonas's world. Welcome to Lois Lowry's *The Giver*.

POST-READING ACTIVITIES RELATED TO *THE GIVER*

The best way to start discussing a book is *freely*. Get in a large circle, or several smaller ones, with others who have read the novel. Use your journal responses to initiate the discussion and keep it going. Make sure everyone has the chance to talk; no one person (this includes the teacher) should dominate. This type of group is known as a *literature circle* or *literature group* (Peterson & Eeds, 1990; Short, Harste, & Burke, 1996), discussed further in Chapter 2.

On your own, please complete the worksheet on page 5.

Once you have completed the worksheet, it's time to debrief. Did answering the questions on the worksheet add to your knowledge or insight? Did they guide your thinking? Did you have to look up any of the vocabulary words? I'm assuming your answers may reflect a rather negative reaction to this worksheet. Now, how would you like to be told you'll be answering similar questions for the next 22 chapters of *The Giver*? You may have read the book in one sitting, and you almost certainly would have resented the interruptions. My students and I generally agree to write "AVOID!" at the top of this worksheet, reminding us there *must* be a better way to help students comprehend a novel. Then, we set out to think of those possible ways.

Anticipation Guide for The Giver

1. Brainstorm to come up with words, phrases, people, and concepts you associate with the word UTOPIA.

UTOPIA

2. List any works of utopian literature, movies, or songs you have read, seen, or heard of:

_____

_____

_____

_____

_____

_____

_____

_____

_____

_____

3. Respond YES or NO to the following statements, and think of a specific situation that exemplifies your position:

_____ Rules are made to be broken.

_____ Money is the root of all evil.

_____ In the interest of fairness, everyone should be treated equally.

_____ It would be a good thing to be able to totally forget bad memories.

_____ If I could eliminate pain from my life and the lives of those I love, I would.

_____ A government should have the right to enforce laws that will make society safer.

_____ A person has the right to choose to die if life has become painful or unproductive or just too long.

Traditional Worksheet for Chapter One of The Giver

VOCABULARY: Look up the following words in the dictionary (if necessary) and write their definitions.

distraught: _____

_____

apprehensive: _____

_____

release: _____

_____

ritual: _____

_____

transgression: _____

_____

COMPREHENSION: Write your answers to the following questions in complete sentences:

1. During what month are jobs assigned in this community?

_____

2. What is the primary mode of transportation?

_____

3. Are certain genders preferred for certain roles in this community? Explain your answer by citing examples from the text.

_____

_____

_____

4. Define *released* as used in Chapter 1.

_____

_____

5. How did you feel about the telling of feelings at the dinner table?

_____

_____

_____

6. Describe the setting of this story.

_____

_____

Some of you might remember that this is exactly the way literature was dealt with in the classrooms you were in as a middle school or high school student. Assigning these worksheets might assure a teacher that a student read and comprehended the text, though you may have memories of friends who were able to get by somehow without actually reading the book. They represent different levels of questioning, which we'll talk about in a later chapter of this textbook. Teacher questioning is valuable and crucial to learning, but you will probably agree that completing this kind of worksheet is not a worthwhile use of your time. It represents the *basalization of literature*, where the teacher actually teaches the novel in the same manner publishers' basal reading series often treat reading instruction in the elementary or middle grades. Such worksheets can reduce the enjoyment a novel can provide. Certainly Lois Lowry did not write this book for the purpose of having students write the answers to hundreds of questions in complete sentences! When I visit classrooms where literature is used this way, I look around at the struggling, bored faces, the students who will have the power of the novel diminished by the very fact that the book is being "taught" like this. I reluctantly conclude that what I see is, like the world of Jonas, a form of *dystopia*.

Are there alternatives to using these traditional worksheets? Many. In Chapter 2, you will read about the reading workshops that are a part of many classrooms. For now, think about the literature circle you participated in on *The Giver*. Did others bring up ideas or pick up on details you hadn't thought of? Were there different interpretations of and reactions to the ambiguous ending of the story? Did the talk extend your thinking about the issues inherent in the novel? Once students get used to being allowed to talk about a text based on *their* responses, there may not be a need for *any* teacher-initiated questions at all. But a teacher *can* provide optional guide questions for the response groups, leading them to areas that might not otherwise get explored.

Throughout this book you'll be shown how to create *reading guides* that serve to aid the comprehension of and thinking about the texts you ask your students to read. That is a very different task from making up worksheets to assess your students' understanding of articles or textbook selections or novels. All of your guides should aim to bring your readers to the construction of thoughtful responses; your goal is to help them acquire knowledge and understand their own positions better.

ACTIVATING PRIOR KNOWLEDGE I.1

Read the Literature Circle Guide for *The Giver* on the following page. Notice that it might lead to some redundancy if you discussed *all* of the questions in the order presented. Talk with your partner or group members again, concentrating on the topics your group didn't already address.

ACTION RESEARCH I.A, I.B

Analyze one of several available published Teacher Guides for *The Giver*. (One is available from Scholastic, another from Novel Units.) Identify the good points and potential drawbacks to using such guides. Discuss with your peers what educational philosophy the questions and structure of the guide represent. (My students were initially impressed by one guide that supplied initiating activities, vocabulary activities, author background information, discussion questions, culminating activities, and an assessment tool, all neatly packaged and well organized. They then discovered that in the guide's Overview, the last chapters were summarized as "Jonas's escape with Gabe: hunger, pain, and then survival at the end" (Green, 1994, p. 2). Survival? This clearly contradicted the interpretation of many of the readers in our class, and pointed to a philosophy of reading not consistent with reader response theory (explained in Chapter 1), upon which our class was predicated. You might show one of these teacher guides to students at the middle or high school level and ask them to talk with you about how they feel about this type of instructional material. They can relate experiences with similar instructional materials and exercise critical-thinking skills as they approve of them, dismiss them, or offer suggestions for improvement.

* * *

Now, find an article that explains how real teachers have used *The Giver* for instructional purposes or how a writer has analyzed the novel, and react to it. Do you like what the teacher and students have done? What educational benefits or curricular connections do you see at work? Do you see any drawbacks to the methods or activities described? Figure I.1 lists some of the many articles relating to *The Giver*.

Literature Circle Guide for The Giver

DIRECTIONS: In your circles, use your journal responses to help you discuss the book. The following questions may help you think about your reading experience. Use as many as you wish; you do not have to go in order. If you wish, use the lines provided to jot down ideas.

1. At what point did you realize what *released* meant in this community? How did you figure it out?

2. At what point did you conclude that Jonas would defect?

3. What symbols can you find in this book? Do you think they're effective? In what ways might the characters' names be symbolic?

4. How do you think Lois Lowry feels about euthanasia? Assisted suicide? Would she say they were morally acceptable practices? Would she say they were good for individuals or for society?

5. The society in *The Giver* is very safe, but that comes about at the cost of freedom. There is always a tension between safety and freedom. Think of ways this plays out in our government and society today. What individual liberties have people given up in return for protection and security? What issues are currently being debated in this area?

6. Did any of you write any favorite sentences down or mark any passages you found significant? If so, which ones? What struck you about them?

(continued)

Literature Circle Guide for The Giver

7. Discuss Lois Lowry's crafting of this book, or her writing style.

_____

_____

_____

_____

_____

8. The Newbery Medal is an annual award given by the American Library Association for the most distinguished contribution to children's literature published in the United States. Do you think this book deserved the 1994 Newbery Medal? Why, or why not?

_____

_____

_____

_____

_____

9. What do you think of the cover art?

_____

_____

_____

_____

10. What would you say to or ask Lois Lowry if she visited our classroom?

_____

_____

_____

_____

_____

11. How might this novel be used effectively in a social studies class? In a science class?

_____

_____

_____

_____

_____

FIGURE 1.1 *Resources showing how teachers can use Lois Lowry's* The Giver.

Corsaro, J. (1994, May). Lois Lowry's *The Giver*. [The Inside Story Column]. *Book Links*, 9–12.

Enriquez, G. (2001). Making Meaning of Cultural Depictions: Using Lois Lowry's *The Giver* to Reconsider What Is "Multicultural" About Literature. *Journal of Children's Literature*, 27(1), 13–22.

Gross, M. (1999). *The Giver* and *Shade's Children:* Future Views of Child Abandonment and Murder. *Children's Literature in Education*, 30(2), 103–117.

Johnson, A. B., Kleismit, J. W., & Williams, A. J. (2002). Grief, Thought, & Appreciation: Re-examining Our Values Amid Terrorism Through *The Giver. The ALAN Review*, 29(3), pp. 15–19.

Lawrence, A. (1999). From *The Giver* to *Twenty-One Balloons:* Explorations with Probability.

Mathematics Teaching in the Middle School, 4(8), 504–509.

Lehman, B. (1998). Doubletalk: A Pairing of *The Giver* and *We Are All in the Dumps with Jack and Guy. Children's Literature in Education*, 29(2), 69–78.

Mahar, D. (2001). Social Justice and the Class Community: Opening the Door to Possibilities. *English Journal*, 90(5), 107–115.

Menexas, V. (1997). Efferent and Aesthetic Stance: Understanding the Definition of Lois Lowry's *The Giver* as Metaphor. *Journal of Children's Literature*, 23(2), 34–41.

Whitelaw, J., & Wolf, S. A. (2001). Learning to "See Beyond": Sixth-Grade Students' Artistic Perceptions of *The Giver. The New Advocate*, 16(1), 57–67.

FIGURE 1.2 *A letter from a reader to an author about a life-changing book.*

Dear Ms. Lois Lowry,

Your book *The Giver* was very thought-provoking. It made me kind of sad and confused. Usually, I read a book two or three times, but I was so upset by *The Giver* that I returned it to the library the very next day.

I've given it a lot of thought, and I see now that *The Giver* made me really angry. I couldn't understand the hero's reluctance to intervene when he saw and understood all the injustices being done in the community. It was horrible.

The truth is, the giver in the story and I have a lot in common. I hold some strong views that I really believe in, but I rarely stand up for them. I'm just too scared to stick out or to expose my ideas to criticism. I can't be angry at the giver in the story for something that I myself do.

I live in a small town in Oregon, where I see bigotry, prejudice, and discrimination every day. We also have strong [proposed anti-gay legislation] here, something I'm firmly against. Still, I'm reluctant to voice my arguments, because some adults and friends of mine have different views.

I understand now that anything I can do is better than doing nothing. My voice is only one, but one voice can sometimes be just enough. As long as I am true to myself, I have nothing to be embarrassed or ashamed about.

From now on, I'm going to take sides on things I feel strongly about and won't let others intimidate me. I've learned, like the giver, that no thing or cause is hopeless, as long as people believe in it and stand up for their beliefs.

Ginger Bandeen, 16
Warrenton High School, Warrenton, OR
Teacher: Kay Rannow

Excerpted from *Dear Author: Students Write about the Books that Changed their Lives* by the Weekly Reader's *Read Magazine*, copyright © 1995, by permission of Conari Press.

ACTION RESEARCH   I.C

Interview people of various ages about their reactions to and interpretations of *The Giver*. You will be amazed at the variety and the intensity of responses and even arguments. One of my students told her son that she thought Jonas and Gabe found a new community by sledding down the hill to where they saw lights on Christmas trees. He confidently retorted, "If you read it carefully, Mom, you can tell they *do* die. They were almost unconscious and were delusional. Jonas thought the moon and stars were colored lights." He tried to convince her further, "Well, Mom, think of this . . . Jonas and Gabe *really* saw heaven with all of the family memories they never had and the music, too. They died when they got on the sled. The sled trip was the trip to heaven. That's what *really* happened" (Margaret Carey, used with permission). His mother then showed him Lois Lowry's Newbery Medal acceptance speech to point out that the author herself says there is no *true* ending or *right* interpretation; rather, "There's a right one for each of us, and it depends on our own beliefs, our own hopes" (Lowry, 1994, p. 420). Lowry includes a few excerpts from readers who have written to her. A sixth grader saw Jonas and Gabe traveling in a circle: Elsewhere was their old community, except now the people had come to accept memories and feelings. Another compared Jonas to Jesus, taking on the pain for everyone in the community so they wouldn't have to suffer; not surprisingly, he interpreted the Elsewhere at the end to be Heaven.

I've found, and I believe you will find as you talk with people, that some readers have actually changed their thinking and their values as a result of being affected by what for them was a powerful book. Figure I.2 contains an example from a book called *Dear Author: Books That Have Changed Readers' Lives* (1995).

> *Getting Ready to Teach I.1* (see page 13)

> *Getting Ready to Teach I.2* (see page 13)

BookTalk   I.2

When my students express disbelief about a society getting to the point of the one in *The Giver*, having given up so much freedom and choice and not realizing what is missing, or when they wonder how the Nazi regime was able to come into power, I read them the novella *The Children's Story: But Not Just for Children* by James Clavell (1981). It's an allegory that describes a morning when the new leaders of a conquered country replace the teachers in a school, and in under a half hour are able to convince the children that the beliefs and values they've been taught by their parents are wrong. It's a simply told, chilling depiction of brainwashing. Clavell adds a note at the end telling about the day his daughter came home from school having been taught the Pledge of Allegiance but not its meaning, instigating his reflection and writing. I urge you to read this story to ponder the potential influence you'll have as a teacher, and the awesome responsibility that entails.

ACTIVATING PRIOR KNOWLEDGE   I.2

I invite you now to connect the idea of utopia to schools. First, take a few minutes to work alone or with a partner on the following: List the characteristics of "the perfect school." One way to do this is to think about the schools you went to, then highlight the good points and change or get rid of the bad. Imagine such power!

Activating Prior Knowledge I.2 is not merely a fantasy exercise that could never be realized. When a new school is opened, or when a new administrator arrives, or when restructuring within a district occurs, people think about *ideal* learning environments and teaching practices. For teachers or preservice teachers, each new school year brings with it great hopes and possibilities. But too often, we hear students referring to school as a jail, or worse. Much of the literature on schools, such as Kozol's *Savage Inequalities* (1991), reports on atrocities within our educational system. Have some of our schools turned into dystopias?

On the other hand, there are books aiming for certain philosophical and educational ideals. B. F. Skinner's title *Walden Two* (1948) recognizes this utopian theme. John Holt's books with titles such as *How Children Fail* (1982) and *Teach Your Own: A Hopeful Path for Education* (1981) point out what he considers bad about the institution that American education has become, and offer his picture of what the ideal would look like. Neil Postman's prophetic-sounding *The End of Education* (1995) has as its subtitle *Redefining the Value of Schools*. E. D. Hirsch, Jr. has convinced some policy makers and educators that what he proposes in *The Schools We Need and Why We Don't Have Them* (1996) can turn around what has become a dismal situation. (We'll hear more about his Core Knowledge Schools and critiques of them in a later chapter.) *Shooting for Excellence: African American and Youth Culture in New Century Schools* (Mahiri, 1998) offers a vision of a school not dominated by disciplinary boundaries. You can explore books and articles as you reflect on your ideal school, your educational utopia, and then use the information as you visit schools and classrooms, as you talk with teachers and administrators and students, and as you take other education courses. Aim for connections at all levels. This helps you develop a strong personal philosophy of education and grounds you as you explore what it means to teach literacy in your content area.

Throughout this book, you meet content area teachers who are striving for an ideal classroom that meets their students' needs in terms of both curriculum and literacy; you are introduced to some of the best practices of content area teachers. In the final chapter, we return to the concept of visionary schooling; for now, here's one person's vision that might help you as you begin your teaching career:

> In an ideal world every teacher would be a teacher of reading. Every history teacher would work to help students understand the typical structure of discourse in historical texts. They would model and demonstrate how historians think as they read and write texts. They would offer powerful instruction that fostered the development ——— And biology teachers

LA - P V133c 1999

LA - P K134 2003

——— the read-
——— ogy. They
——— write, and
——— tent teach-
——— t were well
——— complexity
——— as well as
——— If this were
——— "win–win"
——— not just bet-
——— they would
——— . (Allington,

ACTIVITIES FOR YOUR STUDENTS

You could modify most of the earlier exercises to use with your students in middle and secondary grades, and you can adapt them to use with other texts relevant to the curriculum you'll be responsible for teaching. Throughout this book, you are introduced to trade books and other resources that you can use to teach the content of your discipline at the same time you enhance your students' literacy development. I am using *The Giver* as a model; you can apply the strategies to readings that work well for your classes.

The Giver can be used in an unlimited number of ways to initiate post-reading projects that lead to more learning, as well as enjoyment. Students who are dissatisfied with the ending might write a final chapter that they feel brings more closure to the story. Some can write poems or songs, or create dioramas, collages, or graphic organizers (diagrams illustrating relations among ideas). One of my students made a poster with the final scene, surrounded by actual blinking Christmas tree lights. Another came in with a list of meanings for all of the characters' names in the story.

Following are some examples of choices you could offer students as ways to further explore the issues raised in the book or their responses to the text. I encourage you to try out one or more yourself as a way of actively engaging with the pedagogical information in this textbook.

TEACHING SUGGESTION 1. Ask your students to write a journal entry imagining how Lois Lowry might have come up with the ideas that came together for the creation of her utopian novel. Then find, read aloud, and have the students respond to Lois Lowry's Newbery acceptance speech for *The Giver*. (It can be found in *The Horn Book Magazine*, July/August 1994.) She crafts her speech using, not surprisingly, *memories* that led to the writing of the book. They include family relationships, learning from special mentors, mistakes she made growing up, and personal reactions to problems within our society. She also acknowledges the ambiguity of the ending of *The Giver*, and shares some responses she has received from her readers. Readers can see that they are part of a community of literary people who are all in this together. Perhaps some students will want to write to Lowry using her website or through her publisher, or join a literary chat room to add to their interpretations of or responses to the book.

TEACHING SUGGESTION 2. There are several readily available published reviews and critical interpretations of *The Giver*. For example, in her article "In the Belly of the Whale," Patricia Lee Gauch (1997) dis-

UTOPIA

Callenbach, E. (1990). *Ecotopia: The Notebooks and Reports of William Weston.* New York: Bantam Books.

Carden, M. L. (1998). *Oneida: Utopian Community to Modern Corporation.* Syracuse, NY: Syracuse University Press.

More, T. (1965). *Utopia.* New York: Simon & Schuster.

Murphy, J. (1998). *West To a Land of Plenty: The Diary of Teresa Angelino Viscardi: New York to Idaho Territory, 1883.* New York: Scholastic.

Snodgrass, M. E. (1995). *Encyclopedia of Utopian Literature.* Santa Barbara, CA: ABC-CLIO.

Streissguth, T. (1999). *Utopian Visionaries.* Minneapolis, MN: Oliver Press.

MEMORY

Greenfield, S. A. (1996). *The Human Mind Explained.* New York: Henry Holt.

Lopez, B. (1998). *About This Life: Journeys on the Threshold of Memory.* New York: Knopf.

Meltzer, M. (1987). *The Landscape of Memory.* New York: Viking Penguin.

Neisser, U. (1982). *Memory Observed: Remembering in Natural Contexts.* New York: W. H. Freeman.

Pinker, S. (1997). *How the Mind Works.* New York: Norton.

Rupp, R. (1998). *Committed to Memory: How We Remember and Why We Forget.* New York: Crown Publishers.

Sacks, O. (1995). The Last Hippie. In *An Anthropologist on Mars: Seven Paradoxical Tales.* New York: Knopf.

Stine, J. M. (1997). *Double Your Brain Power.* Upper Saddle River, NJ: Prentice Hall.

Wartwick, N., & Carlson-Finnerty, L. (1993). *Memory and Learning.* New York: Chelsea House Publishers.

---

cusses the novel along with others in relation to the well-known archetype of the hero's journey. In contrast, John Noell Moore (1997) applies a type of literary criticism known as *deconstruction* to the book. Have students read one or more examples of this type of commentary and respond by connecting the information with their previous personal response to the book. Do these supplemental materials add to their insight and deepen their knowledge? What would they say in response to these writers and critics?

TEACHING SUGGESTION 3. *The Giver* deals with topics related to science, government, English, and ethics; it is, therefore, ideal for interdisciplinary study or for exploration in a number of content areas. Encourage students to read further about a theme or topic dealt with in the novel and synthesize their new knowledge with that gained from the original source. Suggestions for exploration include memory, utopia, government control versus individual rights and freedoms, genetic engineering, capital punishment, infanticide, medical ethics, and surrogate motherhood. Figure I.3 contains sample bibliographies for the topics of memory and utopia. All of the suggested topics can be researched on the Internet.

TEACHING SUGGESTION 4. Check the Internet for websites containing information about Lois Lowry. Suggest that students join a chat room to discuss their reading of *The Giver* with readers from other places. It might be especially interesting to listen to readers from those countries with different types of governments and societal rules.

BookTalk 1.3

Has *The Giver* piqued your interest in Lois Lowry's body of works or in utopian/dystopian literature? If so, consider exploring another futuristic society she created in *Gathering Blue* (2000). As in Jonas's society, people with differences and defects are not appreciated; they are eliminated. Kira has a twisted leg, so must fear for her life. Even as her gift for weaving is put to use by the Guardians controlling her fate, there are dark forces at work. As you read this book, note the recurring theme of the importance of memory, and keep your eyes open and imagination ready in case you might sight someone from *The Giver*.

I hope that the variety of activities has helped you realize the many ways a rich core text can be used in the classroom. You've expanded your background knowledge and constructed a base that will serve you well as you connect ideas from the following chapters to your personal experiences. That's why I wanted you to read a young adult book and try some of the suggestions before we got into the actual theories related to literacy. Now, it's time to do just that.

INTRODUCTION

Getting Ready to Teach

I.1 Did you come across any passages in *The Giver* that struck you as particularly effective or that evoked a strong emotional or intellectual response? Did you find yourself paying attention to the language itself at some points? Did any of your classmates underline a key sentence or copy a quote from the book to their journals? Many readers find a way to organize, record, and track text they find meaningful and memorable. I keep a folder that I call my "Favorite Sentence File." You can start one too; start gathering sentences from your personal reading for your unique collection. You may share some entries with others and compare what works for you with what others choose.

I.2 I also keep folders labeled with the titles of the books I use in my classes, as well as the topics within my curriculum. In them I collect articles that connect current events with issues inherent in the literature and in my lessons. For example, in my folder for *The Giver*, I have a newspaper article describing how Sweden sterilized a huge number of people—those considered undesirables—without their knowledge or consent, up until 1976. I also have an article about the Oneida

Community that existed in Central New York in the late 1800s as a real utopian experiment. I have a review of the children's autobiography *Red Scarf Girl: A Memoir of the Cultural Revolution* (Jiang, 1997); it contains striking parallels with the society represented in *The Giver*. I invite you to start your own folder system so that you will have interesting and relevant applications as you teach various topics. Read newspapers and magazines with scissors in hand or a copier available; you'll be amazed at the connections you make once you start reading as a teacher on the hunt for knowledge to enhance your students' learning. Encourage your students to bring in news items and stories they find that connect to curricular topics.

Literacy, Content Area Teaching, and Learning Standards

This chapter helps you to think about and understand what *reading* is, then to consider the ever-broadening concept of *literacy*. You are introduced to the concept of learning standards, and you are asked to consider what it means for you to be a *teacher of literacy* in your chosen content area.

THINKING ABOUT READING PROCESSES

If this is your first literacy or reading education course, or if you are a preservice teacher, chances are you haven't given much thought to what actually goes into the *process* of reading. Entire books can be, and are, devoted to this subject. To begin, there are a few concepts to think about that relate to your students' reading, as well as to issues that are discussed in subsequent chapters.

Researchers and theorists have made great progress defining the act called *reading* and explaining how it works. Smith (1985) writes: "Researchers are discovering that in order to understand reading they must consider not just the eyes but also the mechanisms of memory and attention, anxiety, risk taking, the nature and uses of language, the comprehension of speech, interpersonal relationships, sociocultural differences, learning in general, and the learning of young children in particular" (p. 3). There is not, however, universal agreement among experts as to how reading happens, how it is first learned, or the best way to teach it. The various approaches are described as being *bottom-up* (*text-based* or *part-to-whole*), *top-down* (*reader-based* or *holistic*), and *interactive* (*constructivist* or *generative*).

The *bottom-up* view begins with the smallest parts of a text: the letters and their corresponding sounds. Once readers decode the symbols and letters (and their combinations), they attend to words and their meanings. Words are combined into phrases and then into sentences, paragraphs, chapters, and books. Syntax, involving word order and grammatical constructs, then becomes important. Discourse knowledge, which Leu and Kinzer (1999) define as "the knowledge that readers have of the language organization that determines meaning beyond the single sentence level" (p. 396), pertains to patterns of organization such as cause–effect or sequence and larger structures of text. For example, proficient readers know that stories generally have an initiating episode, characters in some kind of conflict or challenging setting, and a resolution of some sort by the end. Textbooks usually have headings, main ideas, details, references, and study guides. According to those people who subscribe to the bottom-up view, the reading process is largely text-driven, and the reader's job is to discover the meaning that is there through use of decoding skills and comprehension strategies (Flesch, 1955; Gough, 1985). Weaver (1994), while not advocating this position, describes this as a "commonsense" or "person on the street" model because it seems so natural to assume that

> *of course* we read and comprehend by working from smaller parts to increasingly larger parts; by sounding out words and thus identifying them, by combining the meanings of individual words to get the meaning of a sentence, by combining the meanings of sentences to get the meaning of the whole text. (p. 41)

The *top-down* approach to explaining literacy basically reverses this order. Readers go from the global to the specific, bringing their background knowledge and expectations to a text and applying strategies to *bring meaning to* the text, largely through prediction and confirmation. They still require vocabulary knowledge, of course, and they use phonics and a knowledge of word structure to decode as needed (especially when the text contains unfamiliar terms), but this isn't the starting place, or the most important part of comprehension (Goodman, 1967; Smith, 1985).

The view that has prevailed is that reading is neither strictly top down nor bottom up; rather, it is *interactive* (Adams, 1990; Anderson, Hiebert, Scott, & Wilkinson, 1985; Rumelhart, 1976; Stanovitch, 1980). A sociocultural, transactional model of reading involves parts of both the bottom-up and top-down approaches, with part-to-whole and whole-to-part occurring as reading proceeds. Not all readers approach text or reach comprehension the same way, and an individual might stress the different components mentioned at different times, depending on the text type and the reading purpose. Some readers are very aware of the strategies they use as they construct meaning, while others may be very efficient readers but haven't analyzed what for them seems like a natural process.

Gee (2000) shows through an analysis of discourse and sociocultural studies that the long-standing dichotomies in reading theories and research no longer make sense. Reading is complex, and comprehension and response are based on the combination of many factors. Gee explains the reading process not as one thing but many, always situated in contexts and cultural communities; ultimately, "There is no 'reading in general,' at least none that leads to thought and action in the world" (p. 204).

If there is no reading in general, let's turn to some particular cases. As you think more about how you read and as you observe and talk with your students, you will discover that there are numerous ways that individual readers process print and construct meaning from text. Contrasting examples of how real people describe their reading processes are presented in Figure 1.1.

The reading approaches described earlier have implications for the teaching of reading, both in the early grades and beyond. There is a continuing struggle among experts, coined *The Great Debate* (Chall, 1967), that centers largely on whether teaching specific reading skills, especially those having to do with phonics (sound–symbol relationships), should be learned *first* through direct instruction and then applied to stories and other text. Although the more holistic theorists and teachers believe that children learn to read by reading, the majority are positioned somewhere in the large middle section of the continuum and advocate a balanced program. Routman (2000) defines the term as she used it in the 1990s:

> By *balanced* I meant that all aspects of reading and writing received appropriate emphasis and that guided contexts were used to help readers and writers become critical thinkers, independent problem solvers, self-monitors, self-evaluators, and goal setters. The knowledgeable teacher was the decision maker who, based on students' needs, interests, and experiences, determined when, how, and how much to intervene. (p. 15)

However, Routman notes that by the late 1990s the word *balance* was taking on a different and disturbing meaning. "Instead of denoting a state of equilibrium between all the parts . . . , *balance* is now often synonymous with the belief that learning proceeds in a skills-based hierarchy (usually determined by a published program), a view not supported by research" (p. 15). Routman now prefers the term *comprehensive* to refer to the type of literacy program she espouses. You can see that the way reading is thought of and talked about is dynamic. The field is always developing, and there are a number of ongoing philosophical and political debates.

Throughout this book, various aspects of reading are explained and explored and teaching suggestions are provided. Skills and strategies are always present-

FIGURE 1.1 *Readers talking about their reading processes.*

"I'll read about a hundred pages of a book to get the big picture, then go back and read it a second time, for details."
—*Gerald Eisman in Rosenthal, 1995, p. 163*

"As an autistic, I think totally visually . . . I could have never memorized a whole bunch of words. Instead, I memorized the fifty phonetic sounds. . . . I assign a visual picture to each sound . . ."
—*Temple Grandin in Rosenthal, 1995, p. 187*

"I can't stand description since I don't visualize, but I absolutely love the dialogue. . . . I skip all the description. But when I get to the dialogue, I slow down and read at a luxurious pace, savoring every sentence. . . . I glance at everything and pick up two or three key words on a page in the boring parts . . . if I get lost, I do not go back."
—*Martha Lane in Rosenthal, 1995, p. 190*

"I find reading a challenge. I need to read things twice, maybe three times, before I actually comprehend it. So it takes me a long time. I feel as if reading is a job, not a relaxing thing to do."
—*anonymous college student*

"I was so deeply inside the book that I could have been at the bottom of the sea. There was no way to quickly resurface without getting the bends."
—*Wilhelm, 1997, p. 4*

"You take your books and bring them up with your pencils. You do your papers and get reading seatwork when you are done. Then you go back to your seats. Then you go back to the paper you are working on when you're done writing your name. After that paper, you go to the next one. When you're done with those, you go on to the next one until the last one is done. Then put them in her basket. That's what reading in school is."
—*Stephanie, a first grader, in Michel, 1994, p. 36*

ed in authentic contexts. For now, remember that reading is a meaning-driven process—readers must actively construct meaning and work toward fitting new information into the knowledge they already possess. The next section introduces you to a particular way of thinking about readers and text called *reader response theory*. It often is discussed more in relation to literature than to other types of text, and you may wonder why you might find that helpful as a content area teacher. One reason is that you are encouraged throughout this book to use literature, as well as many other resources beyond the textbook, regardless of your subject area. Also, you can apply some aspects of this theory as you deal with all types of text, readers, subjects, and situations. A knowledge of reader response theory may help you as you ponder your own reading; it may answer questions that have puzzled you for a long time.

Getting Ready to Teach 1.1 *(see page 28)*

READER RESPONSE THEORY

ACTIVATING PRIOR KNOWLEDGE   1.1

Think of a book you have read at least twice. Perhaps you read a book as a child and became reacquainted with it recently. Maybe you have a favorite book that you return to often. My questions for you are: Did you have an identical experience each time you read it? If not, what was different? And what was the cause of the change? Write for a few minutes in your learning log or journal before continuing.

Obviously, the context of the text you selected in your reflection did not change. The same words appear in the book—*The Hobbit* (Tolkien, 1982), *The Bible*, *Chicken Soup for the Soul* (Canfield & Hansen, 1993), *Where the Wild Things Are* (Sendak, 1963), *Catcher in the Rye* (Salinger, 1951), *Walden* (Thoreau, 1992), *Leaves of Grass* (Whitman, 1992)— each time you read it. But, inevitably, *you* changed. It's impossible for two readings of a text to be identical even if one occurs immediately after the other; the second time around, you know "whodunnit." Knowing the ending causes you to think differently about the ideas, events, and conversations that occur earlier in the text. If you read *The Giver* concurrently with this book's Introduction, I can say with certainty that if you reread the first chapter now, you would agree that the experience was quite different from your first reading.

Reader response theory explains why two readers can have widely varying interpretations of a character's motives or a story's theme. It also calls into question the common educational practice of asking students what a poem *means*, or what a certain symbol represents, or what an author intended, as though there were only one correct answer that could be put into a multiple-choice test. Some of you may have memories of having had literature, or at least some genres or works, ruined for you because of this method of teaching and testing.

Louise Rosenblatt began championing what later came to be known as reader response criticism with her groundbreaking work *Literature as Exploration* (1938/1995). *The Reader, the Text, the Poem* (1978) expounded on her theoretical premises. She viewed the reader as transacting with a text to create what she called the *poem*, the meaning that emerges from the transaction at a given time. Feelings are evoked not just by the text, but by the text combining with the reader's prior experiences with life and literature, as well the reader's present mood and purposes. "The reader's creation of a poem out of a text must be an active, self-ordering and self-corrective process" (Rosenblatt, 1978, p. 11).

Applying Reader Response Theory in the Classroom

Note: You may want to read *The Butter Battle Book* (1984) by Dr. Seuss and *Snow White and the Seven Dwarfs* (1972) by the Brothers Grimm before reading the next section.

I'll use two examples from my own work to exemplify reader response theory. First, a colleague and I set out to examine the responses of readers of different ages to Dr. Seuss's *The Butter Battle Book* (1984), an allegorical tale with multiple themes that is often used in social studies classes. We asked all participants to write a free response and then to state the main idea (or theme, or author's message, or moral of the story). We found that the third graders in our sample, in addition to drawing pictures in response to hearing the book read aloud, tended to have a literal interpretation of the story: there is a right way and a wrong way to butter one's bread. (This premise was the impetus in the story for the Yooks and Zooks to embark on an arms race.) A typical main idea statement was

"Never trust a Zook that had toast with butter on the bottom."

Many fifth graders responded by being upset over the lack of closure to the story. Dr. Seuss leaves Grandpa and his enemy Van Itch standing on a wall, each with a bomb poised to drop. The students resolved this departure from the story structure they were used to by supplying their own endings. One youngster's story had the bombs drop, blowing the troublemakers Grandpa and Van Itch up to Mars, leaving the rest of the community perfectly able and willing to get along. Another's ending described the bombs dropping, causing the wall to crumble, and the Yooks and Zooks cooperating in order to pick up the debris. Main ideas stated by fifth graders included "People should be able to eat bread and butter either upside down or right side up" and "Dr. Seuss was trying to tell people that people have differences."

Do you know any eighth graders? When we asked students at this grade level to write the main point of the story, one wrote, "Who gives?" Isn't that a perfect eighth grade response? Actually, many of our respondents did "give." They wondered how each side matched and outdid the weapons of the other; they concocted elaborate theories about spies and counterspies working in those back rooms referred to in the story. This age group was the first where the majority understood that the Yooks and Zooks represented nations, that the story was an allegory. One person lamented, "It's just showing that the wars of building weapons will keep on going."

Some of the most intriguing responses were the outliers, the unique answers, those we might perhaps call *wrong* answers, calling into question how reader response theory can work in our classrooms and what its limits are. A tenth grader wrote emotionally, "For stupid reasons we want to fight other people. We spend money and energy on weapons that we don't want to use. When we should use it for other useful things." Her response goes beyond the text, which never mentioned the economic aspects of the arms race, but we can certainly see the connection. What should we do with the tenth grader who wrote that the main point of the story is that the right way to eat butter is on the top of bread? Such a literal interpretation can be considered cute and appropriate from a third grader, but most teachers expect students by adolescence to understand allegory and symbolism. Another wrote, "The story conveys a feeling of hate for people who are different. I don't think children should be told to do this at such a young age." She might be considered to have misunderstood the author's intention, the text's purpose. As teachers, we should try to help this reader read between the lines, to understand the genre of satire. We might model how we put pieces together to arrive at comprehension.

So, reader response theory does not say that *anything goes*; although idiosyncratic responses might be very interesting, the responses to a text must be plausible and defensible by using evidence within the text. We explore reader response theory and its application to content area literacy throughout the chapters of this book; whether you teach math, science, art, history, or another subject, it will help both you and your students to understand that readers construct meaning from the texts they read based on their own purposes, background knowledge, emotional states, literacy abilities, and so on. This will become clearer as more discussion and examples including nonfiction, primary sources, and textbook selections are provided. Meanwhile, I'll end this example with a fifth grader's poetic free response to *The Butter Battle Book*:

> Grandpa was in danger, and so was I,
> If one dropped a bomb, you could kiss us good-bye.
> Grandpa was mad, and so was Van Itch,
> My Grandpa yelled, "Don't drop it, you snitch!"
> The tree I was on started to shake,
> It fell on Van Itch; I yelled, "For Goodness sake!"
> Me and Grandpa were very afraid,
> If the bomb hits the ground, I will die, afraid.
> Grandpa caught Van Itch and his bomb, too.
> The Yooks were safe, hip, hip, you-too-hoo.
> Grandpa made friends with weird Van Itch,
> He turned out nice, he's not a snitch.
> The Zooks became friends with all the Yooks,
> You can read this story in special books.
>
> *(Kane & Gentile, 1989, p. 234)*

Surely, a multiple-choice or true–false quiz could never elicit this type of creative, thoughtful writing.

Using Reader Response Theory to Guide Instruction

A second demonstration of reader response theory involves an activity I created for my own teaching. Each semester, I form seven groups, then pass out copies of The Grimm Brothers' *Snow White and the Seven Dwarfs*. I particularly like the version translated by Randall Jarrell and illustrated by Diane Burkholm (1972). I ask students to read the text with their group members, look at the pictures, discuss the story, and write a group response. As they read, I unobtrusively hand each group one of the following prompts:

- You are parents of preschoolers. You found this book in your child's nursery school classroom.
- You are six-year-old children.
- You are people who inherited the gene that causes dwarfism. You are under four feet tall, and are politically active in the organization "Little People of America."
- You are feminists.
- You are librarians who are on the American Library Association committee that awards the Caldecott Medal to an illustrator for the best picture book of the year.
- You have recently married someone who was divorced. You are a stepparent to your spouse's children who live with you.
- You are enrolled in a course called "The Bible *as* Literature and the Bible *in* Literature." *Snow White and the Seven Dwarfs* is a required text for this course.

When the groups finish writing, I ask a spokesperson from each to read their response to the fairy tale and I write key words I hear on the board. Not surprisingly, we often end up with seven quite different responses in front of us. The students playing the role of the Caldecott Selection Committee notice details about the illustrations and their relation to the text. The parents of preschoolers discuss age appropriateness and voice concern in terms of the violence, sexism, witchcraft and occult symbols, and word and concept difficulty. The group looking for biblical allusions usually has no trouble finding them: the apple as a symbol of temptation, the dying after disobedience, the rescue and resurrection by a savior. The group representing stepparents is outraged by the stereotypical depiction of the evil stepmother. Aren't their jobs hard enough without having to combat images in children's stories?

If you use such an activity in your classroom, you'll find that students use language that affects the voice and tone in their responses to help convey their message and their assumed identities. You can tell which of my groups wrote the following stream-of-conscience reaction: "Yay, Snow White lived and the Queen died. The Queen was bad. She was mean to Snow White. The pictures were pretty. Why was the Queen so mean to Snow White? What's a 'paragon of beauty'? Where can I get a mirror like that? The witch was scary and Snow White was pretty, but I liked the movie better. The dwarfs were ugly, not cute like in the movie. In the book, they didn't go 'Hi ho, hi ho, it's off to work we go.'"

Anger and frustration are evident in this group's response: "The author is obviously uneducated and has no idea about the Little People of the world. He has us mining ore. This gives people the idea that we are ostracized from society because of our appearance. The author didn't even give the dwarfs names. He referred to them as 'the first one,' 'the second one,' and so on, dehumanizing them. The dwarfs are depicted as simple people with simple minds and this directly reflects on their stature." (It's interesting that this entire response focuses on the depiction of the dwarfs, while other groups don't even mention the dwarfs!)

A final example also shows anger, but for a different reason: "Snow White was cast out of the castle because she was beautiful. This shows a lack of regard for her personality and her character. The dwarfs were male chauvinists. 'If you'll look after our house for us, make the beds, wash, sew and knit, and if you'll keep everything neat and clean, then you can stay with us, and you shall lack for nothing' (Grimm, unpaged). It was assumed, of course, that she would do this instead of, say, working in the mines. The prince didn't even care if Snow White was alive; he just wanted to look at her like some ornament."

In this exercise, I used a bit of manipulation to ensure that there would be major differences in the students' readings due to *interested* points of view; but to some extent every person's reading of every text is different. As noted earlier, an individual can't even read a text the same way twice at the same sitting. The first reading, along with many other factors, colors the second experience; one may recognize foreshadowing that she hadn't noticed initially; having comprehended the main idea may free up one's energy to notice beauty of language or precision of organization.

KINDS OF READING: STANCES AND PURPOSES

Did you read *The Giver* for pleasure or for information? Do you read the newspaper for pleasure or for information? You may have said both, and that's fine, but if you had to say which was your primary purpose, you'd probably be able to decide. And for some texts the answer is easy—you read romance or detective thrillers almost totally for pleasure, not intellectual enhancement, and you read a required college chemistry text the day before the midterm almost totally for an understanding of the principles and facts. Rosenblatt has categorized the reader's relationship to the text, the stances a reader takes, as either *efferent* or *aesthetic.* With efferent reading, the reader's primary concern is to gain knowledge or information, to carry something away from the reading. She gives the extreme example of a mother read-

ing a label on a bottle of poison because her child has just ingested its contents. With aesthetic reading, on the other hand, the reader's main concern is with what happens *during* the reading event. "Though . . . the reader of Frost's 'Birches' must decipher the images or concepts or assertions that the words point to, he also pays attention to the associations, feelings, attitudes and ideas that these words and their referents arouse within him. . . . *the reader's attention is centered directly on what he is living through during his relationship with that particular text"* (Rosenblatt, 1978, pp. 24–25).

The same text can be read by two people, or the same person at different times, for different purposes. Rosenblatt conceptualizes the two stances as being on a continuum, or a spectrum, involving complexity. I also like visualizing the stances as intersecting circles. I read professional education journals to gain knowledge of new research, find out which theorists are debating, and learn about innovative practices teachers are developing. That's efferent reading. But I experience a great amount of pleasure doing this, and often let other duties slide when a new issue of *English Journal* or the *Journal of Adolescent and Adult Literacy* or *The Horn Book Magazine* arrives in the mail. That's aesthetic reading. Ben Burtt, winner of four Academy Awards for his creation of the sound effects in *Star Wars* and other movies and producer of documentaries, states, "Reading to do research for a film is actually a form of entertainment for me" (Rosenthal, 1995, p. 169). You may read a book like Annie Dillard's *Pilgrim at Tinker Creek* (2000) because you love her writing style and the book relaxes you, yet find that you have picked up a lot of information about insects that you can carry over into your entomology class! About this example, I'd say that the two circles representing the efferent and aesthetic reading stances in a Venn diagram could be almost entirely overlapping.

One problem that occurs in schools is that the stances can get seemingly reversed. Most of us can name a classic that was spoiled for us because, instead of reading it for pleasure and for personal reasons, as authors intend, we were required to read it for school and were constantly tested to check our comprehension. Then, we were required to write an essay based on it, the purpose of which seemed to be to conform to what was already in the teacher's head. Ask a first grader what reading is, and she'll ask if you mean *home reading* or *school reading* (Michel, 1994). Ask a seventh grader about reading, and he'll also differentiate home reading and school reading (Worthy, 1998). Too often, home reading equates with pleasure reading and school reading is perceived as distasteful, or at least artificial. One of the aims of this book is to help you change that situation for your future students: to promote their natural curiosity, problem-solving ability, and general intellectual growth by providing real opportunities to interact with many types of text.

DEFINING LITERACY (OR SHOULD WE SAY LITERACIES?)

Now that you've started thinking about reading, let's broaden the topic to that of *literacy* in general. How do the two concepts differ? What does literacy mean?

ACTIVATING PRIOR KNOWLEDGE   **1.2**

Imagine that you are being interviewed for a teaching position. An administrator interviewing you asks you to define the word *literacy*. What do you say?

As a follow-up question, the interviewer asks you to define literacy as it applies to the subject you will be teaching. How do you expand your answer?

Finally, another person on the search committee hands you a card that has "_____ literacy" on it and asks you to fill in the blank with as many appropriate words as you can. Take a moment to make a list of the phrases containing *literacy* that come to mind.

Figure 1.2 contains some of the phrases my students have contributed in response to the last question. These, combined with your own, indicate how widely used the word *literacy* is at present.

Traditionally, *literacy* has referred to the ability to read and write. In fact, the glossary of the *Standards for the English Language Arts* (1996) points out, "Until quite recently, literacy was generally defined, in a very limited way, as the ability to read or write one's own name" (p. 73). But the term has broadened to include "the capacity to accomplish a wide range of reading, writing, speaking, and other language tasks associated with everyday life" (p. 73). In the body of the Standards document is an even more expanded definition: "Being literate in con-

temporary society means being active, critical, and creative users not only of print and spoken language but also of the visual language of film and television, commercial and political advertising, photography, and more" (p. 5).

Morris and Tchudi (1996) also "prefer to view literacy in a broader context, one that takes into account far more than literacy in the 3Rs, encompassing an individual's ability to interpret and create texts, to function capably in a vast array of settings, and to operate effectively in society" (p. 12). Alvermann, Hinchman, Moore, Phelps, and Waff (1998) deliberately chose in the title, as well as the body, of their work to pluralize the word; hence, *Reconceptualizing the Literacies in Adolescents' Lives.*

Now, think about the following definition relative to literacy in a particular content area:

> The scientifically literate person knows the social implications of science and recognizes the role of rational thinking in arriving at value judgments and solving social problems. The SLP knows how to learn, to inquire, to gain knowledge, and to solve new problems. Throughout life the SLP continues to inquire, to increase his or her knowledge base, and uses that knowledge to self-reflect and to promote the development of people as rational human beings. (Victor & Kellough, 1997, p. 16)

If your answer to the interviewer's question in Activating Prior Knowledge 1.2 about literacy in your content area doesn't quite match this one, take comfort in knowing you are not alone. In the aptly named article "Exploring Reading Nightmares of Middle and Secondary School Teachers," Bintz (1997) reported on research showing that content area teachers " . . . feel betrayed because they were given no formal knowledge of reading in their teacher education training, frustrated because they have no personal experience with the teaching of reading, . . . overwhelmed because they were trained and hired to teach content, but are now being asked to also teach reading" (p. 210). The intent of this book is to develop your knowledge of content area literacy, as well as to provide you with instructional strategies that can increase your students' multiple literacies.

FIGURE *Phrases showing some current uses of the term* literacy.

cultural literacy	scientific literacy	media literacy	community literacy
civic literacy	computer literacy	critical literacy	functional literacy
mathematical literacy	digital literacy	geographic literacy	political literacy

In 1999, the International Reading Association (IRA) disseminated a position statement on *adolescent literacy*. Noting that "adolescents entering the adult world in the 21st century will read and write more than at any other time in human history," and that "they will need advanced levels of literacy to perform their jobs, run their households, act as citizens, and conduct their personal lives" (Moore, Bean, Birdyshaw, & Rycik, 1999, p. 99), the IRA's Commission on Adolescent Literacy offers seven principles for supporting adolescents' literacy growth, including "Adolescents deserve expert teachers who model and provide explicit instruction in reading comprehension and study strategies across the curriculum" (IRA, 1999, p. 104) and "Adolescents deserve teachers who understand the complexities of individual adolescent readers, respect their differences, and respond to their characteristics" (p. 105). Again, my goal is that this book will serve you as you strive to become the expert, understanding teacher called for here.

Rather than inundate you at this early point with more definitions, let me promise that throughout this book, I provide perspectives that will help you think about the aspects of literacy discussed in the chapters.

CONTENT AREA TEACHERS AND LITERACY

The mathematician John Allen Paulos (1988) coined the term *innumeracy* to refer to lay people's inability to read, write, talk, and think mathematically; in other words, their lack of mathematical literacy. Literacy plays a crucial role in learning within the disciplines. Yet, I find that students preparing to teach subjects at the middle and high school levels are often initially resistant to taking a literacy education course. Similarly, teachers already in the field frequently express frustration because they expect students to come into their classes as proficient readers, ready to use reading to learn algebra, global studies, or earth science. These teachers didn't realize when they were hired that teaching reading came with the territory. For numerous reasons, every teacher must be both a reader and a teacher of reading.

In actuality, many of your students will come to you unable to read well enough to learn from your course materials. Some may be new to the country and the English language; perhaps others didn't learn basic reading skills in the elementary grades due to inappropriate instruction, sickness, emotional obstacles, moving from place to place, learning disabilities, immaturity, social and economic disadvantages, or family turmoil. The list of causes is not as important as your realization that it is futile to blame students, teachers in prior grades, television,

BookTalk   1.1

A wonderful book illustrates the concept of subject area literacy. *Math Curse* (1995), by Jon Scieszka and Lane Smith, is narrated by a child whose math teacher, Ms. Fibonacci, announces, "YOU KNOW, you can think of almost anything as a math problem" (unpaged). The student indeed looks at all aspects of her life mathematically from that point on; she thinks in terms of measurements, graphs, and percentages as she hurries to the bus, eats, and sits in social studies class. She finally breaks what she has come to think of as this math curse, only to have another teacher, Mr. Newton, the next week muse, "YOU KNOW, you can think of almost everything as a science experiment . . . " (unpaged). This book is for all who have ever wondered what math has to do with real life.

or circumstances. It is your responsibility to accept each child as he comes into your class and help him to grow in learning as much as possible. This inevitably involves teaching literacy strategies, and research at the secondary level suggests that such teaching can have a positive impact on reading achievement when students face complex material (Bean & Readence, 1996, p. 23).

Even if all 120 students you see each day are reading and writing on grade level, this does not mean you are free of the responsibility to teach literacy skills. For one thing, the construction of sentences and the vocabulary used increase in difficulty in upper grade and adult-level texts, as concepts and information become more complex. Also, reading really *is* different in specific disciplines. Children who had a wonderful background in the primary grades and who comprehend stories very well often falter when they have to tackle expository text. The expectations of readers by authors are different in various fields; therefore, reading behaviors and attitudes must change accordingly. There are generic reading skills, and others that serve across a number of disciplines. Finally, there are some subject-specific reading skills that exist and must be taught. These skills are discussed in more detail throughout the book.

Whenever I supervise student teachers in a math classroom, I ask them, "Are you a mathematician?" They look at me with a puzzled expression; they've never asked themselves that question. But shouldn't the answer have to be *yes*? You wouldn't send your child to a violin teacher who didn't play the violin; neither would you take lessons from a yoga instructor who didn't practice the art herself. Maybe you won't ever be employed as a scientist or historian, but at some level you have to identify yourself as a practitioner in your field—at least as an active knowledge seeker and sharer. In other words, you have to be highly math literate, science literate, art literate, in order to be an excellent teacher within your discipline. You have to belong to the discourse community. You have to read in your field in order to keep current. You'll have much more credibility with the students you're asking to read and write if they recognize that you are a reader and writer, also. Routman (1995) advocates " . . . using our literate selves as models for teaching" (p. 177).

Numerous real-life examples illustrate academic ways of thinking and living within one's discipline. It has been noted of Einstein:

> No matter what he was doing, science was always present in his mind. When stirring tea, he noticed the tea leaves congregating at the center and not the circumference of the bottom of the cup. He found the explanation and linked it to something unexpectedly remote: the meandering of rivers. When walking on sand he noted with wonder what most of us have known unthinkingly; that damp sand gives firm footing although dry sand and sand immersed in water do not. Here, too, he found a scientific explanation. (Gardner, 1993, p. 127).

That's our goal: to help our students think like geographers, historians, economists, ecologists; to feel like they belong to the discourse communities related to the subjects they are studying. Wide and varied reading is the means to accomplish the goal. More reading correlates with better readers (Foertsch, 1992; U. S. Department of Education, 1999). Adolescents broaden and deepen their content knowledge when they read more (Allington, 2001), and, as they go through the grade levels, the gap widens between children who read a lot and those who read little (Stanovitch, 1986). It makes sense. The readers are getting practice time in; their skills are becoming automatic, like dribbling becomes for the kid who plays basketball hours each day, like finger movement becomes for the guitar player who chooses to spend significant amounts of time playing the instrument.

In this book, you'll meet children and adolescents, fictional and real, who practice their crafts and live an intellectually curious life. Our students can become proficient at performing in the disciplines we teach if we provide a rich environment for in-school exploration, motivation and resources for outside work and play related to our topics, and the skills needed to achieve growth and independence in the discourse community.

Frank Smith wrote of emerging readers "joining the literacy club" (1988). I invite you to join the ranks of teachers interested in pursuing effective ways of teaching literacy concurrently with and through their subject areas. There are wonderful regional and national professional educational organizations for whatever discipline you are preparing to teach. You might also consider obtaining a student membership in the International Reading Association, which includes a subscription to *The Journal of Adolescent and Adult Literacy* (or another journal of your choice). Through your own wide reading of texts in your field, plus educational literature and children's and adolescent literature, you will be on your way to becoming more *literacy literate.*

> **Getting Ready to Teach 1.2** *(see page 28)*

PREPARING TO TEACH LITERACY IN THE CONTENT AREAS

At this point I'd like you to try your hand at preparing materials and strategies to use with students in your content area classrooms. The next two exercises will help you begin.

First, create an anticipation guide for a text in your content area. The text can be a whole book, such as the one I provided for *The Giver,* or it can be a chapter in a textbook, or a newspaper or magazine article. The following page shows a sample of an anticipation guide prepared by Jeffrey S. Waldron, one of my college students, for a class on government.

Next, try giving a booktalk, perhaps modeled on the BookTalks in the introduction and this chapter, to your peers or to a group of middle or high school students. Choose one of your favorite books or a book you consider important in the discipline you will be teaching. Decide on your target audience. Do you want to convince your fellow college classmates, or seventh graders, or the parents of your tenth graders to read this book? What can you say that will entice them, make them want to go right home to start the book? You have a great deal of freedom for this experience; you can use props, ask for writing, invite dialogue, dance on your desk. In my classroom, I do insist on three rules for a booktalk:

1. Keep it short. Hold yourself to a maximum of three minutes if you don't require interaction from your audience. (Look back at my BookTalk for *The Giver*—I didn't require you to actually answer any questions; I just talked to you at that point.) If you

Anticipation Guide for Nothing But the Truth

by Avi

1. What do you think are some good reasons for suspending a student from school?

   _____

   _____

   _____

   _____

2. Is there ever any time when it is okay for a student not to follow rules in a school setting? If so, when? If not, why?

   _____

   _____

   _____

   _____

3. Respond *Agree* or *Disagree* to the following statements:

   _____ Students should always listen to the teacher, even if they think the teacher is wrong.

   _____ Some children are just bad, for no reason.

   _____ If children are bad, it is usually because of their parents or guardians.

   _____ Some teachers are just bad teachers.

   _____ You should be able to sing (or hum) our national anthem wherever and whenever you desire.

   _____ No matter what the situation, there are always better ways to discipline a student than suspension from school.

   _____ If a student has one bad grade on a report card, he/she should not be allowed to participate in school sports.

Now we are going to read the documentary novel *Nothing But the Truth* by Avi. After reading the book, you may want to rethink your answers. You can decide for yourself, in this story's conflict between a teacher and a student, who is in the right and who is in the wrong.

FIGURE 1.3 *Sample interactive booktalk.*

I've got some paper cups right here. And I've got this bottle of water. And I've got a promise. If you drink a single sip of my magic water, you will remain at your present age forever. You will never die. Take a paper cup if you want some. [Pass out cups.] I see some of you refused my offer. Why? People have searched for centuries for the Fountain of Youth! [Your remarks will depend on the answers you get, but the following are possibilities.] Oh, you don't want to survive all the people you love? Take enough for them, too. You feel that you're too young right now? Ok, take some for later; it will retain its magic for several years. Don't worry, it doesn't stop you from growing, learning, expe-

riencing new things. It merely prevents you from *aging.* [Allow for more discussion.]

As you may have guessed, I've lied to you. I got the water from the drinking fountain outside the door. But the book I have here, *Tuck Everlasting* by Natalie Babbitt (1975), has a spring with the property I've tried to tempt you with. The 11-year-old protagonist, Winnie Foster, finds the spring and a family who drank the water—87 years ago. Now, she has a decision to make. If you've ever wondered why things have to die, if you've ever pondered the mysteries of the life cycle, if you've ever thought about the concept of "forever," read this book to find out if and when Winnie drinks the water.

get the audience involved, as I model for you in Figure 1.3, use your discretion in deciding a time limit because there may be other objectives to accomplish simultaneously.

2. Do not start with the sentence, "The book I chose is _____." I know you can be more interesting than that. It's a good idea to get your audience thinking initially about a time, a place, an issue, a person, or a feeling, before you introduce the title of the book. They'll have something to connect the book *to* if you've already got them thinking.

3. Do not give a summary of the plot. Not only is this boring, it can actually *decrease* the listener's need and desire to read the book, which is exactly the opposite of your goal. And don't give away the ending. Most likely, the author can do a better job.

LEARNING STANDARDS

Standards is a term that is proving to be almost as complex and multidimensional as *literacy.* If someone should ask you which camp you're in, the one *for* or the one *against* mandated learning standards, beware! What exactly does this pollster mean by *standards?* And whose standards, which standards? Currently, there are local, state, and national standards representing a variety of content areas. Gratz (2000) points out two primary purposes of standards: "The first is economic: to address the concern that America is losing its competitiveness and the belief that both the country's and the students' best interests require demanding more from each child and each school. . . . The second . . . is to address the disparity between high- and low-achieving students" (p. 682).

He then distinguishes between content standards—what students should *know* in the core academic disciplines—and performance standards—what they should be able to *do.* He then cites several unintended negative consequences that resulted as standards were implemented, but concludes with a hopeful metaphor, "It is not too late to slow down the runaway train that is the standards movement" (p. 687). Similarly, Brady (2000) worries that " . . . behind the standards juggernaut and impelling it forward is the single, primary, simplistic and unexamined assumption that what the next generation most needs to know is what this generation knows" (p. 651).

The major national professional organizations representing the core academic disciplines developed standards to serve as *guidelines* for content area teachers. It is important to note that the standards for every one of the subject areas recognize the importance of literacy. For example, the National Council of Teachers of Mathematics (NCTM) standards contend that problem solving and meaning take precedence over computation and expect students to become "mathematically literate" (Ravitch, 1995, p. 127). At every level, the NCTM standards stress mathematics as *communication.* In order to achieve the standards set forth by the National Council for the Social Studies, which center around 10 themes such as global connections; civic ideals and practices; and production, distribution, and consumption, students must exercise a great number of literacy skills. Similarly, the National Academy of Sciences, noting that the nation has established as a goal that all students should achieve scientific literacy, developed the National Science Education Standards (1996) in order to make that a reality in the 21st century. The Academy states:

FIGURE **1.4** *Resources relating to learning standards.*

BOOKS

Chalker, D. M., & Hayes, R. M. (1994). *World Class Schools: New Standards for Education.* Lancaster, PA: Technomic Publishing Company, Inc.

Dendall, J. S., & Marzano, R. J. (1997). *Content Knowledge: A Compendium of Standards and Benchmarks for K–12 Education* (2nd ed.). Aurora, CO: McREL.

Kohn, A. (1999). *The Schools Our Children Deserve: Moving Beyond Traditional Classrooms and "Tougher Standards."* Boston: Houghton Mifflin.

Ohanian, S. (1999). *One Size Fits Few: The Folly of Educational Standards.* Portsmouth, NH: Heinemann.

Ravitch, D. (1995). *National Standards in American Education: A Citizen's Guide.* Washington, DC: Brookings Institute.

Tucker, M. S., & Codding, J. B. (1998). *Standards for Our Schools: How to Set Them, Measure Them, and Reach Them.* San Francisco: Jossey-Bass.

ARTICLES

Brady, M. (2000). The Standards Juggernaut. *Phi Delta Kappan, 81*(9), 649–651.

Falk, B. (2002). Standards-Based Reforms: Problems and Possibilities. *Phi Delta Kappan, 83*(8), 612–630.

Gratz, D. B. (2000). High Standards for Whom? *Phi Delta Kappan, 81*(9), 681–687.

Merrow, J. (2001). Undermining Standards. *Phi Delta Kappan, 82*(9), 652–659.

Smagorinsky, P. (1999). Standards Revisited: The Importance of Being There. *English Journal,* March, 82–88.

Thompson, S. (2001). The Authentic Standards Movement and Its Evil Twin. *Phi Delta Kappan, 82*(5), 358–362.

All of us have a stake, as individuals and as a society, in scientific literacy. An understanding of science makes it possible for everyone to share in the richness and excitement of comprehending the natural world. Scientific literacy enables people to use scientific principles and processes in making personal decisions and to participate in discussions of scientific issues that affect society. (p. ix)

It's beyond the scope of this book to go into depth about the standards movement, with the promises and hopes of its proponents and the worries and concerns of its critics. Figure 1.4 lists resources that you can explore to learn more and decide where you stand on this complex issue. The resources represent a variety of positions on the standards movement, so you can gather information, understand the arguments for and against the movement itself and certain methods of implementing the standards, and decide for yourself how standards-based teaching and curricula fit into your overall, emerging philosophy of teaching and learning. Chapter 10 discusses the connection between standards and the assessment of student learning.

How can you address learning standards relative to your content area in your long-term plans and daily lessons in a way that does not compromise your educational philosophy, yet meets the expecta-

tions of your school district, state, and national professional organizations? How can you ensure that your instruction is standards-based and still meet your individual students' needs? The strategies for preparing reading guides and for attending to your students' literacy growth provided throughout this book should give you some answers. Be cautious of the ready-made materials publishers provide to give students practice with meeting the various learning standards. Rarely, if ever, should you have to take time from your content instruction to work on achieving standards or practicing skills out of context. For example, plenty of worksheets ask students to answer questions based on maps and time lines, skills students are expected to know to meet social studies standards. But you might prefer to provide your students with a book like Peter Sis's *Starry Messenger: A Book Depicting the Life of a Famous Scientist, Mathematician, Astronomer, Philosopher, Physicist, Galileo Galilei* (1996). This biographical picture book won a Caldecott Honor Medal for its artwork. It contains time lines and maps within the story and in the margins, as well as quotes from Galileo and graphic symbols within pictures. It is a multilayered story that invites a reader to consider many perspectives and to understand Galileo as a scientist, a religious man, a prisoner in his own home, a well-rounded person with a brilliant mind and profound feelings. Students can examine the language and the unusual and provocative writing techniques Sis employs; they can think critically about the relation of religion and science as they read about Galileo's conflict with the authority of the church of his time and his pardon by that church several centuries later.

As you use a rich text such as *Starry Messenger*, you can be aware of what standards are being addressed during the course of this exciting learning experience. For example, national science standards propose that students learn the history of science and its evolution (National Research Council, 1994). Galileo typifies mathematical literacy, as defined by the NCTM, involving " . . . an individual's abilities to explore, to conjecture, and to reason logically, as well as to use a variety of mathematical methods effectively to solve problems" (1989, p. 6). The social studies standards (National Council for the Social Studies, 1994) cite skills such as reading maps and following a time line and a sequence of events. Sis's biography encourages the development of these skills.

A simple test that you can use when you are designing a reading guide or selecting activities from published materials is to ask yourself whether the same type of activity is likely to be used in an authentic, out of school setting. Readers of novels, no matter what age, do not stop after every chapter to write out answers to questions in complete sentences. On the other hand, when we are learning a new skill because we are intrinsically motivated or because we know acquiring that skill might help us get something else we want, we are willing to practice, sometimes repeating steps over and over. It could be anything from aerobics to piano playing to calligraphy. If we apply this test of authenticity, students come to understand that we try not to make them do anything merely for the sake of using up time, or passing tests, or "meeting the standards." They will trust us when we assign something that we've thoughtfully chosen and explain why it was chosen.

> *Getting Ready to Teach 1.3* (see page 28)

CONCLUSION

A goal of this chapter was to stimulate your thinking about—and add to your knowledge of—literacy: What is literacy, and how does it relate to learning standards and other aspects of your teaching? The learner is anything but passive. Elliot Eisner (2002) explains:

> We tend to think that the act of reading a story or reading a poem is a process of decoding. And it is. But it is also a process of encoding. The individual reading a story must *make* sense of the story; he or she must produce meanings from the marks on the page. The mind must be constructive, it must be active, and the task of teaching is to facilitate effective mental action so that the work encountered becomes meaningful. (p. 581)

Throughout the succeeding chapters, we'll be dealing with literacy processes as *constructive*. You'll see how the concept applies to all genres of text and all aspects of learning through literacy in your discipline. And you'll be making meaning yourself as you engage with the text and apply its principles.

CHAPTER ONE

Getting Ready to Teach

1.1 Think of ways to find out what reading means to your students. List some of these ways, or choose one and expound on how you might carry it out. If you're in contact with children or adolescents now, watch them in action and talk to them—get their ideas relating to reading, both in and out of school.

1.2 If, as the IRA's position paper on adolescent literacy says, teens deserve expert teachers who model and provide instruction in reading comprehension across the curriculum, you'll want to be one of those expert teachers. In writing, reflect about one or more ways you'll pay

attention to literacy issues in your classroom. How will you establish credibility as a literate person in your field?

1.3 Ask teachers you know what they think about the various learning standards in your field. How has attention to standards helped and/or hindered their teaching and their students' learning? Or, choose one or more of the national, state, or regional standards established for the subject you expect to teach. Then select a book, as I did with *Starry Messenger* above, and reflect on how it might be used in addressing the standard(s) you chose.

Affective and Social Aspects of Content Area Learning and Literacy

PART ONE

Passion, Motivation, and the Social Nature of Learning

PASSION, MOTIVATION, AND ENGAGEMENT

ACTIVATING PRIOR KNOWLEDGE 2.1

In your learning log or journal, write about something that you have been passionately interested in learning about at some point in your life. It can be from when you were very young, a "passing passion phase," or it can be a long-lasting or present insatiable curiosity. What (or whom) did you want to investigate? Where did you find information about this topic? With whom did you talk about your interest? What initiated your delving into the subject? Share your response with others before reading on.

I often ask my students to write about something they're interested in learning, and I have yet to find a student with nothing to say; pens start flying over paper very quickly, and by the time I announce that time is up, many faces have a bit of a glow. Here are a few samples that reflect the variety of subjects my students have been wrapped up in:

I have always been fascinated with earthquakes, tornadoes, wind. All my life I have picked up books that had anything to do with these topics. To this day I still pick up any book, whether it be a young child's reading book or a meteorologist's handbook.

The space program is something I have been passionate about since I first saw *The Right Stuff*. I thought those guys were the coolest people I had ever seen. So when my third grade teacher gave me a chance to do an extra credit research paper, I jumped at the chance. Since that time I wanted to be an astronaut. I don't have the eyesight for it, but I still love learning about it. I'm the only person I know that can sit through a seven-hour spacewalk and be thoroughly engrossed by it.

"A teacher who is attempting to teach without inspiring the pupil with a desire to learn is hammering on cold iron."

HORACE MANN

I can't tear myself away. I'll sit all day and watch Mission Control on the NASA channel while the astronauts sleep.

No matter your grade level or subject area, you can get to know your students' interests, letting them know you are interested in knowing them. Here is how one twelfth grader responded to her teacher's September survey about reading and writing practices:

In the past, I have written research papers on such topics as the Great Depression, the Ebola virus, and capital punishment. After I begin researching, it is almost like I am so interested in the topic that I forget I am gathering information for a paper, and feel like I'm reading for enjoyment. For example, I wrote the research paper about capital punishment in eighth grade English class, and this summer I was having an argument with one of my friends about why capital punishment was wrong. I could still remember all the information and disgusting facts that I learned while I was writing the paper. Also, after I finished my paper on the Ebola virus, I became so interested that I kept reading all the books even after I finished writing the paper. *The Hot Zone* [Preston, 1994] is still one of my favorite books.

In "Successful Dyslexics: A Constructivist Study of Passionate Interest Reading," Fink (1995/1996) discusses research involving 12 case studies of adults who were very successful in their professions (e.g., a company CEO, a biochemist, a neurologist, a physicist) despite having had major difficulty learning to read. Eleven of the 12 reported learning to read between the ages of 10 and 12, and they "grappled with profound problems with letter identification, word recognition, and sound analysis" (p. 273). Each participant was interviewed extensively in order to learn how they managed to succeed despite their difficulties. The researcher's hypotheses were not confirmed. "I expected to discover extraordinary bypass and compensation strategies. Presumably, continual frustration with basic skills would lead dyslexics to avoid reading. To my surprise, I found that these dyslexics were avid readers. . . . they rarely circumvented reading. On the contrary, they sought out books" (p. 272).

The common theme Fink found was that in childhood each had "a passionate personal interest, a burning desire to know more about a discipline that required reading. Spurred by this passionate interest, all read voraciously" (pp. 274–275). Their passions included biography, math, religion, poetry, novels, business, history, and science. Surely there are instructional implications of this study—we can foster reading and learning if we acknowledge individual interests and build on them as we teach. It doesn't have to be,

as was the case with these dyslexics, that school reading was discouraging and failure producing, while home reading was rewarding and pleasurable.

In this chapter, I provide suggestions for activating and increasing students' passion, engagement, and motivation; they're all connected, so I'll deal a bit with terms first. Csikszentmihalyi (1991) describes engaged reading as "flow," a state of total absorption. The value of engagement in reading is unquestionable; it is strongly associated with reading achievement (Guthrie & Wigfield, 2000), which is what we want for our students. In fact, engaged readers can provide themselves with self-initiated learning opportunities that are equivalent to years of education (Campbell, Voelkl, & Donahue, 1997). Researchers have focused on several aspects of engaged reading. For example, Turner (1995) and Oldfather and Dahl (1994) showed that students' intrinsic motivation, their enjoyment of reading for its own sake, is essential to engaged reading. Cambourne (1995) found engagement in literacy to involve a merger of qualities: holding a purpose, believing in one's capabilities, taking responsibility for learning, and seeking to understand. Cipielewski and Stanovitch (1992) found that students who read frequently and actively improve their comprehension of text.

Reading motivation, which is multifaceted, can be defined as *"the individual's personal goals, values, and beliefs with regard to the topics, processes, and outcomes of reading"* (Guthrie & Wigfield, 2000, p. 405, italics theirs), and can include intrinsic motivation (curiosity, preference for challenge, involvement), extrinsic motivation (external incentives, recognition, or rewards), and social motivation (interpersonal activities), leading to high achievement (Wentzel, 1996). Motivation is what activates behavior, so you can see how crucial it is to learning.

Teachers Can Foster Passionate and Engaged Learning

Bailey White is a first-grade teacher who learned to take advantage of the passion children display for particular themes. She credits maritime disasters for her teaching success. "Give me a man overboard or a good sinking ship, and I can teach a half-witted gorilla to read" (White, 1993, p. 170). She begins by having her class chant old sea chanties as they move their fingers under the words on their song sheets because she discovered that "when children get the idea that written words can tell them something absolutely horrible, half the battle of teaching reading is won" (p. 170). She uses Robert Ballard's *Exploring the Titanic: How the Greatest Ship Ever Lost Was Found* (1988) and though it is written at a fourth-grade reading level,

FICTIONAL CHARACTERS CAN BE PASSIONATE LEARNERS

A wonderful place for students to meet passionate learners their own age is between the covers of a book. I'll introduce you to a few of them in the following booktalks, and the pedagogical strategies discussed throughout this chapter will help you think about how you can use these or other stories about passionate learning and action in your discipline with your students.

BookTalk   2.1

Twelve-year-old Sarny doesn't have a whole lot of learning to be passionate *about* when the novel *Nightjohn* opens. She can't read because she's a slave, and slaves are forbidden to learn to read. She won't *need* book learning anyway; her master is just waiting for her to reach physical maturity so that she can be bred to produce more fine workers for the plantation.

Nightjohn *does* know how to read. The former slave returns from the North, risking limb and life to teach other slaves to read. Sarny accepts the challenge and the risk of becoming literate. To find out the consequences of the passion for learning, and the passion to spread learning, read *Nightjohn* (1993) by Gary Paulsen.

BookTalk   2.2

Meg Murry, the daughter of two scientists, is considered unusual among her peers because she is a girl who is gifted in math. Her little brother, Charles Wallace, is considered unusual in the community because he doesn't talk, at least not outside his home. His family knows that what is *really* unusual about him is his extremely high intelligence—we're talking genius-level intelligence. The siblings get the chance to use their gifts in a most unusual way. They must travel through time and space to rescue their father from the forces of evil on the planet Camazotz, where equality has been achieved by everyone being the same. Read *A Wrinkle in Time* (1962) by Madeleine L'Engle to join this physical, emotional, intellectual, and spiritual adventure. You'll never view *sameness* in the same way again!

BookTalk   2.3

Twelve-year-old Allegra faces a difficult choice. If she wishes to compete in the invitational Mozart competition, all other summer activities must be sacrificed. Her talent and passion for the violin determine her decision, but surprisingly, the areas in which she grows go far beyond the musical. And the people who end up being teachers and mentors to her go far beyond her dedicated music instructor. Is she the winner? Read Virginia Euwer Wolff's *The Mozart Season* (2000) to find out.

These books could be used together as a *text set*, which is explained later in this chapter.

the children display no difficulty with the harder words. White records her guilt-ridden worry that her use of the tragedy is exploitative, concluding, "In my whole career the *Titanic* and I will teach over a thousand children how to read—close to the number of people who lost their lives on that black night. Surely, for the sake of literacy, the spirits of those poor souls will forgive me" (p. 172).

Maria Shriver lists as the first and foremost of her *Ten Things I Wish I'd Known—Before I Went Out into the Real World* (2000), "Pinpoint Your Passion" (p. 1). She relates how her passion for the field of television news was sparked when she was in high school and worked on the Democratic presidential campaign. She advises, "Trust your gut, no matter what you expect your parents or teachers or anyone else will think of your choice. Lots of people don't know where to start. So try to pinpoint the field, the area, the kinds of people you want to be with. It's your life" (Lynnakyla, p. 8).

As teachers, our responsibility is twofold:

1. To nurture our own passion for the subjects we teach, the discipline we've chosen. We must read voraciously to extend our knowledge, refine our thinking, join the literacy club (Smith, 1988) of our field. We must do the same in the area of teaching, the profession we've chosen. Lundberg and Lynnakyla's research (1993) indicates that teachers who are avid readers have students who have higher reading achievement than do the students of teachers who rarely read. Gambrell (1996) hypothesizes that a reason for this is that the teachers who love to read are more likely to be explicit models for their students.

2. To share our passion with our students, hoping to spark interest and fascination in them. Gambrell advocates emphasizing how reading enhances and enriches our lives by reading excerpts of our current reading to our students, and letting students see us as real readers. We must also pinpoint or spark the passions of the students themselves, and help them use literacy to feed those passions and grow in wisdom.

Biographies Can Show Examples of Passion in the Disciplines

A powerful way to build enthusiasm for learning is to use the stories and words of actual people in fields of study. Very often geniuses are eccentric, and anecdotes about the way they work will fascinate your students. For example, math teachers can pass along the legacy of Paul Erdös, a brilliant man who forsook having his own family and home for the sake of mathematics, by reading excerpts from *The Man Who Loved Only Numbers* by Paul Hoffman (1998). Erdos traveled all over the world, staying at other mathematicians' homes, prodigiously publishing proofs that had stymied the best in the field for years or centuries, thinking about math for 18 hours a day. Yet, he had difficulty tying his shoes, cutting grapefruit, following directions, accomplishing mundane tasks. Science teachers can use Barbara McClintock as a role model for students as they try to think and behave in a scientific mode. The biography *A Feeling for the Organism: The Life and Work of Barbara McClintock*, by Evelyn Fox Keller (1983), shows how McClintock's love for the corn she studied helped her make breakthroughs in the field of genetics. Figure

2.1 lists other biographies of outstanding practitioners who show an extraordinary passion for their fields, as well as some who became activists to further their causes.

Two recent titles cleverly highlight ideas rather than people, but the pages capture the zeal, persistence, and enthusiasm of human practitioners: *Zero: The Biography of a Dangerous Idea* (Seife, 2000) and David Bodanis's *E=mc² : A Biography of the World's Most Famous Equation* (2001).

BookTalk 2.4

Imagine a young man so brilliant he earns his Ph.D. in his 20s and is part of the mathematical and scientific crowd based at Princeton in the late 1940s that includes Einstein. Imagine that man then being afflicted with schizophrenia and spending the next 30 years in and out of institutions. Imagine a committee arguing over the fittingness of awarding the Nobel Prize in Economics to a man who is severely mentally ill. These are just a few aspects of the drama that unfolds in *A Beautiful Mind: A Biography of John Forbes Nash* (1998) by Sylvia Nasar. It's loaded with human interest stories—there's a wife who takes care of Nash even after they're divorced; there's a son who eerily plays out the basic story of the early intellectual ascent followed by a plummet into mental illness. In addition, there are plenty of mathematical concepts such as the game theory that Nash was instrumental in conceiving. In terms of math history, you'll join the best of the best at their late afternoon mathematical teas on the Princeton campus. *A Beautiful Mind* is a beautiful book.

After you've enjoyed the book, you might wish to see Nash portrayed by Russell Crowe in the movie of the same name.

ACTION RESEARCH 2.A

Choose one of the biographies listed in Figure 2.1 or mentioned in the preceding section or the BookTalks, or another you find about a practitioner in the discipline you will teach. Read it, responding in your learning log about your own reactions, as well as any thoughts and ideas the text may stimulate in terms of your own teaching. What can you take from this book that will help your students grow in their knowledge of your subject?

FIGURE 2.1 *Stories of and by passionate practitioners and activists.*

Batten, M. (2001). *Anthropologist: Scientist of the People*. Boston: Houghton Mifflin.

Blue, R., & Naden, C. J. (1999). *Madeleine Albright: U. S. Secretary of State*. Woodbridge, CT: Blackbirch Press.

Blue, R., & Naden, C. J. (2001). *Benjamin Banneker: Mathematician and Stargazer*. Brookfield, CT: The Millbrook Press.

Christensen, B. (2001). *Woody Guthrie: Poet of the People*. New York: Knopf.

Dillard, A. (1974). *Pilgrim at Tinker Creek*. New York: Harper's Magazine Press.

Gardner, H. (1993). *Creating Minds: An Anatomy of Creativity as Seen through the Lives of Freud, Einstein, Picasso, Stravinsky, Eliot, Graham, and Gandhi*. New York: HarperCollins.

Giblin, J. C. (1997). *Charles Lindbergh: A Human Hero*. New York: Clarion Books.

Goodall, J., with Berman, P. (1999). *Reason for Hope: A Spiritual Journey*. New York: Warner Books.

Hager, T. (1998). *Linus Pauling and the Chemistry of Life*. New York: Oxford University Press.

Hill, J. B. (2000). *The Legacy of Luna: The Story of a Tree, a Woman, and the Struggle to Save the Redwoods*. San Francisco: HarperSanFrancisco.

Johnson, P. (1988). *Intellectuals*. New York: Harper & Row.

Johnson, R. (1997). *Braving the Frozen Frontier: Women Working in Antarctica*. Minneapolis: Lerner Discovery Series.

Jordan, M. (1998). *For the Love of the Game: My Story*. New York: Crown Publishers.

Kuklin, S. (1998). *Iqbal Masih and the Crusaders Against Child Slavery*. New York: Henry Holt.

Lawlor, L. (2001). *Helen Keller: Rebellious Spirit*. New York: Holiday House.

Loewen, N., & Bancroft, A. (2001). *Four to the Pole!: The American Women's Expedition to Antarctica, 1992–93*. New Haven, CT: Linnet Books.

Markham, L. (1997). *Jacques-Yves Cousteau: Exploring the Wonders of the Deep*. Austin, TX: Raintree Steck-Vaughn.

Matthews, T. (1998). *Light Shining Through the Mist: A Photobiography of Dian Fossey*. Washington, DC: National Geographic Society.

McKissack, P. C., & McKissack, F. L. (1998). *Young, Black, and Determined: A Biography of Lorraine Hansberry*. New York: Holiday House.

Patent, D. H. (2001). *Charles Darwin: The Life of a Revolutionary Thinker*. New York: Holiday House.

Paulsell, W. O. (1990). *Tough Minds, Tender Hearts: Six Prophets of Social Justice*. New York: Paulist Press.

Reef, C. (2001). *Sigmund Freud: Pioneer of the Mind*. New York: Clarion Books.

Rowley, H. (2001). *Richard Wright: The Life and Times*. New York: Henry Holt.

Russell, C. A. (2000). *Michael Faraday: Physics and Faith*. New York: Oxford University Press.

Sacks, O. (1995). *An Anthropologist on Mars: Seven Paradoxical Tales*. New York: Vintage Books.

Selzer, R. (1992). *Down from Troy: A Doctor Comes of Age*. New York: Morrow.

Siegel, B. (1995). *Marian Wright Edelman: The Making of a Crusader*. New York: Simon & Schuster.

THE PROBLEM OF ALITERACY

Learning, wanting to know about the world, other people and ourselves, seems to be as natural as breathing. When do these passions begin? Signs point to "very early." You may have known preschoolers who could tell you more about dinosaurs than you ever thought you wanted to know. Gallas (2001) describes a passionate six-year-old, Emily, whom she was convinced had started her life's work:

> Emily is a scientist. . . . During the year I taught her, in fine weather she spent all of her outdoor time pursuing insects, capturing them, and making containers to keep them in so that she could take them home with her for further observation. . . . She drew the insects and bugs she collected, wrote about them avidly, and offered a wealth of information about most of them to anyone who was interested. . . . At home she insisted on being read only nonfiction. . . . When she was left to herself, her interests in life were exclusively in natural science and/or things that were "real." I was surprised, therefore, to find out early in the school year that Emily believed she could talk to insects (and who am I to say she can't?) . . . she could be seen walking around engaged in serious conversation with whatever poor creature she had happened upon. (pp. 457–458)

BookTalk 2.5

Who painted *Irises,* which sold in 1988 for $49 million, while a patient at an asylum for the mentally ill? Who covered his walls with enormous cutouts in colors that were so bright he had to wear sunglasses to see them? Who spent time while she wasn't painting chopping rattlesnakes' heads off and collecting skulls? What artist almost suffocated while giving a lecture in a deep-sea diving suit? Whose nickname was Drella (combining Dracula and Cinderella)? Who developed ailments after four years of painting while 60 feet in the air with his head bent back? Whose first important commission was a portrait of surgeons dissecting a body? You can get the scoop on many famous and unique geniuses in *Lives of the Artists: Masterpieces, Messes (and What the Neighbors Thought)* by Kathleen Krull (1995). You'll find equally fascinating tidbits in its companion books: *Lives of the Writers: Comedies, Tragedies (and What the Neighbors Thought)* (1994), *Lives of the Presidents: Fame, Shame (and What the Neighbors Thought)* (1998), *Lives of the Musicians: Good Times, Bad Times (and What the Neighbors Thought)* (1993), *Lives of the Athletes: Thrills, Spills (and What the Neighbors Thought)* (1997), and *Lives of Extraordinary Women: Rulers, Rebels (and What the Neighbors Thought)* (2000).

BookTalk 2.6

Some of your students will love trees. They will also love Julia Butterfly Hill, the young woman whose memoir, *The Legacy of Luna: The Story of a Tree, a Woman, and the Struggle to Save the Redwoods* (2000), tells of her two-year stay atop a giant redwood to protest the destruction of the environment. After they read about her life on a platform 18 stories off the ground, writing and receiving hundreds of letters weekly from youthful supporters around the world, fighting with industrialists and politicians, they may be motivated to pursue more knowledge about nature and to take action in their own communities where nature is at risk.

As a result of interacting with Emily and other students, Gallas began to view imagination as a critical component of literacy learning. She let her discoveries guide her research on scientific imagination and her pursuit to take her students beyond basic skills, to move them "toward a deeper understanding of the texts, talk, and semiotic tools that lie at the heart of each discipline" (p. 461).

If passion for learning is so common in youngsters, I wonder why so many of our students can identify with the following passage from the first page of Norton Juster's childhood classic *The Phantom Tollbooth:*

> "I can't see the point in learning to solve useless problems, or subtracting turnips from turnips, or where Ethiopia is or how to spell February." And, since no one bothered to explain otherwise, [Milo] regarded the process of seeking knowledge as the greatest waste of time of all. (1961, p. 1)

And I wonder why it's so easy to find data from adults, even from authors, telling about their lack of learning, and specifically lack of reading, in school.

See if you can think of someone you know who could identify with popular young adult author Chris Crutcher's words:

> I still remember my two correct answers on my ninth-grade exam for *The Scarlet Letter.* I nailed the color, and the actual letter. The first answer was legitimate, since I had read far enough into the title to ferret it out. The second was luck; I began my guesses at the front of the alphabet. . . . The story wasn't about anything I knew. My teacher didn't give me anything contemporary with which to compare the complex issues addressed in the book, something that would have helped me relate those issues to my life. With that assignment, reading became something that was no longer fun for me. When it stopped being fun, I stopped doing it. (Monseau, 1996, p. x)

Crutcher read "a grand total of one book from cover to cover during my entire four years of high school, opting rather to invent titles for book reports, as well as stories to go with them" (p. 1).

Tamara, the senior you met earlier who loves reading for research papers, echoes Crutcher's sentiments:

> . . . A book is ruined by making us take every little thing apart. I understand that it is supposed to help us understand the book better, but when we have to answer a million questions about each tiny detail in the book, it is hard to enjoy the reading. I remember reading *The Good Earth* in ninth grade and not even being able to enjoy it because I had to answer five essay questions about each chapter. I think that it made it hard to concentrate on the book because I was just searching for answers to the questions. Looking

back, I think that I would have really liked the book had I not been so preoccupied with writing five essays per chapter.

ACTIVATING PRIOR KNOWLEDGE 2.2

"Are you a reader?" Ponder this question before you read on. Also, list some titles of books, magazines, poems, or short stories you have read for pleasure (not assigned for courses, not required for a job) over the past few years.

You may or may not have answered the question posed above in the affirmative. Certainly some of my students can fill pages with titles of books they've read, but these students are the exception. Here are some admissions from others (and remember, I don't have a random sample in my class; these are people who are preparing to spend their careers in classrooms):

- I must be pushed into reading a book.
- I am embarrassed to say I do not consider myself a reader.
- My first choice would not be to pick up a book and read, although I'd love to know all the information inside the book.
- All the way through school I got by reading as little as possible.
- To say that I am a reader would be a reach at best.

There is ample evidence that *aliteracy*, the phenomenon of people who are able to read perfectly well choosing not to, exists at all levels of our society (Cramer & Castle, 1994; Harris & Hodges, 1981). It's not just the children, it's not just the poor, it's not just the less educated. Some research has shown that many *teachers* do virtually no pleasure reading, maybe a book a year (Gardner, 1991). What can be done to reverse this unfortunate trend? How can we convince our students of the validity and worth of Merlin's advice in *The Once and Future King* (White, 1958) to the boy who would become King Arthur:

> The best thing for being sad . . . is to learn something. That is the only thing that never fails. You may grow old and trembling in your anatomies, you may lie awake at night listening to the disorder of your veins, you may miss your only love, you may see the world about you devastated by evil lunatics, or know your honour trampled in the sewers of baser minds. There is only one thing for it then—to learn. (p. 183)

FOSTERING CONTENT AREA LITERACY AS A SOLUTION TO ALITERACY

You might be wondering at this point what all this has to do with you; you may be in an education program because you want to teach high school math or music or health or art or science. I'll assume you are passionate about, or at least interested, in continuing to learn in the field you plan to teach. If you're going to be a social studies teacher, I'll assume you read the newspaper, follow current events and politics, read history books, and so on. But try this out. Ask the other people in your class, those planning to teach subjects other than the one you have picked, whether they read anything that will further their learning in *your* chosen field. Even your colleagues are often less than moderately interested in your area of knowledge! Can you imagine how many of your high school geography students or middle school math students will initially desire the treasure you have to offer and come to your class willing to work for it?

So, it appears you have a double problem. Many of your students will care virtually nothing for the subject area you love, and they may be aliterate to boot. Am I trying to discourage you before your idealism has even been given a chance in the schools? Far from it. You hold the key to the solution to both halves of the dilemma. Research shows that instructional practices can increase or contribute to a decline in students' reading motivation (Guthrie, Cox, Anderson, Harris, Mazonni, & Rach, 1998). Subsequent chapters explain how you can help your students acquire a variety of literacy strategies and study skills relevant to content areas. This chapter, however, concentrates on how you can get and keep your students *wanting* to read and to learn more about physics, English grammar, art history, ancient cultures, number theory—any and all aspects of the curriculum you may be responsible for teaching. We face a huge challenge, but, as Milo discovered after rescuing the princesses Rhyme and Reason in *The Phantom Tollbooth*, "so many things are possible just as long as you don't know they're impossible" (p. 247).

The first step toward a solution to student apathy or disinterest can be to increase the breadth and depth of the reading and writing and learning that *teachers* and *preservice teachers* do. In a classic study (Rieck, 1977), 300 students of 14 content area teachers were asked whether their teacher liked to read: 20 percent said yes, 33 percent said no, and 47 percent didn't know. If you recall some of your own high school teachers and ask yourself that same question, you'll get some idea of whether the situation has changed over the years. My goal is to challenge, convince, and help you to become, if you are ready, a person who is such an avid reader that you cannot help but enthusiastically share the wealth with your students. Teaching and promoting literacy is not about telling students to read and checking to see that they're doing it; rather, you can show them what you're reading and explain how you find and select material, make choices as you're reading, and work to comprehend and evaluate ideas.

Let me talk for a moment with the prospective math teachers in the class; if this is not your area, know that what I say can be generalized to your subject also. I chose math because my personal conversion to lifelong learning in this discipline has been the most recent and most surprising to me.

I was a fine math student in high school, not particularly math-phobic or math-anxious. I studied hard, I tested well, and, when I did think about math, it was as something separate from anything else I did. For a long time, I got along in my adult life with a minimum of mathematical activity. It wasn't until I began teaching college education courses in Content Area Literacy that I made a magnificent self-discovery. I loved math! Math was enticing, beautiful, fascinating, aesthetically exhilarating! What caused this revelation? When I went looking for books to help my math education students see the value of teaching reading and having classroom libraries like the rest of the disciplines, I encountered math books that were written in words rather than in symbols and school-type exercises. I met people who devoted their lives to the love of the discipline; in books I met geniuses who had friends, enemies, ambitions, and failures. I bought myself a treat that proved to be the start of my personal math library, *Five Equations that Changed the World: The Power and Poetry of Mathematics* by Michael Guillen (1995). Such books changed my world, and my outlook on the world of math. No one had ever told me about the relationship of math to music, to art, to philosophy, to language. Figure 2.2 lists examples of books now in my

---

FIGURE 2.2 *Math titles for a classroom library.*

Benjamin, A., & Shermer, M. B. (1998). *Mathemagics: How to Look Like a Genius Without Really Trying*, (2nd ed.). Los Angeles: Lowell House.

Berlinski, D. (1995). *A Tour of the Calculus.* New York: Pantheon Books.

Berlinski, D. (1999). *The Advent of the Algorithm: The Idea that Rules the World.* New York: Harcourt Brace.

Burns, M. (1978). *This Book Is About Time.* Boston: Little, Brown.

Carroll, L. (2000). *The Annotated Alice.* New York: Norton.

Cole, K. C. (1998). *The Universe and the Teacup: The Mathematics of Truth and Beauty.* New York: Harcourt Brace.

Hardy, G. H. (2001). *A Mathematician's Apology.* Cambridge: Cambridge University Press.

Hersh, R. (1997). *What Is Mathematics, Really?* New York: Oxford University Press.

Hoffman, P. (1998). *The Man Who Loved Only Numbers: The Story of Paul Erdös and the Search for Mathematical Truth.* New York: Hyperion.

King, J. P. (1992). *The Art of Mathematics.* New York: Fawcett Columbine.

Kuhn, H. W., & Nasar, S. (Eds.). (2001). *The Essential John Nash.* Princeton, NJ: Princeton University Press.

Lesmoir-Gordon, N., Rood, W., & Edney, R. (2001). *Introducing Fractal Geometry.* Lanham, MD: Totem Books.

Maor, E. (1998). *Trigonometric Delights.* Princeton, NJ: Princeton University Press.

Pappas, T. (1993). *Fractals, Googols, and Other Mathematical Tales.* San Carlos, CA: Wide World/Tetra.

Pappas, T. (1994). *The Magic of Mathematics: Discovering the Spell of Mathematics.* San Carlos, CA: Wide World/Tetra.

Paulos, J. A. (1980). *Mathematics and Humor.* Chicago: The University of Chicago Press.

Paulos, J. A. (1995). *A Mathematician Reads the Newspaper.* New York: Basic Books.

Perl, T. (1993). *Women and Numbers.* San Carlos, CA: Wide World Publishing.

Peterson, I. (2001). *Fragments of Infinity: A Kaleidoscope of Math and Art.* New York: Wiley.

Peterson, I., & Henderson, N. (2000). *Math Trek: Adventures in the Math Zone.* New York: Wiley.

Schmante-Besserat, D. (2000). *The History of Counting.* New York: Scholastic.

Singh, S. (1997). *Fermat's Enigma: The Epic Quest to Solve the World's Greatest Mathematical Problem.* New York: Walker.

Wright, R. (2000). *Nonzero: The Logic of Human Destiny.* New York: Pantheon.

BookTalk   2.7

Toward the end of the nineteenth century, a book was published that has remained a mathematical classic: *Flatland* by Edwin Abbott. The main character, A. Square, lives pretty comfortably in a two-dimensional world, not thinking beyond that until he's taken on a journey to other dimensions with societies of their own. It's a book that really exercises the brain while providing lots of playful situations, and it's a satire of Victorian society to boot. If you explore *Flatland*, you'll be able to join a contemporary community of fans who will delight you with their websites and their interpretations and puzzles. And now, more than a century later, a sequel has appeared. It seems that A. Square's great-great-grand-daughter, Victoria Line, has come across his diary in her attic, leading her to an adventure through 10 dimensions. Read Ian Stewart's *Flatterland: Like Flatland Only More-so* (2001) to travel through *mathiverse* with Victoria.

about life, or about what happens when one loves to read. A spontaneous dialogue usually emerges at the close of each book talk; students see the presenter as a fellow learner" (Morley, 1996, p. 131). Students keep track of their guests and the titles they recommend on a student-designed "faculty family tree" with each of the disciplines delineated and photos of the speakers on the branches. Morley tries to obtain the discussed books for the classroom library.

THE SOCIAL NATURE OF LEARNING

ACTIVATING PRIOR KNOWLEDGE   2.3

In your learning log, take a moment to respond to the following assertion: "Learning is social." What does that short statement mean to you? Do you agree with it? Was the assertion borne out in the biography you read for Action Research 2.A? How does it relate to your own learning and to how students are taught in classroom settings?

classroom library. I also recommend *The Journal of Recreational Mathematics.*

We hear so much about math anxiety and see evidence of innumeracy and math avoidance in our schools, but I rarely see a classroom library in a math teacher's room with books that could make an enormous difference in a child's life. You can change this scenario as you enter the field of teaching. If we all work together to enable our students to be wide readers, they'll come to you able to learn the math you are ready to teach them. If our students have technology teachers, economics teachers, earth science teachers, physical education teachers, and administrators who are readers themselves, readers of materials both within and beyond the confines of their disciplines, they will profit in ways we cannot even predict right now. We, the teachers, are models for our students; there must be no aliteracy among the faculty of the schools to which we send our children. Learning will come alive for all. Teacher burnout will become a virtual impossibility.

Sharon Morley is a high school English teacher who lives this philosophy. She invites fellow teachers of various subjects, plus principals, her superintendent, and people from the community, to visit her classes and discuss their pleasure reading. Students might be surprised to know that their principal is a Civil War buff, that the gym teacher reads poetry. Morley explains, "Some presenters use 5 or 10 minutes; some use the entire period, spinning the book talk into an accompanying lesson about history,

Current theories of motivation recognize how learning is fostered by social interaction (McCombs, 1989; Oldfather, 1993). Research indicates that collaboration promotes higher-level cognition, desire to read, and achievement (Almasi, 1995). When students have a sense of belonging in the classroom, along with a caring teacher, they are more likely to be motivated to read (Wentzel, 1997). From a body of research, Gambrell (1996) concludes that opportunities for talking with others about books are an important factor in developing motivated readers, and supports the contention that social interactions, as well as teachers who explicitly model reading behavior and provide appropriate reading-related incentives, have a positive influence on reading achievement.

Psychologist Lev Vygotsky set forth a theory of learning and instruction predicated on the assertion that learners could not be separated from the cultural, historical, and social context of what they were learning, and that learning resulted from interactions. He coined the phrase *zone of proximal development*, defined as "the distance between the actual development as determined by independent problem solving and the level of potential development as determined through problem solving under adult guidance or in collaboration with more capable peers" (1978, p. 86). Think about times when you have been frustrated by a task because it was simply too difficult, way beyond your present capabilities. Now, think of times, perhaps in school, when you complete assignments or solve problems that were extremely easy for you. Neither scenario is good for the learner. Vygotsky recognized that "what the child can do in cooperation today he can do alone tomorrow" (1962, p. 104). The teacher's responsibility is to assess where the student is and to *scaffold* instruction so that what is being taught is beyond the student's independent level, but not so far beyond that it can't be done with assistance. To understand the concept of scaffolding, think of the image of a scaffold on a building, providing support for as long as it is needed; teachers can help students stretch, grow, and accept academic challenges that are within their reach providing they have the resources to support their efforts.

Scaffolding is not an easy task, but when teachers teach to the middle, neither the high achievers nor the struggling readers are being taught in their zone of proximate development. When you provide a range of materials and options for students, and let them have some choice in selecting what materials they will use and how they will achieve goals, you can teach them to find materials that are within the range that is right for them, neither too hard nor too easy (Ohlhausen & Jepson, 1992; Roller, 1996).

There are many ways you can organize your courses and lessons to put Vygotsky's ideas into practice. McMahon (1996), for example, explains how she and her colleagues designed the Book Club Program, which viewed the teacher's instructional role as crucial, yet also incorporated the practice of students acting as more knowledgeable others for their peers. The Book Club consisted of daily, small, student-led discussion groups guided by the students' log entries; the issues to be discussed were initiated by the students themselves. The teachers taught the students how to handle the authority involved in leading discussions, and they monitored peer interactions continually in order to determine how best to provide support and further instruction. The learning and the products that resulted from this teaching method showed the teachers that the students were learning a lot from social interaction.

You will be able to think of ways to use Vygotsky's theory as you design your courses and plan the instruction of your curricular content. Collaborative groups, peer tutoring, projects involving social interaction are all appropriate and helpful. Many of the strategies and instructional methods introduced and developed next stress the social nature of learning.

PART TWO

Classroom Organization and Practices that Foster Passionate Learning, Social Interaction, and Motivated Literacy

In *Beyond Numeracy: Ruminations of a Numbers Man* (1991), author John Allen Paulos, during what he calls a "mathematical stream of consciousness," made connections between what he saw while driving into New York City one day with mathematical concepts such as averages, logic, probability, and estimation. He concludes:

> For most non-scientists, what's most important in science education is not the imparting of any particular set of facts (although I don't mean to denigrate factual knowledge) but the development of a scientific habit of mind: How would I test that? What's the evidence for it? How does this relate to other facts and principles? The same, I think, holds true in mathematics education. Remembering this formula or that theorem is less important for most people than is the ability to look at

a situation quantitatively, to note logical, probabilistic, and spatial relationships, and to muse mathematically. (p. 6)

The same principle holds true for English, social studies, foreign language study, music, health studies, business, technology, physical education, and art. We content area teachers have the responsibility

---

"It is easier to enhance creativity by changing conditions in the environment than by trying to make people think more creatively."

CSIKSZENTMIHALYI, 1996, P. 1

and challenge of helping our students to think in ways conducive to the learning of our respective subjects long after they have left our classes and may have forgotten what element follows zinc on the periodic table. It is the organization and atmosphere of our classrooms, in addition to our methods of instruction and the materials we use, that can help us achieve the goal for our students that Paulos helps us visualize. The next sections introduce structures and strategies to help make our classrooms places where students are enticed, intellectually stimulated, and motivated to learn with others and independently.

CREATING A CONTENT LITERACY WORKSHOP SETTING

Some teachers have chosen to turn their classrooms into *workshops.* This seems sensible because through the centuries, artists have had studios where interns and fledgling artists have learned alongside the masters, observing, experimenting, practicing the craft, asking questions, socializing. Picture your students studying your subject that way with you.

Perhaps the most widely read book on reading and writing workshops is Nancie Atwell's *In the Middle: Writing, Reading, and Learning with Adolescents* (1987), which describes the author's experience transforming her eighth grade English classroom into an inviting place for young people to explore literacy. It's not a how-to book explaining the one right way to implement a workshop approach; rather, it draws a picture of vibrant learning as students self-select books from various genres from the classroom library, choose to write for authentic purposes, talk freely with each other and their teacher, participate in mini-lessons, and grow in knowledge and skill. Atwell gives examples of how she conferenced with students, planned mini-lessons based on her ongoing assessment of the students' work, and struggled with daily planning and organizational decisions. In 1998, Atwell updated her experiences in *In the Middle: New Understandings about Writing, Reading, and Learning*, detailing her reflections, growth, new areas of exploration, and more examples of students' workshop products. The reading–writing workshop approach has been shown to work with other grade levels (Atwell, 1990) and other content areas, including science (Saul, 1994), social studies (Brown, 1994; Kneeshaw, 1999; Shafer, 1997), and math (Borasi & Siegel, 2000).

A few of the elements common to all or most workshop classrooms include:

STUDENT CHOICE. A classroom workshop is student-centered. The teacher knows the students as individuals, so can suggest particular books and materials to fit their needs and match their learning styles. Seldom will you walk into the room to find all of the students reading the same thing at the same time. A classroom library containing a variety of genres of trade books, as well as reference materials and magazines, is arranged invitingly, because there is a relatively high association between the size of a classroom library and student reading achievement (Elley, 1992).

STRUCTURE. It might appear to an outsider that the structure of a workshop classroom is quite loose because some students might be walking around or talking, while others are writing, reading, or listening to the teacher or exploring the Internet. Actually, there must be consistency and an organization that matches the goals of the class. Students have to know what to expect from the teacher and their classmates and what is expected of them. Time blocks for various responsibilities and a list of rules are likely to be posted in the room; routines can be depended upon.

TALKING AND LISTENING. Talk is valued and necessary in a workshop. Individual conferences between student and teacher are common, as are small group conferences among students. Students share information they've discovered, read drafts of their work to classmates, question each other, formulate projects, and talk out ideas. Literature circles, explained later in more detail, are a familiar occurrence in workshop classrooms. Social interaction is encouraged as a way for learners to develop. Chapter 8 focuses on these aspects in more detail.

WRITING. As stressed throughout this book, the language components of reading, writing, talking, and listening are interrelated—good literacy education does not separate them or treat them in an isolated manner; neither is writing confined to English class. Although Chapter 7 focuses specifically on the topic of writing in the content areas, I hope that the book as a whole helps you see all aspects of literacy working together. Very often teachers refer to reading–writing workshop as one entity. Other teachers incorporate more writing than reading, or vice versa, which may be appropriate for their particular teaching situation. In any event, many types of writing occur in a workshop classroom for many purposes.

In the Middle (Atwell, 1987) struck a chord with thousands of teachers at all grade levels; hundreds of books, articles, and conference presentations have

FIGURE 2.3   *Professional resources dealing with a workshop approach.*

Brown, C. S. (1994). *Connecting with the Past: History Workshop in Middle and High Schools.* Portsmouth, NH: Heinemann.

Cordeiro, P. (1994). *Whole Learning: Whole Language and Content in the Upper Elementary Grades.* Katonah, NY: Richard C. Owen Publishers.

Graves, D. (1993). *A Fresh Look at Writing.* Portsmouth, NH: Heinemann.

Hansen, L. (1987). *When Writers Read.* Portsmouth, NH: Heinemann.

Hornsby, D., Sukarna, D., & Parry, J. (1986). *Read On: A Conference Approach to Reading.* Portsmouth, NH: Heinemann.

Hornsby, D., Sukarna, D., & Parry, J. (1986). *Write On: A Conference Approach to Writing.* Portsmouth, NH: Heinemann.

Roller, C. M. (1996). *Variability Not Disability: Struggling Readers in a Workshop Classroom.* Newark, DE: International Reading Association.

documented how teachers at all grade levels and in all subjects have adapted Atwell's principles to match their students' needs and their own philosophies and curricular demands.

Linda Rief, an eighth-grade language arts teacher who modified Atwell's methods to make them her own, described her experience with instruction and learning in a workshop setting in *Seeking Diversity* (1992). She incorporated a lot of art as students explored ideas in and created responses to novels they read. The book has color photographs of some finished products and works in progress, along with quotes from the students showing their reflection, their choices, their revision processes, and their feelings about their accomplishments and struggles.

Connecting with the Past: History Workshop in Middle and High Schools (Brown, 1994) relates the collaborative efforts of a classroom history teacher and a college professor to convert a conventional history class into a studio where students could imitate the role of professional historians. The students used primary resources and wrote stories rather than traditional reports. Multiple perspectives and many interpretations of the past were presented, and students were encouraged to reflect, think critically, form opinions, take stances. Students belonged to history talk groups, and they were taught about various stages of the writing process and were mentored as they revised major pieces of writing in a variety of genres. The book explains how a unit on the Holocaust proceeded using a workshop approach, complete with quotes from students and examples from their creative work.

Figure 2.3 lists resources that describe various ways teachers have implemented a literacy workshop in content areas.

It's true that teachers work within constraints, and that not every one of you could or should have a classroom turned totally over to a studio approach and a workshop setting. But there are all sorts of variations on the theme; some of you may choose to have a workshop once a week, or for one month out of the year, or for part of each class if you have block scheduling. There may be certain aspects of the studio classroom that you like and can apply to your particular style of teaching and the organization of your course. Perhaps the most important thing you can take away from reading about workshop classrooms is the enthusiasm, liveliness, and love of learning so evident in the educational literature on the topic.

LITERATURE CIRCLES

Literature circles, which can be part of a workshop approach or used on their own, give students the opportunity to share responses to what they read as they learn from classmates' insights and reactions. The teacher might or might not participate, and there may or may not be guide questions, depending on the purposes and needs of the participants. (Recall the literature circle guide questions I supplied for *The Giver* in the Introduction.) Questions about and suggestions for discussion topics can be very helpful to get the talk going in certain groups, especially for students who are new to learning via sharing and listening, but may be totally unnecessary or even impede the progress of veteran discussion group participants. Teacher decision making in terms of how much and what kinds of facilitation and guidance to provide is crucial.

The size of literature circles can vary, from the whole class to pairs of students. Usually the circle consists of people who have read and responded to the same work of literature, and sometimes the group may then share its knowledge with the whole class. Figure 2.4 provides guidelines for teaching with literature circles.

The following box offers an example from my own teaching to help you see how literature circles can work in a history class that is studying Europe during World War II, and Figure 2.5 is an example of a *text set* (Harste & Short, 1988; Weaver, 1994)—copies of several related texts put together for the purpose of sharing and discussion—consisting of stories about or memoirs written by people who learned English as a second language. These books contain personal stories of struggles, triumphs, losses, and insights that can help all of the students in your classes better understand language, culture, and the human

CONTENT AREA LITERATURE CIRCLES IN ACTION

I begin by giving booktalks, with the aid of a classroom wall map of Europe, for several books that take place during the time period we're studying. Notice how I work in some geography knowledge and map reading as I introduce the books:

> Look at this map of Europe and locate Denmark. If you were living in Denmark during World War II and needed to help a Jewish family escape the country, what might be a logical plan? The Danish people did what was reasonable given their geography; they hid people on boats and sent them north to Sweden. But of course the Nazis were logical and knowledgeable about geography, too, so this method became increasingly difficult and risky. *Number the Stars*, by Lois Lowry (1989), is a Newbery Medal winner that tells of one young girl's courage as she tries to help her best friend flee the country.

> Here's a different scene. *Waiting for Anya*, by Michael Morpurgo (1990), also involves helping Jewish children flee for their lives. But the action takes place in France, and the geography is different. See these mountains between France, which was occupied by the Germans during World War II, and Spain, which was not? There are children hidden in these mountains. There are border patrols to be evaded. Read this work of historical fiction to learn about the intelligence, skill, and bravery necessary for the rescue operations that really happened here.

> Tiny Holland. Picture one family here, the Ten Booms—Christians who are hiding Jews. Christians who get caught and sent to Ravensbruck. Exactly one member of the family leaves alive, and she subsequently writes *The Hiding Place* (1971). This is a nonfiction account of Corrie Ten Boom's experiences and her struggle to understand them in terms of her future, her religion, her humanity. You can learn from this humble woman if you'll enter her hiding place by reading this book.

> Then there's Germany itself; its Jewish citizens were trapped. *Four Perfect Pebbles*, by Lila Perl and Marion Blumenthal Lazan (1996), is a biographical account of the Blumenthal family's six and a half years in refugee, transit, and prison camps. Marion was nine years old when she arrived at Bergen-Belsen, the terrible concentration camp where Anne Frank and so many others died. If you choose this book, you'll learn how the child used her imagination and a game she made up to keep hope alive amidst the despair.

My students choose from these selections—the books represent a range in terms of difficulty and maturity level. After independent reading and responding in learning logs, I ask my readers to form circles in the four corners of the room to talk over what they have read and written. Without exception, students tell me they learned from listening to other readers. Reactions to the texts vary, but they are usually strong. Different parts of the stories have an impact on different students; some pick up details or nuances that others miss, some talk about their own discoveries and feelings during the reading process, some make connections with other works of literature or with information from their history textbooks. One reader might bring up the author's writing style, which others hadn't noticed; someone else may tell of a personal experience the book made her remember and think about in a new way. Insights lead to more insights as the students talk with each other.

As a follow-up activity to the discussion circles, I ask each group to select a member to role play a character from the book its members read; we hold a "talk show" with the panel that sits in the front comparing and contrasting experiences while fielding questions from the audience. The result is that some of my students later read at least one of the other books from this text set on their own. All of the students end up understanding more about Europe during World War II, and come to a social studies textbook better able to comprehend the content of the chapter on World War II. They are willing to explore primary documents and other resources related to this segment of the curriculum. Literature circles cause ripples that last a long time.

FIGURE 2.4   *Guidelines for teaching with literature circles.*

1. Prepare a text set of books, magazines, or other sources on one topic or theme.
2. Prepare a study or discussion guide for the materials (optional).
3. Give booktalks to introduce each of the books and important content concepts.
4. Allow students to select from the texts.
5. Have students read independently and respond in learning logs.
6. Ask students to join discussion circles with others who have read the same text.
7. Have student representatives from each group share an aspect of the text with the whole class in some format (e.g., talk show, role play a character).

FIGURE 2.5   *A text set containing fiction and nonfiction books about the experience of learning English.*

Aliki. (1998). *Marianthe's Story: Painted Words and Spoken Memories.* New York: Greenwillow Books.

Alvarez, J. (1992). *How the Garcia Girls Lost Their Accents.* New York: Plume.

Anzaldúa, G. (1987). *Borderlands = La Frontera: The New Mestiza.* San Francisco: Spinsters/Aunt Lute.

Hoffman, E. (1989). *Lost in Translation: A Life in a New Language.* New York: Dutton.

Kingston, M. H. (1976). *The Woman Warrior.* New York: Knopf.

Kopelnitsky, R., & Pryor, K. (1994). *No Words to Say Goodbye.* New York: Hyperion.

Little, J. (1987). *Little by Little: A Writer's Education.* Ontario, Canada: Viking Kestrel.

Medina, J. (1999). *My Name Is Jorge: On Both Sides of the River.* Honesdale, PA: Wordsong/Boyds Mills.

Na, A. (2001). *A Step from Heaven.* Asheville, NC: Front Street.

Rodriguez, R. (1982). *Hunger of Memory: The Education of Richard Rodriguez, an Autobiography.* Boston: D. R. Godine.

spirit. If you have single copies of these titles, a group can use them to read individually with the purpose of sharing the information with others.

ACTIVITIES INVOLVING COLLABORATION AND COOPERATIVE LEARNING

Literacy workshops and literature circles in content area classes capitalize on the social nature of learning. Another way to incorporate positive social interaction while building enthusiasm is through the use of collaborative projects using cooperative learning. If you look back at the activities suggested in the early chapters, you'll see that many ask readers and writers to communicate, collaborate, and learn from each other in various ways. Intellectual development comes with and through interaction with others, both peers and those more accomplished in a skill or knowledge area. Therefore, teachers should encourage students to *collaborate*—to work together to solve problems and discuss curricular issues and readings. During the last

several decades, researchers have implemented and studied a number of techniques for *cooperative learning*, where students are given roles and assignments that require the cooperation of group members to achieve a learning goal. Research confirms that thinking becomes deeper and responses grow more complex when students are encouraged to defend positions, ponder, and listen during a discussion (Almasi, 1995). Cooperative learning has been linked to increased academic achievement at all ability levels (Stevens & Slavin, 1995). Vermette (1998) provides evidence that supports the positive effects of cooperative learning on achievement, as well as motivation and self-esteem. This is true for both genders and all ethnicities, and includes those students with various disabilities. Cooperative learning outcomes include retention, application and transfer of principles and concepts, verbal abilities, problem-solving abilities, creative ability, divergent thinking, productive controversy, awareness and utilization of individual capabilities, and the ability to understand and take on others' perspectives (Johnson & Johnson, 1999).

Cooperative learning focuses on both the curricular or discipline knowledge students need, and the social interactions among students as they explore and debate ideas, share information with peers, and take on responsibility for a group's success and accomplishments, as well as individual learning. Many teachers have students working in small groups, but in order to qualify as cooperative learning, the criteria represented by the mnemonic PIGSS must be met:

Positive interdependence (students must be able to work together); Individual accountability (each student is still assessed on what he or she knows); Group processes (a structure exists for how students will work together); Social skills (particular social skills are emphasized during group work); and Specific tasks (students work together to achieve a particular goal). (Lasley, Matczynski, & Rowley, 2002)

Jigsaw (Aronson, Blaney, Stephan, Sikes, & Snapp, 1978) and Jigsaw II (Slavin, 1986), specific cooperative learning strategies, involve dividing a text or project into manageable parts and having individuals learn from and teach each other. I'll give an example from my own teaching of preservice secondary teachers. If a curricular goal is for middle school science students to understand the workings and interconnections of the body's organs, I divide the class (let's say 16 students) into four heterogeneous "base groups" of four. I pass out copies of the following books by Seymour Simon: *The Heart*, *Muscles*, *The Brain*, and *Bones*. Each base group decides who will become the "expert" on which subtopic, and the "experts" read the appropriate book for homework that night. The following day, the class regroups into "expert groups," so that, for example, all the students who have chosen *Muscles* meet together to discuss the text, highlight main points, ask others for clarification, and decide how best to teach the topic to their base group. The *Heart* group meets in another corner, doing the same, and so on. Then, the base groups meet once again, where each "expert" is responsible for teaching about one organ to the group. The teacher provides needed materials, facilitates the discussions, is available for consultation and troubleshooting, and encourages the presenters. At the end of the lesson, all 16 students should understand the main points from all of the books and have had the opportunity to synthesize information and make connections with their peers. Their speaking and listening skills are enhanced simultaneously.

The rewards of working together can be great. I introduce my students to artists Diane and Leo Dil-lon, who have worked jointly for over 40 years, developing the concept of "the third artist"—the fusion of their separate talents into a greater collaborative genius. "The third artist is that place in every collaboration; the crystallization of different vantage points, a place neither of us would go by ourselves. It took practice, patience, and trial and error. The challenge was to let the art evolve freely as it went from person to person without trying to control it from our separate point of view" (Pavonetti, 2001, p. 47).

Before putting students in collaborative groups, teachers can tell stories and provide resources about scientific advances that occurred as a result of teamwork. It's important that the students realize they are modeling their learning processes after the real thing. So, for example, a classroom library could contain a biography of the Curies; Richard Feynman's memoirs of working at Los Alamos with the team studying the nuclear bomb; James Watson's *The Double Helix* (1980), along with Francis Crick's reflective *What Mad Pursuit* (1988). Or a teacher could institute math or science "teas" to discuss principles and dilemmas, perhaps recalling the Princeton afternoons of the late 1940s, as Einstein, Nash, Oppenheimer, von Neumann, Gödel, Wigner, Lefschetz, Church, Steenrod, and other brilliant teachers and students gathered to take part in mathematical gossip and share readings of papers, to participate in a true learning community. Collaborative strategies can create an atmosphere conducive to great discovery and contributions in any field.

As you read the following scenario, imagine how you can apply some aspect of cooperative learning to a curricular area you might teach.

Mr. Yang is a high school teacher who has decided to address the English language arts standards, as well as several in other areas, through an interdisciplinary, exploratory unit focusing on gambling. He begins by asking his class to construct a *mind map*, a visual representation of their thoughts, with "gambling" at the center. Anything that comes to mind is acceptable for this map. When students have finished brainstorming, he helps them categorize their ideas. Based on the categories they develop, six groups form around the following self-selected topics: the mathematics of gambling, the economics of gambling, the psychology of gambling, gambling in literature, the moral and ethical dimensions of gambling, and the political aspects of gambling. Mr. Yang has, with the assistance of the school librarian, gathered books and other materials that the students can use. He also encourages them to use interviewing and to explore the Internet for information. After several

FIGURE 2.6 *Resources relating to cooperative learning strategies and social interaction of learners.*

Anderson, R. P. (2001). Team Disease Presentations: A Cooperative Learning Activity for Large Classrooms. *The American Biology Teacher, 63*(1), 40–43.

Koprowski, J. L., & Perigo, N. (2000). Cooperative Learning as a Tool to Teach Vertebrate Anatomy. *The American Biology Teacher, 62*(4), 282–284.

Muniz, J. (2001). *The Effects of Cooperative Learning in a High School Mathematics Class.* Dissertation. St. Louis: Maryville University of St. Louis.

Neamen, M., & Strong, M. (2001). *More Literature Circles: Cooperative Learning for Grades 3–8.* Englewood, CO: Libraries Unlimited.

Putnam, J. W. (Ed.). (1993). *Cooperative Learning and Strategies for Inclusion: Celebrating Diversity in the Classroom.* Baltimore: Paul H. Brookes.

Quann, S., & Satin, D. (2000). *Learning Computers, Speaking English: Cooperative Activities for Learning English and Basic Word Processing.* Ann Arbor: University of Michigan Press.

Rogers, E. C., Davidson, N., Reynolds, B. E., & Thomas, A. D. (2001). *Cooperative Learning in Undergraduate Mathematics: Issues that Matter and Strategies that Work.* Washington, DC: Mathematical Association of America.

Schwartz, L., & Willing, K. (2001). *Computer Activities for Cooperative Learning.* Ontario, Canada: Pembroke Publishers.

Slavin, R. E. (1990). *Cooperative Learning: Theory, Research and Practice.* Englewood Cliffs, NJ: Prentice Hall.

Vermette, P. J. (1998). *Making Cooperative Learning Work.* Upper Saddle River, NJ: Prentice Hall.

days of facilitating the groups' investigations, discussions, and writing, he allows each group to share their research results and their positions and opinions on the aspect of gambling they read and learned about. On the class website, each group contributes a section of a class report on gambling, outlining the main points and synthesizing the groups' learning.

For a fuller understanding of how you might use cooperative learning strategies in your content courses, consult some of the sources listed in Figure 2.6.

ORAL READING IN CONTENT AREA CLASSROOMS

ACTIVATING PRIOR KNOWLEDGE　　2.4

Think for a moment about those times in high school or elementary school when your teacher may have instructed you to open to Chapter 5 of your science textbook. He began calling on people to read a few paragraphs at a time. Before your turn, what were you doing? After your turn, what did you do? How well did this classroom activity help you comprehend the material? Do you remember any amusing or embarrassing moments connected with this procedure? Reflect in writing for a moment.

Sometimes, I actually try having my education students take turns reading orally. I use an encyclopedia entry on Africa, and I give no purpose for the reading or any background to set the stage. I simply start asking people to read. It's not long before I notice students trying to figure out my pattern of calling on people. They read a bit ahead to practice those hard names of places and rivers that are listed. After they have a turn, they relax and may start looking at the pictures or out the window; they're very surprised if I call on them again before everyone else has had a turn—that's against the unwritten rules of the game! Virtually everyone who has gone to school can identify with this: Linguist Stephen Krashen wrote, "I do remember reading ahead while the rest of the class was taking turns reading out loud, and so not knowing the place when the teacher called on me" (Rosenthal, 1995, p. 179).

After a few (usually deadly) minutes of this *round-robin reading,* I ask the students to write down all they recall from the passage. The results are abysmal, but the mini-fiasco offers us an opportunity to debrief. Some students share that they were so anxious about being called on that they couldn't direct their energy toward comprehending the text either before or during their turn. Others got bored with classmates who stumbled or mumbled. The pace of the activity was right for no one. We couldn't think of anything good to say about this instructional method. So, why do teachers use it? We conclude that it's easy (though teachers will also admit to boredom while listening to students read) and it's what has come to be expected all too often.

This doesn't mean that oral reading doesn't have its place in content classrooms. Good oral reading is a wonderful skill for people, and especially for teachers, to cultivate. But in almost every setting where oral reading is required, with the exception of school, we do not expect people to read aloud in front of people from material they were just handed. Reading silently first is a help. Then, if a teacher or the students think the reinforcement of hearing the material might be beneficial, partners or small groups could form. Everyone gets more practice that way, and students can actually *hear* their classmates—not always the case when a class of 28 is participating in round-robin reading, especially if the desks are in rows and you can't even see the person who is reading.

Certain materials lend themselves to oral reading. Students at times choose to read something aloud to the class, perhaps a text they've composed or selected. Certainly play scripts are meant to be read aloud, and students usually enjoy taking part and playing with their voices and roles. Poetry can be appreciated if it's read aloud to the whole class, with expression and appropriate tone. But for reading content area material in class, my usual recommendation is silent reading or partner reading. When pairs of students read aloud to each other, alternating turns, they can hear and help each other.

Teacher Read-Alouds

Teacher read-alouds can be effective in terms of motivation and learning. Imagine a math teacher beginning a lesson on word problems by rapidly reading this excerpt from *The Phantom Tollbooth:*

> If a small car carrying three people at thirty miles an hour for ten minutes along a road five miles long at 11:35 in the morning starts at the same time as three people who have been traveling in a little automobile at twenty miles an hour for fifteen minutes on another road exactly twice as long as one half the distance of the other, while a dog, a bug, and a boy travel an equal distance in the same time or the same distance in an equal time along a third road in mid-October, then which one arrives first and which is the best way to go? (1996, p. 174)

The teacher, of course, reads the problem in such a way as to let the students know it's a *parody* of the word problems they will encounter. She laughs along with the students and assure them that no

problem on a test will be that complicated and cumbersome; yet, she actually uses the problem to teach students how to discriminate between relevant and irrelevant data. In authentic contexts, situations can indeed be complicated and many-faceted, and problem solvers may have to consider a lot of input. Doctors, military leaders, teachers, inventors, lawyers, and parents can attest to that.

Richardson (1994) bemoans the resistance to read-alouds that secondary teachers exhibit, and shows how reading aloud can be fun and beneficial both affectively and cognitively. She measured her tenth graders' interest by noting their increased attention span and appreciative comments, and found that test responses to those questions based on the read-alouds were better than other responses. Richardson promoted the use of read-alouds that are integrated into lessons, not presented as an added, extraneous activity. Teachers can reassure high school students that read-alouds are not "baby stuff" by explaining the strategy in the context of their lesson objectives.

Richardson recommends that the major resource for finding read-alouds be the teacher's personal reading. She also suggests newspapers and magazines, as well as sources offered by librarians and professional organizations (e.g., International Reading Association). She has authored several articles that give concrete suggestions of materials and ways to use them as read-alouds (see Figure 2.7).

Usnick and McCarthy (1998) provide practical ways teachers can read aloud from popular children's classics to engage middle school students in a highly motivating exploration of mathematical concepts. Stressing that it is not necessary for math teachers to have students read entire novels, they give examples of excerpts containing relevant stimuli for thought, including particular scenes from *A Wrinkle in Time* (L'Engle, 1962) to study such topics as nonstandard units of measure, estimation, operations on integers, measures of central tendency, combinatorics, and probability. Opportunities abound, they point out, in *The Witch of Blackbird Pond* (Speare, 1958) for demonstrating the use of math in real-life situations. There are connections between geometry and navigation, architecture and construction. Usnick and McCarthy had students who informally investigated trigonometric concepts and calculus uses after hearing scenes about the steepness of stairs and the sky reflected on the water in a well.

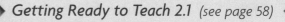

Getting Ready to Teach 2.1 *(see page 58)*

FIGURE 2.7 *Resources for read-alouds in middle and secondary content area classrooms.*

Erickson, B. (1996). Read-alouds Reluctant Readers Relish. *Journal of Adolescent and Adult Literacy,* 40, 212–214.

Pellowski, A. (1990). *Hidden Stories in Plants: Unusual and Easy-to-Tell Stories from Around the World, Together with Creative Things to Do While Telling Them.* New York: Macmillan.

Richardson, J. S. (1996). A Read-aloud for Cultural Diversity. *Journal of Adolescent and Adult Literacy,* October, 160.

Richardson, J. S., & Breen, M. (1996). A Read-aloud for Science. *Journal of Adolescent and Adult Literacy,* March, 504.

Richardson, J. S., & Carleton, L. (1997). A Read-aloud for Students of English as a Second Language. *Journal of Adolescent and Adult Literacy,* October, 140.

Richardson. J. S., & Forget, M. A. (1995/1996). A Read-aloud for Algebra and Geography Classrooms. *Journal of Adolescent and Adult Literacy,* Dec/Jan, 322.

Richardson, J. S., & Gross, E. (1997). A Read-aloud for Mathematics. *Journal of Adolescent and Adult Literacy,* March, 492.

Richardson, J. S., & Smith, N. S. (1996/1997). A Read-aloud for Science in Space. *Journal of Adolescent and Adult Literacy,* Dec/Jan, 308.

Trelease, J. (Ed.). (1993). *Read All About It!: Great Read-Aloud Stories, Poems, & Newspaper Pieces for Preteens and Teens.* New York: Penguin Books.

BookTalk 2.8

Scientists and children have wondered for centuries about how insects think and feel as they busily go about their work. Can they tell us their stories? In *Joyful Noise: Poems for Two Voices,* by Paul Fleischman and E. Beddows (1988), they can and do, in powerful verse no less. Every poem offers students the opportunity to perform with partners as they learn content from the field of entomology. Fleischman and Beddows' earlier work, *I Am Phoenix: Poems for Two Voices* (1985), deals with ornithology in a similar fashion, thus making a great companion piece.

BookTalk 2.9

The year is 1949. Two sixth-grade softball teams meet on the field. What makes this particular game unique is that on one team is a girl whose family spent the war years imprisoned in a Japanese internment camp. On the opposing team is a girl whose father was killed during the attack on Pearl Harbor. Multiple narrators tell their perspectives of the fateful game in Virginia Euwer Wolff's *Bat 6* (1998). This book could be read aloud in class, with students taking on the voices and personas of the players.

Providing Access to Books and Opportunities to Read, Talk, and Write About Content

There is much documentation of passionate reading on the part of learners, but much of this reading has historically taken place outside school walls. Stephen Krashen, a linguistics professor and author of more than 120 articles (now there's passion!) recalls:

> When I was in second grade, I was in the low reading group, the "Bluebirds." My father brought home some comics for me to read, and within weeks, I became an "Oriole." It was a definite turning point in my life. From then on, I became an obsessive reader. . . . The research also says that free voluntary reading is our major source of competence in reading comprehension, writing style, grammar, vocab-

ulary, and spelling. . . . I remember what I considered to be pointless exercises in grammar, spelling, and punctuation. I think I knew then that these practices were things you did in school, and that they had nothing to do with real literacy development. (Rosenthal, 1995, pp. 179–180)

Kosta Bagakis tells a similar story:

> I was passive in school; teachers imposed readings on me and I accepted them. My school life was separate from my private life. When I read something that was directly related to my private life, I came alive and I still do. Right now I'm reading about the Trojan War, and since I'm Greek, that era is part of my heritage. Those heroes are a part of me, and I want to make them clear in my mind so I can understand myself better. (Rosenthal, 1995, p. 194)

We must provide the materials and the opportunities for students to explore them if we want to stimulate their intellectual curiosity and desire to delve deeply and passionately into the curricular topics your course involves. Studies support the benefits of book-rich classroom environments (Elley, 1992; Koskinen et al., 2000; Morrow, 1996). Gambrell (1996) asked students to speak about the most interesting book they had recently read, and found that the overwhelming majority chose to talk about a book they had selected from the classroom library, not the community, school, or home libraries. You can begin to build your classroom library now—visit used book sales or request donations from friends and family.

Another way we can make our classrooms conducive to engaged and passionate learning is to provide opportunities for students to share their excitement and newfound knowledge. Discussion groups can provide an audience. We can also encourage students to write to authors or to people in the field. The box below shows another example from *Dear Author: Students Write about the Books that Changed Their Lives* (*Read Magazine*, 1995).

Dear Elie [Wiesel],

I must honestly say that I did not enjoy your tragic novel *Night*, but then I doubt you wrote it to be enjoyed. I was assigned to read *Night* and literally groaned when I discovered it was about the Holocaust. I felt I had heard enough about this horrible time period and didn't understand why teachers persisted in making us read such graphic accounts. I thought I realized the terror and didn't want to hear one more awful story. Throughout the entire novel, my stomach was tight and my eyes watered. At times I had to set the book down and walk away to relieve my mind and heart of the agony I was constantly feeling for Elle. I hated every page and every word that was a continual reminder of the depravity of man.

I tried to relate with what Elle was going through, but obviously I could not. There was no common ground whatsoever. *Night* forced me to realize there was no way I could ever truly comprehend the horror. I believe it was this that made me even more frustrated with the novel. After all the years I had been taught about the Holocaust and all the stories I had read, nothing compared to yours. Never had I read such a powerful account in my life. *Night* assaulted me with the graphic details others were afraid to tell, and it was this that opened my eyes.

As I finished the book, I threw it across my room, angered and disgusted. I recall looking at it lying on the floor and never wanting to think about its contents again. I froze, and cringed as the realization of my thought sunk in. The reason I hated the book, the reason I didn't want to read the book in the first place, was that I didn't want to think about it. I convinced myself I already knew everything. I told myself I didn't need to hear any more. I tried as hard as I could to protect myself from the full terror of the truth. But I hated myself and the way I was hiding. My actions were as ignorant as those of the average passive citizen during the Holocaust. Like them, I didn't want to know everything, but your emotional and frighteningly true novel forced me to see.

Looking back, I'm glad I read *Night*. Not only did it make me aware of the wall of ignorance I was trying to build around myself, but it helped me to take that wall down. I will never look forward to reading such heart-wrenching novels as yours, but I will do it if only to educate myself. Thank you for the courage you had to write *Night*. Never again will I shut myself off from reality. I will try my hardest to face it and learn from the truth.

Emily Judge, 15
Wheaton-Warrenville South High School, Wheaton, IL
Teacher: Mrs. McKenna

Excerpted from *Dear Author: Students Write about the Books that Changed their Lives* by the Weekly Reader's *Read Magazine*, pp. 174–175, copyright © 1995, by permission of Conari Press.

PAYING ATTENTION TO THE AFFECTIVE DOMAIN

It's a given that content area teachers are responsible for the *cognitive* development of students; we help our students understand the concepts and knowledge base of our subjects, as well as teach them to analyze texts and think critically about course material and current events in the field. It's equally true that we must pay attention to our learners' attitudes, interests, values, and emotions, all of which are considered to be in the *affective domain* (Krathwohl, Bloom, & Masia, 1964) of learning. As students grow in each of these domains, the other can be affected positively. It's one of those cyclical processes, where a person's interest can lead her to learn more about a subject, and the newfound knowledge increases her curiosity and willingness to pursue the subject in more depth, which in turn makes the topic even more fascinating and inviting. You've probably listened to people talk excitedly together, sharing details and opinions, about something you have little interest in, whether it be sports, computers, horses, or the stock market. Similarly, the subject you teach may not be inherently interesting to your September students, but by June they may belong to the discourse community you've helped create and have the attitude and motivation necessary to continue learning the subject independently. Your goal is to replace apathy and indifference with zeal and intellectual curiosity.

Nell (1988) points out that there are certain preconditions that must be met before one becomes a person who chooses to read for pleasure. The person must possess adequate reading skills and fluency, so that texts are not too tedious and slow to be rewarding. Second, there must be the expectation that reading will be a pleasurable experience. Finally, the text selection must be appropriate. In the absence of any of these antecedents, reading for pleasure is either not attempted at all or the attempt fails.

Think about the teacher's role in relation to Nell's assertion. It is your responsibility to increase and enhance your students' reading skills and strategies as they read materials related to your curriculum. Your obvious love of reading and enthusiasm for particular genres or works can lead to the students' expectation that reading what you require or recommend will be worthwhile. As for the third precondition, you should select appropriate texts after determining the needs and interests of individuals and groups, as well as help the students develop and hone the skill of finding and selecting texts that will be worthwhile and rewarding. Many of your students may later credit you as the teacher who turned them on to reading, who helped them discover the treasure in books and other texts. Every chapter in this text involves both the cognitive and affective realms, often together, as we deal with various components of literacy and develop teaching and learning strategies.

Assessing Attitudes

How do your students feel about algebra, or economics, or learning a foreign language, or art history, or poetry? And what are their attitudes about reading and writing, particularly in your subject area? Both questions elicit information that is important for you to know. Perhaps you have some students who like American history but tell you they couldn't care less about world history. Or students who tell you they find all science boring, but they love to read novels for English class. Some students may like to read but resist writing, or vice versa. Whatever your students tell you about their values and attitudes relative to your subject, you can capitalize on the positives they bring with them and accept the challenge to change some of the negative perceptions they have.

Interest Inventories

How should you go about finding out about students' interests, attitudes, and values? You could create an inventory, asking the questions you want to know about. It could be as simple as having your math students write out answers to these questions:

1. What would you like me to know about you as a math student? Tell me anything that might help me know you as a learner and provide what you need to enjoy this class.
2. If you like math, try to explain why or tell what really interests you about it. If you don't like math or are afraid of it, try to explain why and relate any negative experiences you have had with math in the past.

There are also published inventories you can use. For example, Kear, Coffman, McKenna, and Ambrosio (2000) developed a Writing Attitude Survey that can be used throughout the grades, and they explain how the information gained can be used to plan instruction so that "effective teaching strategies and engaging opportunities to write successfully can make real inroads in student perspectives" (p. 15). Examples of questions in the survey include, "How would you feel writing a letter to the author of a book you read?" (p. 16), "How would you feel writing to someone to change their

FIGURE **2.8**   *Using listening questions.*

The following is a conversation between a health teacher and a group of students who have been reading books and articles about child abuse. Notice how the teacher uses listening questions.

Jessica: Angelo and I read *Tangerine* [Bloor, 1997] and we've talked about it, but we can't come up with an idea for our wall poster showing what it meant to us.

Mr. Peng: Mmmm. Did it mean the same thing to both of you?

Jessica: Well, it's such a boy's book!

Mr. Peng: (laughs) A boy's book?

Jessica: Yeah, Angelo loved it; it had the football star, it had violence, it had sibling abuse, it had boys as characters . . .

Ryan: Well, Manuel and I read *When She Was Good* [Mazer, 1999], and that had wicked bad sibling abuse, and death! And it had two girl characters, and we loved it.

Mr. Peng: Oh, thanks for that input! So it's not just the sex of the characters that would make Jessica think that a book might appeal more to boys?

Jessica: Well, actually, I have to admit that I kind of liked *Tangerine*, too. And it did make me think about how sibling abuse would change the whole family. Like, how could those parents

not have told Paul the truth about what Eric did to him when he was little?

Mr. Peng: You found that unrealistic?

Angelo: No, think about it. If they admitted the truth, they'd have to report their own kid for a crime! And once they started the lying, it was harder and harder to get back to the truth. They probably rationalized that covering up would be better. Then Paul wouldn't grow up hating his brother, you know? I mean we as readers know they're wrong, but they're in the middle of a really messed up situation.

Jessica: I think I have an idea for our poster. You know Paul's thick glasses? I think they're kind of symbolic. I think Paul might actually be the *least* blind member of that whole family. The parents are choosing not to see the trouble Eric's in, everyone is blind to what a great kid Paul is and the talents he has. . . .

Angelo: Cool! I like it!

Mr. Peng: Sounds like you're building from each other's ideas. Go for it!

---

opinion?" (p. 17), and "How would you feel writing about something you did in science?" (p. 17).

Listening Questions

One strategy all teachers should use, whether or not you also create an inventory, is to listen carefully to the students. You might ask a question before each day's lesson that elicits their concerns and hopes. Bruns (1992) recommends:

> There is probably no better way to convey interest and nurturance than through listening. Most teacher–student social exchanges are momentary—just a few words and a smile. But sometimes the opportunity presents itself to be with a student in a situation that has nothing to do with schoolwork. Exploit such opportunities to be attentive to remarks about the student's interests. The act of really listening is a tremendous compliment and a powerful tool in building a relationship. (p. 43)

Michel, in *The Child's View of Reading: Understandings for Teachers and Parents* (1994), presents a

model interview with a child and gives suggestions for conducting informal interviews using what she calls *listening questions.* She recommends being nondirective, and suggests that the adult's questions should be based on the students' remarks to bring out more from them. Although her subjects were first graders, the advice and techniques she offers can serve secondary teachers well. If you informally interview students often as they work, taking cues from them and asking questions about the process they are using as they discover information, compose, solve problems, respond to literature, or comprehend reading material, they become comfortable talking about their thinking, attitudes, and working processes. These conversations will lead to increased knowledge for you about what and how to teach, as well as *metacognitive* thinking on the students' part. Metacognitive thinking involves conscious thinking about and monitoring of what one is doing, so that readers are aware of the process they are going through. Metacognition is explored further in Chapter 4. Figure 2.8 shows an informal classroom conversation that exemplifies a high school teacher's use of listening questions.

PREPARING STUDENTS FOR READING

ACTION RESEARCH   2.B

Interview a teacher in your content area to find out how he motivates students to read and write. The interview can be very open-ended, going in whatever direction the teacher chooses, or you could use specific questions such as: "Do you read aloud to your students? Do you use pre-reading activities or anticipation guides? Do you give booktalks? How do you encourage students to read beyond the textbook? What kinds of reading do you do for pleasure?"

Getting Ready to Teach 2.2 (see page 58)

What you do in class to set a purpose for reading a text and to activate the students' conscious awareness of their attitudes and values relative to the topic has enormous potential to enhance motivation and a willingness to engage with the author's ideas. Figure 2.9 shows an activity a preservice math teacher designed for her students to complete before they received their course textbooks.

Throughout this book there are examples of anticipation guides that can fulfill the purpose of engaging students' minds in preparation for content area reading and learning. They don't have to be elaborate. Imagine a teacher getting students ready for reading selections by popular young adult fiction writer Robert Cormier. She might have questions she asks students to reflect on in writing before they begin. Before assigning *The Chocolate War* (1986), she might ask them to respond to one of the following prompts: "Can there be evil, immorality, or unethical behavior within a school administration? What should students do if they discover this?" or, "Do I dare disturb the universe?" In another case, she could ask students to brainstorm situations where a person might have to start life over with a new identity (e.g., participants in a witness protection program or a person fleeing from the Nazis during the Holocaust), and then to imagine what it would be like to have to reject or hide your past and learn to live with a new name, family, country, and so on. This prepares the students to read Cormier's *I Am the Cheese* (1977).

LITERARY FIELD TRIPS

You probably entered the field you are teaching because of a love for or a fascination with your sub-ject area. Your students, however, may not come to you with an inherent interest in the subject matter, and some may even resist learning any academic topics. So, as you plan to teach your curriculum, you'll have to figure out ways to pique their interest. There are many ways to motivate students, including hands-on experiences, guest speakers, and field trips—things that make a subject come alive and make the students part of the real experience. You probably can't take your students on too many field trips—you'll be constrained by geography, time, finances. But you can go anywhere in place or time with the help of literature, primary documents, and a strategy I call *literary field trips*. Come along as American history teacher Ms. Maina applies the strategy.

Ms. Maina is about to begin a unit on the Civil Rights movement. Last year she struggled with the first few lessons because her students were memorizing terms like *Jim Crow laws*, *desegregation*, and *bus boycott*, but not really appreciating the courage of the people who worked for justice and equality. So this year, she spent part of her limited materials budget to purchase 10 paperback copies of *The National Civil Rights Museum Celebrates Everyday People* by Alice Faye Duncan (1995). As an introduction to her Civil Rights unit, she announced to the class that they would be visiting the National Civil Rights Museum. She asked if anyone knew where it was located. Students guessed Washington, DC; Atlanta; Montgomery. She affirmed their hypotheses as logical possibilities, then asked them to brainstorm a list of things they might expect to see there. A student volunteer compiled a list as students called them out: Rosa Parks' bus, stuff from the March on Washington, drinking fountains with signs saying "White Only" and "Negro," a copy of Martin Luther King's "I Have a Dream" speech.

Ms. Maina proceeded to ask her students what questions they might ask a tour guide at the museum. Students thought they'd like to know what the beginning and ending dates of the Civil Rights movement were, what the museum contained on Malcolm X, and what it was like working at the museum. They were ready to head out.

Ms. Maina explained that they would be going on a literary field trip and should stay with their groups of three. As they explored the museum and the Civil Rights movement through their reading, they could talk among themselves, ask new questions, and respond to the pictures and text freely. She passed out a copy of Duncan's book to each group and allowed class time for the students to explore it.

After about 20 minutes, Ms. Maina directed the groups to take a sheet of paper, fold it in half lengthwise, and label the two columns "What we learned

RATIONALE: High school mathematics students often ask, "Why do we need to know this?" and "When are we ever going to use this outside school?" Many students believe that if what they are taught has no relevance to their lives, then there is no real reason for learning it. It is important that teachers help students make connections between mathematics and activities and contexts beyond the school setting.

DIRECTIONS FOR STUDENTS: You are to complete the mind map provided. Take a few minutes to brainstorm before writing anything down. If you need some help, refer to the following websites:

> www.looksmart.com/eus1/eus317829/eus317865/eus76271/r?lm&
>
> www.bhs-ms.org/projects/kapraun/hp.htm

I've also provided a word bank at the bottom of the page that may offer further ideas or suggestions for filling in the mind map. If you can successfully explain your answers, you do not have to worry about being wrong.

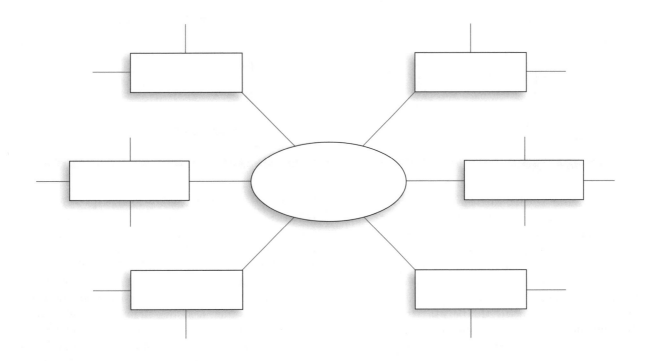

| Business | Distance | Tipping | Area | Sales | Building |
| Weather | Wages | Gambling | Sports | Speed | Checking |

Once you've finished the mind map, reflect on these concluding questions:

1. Did this reading guide help you to gain a better understanding of the uses of math outside the classroom? Explain.
2. Please give me some feedback on the type of graphic organizer, or mind map, used here. Did you like the use of this visual to increase your thinking and brainstorming skills?

Were there any advantages to this approach? Disadvantages?

FOLLOW UP: Now check out some of the books on our display table. Perhaps you'd like to borrow *Great Jobs for Math Majors* (Lambert & DeCotis, 1999), *101 Careers in Mathematics* (Sterrett, 1999), *Careers for Number Crunchers and Other Quantitative Types* (Burnett, 2002), or one of the other books that can help you explore exciting careers related to math.

FIGURE **2.9**   *Continued.*

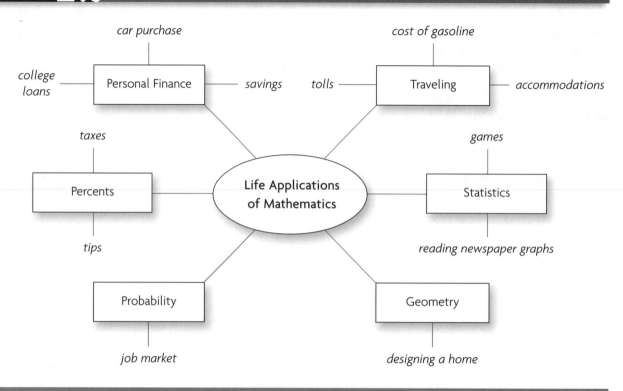

about the National Civil Rights Museum," and "What we learned about the Civil Rights movement." Students had no trouble filling up both sides of the paper. They had learned, for example, that the museum was located in Memphis, Tenn., in the former Lorraine Motel, where Martin Luther King, Jr. had been assassinated. It was designed as a hands-on museum: visitors can feel the bars of a replica of a Birmingham jail cell, crowd into a holding cell modeled after the ones where arrested protesters were kept, get in a bus like the one Rosa Parks rode. They can touch statues of strikers, marchers, and students at restaurant sit-ins. Visitors can stand on the very balcony where Martin Luther King, Jr. was shot. The readers in Ms. Maina's class saw photographs of students participating in an active tour through the museum and read captions about the exhibits. In the second column, they listed many things they learned about the Civil Rights movement. They noted the powerful photographs of Rosa Parks being fingerprinted after her act of protest, lunch counter demonstrators sitting peacefully as white customers poured mustard and sugar on their heads, a burned bus, bruised faces, attack dogs being turned on marchers, the Little Rock Nine walking into Central High and leaving later in caps and gowns.

Ms. Maina's room was noisy as students expressed disbelief and dismay at some of the knowledge they had gained on their literary field trip. They were poised to continue with the unit. The strategy had served to help the students begin to learn content at the same time it provided motivation for learning. Throughout the rest of the unit, Ms. Maina lectured and gave notes, guided them through a textbook chapter, encouraged independent research, and used a variety of other teaching strategies. One strategy included visiting the National Civil Rights Museum's website (www.civilrightsmuseum.org) and taking a virtual tour via the Internet. They could then compare the information found there with that in the book and discuss what processes they used to navigate and comprehend each source.

Once students understand the concept of traveling through time and space via literary and Internet field trips, they can map where they've been—post maps and have the students pin strips of paper to the spots their reading material took them to. They can do the same on a time line. For example, after reading *Hiroshima* (Hersey, 1946), students can make two strips listing the title and author, pinning one on the appropriate area of Japan on the map and the other at the appropriate point on the time line they've made to record their literary journeys.

See Figure 2.10 for guidelines to planning a literary field trip.

FIGURE **2.10**   *Guidelines for literary field trips.*

1. Choose a place or location relevant to a content area lesson you are preparing.
2. Select book(s) and/or other materials relevant to that location.
3. Brainstorm what students might expect to find there.
4. Have students prepare questions for their "tour guide."
5. Divide the students into groups and "tour" the location by reading.
6. Ask students to prepare a summary of the highlights of their tour, telling what they learned about the location and its related content area subject.
7. Have students plot their journeys on a map and/or time line.
8. Discuss where the students' inquiry can go from here, and what other resources they might "tour" next to learn about the topic in more depth and answer any remaining or new questions.

Getting Ready to Teach 2.3 *(see page 58)*

LEARNING CENTERS

Let's stay with Ms. Maina's class for a while. After the whole class experienced the virtual tour of the National Civil Rights Museum via the book *Everyday People*, she spent several days teaching structured lessons on the Civil Rights movement. Now, she felt the students were ready for some independent exploration. So, she introduced them to her learning center, which she had set up in the back of her room at a circular table. There were books representing a variety of genres and levels of difficulty, and sets of directions for assignments. Students could choose from the suggestions or design an independent project of their own. Along the side of the room, there were several computers, and some of the requirements or options for the center involved searching websites, including that of the National Civil Rights Museum. Figure 2.11 lists some of the resources at the learning center.

Project suggestions in Ms. Maina's learning center might include the following:

1. Read one novel by Mildred Taylor. Fill in the wall chart about the Logan family (see Figure 2.12) in the appropriate column. When we finish the chart, we will be able to trace the highlights of the Logan family's saga over the course of several years!

2. Read *The Story of Ruby Bridges* by Robert Coles (1995) and the memoir *Through My Eyes* by Ruby Bridges (1999), then watch the video *Ruby Bridges*. In a review intended for our school literary magazine, compare and contrast the art work, the ways the

information is presented, and the emotional impact of these three nonfiction works.

3. Choose several of Langston Hughes' poems and discuss them in relation to the things you have learned about the Civil Rights movement from your textbook and other sources.

4. Explore Internet sites and recent issues of newspapers and magazines to find examples of ongoing work for civil rights and social justice. Create a collage or other art project, or write a letter or story that represents your response to the issues and events you learned about.

When you design a learning center, there are many possible ways to use it. Because the purpose is to encourage independent exploration, as well as creativity, make sure your directions are clear so the students can proceed with their reading, writing, and art projects without too much assistance (although you should certainly let them know that they can use you and their peers as needed). You can allow pairs of students or small groups to collaborate on the assignments. One group at a time could use the center while you work on different aspects of a unit with others. Or you could have more than one center set up at a time—the students can either choose a center in line with their interests or rotate through them according to your directions.

The center could contain works of a single author instead of works around a theme. Figure 2.13 lists resources for an author center on Russell Freedman. A center might be interdisciplinary, and perhaps be housed in a hall or library. A core team of English, math, social studies, and science teachers could create project ideas using a biography theme, with books representing heroes and masters from all the disciplines. The English focus might be on the

FIGURE 2.11 *Resources for a learning center on the Civil Rights movement.*

Allen, Z. (1996). *Black Women Leaders of the Civil Rights Movement.* Danbury, CT: Franklin Watts.

Bridges, R. (1999). *Through My Eyes.* New York: Scholastic.

Bullard, S. (1993). *Free At Last: A History of the Civil Rights Movement and Those Who Died in the Struggle.* New York: Oxford University Press.

Coles, R. (1995). *The Story of Ruby Bridges.* New York: Scholastic.

Fradin, D. B., & Fradin, J. B. (2000). *Ida B. Wells: Mother of the Civil Rights Movement.* New York: Clarion Books.

Hampton, H., & Fayer, S. (1990). *Voices of Freedom: An Oral History of the Civil Rights Movement.* New York: Bantam Books.

Hughes, L. (1986). *The Dream Keeper and Other Poems.* New York: Knopf.

King, M. L. (1994). *Letter from Birmingham Jail.* New York: HarperCollins.

Levine, E. (1993). *Freedom's Children: Young Civil Rights Activists Tell Their Own Stories.* New York: Putnam.

Levy, P. B. (1992). *Let Freedom Ring: A Documentary History of the Modern Civil Rights Movement.* New York: Praeger.

Medearis, A. S. (1994). *Dare to Dream: Coretta Scott King and the Civil Rights Movement.* New York: Dutton.

Meltzer, M. (2001). *There Comes a Time: The Struggle for Civil Rights.* New York: Random House.

Myers, W. D. (1993). *Malcolm X: By Any Means Necessary.* New York: Scholastic.

Taylor, M. (1975). *Song of the Trees.* New York: Dial Press.

Taylor, M. (1976). *Roll of Thunder, Hear My Cry.* New York: Dial Press.

Taylor, M. (1981). *Let the Circle Be Unbroken.* New York: Dial Press.

Taylor, M. (1992). *The Road to Memphis.* New York: Puffin Books.

Walt Disney Home Video. (1998). *Ruby Bridges.* Buena Vista Home Entertainment.

X, M. (1992). *The Autobiography of Malcolm X.* New York: Ballantine Books.

Young, A. (1996). *An Easy Burden: The Civil Rights Movement and the Transformation of America.* New York: HarperCollins.

FIGURE 2.12 *Sample wall chart.*

	Roll of Thunder	Song of the Trees	Let the Circle Be Unbroken	The Road to Memphis
What years are covered in the book?				
What is the status of the Logans' land?				
What conflicts do the family members face?				
How does a main character change or grow?				
What examples of racial prejudice are there?				
What examples of racial harmony and/or social justice are there?				

| FIGURE 2.13 | Resources for an author center on Russell Freedman. |

Freedman, R. (1980). *Immigrant Kids.* New York: Dutton.

Freedman, R. (1983). *Children of the Wild West.* New York: Clarion Books.

Freedman, R. (1987). *Indian Chiefs.* New York: Holiday House.

Freedman. R. (1987). *Lincoln: A Photobiography.* New York: Clarion Books.

Freedman, R. (1988). *Buffalo Hunt.* New York: Holiday House.

Freedman, R. (1988). Newbery Medal acceptance speech. *The Horn Book Magazine,* 64(4), 444–451.

Freedman, R. (1990). *Franklin Delano Roosevelt.* New York: Clarion Books.

Freedman, R. (1991). *The Wright Brothers: How They Invented the Airplane.* New York: Holiday House.

Freedman, R. (1992). *An Indian Winter.* New York: Holiday House.

Freedman, R. (1993). *Eleanor Roosevelt: A Life of Discovery.* New York: Clarion Books.

Freedman, R. (1994). *Kids at Work: Lewis Hines and the Crusade Against Child Labor.* New York: Clarion Books.

Freedman, R. (1996). *The Life and Death of Crazy Horse.* New York: Holiday House.

Freedman, R. (1997). *Out of Darkness: The Story of Louis Braille.* New York: Clarion Books.

Freedman, R. (1998). *Martha Graham: A Dancer's Life.* New York: Clarion Books.

Freedman, R. (1999). *Babe Didrikson Zaharias: The Making of a Champion.* New York: Clarion Books.

Marcus, L. S. (Ed.). (2000). *Author Talk: Conversations with Judy Blume . . . et al.* New York: Simon & Schuster.

| FIGURE 2.14 | Guidelines for setting up a learning center. |

1. Designate a certain area of the classroom as the learning center.
2. Provide a variety of fiction/nonfiction and print/nonprint materials in various genres and at varying levels of difficulty that focus on a particular author or theme.
3. Offer students the option of working on suggested assignments or on projects of their own.
4. Provide clear directions so that students can work on projects independently.
5. Allow one group to work in the learning center while you work with other students.

writing style and structure of the books, as well as on character development. The science, social studies, and math teachers can create questions to help students think about the inventions or accomplishments of the profiled people and draw attention to the content knowledge that can be gained and constructed as students read several choices. Figure 2.14 provides guidelines for setting up a learning center.

REWARDS AND REINFORCEMENTS AS MOTIVATORS

Every few weeks, I read an article in my local newspaper about a school where the students have met the goals of a special reading program. One principal kissed a pig when her students had read an agreed-upon number of books. Another ate a worm; another took fourth graders (the class with the most books read) to McDonald's in a limousine. Alfie Kohn (1998) presents a somber warning about such rewards, along with the excessive use of grades, test scores, or competition, which can lead students to value reading less. He exhorts teachers to:

> Steer clear of reading incentives, particularly in the form of corporate programs like "Book It," which attempts to train kids to open books by dangling pizzas in front of them. Worse still is something called "Accelerated Reader." Not only does it get kids to think that the objective of reading is to earn points and prizes, and not only does it limit the number of books that will "count," but it makes students answer superficial, fact-based questions about each text to prove they've

read it, thereby changing—for the worse—not only why they read but also how they read. (p. 171)

What about praise? Is that a good motivator and reinforcer? It depends. Holt (1989) warns that continued praise, even when given with the positive intention of increasing self-esteem, can be destructive and actually decrease self-confidence. "I think of countless teenagers I have known who hated themselves despite having been praised all their lives. . . . Many children are both cynical about praise and dependent on it, the worst possible mixture" (p. 140). Warning that any kind of external motivation, positive or negative, submerges or displaces internal motivation, he advocates giving students thoughtful attention as they work rather than praise.

Caine and Caine (1991) point out that under conditions of continuous stress, internal motivation becomes more and more difficult to generate as people begin to see themselves as fulfilling only goals formed by others. Amabile (1983) extensively documents the harmful effects of extrinsic motivation on creativity and problem solving. Gazzaniga (1985) found that people who are learning to perform a skill under external conditions begin to perform that skill only when the reward possibilities continue to be presented. Internal motivators, on the other hand, are developed when people participate in goal setting and problem solving (Howard, 2000, p. 657).

We'll deal with grades as motivators in Chapter 10, which focuses on assessment. For now, I'd like to encourage you to rely on internal motivators and on the interesting, sometimes enticing, texts themselves as much as possible. Many a reader can attest to reading being its own reward because texts give us the knowledge we seek and invite us deeper into the realms of intellectual treasure. The immunologist and Nobel laureate Baruj Benecerraff, one of the highly successful dyslexics discussed earlier, explains his reading habits in elementary school:

> I read a lot, especially about the lives of famous scientists. I had a special dictionary with pictures, and it told about the lives of famous people. Famous scientists and artists, too. I spent many, many hours reading this book as a child. (Fink, 1995/1996, p. 275)

Similarly, another participant in the study, biochemist and Stanford professor Ronald Davis, discusses curiosity as a motivator for reading:

> You read science for how things are put together. . . . My interest in chemistry just came—it started with my interest in airplanes in grade school . . . that quickly converted to propellant systems in seventh and eighth grades. . . . I became

fascinated with nitrogen chemistry. So the way to understand that was to start reading chemistry books. So I got organic chemistry textbooks. (Fink, 1995/96, p. 275)

Gambrell (1996) offers a "reward proximity hypothesis: the closer the reward to the desired behavior (for example, books to reading), the greater the likelihood that intrinsic motivation will increase." How sensible.

MOTIVATING ALL STUDENTS

The described activities can be used to motivate learners with a range of abilities and learning styles. Yet, you may find that you have students who seem to remain unmotivated and distant despite your best efforts at interesting them and inviting them into your field of study. There are many possible reasons for such a case, and each student might require a different course of action on your part. If something outside school is causing the difficulty (e.g., problems at home, lack of sleep, or the need to work a part-time job), then your role might be listening to the student, sympathizing with her obstacles, and suggesting resources or support personnel who can help alleviate the situations preventing the student from committing energy to academic growth. At times a student's distaste for your subject area could be the result of an earlier failure or a boring year of study preceding your class. Again, talking to the student, reassuring and encouraging him, coupled with practical suggestions of techniques or materials that will help him catch up and regain confidence, is in order.

Some of the brightest students you teach will be a challenge because they stopped learning during school hours due to the cumulative effect of boredom in too many classrooms for too many years. Lloyd (1998) offers suggestions that engage students at the top of the ability range without leaving the rest of your class behind. She provides examples of role-playing activities, individual research projects, and interdisciplinary explorations that can reawaken and stretch minds and help the students learn to go as far as they can in content area courses, rather than merely completing the minimum requirements and then stagnating. The strategies, activities, and texts suggested throughout this book will add to your repertoire of skills that you can use flexibly to engage your intellectually gifted students.

Another challenge awaits you. Bruns (1992) reports on a phenomenon he calls *work inhibition*, involving students who have the intellectual capacity and other conditions necessary for succeeding academically yet "have extreme difficulty engaging in the work of school" (p. 38). Neither outstanding teachers nor parental support make a difference. Bruns' research shows that up to 20 percent of students may fit this picture. He found in his study that nearly three of every four work-inhibited students were boys, and that most had good cognitive abilities and above average thinking skills and were generally not disruptive in the classroom. The personality characteristics he found to be fairly common among work-inhibited students included dependency (they did the work if a teacher was sitting next to them), poor self-esteem, and passive aggression. A passive-aggressive child might want to please, but hidden anger might cause him to forget to do assignments or take seemingly forever to accomplish a task. What can teachers do to turn this behavior around? Bruns suggests building a nurturing relationship, listening, teaching strategies for completing tasks in incremental steps, recruiting volunteers to assist the student, providing effective feedback, creating a climate of encouragement, and empowering the student by promoting autonomy.

What about the students in our classes who are behind their peers in reading abilities, weak in

BookTalk 2.11

Just how passionate can one be about the activity of reading? Well, the title of Daniel Pennac's book, *Better Than Life,* gives his answer. This reflection on how the passion for knowledge, language, and literacy can be shared discusses the potential damage that can occur as a result of reading being institutionalized as a school subject. But Pennac recognizes the power of a teacher: "It does happen that a student meets a teacher whose enthusiasm helps turn mathematics, for example, into a field of pure study, practically into a branch of the arts. . . . It is in the nature of living beings to love life, even in the form of a quadratic equation" (p. 92). One of the most popular parts of the book is "The Reader's Bill of Rights" (pp. 170–171). Pennac recommends that we grant to our students the same rights we exercise ourselves as readers, including the rights to skip pages, reread, read for escape, and abandon books.

BookTalk 2.10

Can academic passion be the topic of one's academic passion? The answer is yes in the case of Robert L. Fried, who authored *The Passionate Teacher* (2001) and *The Passionate Learner* (2001). His philosophy is that caring is at the heart of learning; a student must care before she will invest in what it takes to learn curricular material. Therefore, caring should also be at the center of pedagogy. Fried's accounts of wonderful learning experiences in all kinds of school settings are inspiring. For example, in *The Passionate Learner,* he tells the story of Malcolm Mitchell, a sixth-grade teacher of African American and Asian-American children in Boston, who tabbed gripping passages in his college texts and put them in his classroom closet. Before long, his students would come in, head for his closet, and read for half an hour, where before they didn't want to read at all. The personal connection made the difference—they wanted to learn what their teacher was passionate about. Fried's companion books will make you eager to share your own passion about your subject area with students, and will show you how to be successful doing it.

decoding and/or comprehension skills, or struggling in other ways? Roller (1996) shows through her research and experience that workshop settings are ideal for offering variable instruction to variable children. While recognizing the difficulty of creating an environment where all students' efforts are nurtured and respected, regardless of how wide the range of abilities might be, Roller shows how the structure of a workshop classroom can allow for differentiation. "The choice that forms the base of the workshop assumes that everyone will read different material and write different stories and approach classroom themes in their own way. Choice is a powerful mechanism for accommodating variability" (p. 135).

Atwell (1991) documents how students with special needs can flourish in a workshop setting. She relates the story of one eighth grader, Laura, who had spent the previous six years in a special education class, whose skills and motivation were greatly enhanced once she joined Atwell's community of learners. She gained confidence as a reader and a writer, even writing a letter to her favorite author, Judy Blume. She listened in rapt attention to her teacher's mini-lessons about how to get ideas and resources for writing. Atwell describes her as "a sponge, soaking up everything. After years of programmed reading instruction, activities and exercises designed to remediate her poor memory and deficient oral reading, she was getting help that she could use" (p. 26). Laura learned to trust and use her peers' suggestions for reading and their feedback as she revised her drafts, and she learned some real purposes for writing. After composing a beautiful free verse poem about the Challenger tragedy, she explained, "I really liked that Christa McAuliffe. I was upset and mixed up, and this is the way I expressed my feelings" (p. 31).

Atwell credited Laura with showing her Vygotsky's theories in action. In eighth grade, with the help of teacher and classmates in a workshop setting, she read 31 novels and completed 21 pieces of writing, spanning many genres. Atwell concludes:

> The environment marched ahead of Laura and led her. . . . Laura was surrounded by people writing and conferring and publishing, by high expectations, by good children's literature, by energy, commitment, and a willingness on the part of her teacher to be patient and give the time and response that special writers need. (p. 36)

CONCLUSION

This chapter was meant to get you thinking about your own and your students' passion for learning and motivation to participate in literacy activities that lead to knowledge and comprehension. The affective domain is intertwined with the cognitive, and you can go a long way toward helping your students achieve in social studies, science, math, art, language, music, business—any subject you can name—by sharing your enthusiasm; talking about your own reading and learning; using strategies that increase intrinsic motivation, intellectual curiosity, and engaged reading; and helping students discover the exciting world of learning.

The affective dimensions of learning continue to have an important role in subsequent chapters. Your own passion and literacy skills may increase as you learn more about the texts that are available to motivate your students and the instructional strategies that will improve your students' comprehension, knowledge, and thinking.

CHAPTER TWO

Getting Ready to Teach

2.1 Begin a file for "Content Exploration through Literature." As you read books for your own purposes, keep an eye out for opportunities to connect story happenings or scene descriptions with concepts within your field. Once you start, you'll be amazed at the wealth of possibilities that exist. You can also use this file for professional articles like that of Usnick and McCarthy, where authors share their success in terms of motivating students and teaching concepts through literature. Code those parts that you think might make good teacher read-alouds.

2.2 Look at a course syllabus or state or local curriculum guidelines for a particular course or subject you're interested in teaching. You might use a Teacher's Edition of a required course textbook. Then, create an interest inventory that would help you know the students and make wise decisions about how to engage and motivate them and accomplish the goals of the course.

2.3 Select a book or other text in your content area and plan a literary field trip experience for your students. Using the example given in this chapter as a model, design pre-reading questions and a structure to guide them through the text and help them react to "being there" through reading. You can then add an invitation to take a virtual field trip to an Internet site related to the topic. Refer to Figure 2.10, which provides some guidelines for your planning.

3

The Role of Texts
In Content Area Literacy

A s with the word *literacy*, the definition of the term *text* is constantly evolving and can be used to mean a number of things. In their article "The Role of Text in the Classroom," Wade and Moje define texts as:

> organized networks that people generate or use to make meaning either for themselves or for others. . . . Different views of what counts as text—whether they are formal and informal; oral, written, enacted; permanent or fleeting—lead to different views of what counts as learning, and consequently expand or limit the opportunities students have to learn in classrooms. (2000, p. 610)

This chapter examines several types of texts that can guide you and your students as you strive toward your goal of content area learning, and provides strategies for choosing and using appropriate discipline-related texts as you teach.

Getting Ready to Teach 3.1 *(see page 90)*

Textbooks have historically been a central focus of most content area classes from elementary grades through college (Cuban, 1991; Gottfried & Kyle, 1992). Alvermann and Moore (1991) found that a class set of a single textbook has been the primary reading material in subject area instruction, and these textbooks are rarely supplemented by newspapers, magazines, or library books; more recent research upholds their findings (DiGisi & Willett, 1995; Moje, 1996). Things are changing, however. An article entitled "The Day They Threw Out the Textbooks" (Ryan, 1994) describe a failing intermediate school in Alabama that the faculty restructured by virtually eliminating all textbooks except those used

"Many . . . textbooks, which were a weariness and a stumbling-block when studied, I have since read a little in with pleasure and profit."

THOREAU, 19 FEBRUARY 1854, JOURNAL VI:130

for math and as supplements in other courses. Eight thousand books were purchased and scattered throughout the school's classrooms, and another 8,000 were added to the central library. Teaching, of course, could not remain the same because materials to a large extent determine what and how content is taught. Dunn (2000) reports how four social studies teachers rely on the textbook as a supplementary tool, if at all, with great rewards for students and teachers alike. A school near me, where most students have laptops, is opting for software programs, e-books, and Internet resources more and more.

I advocate the use of multiple texts and genres in every secondary classroom, but I recognize that textbooks, wisely selected and judiciously used, can play a vital role and hold much potential for helping students learn. The first part of this chapter explores the various roles and possibilities of textbooks, along with a discussion of their limitations, and provides suggestions for evaluating and selecting textbooks for particular purposes. The second part of the chapter offers a parallel discussion of non-textbook sources, including several other types of texts that teachers can use to their advantage as they instruct students and lead them toward independent learning in the disciplines. Throughout the chapter and the rest of the book, we explore strategies to help students comprehend all types of text and use them with purpose and with increasing independence.

PART ONE

Textbooks

ACTIVATING PRIOR KNOWLEDGE   3.1

Your own experience using textbooks is a good starting place for thinking about the topic of teaching with textbooks. Think about how you interacted with your textbooks. Did you always read assignments? Why, or why not? Did your teachers actually show you how best to read and use your textbooks? Was it necessary to read the textbooks in order to do well in the classes? Did your teachers know when a significant percentage of students didn't read the assigned material? If so, what was their reaction? Did they do anything about it, or try to find out why the text wasn't read? Were there consequences? What will you do if your students don't read the textbook assignments you give?

TEXTBOOKS IN THE CLASSROOM

Students, as consumers of textbooks, are in some sense the most qualified to judge their usefulness, quality, and ability to promote and enhance learning (and this includes you as a current college student). In general, high school students are not reading much from those textbooks that are so present in their courses (Alvermann & Moore, 1991; Armbruster et al., 1991; Campbell, Voelkl, & Don-

ahue, 1997; DiGisi & Willett, 1995). Some middle and high school teachers have given up expecting students to read the textbooks for their courses. Perhaps the text is too difficult; there is a discrepancy between its readability level (explained later in this chapter) and the actual reading ability of at least some of the students. Often textbooks must stay in the school building because there are not enough to send home with all students taking the courses. Or maybe the students are in a community where extracurricular activities or jobs take up their late afternoon and evening hours. Again, some teachers have changed their teaching as a result. They may outline the chapter during class or give the information from the book in the form of a lecture. I've had students tell me that they don't bother to read their textbooks for some courses because they don't have to: "Mr. Dugan puts everything on the overhead projector, and we copy down what he writes. The tests come right from the notes." Many secondary teachers feel they can cover the content more quickly through lecture or demonstration (O'Brien, Stewart, & Moje, 1995). And when students realize they can rely on teachers' recitations to learn the content, they see little need to read the textbook pages they've been assigned (Hinchman & Zalewski, 1996; Moje, 1996).

Teachers and students too often concentrate on the minimum that must be learned for an assessment, and the textbook really does become unnecessary for that goal to be achieved. So, what happens the next year? Students have not practiced reading a textbook and expect that the course material will be given to them in some other way. They are less prepared and less able to handle the textbook, the difficulty of which has increased because they are in a higher grade. A downward spiral throughout the years can result.

Another limitation of textbooks is that there is so much material to be covered that there simply is not time to go into the depth that could give richness to the various topics introduced. Reduction is the result. Vacca and Vacca (1993) explain:

> One way of thinking about a textbook is that it takes a subject and distills it to its minimal essentials. In doing so, a textbook runs the risk of taking world-shaking events, monumental discoveries, profound insights, intriguing and far-away places, colorful and influential people, and life's mysteries and processes and compressing them into a series of matter-of-fact statements. (p. 298)

These researchers point out that many learners don't view textbooks as significant events in their school lives. "Students generally engage in textbook study to take tests and then proceed to forget some, if not all, of the information they have studied as soon as the test is over" (p. 298).

The authors of newer textbooks and their publishers are now aware that textbook prose can be deadly. They, along with content area experts who criticize textbook-based instruction, ". . . know that obscure, incoherent, dense, impersonal sentences can quickly kill an interest in a topic" (Schallert & Roser, 1996, p. 32). So, authors include material designed specifically to arouse interest in readers—details from a famous person's childhood, perhaps, or a seemingly bizarre characteristic of an animal. The problem with these compensatory measures, research found, is that such passages ". . . can actually undermine readers' ability to learn the more important information presented in a text by drawing readers' attention away from important but less enticing information" (p. 33).

TEXTBOOKS AND POINT OF VIEW

Should textbooks have a point of view? Should we as readers be told the textbook authors' opinions about issues or should the material be presented in an objective, neutral, or balanced manner? Schallert and Roser note, ". . . perhaps because textbook authors are so concerned with their task of mentioning all the necessary topics, they seem to forget to make their prose interesting and to shy away from expressing any particular point of view toward their topic. Textbook language easily takes on a didactic, impersonal tone,

the expression of a reasonable, all-knowing intellect, removed from any emotional commitment to the topic or to the audience" (p. 33). However, when textbook authors do express an evaluation, teachers must help their students recognize this and encourage them to read their texts critically. A student might bring up in a class discussion, for example, "Our textbook refers to John Brown's 'crackbrained scheme' (Bailey, Kennedy, & Cohen, 1998, p. 432) to invade the South secretly. Isn't that a bit judgmental?" The teacher or peers could then give their opinions about whether the textbook's use of that phrase is justified and appropriate.

Some newer textbooks deal with controversial issues by recognizing competing positions and allowing disparate voices to be heard, at least a little. For example, *The American Pageant* (Bailey et al., 1998) includes boxes labeled "Varying Viewpoints," offering a forum for dealing with such questions as "Where Did Modern Conservatism Come From?" (p. 1021) and "The Sixties: Constructive or Destructive?" (p. 961). Opinions and their sources are offered for thought and discussion, as well as for further exploration. Political cartoons representing satiric views are included. Primary and secondary sources listed at the ends of chapters offer more in-depth information than a textbook itself can provide.

CONTINUED RELIANCE ON THE TEXTBOOK

Despite the problems mentioned previously, the textbook is still seen as "the core of the curriculum in most schools" (Duffy & Roehler, 1989, p. 436) and some teachers consider the textbook the "expert" on subject matter, defining curriculum purpose and instructional guidelines. In fact, it has been estimated that between 75 and 90 percent of classrooms in the United States use textbooks almost exclusively, though other types of texts are preferred by learners (Moss, 1991; Palmer & Stewart, 1997). Teachers have relied heavily on textbooks for a number of reasons, including those involving money, convenience, and security (Christenbury & Kelly, 1994). Familiarity and comfort level can also be factors. As Hynd explains, "Traditionally, high school history teachers have felt successful teaching history as a story. Typically, teachers use a single textbook, follow its sequence, and embellish it through skillful storytelling" (1999, p. 429).

SUGGESTIONS FOR USING TEXTBOOKS CREATIVELY

How can you begin to make sense of the seemingly conflicting views on textbook use, weigh the disadvantages and advantages, and decide whether and how to use textbooks? Remember, it is still the teacher who is in control, and a creative teacher can make a less than perfect textbook situation bearable, even beneficial, for herself and her students. Following are some guidelines for helping students use their textbooks.

Provide a Preview Guide

You can prepare students by giving them a guide to preview and help them become familiar with the main textbook they'll be using. Figure 3.1 shows a sample of what I mean. If teachers introduce a textbook well and show students how to use it effectively and efficiently, the students benefit and will grow toward using textbooks independently.

Use Multiple Textbooks

Textbooks can be used as direct sources of instruction or as learning tools in innovative ways. For example, instead of having everyone in your class read the same text, you could make several options available.

Then, students could explore, compare, and contrast. How does one science book compare with another on the topic of evolution theories? How do different publishers and authors treat the era of the Vietnam War? A standard junior high school American history text can be read alongside *Now Is Your Time!: The African American Struggle for Freedom* (1991) by Walter Dean Myers, as well as *We Were There, Too!: Young People in U. S. History* (Hoose, 2001). Using multiple textbooks can turn drudgery into fascination as students explore to find differences and even contradictions.

If you're teaching math concepts, for example, students with various learning styles might require the unique approaches presented by different textbooks. If a student doesn't understand the principles of probability theory, send her to another textbook that might explain it more to her liking or might contain an example that causes the principles to click for her. Textbooks can complement each other, so having several editions produced by various publishers on your classroom shelves makes sense. You can pull versions as needed or have students search independently for alternative explanations and additional examples.

FIGURE 3.1   *A textbook preview guide for* The American Pageant.

Dear Students:

Welcome to our American history course and to your textbook, which will be a constant companion to you, along with lots of supplemental materials, throughout the year.

Treat this activity like a puzzle or a treasure hunt; it will help you become familiar with some of the features of this book. Use your knowledge of the structure of textbooks to answer the following questions. Your answers will help me determine how to best teach you. If you don't know how to find an answer, make an X on that question to let me know. I'll conduct mini-lessons as needed.

1. State two ways the maps of the United States on the inside front cover and the inside back cover are different.
2. What documents can be found in the Appendix?
3. On what page could you find information on James Baldwin? Where did you look to get your answer?
4. What kind of information will you find in the "Makers of America" sections of the text? Give a specific example.

5. Write the page number where you located an example of each of the following:
   - a political cartoon
   - a photograph
   - a treatment of varying viewpoints about a topic
   - a chapter title
   - a sub-heading within a chapter
   - an introduction to one of the major parts (1–6) of this textbook
   - a primary source
6. After the table of contents, you'll find two helpful lists. What are they?
7. After perusing this book, what is your initial reaction? What do you think you'll like about it? What scares you or puts you off? What questions do you have for me about the book or how we'll use it?
8. Do you think the book will be too easy, too difficult, or just about right for you?

Plan to interact with this book; I'll be teaching you ways to read the material actively rather than passively. As we progress, please tell me about any areas of difficulty. If you don't understand something about a topic or about how to use this textbook effectively, let me know.

Tailor the Text and Teaching Materials to Your Class

Van de Walle (1998) offers several criticisms of math textbooks, including their datedness. "There is a significant time lapse between state-of-the-art mathematics education and what appears in textbooks" (p. 498). Another problem is their philosophical stance. "The most recent mainstream books remain very close to the 'teach by telling' model. . . . The mainstream textbook is designed for a teacher who believes that the best teaching is done by following the text and who values a high proportion of drill and practice" (p. 498). Rather than recommending that textbooks be abandoned, he suggested several ways that teachers can use textbooks wisely, including using the alternatives provided in teachers' editions, judiciously selecting only those exercises that truly benefit certain classes or students, and teaching to the big ideas instead of letting the textbook rule the format and pace of the class.

Encourage Students to Think Critically About Their Textbooks

A teacher's assignments and guidance in terms of using the text as one resource along with many others may change the way students perceive and use their textbook. For example, supply students with books and articles that point out flaws in textbooks, such as potential bias or omissions, as well as errors found in textbooks, and help students explore and analyze their own textbooks to see whether they can find examples of problems or even outright misinformation. A thought-provoking book to start with is Loewen's *Lies My Teacher Told Me: Everything Your American History Textbook Got Wrong* (1995). Students can use the Internet, a bookstore, or a librarian to seek out similar resources dealing with textbooks in other areas.

Textbooks aren't going to go away, and in many places, they are mandated. Thus, we should learn to use them creatively, in ways that entice our students to read them. The good news is that textbooks are improving in many ways; publishers have listened to consumers. Perhaps in response to threats from process- and literature-based classrooms that have shown textbooks are not necessary for learning to occur, as well as to the reality that it is now much easier, and possibly cheaper, to access up-to-date information from the Internet, publishers are making textbooks more attractive and user-friendly. Authors understand reading theory better as research proliferates, and so they construct the texts with the readers' needs and learning styles in mind. So, we can take advantage of the improved versions, though we still must know how to use them well, without becoming slaves to them or surrendering our curriculum to them. Teachers must help students become active, engaged, critical readers of their textbooks. Schallert and Roser remind us, "It is the teacher, not the textbook, who is responsible for guiding the process of learning, even of learning from the text" (1996, p. 31). The subsequent chapters in this book, while dealing with specific literacy issues and instructional strategies, continue to provide examples of how you can use textbooks, as well as other types of material, to help your students become more literate in the disciplines you teach.

EVALUATING AND SELECTING TEXTBOOKS

I arrived one morning to visit a student teacher I was supervising and found her in a wonderful frame of mind. I thought her teaching must have been going remarkably well, but she was bubbling about something else. "My cooperating teacher is on a textbook adoption committee that's going to choose a new math series for the district. I got to go out to dinner with her and a publishing representative, and I ordered steak! And I got this calculator free, and look at these manipulatives I get to keep for my own classroom some day!" She sounded as if she was ready to sign on the dotted line had she headed the committee. She hadn't said a word, however, about the quality of the textbooks that publishing company had to offer, or how well the series matched the needs of the students in that district.

Textbooks are big business; school districts spend a lot of money on them and expect them to be used. Earlier, I pointed out the potential advantages and limitations of textbooks in general. In reality, there is a huge range in terms of the characteristics and quality of particular textbooks, as well as the cost, another factor that comes into play. How are textbooks selected? You may have the wonderful opportunity and important responsibility of evaluating textbooks or a series for your classroom or district at a time when you actually have a voice in determining the outcome of the selection process. At other times, you may be teaching within the constraints of being expected to use a textbook that was chosen for you, perhaps even at the state level—far removed from your students and you. In any case, it is extremely important that you gain expertise in evaluating textbooks. Once you know their strengths and flaws or weaknesses, you can teach with those in mind and instruct your students on how to achieve the most from the materials.

Resources for evaluating textbooks include the professional educational journals in your field, which publish reviews of recent textbooks. These reviews, usually written by other instructors, are a valuable resource. They discuss both the strengths and weaknesses of the materials. Read several reviews, familiarizing yourself with common criteria used by reviewers when possible, and the context of their remarks. Compare your own evaluation of publishers' materials you examine with evaluations offered in the reviews you read. Perhaps you'll want to add your own voice to the professional conversation by submitting a textbook review to be considered for publication by a journal you respect.

ACTION RESEARCH   3.A

Go to the website of a major textbook publishing company, such as Scott Foresman, Harcourt Brace, Houghton Mifflin, or Merrill. Read what information is available on a textbook appropriate for the grade level and subject area you wish to teach. If outside reviews are not available, write the company via e-mail and ask whether the textbook has been reviewed in any educational journals. If possible, read the reviews themselves. Respond in your learning log.

In a general review of 10 of the most widely used biology textbooks in U. S. high schools, a group of scientists concluded that all were unsatisfactory (2000). They looked at how the texts explained key concepts in the discipline (e.g., cell structure and function, matter and energy transformations, and natural selection and evolution). They found that the texts, while focusing on easy-to-test trivia, glossed over vital concepts and failed to encourage students to examine their ideas and relate the lessons to life. Students might be able to name the parts of a cell, for example, but not understand how cells work and how that could affect cancer research. None of the books were rated highly in terms of building on what students already know or correcting misconceptions. Similarly, the results of an analysis of nine high school biology manuals showed that they seldom enabled students to use their knowledge to investigate natural phenomena, solve problems, pose questions, or make generalizations (Germann, Haskins, & Auls, 1996). Reports like this can help you examine the textbooks your school uses or is considering and make decisions as to how you use the books and how you should supplement them to address their shortcomings or biases.

Getting Ready to Teach 3.2 (see page 90)

PERFORMING YOUR OWN TEXTBOOK EVALUATION

Textbooks may be examined according to many criteria and using a variety of methods. I discuss four methods, but urge you to use a combination approach because no one procedure is complete in itself.

1. Use Your Own Judgment

You will be, if you are not already, an avid reader and an expert in the content area you teach. Therefore, as you read through and subjectively respond to a textbook, you can learn a lot. Notice your thoughts and feelings as you peruse the book. After you've made an initial judgment, you can use the following questions to guide and refine your evaluation:

- Do you find the information intriguing and enticing?

- Do the authors make your job easy by organizing the material in a coherent manner? Are the chapters and subsections well-organized? Do the chapters contain introductions and summaries? This is called *considerate text* (Armbruster, 1984).

- Do the pictures, graphs, and charts work well with the text itself? Are they clear and meaningful? Are captions present and helpful?

- Do you like the questions asked of the students before, during, or after the chapters? Are they stimulating, thought-provoking? Do they call for mere literal recall, or do they stimulate students to think critically, apply concepts, and synthesize information?

- Does the material's presentation encourage readers to engage in higher-level thinking skills?

- Does the publisher supply supplemental materials such as workbook exercises, and, if so, do they require the students to do things that will actually further their practice of a skill or their knowledge of a subject? Do you consider them a valuable use of your and your students' time or just busywork?

- Are suggestions and resources given for further exploration using primary and secondary sources, and websites?

- Are technical terms highlighted, defined well, and explained adequately?

- Is there a glossary? an index? bibliography? appendices?
- Does the text presume an appropriate amount of background knowledge in relation to what you know about your students?
- Do the illustrations and examples represent race, ethnicity, gender, and class fairly? Are the representations of people nonstereotypical?
- Do the authors use nonsexist language throughout?
- Are the examples ones that students can relate to?

If you are answering in the negative, be as specific as possible in identifying the potential problems. This will help if you have to instruct the students on using the text. You'll know which sections might require that you supply more background knowledge, which parts should be complemented or supplemented with other sources, what information you might challenge in your lectures.

2. Apply a Readability Formula

A readability formula is a ready-made procedure used to approximate the difficulty level of printed material that consists of connected prose. There are several available, including the Flesch "Reading Ease" Formula and the Dale–Chall Readability Formula. The Fry Readability Graph (Fry, 1977), shown with step-by-step instructions in Figure 3.2, is one of the most popular. The resulting scores are represented as grade levels, and they reflect the level at which a child should read with the assistance of a teacher. An advantage to applying formulas is that they are easy and quick to use. Yet, many caveats must accompany any recommendation to use such formulas, for, although they have their place, they have been misused. A readability formula provides no more than a rough guide. It usually uses sentence length, number of syllables, and word difficulty or length as criteria to determine difficulty. We know, however, that many more variables, including a reader's back-

---

FIGURE 3.2   *Instructions for using Edward Fry's Readability Graph.*

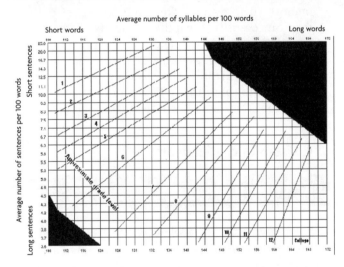

Expanded Directions for Working Readability Graph

1. Randomly select three (3) sample passages and count out exactly 100 words each, beginning with the beginning of a sentence. Do count proper nouns, initializations, and numerals.

2. Count the number of sentences in the hundred words, estimating length of the fraction of the last sentence to the nearest one-tenth.

3. Count the total number of syllables in the 100-word passage. If you don't have a hand counter available,

an easy way is to simply put a mark above every syllable over one in each word, then when you get to the end of the passage, count the number of marks and add 100. Small calculators can also be used as counters by pushing numeral 1, then push the 1 sign for each word or syllable when counting.

4. Enter graph with average sentence length and average number of syllables; plot dot where the two lines intersect. Area where dot is plotted will give you the approximate grade level.

5. If a great deal of variability is found in syllable count or sentence count, putting more samples into the average is desirable.

6. A word is defined as a group of symbols with a space on either side; thus, *Joe, IRA, 1945,* and *&* are each one word.

7. A syllable is defined as a phonetic syllable. Generally, there are as many syllables as vowel sounds. For example, *stopped* is one syllable and *wanted* is two syllables. When counting syllables for numerals and initializations, count one syllable for each symbol. For example, *1945* is four syllables, *IRA* is three syllables, and *&* is one syllable.

Note: This "extended graph" does not outmode or render the earlier (1968) version inoperative or inaccurate; it is an extension.

Fry's Readability Graph: Clarifications, Validity, and Extension to Level 17, *Journal of Reading,* 21 (December 1977), 249. Reproduction permitted; no copyright.

ground knowledge, interest in the topic, and motivation to succeed, may play even more important a part in determining how well a student can handle a text. The formulas do not take into account the use of specialized vocabulary or the abstractness of the concepts being taught. They are absolutely not intended to be used as guides to writing.

A readability formula does provide a good and easy way to estimate the appropriateness of a text in terms of difficulty. However, in individual cases, your professional judgment can and should override the formula's rating. If, for example, after applying the other evaluation procedures explained here, you prefer a certain ninth grade textbook over the other options, even though the formula indicated that it has a tenth grade readability level, you can still choose the textbook—just remember, you'll have to provide more help to make the text accessible to your students. By listening carefully to your students as they use the text, and by actively seeking their feedback, you'll know whether they're struggling and in what ways they're finding the text hard to comprehend.

There are also software packages available that can calculate the difficulty level of texts. One such is Readability Plus, consisting of "Reading Calculations" to determine a grade level and "Vocabulary Assessor" to determine the difficulty of the words used in a passage. Although more expensive than the methods described above, these programs save time, so a district might look into purchasing these tools for use by the faculty and students. Information about Readability Plus can be found at www.micro powerandlight.com/rd.html.

3. Use the Cloze Procedure

Your students' input is necessary to complete the cloze procedure, which has been used for decades to determine texts' appropriateness for instructional and independent use. Type up a passage of 250–300 words from the content area textbook you're evaluating. Leave the first and last sentences intact, and delete every fifth word from the remaining text. Stop deleting words when you have 50 blanks. (Variations on this procedure are recommended by some experts for different subject areas or purposes, but this is the most often-used method.) If the textbook you're using becomes progressively more difficult, you might want to select a middle passage or use two—a fairly early passage and a later selection.

Ask your students to read the passage and fill in the blanks with their best guesses based on semantic and syntactic context. Then, add up the correct responses—count only exact replacements even if a synonym makes sense. Although accepting a synonym as a correct response may seem logical, there is a rationale for the rule of exact replacement: It makes the scoring more reliable. No advantage is gained by accepting synonym replacements because doing so merely increases everyone's score, and requires the use of different percentage bands to interpret the results. (If you use the cloze procedure for instructional purposes instead of assessing the difficulty of the textbook itself, the rules can change.)

Multiply the number of correct responses by two to obtain a percentage score. Students who show a cloze score of 50 percent or higher are at an independent level; they should be able to read the material with no assistance. Those students who score between 30 and 50 percent are at an instructional level—they require teacher guidance but should be able to learn from the text. Students scoring below 30 percent will likely find the textbook too difficult; they are at the frustration level (Pikulski & Tobin, 1982). Because there are variations of this procedure, you might discover a cloze method that uses slightly different percentages to determine the levels of difficulty. Later chapters provide suggestions on how to substitute more accessible texts, use compensatory ways of teaching the material, and help students improve their reading skills and strategies so that they can eventually handle the textbook that gave them difficulty. A sample cloze passage in Chapter 10 focuses on the assessment of students' reading ability and learning. The cloze procedure can be used both to gauge the difficulty of texts and to tell you about the readers as individuals or groups.

4. Listen to the Students

ACTION RESEARCH 3.B

If you have access to adolescents through a practicum connected to your course work or some other avenue, listen to what the current consumers of secondary textbooks have to say about the products. As Lester and Cheek did in their study that was reported in "The 'Real' Experts Address Textbook Issues" (1997/1998), ask one or more students the following questions:

1. Is a textbook available for each of your classes?

2. How often do you use your textbook?

3. Which is your favorite textbook and why?

4. Which is your least favorite textbook and why?

5. If you were writing a textbook, how would you set it up? (p. 284)

Listen carefully to student input, and compare your answers with those of others in your class, if possible. You might be surprised at the wealth and depth of the data you collect. Your middle and secondary students can tell you how they are interacting with their textbooks, what they like and dislike about them, what parts they find particularly confusing or difficult, and how the structure and organization help or hinder their comprehension and ability to retain information.

Lester and Cheek (1997/1998) surveyed students in grades 9 through 11 to find out what they thought about their textbooks in various subjects. The students indicated that they liked math textbooks the least and English texts the most. They offered recommendations to improve the textbooks, including using more graphics and illustrations, dealing with more topics that interest teens, presenting vocabulary in a student-friendly way, and using larger print. Lester and Cheek conclude: "Students are experts because they have consistently been exposed to textbooks as an integral part of their learning process. . . . It is critical to view your students as decision makers in this collaborative process. Their ideas incorporated with yours will result in a more productive learning environment" (pp. 290–291).

Keep your ears open for random or unsolicited comments made by your students about their instructional materials, and feel free to ask them questions so that you know what they think about their textbook. For example, you may have selected a particular textbook partially because you were happy with its metadiscourse—language authors use to ensure that the reader is aware of author intention and perception (Shanahan & Tierney, 1990). Some authors choose to talk directly to their readers (as I do to you) to make purposes clear, to enhance understanding, to contextualize and connect ideas. In some textbooks, this aspect is missing; for example, students might know that they are learning about quadratic equations, but the textbook has not specified why or how that knowledge is useful. Even when metadiscourse is present, in order to know whether this textbook feature is having the desired effect on the students, you may have to ask them. Maybe they're not picking up on the assistance offered through the author's direct communication; maybe they find the tone too chatty or obtrusive. Their responses will help you make wise instructional decisions when guiding them in the use of their textbooks.

It's likely you'll be using the same textbook for several years, so the information you gain from paying attention to your students can help you in subsequent years. Keep notes, perhaps right in your Teacher's Edition of the textbook, to remind yourself of the valuable input you get from your student readers.

Figure 3.3 shows excerpts from a preservice teacher's evaluation of a textbook that she has seen used in courses she hopes to teach some day.

Instructors must strive to keep textbook use in proper perspective. Schallert and Roser (1996) emphasize:

> If there is one area in great need of improvement in the education of future content area teachers, it is in encouraging them to be as innovative and active as guides to textbook reading as they are in other components of instruction. It is the teacher, not the textbook, who is responsible for guiding the process of learning, even of learning from the text. (p. 31)

Textbooks are not the enemy; textbooks should encourage students to be active, continuing learners, rather than viewing textbooks as the stopping point. Teachers should help students see the place textbooks have in the overall scheme of a particular course. For example, I draw a Venn diagram consisting of four intersecting circles for my preservice teachers—the textbook serves as one opportunity for learning, while our in-class activities, their practicum placements, and their experiences as readers and writers serve as others. Sometimes these learning opportunities overlap, and other times, a particular piece of knowledge can only be gained or constructed from one of the sources.

Estes and Vasquez-Levy (2001) suggest viewing textbooks not as the curriculum but as a compendium, to be used like a desk encyclopedia. They describe a situation where one teacher taught a section of American history using only a textbook, a second taught using only Esther Forbes' novel *Johnny Tremain* (1996), and a third used both. The students who used only the textbook learned the least, as determined by an end-of-unit test. The authors found that the sin committed by most textbooks is that of "'mentioning,' the awful tendency to say very little about very much" (p. 509). The textbook is often a necessary component, but it is virtually never sufficient.

FIGURE 3.3 *Excerpts from a preservice teacher's review of a content area textbook.*

The textbook I chose to use, a standard across New York State, is *Course I, Integrated Mathematics*, 3rd Edition, by Isadore Dressler and Edward P. Keenan (New York: Amsco School Publications, Inc., 1998). I applied Fry's Readability Graph to the book, which is commonly used in eighth or ninth grade classrooms. I chose three random hundred-word passages. . . . The average ended up being a seven sentence passage with 153 syllables, which places it at a ninth grade reading level, exactly where it's supposed to be. As far as the usability of this book, I have concluded that it is an excellent book that I would be more than happy to use in my classroom.

Obviously, vocabulary is a big part of the math curriculum. Each year introduces a new set of words for students to learn. This book has every vocabulary term italicized, and it is defined within one or two sentences of the word's initial use.

Each chapter's main ideas or purposes for reading are explicitly stated in the beginning. The first chapter begins with a review of the definition of whole numbers, their uses and where they're found, and why we have them. The chapter ends with a discussion on number lines and graphs. The authors present an organizational structure to guide the student while reading/studying. Each topic is presented along with several examples, which the authors work out, explaining every step along the way. After the topic has been covered, there is a page of exercises for the students to attempt for themselves.

The Table of Contents is excellent, showing a logical development of subject matter. There are lots of graphs, tables, diagrams and pictures, with clearly written captions.

[One weakness is that] there are no outside resources listed as available to the students, or projects for the students to attempt.

So, my overall rating for this textbook is: EXCELLENT.

—*Vanessa Dudley*

TEXTBOOK ADAPTATIONS FOR STUDENTS WITH SPECIAL EDUCATIONAL NEEDS

As noted in Chapter 2, a number of factors cause students to have difficulty with reading. You will have struggling readers in your subject area class, so you must find ways to help them be successful. Middle grade students with learning disabilities are, on average, reading at a level three years behind grade level (Schumaker & Lenz, 1999). So, your eighth grade science textbook will be difficult or impossible for those students without some accommodations. Fortunately, there is much you can do. You can order books on tape for students with particular learning disabilities or vision loss; some students' Individualized Education Plans (IEPs) will require that the text be read to them—there is technology available that can "read" books out loud. Also, it is not necessary that everyone use the same textbook all of the time—textbooks written at an easier level might be a good place for some students to start, and you can fill in any additional information or help students read specific parts of the class textbook that you're using.

Some students must have direct instruction and practice to recognize the textbook's structure and features. For example, you might model how you pre-view a chapter by looking at the headings and subheadings and reading the topic sentences. Ask your students how they're handling the textbook, and identify the specific areas of difficulty from their answers and by watching them. Monitor them as they read, and note where comprehension breaks down in order to determine what strategies might work. Assure them that they will get the support they need in order to comprehend the textbook material.

PART TWO

Beyond the Textbook

Textbooks certainly have their place in content area classrooms, and you may use one or more either as the backbone of your instruction or as a supplementary resource. However, textbooks are not enough. Thus, we now explore materials beyond the traditional textbook, concentrating on several types of trade books and primary sources. Other materials, such as electronic resources and film, are discussed in subsequent chapters.

TRADE BOOKS

Some of the students' complaints about textbooks listed previously (e.g., the book is not interesting, the information is too compacted) can be alleviated or corrected by using *trade books* in subject area classes. Trade books are any books other than textbooks or reference books. Think of the books people buy from bookstores or borrow from libraries; think of children's and young adult literature. Trade books can be narrative or expository, and they span all genres: fiction, poetry, essays, biography, and so on.

The use of trade books in classrooms is growing in popularity; hundreds of articles by teachers at all grade levels describe increased student interest, understanding, and enthusiasm, as well as an increased ability in writing and reading, as trade books replace or supplement textbooks. Alvermann (1994) points out that trade books can increase students' background knowledge in a subject, making the textbook reading more interesting and accessible. She sees a bright future: "Making connections between trade books and textbooks is certain to have a positive impact on teachers' success in motivating and sustaining students' interests in reading and learning across the curriculum" (p. 67). Often trade books provide better material that stimulates a higher level of creative and critical thinking, or expand the students' understanding and provide a deeper dimension of learning, or put information into perspective for students (Savage, 1994). In some cases, they are a better match to individual reading levels, abilities, and learning styles than the standard grade-level textbook chosen by the district or state.

Alvermann (1994) also identifies some concerns about trade books. Some teachers are concerned about the appropriateness (from a literary point of view) of expecting students to read trade books as foundational sources of information for their subject areas. Perhaps some of the pure enjoyment a novel can give, for example, is diminished. This concern is well-founded. It is certainly possible for a teacher to ruin a good book by exercising too much control over how it is read. Recall that in Chapter 1 we thought about the devastating effect of being asked to answer end-of-chapter questions 23 times during our reading of the literary masterpiece, *The Giver*.

Another concern is whether the students can actually transfer the concepts and knowledge gleaned from trade books to their reading of textbooks. Alvermann points out the possibility that trade books, especially multiple books on a topic, add to students' depth of understanding, as well as serve as a bridge to teaching content from textbooks.

As a rule, trade books are superior to textbooks in their ability to tap into the *affective* realm, discussed in Chapter 2. When students' emotions and values become involved, they are more likely to be engaged with the material and remember it longer. Recall from Chapter 1 that Rosenblatt classified reading as having either an *efferent* (the reader is primarily concerned with extracting information from

BookTalk   3.1

Would you like to travel through time? You might think that time travel is merely the stuff of science fiction, but physicists deal with the topic seriously and with respect. One theoretical explanation of the phenomenon is given in Madeleine L'Engle's Newbery winner, *A Wrinkle in Time* (1962). Crossing time barriers is simple compared to the larger problem the story addresses—good versus evil. Travel through time and space with the Murry children as they try to rescue their captive father on the faraway planet of Camazotz, and you'll learn some math and science along the way! (Note that this book was also booktalked in Chapter 2. I want you to learn how to invite readers to come to books in different ways and for different purposes.)

BookTalk   3.2

Debate has continued for over half a century about the necessity and morality of the first wartime use of the atomic bomb. Several picture books can help us understand the consequences to those most immediately and directly affected. *Shin's Tricycle,* by Tatsuhari Kodama (1995), shares the true story of an innocent three-year-old victim of the bomb; you'll see photographs of Shin and of the tricycle he was riding when the bomb fell (on display at the Hiroshima Peace Museum). *Hiroshima No Pika,* by Toshi Maruki (1980), and *My Hiroshima,* by Junko Morimoto (1990), tell of the happenings of August 6, 1945, from the perspective of the city's citizens. *Sadako,* by Eleanor Coerr (1993), relates another true story of a girl dying from leukemia, the "atom bomb disease," a decade after the war; the book includes paintings of the memorial statue of Sadako. The powerful text and illustrations in all of these books will stay with you for a long time. Take a look at these books—reading about wars in your history textbooks will never be the same.

BookTalk   3.3

Are you the type who used to get yelled at for taking alarm clocks and Game Boys apart to see how they worked? Or, like me, are you closer to the type who tends to feel faint when looking at a computer board or under the hood of a car? Wherever you are on the "I wonder how it works?" continuum, you'll enjoy David Macaulay's book *The New Way Things Work* (1998). There's a story line—a woolly mammoth takes readers on a visual trek through history, explaining dozens of inventions; there are also understandable explanations of such principles as fission and fusion. This enjoyable and informative literary experience is also available on CD-ROM.

But wait, there's more! Another book, by Henry Beard and Ron Barrett, followed Macaulay's original version. Theirs is called *The Way Things Really Work* (1993), and includes chapters such as "How Elevators Know to Close their Doors when You Come Running," and "How a 50 Cent Pet Can Cost You $50 by Dying." It's a parody, and it's funny.

a text) or *aesthetic* (the reader is engaged with the material and experiences emotions as she reads and responds) purpose. Trade books can be used for either purpose or for both. The booktalks above relate to texts that teach scientific or historical information while telling engaging stories or otherwise involving the reader.

The next three subsections will help you understand how you might use particular genres of trade books to teach content, as well as enhance your students' literacy.

Picture Books

As middle or high school teachers, you may not have been exposed to the array of wonderful texts in this category—so you may think that using picture books with secondary students is inappropriate because they are too easy or the students may feel insulted by their use. During the past decade, however, many sophisticated and beautiful picture books filled with information and thought-provoking prose were published. Content area teachers can use these books to enhance vocabulary growth; present the facts, theories, and background necessary for new lessons; clarify discipline-related concepts; and show how content knowledge is applied in real life (Bloem & Padak, 1996). Perhaps most important,

having picture books in your classrooms can lead to an increase in the *volume* of reading done by your students, as they peruse your classroom collection during free moments at the beginning or end of class or while waiting for others to finish an assignment. Miller (1998) reports:

> A common, and perhaps surprising, experience of middle-level teachers introducing quality picture books in their classrooms is the delight of many of their early adolescent students (10–14 years old). The combination of stimulating artwork, accessible language, and shortness of text can be very appealing to this age group. Part of the appeal, too, is probably to that side of middle-level students that is not quite ready to completely give up childhood experiences. (pp. 376–377)

Perhaps you can visualize having picture books in your classroom for students to enjoy as an extra, but you're having difficulty thinking of how you could really *teach* from them. The following example might help. Yenika-Agbaw (1997) demonstrates how *Christmas in the Big House, Christmas in the Quarters,* by Patricia and Frederick McKissack (1994), can be read from an aesthetic stance; she notes the power and beauty of the illustrations by John Thompson, the sadness evoked by the story contrasting two very different types of holiday preparation on the plantation, the universal theme of festivity, "... the love that existed among family members in the cultures of masters and slaves as they celebrated Christmas" (p. 448).

Although she accepts that her personal interpretation was rewarding, Yenika-Agbaw goes on to share a postcolonial reading of the book to illustrate how texts can be read for social change. Recognizing slavery as a colonial institution that perpetuated the domination of others, she discusses the book's use of the symbols of whiteness, blackness, and Christmas present; the use of both Standard English (the language of oppression) and slave dialect, and those parts of the plot that helped her gain "insight into an historical past that set the pattern for the social injustices based on race—a history of domination, subjugation, and exclusion of Black people that began a long time ago and continues to shape race relations." (p. 450). Finally, Yenika-Agbaw gives a critical multicultural reading of the picture book, to "uncover the signs of domination (race, class, gender) manifested by the slave masters, pitted against the subtle signs of resistance (words and deeds) from the slaves" (p. 450). She connects the story to what she knows of the political and social chaos present in our day, seeing evidence from both data sources that the oppressed will continue to seek ways to resist domination.

Yenika-Agbaw concludes by providing specific strategies that teachers can use to encourage multiple readings and interpretations. She suggests having students ask questions about the texts they read and then respond to both text-based and life-based questions in literacy journals that can be exchanged with peers. Students can connect new texts with others read previously, and can read critically and reexamine their ideological perspectives. Children's picture books can lead to serious and deep learning and ultimately to actions for social justice.

I encourage you to go to bookstores and libraries to explore the genre of informational picture books, and to enthusiastically recommend your favorites to your students. If *you* do not treat these books as though they're babyish and beneath you, your students will be more likely to respect and use them, also. Figure 3.4 lists examples of high-quality picture books that can be used profitably in content area classes; some are interdisciplinary and so fit more than one category. We deal more with this genre in Chapter 9 when we explore visual literacy.

FIGURE 3.4 *Examples of picture books appropriate for teaching concepts in middle and high school discipline areas.*

MATH, SCIENCE, AND TECHNOLOGY

Ballard, R. D. (1988). *Exploring the Titanic*. Toronto, Canada: Madison Press Books.

Bernardy, C. J. (1999). *Fuel*. Mankato, MN: Creative Education.

Cherry, L. (1992). *A River Ran Wild: An Environmental History*. New York: Dutton.

Collard, S. B., III, & Rothman, M. (2000). *The Forest in the Clouds*. Watertown, MA: Charlesbridge Publishing.

Florian, D. (1998). *Insectlopedia*. New York: Harcourt Brace.

Henderson, D. (2000). *Asteroid Impact*. New York: Dial Books for Young Readers.

Kaner, E., & Stephans, P. (1999). *Animal Defenses: How Animals Protect Themselves*. New York: Scholastic.

Lauber, P. (1987). *Volcano: The Eruption and Healing of Mount. St. Helens*. New York: Dell Publishing.

Locker, T. (1997). *Water Dance*. San Diego, CA: Harcourt Brace.

Markle, S. (1997). *Discovering Graph Secrets: Experiments, Puzzles, and Games Exploring Graphs*. New York: Atheneum.

Ride, S., & O'Shaughnessy, T. (1999). *The Mystery of Mars*. New York: Scholastic.

Sandved, K. B. (1996). *The Butterfly Alphabet*. New York: Scholastic.

Schmandt-Besserat, D., & Hays, M. (2000). *The History of Counting*. New York: Scholastic.

Schwartz, D. (1985). *How Much Is a Million?* New York: Lothrop, Lee & Shepard.

Settel, J. (1999). *Exploding Ants: Amazing Facts About How Animals Adapt*. New York: Atheneum.

Siebert, P. (1999). *Discovering El Nino: How Fable and Fact Together Help Explain the Weather*. Brookfield, CT: Millbrook Press.

Viera, L. (1994). *The Ever-Living Tree: The Life and Times of a Coast Redwood*. New York: Walker.

Wick, W. (1997). *A Drop of Water*. New York: Scholastic.

Wright-Frierson, V. (1998). *An Island Scrapbook: Dawn to Dusk on a Barrier Island*. New York: Simon & Schuster.

(continued)

FIGURE 3.4 *Continued.*

SOCIAL STUDIES

Angelou, M., & Courtney-Clarke, M. (1994). *My Painted House, My Friendly Chicken, and Me.* New York: Clarkson Potter.

Bial, R. (1995). *The Underground Railroad.* Boston: Houghton Mifflin.

Bunting, E., & Diaz, D. (1994). *Smoky Night.* New York: Harcourt Brace.

Coerr, E., & Young, E. (1993). *Sadako.* New York: Putnam.

Corey, S., & McLaren, C. (2000). *You Forgot Your Skirt, Amelia Bloomer!* New York: Scholastic.

McCurdy, M. (2000). *An Algonquian Year: The Year According to the Full Moon.* Boston: Houghton Mifflin.

Hest, A., & Lynch, P. J. (1997). *When Jessie Came Across the Sea.* New York: Scholastic.

Innocenti, R., & Gallaz, C. (1990). *Rose Blanche.* New York: Stewart, Tabori & Chang.

King, M. L., Jr. (1997). *I Have A Dream.* (Paintings by 15 Coretta Scott King Award and Honor Book Artists.) New York: Scholastic.

Lawrence, J. (1993). *Harriet and the Promised Land.* New York: Simon & Schuster.

Musgrove, M., & Yaldez, B. (1976). *Ashanti to Zulu: African Traditions.* New York: Dial Books.

Sis, P. (1998). *Tibet Through the Red Box.* New York: Frances Foster/Farrar.

Ryan, P. M., & Selznick, B. (1999). *Amelia and Eleanor Go for a Ride.* New York: Scholastic.

Tsuchiya, Y., & Lewin, T. (1988). *Faithful Elephants.* Boston: Houghton Mifflin.

Zhang, S. N. (1998). *The Children of China: An Artist's Journey.* Plattsburg, NY: Tundra/McClelland.

FINE ARTS

Houston, J. A. (1998). *Fire into Ice: Adventures in Glass Making.* Plattsburg, NY: Tundra/McClelland.

Lauber, P. (1998). *Painters of the Caves.* New York: Scholastic.

Micklewait, L. (1996). *I Spy a Freight Train: Transportation in Art.* New York: Greenwillow Books.

Monseaux, M. (1994). *Jazz: My Music, My People.* New York: Knopf.

Nichol, B., & Cameron, S. (1994). *Beethoven Lives Upstairs.* New York: Orchard Books.

Richardson, J. (2000). *Looking at Faces in Art.* Milwaukee, WI: Gareth Stevens Publishing.

Rubin, S. G. (2000). *Fireflies in the Dark: The Story of Friedl Dicker-Brandeis and the Children of Terezin.* New York: Scholastic.

Turner, B. C. (1996). *The Living Flute.* New York: Knopf.

Visconti, G., & Landmann, B. (2000). *The Genius of Leonardo.* New York: Barefoot Books.

ENGLISH LANGUAGE ARTS

Blake, W., & Waldman, N. (1993). *Tyger.* New York: Harcourt Brace.

Coville, B., & Sanderson, R. (1994). *William Shakespeare's The Tempest.* New York: Delacorte Press.

Franklin, K. L., & McGirr, N. (Eds.). (1995). *Out of the Dump: Writings and Photographs by Children of Guatemala.* New York: Lothrop, Lee & Shepard.

Lasky, K., & Hess, M. (1997). *Hercules: The Man, the Myth, the Hero.* New York: Hyperion Books for Children.

Lyon, G. E., & Catalanotto, P. (1999). *Book.* New York: DK Publishing.

Wisniewski, D. (1996). *Golem.* New York: Clarion Books.

Poetry

You might be surprised at how much poetry exists that is accessible to young adults and relevant to school subject areas. Although many students and teachers tend to think of poetry as belonging exclusively in English courses because that's where it's typically taught, there's no need to limit it. Poetry is ideal for all areas because there are ways to use it without taking up much instructional time. You may use a collection of poems to start your lessons as a motivational strategy. For example, a science or health teacher might use the following humorous poem at the beginning of a lesson on communicable diseases.

The Germ

A mighty creature is the germ,
Though smaller than the pachyderm.
His customary dwelling place
Is deep within the human race.
His childish pride he often pleases,
By giving people strange diseases.
Do you, my poppet, feel infirm?
You probably contain a germ.

Copyright © 1935 by Ogden Nash, renewed. Reprinted by permission of Curtis Brown, Ltd.

An English teacher might use the following poem as a mini-lesson to emphasize the importance of punctuation before she hands back some student papers that were a bit lacking in that area:

> Call the doctors Call the nurses Give me a breath of air I've been reading all your stories but the periods aren't there Call the policemen Call the traffic guards Give me a stop sign quick Your sentences are running when they need a walking stick Call the commas Call the question marks Give me a single clue Tell me where to breathe with a punctuation mark or two

Reprinted with permission of Simon & Schuster Books for Young Readers, an imprint of Simon & Schuster Children's Publishing Division from *If You're Not Here Please Raise Your Hand* by Kalli Dakos, Text copyright © 1990.

A physical education class can enjoy such poems as "Casey at the Bat" (Thayer, 2000, p. 282) along with sequels: "Casey's Revenge" (Wilson, 1960, p. 284), "Casey—Twenty Years Later" (McDonald, 1936, p. 286), and "Casey's Daughter at the Bat" (Graham, 1988, p. 42).

Chapters 1 and 2 addressed the affective realm of learning, and poetry is a perfect way to help students invest emotionally in the topics they study. For example, compare this textbook excerpt (from *The American Pageant)* on the topic of Reconstruction with the poem narrated by a former Southern soldier that follows it. Consider how a teacher might use the two genres together.

> Beaten but unbent, many high-spirited white Southerners remained dangerously defiant.... Conscious of no crime, these former Confederates continued to believe that their view of secession was correct and that the 'lost cause' was still a just war. (Bailey, Kennedy, & Cohen, 1998, p. 489)

The Rebel

> . . . I won't be reconstructed! I'm better now than them;
> And for a carpetbagger, I don't give a damn;
> So I'm off for the frontier, soon as I can go,
> I'll prepare me a weapon and start for Mexico.
>
> I can't take up my musket and fight them now no mo',
> But I'm not goin' to love 'em, and that is certain sho';
> And I don't want no pardon for what I was or am,
> I won't be reconstructed and I don't give a damn.

Time, or the lack of it, is one of the biggest problems teachers face. Learning content takes time; introducing, practicing, and reinforcing liter-acy skills take time. Of course teachers want, and try, to work in time for pleasure reading, including the enjoyment of poetry. The opportunity for teaching skills plus content is present when you use poems that fit the curriculum. For example, an American history teacher can use a poem or song within a story to help students understand slavery and the Underground Railroad. By reading *Follow the Drinking Gourd* (Winter, 1988), students get invested in the story of Peg Leg Joe, the legendary conductor who taught slaves a seemingly harmless folk song:

> When the sun comes back, and the first quail calls,
> Follow the drinking gourd.
> For the old man is a-waiting for to carry you to freedom
> If you follow the drinking gourd.

From *Follow the Drinking Gourd* by Jeanette Winter. Copyright © 1988 by Jeanette Winter. Reprinted by permission of Alfred A. Knopf Children's Books, a division of Random House, Inc.

Students can be taught that there are "hidden meanings" in this poem—the directions for escape had to be kept a secret from the masters. "The drinking gourd" is the Big Dipper (some science content as an added bonus); the first line refers to spring. Three additional verses contain similar "coded messages" or symbols. When students encounter other poems with symbols, the concept of symbolism may be easier for them to understand because they have understood this song.

Later, when the curriculum involves the era prior to the Civil Rights movement, you might use another poem to help students feel what it must have been like to be the victim of the segregation laws they've learned about in their history books. Langston Hughes has a "colored boy at a carnival" narrating:

> Where is the Jim Crow section
> On this merry-go-round,
> Mister, cause I want to ride?
> Down South where I come from
> White and colored
> Can't sit side by side.
> Down South on the train
> There's a Jim Crow car.
> On the bus we're put in back—
> But there ain't no back
> To a merry-go-round!
> Where's the horse
> For a kid that's black?

From *The Collected Poems of Langston Hughes* by Langston Hughes, copyright © 1994 by The Estate of Langston Hughes. Used by permission of Alfred A. Knopf, a division of Random House, Inc.

The class can discuss the techniques the poet used to make this simple poem so powerful, and they might try to model some of their own writing after this and other favorites. They can experiment with rhyme, repetition, and rhythm, using conversations and questions. Language arts skills are handled very naturally in an authentic context.

We do have to be careful not to overemphasize the skills as our students read poetry because the focus takes away from the enjoyment and wonder. To check ourselves, we might well keep in mind this poem composed and narrated by the character Kate, a middle school-aged child:

> I used to like "Stopping by Woods on a Snowy Evening."
> I liked the coming darkness,
> The jingle of harness bells, breaking—and adding to—the stillness,
> The gentle drift of snow. . . .
>
> But today, the teacher told us what everything stood for.
> The woods, the horse, the miles to go, the sleep—
> They all have "hidden meanings."
>
> It's grown so complicated now that,
> Next time I drive by,
> I don't think I'll bother to stop.

"After English Class," a selection from *Hey World, Here I Am!* Text copyright © 1986 by Jean Little. Illustrations copyright © 1989 by Susan G. Truesdell. Reprinted by permission of HarperCollins Publishers.

Figure 3.5 lists some resources you can explore as you use poetry to enhance your curricular content and your students' understanding of the people, concepts, and events important in your discipline.

Nonfiction

The number and quality of nonfiction trade books have increased enormously over the past several years. Teachers can take advantage of this abundant treasure throughout their curricular units. Students can examine topics in depth while employing critical-thinking skills to synthesize and evaluate the information, and still enjoy the ideas and presentation. A classroom library rich in nonfiction texts also encourages students to practice reading expository text, a skill that will serve them throughout their lives. Attractive and entertaining nonfiction books are tantalizing and motivational; they bring curricular topics to life in a way that textbooks cannot (Young & Vardell, 1993).

Palmer and Stewart (1997) conducted a study of the use of nonfiction in fourth through seventh grade social studies classes. After interviewing teachers and students, as well as analyzing field notes, artifacts, and journal entries, they concluded that the nature of assignments may have to change in order to best use the in-depth topic coverage in information books. They found that sometimes nonfiction was treated as another textbook or encyclopedia, missing a chance to capitalize on the rich potential for meaningful reading. Both teachers and students must learn how to find the treasures of nonfiction titles and use them effectively to learn; interpret the information provided; and appreciate the style, language, and format that makes them literature.

I hope that you see yourself as a member of a community of learners. In order to have credibility as you recommend trade books to students, you have to foster your own growth by reading children's and young adult literature. Fortunately, you will find this a rewarding adventure. Here are two reflections from preservice teachers who discovered this during an education class on content area literacy:

> The first couple of weeks into this class, I was hesitant to believe that any books besides the biology textbook I would use for my class have any space in any of my lesson plans. But I am convinced now that any kind of books in the classroom can and will stimulate students' minds. . . . over the semester my role as a teacher/reader has changed, too. I was put off at first about using children's or young adult books in a classroom setting. . . . But then you pulled out a book [*Standing Up to Mr. O* (Mills, 1998)] in which the storyline was about a child's dislike of dissecting and I thought how well that could be used. . . . I guess my resistance was futile. . . . I can honestly say that when I go to a bookstore or the library, I look for children's or young adult books about biology.
>
> —*Marty Hudson*

Looking back I would have to say that I was the stereotypical math education student. I saw that I had to take a reading course, and said to myself, "John, you're going to teach math. What could reading possibly mean to you as a math teacher?" I walked into class on the first day with skepticism, but on that very day, a change started to occur. Each and every subsequent Monday and Wednesday, I was being transformed into a teacher of reading above all else.

The opportunity to read full books contributed to my transition to a teacher of reading. For the first time ever, I would sit down and read an entire book, not because I could not read before, but because I now had the desire to read. Where did this motivation and desire to read come from? It came from these wonderful things called

FIGURE 3.5 *Sources of poetry for the content areas.*

MATH, SCIENCE, AND TECHNOLOGY

Begay, S. (1995). *Navajo: Visions and Voices Across the Mesa.* New York: Scholastic.

Esbenson, B., & Davie, H. (1996). *Echoes for the Eye: Poems to Celebrate Patterns in Nature.* New York: HarperCollins.

Fleischman, P., & Beddows, E. (1985). *I Am Phoenix: Poems for Two Voices.* New York: Harper & Row.

Fleischman, P., & Beddows, E. (1988). *Joyful Noise: Poems for Two Voices.* New York: Harper & Row.

Klein, M. (Ed.). (1989). *Poets for Life: Seventy-six Poets Respond to AIDS.* New York: Crown.

Nelson, M. (2001). *Carver: A Life in Poems.* Asheville, NC: Front Street.

Prelutsky, J. (1988). *Tyrannosaurus Was a Beast.* New York: Scholastic.

Siebert, D. (1988). *Mohave.* New York: Crowell.

Siebert, D. (1991). *Sierra.* New York: HarperCollins.

Siebert, D. (2000). *Cave.* New York: HarperCollins.

Wong, J. S. (1999). *Behind the Wheel: Poems About Driving.* New York: Margaret A. McElderry Books.

ENGLISH LANGUAGE ARTS

Adoff, A. (Ed.). (1997). *I Am the Darker Brother: An Anthology of Modern Poems by African Americans.* New York: Simon & Schuster.

Armour, R. (1969). *On Your Marks: A Package of Punctuation.* New York: McGraw-Hill.

Carroll, L. (1989). *Jabberwocky.* New York: Harry N. Abrams.

Dillon, L., & Dillon, D. (1998). *To Everything There Is a Season.* New York: The Blue Sky Press.

Franco, B. (2000). *You Hear Me? Poems and Writings by Teenage Boys.* Cambridge, MA: Candlewick Press.

Janeczko, P. (Ed.). (1990). *The Place My Words Are Looking For: What Poets Say About and Through Their Work.* Bradbury.

Jarrell, R. (1963). *The Bat-Poet.* New York: Macmillan.

Kherdian, D. (Ed.). (1995). *Beat Voices: An Anthology of Beat Poetry.* New York: Henry Holt.

Masters, E. L. (1996). *Spoon River Anthology.* New York: Tom Doherty Associates.

Miller, E. E. (Ed.). (1994). *In Search of Color Everywhere: A Collection of African American Poetry.* New York: Stewart, Tabori & Chang.

Okutoro, O. (Comp). (1999). *Quiet Storm: Voices from Young Black Poets.* New York: Hyperion.

Philip, N. (Ed.). (1995). *Singing America: Poems that Define a Nation.* New York: Viking.

Philip, N. (Comp). (1996). *Earth Always Endures: Native American Poems.* New York: Viking.

Seeley, V. (Ed.). (1994). *Latino Poetry.* Paramus, NJ: Globe Fearon.

Sones, S. (1999). *Stop Pretending: What Happened When My Big Sister Went Crazy.* New York: Scholastic.

Willard, N., Provenson, A, & Provenson, M. (1981). *A Visit to William Blake's Inn: Poems for Innocent and Experienced Travelers.* New York: Harcourt Brace.

SOCIAL STUDIES

Boudreau, A. (1989). *The Story of the Acadians.* Gretna, LA: Pelican Publishing.

Bruchac, J., & Locker, T. (1995). *The Earth Under Sky Bear's Feet: Native American Poems of the Land.* New York: Scholastic.

Carson, J. (1989). *Stories I Ain't Told Nobody Yet.* New York: Orchard Books.

Carlson, L. M. (Ed.). (1994). *Cool Salsa: Bilingual Poems on Growing Up Latino in the United States.* New York: Henry Holt.

Clinton, C., & Alcorn, S. (Eds.). (1998). *I, Too, Sing America: Three Centuries of African American Poetry.* Boston: Houghton Mifflin.

Guthrie, W., & Jacobsen, K. (1998). *This Land Is Your Land.* Boston: Little, Brown.

Hesse, K. (1997). *Out of the Dust.* New York: Scholastic.

Hopkins, L. B., & Alcorn, S. (2000). *My America: A Poetry Atlas of the United States.* New York: Simon & Schuster.

Hopkins, L. B., & Fiore, P. M. (1994). *Hand in Hand: An American History through Poetry.* New York: Simon & Schuster.

Katz, B., & Crews, N. (2000). *We the People.* New York: Greenwillow Books.

Longfellow, H. W. (2001). *The Midnight Ride of Paul Revere.* Brooklyn: Handprint Books.

Merriam, E., & Stewart, A. (1968). *Independent Voices.* New York: Atheneum.

Merriam, E., & Diaz, D. (1996). *The Inner City Mother Goose.* New York: Simon & Schuster.

Molloy, P. (Ed.). (1968). *Poetry U.S.A.* New York: Scholastic.

(continued)

FIGURE 3.5 *Continued.*

Myers, W. D., & Myers, C. (1997). *Harlem.* New York: Scholastic.

Paladino, C. (1999). *One Good Apple: Growing Our Food for the Sake of the Earth.* Boston: Houghton Mifflin.

Philip, N. (2000). *It's a Woman's World: A Century of Women's Voices in Poetry.* New York: Dutton.

Philip, N., & McCurdy, M. (Eds.). (1998). *War and the Pity of War.* New York: Clarion Books.

Provenson, A. (1997). *The Buck Stops Here: The Presidents of the United States.* New York: HarperCollins.

Rottmann, L. (1993). *Voices from the Ho Chi Minh Trail: Poetry of America and Vietnam, 1965–1993.* Photos by Thanh, N. T., & Rottmann, L. Desert Hot Springs, CA: Event Horizon Press.

Siebert, D. (1989). *Heartland.* New York: Crowell.

Spier, P. (Illustrator). (1973). *The Star-Spangled Banner.* New York: Scholastic.

Turner, A., & Moser, B. (1993). *Grass Songs: Poems of Women's Journeys West.* New York: Harcourt Brace.

Wood, N., & Howell, F. (1995). *Dancing Moons.* New York: Delacorte Press.

FINE ARTS

Bouchard, D., & Dunfield, R. T. (1997). *If Sarah Will Take Me.* Custer, WA: Orca Book Publishers.

Greenberg, J. (2001). *Heart to Heart: New Poems Inspired by Twentieth-Century American Art.* New York: Harry N. Abrams.

Livingston, M. C. (Ed.). (1995). *Call Down the Moon: Poems of Music.* New York: M. K. McElderry Books.

Nye, N. S. (1998). *The Space Between Our Footsteps: Poems and Paintings from the Middle East.* New York: Simon & Schuster.

Panzer, N. (Ed.). (1999). *Celebrate America in Poetry and Art.* New York: Hyperion.

Shange, W., Bearden, R., & Sunshine, L. (1994). *I Live in Music.* New York: Welcome Enterprises. Distributed by Stewart, Tabori & Chang.

PHYSICAL EDUCATION

Adoff, A. (1986). *Sports Pages.* New York: Lippincott.

Carney, G. (1993). *Romancing the Horsehide: Baseball Poems on Players and the Game.* Jefferson, NC: McFarland.

Glenn, M. (1997). *Jump Ball: A Basketball Season in Poems.* New York: Lodestar.

Janeczko, P. B. (1998). *That Sweet Diamond: Baseball Poems.* New York: Atheneum.

Knudson, R. R., & Swenson, M. (Eds.). (1988). *American Sports Poems.* New York: Orchard Books.

Korman, G., & Korman, B. (1996). *The Last-Place Sports Poems of Jeremy Bloom.* New York: Scholastic.

Macy, S. (Ed.). (2001). *Girls Got Game: Sports Stories and Poems.* New York: Henry Holt.

Smith, C. R., Jr. (2001). *Short Takes: Fast-Break Basketball Poetry.* New York: Dutton Children's Books.

---

booktalks. These sensitive renditions from [my classmates'] personal experience with reading a book gave me a desire to read.

. . . I now uncover the mystery and wonder that is found on every page of a book. . . . I am very happy to have found this alternate world and plan on continuing with my pleasure reading into the future.

—John Turbeville

Figure 3.6 lists some of the many nonfiction books available for incorporation into your content area teaching.

them wisely. Be aware that many trade books, especially older ones, contain inaccurate information or biased presentations of groups. For example, the popular *Little House on the Prairie* series, by Laura Ingalls Wilder, has come under attack from many critics because of the negative way it depicts Native Americans (e. g., Kuhlman, 2001; Mowder, 1992; Romines, 1997; Segal, 1977). Some people recommend avoiding the use of such texts altogether, not having them available in classrooms and school libraries. Others see materials like these as potential teaching tools to motivate student thinking, discussion, and research.

Evaluating and Selecting Trade Books

As is true of textbooks, trade books vary greatly in quality. Teachers who use trade books should select

Getting Ready to Teach 3.3 (see page 90)

SCIENCE, MATH, AND TECHNOLOGY

Adair, R. (1990). *The Physics of Baseball.* New York: Harper & Row.

Akers, C. (2000). *Obesity.* San Diego, CA: Lucent Books.

Allen, J. (Ed.). (1997). *Anthology for the Earth.* Cambridge, MA: Candlewick.

Ashabranner, B. (1982). *Morning Star, Black Sun: The Northern Cheyenne Indians and America's Energy Crisis.* New York: Putnam.

Baker, C. (1997). *Let There Be Life: Animating with the Computer.* New York: Walker.

Carson, R. (1994). *Silent Spring.* Boston: Houghton Mifflin.

Dewey, J. O. (2001). *Antarctic Journal: Four Months at the Bottom of the World.* New York: HarperCollins.

Farrell, J. (1998). *Invisible Enemies: Stories of Infectious Diseases.* New York: Farrar, Straus & Giroux.

Feynman, R. (1995). *Six Easy Pieces: Essentials of Physics, Explained by Its Most Brilliant Teacher.* Reading, MA: Helix Books.

Gallant, R. A. (1995). *The Day the Sky Split Apart: Investigating a Cosmic Mystery.* New York: Atheneum.

Katz, J. (2000). *Geeks: How Two Boys Rode the Internet Out of Idaho.* New York: Villard.

Montgomery, S. (1999). *Once a Wolf: How Wildlife Biologists Fought to Bring Back the Gray Wolf.* Boston: Houghton Mifflin.

National Geographic Society. (1997). *Restless Earth: Disasters of Nature.* Washington, DC: National Geographic Society.

Oleksy, W. G. (1998). *Hispanic-American Scientists.* New York: Facts on File.

Pringle, L. (1993). *Chemical and Biological Warfare: The Cruelest Weapons.* Hillside, NJ: Enslow.

Pringle, L. (1997). *Drinking, A Risky Business.* New York: Morrow.

Pringle, L., & Marstall, B. (1997). *An Extraordinary Life: The Story of a Monarch Butterfly.* New York: Orchard.

Pringle, L., & Moehlman, P. D. R. (1993). *Jackal Woman: Exploring the World of Jackals.* New York: Scribner's.

Smith, R. (1990). *Sea Otter Rescue: The Aftermath of an Oil Spill.* New York: Dutton.

Thomas, L. (1974). *The Lives of a Cell: Notes of a Biology Watcher.* New York: Viking.

Van Meter, V., with Gutman, D. (1995). *Taking Flight: My Story.* New York: Viking.

SOCIAL STUDIES

Able, D. (2000). *Hate Groups.* Berkeley Heights, NJ: Enslow.

Armstrong, J. (1999). *Shipwreck at the Bottom of the World; The Extraordinary True Story of Shackleton and the Endurance.* New York: Crown.

Ashabranner, B. (2000). *A Date with Destiny: The Women in Military Service for America Memorial.* New York: 21st Century.

Ayer, E., Waterford, H., & Heck, A. (1995). *Parallel Journeys.* New York: Atheneum.

Budhos, M. (1999). *Remix: Conversations with Immigrant Teens.* New York: Henry Holt.

Chang, I. (1991). *A Separate Battle: Women and the Civil War.* New York: Lodestar.

Chen, Da. (2001). *China's Son: Growing up in the Cultural Revolution.* New York: Delacorte Press.

Dash, J. (1996). *We Shall Not Be Moved: The Women's Factory Strike of 1909.* New York: Scholastic.

Giblin, J. C. (Ed.). (2000). *The Century that Was: Reflections on the Last Hundred Years.* New York: Atheneum.

Jacobs, T. A. (2000). *Teens on Trial: Young People Who Challenged the Law—and Changed Your Life.* Minneapolis, MN: Free Spirit Publishing, Inc.

Jaffe, S. H. (1996). *Who Were the Founding Fathers? Two Hundred Years of Reinventing American History.* New York: Henry Holt.

Kuklin, S. (1996). *Irrepressible Spirit: Conversations with Human Rights Activists.* New York: Philomel.

Levine, E. (2000). *Darkness Over Denmark: The Danish Resistance and the Rescue of the Jews.* New York: Holiday House.

Murphy, J. (1998). *Gone A-Whaling: The Lure of the Sea and the Hunt for the Great Whales.* New York: Clarion Books.

Ousseimi, M. (1995). *Caught in the Crossfire: Growing Up in a War Zone.* New York: Walker.

Strom, Y. (1996). *Quilted Landscape: Conversations with Young Immigrants.* New York: Simon & Schuster.

Tunnell, M. O., & Chilcoat, G. W. (1996). *The Children of Topaz: The Story of a Japanese-American Internment Camp Based on a Classroom Diary.* New York: Holiday House.

(continued)

FIGURE 3.6 *Continued.*

Warren, A. (1996). *Orphan Train Rider: One Boy's True Story.* Boston: Houghton Mifflin.

FINE ARTS

Aronson, M. (1998). *Art Attack: A Short Cultural History of the Avant-Garde.* New York: Clarion Books.

Beckett, W. (2000). *My Favorite Things: 75 Works of Art from Around the World.* New York: Abrams.

Berger, M. (1989). *The Science of Music.* New York: HarperCollins.

Capek, M. (1996). *Murals.* Minneapolis, MN: Lerner Publications Company.

Carroll, C. (1996). *How Artists See the Elements: Earth, Air, Fire, Water.* New York: Abbeville Kids.

Carroll, C. (1996). *How Artists See the Weather.* New York: Abbeville Kids.

Cobb, M. (1995). *The Quilt-Block History of Pioneer Days.* Brookfield, CT: Millbrook Press.

Cobb, M. (1999). *A Sampler View of Colonial Life.* Brookfield, CT: Millbrook Press.

Collier, J. L. (1997). *Jazz: An American Saga.* New York: Henry Holt.

Cummins, J., & Kiefer, B. (1999). *Wings of an Artist: Children's Book Illustrators Talk About Their Art.* New York: Harry N. Abrams.

Ewing, P., & Louis, L. L. (1999). *In the Paint.* New York: Abbeville Kids.

Greenberg, J., & Jordan, S. (1991). *The Painter's Eye: Learning to Look at Contemporary Art.* New York: Delacorte Press.

Greenberg, J., & Jordan, S. (1998). *Chuck Close Up Close.* New York: DK Publishing.

Pekarik, A. (1992). *Painting: Behind the Scenes.* New York: Hyperion Books for Children.

Sills, L. (2000). *In Real Life: Six Women Photographers.* New York: Holiday House.

HEALTH AND PHYSICAL EDUCATION

Armstrong, L., & Jenkins, S. (2000). *It's Not About the Bike: My Journey Back to Life.* New York: Putnam.

Barbour, S. (Ed.). (1998). *Alcohol: Opposing Viewpoints.* San Diego, CA: Greenhaven Press.

Boitano, B., & Harper, S. (1998). *Boitano's Edge: Inside the World of Figure Skating.* New York: Simon & Schuster.

Gottleib, L. (2000). *Stick Figure: A Diary of My Former Self.* New York: Simon & Schuster.

Hirschfelder, A. (2001). *Kick Butts!: A Kid's Action Guide to a Tobacco-Free America.* Lanham, MD: Scarecrow Press.

Huegel, K. (1998). *Young People and Chronic Illness: True Stories, Help, and Hope.* Minneapolis, MN: Free Spirit.

Ingersoll, B. D. (1997). *Distant Drums, Different Drummers: A Guide for Young People with ADHD.* Bethesda, MD: Cape Publications.

Kent, J. C. (1998). *Women in Medicine.* Minneapolis, MN: Oliver Press.

Macy, S. (1996). *Winning Ways: A Photohistory of Women in Sports.* New York: Henry Holt.

As with textbooks, teachers can use several procedures to evaluate trade books. To assess difficulty, use the cloze procedure or a readability formula to get an idea of a book's appropriate grade level. But remember, a score derived this way is not smarter than the teacher. Let's say you have a student named Chaneta in your eighth grade English class who has severe reading difficulties; reliable assessment instruments (more on these in Chapter 9) have determined Chaneta's reading level to be at about the third grade. She has a passionate interest in biographies of people who have overcome disabilities. You have a book in your classroom library, *Dear Dr. Bell . . . Your Friend, Helen Keller* by Judith St. George (1992), and the back cover indicates that it has a fifth grade readability level (it doesn't say which formula was used). You appreciate the rough estimate

that was supplied, but decide to recommend the book to Chaneta anyway, offering assistance should she need it. She still has the right to abandon it and find a different book if she chooses.

The book *Nonfiction for Young Adults: From Delight to Wisdom* (Carter & Abrahamson, 1990) provides criteria by which we can judge books of that genre. Various chapters focus on interest, accuracy, content, style, organization, format, and uses. Alternate chapters contain conversations with popular writers of young adult nonfiction. In the chapter dealing with accuracy, Carter and Abrahamson recommend examining a nonfiction author's qualifications and scholarship, and examining the book itself for fact and opinion, as well as for flaws such as sensationalism, stereotyping, and anthropomorphism. They use examples from recent titles to demonstrate

FIGURE **3.7** *Resources for selecting and reviewing trade books.*

Adamson, L. G. (1999). *American Historical Fiction: An Annotated Guide to Novels for Adults and Young Adults.* Phoenix, AZ: Oryx Press.

Ammon, B. D., & Sherman, G. W. (1996). *Worth a Thousand Words: An Annotated Guide to Picture Books for Older Readers.* Englewood, CO: Libraries Unlimited.

Association for Library Service to Children. *The Newbery and Caldecott Awards: A Guide to the Medal and Honor Books.* (2002). Chicago: American Library Association.

Benedict, S., & Carlisle, L. (1992). *Beyond Words: Picture Books for Older Readers and Writers.* Portsmouth, NH: Heinemann.

Bamford, R. A., & Kristo, J. V. (1998). *Making Facts Come Alive: Choosing Quality Nonfiction Literature, K–8.* Norwood, MA: Christopher-Gordon.

Castro, R. G., Fisher, E. M., Hong, T., & Williams, D. (1997). *What Do I Read Next?: Multicultural Literature.* New York: Gale.

Christenbury, L. (Ed.) & the Committee on the Senior High School Booklist of the National Council of Teachers of English. (1995). *Books for You: An Annotated Booklist for Senior High Students.* Urbana, IL: National Council of Teachers of English.

Cianciolo, P. J. (2000). *Informational Picture Books for Children.* Chicago: American Library Association.

Day, F. S. (1997). *Latina and Latino Voices in Literature for Children and Teenagers.* Portsmouth, NH: Heinemann.

Dresang, E. T. (1999). *Radical Change: Books for Youth in a Digital Age.* New York: H. W. Wilson.

Estell, D., Satchwell, M. L., & Wright, P. S. (2000). *Reading Lists for College-Bound Students,* (3rd ed.). New York: ARCO.

Freeman, E. B., & Person, D. G. (1998). *Connecting Informational Children's Books with Content Area Learning.* Boston: Allyn and Bacon.

Gillespie, J. T. (2000). *Best Books for Young Teen Readers Grades 7–10.* New Providence, NJ: R. R. Bowker.

Gordon, L., & Tanaka, C. (1995). *World Historical Fiction for Young Adults.* Fort Atkinson, WI: Highsmith Press.

Hall, S. (1990). *Using Picture Storybooks to Teach Literary Devices: Recommended Books for Children and Young Adults.* Phoenix, AZ: Oryx Press.

Hearne, B., with Stevenson, D. (1999). *Choosing Books for Children: A Commonsense Guide,* (3rd ed.). Urbana: University of Illinois Press.

Herald, D. T. (1997). *Teen Genreflecting.* Englewood, CO: Libraries Unlimited.

Howard, E. F. (1988). *America as Story: Historical Fiction for Secondary Schools.* Chicago: American Library Association.

Kennemer, P. K. (1992). *Using Literature to Teach Middle Grades About War.* Phoenix, AZ: Oryx Press.

Krey, D. M. (1998). *Children's Literature in Social Studies: Teaching to the Standards.* Washington, DC: National Council for the Social Studies.

Landrum, J. (2001). Selecting Intermediate Novels that Feature Characters with Disabilities. *The Reading Teacher, 55*(3), 252–258.

Lewis, M. (Ed.). (1996). *Outstanding Books for the College Bound: Choices for a Generation.* Chicago: American Library Association.

Odean, K. (1997). *Great Books for Girls.* New York: Ballantine Books.

Odean, K. (1998). *Great Books for Boys.* New York: Ballantine Books.

Phelan, P. (Ed.). (1996). *High Interest–Easy Reading: An Annotated Booklist for Middle and Senior High,* (7th ed.). Urbana, IL: National Council of Teachers of English.

Rand, D., Parker, T. T., & Foster, S. (1998). *Black Books Galore! Guide to Great African American Children's Books.* New York: Wiley.

Richey, V. H., & Puckett, K. E. (1992). *Wordless/Almost Wordless Picture Books: A Guide.* Englewood, CO: Libraries Unlimited.

Schon, I. (1997). *The Best of the Latino Heritage: A Guide to the Best Juvenile Books About Latino People and Cultures.* Lanham, MD: Scarecrow Press.

Spencer, P. (1999). *What Do Young Adults Read Next?: A Reader's Guide to Fiction for Young Adults,* (Vol. 3). Detroit, MI: Gale Group.

Sudol, P., & King, C. (1996). A Checklist for Choosing Nonfiction Trade Books. *The Reading Teacher* (Feb.), 422–424.

Susag, D. M. (1998). *Roots and Branches: A Resource of Native American Literature—Themes, Lessons, and Bibliographies.* Urbana, IL: National Council of Teachers of English.

Thiessen, D., & Matthias, M. (1993). *The Wonderful World of Mathematics: A Critically Annotated List of Children's Books in Mathematics.* Reston, VA: National Council of Teachers of Mathematics.

(continued)

FIGURE 3.7 *Continued.*

The following journals and periodicals are also extremely helpful for reviews and commentary on relevant trade book issues:

The Horn Book Magazine

The Horn Book Guide

The ALAN Review (The Assembly on Literature for Adolescents of the National Council of Teachers of English)

Books for the Teen Age (New York Public Library)

English Journal (National Council of Teachers of English)

Journal of Adolescent and Adult Literacy (International Reading Association)

Book Links

The New Advocate (Christopher-Gordon Publishers)

their points. For example, they define anthropomorphism as attributing human traits to nonhuman subjects, and provide sample sentences from books about computers that refer to a computer memorizing entire encyclopedias or delivering a joke with perfect timing. Additional criteria can be found in *Checking Out Nonfiction Literature K–8: Good Choices for Best Learning* (Bamford & Kristo, 2000). The authors provide a discussion of and recommendations from several categories of nonfiction, including photographic essays, life cycle books, documents, albums, and reference books, and they suggest ways for teachers to introduce the books to students and use them to teach in content areas.

Fortunately, we do not have to tackle the formidable task of reviewing every trade book that sounds like it might be a profitable addition to our classroom or school library. There are excellent sources of reviews done by experts. Although we won't necessarily agree with each one, they provide an excellent starting place and can help us stay abreast of the recent releases. Figure 3.7 lists some of these resources for teachers, librarians, parents, and students.

When students or inservice workshop participants see my personal traveling library of trade books, I'm often asked whether I spend half my salary at bookstores. There are many ways you can build your personal or classroom collection of discipline-related trade books quite inexpensively. Libraries often sell withdrawn or donated books; I do check out the sale tables at bookstores. Following are the web addresses or phone numbers of several book clubs that cater to the curricular needs of middle and secondary teachers or that are related to disciplines taught in schools:

TAB: The Teen Book Club, www.scholastic.com/tab

Arrow Book Club (for middle grades), www.scholastic.com/arrow

Trumpet Intermediate Years Book Club, 1-800-826-0110

The History Book Club, 1-800-348-7128

Troll Book Club, Grades 6 & Up, www.troll.com

Your school librarian can become your greatest ally as you implement the use of trade books in your content units and projects. Librarians are usually eager to be called upon and are happy to share their expertise and their enthusiasm for content-related literature. They can gather titles and actual books for the teacher, and give booktalks to students.

PRIMARY SOURCES

According to McElvaine (2000), primary sources are:

the raw material of history.... Using primary sources allows us not just to read about history, but to read history itself. It allows us to immerse ourselves in the look and feel of an era gone by, to understand its people and their language.... And it allows us to take an active, hands-on role in (re)constructing history. (p. 8)

In all subject areas, the use of relevant documents can add interest to your lessons, as well as information that will benefit your students as they seek to acquire knowledge in and understand the foundations of the discipline. There's just no substitute for the real thing. For decades, social studies teachers were trained to teach about people, events, ideologies, social movements, and historical eras using published instructional materials. Science teachers taught about the major revolutions precipitated by the discoveries of Copernicus, Newton, Einstein, Darwin, and Watson and Crick the same way. However, current national standards for many content areas now call for students to be exposed to and taught to read and analyze primary sources in the disciplines. They are expected not only to comprehend various texts, but also to react to them; to synthesize information from several places and compare and contrast information from disparate voices. Happily, it is very easy to find documents that support your teaching and your students' scholarly explo-

FIGURE 3.8   *Examples of documentary resources for an American history teacher.*

Commager, H. S., & Cantor, M. (1988). *Documents of American History,* (10th ed.). Englewood Cliffs, NJ: Prentice Hall.

Colbert, D. (Ed.). (1997). *Eyewitness to America: 500 Years of America in the Words of Those Who Saw It Happen.* New York: Pantheon.

Greenwood, T. (2000). *The Gilded Age: A History in Documents.* New York: Oxford University Press.

Lepore, J. (2000). *Encounters in the New World: A History in Documents.* New York: Oxford University Press.

Levy, P. B. (Ed.). (1994). *100 Key Documents in American Democracy.* Westport, CT: Greenwood Press.

McElvaine, R. S. (2000). *The Depression and the New Deal: A History in Documents.* New York: Oxford University Press.

BookTalk   3.4

History textbooks summarize, highlight, and paraphrase important documents. That's their job. But your classroom library can also give students the real words of the people who played roles throughout American history. *Words that Built a Nation: A Young Person's Collection of Historic American Documents,* by Marilyn Miller (1999), provides the complete text or excerpts from such varied pieces as the "Statement on the Causes of Wounded Knee" by Red Cloud, Jane Addams' "Twenty Years at Hull House," Malcolm X's "The Ballot or the Bullet," Cesar Chavez's "Speech to Striking Grape Workers," and *Silent Spring* by Rachel Carson. Students can compare the farewell addresses of George Washington and Ronald Reagan, experience Richard Nixon's letter of resignation, and travel back to 1954 as they read from the U. S. Supreme Court decision in the case of *Brown v. Board of Education of Topeka.* The book offers margin notes that provide context and relevant photographs. It provides a literary fieldtrip to pivotal times and events in our nation's history, and brings together diverse voices on crucial issues.

rations. Figure 3.8 lists titles that an American history teacher might use as material for her lessons or provide to her students.

Newspapers, scholarly journals, government files, Internet sites, autobiographies, and library archives provide fascinating and detailed accounts of events and people's thinking about the topics you teach. This section, by way of example, highlights two types of primary sources, or adapted primary sources, that contain modernized spelling and language and are usually easier to find: letters and personal journals.

Speeches, biographies and autobiographies, and other types of documents are introduced throughout later chapters.

Letters

It's likely your students will be familiar with *epistolary* writing, though they may not know this term and they may not have considered it a real genre or connected to their academic learning. We can change that by using their comfort with writing to their friends and relatives, perhaps via e-mail, as a bridge to other areas of this important category. Teachers can encourage students to explore the preserved letters from real people and examine them in terms of formality, style, and content. You can determine other ways to use these books in your classroom.

Art teachers can use the letters written by Frank Lloyd Wright and Georgia O'Keefe found in *Letters of a Nation* (Carroll, 1997), and one from Vincent Van Gogh to his brother, Theo, found in *Famous Letters: Messages and Thoughts that Shaped Our World* (McLynn, 1993). The personal glimpses into the artists' minds helps students bring more background knowledge and curiosity to the study of their works.

English teachers will have no difficulty finding letters from writers, often to other writers. *Letters of a Nation* contains letters composed by Walt Whitman, Wallace Stegner, Richard Wright, Katherine Anne Porter, William Faulkner, Mark Twain, Ernest Hemingway (to F. Scott Fitzgerald), E. B. White, Sylvia Plath, James Baldwin, John Steinbeck, Jack London, Harriet Beecher Stowe, Nathaniel Hawthorne, Jack Kerouac, and Ayn Rand, among others. McLynn's *Famous Letters* provides epistolary delights from Dante, Mary Shelley, D. H. Lawrence, and Samuel Pepys; and its companion volume, *Famous Love Letters* (Tamplin, 1995), adds correspondence from Elizabeth Barrett Browning to Robert Browning, from Zelda Sayre to F. Scott Fitzgerald, John Keats to Fanny Brawne, and Victor Hugo to

Juliet Drouet. Students will find that romance is not restricted to works of fiction, nor to the present day.

Social studies teachers may have the largest selection of easily accessible letters that will help students get inside the minds of famous leaders and people who initiated, or were affected by, policies and social movements. Letters available in Carroll's *Letters of a Nation* include Meriwether Lewis and William Clark to the Oto Indians (on the purpose of their journey), Abigail Adams to John Adams (exhorting him to "remember the ladies" in their deliberations on the Declaration of Independence), Frederick Douglass to his former master and to Harriet Tubman, Franklin D. Roosevelt's secret cable to Winston Churchill the day after the bombing of Pearl Harbor, John F. Kennedy to Nikita Krushchev on resolving the Cuban Missile Crisis, Malcolm X's letter to his followers about the possibility for peace and good will between blacks and whites, and Elizabeth Cady Stanton to Susan B. Anthony.

Science teachers might share the following letters from *Famous Letters* with students: Galileo Galilei to Belisario Vinta, Louis Pasteur to his family, Albert Einstein to Franklin D. Roosevelt. From *Letters of a Nation*, you can read aloud letters written by Rachel Carson, Albert Einstein, and the American Society for the Prevention of Cruelty to Animals, as well as a letter written to astronaut Scott Carpenter by his father.

Here is an excerpt from a letter written by Albert Einstein to a sixth grade student who had asked him in a letter whether scientists pray:

> . . . everyone who is seriously involved in the pursuit of science becomes convinced that a spirit is manifest in the laws of the Universe—a spirit vastly superior to that of man, and one in the face of which we with our modest powers must feel humble. In this way the pursuit of science leads to a religious feeling of a special sort, which is indeed quite different from the religiosity of someone more naive. (Carroll, 1997, pp. 404–405)

Teachers might use that letter as if it were addressed to all sixth graders, or to their class, and to ask for their response, discussion, and thoughts about science and religion and about a man as important as Einstein taking time to answer a child's letter. Preserved letters are an educational gold mine, treasures just waiting to be put into students' hands.

Journals and Diaries

Lest students think that journals are things dreamed up by teachers to be imposed on students, and nonexistent in the real world, we can assure

BookTalk   3.5

Students love romance, but they, and you, may think that love letters and academic texts are mutually exclusive. Not so! You can provide your students with *Famous Love Letters: Messages of Intimacy and Passion*, edited by Ronald Tamplin (1995). Its contents may give your students enjoyment, inspiration, and modeling at the same time they learn about important people in various fields. They can read letters from Mozart, Theodore Roosevelt, and Winston Churchill to their wives. They'll wonder how Catherine of Aragon, having been rejected, abandoned, and divorced by Henry VIII (who went on to marry one of her ladies-in-waiting, Anne Boleyn) could still write to him just hours before her death " . . . mine eyes desire you above all things. Farewell" (p. 88). The writers in your class might examine the letter from Napoleon to Josephine that begins "I love you no longer; on the contrary, I detest you. You are a wretch, truly perverse, truly stupid," and ends, "I hope to hold you in my arms before long, when I shall lavish upon you a million kisses, burning as the equatorial sun." (p. 46) This book is made even better by the background information and commentary accompanying each love letter. It also includes portraits of the famous lovers and photographs of the letters themselves, of objects such as Henry VIII's writing desk, and of places such as the tomb of those great star-crossed lovers, Abelard and Heloise.

them that this is not the case. In every field, there are wonderful examples of information we would not have now if practitioners had not kept logs. Darwin kept one during his voyages on *The Beagle*; Malcolm X kept one while in prison. Abraham Lincoln poured out his soul in his journal as the Civil War raged. Beatrix Potter created an illustrated journal that led to some very famous children's books. I was in awe when I saw in a museum the open journals of Leonardo de Vinci on display, showing a record of his creative genius and his unique handwriting. Journals allow us into the minds of people as no other source can. On July 15, 1868, Louisa May Alcott wrote in her journal, "Have finished *Little Women*, and have sent it off—402 pages. . . . Hope it will go." (Cheney, 1995, p. 139). Of course, she couldn't have known it would still be in print and in theatres a century and a half later. How lucky we are to have her recorded private thoughts, as well as her published masterpieces.

Students can learn about additional work that resulted from the original journals of people in a variety of disciplines, and the value that people's journals have to future generations. Teachers can use this knowledge about authentic journals to help their students view journal-keeping as potentially valuable to *their* real worlds as opposed to a school assignment that simply must be endured. Students can use published journals as models, for both ideas and formats. In all subject areas, students can get to know people in the field who kept journals to record data, to ask important questions, to reflect on the meaning of life, to gain knowledge through writing. The journals of real people can serve as inspiration to young writers who might be reluctant at first to put their thoughts on paper. Journals can serve as an inspiration for teachers who wish to introduce their classes to the best mentors fledgling journal-keepers could ever have (Kane, 1995).

Journals have the potential to help students learn content, too. They'll remember the horrors of World War II after reading *Anne Frank: The Diary of a Young Girl* (Frank, 1952) or *War Diary 1939–45* (Cavendish, 1995), with excerpts from soldiers' and military leaders' accounts written as the battles raged. Students can meet Lewis and Clark as real people, rather than just as names to be learned for a test on westward expansion, as they read firsthand records of the dangers they faced. Listen in a bit: In the Rocky Mountains, on May 29, 1805, Lewis wrote, "Last night we were all alarmed by a large buffalo . . . that ran up the bank in full speed directly toward the fires, and was within 18 inches of the heads of some of the men who lay sleeping." (Bakeless, 1964, p. 153). On June 16, he worried:

> Found the Indian woman extremely ill. . . . This gave me some concern, as well for the poor object herself—then with a young child in her arms—as from the consideration of her being our only dependence for a friendly negotiation with the Snake Indians for horses to assist in our portage from the Missouri to the Columbia River. (p. 188)

What an opportunity that provides for students to think about how Native Americans were used and viewed by white settlers! On August 18, Lewis was feeling philosophical:

> This day I completed my thirty-first year, and conceived that I had, in all human probability, now existed half the period I am to remain in this sublunary world. I reflected that I had as yet done but little, very little indeed, to further the happiness of the human race, or to advance the information of the succeeding generation. (p. 246)

And on November 7, "Great joy in camp. We are in view of the ocean, this great Pacific Ocean which we have been so long anxious to see, and the roaring made by the waves breaking on the rocky shores . . . may be heard distinctly" (p. 277). This primary source is very different from the textbook account students usually encounter, which simply cannot convey the emotion that a journal entry can.

Figure 3.9 lists books that contain journal entries of real people. Students will find in these examples a wonderful variety of formats and styles, as well as interesting information and glimpses into mathematical, scientific, artistic, political, and poetic minds. The journals can serve as models and as inspiration. More specifically, Figure 3.10 lists resources a social studies teacher might use to give students first-hand accounts of and perspectives on the various wars in which the United States has been involved.

ACTION RESEARCH 3.C

Visit a classroom and note the types of texts in the room. Talk with teachers and students to find out what are considered the main texts and how supplementary or supportive materials are used and viewed.

FIGURE 3.9 *A bibliography of journals relevant to content area learning.*

Carter, J. (1989). *An Outdoor Journal: Adventures and Reflections.* Norwalk, CT: The Easton Press.

Cheney, E. D. (Ed.). (1995). *Louisa May Alcott: Life, Letters, and Journals.* New York: Random House.

Columbus, C. (1987). *The Log of Christopher Columbus.* Camden, ME: International Marine Publishing.

Darwin, C. (1989). *Voyage of the Beagle: Charles Darwin's Journal of Researches.* New York: Penguin Books.

Potter, B. (1966). *The Journal of Beatrix Potter from 1881 to 1897.* (Transcribed from her code writing by Leslie Linder). New York: F. Warne.

FIGURE **3.10** *First-hand accounts of war.*

Boelcke, O., & Hirsch, R. R. (1991). *An Aviator's Field Book: Being the Field Reports of Oswald Boelcke from August 1, 1914, to October 28, 1916.* (Robert Reynolds Hirsch, Trans.). New York: Deutschland Library Co. (Original work published 1917.).

Bircher, W. (2000). *A Civil War Drummer Boy: The Diary of William Bircher, 1861–1865.* (S. S. Sateren, Ed.). Mankato, MN: Blue Earth Books.

Dennes, D. J. (1992). *One Day at a Time: A Vietnam Diary.* Portland, OR: University of Queensland Press.

Forten, C. L. (2000). *A Free Black Girl Before the Civil War: The Diary of Charlotte Forten, 1854.* (C. Steele, Ed.). Mankato, MN: Blue Earth Books.

Jones, J. B. (1993). *A Rebel War Clerk's Diary/John B. Jones.* (Earl Schlenck Miers, Annot.). Baton Rouge, LA: Louisiana State University Press.

Linklater, A. (2001). *The Code of Love: A True Story of Two Lovers Torn Apart by the War that Brought Them Together.* New York: Doubleday.

Roe, A. S. (1904). *The Diary of Captain Daniel Roe, an Officer of the French and Indian War and of the Revolution: Brookhaven, Long Island, During Portions of 1806–7–8.* Worcester, MA: Blanchard Press.

Ropes, H. A. (1980). *Civil War Nurse: The Diary and Letters of Hanna Ropes.* Knoxville: University of Tennessee Press.

Rosenkranz, K. (1999). *Vipers in the Storm: Diary of a Gulf War Fighter Pilot.* Atlanta, GA: Turner.

Sneden, R. N. (2000). *Eye of the Storm: A Civil War Odyssey.* (C. F. Bryan, Jr., & N. D. Lankford, Eds.). New York: Free Press.

Strong, G. T. (1962). *Diary of the Civil War, 1860–1865.* (A. Nevins, Ed.). New York: Macmillan.

USING MULTIPLE GENRES TO STUDY A TOPIC

Whenever you are planning your instruction of a particular topic, ask yourself whether there are materials representing different genres, and, if so, which might benefit your students. Before beginning a math unit on geometry, you might gather historical accounts of its beginnings and the mathematicians who developed and flourished in the field. There are puzzles containing geometric principles and books relating to construction, such as David Macaulay's series *Cathedral* (1973), *Castle* (1977), *Pyramid* (1975), *Unbuilding* (1987), and *Ship* (1993), as well as a few cartoons relating to the subject. Using these materials gives the exercises in the math textbook a context and your students a big picture so that the proofs and skills they're learning won't seem isolated or irrelevant.

ACTIVATING PRIOR KNOWLEDGE 3.2

In your learning log, write down what you know of John Brown. For what is he most known? What places are associated with his name? What causes? When did he live? How did he die? What did your teachers and your American history textbook tell you about this man? Compare your memories and knowledge with that of others before proceeding.

Perhaps your reflection on and discussion of John Brown reveal only a sketchy knowledge—he was an abolitionist, he's connected with Harpers Ferry, he was executed for his violent ways of promoting his cause, he caused dissention before the Civil War. Or there might be some disagreement over whether he was a righteous hero, a murderer, a misguided religious fanatic, or a crazy person. If you had to teach middle school or high school students about John Brown, where would you look for the information to pass on to your students, what materials might you have them explore?

I am no expert on the subject, but I decided to see what genres might help me should I be responsible for teaching about this man and his proper place in history. Here's what I now have in my "John Brown" file.

1. Textbook Treatments

These treatments include excerpts from several textbooks, representing different levels of difficulty and somewhat different perspectives. I have written marginal notes or highlighted particular passages or language I want my students to notice. For example, sentences from *The American Pageant* (Bailey, Kennedy, & Cohen, 1998) such as "The fanatical figure of John Brown now stalked upon the Kansas battlefield," and "[Brown and his followers] literally hacked to pieces five surprised men, presumed to be proslaveryites. This fiendish butchery, clearly the product of a deranged mind . . . " (p. 423), give a different picture to readers than other textbooks that portray Brown in a more sympathetic light. I also include pages from *Lies My Teacher Told Me* (1995), with Loewen's commentary that of 12 recent textbooks he examined, only three used any quotes from John Brown himself. "Our textbooks also handicap Brown by not letting him speak for himself. . . . Brown's words, which moved a nation, therefore do not move students today" (p. 171).

2. Encyclopedia Entries

Students can compare and contrast versions, including some from reference works published long ago. For example, look at how excerpts from two different encyclopedias portray Brown:

> . . . this early abolitionist had all the piety, uprightness, and willingness to die for a cause that marked his Puritan ancestors . . . always brooding with the fervor of an Old Testament prophet on the sin of negro slavery, against which he swore eternal war. . . . In a famous battle at Osawatomie, with only fifteen men, he held off 500 pro-slavery Missourians . . . His bearing at the trial produced an extraordinary impression of heroic simplicity and purity and grandeur of character. . . . his tragic end took on historic significance. (*Compton's Pictured Encyclopedia*, 1931, p. 516)

> During most of his adult years Brown wandered from job to job. Ill fortune, business reverses, and charges of illegal practices followed him. . . . he and five of his sons became embroiled in the struggle between pro-slavery and anti-slavery forces. . . . Brown . . . invaded the Pottawatomie River country and killed five helpless settlers. . . . (*Grolier Encyclopedia of Knowledge*, 1991, p. 332)

3. Letters and Speeches

This section includes copies of letters from John Brown to his pastor and to his children. The first person narrative is powerful and has the potential to help students understand the humanity of the names they learn about in their textbooks. These letters can be found in *The Life and Letters of John Brown* by F. B. Sanborn (1969), as well as on the Internet. I also have this excerpt from the speech he made to the court just before being sentenced to die:

> Had I so interfered in behalf of the rich, the powerful, it would have been all right. . . . I believe that to have interfered as I have done, as I have always freely admitted I have done, in behalf of His despised poor, I did no wrong but right. . . . now, if it is deemed necessary that I should forfeit

my life for the furtherance of the ends of justice, and mingle my blood further with the blood of my children and with the blood of millions in this slave country whose rights are disregarded by wicked, cruel and unjust enactments, I say, let it be done. (Loewen, 1995, pp. 167–168)

4. Biographies and Other Nonfiction Sources

Here, too, in my selection of adult and juvenile biographies, students see variety in how this controversial historical figure is portrayed. My sources include *To Purge This Land with Blood: A Biography of John Brown* by Stephen B. Oates (1984), *John Brown: A Cry for Freedom* by Lorene Graham (1980), and *John Brown: Militant Abolitionist* by Robert R. Potter (1995), which is part of the *American Troublemaker Series*. There is a very easy text, written at a primary level, Streissguth's (1999) *John Brown*, and a powerfully illustrated book, *John Brown: One Man Against Slavery* (Everett, 1993). Jacob Lawrence's paintings are worth examining. Stein's (1999) *John Brown's Raid on Harpers Ferry in American History* goes into much more depth than a textbook or encyclopedia could.

5. Historical Fiction

The young adult novel *Mine Eyes Have Seen* by Ann Rinaldi (1998), narrated by a daughter of John Brown, can help students imagine how others saw Brown. It is well researched and tells the story in an imaginative way. *Lightning Time*, by Douglas Rees (1997), is told from the perspective of a young follower of Brown, and Russell Banks' adult level novel, *Cloudsplitter* (1998), is narrated by Brown's only surviving son years after the event. I could ask my students to use one or more of these books as models as they write a portrait of Brown, or some other historical figure, from the point of view of someone else watching the events and behavior. I also located Bruce Olds' novel, *Raising Holy Hell* (1995), which uses an unusual collage-like structure consisting of songs, folktales, poems, diary entries, scriptural citations, eyewitness recollections, speeches, interior monologues, newspaper articles, and more. As with the biography and nonfiction, the difficulty levels of the texts represent a large range, assuring that the needs of the students are met.

6. Documentary and Secondary Source Information

Students can make connections among people and begin to get a big-picture view of events by reading what other people were saying at the time of Brown's life and death. One example is from Victor Hugo: "The gaze of Europe is fixed at this moment on America. . . . [Hanging Brown] will open a latent fissure that will finally split the Union asunder. The punishment of John Brown may consolidate slavery in Virginia, but it will certainly shatter the American Democracy. You preserve your shame but you kill your glory" (Loewen, 1995, pp. 168–169). Another example describes the interpretation of John E. Dangerfield who was taken prisoner at Harpers Ferry: "During the day and night I talked much with John Brown, and found him as brave as a man could be, and sensible upon all subjects except slavery" (Colbert, 1997, p. 199). Still more interesting information to ponder, involving well-known and respected contemporaries of John Brown:

> When Virginia executed John Brown on December 2 [1859], making him the first American since the founding of the nation to be hanged as a traitor, church bells mourned in cities throughout the North. Louisa May Alcott, William Dean Howells, Herman Melville, John Greenleaf Whittier, and Walt Whitman were among the poets who responded to the event." (Loewen, 1995, p. 168)

7. Internet Sites

The entire text of Thoreau's "A Plea for Captain John Brown" is available at www.msstate.edu/Archives/History/USA/Afro-Amer/john brown.thoreau. The tone of this 13-page work of art is as passionate and accusing as the voices rising against the death penalty today, as is evident in this excerpt:

> Who is it whose safety requires that Captain Brown be hung? Is it indispensible to any Northern man? Is there no resource but to cast this man also to the Minotaur? If you do not wish it, say so distinctly. While these things are being done, beauty stands veiled and music is a screeching lie. Think of him—of his rare qualities!—such a man as it takes ages to make, and ages to understand; no mock hero, not the representative of any party.

8. Songs

John Brown's Body

(sung to the tune of Battle Hymn of the Republic)

John Brown's body lies a-mold'ring in the grave,
John Brown's body lies a-mold'ring in the grave,
John Brown's body lies a-mold'ring in the grave,
His soul goes marching on.

Glory, Glory! Hallelujah!
Glory, Glory! Hallelujah!
Glory, Glory! Hallelujah!
His soul is marching on.

He captured Harpers Ferry with his nineteen men so true
He frightened old Virginia till she trembled
    through and through
They hung him for a traitor, themselves the traitor crew
His soul is marching on.

John Brown died that the slave might be free,
John Brown died that the slave might be free,
John Brown died that the slave might be free,
But his soul is marching on! . . .

I could make a poster of these words to display in the classroom as we study the Civil War. In a way, John Brown will still be present, showing just how true those words carried into battle were!

Can you see how my planning and researching enable me to bring this history lesson to life and to encourage critical thinking and debate from my class? My file will grow as students bring in more information that they've found in additional resources as they investigate the enigma known as John Brown.

Of course, supplying variety in materials is not beneficial unless you teach the students how to use and think about them. Most students do not naturally read intertextually, comparing and contrasting sources and viewpoints. This type of reading strategy must be taught, even at the high school level (Perfetti, Britt, Rouet, Georgi, & Mason, 1994; Stahl, Hynd, Britton, McNish, & Bosquet, 1996). Afflerbach and VanSledright (2001) studied fifth graders who read from two textbooks on the topic of the Jamestown Colony: a traditional history textbook and a more innovative text that had an imbedded poem and excerpt from the Jamestown governor's diary. They found that the embedded texts benefited some students by eliciting an emotional response of empathy, but created obstacles for others who had difficulty shifting from one text type to another, or had trouble understanding the diary's archaic vocabulary and complicated syntax. The researchers concluded:

> . . . the think-aloud protocol of our readers suggests that much additional work remains to determine how reading multiple texts can be a productive experience for students. . . . Embedded texts and sources may create opportunities for students to develop historical thinking, to have enriched interactions with text, and to foster strategies for critical reading practice. However, these interactions and ways of thinking are learned, and many students may need coaching and modeling from teachers and knowledgeable peers around how the texts can be understood as part of a much larger historical evidence chain from which history is constructed. (p. 705)

▶ *Getting Ready to Teach 3.4 (see page 90)* ◀

As you read more within your field, you'll find that this activity becomes easier, and you can develop other folders for your future use with students. You can begin now to organize a set of empty file folders for various topics within the disciplines that you are likely to teach or that you have a special interest in, so that as you come across things in your own reading, you'll be ready with a place to put them. For example, language arts teachers might start folders labeled Reading Lists, Grammar, Letter Writing, Themes in Literature, Censorship, Stories about Authors, Satire and Irony, Journals, Articles about Language, Examples of Metaphors and Similes. Over time, you'll fill these folders with samples of all of the types of texts discussed in this chapter. You can add newspaper and magazine articles, student papers on the topic, Internet addresses, and a list of trade book titles along with where to find them (e.g., your personal collection, the school library, public library). Figure 3.11 provides an example from a teacher's math files.

MATCHING STUDENTS AND TEXTS

Matching materials to students is an important challenge teachers must meet, and collecting resources will help. We've probably all been victims, at one time or another, of a mismatch. Recently, I was observing a student teacher in a seventh grade English class as she taught a lesson on how to write limericks. With no motivational activity, the student teacher simply handed out a worksheet that began by defining a limerick as a short funny poem

in which lines 1, 2, and 5 rhyme; lines 3 and 4 rhyme; lines 1, 2, and 5 have eight to ten syllables; and lines 3 and 4 have five to seven syllables.

The class read the limerick examples, and then students were asked to complete the assignment at the end of the worksheet—write a limerick. The suggestions of people to write a limerick *about* included Willie Mays, Howard Cosell, Ali McGraw, Ringo Starr, Anthony Quinn, Tiny Tim, Princess Anne, Mark Spitz, Bobby Orr, and Geraldine. If you are having trouble identifying some of these people and even more trouble working up the enthusiasm to write poetry about them, you're not alone. The poor 12-year-olds looked up in puzzlement at the student teacher, who appeared a bit insecure herself as she looked my way for guidance. I looked at the bottom of the worksheet—the bibliographic notation showed a copyright date of 1974!

Times change, students change, and teachers and materials must change. Because you are such wide readers yourselves, your files will be current and will match your students' needs. Thank goodness!

Of course, matching texts with students requires that you know your students well; this is not easy for secondary teachers, who often have well over 100 students in their multiple daily classes. Yet, there are many reasons why students need their teachers to know them as individuals, so listening to them; talking informally before and after school and between classes; and paying close attention during a reading or writing workshop, small group work, and whole class discussion are crucial. You might keep a class list handy and jot down notes about things you hear from your students that will help you recommend or supply relevant texts. You might quietly place a book on volcanoes or a newspaper article about a tornado on the desk of a student you know is interested in natural disasters. Or you could write a short note to a student, saying something like, "Reggie, I know you like Gary Paulsen's books. I just got *The Beet Fields: Memories of a Sixteenth Summer* (2000) and *Guts: The True Stories Behind* Hatchet *and the Brian Books* (2001) for our classroom library. If you want to be the first to take them out, let me know today before I put them on the shelves." An efficient way to learn your students' interests is to ask them to fill out a survey. Figure 3.12 has some sample questions, and you can add others relating to particular curricular areas.

A very short read-aloud has the potential of capturing even the most resistant student. Imagine Mario, a student who is discouraged with school and thinks he has absolutely no interest in biology, especially this second time around. Now, picture him perking up when he hears his teacher reading the incredible prose Annie Dillard uses to describe

FIGURE 3.11 *An example of curricular file contents.*

PROBABILITY AND STATISTICS

A. Textbook reading:

"The Probability Formula," pp. 95–101 in Bellman, A., Bragg, S. C., Chapin, S. H., Gardella, T. J., Hall, B. C., Handlin, W. G., & Manfre, E. (2001). *New York Math A: An Integrated Approach.* Upper Saddle River, NJ: Prentice Hall.

B. Titles of resources to introduce, teach, and reinforce the topic:

- *Socrates and the Three Little Pigs* by Mori, T., & Anno, M. (1986). New York: Philomel Books.

- *Do You Wanna Bet?: Your Chance to Find Out About Probability* by Jean Cushman (1991). New York: Clarion Books.

- *Against the Gods: The Remarkable Story of Risk* by Peter L. Bernstein (1996). New York: Wiley.

- *The Universe and the Teacup: The Mathematics of Truth and Beauty* by K. C. Cole (1998). New York: Harcourt Brace.

- DNA Fingers Murderer: Life, Death and Conditional Probability. In *A Mathematician Reads the Newspaper* by John Allen Paulos (1995). New York: Basic Books.

- *A-Plus Notes for Algebra (with Trigonometry and Probability)* by R. Yang (1997). Redondo Beach, CA: A-Plus Notes Learning Center.

C. Newspaper articles:

1. (June 10, 1998) My Summary: Three boys in Central New York, injected with the same batch of chemotherapy medication, became paralyzed, which is normally an extremely rare side effect. It was anywhere from a one-in-a-million to a one-in-a-billion chance for all of the boys to become paralyzed as a known side effect of the drugs. The medical mystery has baffled the National Cancer Institute and the Food and Drug Administration because experts say there was no way a mistake was made at the pharmacy where the drugs were mixed, and there is no evidence of impurities or overdoses. The conclusion is that it was a strange coincidence, a statistical fluke.

TEACHER'S NOTE: I'd like my students to grapple with this mystery. The parents of the victims say that the chances of the three cases being coincidental are so astronomical they won't even consider the possibility. Yet, that's what the medical, governmental, and legal establishments are asking them to accept. I believe this case will help students deal with related issues, such as how this incident might affect future decisions about the treatment of children with leukemia, and how doctors and patients weigh the risk factors of using such medications and treatments against risk factors of *not* using them to fight progressive diseases. Students will see how probability and statistics are used in authentic situations, which will help them understand the more abstract concepts of our unit, and they'll be on the lookout for other examples of statistics at work.

There was another article on January 18, 2001, with an update on the boys' condition and the story of a settlement involving a $6 million payment to the boys. There's definitely more grist for the mill in that story.

2. *Herald American*, 8/2/98, Study: It's Happier and Healthier at the Top. "According to the first international research study examining the links between social rank and mind-body health, every increase in socioeconomic status brings an elevation in physical health and sanity. In other words, a corporate CEO is invariably healthier in body and mind than his middle manager. An administrative assistant is bound to be less fit and more frazzled than the boss, but far more likely to be in better physical and mental shape than a factory worker."

TEACHER'S NOTE: I'll ask students to analyze these opening sentences and apply what we have studied in statistics so far to identify the error in them.

D. Internet addresses:

- gasbone.herston.ug.edu.au (AIC: Statistics Introduction)

- www.learningchoices.com (information on resources)

E. Favorite sentences:
(enlarged and put on overhead transparencies)

1. For a coin to land on heads 50 consecutive times, it would take a million people tossing coins 10 times a minute for 40 hours a week—and then it would happen once every 9 centuries! (found in a seventh grade math classroom posted on a wall)

2. "The probability that a student, guessing randomly, could get 9, four-choice multiple choice answers correct is less than 4 in a million" (Smith, 1994, p. 218).

FIGURE **3.12**   *An interest survey for a content area class.*

Dear Student,

In this course we will be doing a lot of reading beyond the textbook. You'll find a great classroom library from which you can borrow books. I'll be able to supply you with other resources once I get to know you better. This survey will help me to know what kinds of reading you already do and to learn something about your interests. Please answer the following questions, and then add anything else you'd like me to know.

1. What is your favorite subject?
2. What interests and hobbies do you have?
3. Please list the names of any magazines or newspapers you read.
4. What kinds of books do you enjoy reading outside of school?
5. When you go to a bookstore, what section(s) do you head for?
6. List any of your favorite books or authors.
7. Which course topics interest you most? What would you like to learn more about?

her observation of a praying mantis and its mating habits:

> I lay on the hill this way and that, my knees in thorns and my cheeks in clay, trying to see as well as I could. I poked near the female's head with a grass; she was clearly undisturbed, so I settled my nose an inch from that pulsing abdomen. It puffed like a concertina, it throbbed like a bellows; it roved, pumping, over the glistening, clabbered surface of the egg case, testing and patting, thrusting and smoothing. . . .
>
> The male was nowhere in sight. The female had probably eaten him. . . . The mating rites of mantises are well known: a chemical produced in the head of the male insect says, in effect, "No, don't go near her, you fool, she'll eat you alive." At the same time a chemical in his abdomen says, "Yes, by all means, now and forever yes."
>
> While the male is making up what passes for his mind, the female tips the balance in her favor by eating his head. (1998, pp. 58–59).

Mario asks for the book *Pilgrim at Tinker Creek* (1998) and becomes increasingly hooked. His teacher has more Annie Dillard, and other books on insects and pond life, as Mario asks for them. Thoreau waits in the wings. Teacher and student keep talking about texts, about ideas.

Susan Nelson Wood is a teacher who was willing to admit that motivating her reluctant readers was wearying work. According to her article "Bringing Us the Way to Know" (2001), her attitude changed to "Truthfully, I was leaping out of bed in the mornings, eager to get to school" (p. 67) after

she introduced her students to author Gary Paulsen. They could not get enough of him (fortunately, he's written more than 240 fiction and non-fiction books, so the supply did not run out). She witnessed astonishing changes, such as the one in Brad, who was " . . . finishing his fourth year in our two-year school; not prone to talking, much less reading, he was more at home in the school hallway picking a fight than in the library picking a book" (p. 67). Brad was so enthralled with his newfound hero–author that he searched out Paulsen's home phone number. It ultimately resulted in Paulsen visiting the school and sharing stories with Wood's previously resistant eighth grade readers. The success stories are mounting, and yours can be added to the testimonies of students being turned on to reading when teachers match them up with texts that meet their needs.

CONCLUSION

In terms of instructional materials, it's a great time to be a teacher. We've never been better off. There are considerate, up-to-date, and multicultural textbooks; a proliferation of trade books at low prices; online journals; primary sources; TVs; VCRs; and movie rentals. We have access to the Internet and educational software. Students can create their own texts by using desktop publishing. One of my students had this to say in his learning log at semester's end:

> There is no better way to open up this story-world [of history] than by reading stories about the

times. I could not possibly convey the struggles faced by Jews during World War II as well as Anne Frank could. I couldn't give an account on slavery as accurately as Frederick Douglass would. It would be impossible to explain the despair of the Chinese immigrants on Angel Island without sharing the poetry they had written on the detention center walls. One cannot explain history without the voices of the people who lived through it. . . .

Stories, whether fiction or nonfiction, can magically give a reader the feelings of an experience. Books are like time machines that transport us through time and space. They can pull at our heart strings, fill us with anger or remorse, and can make us laugh or cry. These are the experiences I want my students to have. I want them to know what it was like so that they can not only have the knowledge, but also treasure the wisdom. . . .

I also believe that history is an exploration from which each individual can form a perspective. As a teacher, it will become my job to give my students as many resources as possible for them to formulate their own sense of the world and its events. They cannot rely on the textbook alone.

Make it a goal to become a collector of interesting texts of all sorts on the topics in your curriculum, and begin to work toward that goal immediately. Your students may catch your enthusiasm for seeking out information and opinions, and then you can take advantage of the opportunity to teach them how to

- find materials that will enrich their learning
- gain independence
- collaborate with others
- and develop a lifelong love for learning through reading

No matter what texts are used, teachers help students comprehend by what they do before, during, and after the reading. By helping students deal with vocabulary, background knowledge, organization, concepts, and so forth, they make reading and learning enjoyable experiences. Future chapters expand on the strategies that teachers and students can use to aid comprehension and expand thinking.

CHAPTER THREE

Getting Ready to Teach

3.1 Imagine that you are being interviewed for a teaching job in your content area. The search committee, consisting of a principal, a curriculum coordinator, and several teachers, informs you that the school you hope to work in has a policy of using no textbooks! They ask you to surmise what the philosophy underlying this decision might be, and ask you what kinds of materials you would use and how you would teach under these circumstances. Write in your learning log, thinking through how you might envision your job and answer your interviewers.

3.2 Start a file now for book reviews, including textbook reviews. You'll find reviews in professional journals, and you can search for reviews of particular materials on the Internet. Be sure to note who the reviewer is—the study on the science books described in this chapter, for example, was financed by the Carnegie Foundation and conducted by biologists and college and K–12 teachers who had no connection to the publishers of the books they reviewed. Whether the commentaries you find are positive, negative, or mixed, they can help you think about curricular and pedagogical issues as you assess materials and design instruction for your courses.

3.3 Jean Fritz is an award-winning author of historical biographies for children and young adults. She is respected by many experts in the fields of library science and education, and is the winner of the Laura Ingalls Wilder Medal. In 1983, Fritz's *The Double Life of Pocahontas* was published. The biography has several pages of notes and references, as well as a bibliography of scholarly sources and an index. The book was chosen as an American Library Association Notable

Book, and it won the Boston Globe–Horn Book Award, both prestigious achievements. A college content area textbook, in a chapter encouraging the use of trade books throughout the curriculum, considers Fritz's work exemplary. "More than a few high schoolers have had their interest in American history piqued by the style and wit of Jean Fritz, who makes such historical figures as Sam Houston and Pocahontas alive and human without sacrificing accuracy in the telling" (Schallert & Roser, 1996, p. 35). If possible, read this book and think about how you feel about its overall quality and how you think it might work with secondary students, especially those who are struggling readers and need materials that are interesting but not difficult.

Now, read the following review of Fritz's work from *Through Indian Eyes: The Native Experience in Books for Children* (Slapin & Seale, 1992).

Although most historians now acknowledge that John Smith lied when he told of having been saved by Pocahontas, the popular conception remains unaffected. Jean Fritz's "biography" will do nothing to change this. She reproduces the standard version, intact, with enough chunks of history of the Jamestown colony thrown in to make it book-length. There is plenty of speculative padding: "she would have" and "she must have" are common phrases. John Smith is portrayed as a hero, and there is more about him in this book than there is about Pocahontas. . . .

There is considerable emphasis on the trickery, savagery and childish naiveté of the Native people:

" . . . other Indians were not one bit friendly. Once they killed an English boy and shot an arrow right through President Wingfield's beard. Often they lay in the tall grass . . . waiting for someone to come through the gate. . . . Not even a dog could run out safely. Once one did and had forty arrows shot into his body.

And surely it should not *still* be necessary to point out that there has never been such a thing as an Indian king, queen or princess?"

It would serve no useful purpose to go through this book page by page, separating fact from fantasy. Suffice it to say that Fritz has added nothing to the little already "known" about Pocahontas, and that this little is treated with neither sensitivity nor insight. (pp. 157–158)

From B. Slapin and D. Seale (Eds.), *Through Indian Eyes: The Native Experience in Books for Children*. Los Angeles: UCLA American Indian Studies Center. Reprinted with permission.

What is your response to this review? As a teacher, what would you do if confronted with its information and opinions? Should Fritz's biography of Pocahontas be removed from our shelves? Write an argument in favor of this, or write about some ways you could use both the book and the review with students.

3.4 Choose a curricular topic in your subject area and begin a file in which you collect text titles representing the various genres' treatment of the topic. You might research several current or past textbooks to see how they handle the topic, then check the library for fiction and nonfiction sources, as well as reference materials. Explore the Internet, also. You may wish to start with a topic about which you have read widely or a topic you have wondered about and want to investigate more thoroughly. Enjoy!

4

The Reader's Role in Comprehension

PART ONE

Prior Knowledge

We've considered many issues relating to literacy, motivation, readers, and texts thus far. In this chapter, we explore the reader's role in comprehension—what the reader brings to the text and does before, during, and following the reading is crucial. You, as a content area teacher, play a huge role, too. You can activate and build prior knowledge, create reading guides that aid understanding, and teach the students strategies that will help them be aware of and monitor their reading and thinking in and beyond your class.

ACTIVATING PRIOR KNOWLEDGE 4.1

Fold a piece of paper in thirds, and label the columns K, W, and L. For the next few minutes, write down in the K column things you **know** about the topic ROBOTICS. (If absolutely nothing comes to mind, free associate about the word ROBOTS. What do they look like? What are they used for? Who programs them? Have you seen any in movies? In real life?) If you're in class or with other people, share your ideas and build on others' knowledge. Maybe there is a previously unidentified robot whiz among you who can be the hero of the moment. *(continued)*

"A man [woman] receives only what [s]he is ready to receive, whether physically or intellectually. . . . We hear and apprehend only what we already half know. If there is something which does not concern me, which is out of my line, which by experience or genius my attention is not drawn to, however novel and remarkable it might be, if it is spoken we hear it not, if it is written we read it not, it does not detain us."

THOREAU, JOURNAL XIII: 77–78

My students, after the initial "You're kidding, right?" are usually able to start the column with some simple stuff like R2D2 and C3PO, then add some things they've learned from science class, novels, newspapers, or conversations. Once in a while, a student amuses the others with an anecdote, such as knowing a pharmacist who works alongside a prescription-filling robot.

The next part of the activity is often the trickiest for teachers. In the next column, which you've labeled W, write down what you **want** to know about robotics. Now, you can imagine that seventh or eighth graders, when asked by a teacher or textbook what they want to learn about almost any topic—cells, the Industrial Revolution, fractals, Impressionist painters—might feel inclined to answer, "Nothing." And I can understand how you might say the same about this topic; if you were interested in the subject of robotics, you would have explored it on your own. So, I'm going to help you out.

Imagine the following scenario. You have just been informed by your doctor that there is something seriously wrong with you. You have two options. You can have major surgery that will require you to miss school and work for eight weeks. Or, you can agree to having a tiny robot inserted into your body to fix the problem. You will be an outpatient and can resume your normal activities the following day. In the W column, write the questions you want answers to before making your decision.

I'll bet you didn't leave the column blank or answer "Nothing" to the implied question of what you want to learn this time. Typically, my students are suddenly very inquisitive about this robot and the medical procedure. "How big is it?" is often at the top of the list. "Will it hurt?" they want to know. How expensive is this new operation, and will insurance cover it? How many times has it been performed before? How is the robot removed? What are the risks? You've probably listed additional questions.

The third step of the K-W-L strategy (Ogle, 1986) is to read an assigned text and fill in the third column, under L, the things you've **learned**. Have your questions been answered? Was there information you didn't know before? The box below contains the reading I assign my students.

(continued on p. 95)

FANTASTIC VOYAGE: TRAVELING THE BODY IN MICROBIOTIC STYLE

by Steve Nadis

Researchers at MIT's Artificial Intelligence Lab have plans to go where no man, woman, or "mobot" has ever gone before—into a dark, slimy, and winding tunnel known as the large intestine, or colon. The microbot—named Cleo and little more than an inch in width, breadth, and height—was devised by 22-year-old MIT senior James McLurkin, who admits to having "always liked small things." Cleo is about the smallest thing on two treads going these days and it's also among the smartest. It can find a path between obstacles, move toward or away from light, avoid hills, and grasp objects with a small claw. All these actions can be initiated by a person operating a joystick. Cleo can also function on its own, untethered, making its way through a plastic colon maze, for instance, by bumping into a wall, backing up, and shifting its direction ever so slightly.

Cleo is the fourth so-called "ant" created by McLurkin—and the product of an effort certainly dispro-

portionate to its modest size. To gather all its miniature parts, McLurkin pored through catalog after catalog, making a million phone calls, always asking the same question: "Do you have anything smaller?"

The project is funded by the Advanced Research Projects Agency (ARPA) in the Department of Defense which is looking to remote surgery as a long-term goal. According to this vision, [one day] remote manipulators (robot arms) might perform surgery on U.S. soldiers around the world, guided by physicians back home. For the nearer term, the agency regards colon examinations and surgery as the most immediate applications. "A diagnostic task such as looking for cancer is the main motivation," explains ARPA surgeon Richard Satava.

The technology allows the microrobot to work in conjunction with light and a camera; if something unusual is spotted, the controlling physician might take a sample (a biopsy), or possibly snip off little growths or polyps and stop intestinal bleeding with lasers or electricity. "We can do all these things today in a procedure called colonoscopy, but that involves pushing a long tube into a person, which is extremely uncomfortable," Satava says. "A small instrument like a microrobot has the potential to be much less painful and much less dangerous." He predicts that robotic colon surgery could be possible within five to ten years.

Robotic surgery is not altogether new. "Robodoc," for instance, is used during hip replacement surgery to bore a precision hole in the hip bone for an artificial replacement part. Robots have also helped neurosurgeons determine the exact position of brain tumors. But Cleo is among the first to be designed to go *inside* the human body. . . .

It may be quite a few years before anything as futuristic as this high-tech version of the 1966 classic *Fantastic Voyage* is in common use, but McLurkin is optimistic about the future. "This is not pie-in-the-sky," he insists. "Sooner or later, one way or another, robotic surgery is gonna happen." Now that really will be a fantastic voyage.

Omni Magazine, Winter, 1994, p. 9.

ACTIVATING PRIOR KNOWLEDGE, *continued*   4.1

Some teachers add a fourth column to the exercise, changing the name to K-W-L Plus (Carr & Ogle, 1987), when the class maps out what they have learned by creating some kind of graphic organizer. Other teachers use K-W-L-S (What do I STILL have to learn?) (Sippola, 1995). In the fourth column, the reader lists additional questions generated by reading. For example, something a text says might contradict something you thought was true. You might have to look further to clear up any confusion. At this point, I also ask my students to notice the information's source. They realize that the Steve Nadis article, while sounding a bit futuristic to some, is actually quite dated, so they wonder what advances have been made since 1994. A few of my students have observed that although *Omni Magazine* was noted for reporting on scientific breakthroughs, it often featured articles on UFOs and the paranormal, so caution on the reader's part might be advisable.

In this particular situation, I've had students bring in articles from various sources on nanotechnology that confirm, update, or extend the information we've read together. For example, a student presented us with a newspaper article about a hospital using a robotic surgical arm, controlled by a surgeon's voice, that holds and moves a camera around inside a patient during an operation. Another brought in an article on magnetic devices implanted in patients that can reduce or eliminate seizures. We've read of a camera within a pill that can photograph the small intestine. (You'll notice that I've followed my own advice from Chapter 3 about keeping file folders on topics I teach; I have a growing "Robotics" file.)

Students might realize they know more for that first column than they originally thought; perhaps, they just never thought about pacemakers being connected with the field of robotics. My students usually discover that they're more interested in robotics than they had initially thought, and the little bit of information they've acquired enables them to learn more easily when they do encounter new material on the topic.

The simplicity of the K-W-L-S strategy makes it a natural for students to use independently. Some students, after an explanation and some practice in a content area classroom, may find that it's a portable, transferable strategy that helps them manage and comprehend all kinds of texts. But there's a danger. It *can* become artificial, another one of those "workbook" type, please-the-teacher techniques, or simply a way of assessing whether students have read and understood, or busywork. We have to help students experience the real help a strategy such as K-W-L-S can give them as readers of authentic materials. And we have to use our teaching skills as we're planning assignments. So, add a Teacher (T) column for us as we apply the strategy, asking, "What will make K-W-L-S work with this *particular* text, and with our *particular* students?"

BookTalk 4.1

If you found the article on robotics interesting, you might wish to read Isaac Asimov's *The Fantastic Voyage* (1966), to which the article referred. Another related work of fiction is Madeleine L'Engle's second novel about the Murry family, whom readers come to know so well in *A Wrinkle in Time*. *A Wind in the Door* (1973) tells of the mysterious illness of Charles Wallace, the baby of the family, and the courageous voyage his sister Meg and her teammates make into his body to battle the forces trying to kill his mitochondria. Swim alongside the characters while reading this book.

> **Getting Ready to Teach 4.1** *(see page 120)*

Figure 4.1 shows a preservice teacher's application of the K-W-L-S strategy.

THE ROLE OF PRIOR KNOWLEDGE

Stanovitch (1986) coined the term *Matthew Effect* with respect to learning and reading. Readers who come to a text with a rich background in a subject area have a much easier time learning the new information. Think about a hobby or interest you have, and consider how you could comprehend an article on the subject compared to a person uninitiated in the field. Whether we're talking sports, computers, art, the stock market, gardening, or cooking doesn't matter. The rich get richer; the poor give up or turn away. This is extremely important for teachers to understand. Young adult novelist Richard Peck calls the age of six "late in life. Most of what we'll be is already decided before we ever see school. Formal education doesn't build foundations; it builds upon them" (1994, p. 6). Think of the diversity of children

---

FIGURE 4.1 *K-W-L-S guide for science.*

EBOLA			
K	W	L	S

Answer the first two questions before watching the movie *Outbreak* (1995).

1. WHAT WE KNOW: Write down everything you know about Ebola and similar deadly viruses in column 1 (K).
2. WHAT WE WANT TO FIND OUT: What should you know if people in the community you live in came down with one of these viruses, and authorities quarantined your town with you in it? Write your questions in column 2 (W).

Now watch the movie, noting if, when, and how your questions are answered. Then, answer the next two questions.

3. WHAT WE LEARNED: What did you learn from watching the movie about the outbreak, how the virus is spread, and other interesting facts? Write your answers in column 3 (L).
4. WHAT WE WANT TO KNOW NOW: Write down any new questions you've come up with as a result of watching this movie in column 4 (S).

—Brian VanArsdale

entering first grade, a crucial year in terms of learning to read. Some have spent literally thousands of hours listening to family members or others read to them; some have spent virtually none.

"Whoever has will be given more, and [s]he will have an abundance. Whoever does not have, even what [s]he has will be taken from him [her]."

MATTHEW 13:12

By the time those students get to the upper grades and are members of content area classes, the range has widened. But you can't just despair or blame the elementary teachers, parents, television, or society. Despite what Peck says, sometimes teachers *do* have to build foundations, or repair or strengthen them, in order to introduce new curriculum. That's a crucial part of teaching.

The importance of background knowledge, or prior knowledge, to reading comprehension and to learning in general cannot be overstated. Researchers have found that readers spend up to 70 percent of their time interpreting the author's ideas and deciing how those ideas relate to their own prior knowledge on the subject. They engage in an ongoing dialogue with authors as they read (Harste, 1986).

SCHEMA THEORY

When we learn, we naturally connect new information to information we already possess. It's much harder to understand and remember facts in isolation. Research has indicated that there are networks of concepts that seem to trigger each other. *Schema theory* demonstrates how a person's knowledge affects the way new information is comprehended and remembered (Anderson & Pearson, 1984). A reader actually constructs new knowledge by combining textual material with information already possessed. A schema is a set of mental slots used for storing concepts in memory (Rumelhart, 1981). We have *schemata* for many types of knowledge. When I asked you in Chapter 1 to brainstorm a list of words you associate with the word *utopia*, your schema for that concept was activated. You'll probably recall that your classmates shared many of the same associations, maybe phrases like "an ideal place," "a place of peace," "a place with no worries or problems," but some specifics may have been different—one person knew that the term was coined by Thomas More

and means "no place," another had just read *The Handmaid's Tale* (Atwood, 1986), and so on. By having you look at each other's lists of associations, I hoped to increase your background knowledge as you began reading *The Giver.* In general, the richer your background knowledge, the more success you will have understanding new material. Readers with extensive background knowledge tend to focus on broad, relevant concepts at the same time they pick up on important details, while less knowledgeable readers are more likely to fixate on less significant facts, words, dates, and numbers, and later cannot recall what they read (Conley, 1995).

Assimilation

One way that readers use prior knowledge during reading involves the concept Piaget (1952) called *assimilation*, the process by which the reader recognizes and remembers some facts and not others. There is a base upon which new information can be added and comparisons made. For example, middle school students have learned some things in science and social studies about the food chain, the balance of nature, and endangered species. If they read the novel *Who Really Killed Cock Robin?* (George, 1991), they learn more details about how environmental pollutants can cause a chain reaction that upsets the balance of nature. In addition, they learn how politics can affect decisions that are made regarding industry and the environment. Their now-expanded prior knowledge is even more helpful when they encounter related newspaper articles, encyclopedia entries, Internet sites, and so forth. Bill Costello, an avid baseball fan, commented, "Now when I read about baseball, I'm just filling in more little pieces of knowledge to the large mosaic of information I have collected on the subject over the years. I've probably read more books about baseball than anybody on the planet" (Rosenthal, 1995, p. 173). Knowledge breeds knowledge. Stahl, Hynd, Glynn, & Carr (1996) explain, "One must view each fact as embedded in a fabric of other related information. To learn a fact, it is not enough to memorize it; it should be learned as part of an overall schema" (p. 140). A statement by chemist Linus Pauling exemplifies assimilation:

> Whenever I see something that seems to me to be new, or new so far as my memory goes, I ask myself, "Does this fit into my picture of the world that I've developed over ninety-three years?" If it does, that's fine. If it doesn't, then I ask, "Well, why doesn't it? How can it be interpreted to fit into my picture of the world?" (Rosenthal, 1995, p. 152)

Accommodation

A second element of schema theory involves *accommodation*, the process by which schemata are used to interpret and reconstruct information from the text and the reader's mind to form new concepts. Accommodation involves creating new slots in the reader's storage system and sometimes dissolving existing ones.

New material challenges what we thought we knew. In the science area, children often have mistaken theories (e.g., plants get their food from the soil, heavy objects fall faster than light ones, winter jackets make one warm by generating heat). Sometimes the mistaken "knowledge" has actually been taught by parents or by teachers. Fill in the following blank: "Never start a sentence with _____." Chances are you immediately wrote "because" or "and," which indicates that some helpful teacher most likely taught you that rule so that you would not use a sentence fragment in a composition. Then, at some point you notice that some excellent published writers break the rules, and you accommodate that new information by recognizing that the rule you had to follow in fourth or seventh grade does not generalize to all sentences in all circumstances. By using the process of accommodation, you are no longer just a receiver of knowledge; you are a constructor of knowledge. Teachers can help students construct new knowledge by making them aware of any discrepancies between long-held ideas and new ideas and by providing some explicit hands-on experimentation or demonstration when possible.

Sometimes, readers' own views or opinions or beliefs are so deeply entrenched that they are unable to reconstruct their schema; they distort what they read to fit their perceptions rather than modify what they have thought to be true. Successful readers use a conceptual change strategy. "They integrate their prior knowledge with information from the text but use facts in the text to reconstruct their schema. In other words, they adapt or accommodate their schema so that it fits what they read, rather than vice versa" (Gunning, 1996, p. 308).

Accommodation is an intellectually demanding task, and a teacher must take steps to help students make the conceptual change. This chapter provides a number of instructional strategies that teachers can use to activate students' prior knowledge and curiosity, and also help them recognize what they do not know or are unsure of so that they approach the text prepared to learn.

Of course, there may be times when incoming information conflicts with the student's schemata and the text is actually wrong! For example, for a few years after the collapse of the Soviet Union,

BookTalk 4.2

We've all had mistaken notions, and perhaps were even embarrassed when they led us into trouble or were discovered by those more knowledgeable. We might be comforted to know that we're in good company; history is full of examples of errors in thinking, as can be seen in *Shocking Science: 5,000 Years of Mishaps and Misunderstandings* by Steve Parker and John Kelly (1996). Read about how doctors used to relieve headaches by drilling holes into people's brains; how, for decades, 20th century scientists thought they had found the missing link to human evolution, when in fact the "Piltdown Man" was a hoax; how engineers, figuring the more wings a plane had the better, designed the Multiplane, with 20 wings, making the plane look like a flying Venetian blind. This book teaches many scientific principles as it humorously illustrates the risks and hypotheses that are part of discovery and learning. Related books students will enjoy include *Scientific Blunders: A Brief History of How Wrong Scientists Can Sometimes Be* by Robert Youngson (1998), *Voodoo Science* by R. Park (2000), *The Encyclopedia of Pseudoscience: From Alien Abductions to Zone Therapy* by W. F. Williams (2000), and *Mistakes that Worked: 40 Familiar Inventions and How They Came to Be* (1991) and *Accidents May Happen: Fifty Inventions Discovered by Mistake* (1996), both by Charlotte Foltz Jones.

many students were using social studies textbooks that were quite suddenly outdated and no longer accurate. Literacy skills are necessary to deal with the barrage of information in daily newspapers and on the Internet that may challenge a reader's thinking so that inaccuracies and faulty reasoning in text don't cause accommodation that actually lessens knowledge. We must teach students how to check the validity of all text sources, especially those they find on the Internet. Also, you can include books in your classroom library that explicitly deal with misconceptions, such as *Lies Across America* by James Loewen (2000) and *Yes We Have No Neutrons: An Eye-Opening Tour Through the Twists and Turns of Bad Science* by A. K. Dewdney (1997).

The instructional implications of schema theory and the research on background knowledge are enormous. It's very important to help students deal with any inaccurate prior knowledge, or misconceptions, that can actually make comprehension of a text harder than having little background knowledge on the topic (Holmes, 1983; Lipson, 1982; Myhill, 2000; Watson, 2000). The principle of *scaffolding*, as you learned in Chapter 2, involves a teacher starting with a student's knowledge or skills base and building on it. You'll determine how much and what kinds of supports your students need. For example, you might use the tree diagrams and the humorous story of a wolf trying to determine his best chance for nabbing a pig in Mori and Anno's *Socrates and the Three Little Pigs* (1986) to prepare students for a lesson on probability. Vygotsky (1978), as mentioned in Chapter 2, called the range where a student could not function independently but could learn with the help of a teacher or other competent mentor the *zone of proximal development*. He emphasized the social nature of learning, which constructivists have built on ever since. It only makes sense that we assess where our students are, activate their prior knowledge, and then provide supporting structures to take them further on their learning journey. As students improve a skill, such as reading, and are capable of more independence, some of the supports can be removed, and new guidance offered at a higher level.

BookTalk 4.3

Since my discovery of the internment of Japanese Americans, I have found sensitively written accounts that have helped my knowledge grow. *Baseball Saved Us* (1993), by Ken Mochizuki, is a picture book that tells a story of daily life within the camps. Jerry Stanley's nonfiction account, *I Am an American* (1994), includes emotion-provoking and thought-provoking photographs. Equally interesting are some books that tell about Japanese Americans after the war. *Snow Falling on Cedars,* by David Guterson (1995), is a best-seller that tells of lingering racism through a story of a Japanese American accused of a terrible crime and brought to trial. The young adult novel *Bat 6* (1998) by Virginia Euwer Wolff relates through various narrators a story of two girls' softball teams in 1949. On one team is a Japanese American girl who had been in an internment camp; on the competing team is a girl whose father was killed in the Pearl Harbor attack. Read this book to find out if such differences can be reconciled. And Eve Bunting's *So Far from the Sea* (1998) is narrated by a child telling of her family in 1972, revisiting Manzanar, where her father had lived as a child and where *his* father is buried. A lesson has been learned at a very great price.

PRE-READING STRATEGIES TO ACTIVATE AND BUILD PRIOR KNOWLEDGE

There are many ways teachers can assess, activate, and supply background knowledge to provide support as students read relevant texts. This section discusses several strategies that you can employ in your content area classes.

Brainstorming

Brainstorming to call to mind what we know about topics can be done individually or in groups. I used this strategy with you earlier in this chapter in the robotics exercise. Sometimes, I structure whole-class brainstorming sessions by putting up pieces of poster paper with category labels. Before discussing the trade books about World War II introduced in Chapter 1, or a textbook chapter on the same topic, I ask the students to fill in posters that have the following headings: EVENTS, DATES, PEOPLE, PLACES, CAUSES, and RESULTS (WHO, WHAT, WHERE, WHEN, WHY could also be used). I vary the posters as needed for different topics. For example, when I begin my sixth grade Bible Study class each fall, I explain to my new students that I can teach them better once I know what they already know. I ask them to walk around with markers and fill in information on posters labeled PEOPLE IN THE BIBLE, BOOKS OF THE BIBLE, BIBLE VERSES I KNOW, and so on. As the course progresses, the students add information to these posters, and the evidence of new knowledge becomes visible.

Getting Ready to Teach 4.2 (see page 120)

List–Group–Label

For the brainstorming strategy, I provided labels that structured the answers I wanted to elicit. Taba (1967) approached brainstorming a different way. She modified the strategy by asking the students to free associate first, and then to examine their list to see whether the words could be placed into logical groupings—she called the activity List–Group–Label. Students may find that their schema for a topic includes facts that are hierarchical. For example, they may realize that, in preparation for a geography reading assignment, they have brainstormed names of countries, names of states or provinces or regions within those countries, names of cities within those regions, and finally, names of specific sites within the cities.

Before reading Diane Stanley's beautifully written and illustrated biography *Leonardo da Vinci* (1996), I asked my students to call to mind whatever they associated with the name of this famous man. Answers included: "The Last Supper," "helicopters and flying machines," "Mona Lisa," "He wrote backwards," "machine guns and grenades," "He did dissections of human bodies even though they were illegal," "self-portraits," "submarines," "He competed with Michelangelo," "engineering," "Renaissance Man," "He drew that, you know, that human body with all the arms and legs in a circle." Students were able to group their answers into categories representing Leonardo as *inventor, artist, mathematician,* and *scientist,* as well as one containing *personal characteristics.* Further discussion revealed that the categories couldn't be seen as discrete; sometimes a work was both a scientific and artistic achievement, for example. This activity prepared the students intellectually and affectively to delve into the text in order to clarify and extend their knowledge of Leonardo. They loved the book and were amazed at all they learned.

Graphic Organizers

Because we know from schema theory that our prior knowledge is somehow organized in our minds, that the bits of information we have are connected to each other, instructors can make great use of visual representations of connected ideas to activate the knowledge that students can bring to their reading and learning. You may have had experience with these in your own education and might know them by various names, including *graphic organizers, semantic webs, clusters, structured overviews,* or *visual maps.* These organizers have many other instructional uses, as you will learn in the next few chapters, but right now we'll look at how they can be used as a type of structured brainstorming to activate the schemata of individuals and groups in preparation for reading.

A teacher might supply the structure and category labels for the students, as exemplified in the pre-reading organizer for an interdisciplinary inquiry into the topic of gambling in Figure 4.2.

The teacher can find out what students already know, identify misconceptions, and have students share their ideas and learn from others. They should then be ready and motivated to read the chapter to gain new information, and their minds will be keyed in to the superordinate categories of *causes* and *effects,* which can aid comprehension. After the reading, students can go back to change any information that conflicts with their new knowledge

(unless they want to dispute the text and research further) and add more details to the categories.

At times, it might be more appropriate to have the students themselves generate the categories for a class graphic organizer in preparation for a unit of study. Figure 4.3 shows a wall chart that students in an art course might make on the first day of class, representing their combined thinking on the discipline the teacher asked them to brainstorm: art history. Using this chart, the teacher will get a good idea of what the students already know and will be able to use appropriate "hooks" on which to hang the new information they will gain from reading, viewing, and listening to their teacher's lessons. As the weeks proceed, they might consciously or unconsciously look for the characteristics and concepts they addressed on the poster. Again, at intervals during the course, students can add or revise information on the chart, representing their knowledge growth.

> **Getting Ready to Teach 4.3** (see page 120)

Anticipation Guides

You're already familiar with anticipation guides from earlier chapters. Pre-reading guides are very helpful in activating schemata, challenging beliefs and commonsense notions, provoking differences of opinion among classmates that lead to productive dialogue, and modifying misconceptions about a topic.

Alvermann and Phelps (1998) provide concrete steps to help teachers create anticipation guides.

1. Analyze the text to identify key information and major concepts.
2. Find "points of congruence between text ideas and students' prior knowledge" (p. 179), anticipating ideas that might be controversial or counterintuitive, especially possible misconceptions students might hold.
3. Devise several statements that address students' existing prior knowledge.
4. Write an introduction to the assignment, and write directions for the students.
5. Have the students complete the guide after you give a short introduction to the topic.
6. Provide time for small groups to discuss their answers before and after reading.

Alvermann and Phelps warn of a mistake teachers can make when creating an anticipation guide— including statements that are too passage dependent.

FIGURE 4.2 *A pre-reading graphic organizer for a chapter on gambling.*

DIRECTIONS: Before we start our chapter on gambling, I'd like you to brainstorm what you already know (or hypothesize) about various aspects of the topic. Please place information in whatever categories you can. If you're not sure about some ideas, place a question mark after what you write.

CAUSES OF/REASONS FOR GAMBLING

psychological: _____
_____

mathematical: _____
_____

moral/ethical: _____
_____

social: _____
_____

financial: _____
_____

EFFECTS OF GAMBLING

psychological: _____
_____

mathematical: _____
_____

moral/ethical: _____
_____

social: _____
_____

financial: _____
_____

I often see this mistake on my preservice teachers' early attempts. When I write in the margin, "How would I have any idea about this before I read the text?" they say, "Oh, yeah," and eliminate or change the statement. For example, one student asked students to agree or disagree with statements such as "Abner Doubleday created baseball in 1839 at Cooperstown, New York" and "In 1887, all black baseball players were banned from all white teams, and the ban was not lifted until 1946." If students had the level of knowledge necessary to answer these detailed questions, they'd have no need to read the chapter for which the guide was supposedly preparing them.

Figures 4.4 through 4.7 are examples of anticipation guides created by my education students.

FIGURE 4.3 *A graphic organizer showing whole-class brainstorming in art.*

WHAT WE ALREADY KNOW ABOUT ART AND ART HISTORY

Genres of Art We Know:

sculpture	painting	glass blowing/stained glass work
drawing	photography	crafts (maskmaking, jewelry, quilting, etc.)

Types of Painting We Know:

Impressionism	cave drawings	modern art
cubism	surrealism	pop art

Artists We Know:

Picasso	Matisse	Van Gogh	Dali
Michelangelo	Andy Warhol	Jackson Pollack	Monet
Mary Cassatt	Leonardo da Vinci	Georgia O'Keefe	Grandma Moses

Illustrators We Know:

Maurice Sendak	David Wiesner	Leo and Diane Dillon	Allen Say
Barbara Cooney	Chris Van Allsburg	David Diaz	Susan Jeffers
Christopher Myers	Faith Ringgold	Jan Brett	Patricia Polacco

Famous Works of Art We Know:

The Mona Lisa	Starry Night	The Sistine Chapel	Whistler's Mother
The Persistence of Memory	The Thinker	Michelangelo's Pieta	David

FIGURE 4.4 *An anticipation guide for science.*

DIRECTIONS: Before reading the novel *A Wrinkle in Time*, by Madeleine L'Engle, decide whether you agree or disagree with each statement below. After you read the book, decide whether the author would agree or disagree, and record your answers in the right-hand column.

	YOU		AUTHOR	
1. Science is a universal language.	Agree	Disagree	Agree	Disagree
2. Time travel is possible.	Agree	Disagree	Agree	Disagree
3. There is intelligent life on other planets.	Agree	Disagree	Agree	Disagree
4. The shortest distance between two points is a straight line.	Agree	Disagree	Agree	Disagree
5. ESP (Extra Sensory Perception) is not possible.	Agree	Disagree	Agree	Disagree
6. Time is linear.	Agree	Disagree	Agree	Disagree
7. A utopian society would be a good place to live.	Agree	Disagree	Agree	Disagree
8. Love always overcomes evil.	Agree	Disagree	Agree	Disagree

—*Shannon Dearborn*

FIGURE 4.5 *An anticipation guide for geography.*

DIRECTIONS: As you know, we have been studying the climate and geography of various regions of the world. Please answer the following questions in preparation for our next assigned reading.

1. What comes to your mind when you think of Alaska? What do you think it would be like if you visited there? How would you describe it? Climate? Environment? Plant and animal life? What would you pack if you were planning a trip there? Write down any concepts or words that come to mind.

2. Imagine you are standing deep within a tropical rain forest. How would you describe it? What does it look like? Where on the earth might you be? List any words or concepts that come to mind when you think of a tropical rain forest.

3. Have you ever heard a person claim that it was raining or snowing on one side of the house, but not the other? Do you think this is possible? Why or why not?

4. If you were planning a vacation for your family, and one parent wanted to go mountain skiing, while the other wanted to hike through a rainforest, what would you do if you could choose only one destination? Where might you go?

For homework, please read the article "Winter Green," by Jill Shepherd, found in the magazine *Alaska*, February 1999, beginning on page 34. When you finish, review your answers to the questions above. In a different color pen, add information you learned from your reading.

—*Palmyre "Pam" Charron*

FIGURE 4.6 *An anticipation guide for mathematics.*

DIRECTIONS: Before reading Chapter One of *The Broken Dice: And Other Mathematical Tales of Chance* by I. Ekeland, answer the following questions.

1. How many possible outcomes are there if two dice are rolled? How did you arrive at your answer?

2. To the best of your ability, draw a tree diagram that would represent the possible outcomes of rolling two dice, along with their probabilities. If you're not sure, draw something anyway to see if you discover anything.

3. What are some uses of dice?

4. For what purposes do you, personally, use dice?

5. What is meant by the phrase *loading the dice*? What is the effect of loading the dice?

6. What would happen if a die broke while in use? For example, if two faces of a die are facing up, should both numbers count?

Now you're ready to read the chapter. After the reading, we'll have a class discussion of the story, and we'll solve a problem that involves issues of the accuracy of the methods discussed in the story. Then, we'll look at different ways to represent the use of dice to solve problems.

—*Author unknown*

FIGURE 4.7 *An anticipation guide for English.*

1. Think of the phrase "mind over matter." List the first five things that come to your mind:

   a. _____

   b. _____

   c. _____

   d. _____

   e. _____

2. Give a short description of a time when you had to overcome some great obstacle in life.

   _____

   _____

3. What kinds of items would you expect to find in a treasure chest?

   _____

   _____

4. Respond YES or NO to the following statements:

   YES NO   Laws are to be followed so that I can be protected.

   YES NO   Jails are for bad people who are guilty and deserve what they get.

   YES NO   Standing up for what I believe in is very important.

   YES NO   Not sticking to a plan could result in failure.

   YES NO   Parents and teachers are always right.

   YES NO   Just because something an adult says is wrong doesn't mean that I should not obey what he/she says.

   YES NO   Curses, jinxes, hexes, and bad luck are real.

   YES NO   Digging holes is a fun activity.

   Now, read the novel *Holes*, by Louis Sachar, and follow the adventures of Stanley Yelnats as he struggles to survive just being a kid. After you have finished this book, look back at this guide to see how closely you related to Stanley and his friends at Camp Green Lake Juvenile Detention Center. How did you do?

   —*Michael Anderson*

Getting Ready to Teach 4.4 *(see page 120)*

"What Would You Do?"
Pre-Reading Thinking Activity

Imagine you receive the following two letters from friends. How would you reply to them?

> Hi! You'll never believe what happened to me! I found a baby! She's so cute, and I'm taking really good care of her. I can tell she trusts me. I know you'll find this hard to believe because I'm so independent, but I want to keep her. What do you think I should do?

> Hello from your traveling friend! Don't tell a soul, but I'm on a really important mission. I'm transporting some illegal immigrants to a place of safety. It's scary, but exciting and rewarding. What do you think?

The "What Would You Do?" pre-reading activity prepares students to reflect actively on ideas, using prior knowledge of events and relationships in their own lives. It often involves students' values as well as their decision-making skills. The main character in Barbara Kingsolver's *The Bean Trees* (1988) gets involved in situations like the two described. In

FIGURE 4.8 *A "What Would You Do?" guide in preparation for* When I Was Puerto Rican *by Esmerela Santiago.*

1. Brainstorm words, phrases, and people that you associate with the term *imperialism*.

2. List any titles of works of literature, movies, or songs that deal with imperialism that you have read, seen, or heard of.

3. Imagine that you are 10 years old. People from another country come to yours and force their customs, beliefs, and ways of life on you. How would you feel?

4. Imagine also that these people speak another language, eat different foods, listen to different music, and practice a different religion from yours. Would you accept this and change, or would you speak out and try to resist?

5. Now imagine that you were being pressured to move to these people's country in order to help your single mother raise your seven younger siblings. Would you fight to stay with your father and his new family, or would you go along and help your mother?

Now read *When I Was Puerto Rican* to see how Negi reacts to these challenges. Does she do anything that you would have done also? What does she do differently?

—Kelly Gorman

---

preparing to read the novel, your students' knowledge and opinions relating to abandoned babies and illegal immigrants has been activated, as well as their values related to each. This readies readers for engagement with, comprehension of, and response to the story. Your students' opinions might change as they read, and their knowledge might grow. In every subject area there are stories, real or fictional, that involve situations you can ask students to think about prior to reading.

Figure 4.8 shows a preservice Spanish teacher's guide designed to activate knowledge and thinking before reading the autobiography *When I Was Puerto Rican* by Esmerela Santiago.

Previews

Everyone is familiar with the effectiveness of movie previews, letting us in on coming attractions. You can use a similar strategy—read aloud a script you compose to get students ready to read a narrative or expository text that is challenging. This activity provides the scaffolding that enables them to comprehend at a higher level than they could do independently. Previews have been used effectively with second-language learners (Chen & Graves, 1996). You can be dramatic or humorous, but the preview, according to Graves, Prenn, and Cooke (1985) should consist of three components:

1. An introduction that links the text to students' lives or prior knowledge.

2. A summary.

3. Purpose-setting questions.

Ryder and Graves (1998) provide helpful instructions for constructing a preview:

① Read the text selection yourself several times to become familiar with important characters, ideas, or events.

② Ask yourself how you might make the information relevant to your students by linking it to their background knowledge.

③ Write an introduction to the text, ending with a question that draws upon students' prior knowledge.

④ Write a summary of main ideas and supporting details following the order used in the text, being careful not to give away the ending of the story.

⑤ Ask purpose-setting questions.

⑥ Tell students about anything they should watch out for in terms of structure or potentially troublesome parts of the text.

Figure 4.9 shows a preview I wrote for education students who were about to read an article from a professional journal. The circled numbers correspond to the instructions outlined above.

FIGURE 4.9 *A preview lesson.*

① **INTRODUCTION:** The article you are about to read, "They Can But They Don't" by Jerome H. Bruns (1992), will give you valuable information about students who exhibit *work inhibition*, a condition that may affect up to one-fifth of the students you will teach. Before listening to my summary of some of the key points in the article, think about the following questions that will help you link your prior experience with the topic:

② 1. Have you ever experienced difficulty or reluctance when doing a certain job even though you had
③ the *ability* to do it? What might have caused your resistance or struggle?

　2. Do you know people who, though smart and skillful, are sometimes not successful at what others think they *should* be able to do? What characterizes a person who might be labeled an *underachiever*?

④ **SUMMARY OF SOME KEY POINTS:** Bruns begins by defining the term "work inhibited," referring to students who *can* but *don't* do the work required at school. Something unrelated to knowledge, abilities, and skills is blocking them from succeeding. Even excellent teachers cannot get them to engage in the process of learning.

　In one section, Bruns identifies the characteristics of work-inhibited students, including a lack of independence, poor self-esteem, and passive aggression, all of which he explains by the use of examples.

He describes these students as having not developed the emotional skills necessary to do independent work, and states that "while standard educational practices are not in themselves the root causes for work inhibition, these practices typically exacerbate the problem" (p. 42).

　Another section of the text you will read concentrates on how teachers can identify students in this category and help them by building nurturing relationships; encouraging persistence; offering positive, effective feedback; and empowering them. The author ends by discussing specific practices teachers should avoid in their interactions with work-inhibited students.

⑤ **PURPOSE-SETTING QUESTIONS:** As you read this article, ask yourself:

⑥ ■ As a teacher, what should I know about the problem of students who are work inhibited?

　■ How can I identify, assess, and assist the work-inhibited students in my classroom?

　The article is well-structured; the title, headings, and topic sentences, as well as the interesting examples, should aid your comprehension. When you finish, please react to the main ideas in your learning log. We'll discuss the reading and your thoughts on work inhibition in our next class meeting.

Now you try. Choose a text that you think is demanding for the grade level you're targeting and compose a preview that will activate or build on prior knowledge, summarize the selection, set a purpose, and provide guidance for your students.

Introduction of Short Readings as Preparation for Main Readings

When students read two articles on the same topic, their comprehension of the second improves (Crafton, 1983). This should not surprise you, given what you know about the importance of activated prior knowledge. So, one way to prepare your students for a chapter in their textbook or another text is to provide related readings. For example, a teacher introducing the novel *Maniac Magee*, by Jerry Spinelli (1990), with a title character who is a homeless teenager, might bring in a recent article from a local newspaper quoting statistics on homeless teens in the area. Or she could have students peruse pic-

ture books on the topic, such as *We Are All in the Dumps with Jack and Guy* (Sendak, 1993), *Fly Away Home* (Bunting, 1991), or *A Day, A Dog* (Vincent, 2000), and then ask the students to discuss the topic of homelessness.

　The strategy works equally well before a textbook treatment of a major topic. Before students read a chapter from their history text on the Civil War, you can offer them the picture book *Pink and Say* (Polacco, 1994), and read aloud Lincoln's Gettysburg Address or excerpts from soldier's diaries, official papers dealing with buying and selling slaves, or quotes from Southern and Northern newspapers of the times. You can start a file now that matches these short readings with longer ones.

CULTURAL LITERACY AND THE CORE KNOWLEDGE MOVEMENT

ACTIVATING PRIOR KNOWLEDGE   4.2

One of my former students began her Honors thesis in this way:

> As a freshman, . . . I came to the conclusion that I was not prepared for college. [An] instructor was making references to people and works I had never even heard of. He didn't even pause to try to explain those references. He acted as if everyone should just know them. How could that be? I had graduated at the top of my class in high school. It didn't seem like I should be running into ideas that I had never even heard of before so early on in my studies, especially if the professor was not even explaining them. That implied some kind of deficiency on my part. I felt like I had been absent for an important part of high school and I didn't even know it. (DeMartino, 1998, p. 1)

Try to think of times when you have felt lost or clueless because someone was talking about something you didn't have the background to understand. It can relate to a school subject or to your out-of-school acquaintances or experiences. What did you do, if anything, to get to the point where you could learn from, and maybe even contribute to, the conversation? Write in your learning log about your experience and what it shows you about the importance of foundational knowledge to your own education.

For decades, researchers and educators have been concerned about students leaving secondary school without the knowledge to be successful workers, citizens, and college students. For example, the First National Assessment of History and Literature formed the basis for a widely read book called *What Do Our 17-Year-Olds Know?* (Ravitch & Finn, 1987). Based on data obtained from a large sample of students who completed multiple-choice questions, the answer to the title question seemed disheartening. You can look at the list of the specific items tested in the appendix of Ravitch and Finn's book to discover that almost half of the students tested did not know that the spread of slavery was debated before the Civil War, and only 32 percent could place the Civil War between 1850 and 1900. Fewer than a quarter, when given several 20-year time spans, could pick the one during which Abraham Lincoln was president; just 21 percent could pick out the definition of the historical period

known as the Reconstruction. Surely, we can assume that most of those 17-year-olds had been taught this information in history classes. The results on the literature section were no more encouraging. Thirty-five percent couldn't identify Aesop as a writer of fables; 43 percent didn't know that Shakespeare wrote sonnets. Subsequent studies (e.g., Stoltman, 1997; Davis & Klages, 1997; Neal, Martin, & Moses, 2000) have been consistent with this classic one.

You might be thinking, "So what?" What's the big deal about these isolated bits of information, and who's to decide which facts are important? Those are reasonable questions, given that we are now in what some call the Information Age, vulnerable to becoming overwhelmed with *new* facts, never mind the old. More than a thousand books are published daily, information doubles every few years, and one weekday edition of *The New York Times* provides more information than the average seventeenth-century person had to deal with in a lifetime (Wurman, 1989). Yet, there has been a recent rash of books with titles like *Don't Know Much about History . . .* (Davis, 1999), *The Science Class You Wish You Had* (Brady & Brady, 1998), and *Lies My Teacher Told Me* (Loewen, 1995), seeming to indicate that the buying public not only recognizes that they missed some basic knowledge in their school learning, but also that they'd like to "correct" the problem.

Probably the name most associated with the insistence that our students have specific factual content knowledge is that of E. D. Hirsch, Jr. In *Cultural Literacy: What Every American Needs to Know* (1987), he bemoans the decline of literate knowledge and explains that shared information is necessary for us to survive as a society. He cites the lack of wide-ranging background information among young men and women as an important cause of the illiteracy that large corporations are finding in their middle-level executives. "In former days, when business people wrote and spoke to one another, they could be confident that they and their colleagues had studied many similar things in school" (p. 8). Hirsch gives several examples of allusions that cannot be understood without specific background knowledge, and devotes a whole chapter to the topic of schema.

Perhaps the part of Hirsch's book that was the most widely read and discussed, and that drew the most criticism from those who considered the author conservative, simplistic, biased, elitist, or worse, was the appendix (co-authored with Joseph Kett and James Trefil), an alphabetized list of "What Literate Americans Know." Do you wonder how you'd fare with such a list? (I do!) Out of the several thousand names, dates, proverbs, events, places, etc., here are the first several under the letter *m*: Douglas MacArthur, Macbeth, Machiavelli, Machiavellian tactics, Mach number, macho, macrocosm/ microcosm, macroeconomics, Madagascar, mad as a hatter. Scholarly criticism from many quarters attacking Hirsch's premises and allegedly biased choices regarding what should be considered "necessary knowledge" did not seem to lessen sales.

Gardner (1991) makes the following points about the implementation of core knowledge in the curriculum:

> First informally and now with increasing formality and decisiveness, Hirsch has produced lists of cultural references and suggested that they be afforded a central place in the curriculum. Willfully or not, he has provided an almost irresistible plan for many teachers: to teach these lists of terms directly, as they now teach vocabulary lists or mathematical facts, and then to test for them as part of the standard curriculum. Rather than being acquired in the process of a rich diet of reading or through immersion in a culture where such references arise meaningfully in the course of everyday exchanges, cultural literacy becomes the subject matter of rote, ritualized, or conventionalized performances.
>
> To my knowledge, Hirsch did not initially recommend such a rigid educational approach, one that seems destined to deaden, rather than make accessible, the vitality of the culture for most students. Yet his publications and activities in recent years have all pointed toward prepackaging such literacy. Hirsch's initial analysis and recommendations seem well intentioned enough, but an educational policy maker must take responsibility for the uses to which his ideas are put. In this case, it seems to me, the packaged cure is really part of the disease that runs rampant in a sound-bite culture. (pp. 188–191)

From *The Unschooled Mind* by Howard Gardner. Copyright © 1991 by Howard Gardner. Reprinted by permission of Basic Books, a member of Perseus Books, L.L.C.

ACTION RESEARCH 4.A

Find a copy of the latest edition of *The Dictionary of Cultural Literacy.* Examine the entries for several purposes. How culturally literate are *you,* according to the criteria set forth in this book? Does reading these entries interest you? Do you think you'd remember the information over a period of time? Do you consider some of the facts dated or unimportant? Can you think of basic knowledge in the subject area you will be teaching that is noticeably *absent* in this compendium? Now, explore the Internet to see how others are talking about the topic. You might begin with www.coreknowledge.org.

BookTalk 4.4

You're probably familiar with author Pat Conroy through his popular novels *Prince of Tides* (1986), *Lords of Discipline* (1980), and *Beach Music* (1996). Did you know that he began his career as a teacher? In *The Water Is Wide* (1987), which was later made into the movie *Conrack,* he tells of his adventures teaching on an island off the Atlantic coast. He was appalled at his students' lack of basic knowledge. They didn't know the name of the first president of the United States, nor the current one. As a matter of fact, they didn't know the name of our country. They didn't know what the Atlantic Ocean was, despite Yamacraw Island being surrounded by it. E. D. Hirsch, Jr. would be appalled! Much of Conroy's year was spent giving his students the experiences and factual knowledge they needed in order to understand their books and the curriculum he was to teach them. He discovered in this process that the teaching and learning were reciprocal; the students had rich knowledge (though not of the type on Hirsch's lists) that became his as he got to know them and became a part of their community. Sound like a happy ending? One problem—there were (Caucasian) administrators and politicians who disapproved of (Caucasian) Conroy's unconventional teaching methods and his relationship with these black students. Read *The Water Is Wide* to discover who the winners and losers are. Prepare to be stimulated to think about the kind of teacher you want to be.

Figure 4.10 lists examples of reference books that you might consider for your classroom library. They are filled with facts and figures that would thrill the most ardent supporters of the core knowledge movement, yet they are attractive and interesting. My students love perusing them and savoring their illustrations, anecdotes, quotes, and rich statistics, and I think yours would, too. A library containing these works can provide both breadth and depth of knowledge.

PROCEDURAL KNOWLEDGE AND DISCIPLINE-BASED INQUIRY

According to schema theory, the facts, terms, concepts, events, and theories we've just discussed belong in the category of *declarative knowledge* (Ruddell & Unrau, 1994). Another type of back-

FIGURE 4.10 *Reference books for the content areas.*

Adams, S. (1999). *1,000 Makers of the Millennium: Men and Women Who Have Shaped the Last 1,000 Years.* New York: DK Publishing.

American History Desk Reference. (1997). New York: Scholastic.

Barnes-Svarney, P. C. (1995). *The New York Public Library Science Desk Reference.* New York: Macmillan.

Children's History of the 20th Century. (1999). New York: DK Publishing.

Chisholm, J. (1998). *The Usborne Book of World History Dates.* London: Usborne Publishing.

Colman, P. (2000). *Girls: A History of Growing Up Female in America.* New York: Scholastic Reference.

Davis, K. C. (1992). *Don't Know Much About Geography: Everything You Need to Know About the World but Never Learned.* New York: Morrow.

English, J. A., & Jones, T. D. (1998). *Scholastic Encyclopedia of the United States at War.* New York: Scholastic.

Ferris, T. (1991). *The World Treasury of Physics, Astronomy, and Mathematics.* Boston: Little, Brown.

Fritz, J., Paterson, K., McKissack, P., McKissack, F., Mahy, M., & Highwater, J. (1992). *The World in 1492.* New York: Henry Holt.

Grun, B. (1991). *The Timetables of History,* (3rd ed.). New York: Simon & Schuster.

Keenan, S. (1996). *Scholastic Encyclopedia of Women in the United States.* New York: Scholastic.

Owen, J. (1996). *Usborne Mysteries and Marvels of Insect Life.* New York: Scholastic.

Parker, S., Morgan, S., & Steele, P. (1998). *Ultimate Atlas of Almost Everything.* New York: HarperCollins.

Scholastic. (1993). *Scholastic Voyages of Discovery: Paint and Painting.* New York: Scholastic.

Scholastic. (1995). *Scholastic Voyages of Discovery: Architecture and Construction.* New York: Scholastic.

Stolley, R. B. (Ed.). (2000). *LIFE: Our Century in Pictures for Young People.* Boston: Little, Brown.

Suplee, C. (1999). *Physics in the Twentieth Century.* New York: Harry N. Abrams.

Trefil, J. (1992). *1001 Things Everyone Should Know About Science.* New York: Doubleday.

The Usborne Illustrated Encyclopedia: Science and Technology. (1999). New York: Scholastic.

ground knowledge relates to knowing *how* the disciplines work and how people within a discipline think and work; *procedural* knowledge has to do with strategies for using and applying knowledge (Ruddell & Unrau, 1994). As *Math Curse* (see Book-Talk 1.1) shows in a humorous way, people in certain fields really do observe events, interpret data, and talk to others in ways consistent with their work. You'll find that this is true in education. I can't read the newspaper anymore without scissors in hand because I know I'll find something of interest to bring into my content area reading classes. Professional conferences in every field can be stimulating and invigorating because people belonging to the same *discourse communities* enjoy listening to and sharing with others in their fields. I encourage you to join local, state, or national educational organizations in your discipline and to take advantage of the opportunities they provide for enriching your knowledge, as well as for meeting others who love the field you love. The names and addresses of several professional organizations are listed in Figure 4.11.

Stahl, Hynd, Glynn, and Carr (1996) discuss the rich disciplinary knowledge that students need in addition to topic knowledge. "Although we are interested in the ways readers learn what historians and scientists have discovered, our interest is also focused on ways readers learn to think like historians and scientists. Developing such knowledge involves texts, but it involves using those texts differently than when students read and study primarily for the goal of passing a test" (pp. 139–140). Disciplinary knowledge includes knowing how inquiry takes place within a field. Students can learn that scientists use a method actually called the *scientific method*, and that they evaluate hypotheses through research; they measure claims by collecting data and examining evidence. Historians also weigh evidence and draw conclusions. Mathematicians follow steps to test maxims, algorithms, and theories. Professionals often collaborate and sometimes compete with colleagues to arrive at proofs.

Students also can be taught to understand that throughout history, new understandings have replaced prevailing theories that no longer work. The principles of assimilation and accommodation, explained earlier in this chapter, can apply to entire fields, as well as to individuals. Constructing knowledge is not a totally *linear* process, always moving

BookTalk 4.5

Which is more important for students: *breadth* or *depth* of knowledge? Though often debated, these two important types of knowledge really don't have to be viewed as being in opposition at all. You'll strive for both, in your own learning as well as your students'. Two excellent books published in 2000 that exemplify how breadth and depth can be complementary are *LIFE: Our Century in Pictures for Young People,* edited by R. B. Stolley, and *The Century that Was,* edited by James Cross Giblin. The former contains hundreds of stunning, thought-provoking photographs accompanied by a paragraph of enticing text. The latter, subtitled *Reflections on the Last One Hundred Years,* consists of thought-provoking essays written by acclaimed authors of literature for young adults. Nonfiction writer Jim Murphy writes about "One Hundred Years of Wheels and Wings," Penny Colman discusses the strides women made in the 20th century, Walter Dean Myers explains the changing concept of civil rights in America, Eve Bunting comments on immigrants, and Lois Lowry writes about fashion. You can read Milton Meltzer's thoughts on politics, Katherine Paterson's look at 20th-century religious issues, Lawrence Pringle on heroes, and more. Together, these books can help your students celebrate depth and breadth of knowledge.

BookTalk 4.6

You want your students to get the big picture, to be able to put pieces together and think about the whole. That can be difficult for a subject as large and complex as the Holocaust, but a good place to start might be the *Holocaust Biographies Series* published by The Rosen Publishing Group. After initiating and listening to students' questions, such as "How could this tragedy have happened? Could it have been prevented? What was it like for victims? How about for people who helped the Jews and resisted the Nazis? What was life like for survivors?", you might explore the set using a jigsaw approach, with small groups choosing individual biographies to explore, talk about, and understand. Titles include *Adolf Eichman: Engineer of Death; Joseph Goebbels: Nazi Propaganda Minister; Hermann Goring: Hitler's Second- in-Command; Adolf Hitler: A Study in Hate; Oskar Schindler: Righteous Gentile; Hans and Sophie Scholl: German Resisters of the White Rose; Raoul Wallenberg: Swedish Diplomat and Humanitarian;* and *Elie Wiesel: Spokesman for Remembrance.* After the groups present summaries and reactions, the class can decide how to put their new knowledge together. Don't be surprised to find students taking out other volumes long after the original project is finished. They'll want to learn more and more.

FIGURE 4.11   *Professional organizations.*

National Council of Teachers of Mathematics
1906 Association Drive
Reston, VA 20191
www.nctm.org

National Art Education Association
1916 Association Drive
Reston, VA 20191
www.naea-reston.org

National Council of Teachers of English
1111 Kenyon Road
Urbana, IL 61801-1096
www.ncte.org

Council for Exceptional Children
1110 North Globe Road, Suite 300
Arlington, VA 22201-5704
www.cec.sped.org

American Council on the Teaching of
    Foreign Languages
6 Executive Plaza
Yonkers, NY 10701
www.actfl.org

National Council for the Social Studies
3501 Newark Street NW
Washington, DC 20016-3167
www.socialstudies.org

National Science Teachers Association
1840 Wilson Blvd.
Arlington, VA 22201
www.nsta.org

forward; rather, it's a *recursive* one, as new knowledge gets absorbed and debated based on what is already known. Your students can see disciplinary thinking as evolving, yet sometimes involving leaps, and understand that there are various approaches to knowledge. When a new discovery or theory so shakes the foundations of a discipline's knowledge that a totally new way of thinking results, a *paradigm shift* occurs (Kuhn, 1996).

Acquiring Discipline-Based and Procedural Knowledge

It should come as no surprise that I recommend your encouragement and modeling of voluminous, wide, and yes, passionate reading as the best way to help students increase their background knowledge, new content knowledge, and procedural knowledge, to help students learn to think like a practitioner in your subject area. Madeleine L'Engle, author of *A Wrinkle in Time* and several other works of fantasy, warns, "A child denied imaginative literature is likely to have more difficulty understanding cellular biology or post-Newtonian physics than the child whose imagination has been stretched by fantasy and science fiction" (Bloom, 1998, p. 72). Annie Dillard, author of the Pulitzer Prize–winning *Pilgrim at Tinker Creek* (2000), a book full of fascinating scientific knowledge, illustrates L'Engle's point. As a child, she read many genres. "Books swept me away, one after the other, this way and that; I made endless vows according to their lights, for I believed them" (Dillard, 1987, p. 85). A favorite that she reread every year was Ann Haven Morgan's *The Field Book of Ponds and Streams* (1930), which led to her desire for a microscope, which led to her beginning to do work in science and gain knowledge experientially, as well as from continued reading. She had joined the discourse community. Similarly, Linus Pauling, the scientist quoted earlier in this chapter, explains:

> My eldest son says that I'm successful because I have an extraordinary memory, I'm curious so that I often begin reading about a new field in science on my own, and I make the effort to connect the great body of knowledge I have of science as a whole with what I read about in the new field. The result is that I often make an important discovery in the new field. (Rosenthal, 1995, p. 152)

A. E. Cunningham and K. E. Stanovitch (1998) showed that "the very act of reading can help children compensate for modest levels of cognitive ability by building their vocabulary and general knowledge . . . ability is not the only variable that

BookTalk   4.7

Sometimes new knowledge replacing old can be a painful ordeal. What would you do if you made a discovery that people, including powerful authorities, didn't want to believe? Galileo found himself in just such a predicament. Read Peter Sis's 1997 Caldecott Honor winner *Starry Messenger*, which the author calls "a book depicting the life of a famous scientist, mathematician, astronomer, philosopher, physicist" (unpaged). The format is unique, and the illustrations are awesome.

counts in the development of intellectual functioning. Those who read a lot will enhance their verbal intelligence; that is, reading will make them smarter" (p. 14).

Imagine that! You can promise your students that reading will make them smarter. Who wouldn't be happy to know that increasing intelligence is an achievable goal? And you can easily see how this can occur. If your students read several of the World War II books that were booktalked in Chapter 2, they learned many, many facts about the war. For example, Lowry's *Number the Stars* (1990), within the context of the story of two families, tells of King Christian of Denmark ordering that his whole fleet be destroyed rather than allow it to be used by the Nazi conquerors. The stories in the books help students understand which countries were fighting which other countries, who some of the political and military leaders were, causes of conflict, significant dates, how ordinary citizens handled problems and relationships, and how events were interconnected. The knowledge gained can help them in future reading of textbook material, historical documents, and reports of current events that are impacted by the past. In addition, those students may search for other books about World War II, about refugees, about courageous escapes; or they may look for other books by the authors, including Lois Lowry's subsequent Newbery winner, *The Giver*. They'll be acquiring content knowledge plus procedural knowledge in terms of research.

Figure 4.12 lists books appropriate for a classroom library that can provide much procedural knowledge, an understanding of discipline-based inquiry, and background knowledge in various subjects. They can be used as reference tools, or students can peruse them at their leisure. Many are written in a style meant to be enjoyable, intriguing, or humorous.

FIGURE 4.12 *Books providing procedural knowledge.*

Baker, R., & Zinsser, W. (1995). *Inventing the Truth: The Art and Craft of Memoir.* Boston: Houghton Mifflin.

Beil, K. M. (1999). *Fire in Their Eyes: Wildfires and the People Who Fight Them.* New York: Harcourt Brace.

Byman, J. (2001). *Carl Sagan: In Contact with the Cosmos.* Greensboro, NC: Morgan Reynolds.

Caro, R. A., & Zinsser, W. (1986). *Extraordinary Lives: The Art and Craft of American Biography.* New York: American Heritage.

Christolow, E. (1999). *What Do Illustrators Do?* New York: Clarion Books.

Crick, F. (1988). *What Mad Pursuit: A Personal View of Scientific Discovery.* New York: Basic Books.

Fridell, R. (2000). *Solving Crimes: Pioneers of Forensic Science.* New York: Franklin Watts.

Goodall, J. (1999). *Reason for Hope: A Spiritual Journey.* New York: Warner Books.

Goodman, S. E. (1999). *Ultimate Field Trip 3: Wading into Marine Biology.* New York: Atheneum.

Heiligman, D. (1994). *Barbara McClintock: Alone in Her Field.* New York: Scientific American Books for Young Readers.

Jackson, D. M. (1996). *The Bone Detectives: How Forensic Anthropologists Solve Crimes and Uncover Mysteries of the Dead.* Boston: Little, Brown.

Maze, S., & Grace, C. O. (1997a). *I Want to Be an Astronaut.* New York: Harcourt Brace.

Maze, S., & Grace, C. O. (1997b). *I Want to Be a Dancer.* New York: Harcourt Brace.

Maze, S., & Grace, C. O. (1997c). *I Want to Be an Engineer.* New York: Harcourt Brace.

Maze, S., & Grace, C. O. (1997d). *I Want to Be a Veterinarian.* New York: Harcourt Brace.

Pringle, L. (1997). *Elephant Woman: Cynthia Moss Explores the World of Elephants.* New York: Atheneum.

Simon, S. (2000). *From Paper Airplanes to Outer Space.* Katonah, NY: Richard Owen Publishers.

Sola, M. (1997). *Angela Weaves a Dream: The Story of a Young Maya Artist.* New York: Hyperion.

Swinburne, S. R. (1998). *In Good Hands: Behind the Scenes at a Center for Orphaned and Injured Birds.* San Francisco: Sierra Club Books for Children.

Tanaka, S. (1998). *Graveyards of the Dinosaurs: What It's Like to Discover Prehistoric Creatures.* New York: Hyperion/Madison Press.

Thimmesh, C. (2000). *Girls Think of Everything: Stories of Ingenious Inventions by Women.* Boston: Houghton Mifflin.

Watson, J. D. (1980). *The Double Helix: A Personal Account of the Discovery of the Structure of DNA.* (G. S. Stent, Ed.). New York: W. W. Norton.

Of course, just having books and other sources available isn't going to magically increase your students' procedural knowledge. Teacher modeling is a great instructional strategy for the purpose of developing discipline-based inquiry skills. You might demonstrate how *you* go about learning science, history, or an artistic skill, talking aloud as you go through the process, and connecting your process to those of others in the field, especially those your students have already read about. Reading guides that use questions specifically about procedural knowledge also are helpful with particular texts, perhaps chosen from the list in Figure 4.12.

PRIOR KNOWLEDGE AND ENGLISH LANGUAGE LEARNERS

You are aware that the students in the middle and secondary grades come to your subject area courses with varying types and levels of prior knowledge, and that this affects their ability to read and understand the new material that you require. The variability is even greater when you have students who are just learning English or who have a limited proficiency in the English language.

Imagine moving to a country you know little about—Cambodia, perhaps, or Brazil, Russia, Uganda. Now, place yourself in a secondary math, history, literature, or science class there. A large part of your difficulty meeting the expectations of the class has to do with your limited skills in the new language, of course. But you also should notice that you just don't have the background knowledge that the native speakers possess. No matter how knowledgeable you are in your native culture, there are gaps in your knowledge about the new culture that interfere with learning. The support of your teachers and your peers is necessary to help you meet their educational goals. The same is true, of course, for the English language learners (ELL) in your classroom.

When you have students who are learning English, do all you can to make them comfortable and able to learn. By your words, nonverbal expressions, and attitude, express your confidence that they can learn and that you will be patient and helpful as they do so. Get to know them and assess what their educational background is like in their native language. Some students are very literate in their own language, and others didn't have the opportunity to become so. Some Limited English Proficient (LEP) learners have grown up in this country, perhaps speaking Spanish at home, while others are coming from far away where their cultures and lifestyles were extremely different. Your role differs depending on factors like these.

No one expects you to be an expert on second language acquisition issues; rather, you should collaborate with an English as a Second Language (ESL) teacher or use resources your district provides to teach and support the English learners. There are some things content area teachers can do to help build the background knowledge base that these students require in order to be successful. For example, you learned in Chapter 3 about the value of your students using many types of texts, representing a variety of genres and levels of difficulty. Mundy and Hadaway (1999) documented the benefits of using informational picture books with secondary ESL students to help them understand content concepts, as well as to learn new vocabulary.

Thinking of a particular student and course may be helpful here. Imagine that a student named Hao, whose family recently immigrated from China, has joined your eighth grade American history class. The following strategies may help Hao succeed:

1. Allow Hao to self-select books about the United States government and American history from your classroom library. Picture books, such as Jean Fritz' *Shhh! We're Writing the Constitution!* (1987), *House Mouse, Senate Mouse* (Barnes & Barnes, 1996), and Alice Provenson's *The Buck Stops Here: The Presidents of the United States* (1997), provide basic information about how our government came to be and currently runs. (By the way, your library should also contain enticing books about other cultures and types of governing. They will benefit all of your students.)

2. Use audiovisual resources, such as films, to provide context and background knowledge before reading assignments. Literary field trips via the Internet are very helpful to second language learners. Remember, they might need more time to explore or opportunities to revisit sites in order to comprehend what is offered; that's the beauty of interactive programs that allow for unlimited, untimed, and varied ways of navigating the material. Hao can explore the White House, Congress, and the U. S. Supreme Court at the computer along with his classmates and on his own.

3. Provide as much direct experience and as many authentic contexts as you can. Conducting experiments; going on field trips; showing objects; and using maps, charts, pictures, and graphs make the learning concrete and meaningful.

4. Simulation games as pre-reading activities can benefit English learners (Peregoy & Boyle, 1997). The games build background knowledge, provide opportunities for enjoyable social interactions, and help motivate students to read. Having students simulate oral arguments in front of the U. S. Supreme Court before reading about *Brown v. The Board of Education* helps the material come alive.

5. Provide peer support whenever possible. When Hao is involved with other students in a cooperative learning group that is researching the Trail of Tears, which he may have no previous knowledge about, he can listen and watch the others, ask questions, and learn in a safe, comfortable environment. He'll have knowledge and stories that can enrich the other students, also—encourage him to share.

6. Have students write in learning logs, reflecting on content and their own learning processes. You can learn from Hao's entries not only about his writing progress and needs, but about how he's thinking of the material he's encountering, and you'll be able to determine what further scaffolding you should supply. You can also respond in writing to his entries, explaining concepts he shows confusion about, suggesting new resources or strategies, and providing words of encouragement. This shows your interest in and respect for the knowledge he brings with him.

You may be thinking that these suggestions seem like they'd be good for all students, not just for ESL students, and you're correct. Many of the things you do for second language learners are simple extensions or adaptations of what excellent teachers do for all. Because you'll get to know all of your students and their strengths and needs, you'll be used to modifying instruction, learning about how to address new challenges, and collaborating with experts in your district to provide whatever students need. You'll find that the English language learners in your class can make many valuable contributions, and you'll benefit from providing background knowledge and literacy strategies to them. Other issues related to learners with limited English proficiency are addressed in subsequent chapters.

You may have noticed that I've used different terms and acronyms to denote people learning English: ELL, LEP, ESL. All are used in the literature, sometimes differing slightly in meaning. The most current and widely used at present is ELL.

ACTION RESEARCH   4.B

Picture using the novel *The Giver* with a class that has a very diverse student population, one in which a good percentage of the students remember life in another country, or at least have heard their parents talk about the cultures they were a part of before coming to the United States. How might the background knowledge of these students affect their understanding of and response to the novel? Write for a few moments in your learning log, noting specific aspects of the book that might elicit unique responses from your students. (I realize that some of the readers of this text also fit this category of "diverse learners" and might have background knowledge and experiences that make this thinking exercise an easy task, and can share valuable contributions with others.)

Enriquez (2001) conducted research in two intermediate ESL writing courses during a summer school enrichment program. Her teenage students came from 11 different countries. Enriquez asked her students to explore the thematic question, "What does it mean to belong to a culture?" (p. 15) as they read *The Giver*. Her analysis of the data revealed that the students generally engaged in the following sequence as they generated meaning from the book:

1. They identified information about Jonas's culture that was unfamiliar to them and unique to Jonas's world.
2. They used prior knowledge to make sense of Jonas's culture.
3. They reflected on the unique characteristics of their own cultures.
4. They identified the unique characteristics of Jonas's culture.

The students used personal experience as they talked about the text, comparing and contrasting facets of Jonas's community with their own, such as the rule that each family unit can have only two children, arranged marriages, and government control of society. One student wrote, "'In my society we are watched, too, but not by the Elders but by Allah, God, the creater [sic] of heaven and hell. We Muslims . . . believe that God is watching us" (p. 18).

Enriquez found that her students began by using their own cultures to make sense of the fictional one, and then examined their own cultures, often coming to a new appreciation for them. We can learn from the insights provided by this study as we think about reader response theory and issues relating to background knowledge.

PART TWO

Metacognition

Literacy educators attend to many, many aspects of thinking. This chapter has dealt with teachers and students acquiring the knowledge of and beginning to think like members of the disciplines you are preparing to teach. A later chapter focuses on critical thinking, although we've already started on that topic, for thinking like a scientist, or a writer, or an artist, or a mathematician does of course involve thinking critically. Right now, I'd like you to concentrate on the concept of *thinking about thinking* (or *knowing about knowing*) and more specifically, thinking about your own reading and learning processes.

When you read *The Giver*, how did you achieve comprehension? How did you get from those black marks on white pages to the understanding of a story? How did you figure out the special meaning *release* had in the text? How did you deal with the ambiguity of the ending, if indeed you found it ambiguous?

How are you making sense of this chapter right now? Did you take the time to reflect on the questions asked in the previous paragraph? Are you aware of your own background knowledge (about reading, about your content area, and about education) at work as you comprehend new material? Are you questioning or talking back to me as the author, or to any of the researchers I've quoted?

All of these questions involve the concept of *metacognition*, the process of being aware of one's thinking and reading (Flavell, 1976). It's knowing about knowing. And it involves monitoring the process of reading, controlling the cognitive process, and self-control (Paris & Winograd, 1989). If you ask children, adolescents, or adults *how* they read, they'll likely be able to answer you, and some answers may surprise you. Rosenthal did just that and then compiled the book *Speaking of Reading* (1995). Here are sample quotes she obtained during interviews that are rich with metacognitive reflection:

> I'll read about a hundred pages of a book to get the big picture, then go back to read it a second time for details, for examples. . . . I get very involved reading technical material. . . . An hour session gives me a lot to digest, and it can really inspire me. After that hour, I play with the thoughts I've gained and synthesize them into other ideas I may be working on. (Gerald Eisman, p. 164)

> Sometimes I still have difficulty comprehending what I'm reading . . . so I'll have to read it over and over. It may be the linguistic style that creates the problem, or that too many concepts are introduced in too short a span of time. If I don't quite understand the first concept, then the next one that's linked to it will be fuzzier still, until pretty soon I won't be able to digest anything further down the page. (Rich Clarke, p. 33)

As a content area teacher, you can help your students become better comprehenders, and more efficient and productive readers of content area materials, if you teach them to be aware of how they read, and especially to think consciously about what they do when reading breaks down. We've all had the experience of suddenly stopping while reading and saying to ourselves, "Wait a minute! I just read two pages and nothing has sunk in!" Good readers monitor their reading automatically, change their pace when needed, and apply corrective strategies whenever necessary. Struggling readers may not recognize when they don't understand the material, or may not know what to do if they do come to that stopping point (Smith, 1991). They are likely, for instance, just to keep reading (Garner & Reis, 1981). Good readers at times decide to do this, but they also may realize that they're tired and should take a five-minute walk, or that there is some background they're missing that they should look up before reading on, or that they're becoming cognitively blocked by the emotion of failure anxiety and must deal with that first.

You can help your students realize that they have an executive control center that they can activate to help monitor their progress toward goals and make wise decisions, including regulating, monitoring, and taking corrective action when necessary while reading, as well as knowing themselves as learners. Examples of corrective strategies include:

- Put a confusing passage into your own words.
- Use visual aids.
- Reread.
- Read ahead for clarification.
- Slow down.
- Check a reference (e.g., a dictionary).

A statement that you may think goes without saying, but that struggling readers often must be told and reminded of, is that reading should always make sense. Winograd, Wixson, and Lipson (1989) devised steps to teach metacognitive as well as other literacy strategies, consisting of the following:

1. Describe the strategy.
2. Explain why it is important.
3. Demonstrate it.
4. Explain when and where to use it.
5. Explain how and why to evaluate it.
6. Provide guided practice and application.

INSTRUCTIONAL STRATEGIES FOR ENHANCING METACOGNITION

Students must understand what metacognition is and how it can help them comprehend text, and should be taught how to monitor their reading (Miner & Reder, 1996). Most of the reading strategies modeled in this text can be considered metacognitive strategies. When students independently apply the K-W-L-S strategy explained at the beginning of this chapter, for example, they are using the structure to help themselves think about their reading process and comprehension. This section discusses several other metacognitive strategies you can teach and encourage your students to use.

Think-Alouds

The think-aloud method is aptly named because it calls for a reader to express his thoughts aloud as he proceeds. It can involve recalling background knowledge, identifying key points and terms, and putting things into one's own words (Davey, 1983). Teachers can model a think-aloud for students, being sure to include thinking about the actual process of reading and monitoring comprehension, and then can encourage students to use the strategy. Imagine a biology student, Gabi, who has been assigned to read an article called "The Incredible

Sponge" (Genthe, 1998) for homework. Listen in on her think-aloud as she applies the K-W-L-S strategy to the assignment:

> Ok, I've got to "activate my schema," as Ms. Cruz tells us. So, what do I already know about sponges?
> (K) Not much! The first thing I think of is the sponges we use for cleaning, but I know they're artificial. Ok, sponges are living, and they live in the sea. They're probably different colors. They must feed off some little things floating around them. I don't think they move around; they're stationary. (Pause) Well, I guess it's on to Step Two. What do I *want* or *need* to know about sponges? I do want to find out what they eat. And I wonder how they reproduce? Are there really
> (W) female and male sponges, mothers and babies? My mind is kind of chuckling at that. And how do we get them out of the sea? Do we take them dead or alive? And what are they used for?

As Gabi reads the article, she fills out the third category, either in writing or in her head, noting what she's learning and maybe where she's confused, or by talking aloud again. A few of her thoughts may go like this:

> I never knew sponges had poison in them! But I guess they have to defend themselves from other animals.
> (L) And they can be used for medical purposes for humans, how about that. They have such complicated names, *Dysidea frondosa* and *Plakortis simplex*. I hope we don't have to remember those. No, Ms. Cruz told us just to read for the main ideas. Ok, I like this image of the sponge acting as a condominium for all sorts of tiny sea creatures needing a safe haven. I'll remember that. Oh, neat, a sponge acts as a filter, pumping water through and feasting on bacteria and plankton. I guess I was wrong about them never moving. At least the larvae creep about, it says, searching for a place to grow into adults. And now it says sponges can crawl over the seabed, "contrary to long-held popular and scientific opinion. . . . " (Pause) Ok, I'm done. I didn't understand every little scientific detail, but I sure know a lot more about sponges than when I started. Now, for the "Still Need to Know" stage of our strategy, where do I go from here? Well,
> (S) I'd like to learn more about those pharmaceutical properties the article mentioned. I could ask Angel's mother; she's a nurse.

Notice that Gabi reflected on both content and her own reading process. She thinks about sponges, stating new knowledge as she gains it, and she shows metacognitive awareness as she consciously applies the K-W-L-S strategy her teacher has taught her. She monitors her reading and learning. Note also the affective aspects involved—her interest, her chuckling at images.

For further study of the think-aloud process, I recommend Jeffrey D. Wilhelm's *Improving Comprehension with Think-aloud Strategies* (2001). To try a think-aloud for yourself, monitor your thoughts as you read a passage from a text of your choice. Either jot down your thoughts as you proceed or talk into a tape recorder and transcribe your words later. Then, reflect on what you discovered or learned from eavesdropping on your own thoughts. Notice that some of your thinking is about content, while some is monitoring the process of your reading and comprehension; the latter represents metacognition.

Embedded Questions

Readers who have poor comprehension use metacognitive strategies much less frequently than do skilled comprehenders (Duffy, Roehler, & Hermann, 1988). But they can improve their comprehension when taught metacognitive strategies (Nolan, 1991). A teacher gives metacognitive instruction when he embeds questions that simulate the metacognitive strategies that skilled readers use and that activate conscious thinking about reading processes while reading (Walczyk & Hall, 1989). Weir (1998) used *embedded questions* and much classroom discussion to help her middle school remedial readers increasingly use metacognitive strategies independently. Initially, she cut up short stories and required her students to stop at various points in their reading to answer such questions as, "What do you think will happen next?" "What are you wondering about at this point?" and "What was the most confusing part of this story? How did you handle it?" Later, she had the students analyze their work and identify the strategies they used. Finally, students had to read a short story independently and annotate it themselves with predictions and questions. By examining their annotations, Weir could understand the students' metacognitive processes. Test results showed gains in many of her students' reading competency levels, and in a videotaped interview with her students, she received comments like the following from Annie:

> Now, when I read, I try to go into it more like what is he trying to tell us? Why is he writing this book? But before, I just read it. I didn't really care. Now I can go into it more deeper. I can ask myself questions and see if I understand the book. I can question myself and see how I understand it. (p. 466)

Figure 4.13 shows a reading guide that uses embedded questions to aid comprehension, monitoring, and reflective thinking while reading a nonfiction book.

FIGURE 4.13 *A reading guide using embedded questions.*

INTRODUCTION: You've learned through our textbook chapter and my lecture that Denmark holds the unique position of being the only country in Europe that saved the majority of its Jewish population during the Holocaust. We've hypothesized some reasons for this. For homework, you're going to read the chapter "Resistance Begins" in Ellen Levine's *Darkness Over Denmark: The Danish Resistance and the Rescue of the Jews* (2000). You'll find out some fascinating details and meet some heroic rescuers. This reading guide will help you comprehend the text and think about the topic and your reading process as you read.

DIRECTIONS: Stop at the end of each section (indicated in parentheses) and answer the questions before reading on.

AFTER SECTION ONE: Those conquered Danes who favored resistance felt that the policy of *negotiation* with the Nazis was the equivalent of *collaboration*. Do you see their point? Do you agree? Can you see how the gradual increase of concessions they had to make was making the Danish government "Danish in name only" (p. 30)? What questions do you have at this point? If you're confused, reread this section before proceeding.

AFTER SECTION TWO: Why did medical student Jorgen Kielor join the student protest on November 21, 1941? What were the demonstrators protesting about? What resulted from the newspaper pictures that showed the police beating and arresting fellow Danes? How are you feeling at this point? Can you imagine yourself there? Do you think you would have joined the protestors?

AFTER SECTION THREE: Why couldn't the Danes trust official news reports in Danish papers? What other sources of information did they find? What were some examples of passive resistance the Danes used on an everyday basis? Do you think you would have printed or distributed the underground pamphlets urging resistance of your Nazi occupiers? How do you like this chapter so far? Think of a couple of questions you'd like answered in the next chapter, "Resistance Grows."

> *Getting Ready to Teach 4.5* (see page 120)

Process Checks

Moore, Moore, Cunningham, & Cunningham (1994) recommend the use of *process checks*, giving students questions they can ask to monitor their strategies while reading. Before reading, the teacher can ask, or teach the students to ask themselves, "How will you remember this?" "What are some things you might do to learn this information?" (p. 98). After reading, simple questions can be asked: "What led you to that conclusion?" "Why do you say that?" "How did you figure that out?" "How did you approach this?" Similarly, Niles (1985) suggests that teachers first ask questions about the reading process, thus making it visible. Questions can focus on making predictions, confirming or disputing the predictions, or noticing certain text structures such as headings or the organization of paragraphs. Gradually, over time and with practice, students can internalize these questions and learn to use them strategically during their independent reading. It's important that you help the students realize the purpose of these questions in terms of monitoring and enhancing their comprehension; many of them have been inundated for years with questions that seemed purposeless to them, or that they needed to answer to show that they understood content material they had read.

Questioning strategies are important and beneficial before, during, and after reading. Subsequent chapters provide further instruction on creating good questions to enhance discipline-based literacy.

Guest Speakers

An authentic way of helping students understand how people in various fields gain and create knowledge, and how they think about their own learning, is to invite practitioners in to talk with them about how they go about working and learning. Think of your friends and acquaintances who might be willing to share what they do and how they think while doing it. I've invited my neighbor to talk to my classes about his experiences and reflections as an army chaplain in Vietnam. He had to learn many new things and make crucial decisions during his tours of duty. The parents of your students are a rich resource for you to tap. There are most likely parents who have jobs related in some way to math, science, technology, government, literature, education, the arts, business, child development, history, law, social work, and psychology. Some will be delighted to share their learning processes, reading materials, stories, and advice with the next generation. For those who can't come in, you might invite them to share thoughts in a letter to the class. Your students can compose an initial letter to take home to their parents, asking them to visit or write. You can customize the invitation according to your specific needs.

During the talks, you and your students can interact with the speakers, asking specific questions that get at metacognitive issues. Later, your class can analyze the speakers' messages to see whether you can get at how they think about the processes involved in their learning in authentic contexts, how they think on the job to accomplish tasks, solve problems, and originate new ideas. Some speakers are willing to answer follow-up questions via letters, e-mail, or phone calls.

The SQ3R Study Strategy

The term *SQ3R* might sound familiar to you—it's been around since 1946 (Robinson). Perhaps it was a strategy that really worked for you and you still employ it independently in your own reading. A few students in my classes extol its usefulness when I survey them, though most say it was an isolated thing they learned in some class and then forgot when they went on to another teacher; they never recognized it as a useful strategy for other types of reading.

The SQ3R steps are: Survey, Question, Read, Recite, Review. You can help your students preview materials and set purposes for reading, then read the material, recite answers to the questions they had set, and review the material. Readers can systematically apply this strategy in any content area, thus monitoring and assisting their comprehension.

> ► *Getting Ready to Teach 4.6* (see page 120) ◄

METACOGNITION OVERLOAD?

Of course, there may be such a thing as too much metacognition. Practitioners, whether they be musicians, athletes, artists, writers, actors, or readers, often do best when they are not consciously thinking about discrete parts of their performance. Madeleine L'Engle (1972) tells of Dmitri Mitropoulos, who, when asked to explain the effect his con-

---

BookTalk 4.8

You might be wishing at this point that there was a book out there about metacognition and procedural knowledge within the field of education. Actually, there is a wealth of this kind of reflection. Because teachers are often by nature mentors and storytellers, many have shared their thinking, their learning, and their advice in published form, so we can access what good teachers know and do and think about. You might start with Donald Graves' *How to Catch a Shark: And Other Stories about Teaching and Learning* (1998). After reading these thought-provoking life stories, you'll realize you have stories of your own to share with your students and others about your own learning, and possibly teaching. Other reflections on the discipline of education include Jane Tompkins' *A Life in School: What the Teacher Learned* (1996), Vivian Paley's *The Girl with the Brown Crayon* (1997), and Ruth Vinz's *Composing a Teaching Life* (1996).

---

ducting had on orchestra and audience, replied that he wouldn't try for fear of becoming like the centipede who was asked by another bug which of his hundred legs he moved first when he walked. The centipede began analyzing the question and the process and lost the ability to walk. L'Engle concludes, "Bug or centipede, we're apt to get tangled up in legs when we begin to analyze the creative process: what is it? why do people write—or paint—or sing?" (p. 172). Santiago Ramon y Cajal, a Nobel laureate in physiology, considered the field of neuroanatomy an extension of himself, and advised his students, "'Lose yourself in the observation and become the thing you're studying.' For him, this meant becoming a cell neuron and imagining the world of neurons by living among them" (Siler, 1996, p. 5).

Scientist Barbara McClintock has a way of talking about her work process at the point when she is on the brink of a discovery, which represents a marvelous blend of losing oneself in thought, while on some level remaining highly aware:

> It never occurred to me that there was going to be any stumbling block. Not that I had the answer, but [I had] the joy of going at it. When you have that joy, you do the right experiments. You let the material tell you where to go, and it tells you at every step what the next has to be because you're integrating with an overall brand new pattern in mind. You're not following an old one; you are

convinced of a new one. And you let everything focus on that. You can't help it, because it all integrates. (Keller, 1993, p. 125)

Part of the art of teaching reading is to know when to let your students continue on automatic pilot, and when to help them analyze the steps they're taking toward comprehension. You'll find that some students do fine without obvious metacognitive activity, while other students are helped when you provide them with a structure to monitor their reading and thinking processes. Sometimes, as students talk to each other while they are immersed in a learning activity, they naturally analyze the meanings they have constructed, as well as how they got there. One teacher watched and listened as groups of a colleague's art students shared projects, and told him, "This artwork is as sweet a piece of metacognition as you can imagine. The kids are seeing how they think and seeing how other kids' minds work. They can actually be let into their heads and see what others see when they read!" (Wilhelm, 1997, p. 142).

All of the strategies presented and modeled in this text are here for you to use as appropriate for your particular context and your students' varying needs. Occasionally, you may introduce and teach a strategy, support your students' attempts to apply and practice it, and then allow them to decide whether the procedure is helpful. Peters (1996) provided questions in the form of a metacognitive reflective guide that may help students determine how certain reading guides work as comprehension tools. You might try applying these questions to one of the guides you've completed: "How well did the reading guide work?" "How did it help you understand what you were asked to read?" "What changes would you make to improve the guide?" "How might you use the guide with other types of reading assignments you have?" (p. 206).

CONCLUSION

This chapter discussed the importance of background knowledge in terms of your students' reading and learning. As their teacher, you can help the Matthew Effect along. You can devise anticipation guides that tap into the prior knowledge they have on curricular topics and help them to connect that

background to new texts. You'll also provide information and many classroom texts, materials, and resources that can increase their background knowledge of other areas that they will pursue. Your stories, your enthusiasm, your guidance ensure that your students become richer in understanding and intellectual curiosity. You'll be part of the joy of learning. You won't have to worry about "mere facts versus in-depth exploration" because you will find ways to navigate that terrain so that neither breadth nor depth suffers as your students explore the riches of your curriculum.

You've also now begun to explore metacognitive processes—both your own and your students'. Thinking about thinking, learning, reading, and monitoring the processes you use to be more efficient and successful can make a positive difference in academic growth. You can teach your students strategies that tap into metacognitive thinking and model them yourself. It's a fascinating realm to explore, as is the area of discipline-based inquiry. Learning about how practitioners think and act in authentic situations can make your subject come alive for your students. No longer will math, chemistry, English, geography, health, Spanish, and art be topics confined by school walls and academic calendars. You can be a leader in a discipline-based community of inquisitive minds. The remaining chapters build on the ideas presented thus far; more and more you'll see how the topics connect and allow you to grow as a knowledgeable, metacognitive, discipline-based teacher.

CHAPTER FOUR

Getting Ready to Teach

4.1 Find an article or chapter on a topic that you might be responsible for teaching. Create a K-W-L-S activity as a guide for your students as they tackle the text. Help them tap into what they already know about the subject, stimulate questioning, and provide the structure for them to document what they learned from the text.

4.2 Think of a curricular topic you might be responsible for teaching. List categories under which the students can note the information they already have. Try the activity with your peers or with students, and revise your categories based on what you learn from them. Begin a file labeled Group Brainstorming so that you can create these posters for other topics within your content area.

4.3 Choose a text in your curriculum area, whether it be a trade book, newspaper or magazine article, primary source document, or textbook chapter. Create an assignment using brainstorming, webbing, or the "list–group–label" strategy that will activate and extend students' prior knowledge of the topic addressed in the text. If possible, try it out with a group of students or your own classmates.

4.4 Use Alvermann and Phelps' recommendations listed previously, as well as any ideas you want from the sample anticipation guides in Figures 4.4 through 4.7, to create an anticipation guide for a text in your subject area. Ask someone in your class or someone else you know to complete the guide and give you feedback. The answers may tell you if you made any statements too passage dependent, or if any are ambiguous or unnecessary. They may also let you know which ones stimulated the kind of thinking and prior knowledge that could help readers better engage with the author's ideas.

4.5 Choose a text in your curricular area that might be difficult for struggling readers at your chosen grade level. Make a copy of it, and cut and paste to embed questions at certain points to help students make predictions, attend to relevant details, pose questions, think about significant vocabulary, recognize mood or tone, or reflect on points that are implied instead of directly stated. Remember that the purpose of your questions is to guide and help, rather than test, your students' comprehension. Weir (1998) gives these examples of typical embedded questions you might use or adapt:

- What do you think will happen next? Make a prediction.
- What are you wondering about at this point? Write a question.
- Underline the quality about character X that the author emphasized.
- Stop and visualize X. Draw a sketch of your visualization.
- What was the most confusing part of this story? How did you handle it? (p. 461)

4.6 Always try out a strategy yourself before recommending or teaching it to your students. Choose a chapter from a textbook at any level, or another piece of expository text, and apply SQ3R:

- **S**URVEY the piece. Notice headings, topic sentences, accompanying graphs or pictures; read the first and last paragraphs.
- Turn the subheadings into **QUESTIONS**.
- **READ** to find the answers to the questions you composed.
- **RECITE** your answers.
- Actively **REVIEW** the material.

Here's an example of the Questioning step. A heading in this chapter is "Metacognition Overload?" As a reader, you might ask, "What will this section tell me about what that term means? Why does it have a question mark after it?" You'll then read to obtain answers to your questions.

Now reflect on the process you went through. Was the strategy helpful? Are you able to transfer it to other situations? Do you think you'll retain the information longer than if you had simply read the text without applying SQ3R? Do you think SQ3R might be beneficial for the students in your content area classes?

Vocabulary Development and Language Study

In Norton Juster's children's classic *The Phantom Tollbooth* (1961), the king of Dictionopolis sends the young protagonist Milo on a journey, giving him a small box that he claims promises protection:

"In this box are all the words I know," he said. "Most of them you will never need, some you will use constantly, but with them you may ask all the questions which have never been answered and answer all the questions which have never been asked. All the great books of the past and all the ones yet to come are made with these words. With them there is no obstacle you cannot overcome. All you must do is use them well and in the right places." (pp. 98–99)

This chapter explores various aspects of vocabulary and language development, both for yourself and for the students in your content area classes. We'll notice how authors and textbooks use words "well and in the right places" and find ways we can do that also. Keep in mind that, although I'm separating vocabulary from comprehension in order to talk about it, the two are intimately connected. Think about these words of Cox and Zarillo: "We comprehend because we know the meanings of enough of the words in a story to make sense out of what we have read. The converse is also true: We grasp the meanings of the words because we know what the story or the article is about" (1993, p. 13).

ACTIVATING PRIOR KNOWLEDGE 5.1

Before you read on, please take a few minutes to answer the following questions in your learning log. Your answers will help you connect your own experiences with much of the information in this chapter.

1. How many words do you know? (You're not allowed to say "A lot." Take a guess and put down a number.)

Are you happy with the level of your vocabulary knowledge? How's your "vocabulary self-esteem"?

2. How did you learn the words that are now in your vocabulary? List as many ways as you can.

3. How many words do you think a typical child entering kindergarten knows? *(continued)*

4. Try to think of some words you know today that you didn't know a couple of years ago. List them. (Hint: Think of courses recently taken, new developments in your field, new hobbies, words from movies or television or the Internet.)

5. Have you ever been unable to follow or participate in a conversation because you lacked the vocabulary? (A group may have been talking about computers, sports, accounting, etc.) Do you remember any of the words that were tossed around?

6. Define the word *regicide.*

7. Define the word *lexiphile.* I'll even give you some context to help you with this one. "The goal of instruction should be to develop what one lexiphile has termed *word consciousness.* Encounters with words should be playful, so as to provoke curiosity and an interest in word study" (Anderson & Nagy, 1992, p. 46).

8. List at least five of your favorite words.

9. List at least five words little kids think are neat.

10. Write a definition of the word *culture;* imagine you're trying to explain the concept to someone who doesn't know the word. Then, free associate to come up with as many phrases using the word as you can (which may in turn help your explanation).

In their review of research on vocabulary instruction, Baumann and Kameenui (1991) begin by quoting Voltaire as saying, "Language is very difficult to put into words" (p. 604) and conclude that the reciprocal, "Words are indeed very difficult to put into language (instruction)" (p. 627), is even more challenging for educators. I concur. I've divided this chapter into four parts, all of which overlap to some extent. First, I address several aspects of words and vocabulary growth in general. In Part Two, I discuss some of the ways we as teachers can revel in language ourselves and build enthusiasm for language study along with vocabulary growth in our classrooms. In Part Three, I present some specific strategies for teaching vocabulary in relation to literacy in the content areas, and in Part Four I address language issues connected to English language learners.

PART ONE

Speaking of Words

HOW MANY WORDS DO WE KNOW? AND WHAT EXACTLY *IS* A WORD?

Chances are your answer to the first question from the Activating Prior Knowledge 5.1 exercise differs from your classmates' or friends' estimations of their accumulated word knowledge. The variance might have to do with the fact that some of us really do know many more words than others. It also might be due in part to the fact that our concept of large numbers is often far from accurate. I've had students guess they know 1,000 words and others say a billion. Both guesses are way off. Another possible reason for the varied answers has to do with how individuals interpret the question. What do I mean by a *word?* Is *bear,* for instance, one word or many, depending on whether it's used in the phrase grizzly bear, the right to bear arms, bear a child, bear malice, bear a resemblance, can't bear to look, a bear of a man, a bear market, bear with me, and so on? We call such words *multimeaning* words, and they abound. According to *The Top 10 of Everything 1999 Book* (Ash, 1999), *The Oxford English Dictionary* lists 464 meanings for the word *set* alone!

If you know a word fairly well when you encounter it in a text but can't spout its definition out of the blue, can you count it as a word you know? The former is considered *receptive vocabulary,* relating to listening and reading; the words we can actually produce in our own talk are part of our

HOW EARLY (AND HOW) DOES VOCABULARY DEVELOPMENT OCCUR?

Let's go back to Question 3 at the beginning of the chapter, where you guessed the size of a young child's vocabulary. Research shows that from ages two to six children learn around 10 words a day, so by age six they may know 14,000 words (Clark, 1993). Any parent can actually observe children experimenting with words. For example, my three-year-old Christopher was frustrated with me and knew he was not allowed to use the word *hate*. But he needed a word equally powerful and finally blurted out, "I don't like you one *smithereen!*" A couple of years later he led me to a snow fort he and a friend had made, with an entrance he announced was "virtually invisible." Surprised, I asked him what *virtually* meant, and he replied, "I don't know; I just know how to use it." Author Madeleine L'Engle, perhaps best known for her children's classic *A Wrinkle in Time* (1962), recalls how she learned vocabulary by encountering new words in her reading for fun. "I didn't stop to look up the new words; I was far too interested in what I was reading. By the time I'd come across the word in two or three books, the shades of its meaning would automatically become clear, and the word would be added to my vocabulary" (1972, p. 148).

expressive vocabulary, that related to speaking and writing. Experts define word knowledge in a number of ways. Vygotsky (1962), for example, views a word as a unit of "verbal thought" that is "already a generalization" (p. 5); Baumann and Kameenui, in their review of research on vocabulary instruction (1991), answer their own question, "So, what's a word?" with "It depends. It depends upon your purpose for asking the question and your view of thought and language" (p. 605).

Experts disagree on the size of people's vocabularies—of course, it depends on how vocabulary is defined. Crystal (1995), for example, found that adult subjects reported knowing about 25 percent more words than they actually used, reflecting a difference between receptive and expressive vocabulary. Nagy and Anderson (1984), after an analysis of a thousand items of published materials in use in schools, concluded that there are about 88,500 distinct words in printed school English, and that "the average high school senior may well know about 40,000 words and that the average child in elementary school or high school probably learns 2,000 to 3,000 new words each year" (p. 305). They go on to point out the futility of trying to teach the 20 words a day necessary to reach this goal; obviously, most of us must have learned most of the words we know in some way other than vocabulary-building workbooks in school. I'm sure you answered Question 2 with other routes to vocabulary acquisition, perhaps including recreational reading; listening to parents, siblings, teachers, television, and friends; independent study at times when you were self-motivated and set a goal for yourself, perhaps for the purpose of raising your score on the verbal section of a standardized test used by colleges. Experts do agree that the single most effective way to increase vocabulary is by wide and regular reading (Cunningham & Stanovitch, 1998; Johnson, 2001; Krashen, 1989; Nagy, 1989; Nagy, Anderson, & Herman, 1987).

Moore et al. (1994) point out that as content area teachers we had better think broadly about what constitutes a word. "Phrases, symbols, abbreviations, initials, and acronyms all occur in the material students read in content areas. While these terms are not technically 'words,' they are entities for which meanings must be built" (p. 198). So, you can have students create a chart: "Initializations and Acronyms We Know and Love." Challenge the other subject area teachers to see which discipline can claim the most acronyms and initializations. (An acronym is pronounced as a word, while an initialization is pronounced as the letters that form it.) I'll get you started:

Science: DNA, LASER, AIDS, RADAR, NASA, SCUBA, SONAR, TEFLON, EKG, HIV

Math and Technology: CD-ROM, LCD, ANOVA, CPA

Social Studies: IRA, AFL-CIO, NAACP, AWOL, NATO, SWAT, ZIP, CEO, GNP

Education: LD, ESL, LEP, IEP, TESOL, ADA, GPA, IQ, PTA

For further help, you can check out the *Acronyms, Initialisms, and Abbreviations Dictionary*, published irregularly and complete with periodic supplements by Gale Research of Detroit. Also, ask your students for some of the shortcut words they use while talking to their friends via e-mail—their vocabulary will astound you. They might offer TPTB (the powers that be), WYSIWYG (what you see is what you get), EOL (end of lecture), IMO (in my opinion), RSN (real soon now), PMFJI (pardon me for jumping in), MHOTY (my hat's off to you), and TYVM (thank you very much). Students can recognize that language is changing; they're helping to change it!

THE RICHNESS OF WORDS: DENOTATION, CONNOTATION, SHADES OF MEANING, AND SPECIAL MEANINGS

Students should become aware that many words have *connotations*, various associated and evaluative meanings, as well as *denotations*, the explicit, literal, or direct meanings. You can give your students the dictionary definitions of those terms, but examples from real contexts often help more. So, whenever you encounter words with special connotations in authentic contexts, take advantage of the opportunity to share examples with your students. Sometimes, an exaggerated example works best when you are first explaining a concept such as *connotation*. In a "Peanuts" cartoon by Charles Schulz (1995), Sally tells Linus to get off her porch. Linus replies, "This isn't a porch. This is a stoop. A porch has a railing all around it, and a roof over it, and it's all white, and it has a swing and some rocking chairs . . . and a little table with lemonade glasses and warm nights, and fireflies, and crickets, and soft music, and a moon in the sky. . . . " Linus refers to the things that resonate in the minds of listeners when they hear the word *porch*.

Here's another example. In literature, the genre that was formerly known as *adolescent literature* is now more commonly referred to as *young adult literature*. Teenagers were avoiding the books targeted for them because the term "adolescent" has developed a negative connotation. Various groups of people have changed their preferred names because of connotations associated with certain terms, which may have started out as purely descriptive. The book *Talking About People: A Guide to Fair Language* (Maggio, 1997) is full of entries on this subject, with interesting discussions of the reasons for some changes.

Some multimeaning words can have either a positive or negative connotation depending on the context in which they're used. A *bond* can be a negative thing, chaining a prisoner or limiting a person emotionally in some way. But a *bond* between friends, teammates, or family members is usually seen as a good thing. Help your students ponder the complexity and richness of our language by sharing your own fascination with words, by using rich vocabulary in your lessons and conversations, by pointing out interesting language issues in the readings you assign.

Remember how *The Giver* began with Jonas searching for just the right word to describe how he was feeling? After rejecting several, he settled on *apprehensive*; he had struggled for precision and achieved it. It's really important for students to play around with, to manipulate, the essential words of the disciplines and to aim for exactness and thoroughness. Take the word "culture," for instance, a word crucial to social studies, which I asked you to play with in Question 10 of the Activating Prior Knowledge 5.1 exercise. The dictionary definitions, including "the quality in a person or society that arises from a concern for what is regarded as excellence in arts, letters, manners, scholarly pursuits," as well as 11 others (Merriam-Webster, 1996), might help or they might confuse further. We must realize that many students have difficulty deciding which dictionary definition fits their needs. A textbook glossary may also define the word, or the word might be explained in a passage. When students pay attention to all of the various contexts in which they hear and see the word, they gain a deeper understanding, complete with nuances and connotations. Words become known to us in small increments. For some words we read, we move from no knowledge to some knowledge, and for others, we move from some knowledge to a fuller knowledge (Krashen, 1989).

I've asked my students to brainstorm phrases using the term *culture* and its derivatives. In addition to many social studies–related definitions, some students note that in a biology or health setting, the word is used with a quite different, specialized meaning—they supply *throat culture* and scientists growing *cultures* in dishes. Depending on a teacher's purpose, a next step could be arranging those terms into categories, perhaps creating a *graphic organizer*, a visual representation of these associations. Then, student "word detectives" can be on the lookout in their future reading for further examples to add to the list; they can explore websites or library catalogs to find titles incorporating the word. Having consciously played with the word (and hence the concept) and found it exemplified in outside sources, students have a better understanding of their textbook passages dealing with culture. And they can use the concept when they discuss issues themselves—they can apply their concept knowledge as they talk about the culture of the utopian/dystopian society represented in *The Giver*, for example.

We now certainly have a much deeper understanding of the concept *culture* than any dictionary could give us; we've listened to real people, ourselves and experts, grapple with this important word's meaning. You and your students can do the same with many terms in your specific curricular areas.

There is worry that the richness of language is being diminished these days by a number of societal factors. According to Spretnak (1997), over the past 50 years, the working vocabulary of the average 14-year-old has declined from about 25,000 words to a mere 10,000 words. Orr (2000/2001) warns us about the consequences of this decline. "Because we cannot think clearly about what we cannot say clearly, the first casualty of linguistic incoherence is our ability to think well about many things" (p. 28). He suggests ways to combat the problem, including limiting our use of Internet communication and television, as well as restoring the habit of public reading. He exhorts:

> We are never better than when we use words clearly, eloquently, and civilly. Language can elevate thought and ennoble our behavior. Abraham Lincoln's words at Gettysburg in 1863, for example, gave meaning to the terrible sacrifices of the Civil War. Similarly, Winston Churchill's words moved an entire nation to do its duty in the dark hours of 1940. If we intend to protect and enhance our humanity, we must first decide to protect and enhance language and fight everything that undermines and cheapens it. (p. 29)

TYPES OF VOCABULARY WORDS IN CONTENT AREA TEXTS

It is helpful for teachers to recognize that their students will come across different categories of vocabulary words in their reading and study. *General vocabulary* words are those used in everyday language, although they certainly might be unfamiliar to us or to our students. Examples include *ambivalent, miser, serendipity, confirm.*

Content-specific words, or *special vocabulary*, include words that may be part of our students' regular vocabulary, but that take on a specific meaning in a particular content area, such as *culture* in biology, *latitude* in geography, *congestion* in medicine, or *confirm* in religion. *Evolution* takes on a certain meaning in science. Students encountering the word *revolution* in astronomy class and then later in history class must recognize that the word does not refer to the same thing in both textbooks. Students may know what the word *resistance* means in general, but may have to be taught what the *Resistance* was during World War II.

Finally, *technical vocabulary* refers to words that are used only in particular disciplines, such as *fractal, isotherm, pointillism, iambic pentameter.* Much of what people outside a discipline might consider jargon is actually technical vocabulary. Think of words and phrases you've had to learn in your education classes: *metacognition, morpheme, dyslexia, zone of proximal development.* Some of the words you listed for Questions 4 and 5 on the Activating Prior Knowledge 5.1 exercise are probably examples of technical vocabulary.

ACTION RESEARCH 5.A

Johnson (2001) lists words within several discipline categories, giving the following directions to readers, which I pass on to you: "As you read these lists, consider the first meaning that comes to your mind for each word and then think of the meaning that usually is associated with the word in the named discipline" (pp. 97–98).

MATH

foot	solid	root	peck
square	power	product	yard
mean	curve		

SCIENCE

motion	force	fault	degree
wave	current	resistance	host
matter	charge		

SOCIAL STUDIES

key	bill	race	legend
product	plain	ruler	crop
run	cabinet		

ENGLISH

case	mood	tense	article
subject	tone	romance	dash
voice	stress		

From Dale D. Johnson, *Vocabulary In The Elementary and Middle School.* Copyright © 2001. Adapted by permission by Allyn & Bacon.

You might use these words in a game to demonstrate to your students that words take on specialized meanings within subject areas. Present the ones appropriate to your discipline, have the students look at them and think about their usual meanings, then ask them to talk about the special meaning each has in the subject you teach. Lively discussion will ensue as students work together and think of definitions and examples to complete the exercise. You and they may be able to add other words to the list.

In content area instruction, the specific meanings for concepts and words, along with all they imply, are central and must be understood and remembered—the terms are often necessary building blocks for subsequent lessons (Blachowicz & Fisher, 2000). So, as wonderful as the incidental and independent learning of words is in general, a teacher must provide direct vocabulary instruction and teach and model vocabulary-building strategies in many subject-specific lessons.

A CONTENT AREA APPLICATION

Imagining I was a high school math teacher about to embark on teaching a course in statistics to advanced upperclassmen, I looked through the textbook *Statistics by Example* (Sincich, 1990). I found few words that could be considered in the *general vocabulary* category with which I thought students would have difficulty. There were, however, many words that the students might know in their general sense, but that take on a special meaning in the field of statistics—*specialized vocabulary* words, including *frequency, population, sample, reliability, distribution, center, mean, median, mode, uncertainty, event, parameter,* and *frame.* I want to teach these words directly and carefully, helping the students to relate them to their more typical meanings while alerting them to the precise meanings they take on in the context of our course. Finally, I found many words and phrases in the *technical vocabulary* category: those unlikely to be found anywhere outside a statistics setting, but crucial to an understanding of the principles of the course. It is my job to teach the terms *standard deviation, empirical rule, interquartile range, z-score, discrete random variable,* and *confidence coefficient* so that students can comprehend the text and the subject matter.

ACTION RESEARCH 5.B

Look through a middle grade or high school textbook used in the subject area you will teach. Make three columns on a sheet of paper, labeled GENERAL, CONTENT-SPECIFIC, and TECHNICAL. List the vocabulary words you might have to help your students with in each category. Begin to think about ways to explain them so that the students can understand the concepts and remember the terms.

Getting Ready to Teach 5.1 (see page 161)

CONTROLLED VOCABULARY: GOOD IDEA OR BAD?

Basal readers (traditional published reading programs) and textbooks often control the vocabulary used so that students are not confronted with too many difficult words at once. Formulas for determining appropriate grade levels of reading materials, discussed in Chapter 3, usually use the length of words or number of syllables as a criterion. Instructional materials are often created to conform to established reading levels. But many reading experts, as well as authors, disagree vehemently with this practice, and many recently published programs no longer artificially control the vocabulary in reading selections (Hoffman et al., 1994). Thompson (1996b) provides lists of words found in children's classics that are quite a contrast to the types of words typically found in school reading. Examples include "dif-

fidence, placid, adhere, quietus, miscreant, quixotic, reproof, condescend, somber, enigma, phlegmatic, undulate, sublime, resolute, strident, din, amicable, amorous . . . ," all from Barrie's *Peter Pan* (p. 63). He concludes:

> Educational practice has tricked us all into thinking that such vocabulary is not for children, that it is developmentally inappropriate, or that it should be postponed until some imaginary later appropriate time. Well, I think that any little child who can handle a big term such as *Sanfranciscofortyniner* or *teenagemutantninjaturtle* can handle *fastidious*, and that we are committing national intellectual suicide with our age-graded pistol. (Thompson, 1996b, p. 64)

Madeleine L'Engle, speaking as an author who respects children, concurs:

> The more limited our language is, the more limited we are; the more limited the literature we give to our children, the more limited their capacity to respond, and therefore, in their turn, to create. The more our vocabulary is controlled, the less we will be able to think for ourselves. We do think in words, and the fewer words we know, the more restricted our thoughts. As our vocabulary expands, so does our power to think. (1972, p. 149)

PART TWO

Promoting Language Study

Harmon (2000) listened to seventh-grade students of varying reading abilities as they described how they figured out word meanings. She reports that, not surprisingly, the capable, avid reader used the most strategies the most efficiently and flexibly: Lyn attended to syntax and to parts of words, considered context within sentences and beyond sentences, and considered story plot and authors' styles. A much less able and avid reader, Angela, used a narrow range of strategies, focusing only upon the sentence containing the targeted word; she did not consider using a dictionary, preferring to skip words or ask for help. (Skipping words and asking for help are both fine avenues for you and your students to use at certain times, but must not be the only or necessarily the first means you employ.) Harmon uses her data to conclude that some students require support, encouragement, and access to challenging materials and opportunities to read widely. Others need more explicit instruction to develop more efficient and effective independent word learning strategies, and, perhaps more important, the knowledge and confidence that they can become strategic learners and make good decisions about unfamiliar words they encounter.

Your students can learn more of what they have to in your subject area if you help them to realize the importance of vocabulary and to be aware of vocabulary issues, and teach them a variety of strategies to deal with new words they encounter. The following sections detail some ways to expand the vocabulary necessary for your students' understanding of texts in your field, and ways that you can encourage students to explore language and increase their vocabulary independently. The resources provided also help *you* increase your store of words and concepts and become an enthusiastic model and resource for your students.

TEACH STUDENTS TO USE STRUCTURAL ANALYSIS

Were you able to define *regicide* in the opening exercise? If so, do you know *why* or *how* you know that word? If not, can you come close, or can you at least guess what it might have to do with? Can you identify its part of speech? Think of other words you know that end in *-cide. Suicide,* you say? *Homicide, herbicide, pesticide, genocide, infanticide?* If you've

taken Latin, you'll probably add *fratricide, patricide, matricide.* (I've had some kids guess that this last word means the killing of a mattress, which is okay; word play is good.) To help students understand the word *regicide,* have them think of the word *regal* and use the target word in context: "*Hamlet* is a play about regicide." Through induction, the students can now conclude that *regicide* refers to the killing of a king. Interestingly, a new word, *medicide,* has recently entered our language to refer to doctor-assisted suicide.

Question 7 of the Activating Prior Knowledge 5.1 exercise was included to help you realize how we learn language and generalize and hypothesize about new words based on what we already know. You may have tackled the unfamiliar word *lexiphile* by comparing it to similar words you do know. *Lexicon* and *lexicographer* may have helped, combined perhaps with *bibliophile, pedophile, Anglophile,* or *Francophile.* "A person who loves words, who studies language" is a very good guess, but a "wrong" one—Anderson and Nagy (1992) tell us that looking up the word *lexiphile* in the dictionary will not help because "it is a word we made up" (p. 47).

Breaking Words Into Meaningful Parts

Teaching your students the strategy of breaking words into meaningful parts, or *morphemes,* is a tremendous way to help them understand terms and concepts they must know and discover the meaning of new words. Morphemes include *root words,* as well as *affixes* (*prefixes,* which come before roots, and *suffixes,* which follow them). Research shows that a morphological awareness on the part of students makes a significant contribution to reading ability (Carlisle, 1995; Carlisle & Nomanbhoy, 1993). It has been estimated that about 60 percent of the new words that students encounter can be analyzed into parts that give substantial help in determining their meaning (Nagy & Anderson, 1984). See Figure 5.1 for some common word parts.

Etymology

An expedient way to enlarge your own vocabulary and that of your students is to learn a bit about *etymology,* which involves the history and derivation of words. You might be pleasantly surprised at how

FIGURE 5.1 *Common word parts.*

PREFIXES	ROOTS	SUFFIXES
1. auto (self)	graph (writing)	mania (madness for)
2. anti (against)	phon (sound)	phobia (fear of)
3. tele (far)	hydr (water)	itis (inflammation)
4. bi (two)	therm (heat)	ist (one who)
5. dia (through)	meter (measure)	ic (pertaining to)
6. con (together)	dic (say)	ism (condition of)
7. trans (across)	vit (life)	able (able to)
8. re (again)	port (carry)	ment (state of)
9. in, im, un (not, in)	pen, pun (punish)	er (one who)
10. pre (before)	vert (turn)	ion, tion (act of)

Source: N. L. Cecil, Striking a Balance: Positive Practices for Early Literacy. Copyright © 1999, Holcomb Hathaway, Scottsdale, AZ. Used with permission.

much enthusiasm young people can show about the so-called *dead* languages, Greek and Latin. Boyce (1996) tells the story of a verbally gifted child whose life was changed by Latin:

> Not until she took Latin in high school did Nadine find the intellectual substance about words that matched her voracious appetite. Nadine says, "In Latin, I enjoyed memorizing vocabulary; I could memorize it instantly. My favorite Latin root is sesqu—consequence, sequel, consecutive, sequence —a cool word!" Nadine's only memory of vocabulary study throughout her school career is of her Latin classes. Her own voracious reading and her constant compiling of word lists nurtured the ability that school neglected. (p. 262)

Boyce highly recommends that vocabulary study include learning Greek and Latin etymology, "with special attention to the aesthetic and intellectual surprises that are not apparent from dictionary definitions" (p. 173). This kind of delight happened to me with the morpheme *nano-*. I recently noticed how often I come across words beginning with this word part—*nanoseconds* and *nanobes* (organisms ranging from 20 to 150 *nanometers* in length). I looked up *nano-* in an old dictionary and found it there with the definition of one-billionth, or 10 to the −9 power. Then, I looked it up in a newer dictionary, where I found the previous definition, plus "a combining form with the meaning 'very small, minute' used in the formation of compound words" (Merriam-Webster, 1996). Scanning the page, I found the words *nanogram, nanoid, nanomole, nanoplankton,* and *nanotechnology,* which entered the dictionary,

not surprisingly, in the late 1980s. An added treat was reading that *nano-* came from the Greek word meaning *dwarfish.*

Finding out where words originated can be fascinating, as well as helpful in terms of understanding their meanings. Some words, including terms students must know for the disciplines they study, have interesting beginnings. For example, the math term *integer* comes from the Latin for "untouched"—a good word for something that is intact, whole. Students could connect *integer* to a related word, *integrity.*

Hennings (2000) recommends several instructional principles for content area teachers to use when adolescents are "analyzing and sorting words into groups based on shared elements, searching for structurally and etymologically related words, and discovering generalizations about word connections—all at the point of use, when study is most relevant and meaningful" (p. 269). Teachers can:

- Highlight Latin and Greek roots across the curriculum.

- Associate and visually highlight new terms derived from a root with words the students know that share the root.

- Give attention to prefixes that carry a negative message (such as *anti-, dys-, counter-/contra-,* and *in-/im-/ig-*).

- Encourage students to explore meanings and etymologies using dictionaries and online sources such as the Merriam-Webster website (www.m-w.com) or www.word-detective.com.

FIGURE 5.2   *Useful Latin and Greek roots.*

LATIN NUMBERS

CARDINAL NUMBERS		ROMAN NUMBER	ENGLISH COMBINING FORM	EXAMPLE
1	unus	I	uni-	uniform
2	duo	II	duo- or du-	duet
3	tres	III	tri-	triangle
4	quattuor	IV	quadri-	quadrilateral
5	quinque	V	quinqu-	quinquennial
6	sex	VI	sexi- or sex-	sextet
7	septem	VII	sept-	September
8	octo	VIII	oct- or octa-	octet
9	novem	IX	novem- or noven-	November
10	decem	X	decem-	December
100	centum	C	centi- or cent-	centigrade
1,000	mille	M	milli- or mill-	millennium

OTHER COMMON ROOTS

ENGLISH WORD	LATIN WORD	GREEK WORD	GREEK COMPOUND FORM
heart	cors, cordis	cardia	cardio-
lung	pulmo, pulmonis	pneumon	pneumo-
stomach	stomachus, stomachi	gaster, gastros	gastro-
	abdomen, abdominis	eneron	entero-
liver		hepar, hepatos	hepato-
kidney	renum, reni	nephros	nephro-

Source: T. M. Green, *The Greek and Latin Roots of English* (2nd ed.). Copyright © 1994 by Ardsley House. Used with permission.

Hennings concludes:

> Some content area specialists may be fearful of "wasting" instructional time allocated to their discipline on word study investigations. Just the opposite is likely; time spent in meaningful, contextually relevant word study facilitates students' understanding of the subject discipline. . . . To this end, content area specialists must keep alert for "teachable moments" when they can integrate word study into ongoing content area lectures and discussions. To do this successfully, they must become knowledgeable about word relationships, especially connections based on Greek and Latin roots, prefixes, suffixes, and suffixlike elements. (p. 278)

Though you might associate general vocabulary development with English classes based on your own schooling, I agree with Victor and Kellough (1997) that "regardless of their primary teaching subject, all teachers are teachers of language arts" (p. 94), and I'm convinced that all content area teachers should do their part to spread the good news that Latin and Greek roots are both helpful and fun. Figure 5.2 has examples of charts I'd like to see during a tour of a language-rich high school. Students can add to these charts as their courses progress and their encounters with more examples multiply.

ACTIVATING PRIOR KNOWLEDGE   5.2

Examine the following list of Latin words and their English meanings that are associated with the topic of law. Write words you know that are derivatives of the Latin words. If you're not sure whether there is a connection, look the word up in a dictionary to learn its origin. You can also search a dictionary to add to your original list. Then, think about how you might use this information with middle school or high school social studies classes.

LATIN WORD	ENGLISH MEANING
lex, legis	law
jus, juris	right, law, justice
judex, judicis	judge
cohors, cohortis	enclosure; group, company
crimen, criminis	accusation; the crime of which one is accused
codex, codicis	book

Source: T. M. Green, *The Greek and Latin Roots of English* (2nd ed.). Copyright © 1994 by Ardsley House. Used with permission.

The study guide *Civil Service Arithmetic and Vocabulary* (Erdsneker, Haller, & Steinberg, 1998), after explaining that one of the most efficient ways of increasing vocabulary is to pay attention to etymology (how words are formed), guides the reader through some examples:

> The word *biography* is made up of two important parts. *Graphy* comes from a Greek word meaning "writing." Many English words use this root. *Graphology*, for instance, is the study of handwriting. *Graphite* is the carbon material used in "lead" pencils. The *telegraph* is a device for writing at a distance. The *bio* part, also from Greek, means "life." It too is at the root of many English words, such as *biology* (the study of life) and *biochemistry* (the chemistry of life). When we put *bio* and *graphy* together, we get a word meaning "writing about a person's life." We can make another word by adding another part, this time from the Latin word *auto*, meaning "self." An *autobiography* is "a person's written account of his [sic] own life." (p. 156)

You can show the same enthusiasm as you guide your students through the combinations of roots that make up some essential or interesting words within your discipline. Encourage them to take notice of, collect, use, and point out words they come across, so that everyone's vocabulary and interest in language grow. Moore et al. (1994), however, warn, "Students are often turned off to vocabulary instruction by being taught obscure Latin and Greek derivatives that have few examples in common use today. . . ." (p. 156). They suggest using what they call the *Five Test*. If you can't readily think of five words that use the word part without running to a dictionary, it may not be worth alerting students to the meaning of the word part. They apply the test to the prefix *mal-* and after citing the words *malpractice, malice, malignant, malfunction,* and *malcontent,* conclude that *mal-* is indeed a valuable morpheme to teach. Try this with such morphemes as *mega, circum-,* or *chrono-*. One morpheme that passes the Five Test with flying colors is *-phobia.* Johnson (2001) lists about 100 words in which *-phobia* combines with other morphemes to give us words about fears in many categories, including travel, food, health, animals, and the elements.

Structural analysis does not help figure out vocabulary words 100 percent of the time. Occasionally, something a student might think is a prefix, root, or suffix isn't (e.g., *decide* does not belong with the other *-cide* words we brainstormed previously; *silver* ends in *-er,* which functions as a suffix in many words, but not in this case; *lens* ends in *-s* but is not a plural). And a morpheme may have multiple meanings: *homo-* from Latin means *man,* while *homo-* from Greek means *same*). Help your students realize that paying attention to word structure is very beneficial, but is only one of many strategies they'll use to figure out word meanings.

TEACH STUDENTS TO USE CONTEXT CLUES

Authors want their readers to understand the terms they use. You can help students to realize that authors often define words as they go along; that is, in the *context* of their piece. Students might panic when they see words unfamiliar to them, but if they just keep reading, they'll find that the meaning has been supplied. Authors typically have a targeted audience—they address readers they assume know most of the words they use. But often, authors are trying to introduce new concepts, at least new to their targeted readers, so they define words at appropriate times. Biologist E. O. Wilson's *Consilience: The Unity of Knowledge* (1998) contains this example: "Scientific evidence is accretionary, built from blocks of evidence joined artfully by the blueprints and mortar of theory" (p. 59). Two sentences later the word that was just defined is used again: "Only very rarely, as in the theories of natural selection and relativity, does an idea change our conception of the world in one quantum leap. Even the revolution of molecular biology was accretionary, building upon but not fundamentally altering physics and chemistry" (p. 59). The repetition helps; this is *considerate text*, as was discussed in Chapter 3.

If I as a reader had not known the word *accretionary*, I didn't have to stop and look up the word or use structural analysis (though I could have done either). The strategy of simply reading the sentence worked well. You as an adult, fluent reader use this strategy naturally all of the time without even realizing it; it has become automatic. It may, however, be necessary to directly teach your students the strategy of reading ahead to get more information or context; reinforce this strategy using real examples that they find in textbooks, trade books, and primary sources. "Think aloud" to show them how you use clues and put information together to figure out the meanings of terms as they are used in particular contexts.

Another device authors may use is supplying, not the definition, but an example that leads to the reader's knowing the meaning of the word. E. O. Wilson (1994) uses the word *paradox*: "Gene-culture co-evolution may seem to create a paradox: At the same time that culture arises from human action, human action arises from culture" (p. 166). He then further clarifies the word by using a synonym in the following sentence: "The contradiction evaporates, however, if. . . . " (p. 166). Again, not necessarily easy reading, but considerate text.

Finally, there are times when the author gives neither the definition nor an explicit example, but readers can still figure out, or take a pretty good guess at, a word's meaning by its use in a sentence or a passage. They may only get an approximate meaning at any one time, but when they encounter a word repeatedly, the meaning is confirmed and refined. For example, take the word *formidable*. During one lesson on vocabulary development, my class read an article containing the following sentence: "If the average high school senior knows forty thousand words . . . , you would have to teach twenty words a day to cover them, a . . . formidable task" (Anderson & Nagy, 1992, p. 14). The very next article we read contained a list of words the author selected from a children's classic, followed by "Impressive, don't you think? . . . These are formidable and advanced words—erudite even" (Thompson, 1996b, p. 63). The following week, these students were reading the young adult novel *Summer of My German Soldier* (Greene, 2000) when they came across the word again. As we hear or see a word in a variety of contexts, the word is added to our receptive vocabulary, and eventually to our expressive vocabulary. It's easy to see why so many experts recommend wide reading as the single best way to increase vocab-

BookTalk   5.1

Would you rather study vocabulary for a standardized test, such as the SAT, or read a novel? Which do you think your students would prefer? You can do both simultaneously when reading *Tooth and Nail: A Novel Approach to the New SAT* by Charles Herrington Elster and Joseph Elliot (1994). They've written a mystery that just happens to include words they found through an analysis of SAT tests. The reader encounters each highlighted word in the context of a sentence within a story. Try it; although it may not win any awards for being great literature, it really is fun—as the authors promise.

ulary. The chances of learning much about a word from a single encounter in a natural context are slim (Nagy, Anderson, & Herman, 1987; Schatz & Baldwin, 1986), but repeated encounters help refine and reinforce the meaning of words.

Using context clues is a skill that can be taught. But to be effective, the instruction should be explicit and well-scaffolded, and provide practice and feedback (Blachowicz & Fisher, 2000; Buikema & Graves, 1993). Readers must have a repertoire of strategies to choose from and the persistence to try another when one doesn't help. Students must be taught that they can use multiple strategies to figure out words. Also, a metacognitive component should be included. You'll recall from the last chapter that metacognition involves an awareness of and control over one's cognitive processes. Students exhibit *metalinguistic* ability when they reflect on and monitor their learning about words and language.

TEACH STUDENTS TO USE REFERENCE MATERIALS

When the interdisciplinary discussion group I belong to met recently to discuss the book *Unto Others: The Evolution and Psychology of Unselfish Behavior* (Sober & Wilson, 1998), a biologist brought along a glossary of terms relating to genetics for those of us, like myself, who were not scientists. This colleague realized that we did not represent the author's target audience, and might need help with the vocabulary and concepts that the authors assumed readers would know. The glossary was a much appreciated tool. Help your students learn that references, such as dictionaries, atlases, and compilations of facts and terms, can greatly aid their reading and understanding. Too many students consider dictionaries boring and deadly because they have been subjected to seemingly endless assignments such as "Look up these 10 words in the dictionary and copy the definitions. Use each word in an original sentence." Moore et al. (1994) state:

> The most common vocabulary activity in classrooms at all levels is to assign students to look up words and write their definitions. This frustrating practice is like expecting that you could get to know some new people by looking them up in *Who's Who* and writing down their distinguishing characteristics. Such an activity is helpful only if you already know something about the people and want to find out more. In the same way, dictionaries are wonderful resources for adding to or clarifying a word's meaning. (p. 224)

Out of context, few of us learn words by looking them up and memorizing someone else's definition. In fact, this practice can lead to misunderstandings. I supervised a student teacher who developed a multiple-choice vocabulary test for her middle school students that consisted of sentences she had made up herself. The test was terrible, and only added to her students' confusion. One question stated:

> The ocean was *lackadaisical*, which was perfect for Casey's swim.
>
> a. lukewarm b. freezing c. hot d. ice

I pointed out to Nina that the sentence was not likely to be used in an authentic situation. She explained that she had looked up the words in a thesaurus to find out what they meant; then, armed with synonyms, she created the test, adding some non-synonym answers as distractors. Though *lukewarm* can be substituted for *lackadaisical* in *some* sentences, it did not work for her here because she did not own the word herself. She had to work on her own vocabulary, and looking up words in a dictionary or thesaurus was not going to be enough. Wide reading of rich text and attention to language will improve Nina's ability to enhance word study in her classroom.

When our students realize that reference sources are meant to be used when needed, when they hear or see a term they don't know and want to know, and when they are taught how to use reference tools by using the real thing (not a publisher's workbook sheet simulating a dictionary page), worlds, as well as words, open up to them. With encyclopedias, dictionaries, and other reference materials available online or on CD-ROM, using the tools has become easier and, for many, much more enjoyable.

At the risk of seeming to contradict myself, I do suggest that you keep lots of reference materials on hand as part of your classroom library for your stu-

BookTalk 5.2

How do dictionaries get written? Who does the work so that we can open to a page and find the meaning we're looking for? There are fascinating stories that answer these questions. *Dictionaries—The Art and Craft of Lexicography,* by Sidney Landau (2001), explains the principles underlying the making of "wordy" reference books. *Caught in the Web of Words,* by K. M. Elizabeth Murray (2001), is a biography of the author's grandfather, James Murray, the man most responsible for the creation of the *Oxford English Dictionary,* the definitive source for word lovers. Then, there's *The Professor and the Madman* by Simon Winchester (1998). This best-seller's subtitle is enticing: *A Tale of Murder, Insanity, and the Making of the Oxford English Dictionary.* Enjoy!

dents' perusal. When they *choose* to leaf through a dictionary, or explore an atlas, even though the terms and information they read is not within the wider context of a passage or book, learning can take place. Some people really do choose reference books for pleasure reading, and certain of your students might prefer reading from a book of phrases to reading a few paragraphs from a novel or a textbook assignment if they only have a few minutes before the bell rings. Encourage this independent pastime, and listen actively should your students choose to share their discoveries with you. I have included a bibliography of reference books pertaining to language in Figure 5.3. Peruse them, enjoy them, and add excerpts that relate to topics in your curricular area to your repertoire of stories. You can also give booktalks to entice your students to read about the living, lively language they use.

WORD WALLS

No matter what your subject area, have your students post new words they acquire in visible places around the classroom—alone or with definitions, examples, or sample sentences. They can be in list form, in random order, in semantic webs, or arranged in categories; they can be accompanied by pictures or placed within student art work. The words can be selected by the students from their textbooks, or they can represent new words found in outside reading. The word walls serve to reinforce terms and concepts you have taught, as well as introductions to new words. Students may use them in their writing, to ask questions, to share proudly with others their

Asimov, I. (1969). *Words of Science and the History Behind Them.* New York: New American Library.

Brook, D. (1998). *The Journey of English.* New York: Clarion Books.

Chapman, R. L., with A. Kipfer (1995). *Dictionary of American Slang* (3rd ed.). New York: Harper-Collins.

Fry, B. F., Kress, J. E., & Fountoukidis, D. L. (2000). *The Reading Teacher's Book of Lists* (4th ed.). Paramus, NJ: Prentice Hall.

Hendrickson, R. (1994). *Grand Slams, Hat Tricks, and Alley-Oops: A Sports Fan's Book of Words.* New York: Prentice Hall.

Hobbs, J. B. (1999). *Homophones and Homographs: An American Dictionary* (3rd ed.). Jefferson, NE: McFarland.

Kahn, J. E. (Ed.). (1990). *Illustrated Reverse Dictionary: Find the Right Words on the Tip of Your Tongue.* Pleasantville, NY: Reader's Digest Association.

Klausner, J. (1990). *Talk About English: How Words Travel and Change.* New York: Crowell.

Lang, P. (1995). *The English Language Debate: One Nation, One Language?* Springfield, NJ: Enslow.

Lederer, R., & Dowis, R. (1999). *Sleeping Dogs Don't Lay: Practical Advice for the Grammatically Challenged.* New York: St. Martin's Press.

Lewis, T. (1990). *Et Cetera, Et Cetera: Notes of a Word Watcher.* Boston: Little, Brown.

Morris, E. (2000). *The Word Detective.* Chapel Hill, NC: Algonquin Books of Chapel Hill.

O'Connor, P. T. (1996). *Woe Is I; The Grammarphobe's Guide to Better English in Plain English.* New York: Putnam.

O'Connor, P. T. (1997). *Words Fail Me: What Everyone Who Writes Should Know About Writing.* New York: Harcourt Brace.

Randall, B. (1997). *When Is a Pig a Hog?: A Guide to Confoundingly Related English Words.* New York: Galahad Books.

Safire, W. (1997). *Watching My Language: Adventures in the Word Trade.* New York: Random House.

Safire, W. (1999). *Spread the Word.* New York: Random House.

Sommer, E. F., & Sommer, M. (1998). *Similes Dictionary.* Detroit, MI: Visible Ink Press.

Soukhanov, A. H. (1995). *Word Watch: The Stories Behind the Words of Our Lives.* New York: Henry Holt.

Walsh, B. (2000). *Lapsing into a Comma: A Curmudgeon's Guide to the Many Things that Can Go Wrong in Print—and How to Avoid Them.* Chicago: Contemporary Books.

FIGURE 5.3   *A sampling of books on language.*

knowledge and discoveries of new words, to discuss relations between words or shades of meanings. Word walls don't have to use any of your precious teaching time; they are simply there adorning your walls and adding interest to the surroundings.

Figures 5.4, 5.5, and 5.6 illustrate various types of word walls. The possible variations for you and your students, however, are endless!

> **Getting Ready to Teach 5.2** (see page 161)

SCHOOL AND COMMUNITY-WIDE VOCABULARY FOCUS

The growth of vocabulary is a noble goal for individuals and groups. Most people, as you learned from Question 1 on the Activating Prior Knowledge 5.1 (APK) exercise, would like their vocabularies to be larger than they are presently. Some schools have made this goal a focus for the school year or at least some part of it. Several sixth-grade students I teach in a weekly religion class told me of the "Vocabulary Celebration Week" their middle school was promoting. Every teacher had thought of some way to bring words and language to the fore. Students all carried new words in their pockets throughout each day. They could be stopped in the hall by upperclassmen and teachers who were part of the "Vocabulary Patrol," ready to reward with small prizes those students who could pull out a word from their pockets and give its definition. There were word walls and posters in stairwells, there were challenges from the principal over the loudspeaker each morning, teachers made banners proclaiming great new words. The students were excited, and when I questioned them several months later about the words they had learned, their recall proved strong. Although extrinsic rewards and designated "weeks" or "celebrations" like this one are certainly not the entire answer to

FIGURE 5.4   *Words we found that connect to the concept of thinking.*

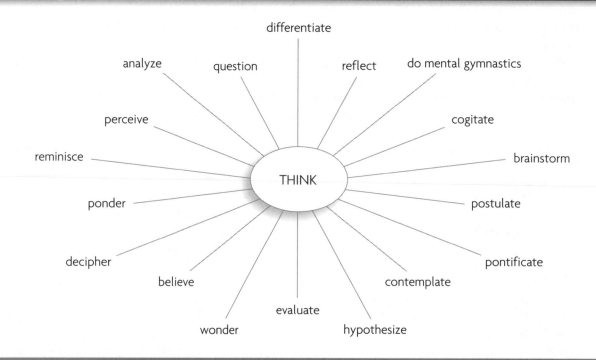

differentiate

analyze   question   reflect   do mental gymnastics

perceive   cogitate

reminisce   brainstorm

THINK

ponder   postulate

decipher   pontificate

believe   contemplate

wonder   evaluate   hypothesize

FIGURE 5.5   *Math words we know and love.*

dodecahedron
triskaidekaphobia
game theory
topology
exponential
googol
parabola
tangram
fractal
pi
calculus
factorial
geometric
quadratic
histogram
symmetry
coefficient
Fibonacci
complementary
polynomial

FIGURE 5.6   *Ms. Morley's morpheme magicians.*

MORPHEMES

A *morpheme* is the smallest meaningful linguistic unit. We've found these words that combine morphemes. Can you figure out their meanings?

pseudoscience

postmodern

prenatal

neoclassic

hydroelectric

megabyte

postnasal

socioeconomic

subterranean

chronology

anti-establishment

parisitophobia

enhancing the student body's collective vocabulary, they can raise the students' consciousness about words and language and may help them see their elders learning as well. As one of many ways to encourage language growth, school-wide efforts can be fun and productive. As an individual teacher, you can continue the celebration throughout the year.

"Read a Million Minutes" is a month-long program that has fostered and encouraged wide reading in several states for two decades. Students set individual goals and read independently from a variety of genres, sometimes connected to a theme, to contribute toward the statewide goal of reading a total of 60 million minutes. Special community activities add to the enthusiasm, and teachers report an increased interest in reading among students. Johnson (2001) connects this to vocabulary development. "Imagine the number of new words learned by the students of a state who read a combined total of sixty million minutes in a month" (p. 42).

EXPLORING AND PLAYING WITH LANGUAGE

Question 1 of the Activating Prior Knowledge 5.1 exercise, designed in part to help you bring to a conscious level how you feel about your personal vocabulary achievement at present, has resulted in my students, future teachers, admitting to being discouraged about their own vocabulary level and

---

"For students who have learned to play with words, literature and all language become the playground."

(BOYCE, 1996, P. 269)

---

growth. They complain of having forgotten the words they learned in high school for the SATs and final course exams and find learning the vocabulary associated with all of their college courses a daunting task. Some have even developed a fear of words: *logophobia!* Yet, their answers to Questions 8 and 9 (APK 5.1) show them that they have not entirely lost the ability to appreciate the beauty and interest of words or the ability to play with language. Take a moment to listen to the words your classmates picked as favorites, and share your own. You'll be able to categorize them according to why they were picked. My students always come up with words they like because of the way they sound: *happenstance, cornucopia, passé, incorrigible, sophisticated, exquisite, onomatopoeia, Mississippi.* Others are

favorites because of their meanings or associations: *love, payday, peace, chocolate, family.* Once in a while someone offers a word, such as *serendipity, lullaby,* or *bubble bath,* that fits in both the sound and association categories. I look around at this point in our sharing and notice that my students are smiling and nodding as they hear and savor the words being mentioned. This increases as we share words that young children tend to love: *mine, why, candy, Mommy, Tyrannosaurus Rex, NO, Dad, Tigger, awesome, supercalifragilisticexpialidocious.*

You are given ways in this section to improve your own vocabulary, as well as those of the students in your content area classes. You'll become attuned to noticing the language in the texts you read (called developing *word consciousness*), and you'll find new ways to play with and have fun with words.

Children pick up words easily and are very curious. One day I had some neighborhood children in my house; they like to play library with my hundreds of books and thus, help me keep them in some order. I said to 11-year-old Jeff, "Here's a book on the Industrial Revolution I think you might like." Alex, my six-year-old niece, piped up, "I already know what that is. Animals turned into people." I replied, "I said *revolution.* Where did you learn about *evolution?*" She responded casually, "I read it in a book." My attention went back to Jeff, and I forgot about the incident until Alex's mother told me that when she got home from work that night, Alex greeted her with, "Mom, what's *revolution?*" and then went around the house that night singing "evolution-revolution" under her breath. She was playing and learning.

Somehow, we have to keep that level of curiosity high in our students, and of course in ourselves, too. Actually, researchers have found that verbally gifted students, while able to comprehend and use humor to a greater degree than others, sometimes are *not* appreciated by their teachers or their peers, who discourage verbal play (Shade, 1991; Ziv & Gadish, 1990).

Boyce (1996) offers both reasons and resources for encouraging students to engage in word play in order to "master the game of language" (p. 261). She describes verbally talented individuals as having "a love affair with words—relishing images and sounds, striving to understand a word's origin and history, collecting words, making people laugh with parodies and outrageous use of words, searching for meaning, and honing the ability to make an exquisite word choice." In a delightful chapter entitled "In the Big Inning Was the Word," she discusses resources for teachers such as specialized dictionaries, books about the origins of words, books that play with all types of words, and books that provide teachers with word games. She promises that word collecting can become a passionate hobby.

Word Games

Word games have always been popular, in every age and at every age. Children love to rhyme, to try out new words, to invent new languages with their friends. Every generation coins terms and uses words in ways their parents didn't. But some word games can bring family members of various ages together and prove that everyone can learn new words. SCRAB-BLE®, for instance, has been popular for decades and is still going strong (now also in electronic format on CD-ROM). Supplying your classroom with games and books that employ and play with words can only help your students. These materials might not relate direct-

---

BOOKS WITH CHARACTERS WHO LOVE WORDS

We don't see many characters in children's and young adult books learning new words by studying lists for midterm exams—perhaps because that is not the stuff adventures are made of. But readers who pay attention, as we can help our students do, can see vocabulary acquisition at work as they read literature. For example, in Antoine de Saint-Exupéry's classic fantasy, *The Little Prince* (1943), a geographer, while recording everything from mountains to seas, explains to the little prince that he does not record flowers because they are ephemeral. Our protagonist asks:

> "But what does that mean—'ephemeral'?" . . . "It means, 'which is in danger of speedy disappearance,'" replies the geographer. "My flower is 'ephemeral,' the little prince said to himself, "and she has only four thorns to defend herself against the world. And I have left her on my planet, all alone!" (pp. 65–66)

He has his first moment of regret; both the character and the reader are emotionally involved with the flower at this point. Thus, *ephemeral* is likely to be remembered, especially if the teacher or student uses it in other applications soon after.

Kevin, one half of the inseparable duo known as *Freak the Mighty* (Philbrick, 1993), is a boy who has known since he was seven, when he looked up the name of his disorder in a medical dictionary, that he wasn't going to have a very long life—his bones won't grow, but his internal organs continue to enlarge. His heart will grow too big, literally, for his body. What *does* grow at a rapid rate is Kevin's knowledge, particularly his vocabulary. He carries a dictionary with him and uses it when his overgrown friend Max becomes confused when he talks about such things as *archetypes, relativity,* and *ichthyology.* "Freak's Dictionary" is included at the end of the book. Students will laugh at Kevin's spin on some of the definitions.

The ambitious 12-year-old narrator of Bette Greene's *Summer of My German Soldier* (2000) is working her way through *Webster's Collegiate Dictionary* in order to meet her goal of someday knowing the meaning of every word in the English language. She knows all kinds of words, "thin ones like ego and ode. Fat ones like harmonic and palatable . . . beautiful ones like rendezvous and dementia praecox . . . ugly ones like grief and degrade" (p. 72). Like our friend Jonas in *The Giver,* she's concerned with the precision of language. She explains to a reporter, "Like a moment ago you used the word aptitude, and because you didn't think I understood, you substituted the word ability. But you didn't actually mean ability. We both know that I don't have the ability to be a reporter today, but I just might have the aptitude" (pp. 92–93). Readers of this historical novel will see how Patty's knowledge of words and concepts becomes armor and solace when her family and town turn against her for harboring an enemy prisoner of war.

You may come across many other books in your own reading that have characters who love language and use words carefully, purposely, or playfully. Share them, and encourage your students to do the same. You might have a poster on your classroom wall devoted to titles and examples related to the topic of language use by characters, fictional and real. To get started, check out *Multiple Choice* by Janet Tashjian (2001), *The Mozart Season* (2000) by Virginia Euwer Wolff, and *Silent to the Bone* (2000) by E. L. Konigsburg.

BookTalk 5.3

The Music of Dolphins (1996), by Newbery Medal winner Karen Hesse, doesn't exactly fit the category "Characters Who Love Words," because language is an uncomfortable fit for Mila, a feral child who spent most of her life with dolphins before coming to the Language Institute. But you'll certainly be stimulated to ponder the relationship between thought and language, as well as what it means to be human, as you experience Mila's struggle to become vocal and literate, and to acquire the culture of her new environment. You'll witness the frustration of her teachers, and, with the characters, you'll face some ethical dilemmas regarding freedom and control.

FIGURE 5.7	*Language-based games, books, and websites.*

Agee, J. (1999). *Sit on a Potato Pan, Otis: More Palindromes.* New York: Farrar, Straus & Giroux.

Augarde, T. (1984). *The Oxford Guide to Word Games.* New York: Oxford University Press.

Carroll, L. (1982). *Alice's Adventures in Wonderland.* (S. H. Goodacre, Ed.). Berkeley: University of California Press.

Farb, P. (1993). *Word Play: What Happens When People Talk.* New York: Vintage.

Frasier, D. (2000). *Miss Alaineus: A Vocabulary Disaster.* New York, Harcourt Brace.

Garrison, W. (1992). *Why You Say It: The Fascinating Stories Behind Over 600 Everyday Words and Phrases.* New York: MJF Books.

Gwynne, F. (1970). *The King Who Rained.* New York: Simon & Schuster.

Gwynne, F. (1976). *A Chocolate Moose for Dinner.* New York: Simon & Schuster.

Gwynne, F. (1988). *A Little Pigeon Toad.* New York: Simon & Schuster.

Heller, R. (1987). *A Cache of Jewels: And Other Collective Nouns.* New York: Scholastic.

Heller, R. (1988). *Kites Sail High: A Book About Verbs.* New York: Scholastic.

Heller, R. (1989). *Many Luscious Lollipops: A Book About Adjectives.* New York: Scholastic.

Heller, R. (1990). *Merry-Go-Round: A Book About Nouns.* New York: Scholastic.

Heller, R. (1991). *Up, Up, and Away: A Book About Adverbs.* New York: Scholastic.

Heller, R. (1995). *Behind the Mask: A Book About Prepositions.* New York: Scholastic.

Heller, R. (1997). *Mine, All Mine: A Book About Pronouns.* New York: Scholastic.

Heller, R. (1997). *Fantastic! Wow! And Unreal!: A Book About Interjections and Conjunctions.* New York: Scholastic.

Lederer, R. (1990). *The Play of Words: Fun & Games for Language Lovers.* New York: Pocket.

Lederer, R., & Dowis, R. (1999). *Sleeping Dogs Don't Lay: Practical Advice for the Grammatically Challenged.* New York: St. Martin's Press.

Lipton, J. (1991). *An Exaltation of Larks: The Ultimate Edition.* New York: Viking.

Maizels, J., & Petty, K. (1996). *The Amazing Pop-Up Book of Grammar.* New York: Penguin Books.

McQuain, J., & Malless, S. (1998). *Coined by Shakespeare: Words & Meaning First Penned by the Bard.* Springfield, MA: Merriam-Webster.

Merriam-Webster's Word Crazy: The Action Word Game on CD-ROM. Springfield, MA: Merriam-Webster.

Rice, R. (1992). *English Teacher's Book of Instant Word Games.* West Nyack, NY: Center for Applied Research in Education.

Shepherd, R. (1991). *Playing the Language Game.* Philadelphia: Open University Press.

Sperling, S. K. (1985). *Murfles and Wink-a-Peeps: Funny Old Words for Kids.* New York: Clarkson Potter.

Stein, L., & Voskovitz, B. (1999). *The Buzzword Bingo Book: The Complete Definitive Guide to the Underground Workplace Game of Corporate Jargon and Doublespeak.* New York: Villard.

Thompson, M. C. (1990, 1991). *The Word Within the Word,* (Vols. 1 & 2). Unionville, NY: Trillium.

Thompson, M. C. (1991). *The Magic Lens.* Unionville, NY: Trillium.

A.Word.A.Day—www.wordsmith.org/words/yester.

Word Puzzles—www.vocabulary.com/VUlevelone.html.

ly to the topics you're teaching, but they can make your students eager learners and sharper thinkers; perhaps yours will be the classroom that students love to visit after school to have competitions with students from other class periods. You'll have the opportunity to talk informally with students, to chat and laugh while you observe them play language games or play along with them. In addition, you can use the formats of these games or books to create, or encourage the students to create, similar challenges using subject-related words. Figure 5.7 offers some language-based games, books, and websites.

Maybe you're thinking that, as a content area teacher, you really don't have time for playing with words in general. In that case, I encourage you to make up activities and games that promote word study (and simultaneously play) to help your students remember the concepts in your subject. For example, you can make cards with definitions on the top and vocabulary terms (for different definitions) on the bottom. Make enough cards for each student to have at least one. You read the first definition, and whoever has the card with the answer calls it out; then, that person reads the definition

FIGURE **5.8**   *Examples of vocabulary game cards for an algebra class.*

Definition: The sum formed by changing the sign of the subtrahend in a subtraction problem and then adding.

[*Another card has "algebraic subtraction" on the bottom.*]

Term: Conditional equation

[*Another card will have the definition to match this.*]

Definition: A number or quantity placed before and multiplying another quantity.

[*Another card has "coefficient" on the bottom.*]

Term: Variable

[*Another card will have the definition to match this.*]

on her card, and another person answers. This routine continues until all terms are matched with definitions. (The last answer should be on your card.) You can also play the game by saying the term first, with the answer being the definition. It works well as a review at the end of a unit. Figure 5.8 gives examples of these cards.

Alphabet Books

Another way to play with words and enhance vocabulary is through the use of alphabet books. "Alphabet books?" you say. "Aren't they just for little kids?" Absolutely not. You'll be amazed at the sophistication and the instructional potential of many alphabet books once you start exploring them through your new lens as a content area literacy teacher. They can help your students grasp concepts, encounter new terms, and appreciate the creativity and artistry of the authors and illustrators within the genre. For example, readers may pore over the detailed artwork in Graeme Base's *Animalia* (1986) while having the concept of alliteration reinforced; and as they explore the "I" page and read "Ingenious Iguanas Improvising an Intricate Impromptu on Impossibly Impractical Instruments," they may note parts of speech, prefixes, and suffixes.

Students can hone critical-thinking skills as they argue issues of censorship and the appropriateness of Eve Merriam and Lane Smith's *Halloween ABC* (1995) for elementary or secondary school students. It starts off with the letter A being represented by *apple*, which couldn't be more traditional, but the poem accompanying the letter ends by describing the delicious apple as being *malicious*, as well as delicious, causing death with one bite. D stands for *demon*, N for *nightmare*, R for the *rope* that forms a hangman's noose. I've listened to teachers argue about this alphabet book; some say their students

have great fun with it, while others call it dark, disturbing, unwholesome, subtly dangerous.

Science teachers can tap into the affective realm when teaching about the destruction of habitat and extinction of species by using books such as *V for Vanishing, The Extinct Alphabet Book* and *Aardvarks, Disembark!* Figure 5.9 provides a sampling of alphabet books you could choose from as you create a classroom library that matches your curricular topics and goes beyond them. You might also choose some alphabet books just for their beauty, innovation, cleverness, and aesthetic appeal.

BookTalk   5.4

When we have something unpleasant to tell someone, we sometimes try to soften the news by using *euphemisms*. Some people avoid the hard word *dead* by using *passed away* or *departed*; workers get *laid off* or *transitioned*; companies *downsize*. William Lutz coined the term *doublespeak* to explain the ridiculous extent to which politicians, economists, lawyers, and business executives have taken this practice. In *Doublespeak: From Revenue Enhancement to Terminal Living* (1990) and *The New Doublespeak: Why No One Knows What Anyone's Saying Anymore* (1996), you can learn about and laugh about the terms that have been created to distort the truth, as well as learn how to fight doublespeak on an individual and societal level. Reading these books may prove the first step toward joining a language-consumers movement! You can also check out recent annual winners of the Doublespeak Award, given each year at the NCTE convention, in the *Quarterly Review of Doublespeak*.

FIGURE 5.9 *Content-relevant alphabet books appropriate for middle and high school students.*

MATH, SCIENCE, AND TECHNOLOGY

Crosbie, M. J., Rosenthal, K., & Rosenthal, S. (2000). *Arches to Zigzags: An Architecture ABC.* New York: Harry N. Abrams.

Jonas, A. (1990). *Aardvarks, Disembark!* New York: Greenwillow Books.

Markle, S., & Markle, W. (1998). *Gone Forever: An Alphabet of Extinct Animals.* New York: Atheneum.

Mullins, P. (1994). *V for Vanishing: An Alphabet of Endangered Animals.* New York: HarperCollins.

Munro, R., & Maddex, D. (1986). *Architects Make Zigzags: Looking at Architecture from A to Z.* New York: Wiley.

Palotta, J. (1989). *The Yucky Reptile Alphabet Book.* Watertown, MA: Charlesbridge Publishing.

Palotta, J. (1993). *The Extinct Alphabet Book.* Watertown, MA: Charlesbridge Publishing.

Poortvliet, R., & Huyben, W. (1989). *The Book of the Sandman and the Alphabet of Sleep.* New York: Harry N. Abrams.

Rosen, M. J., & Butler, D. (2000). *Avalanche.* Cambridge, MA: Candlewick Press.

Schwartz, D. M. (1998). *G Is for Googol: A Math Alphabet Book.* Berkeley, CA: Tricycle Press.

Schwartz, D. M. (2001). *Q Is for Quark: A Science Alphabet Book.* Berkeley, CA: Tricycle Press.

ENGLISH

Base, G. (1986). *Animalia.* New York: Harry N. Abrams.

Bourke, L. (1991). *Eye Spy: A Mysterious Alphabet.* San Francisco: Chronicle Books.

Harley, S. (2000). *Fly with Poetry: An ABC of Poetry.* Honesdale, PA: Wordsong.

Yolen, J., & Mills, L. (1990). *Elfabet: An ABC of Elves.* Boston: Little, Brown.

FINE ARTS

Anno, M. (1975). *Anno's Alphabet.* New York: Crowell.

Cox, P. (2001). *Abstract Alphabet: A Book of Animals.* San Francisco: Chronicle Books.

Horenstein, H. (2000). *A Is for ?: A Photographer's Alphabet of Animals.* New York: Scholastic.

J. Paul Getty Museum. (1997). *A Is for Artist: A Getty Museum Alphabet.* Los Angeles, CA: Author.

Johns, S. (1999). *The Alphabet Book: Alphabets for Design and Decoration.* London: Aurum.

Johnson, S. T. (1995). *Alphabet City.* New York: Viking.

Kelly, J., & Koeth, A. (Eds.). (2000). *Artist and Alphabet: Twentieth Century Calligraphy and Letter Art in America.* Boston: D. R. Godine in association with the American Institute of Graphic Arts and the Society of Scribes.

Mayers, F. C. (1988). *ABC: Musical Instruments from the Metropolitan Museum of Art.* New York: Harry N. Abrams.

Mayers, F. C. (1998). *ABC: Egyptian Art from the Brooklyn Museum.* New York: Harry N. Abrams.

Pelletier, D. (1996). *The Graphic Alphabet.* New York: Orchard.

Rubin, C. E. (Selector). (1989). *ABC: Americana from the National Gallery of Art.* Orlando, FL: Harcourt Brace/Gulliver.

Wilks, M. (1986). *The Ultimate Alphabet.* New York: Henry Holt.

SOCIAL STUDIES

Aylesworth, J. (1992). *The Folks in the Valley: A Pennsylvania Dutch ABC.* New York: HarperFestival.

de Mejo, O. (1992). *Oscar de Mejo's ABC.* New York: HarperCollins.

Der Manuelian, P. (1995). *Hieroglyphs from A to Z.* New York: Scholastic.

Hall, F., & Oehm, K. (1998). *Appalachian ABCs.* Johnson City, TN: Overmountain Press.

Hudson, W., & Wesley, V. W. (1997). *Afro-Bets Book of Black Heroes from A to Z: An Introduction to Important Black Achievers for Young Readers.* East Orange, NJ: Just Us Books.

Johnson, J. (1988). *Sanitation Workers A to Z.* New York: Walker.

Jordan, M., & Jordan, T. (1996). *Amazon Alphabet.* New York: Scholastic.

Kreeger, C., & Cartwright, S. (1991). *Alaska ABC Book.* (Last Wilderness Adventures). Wasilla, AK: Alaska ABC Book.

Musgrove, M., Dillon, L., & Dillon, D. (1976). *Ashanti to Zulu: African Traditions.* New York: Dial Press.

Paul, A. W. (1991). *Eight Hands Round: A Patchwork Alphabet.* New York: HarperCollins.

Paulson, T. (2000). *Rainforest ABC.* New York: Winslow Press.

Yorinks, A. (1999). *The Alphabet Atlas.* Delray Beach, FL: Winslow Press.

(continued)

FIGURE 5.9 *Continued.*

INTERDISCIPLINARY AND MISCELLANEOUS

Ada, A. F., & Silva, S. (1997). *Gathering the Sun: An Alphabet in Spanish and English.* New York: Lothrop, Lee & Shepard Books.

Alexander, R. (1997). *Alef Is Silent: A Hebrew Alphabet.* Seattle, WA: Inksleeves.

Bruchac, J., & Goetzl, R. F. (1997). *Many Nations: An Alphabet of Native Americans.* Mahwah, NJ: Bridgewater Books.

Brustad, K., & Al-Batal, M. (1995). *Alif Baa: Introduction to Arabic Letters and Sounds.* Washington, DC: Georgetown University Press.

Edwards, M. (1992). *Alef-Bet: A Hebrew Alphabet Book.* New York: Lothrop, Lee, & Shepard Books.

Ford, J. G. (1997). *K Is for Kwanzaa: A Kwanzaa Alphabet Book.* New York: Scholastic.

Hepworth, C. (1992). *Antics!: An Alphabet Anthology.* New York: Putnam.

Humez, A., & Humez, N. (1983). *Alpha to Omega: The Life and Times of the Greek Alphabet.* Boston: David R. Godine.

Jacobs, L., & Ohlsson, I. (1994). *Alphabet of Girls.* New York: Henry Holt.

Mayers, F. C. (1996). *Basketball ABC: The NBA Alphabet.* New York: Harry N. Abrams.

Rankin, L. (1991). *The Handmade Alphabet.* New York: Dial Books.

Roberts, P. L. (1987). *Alphabet Books as a Key to Language Patterns: An Annotated Action Bibliography.* Hamden, CT: Library Professional Publications.

Royston, A., & Pastor, T. (1993). *The A-to-Z Book of Cars.* New York: Scholastic.

Ruiers, M. (1996). *A Mountain Alphabet Book.* Toronto, Canada: Tundra Books.

Russell-McCloud, P. (1999). *A Is for Attitude: An Alphabet for Living.* New York: Harper-Collins.

Viorst, J., & Hull, R. (1994). *The Alphabet from Z to A: (With Much Confusion on the Way).* New York: Atheneum.

My preservice teachers enjoy creating alphabet books to teach vocabulary terms related to their curriculum. Figures 5.10 through 5.12 show examples of their products.

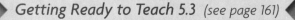

Getting Ready to Teach 5.3 *(see page 161)*

CELEBRATE THE BIRTH OF NEW WORDS

People coin new words as needed, sometimes by combining two existing words or morphemes, as in *cognitive science, bioethics, sociobiology, neuroscientist, pseudoscientist, psycholinguist, biochemical, computer science, psychophysiological, neurobiologist, Social Darwinism.* In Chris Crutcher's young adult novel *Stotan!* (1986), we learn that a *Stotan* is a very special kind of athlete, combining the characteristics of a *Stoic* and a *Spartan* (p. 27). Wilson, in *Consilience*, uses a Scottish term, *satisficing*, joining the meanings of *satisfying* and *suffice*, to discuss how humans make choices (p. 136).

Sometimes authors include word origins as part of a more extended explanation of new or difficult concepts. Note the following example:

The term "meme" was introduced about twenty years ago by the British biologist Richard Dawkins, who used it to describe a unit of cultural information comparable in its effects on society to those of the chemically coded instructions contained in the gene on the human organism. The name harks back to the Greek word *mimesis*, or imitation, for as Dawkins pointed out, cultural instructions are passed on from one generation to the next by example and imitation, rather than by the shuffling of genes that occurs between sperm and ova. Perhaps the best definition of a meme is "any permanent pattern of matter or information produced by an act of human intentionality." (Csikszentmihalyi, 1993, p. 120)

If students are taught to be aware of strategies like this that authors use, they can apply good reading strategies to learn the word, connecting it to its origin if that's helpful. Comprehension, as well as vocabulary development, may be increased.

One type of language study involves understanding how a word can be misused and misunderstood. For example, take the technical term Einstein used to describe his famous theory, *relativity.* K. C. Cole tells us in *The Universe and the Teacup* (1998), "Somehow relativity managed to slip

FIGURE 5.10   *An excerpt from an alphabet guide for world history.*

Allies were countries that fought with the United States against the **A**xis powers. The **A**llied powers included Britain, France, and Russia.

Blitzkrieg is a German word that means lightning war, which was one of Germany's attack methods.

Collective farms were government-run farms that Joseph Stalin ordered peasants to join prior to WW II.

D-Day was June 6, 1944; that was the day the Allies began the invasion of Europe during WW II.

Enola Gay was the American bomber that dropped the atomic bomb on Hiroshima, Japan.

France was one of the Allied powers; it surrendered early in the war.

GI Bill of Rights was an Act passed in 1944 to help returning veterans of WW II.

—Russell Hartwell

FIGURE 5.11   *Pages from an alphabet book for high school mathematics.*

Letters in Math?!

A is for Algebra, the study of

B is for Base angles, the bottom angles of a triangle.

C is for Congruent, a term meaning equal.

D is for Dilation, the size of a shape.

E is for Ellipse, a circle squashed in the center.

F is for Function, sometimes seen as a machine.

G is for Geometry, the study of shapes.

H is for Hyperbola, the set of all points that looks like this:

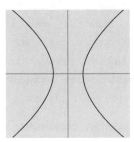

I is for Imaginary number, a number that does not exist— but does in an imaginary context!

J is for Joining line segments, two or more nonparallel line segments.

K is for Kite, a geometric figure with two congruent sides.

L is for Logarithm, another way to write an exponential equation.

M is for Monomial, an expression with one term.

N is for Negation, meaning the negative of a statement.

O is for Octagon, an eight-sided figure.

P is for Parallel lines, two lines that never meet.

Q is for the Quartic function, a function of degree 4.

R is for the Radical numbers, numbers that have decimals.

S is for Slope, the elevation of a straight line.

T is for Trinomial, an expression with three terms.

U is for Undefined, occurs when dividing any number by 0.

V is for Vector, a quantity with both direction and magnitude.

W is for Width, the thickness of an object.

X is for the X-axis, the horizontal axis in a plane.

Y is for the Y-axis, the vertical axis in a plane.

Z is for the Z-axis, which makes a plane three dimensional.

—Alisha James

into conventional wisdom with a meaning opposite to its true message. While Einstein's theories focused on invariant properties of things that do not change, no matter what, the popular translation came out as some version of 'There is no truth; truth depends on how you look at it'; or simply, 'Everything is relative'" (pp. 172–173). Student word detectives can research to find more examples of this type.

FIGURE 5.12   *An alphabet book for American history.*

An Alphabet of Indians*

A is for Apache, who know the desert well.

B is for the Blackfeet. In the northern plains they dwell.

C is for Cheyenne. They are always counting coup.

D is for Dakota, sometimes called the Sioux.

E is for the Erie, a people near the lake.

F is for the Flathead; strong cradles do they make.

Gabrielino starts with G. They live along the Bay.

H is for the Hopi. They make things out of clay.

I is for the Iroquois, 6 tribes or 5 at least.

J is for Jicarilla, Apaches in the East.

K is for the Kickapoo. They live in many places.

L is for Laguna. Kosharis[+] paint their faces.

M is for the Mohawk. They protect the northern door.

N is for the Navajo, "code talkers" in the war.

O is for the Osage, out on the southern plains.

P is for the Pima; remember Ira Hayes[+].

Q is found in Quapaw. They're related to the Sioux.

R is for the rivers that provide for me and you.

S is for the Seneca. They live in New York State.

T is for Tuscarora. They arrived a little late.

U is for the Ute, surviving on the basin.

V is for the vision quest, known to many nations.

Wompanoag starts with W; so does where, and when, and why.

Nothing starts with X; I'm not even going to try.

Y is found in Yaqui, way down in Mexico.

Z is for the Zuni, a good Pueblo tribe to know.

[*] The author, who is a member of the Mescalero Apache Nation of New Mexico, prefers the term "Indians" to "Native Americans."

[+] Kosharis—ceremonial clowns among the Pueblo nations

[+] Ira Hayes—a member of the Pima Nation; he was photographed holding up the flag at Iwo Jima (the man in the back)

—*Stephen Crawford*

ACTION RESEARCH   5.C

What were your answers to Question 4 in the Activating Prior Knowledge 5.1 exercise, which asked you to think of words that you recently acquired in your vocabulary from courses, hobbies, and so on? Combine your answers with those of your classmates, search for other words that have recently come into being, and create a chart for your classroom. This can then be used as a model when you have your own students explore new words in your discipline. The book *Neo-Words: A Dictionary of the Newest and Most Unusual Words of Our Times* (Barnhart, 1991) can serve as a resource for this activity. Also, the "English in the News" section of the January 2001 issue of *English Journal*, noting that hundreds of words appear for the first time in the latest edition of the *Random House Webster's College Dictionary*, offers this sampling (taken from the *San Francisco Chronicle*, June 21, 2000):

High tech terms include *dot-com, antiglare* (as in headlights), *slamming* (changing long-distance service without the customer's permission), and *zetta-byte* (one sextillion bytes). Other terms include *24-7, energy bar, megaplex, fashionistas, Gen Y'ers,* and *senior moment.* Slang phrases include *dead-cat bounce* (a temporary recovery in stock prices after a steep decline), *eye candy* (attractive person of limited merit), and *my bad!* (whoops!).

The article continues with a few historical examples:

In the 1940s, new words included *apartheid, atom bomb, baby-sit, barf, cheeseburger,* and *gobbldygook.* New words in the 1980s included *AIDS, caller ID, channel surf, dis, trophy wife,* and *wannabe.* The 1990s added *anatomically correct, bad hair day, carjacking, soccer mom, step aerobics,* and *World Wide Web.* (p. 413 of *English Journal*)

FIGURE 5.13   *Group language exploration.*

Similes We Found in Barbara Kingsolver's
High Tide in Tucson: Essays from Now or Never

"A magazine piece is meant to bloom like an ephemeral flower on the page, here today and recycled tomorrow . . . " (p. ix).

"*Want* is a thing that unfurls unbidden like a fungus, opening large upon itself, stopless, filling the sky. But needs, from one day to the next, are few enough to fit in a bucket, with room enough left to rattle like brittlebush in a dry wind" (p. 13).

"The schoolhouse's plaster ceilings are charted with craters like maps of the moon and likely to crash down without warning" (p. 35).

"The part of my soul that is driven to make stories is a fierce thing, like a ferret—long, sleek, incapable of sleep, it digs and bites through all I know of the world" (p. 43).

BookTalk   5.5

Have you ever felt insecure because you know a word from seeing it in print, but you're not really sure how to say it? *The Big Book of Beastly Mispronunciations: The Complete Opinionated Guide for the Careful Speaker,* by Charles Harrington Elster (1999), can come to your rescue! In his introduction, the author sort of gives his own booktalk, promising:

> The Big Book of Beastly Mispronunciations *is much more than a dry list of acceptable and unacceptable pronunciations. It provides historical background. It reports the opinions of numerous authorities. It offers pithy explanations and passionate opinion . . . a concise and accessible discussion of past and present usage, alternative pronunciations, levels of acceptability, analogies and tendencies, the vicissitudes of human nature, the terrible swift sword of phonetic justice. (p. xi)*

I've read lots of entries and received confirmation on pronunciation, as well as entertaining commentary on words such as *gondola, awry, en route, entrepreneur, remuneration, albeit, schism, eschew, assuage,* and *diaspora.* I chuckled throughout as I learned. And I'm much more secure about speaking in public! So, I recommend this book to you.

USE LANGUAGE EXPLORATION CENTERS

Some teachers set aside a corner of the classroom or some other space and fill it with resources, including those mentioned previously. In a class where several kinds of activities are going on (e.g., a reading–writing workshop), a learning center like this could offer opportunities for individuals or small groups. You might have project suggestions, or students could simply set their own goals and use the learning center to meet them. The results of their explorations can be posted on your word walls, or students can present their findings to the class. For example, in a high school English class, a study group might explore the use of metaphoric language and similes in nonfiction and post the findings as shown in Figure 5.13.

BookTalk   5.6

After you take care of any potential pronunciation problems by reading Elster's book (see BookTalk 5.5), you'll be ready to tackle issues of style, spelling, usage, and grammar by reading Karen Elizabeth Gordon's *Torn Wings and Faux Pas* (1997). She explains and illustrates the differences between confusing pairs of words such as *imply/infer, fewer/less, all together/altogether, reluctant/reticent, compliment/omplement,* and *tortuous/torturous.* She uses humorous examples to teach lessons on such topics as parallel constructions, split infinitives, and double negatives. This book makes grammar lessons painless.

HIGHLIGHT LANGUAGE CONNECTIONS IN YOUR DISCIPLINE

You may get the occasional student who tries to tell you that talk about language should be left in the English classroom. You can assure him that is not the case, nor should it be. People in every field take words seriously. Language issues are central to every subject area; it's up to you to show the students how to capitalize on the benefits language study can provide them as they learn the discipline you teach. Dial and Baines (1998) point out that "the mere mention of mathematics is enough to strike terror in the hearts of many language teachers" (p. 112), but considering that mathematics is a language, they think it's time for this to stop. They call on secondary language teachers to present specific lessons to enhance the learning of math vocabulary and concepts, teach the history of numbers and how our words and symbols for numbers developed, and collaborate with math teachers on cross-curricular lessons. So, I'll use math for the purposes of our discussion.

The battle in Norton Juster's *The Phantom Tollbooth* (1961) was fought between the residents of Digitopolis and Dictionopolis over the superiority of numbers or words. Although the book ends with a happy resolution, in our schools, math and language still too often represent two distinct camps, with walls separating classrooms and artificial boundaries separating ideas. Teachers add to the dilemma when they present the two subjects as opposing systems (Bullock, 1994; Dial & Baines, 1998).

In fact, there is a vital connection between learning the two subjects. The greater the students' ability to read and write, the greater their comprehension of math is likely to be (Maida, 1995). Students sometimes fail at math because of a difficulty understanding the word problems used to show the application of math skills. Students need to understand that math is a language and that language is used to teach math (Miller, 1993). Vocabulary is essential to math; there are concepts and terms that are prerequisite for understanding many math principles.

Some textbook authors recognize the need to help students understand math through the use of language. They may highlight or box definitions and key words, or explain terms further in marginal notes. Teachers, of course, must make sure their students take advantage of and use the language aids the textbooks supply. Math textbooks might also help students see and make connections beyond numbers and math theories by using language to present cases and real-world applications. Sincich (1990), in *Statistics by Example*, points out that his text differs from most in that it uses real data sets, such as the set of starting salaries of college graduates, and that concepts and statistical methods are motivated by and based on these real data sets. Think about how you could interest students in studying and applying statistical principles to case studies such as "The SAT Pill," "New Coke Is It," "Lottery Buster!", "Statistics Can Scare You to Death," "The M*A*S*H Generation's View of the Business World," "Moral Development of Teenagers," "The Lonely Hearts Club," "Mental Imagery and the Third Dimension," and "Birth Order and Car Salesmen: Is Last Best?" That's just a sampling of what this math textbook offers.

You'll be well prepared to begin a discussion of transdisciplinary math projects if you read books on math topics yourself. For example, I found the table of contents of *The Universe and the Teacup: The Mathematics of Truth and Beauty*, by K. C. Cole (1998), to be quite inviting. I wasn't intimidated by chapters with names such as "The Signal in the Haystack," "Fair Division: The Wisdom of Solomon," and "Emmy and Albert: The Unvarying Nature of Truth." Math and language work beautifully together.

EXPLORE VOCABULARY WITHIN LITERATURE CIRCLES

When small groups of students are discussing texts and learning from each others' responses, vocabulary enhancement can be quite naturally worked in. Daniels (1994) suggests assigning the role of "vocabulary enricher" to one of the members of the group;

BookTalk 5.7

Want to learn more than 100 math terms and have fun in the process? Check out David M. Schwartz's *G is for Googol: A Math Alphabet Book* (1998). For each letter of the alphabet, Schwartz explains a mathematical concept, mathematician, or application. He includes stories, history lessons, problem-solving techniques, and problems for readers to try. Hilarious pictures by Marissa Moss accompany his mini-lessons on topics ranging from the abacus to the concept of a zillion. In addition to the targeted word, he adds lists of other mathematical words beginning with each letter, which are later defined in a glossary.

One of my favorite chapters is "M Is for Möbius Strip." Schwartz teaches the meaning of the term inductively by instructing readers to make a loop from a strip of paper, give it a twist, and tape the ends together. In the course of his explanation, Schwartz defines *topologists* as "mathematicians who study what happens to various shapes and solids when they are pushed and pulled and twisted and cut and contorted in different ways" (p. 26) and states that a topologist would say that a Möbius strip has only one side. He gives an example of a kind of conveyor belt being an industrial application of the principle, and he gives suggestions for experiments that readers can do to examine the properties of the concept.

If you teach a subject other than math, you could use this book, along with its companion, *Q Is for Quark: A Science Alphabet Book* (2001), as a model and encourage your students to make an alphabet book using words from history, science, art, physical education, and so on.

FIGURE 5.14   *A literature group vocabulary project.*

New and Interesting Words Our Literature Groups Found in Books About World War II

Number the Stars

Resistance, rationed, insolently, synagogue, exasperated, congregation, haughtily, implored, appliquéd, dubiously, protruding

Darkness Over Denmark: The Danish Resistance and the Rescue of the Jews:

tribunal, covert, sabotage, cryptic, Torah, Aryan, martial law, haven

The Devil's Arithmetic

Seder, prophet, Yiddish, portents, cauldron, tremulous, discernible, rabbi

The Hiding Place

Gestapo, barracks, Gentile, imperceptibly, yearning, deportation, threadbare, interminable, recurrent

The Good Fight: How World War II Was Won

infamy, isolationists, relocation center, blitzkrieg, bunkers, pillboxes, authoritarian, ex post facto, embargo, kamikaze

I Have Lived a Thousand Years

intolerable, desperation, straggle, liquidated, infirmary, stamina, interrogation, internment, inexplicably, confiscate, pandemonium, deportation, liberate

---

the other students have different roles and responsibilities. Harmon (1998) conducted a case study of vocabulary teaching and learning in a seventh-grade literature-based classroom. She reported rich examples of the vocabulary enrichers choosing words from texts to discuss and employing a variety of tactics, including defining words they had looked up before the literature circles met, asking group members for definitions and ideas, and reading aloud from passages containing targeted words. They sometimes modeled their behavior on their teacher's actions, using synonyms, constructing word meanings, asking for comments. Harmon notes, "These reflections about new words were springboards for critical discussions about important new concepts and literary elements in the readings" (p. 522). Figure 5.14 shows a poster created by literature groups that read books about World War II and, among other things, kept a record of words from the books that they added to their vocabulary.

MODEL AND ENCOURAGE VOLUMINOUS SELF-SELECTED READING

Have I mentioned that I'm a proponent of wide reading? The importance of pleasure reading can't be overemphasized. Research shows that vocabulary knowledge is an important predictor of reading comprehension, and that from 25 to 50 percent of the estimated growth of students' vocabulary can be attributed to incidental learning from context while reading (Baumann & Kameenui, 1991; Nagy, Anderson, & Herman, 1987; Nagy, Herman, & Anderson, 1985). Cunningham and Stanovitch (1998) explain:

> If most vocabulary is acquired outside of formal teaching, then the only opportunities to acquire new words occur when an individual is exposed to a word in written or oral language that is outside his current vocabulary.... this will happen vastly more often while reading than while talking or watching television. (p. 10)

Their research demonstrated that "reading yields significant dividends for everyone—not just for the 'smart kids' or the more able readers. Even the child with limited reading and comprehension skills will build vocabulary and cognitive structures through reading" (p. 14).

William F. Buckley, Jr. (1996) gives a great example of the value of practice and voluminous reading in terms of vocabulary development. He tells a humorous story of a man who complained to him about his use of too many long words in *National Review*, which the man had just subscribed to the month before. A year later, he met the man again, who commended him for taking his advice, for he was bothered less and less by difficult vocabulary. In reality, Buckley says the law of the flexed muscle was at work:

> The moral here is really liberating. The unused muscle begins to work out. In January it hurts awfully, looking at all those unfamiliar words—like the first day of skiing, or tennis. In February, the incidence of such words is a little less, and you feel the relief. In March it still happens to you, but only now and again. By June?—Yes. You feel no pain at all. (p. 40)

Buckley goes on to explain the analogy:

> It isn't necessarily that your vocabulary has increased at a geometric rate. It is that the words you used to think of as alien and intimidating are less and less that, as they continue to crop up and your mind and imagination are gradually includ-ing them in your immediate-visibility range. If you are assigned the job of sportswriter . . . , you gradually get to feel at home with any number of words you simply could not have defined before. Exactly the same thing happens, or has happened, to the reader of the Sports Section. Or of the Financial Section. After a while you feel quite at home. (p. 40)

Encourage your students to read independently. Share with them the benefits to their vocabulary and comprehension. Perhaps more important, model the practice yourself and share information about what you are reading with them. Give regular booktalks, build a classroom library, provide time for reading, and listen to students as they talk about what they're reading and show that they are indeed reaching your goal of having them become more conscious of the language and concepts in your subject.

PART THREE

Specific Strategies for Teaching Vocabulary in Content Area Lessons

Part Two dealt with various ways you can help your students become language enthusiasts and independent word explorers. This section focuses on ways you can help your students learn the vocabulary necessary for particular lessons, curricular topics, and reading materials in your discipline. As usual, my categories are not entirely discrete; you'll find them overlapping.

DIRECT TEACHING OF DEFINITIONS

Although a great deal of vocabulary knowledge can be and is gained incidentally from context (Schatz & Baldwin, 1986), research shows that "if you want a student to know what a particular word means, explaining it is unquestionably more effective than waiting for the student to encounter it numerous times in context" (Nagy & Scott, 2000, p. 277). There will be many times when you'll have to point out to students that, in order to comprehend a certain reading, whether it be a textbook section, a primary document, a literary selection, or an article, they'll have to know the meaning of certain words, possibly vocabulary they have not previously encountered.

Specialized and technical words, explained earlier, usually require direct instruction. Often you'll do this before students begin reading an assigned text. Similar to the preview strategy modeled in the last chapter, the teacher can script an introduction calling attention to key terms. Or she can hand out a list of words and definitions the students can keep handy as they read. The following scenario illustrates what direct teaching of a vocabulary term for an English lesson might sound like:

> For the next few weeks we'll be reading and writing memoirs, so I want to begin by making sure you understand the term itself. Does anyone want to define the word for us? (Silence.) Ok, that's fine. Think of the word *memory*. A memoir is a crafted account of a person's memories of past events or of a particular time in his or her life. It comes from the French *memoire* and from the Latin *memoiria*, meaning memory. So, that makes sense, right?
>
> Charlotte, would you be the recorder at our word wall as we brainstorm words that might be related to memory and memoir? (Students call out *memo, memorabilia, memorial, memorable, memorize,* and *memorandum.*)

Great! Now, you already know the term that applies to a first-person account of someone's life, right? (She looks at Richard, who says, "Autobiography?") That's right! We talked about the parts of that word: auto- means self, bio- means life, -graph means write, so that word makes perfect sense. Well, a memoir is similar to an autobiography because it does involve a person recalling autobiographical information. But it doesn't attempt to be complete; it's selective; it focuses on one memory or one area or one part of a life. For example, one of your reading choices will be Annie Dillard's *An American Childhood*. Dillard is an author who won a Pulitzer Prize for her book *Pilgrim at Tinker Creek*, which is a detailed account of her observations of nature while living alone for a time. Beth, you read that as an independent choice, didn't you? But in her memoir, Dillard concentrates only on her growing up, her school years; she deliberately ends it as she's on the brink of adulthood.

Here's another book you might choose to read. You're familiar with the novels of Betsy Byars; we read *The Pinballs* as a class, and we've got several of her other books in our classroom library. Well, look at the cover of this book, *The Moon and I*. The bottom of the cover identifies the book as a memoir. The chapters tell various stories about the author, all relating in some way to her becoming or being a writer. There are many other things she'd have to include if she were writing an autobiography, telling the story of her life. She's chosen instead to write this as a memoir.

So, *memoir*. You know the definition. After we read and write several memoirs, you'll have a richer understanding of the term and of this very popular genre. Tonight, I'd like you to ask a few family members or friends if they can define memoir, and if they've read any memoirs or written one. We'll talk about your discoveries tomorrow.

Figure 5.15 shows how a teacher plans to provide and teach vocabulary in preparation for her students reading *The Phantom Tollbooth*.

VOCABULARY GUIDES TO ACCOMPANY TEXTS

You should become really strong in this area as you teach your subject and assign various readings, both in and beyond textbooks, to your students. If you identify the vocabulary that students will need or that you anticipate they may have trouble with, you can help them to prepare for their reading by completing a guide you create, or let them complete the guide as they progress through the text. Having your reading guide as a tool will in some way be like having you with them, even if they're reading outside class.

Figures 5.16 through 5.18 are examples of vocabulary guides created by preservice education students for discipline-specific texts. Critique them and think of ways to modify them for the texts your students use.

USE OF ANALOGIES

Creating analogies and constructing images can be effective tools to forge lasting links between words and their meanings. Do you recognize when you, your students, people you talk with, or authors utilize analogy, connecting ideas and images by way of comparison?

You're familiar with the first sentence of Lincoln's Gettysburg Address: "Fourscore and seven years ago, our forefathers brought forth, upon this continent, a new nation, conceived in liberty, and dedicated to the proposition that all men are created equal." Try saying it out loud, really listening to the sounds and cadence of the sentence. Here's how Thompson (1996a) describes what he hears:

> Lincoln was using the music of the voice to enhance and support his meaning, and only by hearing the music can we understand the grammar. For the first 14 words, Lincoln is playing the bass notes, the *o*s and the *u*s enriched by the *r*s. Hear the sounds: *four score, year, ago, our, forefather, brought, forth, upon, continent.* Lincoln is playing an oboe or a bassoon. And then suddenly, rising above the low tones, we have sounds, alliterated with *n*s, that are higher and lighter—a flute: *new, nation.* And all of this leads to the finale: the most important word, uttered last so that it echoes in the silence at the end of the sentence: *equal.* Equal. (p. 166)

Thompson goes on to interpret the language of the speech in terms of assonance, consonance, and alliteration, but he has begun with a comparison, utilizing an analogy to music made by instruments that helps readers understand what he means by those words.

Sometimes, we can begin to comprehend a new concept by comparing it to something we already know. When we use relationships, and point out how an unfamiliar concept is like and unlike a familiar one, we can help students learn and remember new information and terms. We can also listen carefully for the images our students create naturally and encourage them to strive consciously to create metaphors that help them understand and remember concepts. For example, Whitin and Whitin (1996), after teaching the concept of geometric progressions in an intermediate grade math

FIGURE 5.15 *A graphic organizer and word list for* The Phantom Tollbooth.

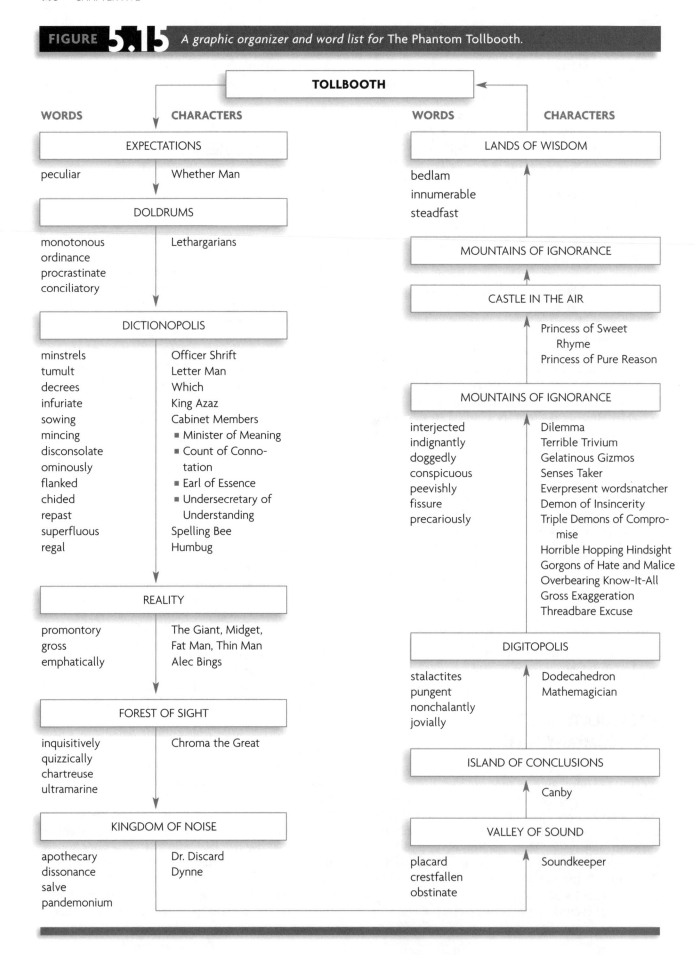

TOLLBOOTH

WORDS	CHARACTERS

EXPECTATIONS

peculiar   Whether Man

DOLDRUMS

monotonous   Lethargarians
ordinance
procrastinate
conciliatory

DICTIONOPOLIS

minstrels   Officer Shrift
tumult   Letter Man
decrees   Which
infuriate   King Azaz
sowing   Cabinet Members
mincing   ▪ Minister of Meaning
disconsolate   ▪ Count of Conno-
ominously   tation
flanked   ▪ Earl of Essence
chided   ▪ Undersecretary of
repast   Understanding
superfluous   Spelling Bee
regal   Humbug

REALITY

promontory   The Giant, Midget,
gross   Fat Man, Thin Man
emphatically   Alec Bings

FOREST OF SIGHT

inquisitively   Chroma the Great
quizzically
chartreuse
ultramarine

KINGDOM OF NOISE

apothecary   Dr. Discard
dissonance   Dynne
salve
pandemonium

WORDS	CHARACTERS

LANDS OF WISDOM

bedlam
innumerable
steadfast

MOUNTAINS OF IGNORANCE

CASTLE IN THE AIR

Princess of Sweet
Rhyme
Princess of Pure Reason

MOUNTAINS OF IGNORANCE

interjected   Dilemma
indignantly   Terrible Trivium
doggedly   Gelatinous Gizmos
conspicuous   Senses Taker
peevishly   Everpresent wordsnatcher
fissure   Demon of Insincerity
precariously   Triple Demons of Compromise
Horrible Hopping Hindsight
Gorgons of Hate and Malice
Overbearing Know-It-All
Gross Exaggeration
Threadbare Excuse

DIGITOPOLIS

stalactites   Dodecahedron
pungent   Mathemagician
nonchalantly
jovially

ISLAND OF CONCLUSIONS

Canby

VALLEY OF SOUND

placard   Soundkeeper
crestfallen
obstinate

FIGURE 5.15 *Continued*

Structured Overview (Graphic Organizer)

For *The Phantom Tollbooth* by Norton Juster

Included here are a structured overview on the entire book and a word list. The overview is to be made into a transparency and presented on an overhead projector. The structured overview is to be presented before the students read the book. The word list will be handed out after the following discussion. The word list was put together to assist the students while they read.

When the structured overview is presented I will **ask the students to observe** the different areas that the main character travels to, the characters he encounters in each area, and the vocabulary that is present in each section of the book. I will then start with the vocabulary listed for Expectations on the overview. I will **ask for definitions** in the students' own words. If students do not come up with a definition for a certain term, I will try to give clues. If students are still puzzled about a certain term or terms, I will skip over them because the students will become familiar with all the meanings when they receive the accompanying guide. Then I will **ask if anyone can try to describe an area based upon the name of the area** and the characters listed for each area.

Some examples of questions that I can ask to stimulate background knowledge and increase the classes' interest and curiosity in reading the story:

What is the purpose of a tollbooth?

What is a Witch? What do you think a Which is? The two names sound the same; how do they differ in meaning? Describe what you believe the behavior and appearance of a Which would be.

Word List

For *The Phantom Tollbooth* by Norton Juster

peculiar (1) exclusively individual; distinctive. (2) odd; strange.

monotonous (1) continued in the same unvarying tone. (2) unvarying. (3) wearisome because of this.

ordinance (1) an established rule, rite, or law. (2) a statute or regulation, especially one of a local government.

procrastinate to put off to a future time; defer.

conciliate (1) to win or gain the affections of. (2) to reconcile.

minstrels (1) in medieval times, any one of a class of men who traveled about singing their compositions to the accompaniment of a harp or a lute. (2) a performer in a minstrel show (a variety show).

tumult (1) the noisy commotion of a number of people; uproar. (2) great confusion or disturbance of the mind or emotions.

decree (1) an ordinance, law, or edict. (2) a judicial decision: to determine, settle, command, or establish by decree; ordain: to make or publish a decree.

infuriate to enrage; madden.

sow (1) to scatter or plant in or on. (2) to instill as an idea, or disseminate, as propaganda.

mincing affectedly elegant.

disconsolate (1) sad; inconsolable. (2) cheerless.

ominous foreboding evil; inauspicious.

superfluous more than enough or necessary; excessive.

flank (1) a side of anything. (2) the right or left side of a formation, army, etc.: to be located at the side of.

chide to reprove, usually mildly.

repast a meal; food and drink.

regal of or pertaining to a king; royal.

promontory a headland; high peak jutting into the sea.

gross flagrant, bad, unrefined.

emphatic (1) uttered with emphasis. (2) forcible; significant.

The vocabulary guide below, based on the "Knowledge Rating Strategy" (Blachowitz, 1986) is accompanied by a real newspaper article middle school math students may find interesting. Complete the chart, then answer the questions based on your reading. Think about whether students could be helped by having this vocabulary strategy accompany their reading of the text.

DIRECTIONS: The chart lists several words that you'll encounter in the article "Student Shows Big Interest in Math." For each word, check the column that indicates your level of knowledge about it.

Word	I can define	I can use	I've seen it	Clueless
nought	○	○	○	○
centrillion	○	○	○	○
mere	○	○	○	○
googol	○	○	○	○
centrillionth	○	○	○	○
Timillion	○	○	○	○
cryptography	○	○	○	○
googolplex	○	○	○	○

As you read the article, see how many of the unfamiliar words you can determine the meaning of. Which ones are defined in the text? Which can you figure out by using the context? Do you need to know every word in order to comprehend the passage? Write down a brief definition or synonym for the listed words. There's at least one word you may have to look up in the dictionary or ask someone the meaning of. Can you think of other words named after their discoverers or inventors?

STUDENT SHOWS BIG INTEREST IN MATH

By Larry Richardson

CAZENOVIA—Tim Gioncchetti's effort was all for nought. Nearly 92,000 noughts, in fact.

Inspired by a discussion of large numbers in his seventh-grade math class, Tim spent a month printing and taping together a number that's 735 feet long.

That's longer than the Washington Monument (555 feet) is tall. It's longer than 2 1/3 football fields (at 100 yards apiece). And it's nearly as long as Tim's favorite ill-fated ocean liner, the Titanic (882 feet).

His number, which doesn't have a name, is a 1 followed by 91,809 zeroes. The largest named number, according to one dictionary, is a centrillion, which has a mere 303 zeroes.

Tim recently showed up in math class with his number wrapped around a spool. Barry Parker, his math teacher at Cazenovia Middle School, said the project started innocently enough.

"We were discussing large numbers, and we were talking about a googol, which is a one followed by 100 zeroes," Parker said. "I stated it would be impossible to write a googol to the googol power, or a centrillion to the centrillionth power.

"Tim took that as a challenge to create a huge number, larger than he had ever seen before or that we had ever talked about."

Tim said he took a centrillion and raised it to the 303rd power. Then he calculated that he needed to print 26 pages—with 54 rows of zeroes on each page—on his home computer to tape the number together. He cut each horizontal row of zeroes into separate strips and attached them with cellophane tape—six rolls of it.

He said he spent up to an hour a day for a month cutting out the zeroes and taping them together.

Tim said he will call his number a Timillion until someone gives the number an official name.

"That could take a long time," said Andrew Odlysko, who heads the mathematics and cryptography research department at AT&T Labs in Slorham Park, NJ. "There is no official organization in charge of naming numbers," he said.

"While the dictionary stops at a centrillion, some huge numbers have been named," said Odlyzko. "A googolplex, for example, is a one followed by googol zeroes," Odlyzko said.

"That is a lot larger than your chap's number," he said.

Odlyzko said Tim's project is good for someone that age to do. "It's nice to encourage people to play around with numbers," he said.

Parker displayed the spool holding the Timillion in his classroom.

"We will take Tim's word for it that there are 91,809 zeroes," he said. "We didn't count them."

The Herald Co., Syracuse, NY © 1998/1999 *Herald-Journal/The Post-Standard.* All rights reserved. Reprinted with permission

This reading exercise serves several purposes. It can help students acquire technical vocabulary and concepts in the field of math. It provides practice reading the newspaper genre. It can help students gain confidence in the strategies they can use to figure out new words in math and other areas, and it may serve as motivation to spark their own mathematical reasoning and curiosity. You might connect it to the search that is currently being conducted by mathematicians to identify the largest prime number. You could give booktalks for *How Much Is a Million?* by D. Schwartz (1985) and *Anno's Mysterious Multiplying Jar* by M. Anno (1983). You could ask a couple of actual math questions based on the text.

FIGURE 5.16 *A vocabulary guide for science.*

Name _____   Date _____   Biology   Mitosis

Envision it. A sphere, and inside it lies a structure that looks like a small X. You notice that the X now duplicates itself to form a mirror image (XX). They move to the **middle** of the sphere and then each X moves **back** (X X) from the other. The sphere isn't large enough for the two of them, so it begins to split. Eventually, the cell pinches in two, and there is a **distance** between them now. You have just witnessed *mitosis.*

Not impressed? How about this? Mitosis is occurring thousands of times every minute in your body. In fact, by this time tomorrow, your body will have made more cells than there are hairs on your head. This process is what makes us grow, heals our wounds, and keeps us healthy.

Fortunately, such a complicated process as this can be broken down into six easy steps. It's easier to understand if you know what the names of the steps mean.

Before you read the section from your textbook on mitosis, I want you to consider these definitions.

WORD PART	DEFINITION
phase-	stage
inter-	between
pro-	before
meta-	change/middle
ana-	back
telo-	distant

You may have heard other words that contain these word parts. Jot down examples as you think of them. Now, reread the opening paragraph of this guide, and then read the textbook section on mitosis, noting especially the explanations for the words listed. Write the definitions, using the words in the text or your own words to explain the term.

Interphase: _____

_____

_____

Prophase: _____

_____

_____

Metaphase: _____

_____

_____

Anaphase: _____

_____

_____

Telophase: _____

_____

_____

—Dan Mainville

FIGURE 5.17 A vocabulary guide for literature.

On Monday, we will start reading *A Separate Peace* by John Knowles. This reading guide is to help you understand words that you will encounter and may not be familiar with. This exercise offers you another way to learn and grasp new words. For Monday, fill out the rest of the columns for each word listed. I have given you an example to get you started.

I will collect the guides to see how well they work for you, and then you will enter this into your learning log. Have fun!

*Helpful Hint: It is okay to talk with parents or friends for ideas. It is actually encouraged and will most likely heighten your understanding of the new vocabulary.

NEW VOCABULARY	WHAT IS IT?	WHAT IS IT LIKE?	WHAT ARE EXAMPLES?	WHAT OTHER CONCEPTS FIT IN THIS CATEGORY?
Contemplate	*Verb: to view or consider with continued attention*	*talking to yourself, in your head, about something*	*staring into your closet, trying to decide what to wear*	*thinking, rationalizing, figuring out*
interval				
convalescence				
prodigious				
reverberant				
inanimate				
primitive				

—*Donna Johnson*

FIGURE 5.18   *Reading guide for a mathematics lesson on numbers, averages, and infinity.*

DIRECTIONS: Before reading the book *The Phantom Tollbooth*, by Norton Juster, complete Steps 1–3. Complete Step 4 during your reading, and after reading the book, complete Step 5.

BEFORE READING

Step 1. Look up each of the following words in a dictionary; they will help you with the reading.

doldrums: _____

(Hint: This word has more than one meaning. Look for the definition that is similar to the idea of lethargy.)

infinite: _____

average: _____

Step 2. I've put a couple of words into sentences. See if you can figure out their meanings based on the contexts in which they are used.

"I really wish that baby would stop screaming; he's making an awful *din.*"

din: _____

"After watching a scary movie, Laurie 'saw' a ghost sitting on her bed, but when she turned on the light, it was gone. She realized it was only an *illusion.*"

illusion: _____

Step 3. This book follows the adventures of a young boy as he travels through many strange lands, including both Dictionopolis and Digitopolis. Provide a guess (hypothesis) as to what distinguishes these two cities.

Dictionopolis: _____

Digitopolis: _____

DURING READING

Step 4. While you are reading, keep a vocabulary journal. Jot down new words you come to and play with them. Guess what they might mean from the way they're used, write down other words they remind you of, or look up their definitions. Star your favorites.

AFTER READING

Step 5 (Reflection). Please respond to the following questions in your dialogue journals.

1. Which city would you prefer to live in: Dictionopolis or Digitopolis? Why?
2. Now which do you feel is more important for wisdom: words or numbers?
3. How did the vocabulary presented in this guide assist you with the reading?
4. What do you think of Milo trying to find *infinity*? Do you believe that real numbers are infinite, or is *infinity* just an *illusion*?
5. Think of ways you might use an *average* in your life.
6. Write one or more words you added to your vocabulary independently through reading this book. How might you teach the meaning of this word to your classmates?

   —*Erika Moshier*

class and having students experiment with some on their calculators, asked, "What do these numbers remind you of? What pictures do you have in your mind as you see numbers like these getting larger and larger?" (p. 62). One child, Andrew, wrote, "It reminds me of an avalanche because the numbers are snow fall[ing] down a mountain" (p. 62). Other children went on to interpret the meaning of his analogy. Danielle said, "An avalanche starts off . . . it pours down. The avalanche starts kind of small, and then starts getting bigger and bigger and bigger" (p. 63). Language play helped the students comprehend a mathematical concept.

A high school biology teacher (Middleton, 1991) suggests ways to encourage students to generate analogies to help them understand and remember key vocabulary terms. A copy of a guide he devised to use with vocabulary words that the students had been exposed to is shown in Figure 5.19. Its purpose is to further the students' understanding and application of the terms, as well as make the concept more relevant and easier to remember. Any of the association levels listed on the top right can be used; Middleton asks his students on the first day to use *appearance* as the criterion for the analogy, and *function* on the next day, and so forth. For Association Level 1, students might fill in "jigsaw puzzle" in the second column for the vocabulary term *enzyme*. They then draw the puzzle piece in the third column box. For Association Level 2, students might take the word *transpiration* and relate it to water going up a straw. An example of Association Level 3 is students comparing the vocabulary word *nucleus* to a brain.

Middleton describes an extension of the analogy strategy in his use of metaphorical sketches. He gives groups of students large sheets of paper and asks them to show a biological concept in terms of everyday topics. Students, whom Middleton notes generally put much humor and enthusiasm into this project, have come up with the following sketches:

- Cells (with organelles)—a city with a government, roads, and businesses
- Body Systems—factories processing and transporting materials
- Drugs and Alcohol—pollution in the environment to cause environmental problems
- Classification—sorting baseball cards in a collection

USE OF VISUALS

A similar instructional strategy involving verbal–visual associations is used successfully by high school teacher Gary Hopkins (Hopkins & Bean, 1998/1999)

in the Native American community where he teaches. He has his students draw a "Vocabulary Square," further divided into four boxes. In the upper-left, the student writes a content term or a root, prefix, or suffix. Next to it goes the definition. In the third box, the student puts an example of the concept, and in the final box, she draws a picture of the example. Students showed engagement with this type of word study, which led to lively class discussions, use of independent problem-solving skills, and good performance on tests (see Figure 5.20).

Pictures and illustrated texts can be most helpful to students learning new terms. Labeled pictures and diagrams make concepts clearer and help students retain the information. There are many well-done illustrated informational books that are full of vocabulary. Figure 5.21 lists some *visual dictionaries* and related material. As with alphabet books, you and your students can use these as models and create visual dictionaries for your own classroom library. We'll explore visual literacy and visual texts more thoroughly in Chapter 9.

SEMANTIC FEATURE ANALYSIS

Semantic feature analysis, developed by Johnson (Johnson & Pearson, 1984), can be used to clarify and enrich the meanings of known words, as well as to pre-teach words that are important to the comprehension of an assigned reading. It uses a grid that relates words in a category based on identifying characteristics; it invites comparison and contrast. Along the side, the teacher or students list terms that fall within the category being examined. Across the top are features that the listed concepts either have (+) or lack (−). Students complete the grid based on prior knowledge, listening to the teacher and others, or reading the passage. Figure 5.22 shows a student's feature analysis strategy used during a chapter on the Middle Ages.

USE OF VOCABULARY THINK-ALOUDS

Recall the discussion of think-alouds in Chapter 4, a strategy that can help students verbalize the mental strategies they use as they read. Think-alouds can be very helpful in terms of understanding and improving the strategies that students use as they tackle unfamiliar words in their reading. The use of vocabulary think-alouds has multiple benefits. Listening to the students helps you to know which strategies they use, how well the strategies are working for them, and what instruction or further guidance you can provide. They also help students reflect on their think-

FIGURE 5.19 *A vocabulary guide for science.*

Biology Analogies Worksheet

Name _____   Period _____   Date _____

Unit: _____

Association Level: _____

ASSOCIATION LEVELS

1—Appearance (shape, size, color)
2—Function or process
3—Another biological structure or process

VOCABULARY TERM	IS LIKE: (everyday object or process)	HOW? (make a sketch or explain briefly)
1.		
2.		
3.		
4.		
5.		
6.		
7.		
8.		
9.		
10.		
11.		
12.		
13.		
14.		
15.		
16.		
17.		
18.		
19.		
20.		

By James L. Middleton. Published in *The American Biology Teacher,* Vol. 53, No. 1 (Jan. 1991). Reprinted by permission of the author.

FIGURE **5.20** Vocabulary square for science.

WORD:	DEFINITION:
marsupial	a mammal whose young stay in a pouch on their mother's body for months after birth
EXAMPLES:	ILLUSTRATION:
opossum kangaroo	

ing, bringing their processes to a conscious level that makes them more aware of their skills, their problem areas, their active participation in bringing meaning to text. This, in turn, may make them more likely to employ the strategies you've taught them, including using structural clues, context, and reference materials, as they continue to read materials that are assigned or that they pursue independently.

Getting Ready to Teach 5.4 (see page 161)

ADAPTING STRATEGIES FOR STUDENTS WITH READING DISABILITIES

Strategies for figuring out new words and building vocabulary do not work equally well for all students. And the adaptations you make for the struggling readers in your classes depend on individuals' strengths and specific disabilities. Carlisle (1993) discusses approaches that may be most helpful for students with varying reading disabilities. Students with weak verbal abilities will probably not be helped by your merely supplying plenty of reading

FIGURE **5.21** Samples of visual dictionaries available for content area learning.

Berger, M., & Bonner, H. (2000). *Scholastic Science Dictionary*. New York: Scholastic.

Carley, R. (1997). *The Visual Dictionary of American Domestic Architecture*. New York: Henry Holt.

Challoner, J. (1996). *Visual Dictionary of Chemistry*. New York: DK Children's Books.

Corbeil, J., & Archambault, A. (2000). *Scholastic Visual Dictionary*. New York: Scholastic.

Dorling Kindersley. (2001). *Dorling Kindersley Ultimate Visual Dictionary 2001*. New York: Author.

Reynolds, D. W., Bies, P., Hall, N., & Ivanov, A. (1998). *Star Wars: The Visual Dictionary*. New York: Dorling Kindersley.

Stanchak, J. (2000). *Visual Dictionary of the Civil War*. New York: Dorling Kindersley.

The Visual Dictionary of Ancient Civilizations. (1994). New York: Dorling Kindersley.

FIGURE 5.22 *Example of semantic feature analysis for social studies.*

Category: Males in the Feudal System

	OWN LAND	WORK LAND	DEFEND LAND	ARE LIKE SLAVES
King	+	–	–	–
Lords	+	–	+	–
Lesser Lords	+	–	+	–
Knights	+	–	+	–
Serfs	–	+	+	+

—*Matt Wieczorek*

materials and opportunities for reading. They require direct instruction of such strategies as semantic mapping and semantic feature analysis to make connections and distinctions between words. You can provide modeling and practice, and then gradually allow your intervention to fade as these students show more independence in applying and using a strategy to understand concepts.

Carlisle provides strategies appropriate for those students with reading disabilities who have good verbal ability. These students' comprehension problems often stem from difficulties with word recognition. So, instruction in decoding and word recognition, along with vocabulary learning strategies, are necessary. Carlisle concludes:

> One point that becomes very clear in reviewing the array of instructional approaches is that several may be used for the same students. Different approaches may provide students with complementary systems of vocabulary growth. . . . Vocabulary development may be taught in different ways in different school courses. For example, while a program of semantic enrichment is underway in language arts, the science teacher may be using semantic mapping and the reading specialist may be working on the student's access to words through analysis of the morphological structure. Thus, different methods may be appropriate for different educational goals, and the exposure to a variety of approaches could be natural and effective. (pp. 103–104)

So, be ready to teach your students with reading disabilities a repertoire of vocabulary strategies that fit their particular strengths and needs. Don't overwhelm them with too many new words at a time, and give encouragement, opportunities for practice, and instructional support.

PART FOUR

Language Issues Relating to English Language Learners

I think it's appropriate to begin this section with a vocabulary mini-lesson, one author's explanation of the important difference between two words that on the surface seem quite similar. Beginning a chapter section with the heading "Mainstream Empowerment Acculturation," Cortez (1994) states:

> Notice I use the word acculturation, not assimilation. As I employ the two terms, acculturation means learning to *adapt* to mainstream culture, while assimilation means attempting to *adopt* it as yours. While assimilation is subtractive—as when schools encourage students to leave their ethnic and cultural differences behind and sometimes even to hide or escape from those differences—acculturation is additive because it involves encouraging students to learn to operate within the mainstream while at the same time participating, if they wish, in their various cultures. (p. 26)

Gunderson (2000) believes that "teachers, particularly those who teach 'academic' classes, must know about culture" (p. 693). He is dismayed because:

> We teachers as a group tend to view immigrant students as inferior because their English is not standard. . . . Teachers who judge students by their English development are trapped in views that are uninformed and destructive. Limited English proficiency does not mean limited intelligence. . . . [Immigrants'] chances of surviving in the content-based worlds of English, social studies, and biology are diminished by their teachers' attitudes and beliefs about ESL students and their cultures. (p. 694)

You must ensure that you don't become a teacher who is "trapped in views that are uninformed and destructive." One way you can show appreciation for your students' culture is to show an interest in their language, even as you teach your subjects. For example, a 16-year-old student in Gunderson's study bemoaned the fact that the class studied poetry, but always *English* poetry: "I try to talk about Spanish poetry, we have beautiful poems in Spanish in Honduras, but the teacher and the students were not interested" (p. 701). It would take very little time and would benefit everyone in the class to accommodate this student's desire. In addition to the poems the students contribute, the teacher might

add *Cool Salsa: Bilingual Poems about Growing Up Latino in the United States*, edited by L. M. Carlson (1995), to her classroom library.

You've learned that all of your students require varying degrees of help from you as they learn the general, specific, and technical vocabulary that allows them to progress in their understanding of and exploration in the subject you teach. In the last chapter, you were asked to think about how issues relating to prior knowledge might affect how your students with limited English proficiency would learn, and how scaffolding your instruction would be different as you helped them acquire the background knowledge the English speakers would likely already have. Now, I'd like you to think about vocabulary and grammar in relation to those students who are learning English. At first, it might seem that they (and you) are faced with an insurmountable task. How can you teach them all of the English words the other students have acquired over 12 or 16 years? And if they don't speak English fluently, how will you ever get them to comprehend the sophisticated concepts and specialized vocabulary of your curriculum? How will they be able to read the textbook, and write reports and journals and test answers?

As I've said before, you are not alone as you face this task, and no one expects you to be the expert on ESL issues. Get to know your students, help them feel comfortable, find out what they know in terms of English and in terms of your subject area. They may come with a lot of content knowledge in their native language, even more than your English speaking students. Depending on their first language, there might be words that are similar to the English words you'll be using as you teach. So, keep in mind that a deficit model must be avoided. ELLs do not have a *problem*, or something *wrong* with them, just different needs because of their unique circumstances. Help them to rejoice in the wonderful words they bring with them, even as you teach them wonderful new words in English. Learn some of *their* words, and have some content materials and recreational reading materials in the students' first language. It's appropriate to have reference books such as *NTC's American English Learner's Dictionary: The Essential Vocabulary of American Language and Culture* (Spears, 1998), and to teach the students how to use it along with other reference books in the library. Students learning English recognize and say that vocabulary is an issue for them. Gunderson (2000) found, "A large majority of students suggested that their learning of academic content in English would have been improved if they were allowed to consult their bilingual dictionaries or bilingual classmates who could explain difficult vocabulary" (p. 702). As one 16-year-old boy plainly put it, "We know hard words, chemistry and physics words, in Polish, but not English" (p. 702). So, do whatever makes sense to bring the two languages together as English learners grapple with concepts and content in your classes.

In addition, have books at hand, such as some of the alphabet books discussed earlier, that celebrate the beauty of language and will intrigue all students to learn at least a bit about a variety of languages. Encourage students to share words from various languages with each other. Convey the message and attitude that bilingualism is an asset; we do not want students who are learning English to lose their first language—developing and growing in both can go hand in hand.

You may find this list developed by Hatch and Brown (1995) helpful. Their research determined five essential steps that ESL students must complete in order to learn vocabulary, including:

- having sources for encountering new words,
- getting a clear visual and/or auditory image for the forms of new words,
- learning the meaning,
- making a memory connection between the forms and meanings of the words, and, of course,
- using the words.

Reflect on whether and how you provide instruction or assistance at each of those stages. Do you provide opportunities for the steps to occur? Do you model and teach strategies for learning words?

Keep several things in mind as you teach vocabulary to students with diverse language backgrounds. Because most textbooks are written for native speakers of English, they may use figures of speech, idioms, and words with multiple meanings that can cause ESL students difficulty. As you plan your lessons, read the text with the purpose of spotting some of the things you think may require explanation or clarification. Also, encourage the students to tell you when a term confuses them—and then teach it gladly.

As much as possible, teach concept development before vocabulary. If students experience a concept through a demonstration, hands-on experiments, simulation, role-playing, games, or the use of visuals,

if they first acquire an understanding of a principle or idea, it's easier to learn the word for it. For example, a science teacher can demonstrate the concept of *condensation* before or while teaching the term. Aim for knowledge and understanding of vocabulary rather than just memorization. Many of the activities described previously, such as the use of graphic organizers and semantic feature analysis, work well with ESL students. You'll note that many of the teaching strategies mentioned are examples of good teaching in general, benefiting all learners. So, choose meaningful activities that foster language growth and conceptual development simultaneously.

Of course, these students' vocabulary and knowledge of and ability to use grammatical structures of English is enhanced as they learn in authentic contexts with a lot of social interaction with their peers. A language-rich environment helps them flourish. But keep in mind that, although it only takes a couple of years for English learners to reach a level of proficiency in terms of conversational skills, it takes several years for many ESL students to reach a level of academic proficiency in English comparable to their native English-speaking classmates (Cummins, 1994). Teachers in content areas must be patient and persistent, and schools must make a long-term commitment to ensuring the academic progress of diverse learners. Vocabulary development is one aspect of this progress, and middle and high school teachers will do well to internalize these words of Cummins:

> The teaching of English as a second language should be integrated with the teaching of other academic content that is appropriate to students' cognitive level. By the same token, all content teachers must recognize themselves also as teachers of language. (1994, p. 56)

Figure 5.23 summarizes recommendations for teaching vocabulary to English language learners.

CONCLUSION

Blachowicz and Fisher (2000) summarize the main principles that research suggests should guide vocabulary instruction as follows:

1. Students should be active in developing their understanding of words and ways to learn them.
2. Students should personalize word learning.
3. Students should be immersed in words.
4. Students should build on multiple sources of information to learn words through repeated exposure. (p. 504)

FIGURE 5.23 *Recommendations for teaching vocabulary to English language learners.*

- Get to know your students and help them feel comfortable.
- Find out what they know about English and your content area.
- Avoid thinking of them as having a problem.
- Learn some of their words.
- Have some content and recreational reading materials in the students' first language.
- Provide bilingual dictionaries.
- Allow them to consult with other bilingual classmates.

- Make available alphabet and other books that celebrate language.
- Convey the message and attitude that bilingualism is an asset.
- Read the textbook looking for figures of speech, idioms, and words with multiple meanings that can cause problems.
- When possible, teach concept development through hands-on activities before vocabulary.
- Provide authentic contexts for vocabulary use and a lot of social interaction with peers.

The ideas and suggestions in this chapter are consistent with these principles. After reading this chapter, you should have many vocabulary and language issues to think about. We talked about various types of vocabulary that enable your students to learn, read, and flourish in your content subjects. You've been given language issues to ponder and reflect on as you pursue your own studies and prepare to teach. I've provided examples of specific strategies that you can use to enhance your students' vocabulary and teach terms and concepts, and you now know of many resources that will help your classes explore language in general and within your field of study. You've had opportunities to apply instructional strategies to lessons and texts that contain crucial vocabulary or involve issues relating to language. The final section expanded your understanding of how you can help students with limited English proficiency, being a good teacher of language and content simultaneously.

I'm sure you realize now what an enormous and important part vocabulary will play in your students' learning. And there is no one best way to build the content-specific vocabulary your students must have to thrive in your courses. At times, you might employ direct instruction, connecting new words through examples, nonexamples, and definitions to concepts or other words already known; you'll respond to students' questions and needs, provide structure through vocabulary guides, and also encourage independent language play and exploration. Your methods will vary based on particular texts, classes, situations, individuals. Model inquisitiveness and provide opportunities for social interaction and collaboration focusing on language issues within your subject area. Show students how to be metacognitive as they employ strategies to learn technical vocabulary and figure out new words based on structure or context.

CHAPTER FIVE

Getting Ready to Teach

5.1 Cartoons and comics have wonderful vocabulary representative of all three vocabulary categories, that connects to content areas. My folder labeled "Vocabulary in Comics" holds many examples from "Peanuts," "Dilbert," "Calvin and Hobbes," and so forth. Begin your own file of cartoons that involve general, specific, or technical vocabulary words for your subject area, as well as other areas. Your colleagues will thank you as you pass appropriate cartoons to them, and you'll show your students you can go beyond the boundaries of your subject. You can share these comics using a bulletin board, to which students can add any time they find an appropriate comic fitting the category.

5.2 Our students, like the book characters mentioned earlier, can be taught and encouraged to pay attention to the words they hear and find through their life journeys. But we must start with ourselves. So, begin a vocabulary list or journal or notebook of your own. Collect words from your friends and family, from your reading, from lectures and conversations. Notice language-related issues and practices in your classes, work settings, and schools you visit. You might organize the words by categories, perhaps related to your content area topics. Be alert and ready to be surprised, by words that are perfect to describe something you are thinking or feeling. Share your discoveries with others, and know that you'll be able to share your enthusiasm with your students, as your vocabulary and theirs are enhanced.

5.3 Using the student-made examples in Figures 5.10, 5.11, and 5.12, or any of the books from the bibliography of alphabet books, create an alphabet that teaches or reinforces terms related to a topic in your subject area. You can illustrate it if you wish. Be sure to begin a file of alphabet books, so that as you and your students compose others, you'll have an organizational plan. Think of the wonderful display you can make when you have multiple teacher and student-made alphabet books.

5.4 Choose a text, perhaps a chapter of a textbook or an article, and make a list of the key terms and concepts necessary for the comprehension of the material. Create a vocabulary guide using one of the strategies modeled in this chapter, or write a narrative (perhaps accompanied by a picture or graphic organizer) explaining how you would teach the vocabulary in preparation for or in conjunction with the reading material.

Comprehension and Critical Thinking

PART ONE

Teaching Comprehension

The terms in the title of this chapter should already be familiar to you; previous chapters certainly dealt with both comprehension and critical thinking. Now, these concepts become the actual focus of discussion, and you'll learn how you can teach and enhance skills that will lead to your students' understanding of increasingly complex texts in your subject areas, as well as to their being able to join conversations begun by such texts.

How about if you were a parent and had to choose one of these teachers for your middle school child: Teacher A or Teacher B?

How about if you were an administrator (a principal, curriculum coordinator, or department chair) and had to hire one of these teachers for your high school: Teacher A or Teacher B?

Discuss your answers with your classmates. Then, read the following two quotes, and see if your thinking changes at all:

"As a recent graduate of a teacher education program, I can tell you the profession is in danger of being overwhelmed by hordes of candidates who are well schooled in innovative methods of instruction, brimming with creativity, idealistic and sensitive to students' feelings, but who know little about what they are teaching." (T. R. Burns, 1995, p. 2)

"More important than the information a teacher acquires about science is a teacher's knowing how to inquire, how to find answers, how to use material and human resources, and how to model these in a science classroom." (Yager & Penick, 1990, p. 663)

ACTION RESEARCH 6.A

Write in your log for a moment answering the following "Forced Choice" questions, giving a reason for your choices.

You must take a required course in your major or the content area you plan to teach. There are two sections offered by different teachers. Teacher A is very knowledgeable in her content area, but is weak when it comes to pedagogical skills. Teacher B is very strong in her knowledge of teaching and motivational strategies, but is weak when it comes to content. Which would you choose: Teacher A or Teacher B?

I suspect you and your colleagues found this a hard choice because you would surely prefer in each of the three scenarios to choose a hypothetical Teacher C, who is strong in both areas. Now that you've been reminded of the ideal combination and maybe recommitted to becoming that Teacher C, I'd like you to look more carefully at the construction of the quotes I supplied. Each takes the teaching components of pedagogy and content knowledge and relates them in some way. I went a step further by juxtaposing them, hoping to provide you with somewhat contrasting statements on the topic. This chapter discusses the type of comprehension requiring *discourse knowledge*, that knowledge of organization and connections that enables us to understand text beyond the single sentence level (Beck, McKeown, Omanson, & Pople, 1984; Leu & Kinzer, 1999a). That's what helped you know that there was a relation between content knowledge and pedagogical knowledge in each quote, as well as a connection between the two quotes as used in this chapter. Those readers who can decode and recognize the meaning of every word in those quotes will still have great difficulty with comprehension if their discourse level knowledge is not adequate.

Block (1999) uses metaphoric language to explain comprehension, calling comprehension a crafting process and students sculptors, rather than molds to be filled. "Thus, if students are to craft a more enriched understanding they must be taught how to experience a broad continuum of thoughts, bordered on one side by authors' intended meanings and on the other by their personal applications of text to their lives" (p. 99). However, Durkin's classic study (1978/1979) showed that, although teachers recognized comprehension as important and talked about it, there was little explicit teaching of how to do it. Subsequent studies (Beck, McKeown, & Gromoll, 1989; Pressley, Wharton-McDonald, Hampson, & Echevarria, 1998) show evidence leading to similar conclusions. This book attempts to give you a repertoire of ways to guide your students to process text beyond the word and sentence level and to respond actively and thoughtfully, giving students strategies to analyze, synthesize, and critique texts of all sorts. You, the content area teacher, can learn how to follow Block's advice to demonstrate how students can use authorial clues and comprehension strategies interactively to craft meaning.

AN EXAMPLE OF TEACHING COMPREHENSION

To make the concepts of reading at the discourse level and teaching comprehension clearer, I'll use Carmen Agra Deedy's *The Yellow Star: The Legend of King Christian X of Denmark* (2000) as an example. In this book, the reader is let in on a series of decisions the king has to make after his country is conquered. When the Nazi flag is hung at the palace, the king sends a Danish soldier to remove it. Subsequently, when a Nazi officer threatens to shoot the next man who takes down the flag, the king counters with a warning that he himself would be that man. "The Nazi flag did not fly from the palace again. The missing flag became a powerful symbol of resistance . . ." (unpaged). The reader is expected to comprehend that the flag did not fly because of what the king said; the cause–effect relationship is implied, rather than stated directly.

What follows is a transition sentence that can help a reader make connections and predictions and be ready to comprehend what comes next. "Yet it was only a small victory; the king and his people's greatest test was still to come." The next few pages tell of the edict ordering all Jews to sew a yellow star onto their clothing. There is a picture of the king deep in thought, with images of war surrounding him, and the text helps us visualize the problem-solving process he uses:

> If King Christian called on the tiny Danish army to fight, Danes would die. If he did nothing, Danes would die. . . . "If you wished to hide a star," wondered the king to himself, where would you place it?" His eyes searched the heavens.
>
> "Of course!" he thought. The answer was so simple. "You would hide it among its sisters."
>
> The king summoned his tailor. (unpaged)

The book never says directly what the king requested of his tailor, but the picture on the next page shows him riding alone on a horse through Copenhagen, wearing a yellow star. "As they watched him pass, the subjects of King Christian understood what they should do." The following page shows Danish citizens, all wearing a Star of David.

Comprehension of this text is dependent on the reader being able to read beyond the words. A teacher could teach and model the skill of making inferences using this story as an example, putting together text and picture cues to reach understanding. She could then draw attention to the Author's Note following the story, where Deedy provides the dictionary definition of the word *legend* and explains that in her research she found only unauthenticated references to King Christian's legendary defiance. Yet, she defends its telling, noting that among the Nazi-occupied countries, Denmark was the only one that rescued the overwhelming majority of its Jews.

Asking "What if . . . ?" is a good way to get students' imaginations actively engaged in a topic. The author's final words to the reader are a perfect example of this thinking prompt:

> What if it *had* happened? What if every Dane, from shoemaker to priest, had worn the yellow Star of David?
>
> And what if we could follow the example today against violations of human rights? What if the good and strong people of the world stood shoulder to shoulder, . . . saying, "You cannot do this injustice to our sisters and brothers, or you must do it to us as well." (unpaged)

You might choose to have the students read the story first, and then point out things like the connection between sentences, as well as the convention of the Author's Note at the end, which supplies more historical statistics and leaves the reader with questions. Or you might tell them what to watch for before they begin and help them connect what's coming with the background they have from previous lessons or from your introductory lecture on the topic. You could supply an anticipation guide, or a K-W-L-S exercise, or stop students at predetermined points to illustrate how a reader "reads between the lines." You might employ one instructional strategy with some students and a different one with others. There are no magic answers to teaching comprehension; you decide based on the assessed needs of individuals in your class. But what you *won't* do is just leave comprehension to chance or assume that if the students can decode words and know their meanings, comprehension will naturally follow.

Research has shown that comprehension instruction should be multicomponential (Pressley, 2000). Comprehension development should increase as a result of extensive reading of excellent literature and expository material because, for one thing, literature exposure increases a reader's knowledge (Cunningham & Stanovitch, 1998), which should in turn improve the comprehension of related content in the future (Pressley, 2000).

But that's not enough. Students should be taught explicitly to use comprehension strategies; the self-regulated use of such strategies can be seen in the reading of skilled adult readers (Pressley & Afflerbach, 1995), and studies have shown an improvement in text comprehension after instruction. For example, transactional strategies instruction (Pressley, El-Dinary et al., 1992), involving direct explanation, teacher modeling, and guided practice, as well as lively interpretive discussions of texts, showed striking effects in studies with intermediate grade students (Collins, 1991) and middle and high school students (Anderson, 1992).

The following sections discuss various aspects relating to comprehension and give you lots of ideas as to how you can incorporate instructional strategies at the discourse level into your teaching.

TEXT STRUCTURE AND GENRE

As you learned in Chapter 3, your students must understand that there are different types of texts and recognize into which type a particular piece of writing falls (Armbruster, Anderson, & Ostertag, 1989; Graesser, Golding, & Long, 1991; Roller, 1990). Writers of various types of texts have differing expectations of readers, and readers must approach different types of texts in the most effective way. Texts can first be divided under two major headings: (1) *expository*, or explanatory, and (2) *narrative*, using a story form. Typically, children in the primary grades are taught to read primarily through the use of narrative text, but that is changing. Some say that expository text is more demanding than narrative text, but actually, I've found that varies depending on a number of factors. Some nonfiction pieces can be quite straightforward, while some narratives are quite complex, having perhaps several strands that intersect. A sixth-grade teacher I know told me her class wouldn't be able to comprehend the 1997 Newbery winner *The View from Saturday* (Konigsburg, 1996) because the story line was not linear; the four or five interconnecting stories would be too confusing. The sequence of events in a story may also be recorded in a nonlinear way, with flashbacks, changes in verb tense, dream retellings. Some narratives are told from more than one character's point of view. In fact, Paul Fleischman's *Bull Run* (1993) has 16 narrators, and *Bat 6*, by Virginia Euwer Wolff (1998), has 21!

Rather than sigh about our students' lack of skills necessary to decipher the structure of complex texts, we must address their needs and give them guided experience with increasingly sophisticated yet well-written material. If they can't read *The View from Saturday* in middle school, how will they be able to tackle Toni Morrison's *Beloved* (1987), Amy Tan's *The Joy Luck Club* (1989), or James Joyce's *Ulysses* (1992) later? How will they learn to navigate the huge number of formats and styles and conventions used on the Internet?

The categories of expository and narrative are not mutually exclusive. Especially recently, there have been a number of books published that combine the two. The *Magic School Bus* series, by Joanna Cole and Bruce Degen, takes readers on imaginary adventures with Mrs. Frizzle and her class as they explore the human body, the solar system, the age of dinosaurs, and hidden mysteries beneath the earth's crust. Explanations of facts and scientific principles, whole lessons, are embedded in the story. David Macaulay's *The New Way Things Work* (1998) uses a similar format. In the middle of a very informative article on sponges in the *Smithsonian Magazine* (1998), the author invites, "To best understand them, come with me on a scuba dive. Let your imagination take over. Shrink to microscopic size and roll off the dive boat's gunwale into the warm waters washing over a coral reef somewhere tropical. Exhale, sink down and swim over to that bright red sponge" (Genthe, 1998, p. 54). A combination of narrative and expository styles help make this information-packed article an enjoyable read.

When you see or hear the sentence, "It was a dark and stormy night," what kind of story do you expect to hear? If you predicted a scary story, you have come to your conclusion using *discourse knowledge*. (You may have recognized it as the opening of the 1963 Newbery winner *A Wrinkle in Time*.) Within the major categories of narrative and expository, there are several genres, each with its own characteristics and conventions and demands upon the reader, though categories can overlap or a certain text may break some of the genre's rules. It's crucial that we help our students recognize, appreciate, and interact appropriately with particular genres and text structures. Expository writing is not all alike, nor is it always accurate or "true." A daily newspaper contains editorial essays, human interest stories, movie reviews, and political cartoons in addition to "the news." Biographies and autobiographies differ; memoirs often combine elements of expository writing and narrative. Technical reports are common in all fields, from science to business to politics. Students also should know that fiction consists of short stories as well as novels, and that there are further subdivisions such as young adult literature, fantasy, realistic fiction, historical fiction, horror, satire. When readers are aware of the conventions of various types of writing, comprehension is aided. Students who approach the comprehension of all genres and formats in the same way, on the other hand, can find themselves in trouble.

Even textbooks vary their formats and structures. Some are totally formal, while others may contain anecdotes and vignettes, letters from experts, cartoons. As a literature-based and primary source–based teacher of your content area, you should create many opportunities for students to do wide reading within and across many genres, and guide them in that reading. Introduce them to examples of different text structures, and teach them how to actively engage with them.

ACTION RESEARCH 6.B

Is satire within the fiction or nonfiction category? Is it narrative or expository writing? What examples of satire can you think of? Compare your answers with your classmates.

Now, read the following paragraphs, the beginning of a newspaper editorial.

SUMMER READING REQUIREMENT

How cruel can teachers get?

Corporal punishment is no longer allowed in public schools. But that doesn't mean school officials have no alternatives for indulging their brutal instincts and inflicting misery on their vulnerable charges.

Take the heart-breaking case of the poor waifs at Cicero-North Syracuse High School. After huffing and puffing to the finish line of the school year, they were looking forward to a well-earned 10-week break.

Not so fast, said their tormentors, with a sinister laugh borrowed from Snidely Whiplash. The kids' vacation would not be entirely their own. [They] would be required to perform a painfully arduous task before returning to class after Labor Day. Or else.

They have to read a book. . . .

How in the world are these disciples of the Marquis de Sade allowed to get away with such torture? Why haven't higher authorities intervened? There oughtta be a law.

One 11th-grader explained . . . , "You're not supposed to have to work over vacation. [Reading] . . . takes too much time."

How much time? Well, to get through a 200-page book during the course of a summer, a student would have to read at the pace of nearly three pages a day. Oh, the inhumanity!

Teachers and administrators . . . want to improve students' performance on college entrance and Regents exams.

Those are noble goals, but at what cost? Are they worth the trauma being inflicted upon the tender sensibilities of these young scholars? Why, they might have to miss the rebroadcast of an episode of "Seinfeld" in order to meet the requirement. . . .

By James L. Middleton. Published in *The American Biology Teacher*, Vol. 53, No. 1 (Jan. 1991). Reprinted by permission of the author.

At what point did you realize that the editors did not mean for this text to be taken literally? What clues or signs did they give the reader? What techniques were

(continued)

used to create a satiric text? Now, think what would happen to comprehension if a reader did not possess the discourse level knowledge that enabled her to appreciate the spoof. How and where and when does this skill or ability develop, and whose responsibility is it to teach and reinforce it? This chapter helps you think about and begin to answer these questions and understand the higher-level thinking skills necessary for reading and evaluating various content area-related materials.

PATTERNS OF ORGANIZATION

Regardless of what overall genres authors use, all texts also structure the ideas within them in certain ways; sentences relate to each other according to discernable patterns of organization. That's what makes paragraphs and chapters *coherent*. It's important for readers' comprehension to recognize organizational structures and patterns in the text (Alexander & Jetton, 2000; Goldman & Rakestraw, 2000). This section addresses five major types of relations: time order or sequence, cause–effect, compare–contrast, problem–solution, and enumeration. I give examples of each from various genres and offer possible ways that you can guide your students to use their knowledge of the patterns to comprehend and remember information. Keep in mind that these categories are not necessarily discrete; rather, they can overlap. Authors can use more than one simultaneously; in fact, good writers almost always do.

Think of the subject you're planning to teach. How is time order important in that discipline? What will you teach that relates to time or sequence? How are time issues dealt with in texts you and your students might be reading? Now ask yourself these same questions with regard to cause–effect, compare–contrast, problem–solution, and enumeration (listing things). Compare your answers and examples with others if possible. This will activate your thinking about what you already know about the topic of relationships used in texts, speech, and thinking, and help you reflect on the information that's coming up.

Sequence

I'd be surprised if any teacher in any subject said sequence was not important. It may be most immediately apparent in history, where dates and time lines come with the territory. But math teachers point out that order of operations is crucial to arriving at correct answers; science teachers tell of disasters that occur if experiments are done with the steps out of order, or cite the importance of time in geological and archeological discoveries and theories. Artists do some things before others as they create; so do cooks, market researchers, attorneys, computer programmers. Teachers plan, thinking through objectives, examining materials, assessing students' prior knowledge, before they instruct. Fiction writers pay great attention to sequence. They

HOW EARLY CAN CHILDREN DEAL WITH VARIED GENRES?

A literacy textbook asks, "Are you surprised that the reading materials first grade children are introduced to are stories? Can you imagine passing out science books and welcoming children to their first readers?" (Brozo & Simpson, 1999, p. 32). My answer to the latter question is a resounding YES! It's true, as the authors say, that "We begin teaching children to read with stories because they are already familiar with the structure of stories" (p. 32). But many are also familiar with, and may even have a preference for, nonfiction of various sorts. Children will pore over toy catalogs; Turtle, a toddler in Barbara Kingsolver's *The Bean Trees* (1988), is very attached to seed catalogs!

I've known youngsters who had short attention spans when it came to stories, but who could attend to texts on manatees, baseball statistics, cars and trucks, or black holes for an unlimited amount of time. As teachers, we can encourage children's parents to provide varied experiences and reading materials, and we can continue at all grade levels to introduce and supply nonfiction texts and help students actively engage with them. The book *Informational Picture Books for Children*, by Patricia J. Cianciolo (2000), has recommendations and annotations of books exemplifying expository writing ranging from the primary level to books appropriate for teens.

BookTalk 6.1

Some books have more than one story going on at a time. *Walk Two Moons*, the 1995 Newbery Medal Winner by Sharon Creech, uses a journey motif to tell the story of Salamanca coming to terms with the fact that her mother left her. As she and her grandparents retrace the route across the country her mother took when she left, she fills the time by telling them about her friend Phoebe, whose mother also disappeared, but for very different reasons. This embedded story is a mystery, complete with a suspicious stranger, notes seemingly written in code, and the girls' adventures as sleuths trying to put all the pieces together. The "story within a story" structure is fascinating; readers can appreciate the crafting even as they become emotionally involved with these two very likeable teenaged characters who have lost their mothers and have the courage and imagination needed to do something about it.

either tell a story chronologically or deliberately manipulate time through flashbacks, time travel, or other literary devices. Readers must pay attention to clues that let them know when things are happening, how much time is passing during the story, how time relates to other aspects of the story.

Writers use any number of words to alert readers to sequence, including the following: *first, second, then, finally, after, before, following, subsequently, previously*. Your reading guides, your instruction, and your questioning during the reading of texts in your class can help students pay attention to clue words and important points about time and sequence. You might be surprised to learn that the students in your class have less knowledge and understanding of time issues than you might have expected. For example, in the classic study "What Do Our Seventeen-Year-Olds Know?" (Ravitch & Finn, 1987), a wide survey of students found, among many other things, that only 35 percent of the sample could place the Civil War within the correct 50-year time period given in a multiple-choice question. It's up to you as a teacher to help your students comprehend their texts and your subject relative to sequence issues.

Some texts are very explicit in their treatment of time order. The table of contents in the book *Extraordinary Women of Medicine* (Stille, 1997) consists of a chronological list of names, birth and death dates, and fields of influence, accompanied by photographs of the women highlighted in the chapters. There are other types of sequence also, such as step-by-step

instructions for assembling something or completing a procedure. In *Why Greenland Is an Island, Australia Is Not—and Japan Is Up for Grabs* (Davis, 1994), the author outlines a sequential strategy for readers to follow in order to become geographically literate:

> Step #1: Immediately identify the geographical issue . . .
>
> Step #2: Study closely all maps reproduced in or accompanying the reading material you're using . . .
>
> Step #3: Compare the maps you're given with more *detailed* maps in an atlas . . .
>
> Step #4: Compare the maps you're given with *large-area* maps showing how the area in question fits into a broader geographical context . . .
>
> Step #5: Combine what you now know about the geography with the other facts involved in the situation . . .
>
> Step # 6: Close your eyes and try to picture the scene you've been studying. (pp. 21–22)

Davis is just as considerate to the reader in terms of time order in the section under the subtitle, "What Exactly Happened to the USSR?" She uses phrases such as "As you read through this sequence of events" and "This scenario, presented in chronological order," and then recounts:

> **Event One:** *Lithuania* makes a declaration of independence from the USSR on March 11, 1990 . . .
>
> **Event Two:** *Georgia* begins to seek independence in late 1990 . . .
>
> **Event Three:** A coup is attempted by military leaders on August 19, 1991, against USSR President Mikhail S. Gorbachev . . .
>
> **Event Seven:** On December 21, 1991, eleven of the twelve former republics of the USSR . . . join the Commonwealth of Independent States.
>
> **Event Eight:** The USSR is formally dissolved on December 25, 1991. (pp. 24–25)

Other texts are not so explicit and reader-friendly; for texts that do not use a clearly discernible time sequence, teachers have to help students do more of the constructing of the events' times and sequences. Making time lines to be posted in the classroom is an ideal strategy to accomplish this purpose or to help students who have to visualize the sequence of events in any text.

No matter what your subject area, you might begin a discussion of time issues with your class by having them brainstorm the titles and lyrics of songs that deal with this popular theme. Or you

FIGURE 6.1 *Books about time and sequence.*

Babbitt, N. (1975). *Tuck Everlasting.* New York: Farrar, Straus & Giroux.

Burns, M. (1978). *This Book Is About Time.* Boston: Little, Brown.

Chisholm, J., & Addario, S. (1998). *The Usborne Book of World History Dates.* New York: Scholastic.

Cole, K. C. (1998). *The Universe and the Teacup: The Mathematics of Truth and Beauty.* New York: Harcourt Brace.

Denman, C. (1995). *The History Puzzle: An Interactive Visual Timeline.* Atlanta, GA: Turner Publishing.

Fritz, J., Paterson, K., McKissack, P., McKissack, F., Mahy, M., & Highwater, J. (1992). *The World in 1492.* New York: Henry Holt.

Glennon, L. (Ed.). (1995). *Our Times: The Illustrated History of the Twentieth Century.* Atlanta, GA: Turner Publishing.

Grun, B. (1991). *The Timetables of History: A Linkage of People and Events.* New York: Simon & Schuster.

Hawking, S. (1988). *A Brief History of Time.* New York: Bantam Books.

Hawking, S. (2001). *The Universe in a Nutshell.* New York: Bantam Books.

Jackson, E. B. (1998). *The Turn of the Century.* Watertown, MA: Charlesbridge Publishing.

L'Engle, M. (1962). *A Wrinkle in Time.* New York: Farrar, Straus & Giroux.

Rubel, D. (1994). *Scholastic Encyclopedia of the Presidents and Their Times.* New York: Scholastic Reference.

Wells, H. G. (1988). *The Time Machine.* New York: Ace Books.

---

could make a class chart of proverbs and common sayings about time to stimulate discussion and activate thinking about this important concept.

Figure 6.1 lists examples of texts about time that cross various disciplines. You and your students can add to this chart as you make new discoveries in your reading.

> *Getting Ready to Teach 6.1 (see page 197)*

Cause–Effect

As you completed Action Research 6.C, did you have any trouble thinking of how your subject area uses cause–effect relationships? I doubt it. Purposes for actions and consequences of actions have been with us since early childhood in all aspects of our lives; it's almost impossible to get through a day without thinking or speaking in terms of cause and effect. We wonder why things happen or people act the way they do, and we explain our thoughts and actions starting with "because." Science teachers help students understand why certain reactions occur, and can predict or debate what the results of particular behaviors and actions will be. Readers apply their knowledge of cause–effect in order to understand characters in fiction, as well as the heroes and villains of biographies. Math teachers must be ready to answer such student questions as "Why do we have

BookTalk 6.2

When I ask my students what happened in 1492, I get an immediate poetic response: "In fourteen hundred and ninety-two, Columbus sailed the ocean blue." When I follow this with, "What else?" I draw silence and blank or quizzical stares. That's when I introduce *The World in 1492* by Jean Fritz et al. (1992). This collaborative effort by a number of popular children's authors and illustrators gives a global perspective of that particular point in time. Katherine Paterson tells of Asian nomads who belonged to the most sophisticated army in the world; Patricia and Frederick McKissack describe the art, religions, and storytelling traditions flourishing in Africa at the time. Margaret Mahy depicts the rich family life of aboriginal people of Australia, and Jamake Highwater recounts the accomplishments and lifestyles of the Aztecs, Incas, Plains Indians, and other cultures already present in the Americas at the time of Columbus's "discovery." Your students can learn much information from this book, then use the same procedure and format for doing research and making their own books or posters covering other points in time. Cooperative learning groups might produce texts about the world in 1776, 1865, 1929, 1968, 2010.

FIGURE 6.2 *A graphic organizer depicting a cause–effect pattern in the novel* Ironman *by Chris Crutcher.*

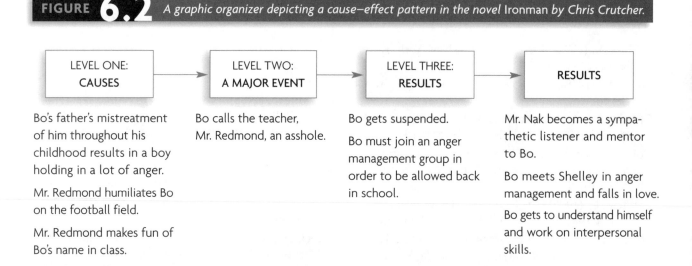

LEVEL ONE: CAUSES	LEVEL TWO: A MAJOR EVENT	LEVEL THREE: RESULTS	RESULTS
Bo's father's mistreatment of him throughout his childhood results in a boy holding in a lot of anger. Mr. Redmond humiliates Bo on the football field. Mr. Redmond makes fun of Bo's name in class.	Bo calls the teacher, Mr. Redmond, an asshole.	Bo gets suspended. Bo must join an anger management group in order to be allowed back in school.	Mr. Nak becomes a sympathetic listener and mentor to Bo. Bo meets Shelley in anger management and falls in love. Bo gets to understand himself and work on interpersonal skills.

to do it that way?" and "Why do we have to know this, anyway?" and "What would happen if we solved the problem this way?" Psychology texts deal with why people behave certain ways under certain circumstances, and what the consequences of various medicines, nurturing styles, stresses, and heredity are.

Chris Leahey, a first-year teacher in a workshop I led, challenged the group to name any event and promised he could make a cause–effect poster of it. A veteran teacher called out, "The bombing of Nagasaki," and Chris wrote it in the middle of the paper. He drew lines upward and wrote causes as the rest of us called them out, and then did the same downward as we contributed results. I was impressed both with the teacher's confidence and with how pervasive the cause–effect pattern is. But what really stimulated us was his showing us that the causes we had listed could be clustered into categories that he labeled *political, social, ideological, scientific,* and *economic;* the results fell into the same categories. He uses this strategy with his social studies students; although they consider it a game, it aids them in understanding the content, reading texts, and studying and remembering connected details. It organizes their knowledge.

You can apply the cause–effect strategy to literature, also. Choose a crucial happening or decision by a character. Then, depict the causes leading to it and the results stemming from it. Categorize them if appropriate. Or create a graphic organizer to map out the connected ideas in a cause–effect relationship. Figure 6.2 shows an example of a visual representing the cause–effect pattern running through the plot of Chris Crutcher's *Ironman* (1995).

Because we naturally think so much in terms of the cause–effect pattern, because it is so important

(I'm using it right now), it should come as no surprise that writers of many genres, including textbooks, use it often. The following is an example from an education journal with teachers, administrators, and education policy makers as its target audience. Before you read it, you might ask yourself how you think your students' parents perceive teachers, and what causes them to have the impressions and expectations they do.

> Demanding teachers awaken parental memories of the English teacher who made them memorize the "General Prologue" to the *Canterbury Tales* in Middle English. They conflate intellectual rigor with disciplinary zeal, recalling despotic teachers who forced them to pluck gum from their mouths and stick it on their noses, then write "I will not chew gum in class" several hundred times for homework. The use of writing as punishment taught many a student to loathe the activity. People who are slaves to such memories have difficulty thinking of teachers as professionals. So they don't. Instead, they alternate between the conceptions of the teacher as tyrant and the teacher as servant. Their memories of childhood make us tyrants; their desire for retribution as adults encourages them to treat us like servants. (Burniske, 1999, p. 124)

Such text is much easier to comprehend, and react to, if you zero in on the cause–effect pattern it relies on. Good readers do this naturally, paying attention to clue words and understanding that some sentences connect to others using this relationship. But some of your students may treat each sentence as an entity separate from those before and after, losing much of the paragraph's message. Good teaching and guidance on your part can capitalize on this dis-

FIGURE **6.3** *A "during reading" text pattern guide focusing on cause–effect.*

DIRECTIONS: Some Native Americans believe that one's actions affect the people and the environment for seven generations. As you read "Plenty Kill," Chapter One of Luther Standing Bear's autobiography, *My People, the Sioux* (1983), fill in what you think are the causes for these cause–effect relationships. After you've finished, reflect on the questions with honesty and sincerity. We will be discussing them in class tomorrow, and your thoughts and opinions are anticipated.

1. Cause: _____
   Effect: "White man" could take control of land and push Native Americans out easily.

2. Cause: _____
   Effect: Native Americans did not fear "white man."

3. Cause: _____
   Effect: Members of the Sioux Nation thought they could get water at the railroad station.

4. Cause: _____
   Effect: A council was called, and members of the Sioux Nation decided to take action.

5. Cause: _____
   Effect: A train was derailed.

6. Cause: _____
   Effect: Beads were introduced to the Sioux culture.
   Effect: Tensions grew between the Sioux and "white man."

ANTICIPATION QUESTIONS:

1. Form a hypothesis about how you think these relations, which affected members of the Sioux and the dominant culture in the late 1800s, made an impact on today.

2. Thinking ahead to the next few chapters: "White man" killed buffalo (an animal that the Plains Indians relied on for food, clothing, and shelter) for sport, not really thinking of the end result until it was too late. Think about the following items and how your attitude and actions toward them may affect generations to come:

   water   pesticides   violence in film
   trees   urbanization

   —*Branden Wood*

BookTalk   6.3

If the birds from your community disappeared, wouldn't you wonder why? Wouldn't you worry? What might you do to find out the cause? A group of youngsters decides to investigate their town's diminishing bird population in Jean Craighead George's 1991 environmental mystery *Who Really Killed Cock Robin?* The result is a further mystery: why won't the town's mayor cooperate with them? Join your efforts to theirs as they solve the mystery and battle the dire consequences that greed and corruption can cause. The author has two more environmental mysteries: *The Missing Gator of Gumbo Limbo* (1992) and *The Case of the Missing Cutthroats* (1996). You and your students can exercise your cause–effect and problem-solving skills as you vicariously experience the mysterious circumstances and clever solutions of fictional characters.

course level of comprehension. You can also have a chart posted listing clue words to the cause–effect relationship, such as *because, therefore, why, thus, as a result, so, consequently,* and so on.

One straightforward strategy that can aid comprehension involves readers asking themselves why the facts in a text are sensible. Why-questioning has been shown to have significant effects on learning material in factually dense text (Pressley, Wood et al., 1992). You might try this out yourself as you read this text or the curricular materials you use in your content area. Then, create and take advantage of opportunities to show your students how you ask the why-questions and how they lead to understanding.

Figure 6.3 shows a preservice teacher's reading guide prepared to facilitate students' understanding of the cause–effect patterns during their reading of a text.

Compare–Contrast

In Roald Dahl's *Matilda* (1988), the novel's gifted title character meets two educators on her first day of kindergarten, and I'd like you to meet them too:

> Their teacher was called Miss Honey . . . She had a lovely pale oval madonna face with blue eyes and her hair was light brown. Her body was so slim and fragile one got the feeling that if she fell over she would smash into a thousand pieces, like a porcelain figure. . . .

Miss Trunchbull, the Headmistress, was something else altogether. She was a gigantic holy terror, a fierce tyrannical monster . . . you could almost feel the dangerous heat radiating from her as from a red-hot rod of metal. . . . When she marched along the corridor you could actually hear her snorting as she went. (pp. 66–67)

Dahl makes his use of contrast explicit by using the phrase "something else altogether." Teachers and students can also notice—and judge—particular traits the author uses in his comparison. Some astute readers might be bothered by Dahl's use of stereotypes; the nice teacher is pale, slim, blue-eyed and young, while the meanie is overweight and animal-like. Here's an opportunity for teachers to help students recognize and consider the effects of the use of such devices.

When we try to explain something to another person, we often compare a new idea to something familiar to our listener. Writers do the same, sometimes very beautifully, through the use of analogies. I'd like to suggest that you and your students start an "Analogy File," collecting examples from texts you read in your discipline. Comparisons can be as short as a phrase, as in a simile, or in a sentence such as the following from a novel: "The air was so humid that the backyard felt as if God had turned on a giant vaporizer for a world full of asthma sufferers (Konigsburg, 1993, pp. 37–38). Thompson (1996b) employs a comparative structure to make a point about the basic grammar of a sentence:

When Crick and Watson were searching for the secret of life in the structure of the DNA molecule, they let their search be guided by the strong conviction that the guiding molecule of life would not be an ugly, amorphous molecule, a misshapen tangle, but would be something beautiful—and so it was. The double helix with its twin spirals is both a biological and aesthetic miracle, a gorgeous secret to the vast biological complexity of our planet. In a precisely similar way, the vast complexities of human thought structures have in common the beautiful subject/predicate nucleus which, if it is understood and appreciated, yields understanding of the very essence of clarity. (p. 155)

Students can learn, as a result of your instruction and modeling, to recognize when writers are making comparisons or contrasts, to ponder the aptness of analogies, and to pay attention to helpful cues. An author or character may make an extended analogy. Note the comparisons used in Granddaddy Opal's explanation of a black hole to Miracle, the protagonist in *Dancing on the Edge* by Han Nolan (1997):

"You know what a star is, don't you? . . . Did you know stars can run out of gas?"

"Like a car, you mean?"

"Kinda. . . . The star just gets so hot and gives off all that gas until it uses it all up and then guess what? . . . See, what happens is the star, once it loses all its fuel, starts to cool off and shrink, like the light on your TV set, and then once it shrinks enough, gravity pulls on the star. . . . Now here's where it gets interesting. The gravity is pulling on the star so much that the light, instead of being sent out in the universe so's we can see it, gets turned inward, like pulling on a sock and turning it inside out. See, and if you pull that sock inside out and all the light was on the outside of the sock and now it's on the inside, well, then you have a black hole, because without the light you can't see it, and the light can't escape back out the hole. It's invisible. Just like staring into a TV set when it's off. (p. 87)

You can have your students contrast the explanations and analogies in various nonfiction texts, such as *Black Holes and Baby Universes* by Stephen Hawking (1993). Here's an excerpt from the nonfiction book *Star Crossing* by Judith Herbst (1993); notice both cause–effect and compare–contrast relationships at work:

Black holes do not sit idly by minding their own business. They can't. Their gravity is much too intense and has disastrous effects on everything in the neighborhood. Careless stars that stray too close are gobbled down whole, while those a little farther away are held captive like flies in a spider web. As the prisoner star orbits the black hole, it slowly loses material to the black hole's deep gravity well. The star's gas is sucked down into the black hole, similar to the way crumbs and other debris are pulled toward a vacuum cleaner nozzle. The gas spirals around the perimeter, forming a glowing ring called an accretion disk, before it vanishes forever into the black hole's hungry jaws. (p. 146)

It's easy to see how reading well-written text and noticing, delighting in, creative language that exhibits patterns of relationship such as compare–contrast takes students a long way toward true and lasting comprehension. The information they learn in your classes need not be spewed out onto a test and then sucked forever into a black hole.

Textbooks and nonfiction books use compare–contrast to teach concepts and make points. Student readers can be taught to notice this pattern and use it as an aid to comprehension. Rather than learn all of the facts about the North and the South before, during, and after the Civil War as separate

BookTalk 6.4

Would you volunteer to be a passenger on a space ark headed for another galaxy? Would you like to visit a black hole? Would you allow yourself to be cryonically frozen if you had a terminal illness, with the promise that you'd be thawed out once a cure was found? *Star Crossing: How to Get Around in the Universe,* by Judith Herbst (1993), will help you make informed decisions about these and many other possibilities. Its entertaining style, references to historical quotes and science fiction movies, and fascinating facts (such as the existence of the "forever flask," a giant thermos bottle offered by the Trans Time company to those willing to pay $100,000 to be frozen in liquid nitrogen at the moment of death) will appeal to readers of all ages. It does a marvelous job of teaching physics and astronomy, while helping the imagination soar as high as the rockets it explains. I loved this book, from the dedication page ("This book is dedicated to the memory of my physics teacher at Bayside High School, who thought I'd never understand this stuff.") to the last page, where the author imagines the reaction of aliens as they greet human space travelers on their home planet:

> A hand will reach out to touch. A moment, poised, like an angel on the head of a pin.
> "We come from a place called Earth," we will whisper. "A blue planet with a yellow sun. It's not very far."
> They will not know our words, but they will know our souls, for they too will have been waiting, wondering if they were all alone. (p. 178)

so. Listen in as teacher Ms. Beyerbach gives book-talks in her seventh-grade humanities class:

> This week in reading workshop you'll have your choice of reading one of two novels that have several similarities yet several differences. I've made a Venn diagram to illustrate this. First, they're both Newbery Medal winners. *Walk Two Moons,* by Sharon Creech (1994), won the gold in 1995, and *Holes,* by Louis Sachar (1998), won four years later. Both contain a story within a story, and both contain surprises. You'll find some humor, some sadness, some symbolism, much friendship, and some mystery, no matter which you pick. However, *Walk Two Moons* has a female main character, while *Holes* has a male. The settings are very different—while Salamanca Tree Hiddle travels across the country to find answers about life, Stanley Yelnats' adventure takes place in a juvenile detention facility called Camp Green Lake (though it isn't green and it has no lake). So, look at the diagram I've shown you, examine the books, sign up to read one of them, and then participate in a literature circle. Enjoy!

Getting Ready to Teach 6.2 (see page 197)

BookTalk 6.5

As you prepare for a holiday, you probably realize that your family does certain things that many others do also, while some of your traditions might be unique to your own family. In *Christmas in the Big House, Christmas in the Quarters* (1994), Patricia and Frederick McKissack take us back to 1859 as a plantation family merrily gets ready for Christmas. On alternate pages, the text and illustrations show the slaves of this plantation preparing for *their* celebration of the holiday. Readers will long remember the contrast. The time of this story is important, too; as the story comes to a close, the plantation owner promises his daughter that when she turns 16, she can get her own personal slave for Christmas. The daughter thinks that's a long time to wait; it will be 1864! The reader is in on a historical secret that the characters do not yet know.

An informational picture book that may serve as a companion text is *Daily Life on a Southern Plantation 1853,* by Paul Erickson (1998). Based on a real plantation house in Louisiana, it's full of photographs of the mansion, the slave quarters, and artifacts such as a chimney brush, washboard, schoolbooks and slates, blacksmiths' tools, clothing, picture frames, and guns. Perfect for a literary field trip!

entities, if they compare each side in terms of society type, population, positions on slavery, position on states' rights, they will have an easier time understanding and remembering the issues and information. You can teach students to be alert to clue words indicating the pattern is at work, including: *like, on the other hand, differ, in contrast, but, similarly, however, contrary to, more than, less than, fewer than.* Figure 6.4 depicts a preservice teacher's construction of a reading guide to aid comprehension of a work of historical fiction using the compare–contrast pattern. Figure 6.5 shows a semantic map prepared by a preservice teacher to help students relate ideas after reading two novels.

One way you can help your students become increasingly aware of compare—contrast relationships is to use the pattern in your teaching, drawing their attention to your use of clue words as you do

FIGURE 6.4 *Compare–contrast guide for a historical novel.*

DIRECTIONS: The book *Nightjohn*, by Gary Paulsen (1993), takes place on a plantation in the American South prior to the Civil War. In Columns A and B, write down all of the aspects of slavery and the Southern plantation system that you can recall. Think about the lifestyles that differentiated the lives of the slaves and their owners. To help you begin, think about the food, living arrangements, level of education, and material possessions that each group might have had.

A. LIFE OF A SLAVE

_____

_____

_____

_____

B. LIFE OF A PLANTATION OWNER

_____

_____

_____

_____

Now that you have filled in the chart, read the book *Nightjohn*. When you have completed the book, go to Columns C and D and write down any new information that you learned in these categories. Did anything surprise you? What new ideas or facts did the book introduce you to that you had not thought of before?

C. LIFE OF A SLAVE

_____

_____

_____

_____

D. LIFE OF A PLANTATION OWNER

_____

_____

_____

_____

—*Kevin Palkovic*

Problem–Solution

Once again, I'll wager that no preservice or in-service teacher answering the questions in Action Research 6.C had any trouble seeing how the problem–solution pattern is evident in his discipline. Literature is based on conflict; if a protagonist does not have to come up against some force, human or otherwise, there simply is no story. So, the most common story structure is that of a struggle building, reaching a climax, and being resolved in some way. Math students, as well as math textbooks, refer to the work they have to do as "math problems"; they search for "solutions," although there have been problems, such as Fermat's last theorem, that have taken centuries to solve. History is often relayed through explanations of problems and at least attempted solutions, though one group's solution doesn't always please another, which can lead to more problems. Artists, athletes, and scientists encounter problems in their projects, as well

as in their lives. Paying attention to the problem–solution patterns in a text can aid comprehension; in fact, readers can predict the solutions to problems and read to confirm or disconfirm them.

Your reading guides, your modeling, and your instructions regarding reading will teach students to recognize and to think using this important pattern. They can also react to the problem solving evident in their curriculum. For example, Josten (1996), in an article aptly titled "Students Rehashing Historical Decisions—and Loving It!" explains a structured strategy she teaches her students called Concerns and Decision Making (CAD) so that they can discuss and evaluate the real decisions they learn about in their textbooks. The article illustrates how students used the question, "Did the Continental Congress make a good or a poor decision when it adopted the Ordinance of 1785 and the Northwest Ordinance of 1787?" (p. 571). After reading and discussing the data, they agreed with the decision. Imagine using

FIGURE 6.5 *A semantic map showing similarities and differences in two novels relative to the concept of grieving.*

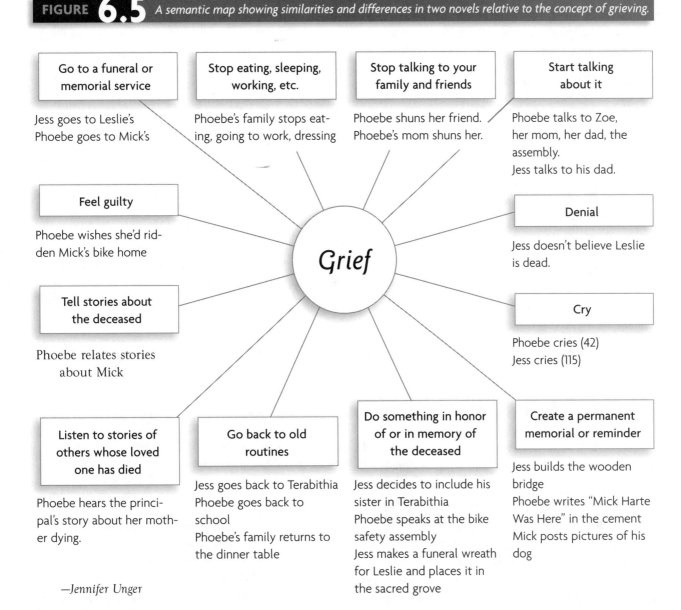

—*Jennifer Unger*

this strategy to think about recent U. S. Supreme Court decisions, presidential acts, or decisions made by scientific research organizations or by characters in works of fiction. As students repeat the strategy in several disciplines with a variety of text samples, they will rely less on teacher guidance and become independent users of the strategy—they'll own it, and they'll determine when it will help them comprehend and evaluate texts in different contexts. It can also help them as they confront problems, academic and otherwise, and seek viable solutions.

By giving students ways to grapple with problems in texts and problems in their lives, as well as in your field of study, and to recognize and utilize the problem–solution pattern, you enable them to become active constructors of knowledge. You open up new worlds to them within and beyond the texts they're reading. Figure 6.6 depicts what a literature circle's analysis of a biography using this relationship might look like.

Enumeration

On the first page of Barbara Kingsolver's *The Poisonwood Bible* (1998), one of the five female narrators describes the jungle of the Congo in 1960 by listing vivid details that help the reader visualize the setting:

FIGURE 6.6 *A problem–solution timeline.*

Timeline based on *Restless Spirit: The Life and Work of Dorothea Lange,* by Elizabeth Partridge (2002).

PROBLEM: 1936. Dorothea knows she has to help the starving migrant workers at the pea-pickers' camp at Nipoma, California.

SOLUTION: She brings her photos to the *San Francisco News,* and they are published. "Seeing the desperate, helpless mother unable to feed her children shocked Americans. . . . The federal government acted immediately, shipping twenty thousand pounds of food to the California fields" (p. 5).

PROBLEM: 1942. Dorothea is conflicted about working for the War Relocation Authority, since she disagrees with Executive Order 9066, which calls for the forcible removal of people of Japanese descent living on the West Coast, taking away basic freedoms guaranteed by the Bill of Rights.

SOLUTION: Though she hasn't the power to provide a real solution, she decides, "The best she could do was to photograph the process, so there would be a clear record of what was actually happening" (pp. 83–84).

PROBLEM: 1964. Dorothea is diagnosed with incurable cancer of the esophagus. She longs for the peace and care that her doctor recommends, and must decide how to spend her final months of life.

SOLUTION: She chooses to do a retrospective show at the Museum of Modern Art in New York, covering her lifetime of photography. "In this show, I would like to be speaking to others in the sound of my own voice, poor though it may be . . . I don't care how wide I lay myself open, this time" (p. 108).

BookTalk 6.6

The books in the series *Scientists in the Field,* produced by Houghton Mifflin, provide authentic examples of how scientists operate in the problem–solution mode. Take, for instance, *Once a Wolf: How Wildlife Biologists Fought to Bring Back the Gray Wolf* by Stephen R. Swinburne (1999). This book, containing exquisite photographs, details how the deliberate killing of the wolves and altering their habitat caused an upset in the balance of nature (problem), then gives a fascinating account of scientists tracking and studying wolves, rethinking the importance of predators in ecosystems, educating the public, and diligently working for years to bring wolves back to roam free in Yellowstone National Park for the first time since 1926 (solution). "Wolf biologists believe that their work with the wolves is about fixing what humans have destroyed in the past, righting a long-standing wrong" (p. 44). That's problem–solution at its best, but biologist Doug Smith insists, "All credit is due the wolves. They are supremely adapted to life in the wild. Our plan was good, but once the wolves hit the ground, they did it. Wolves are great at being wolves" (p. 43). This book is great at helping us appreciate that.

Every space is filled with life: delicate, poisonous frogs war-painted like skeletons, clutched in copulation, secreting their precious eggs onto dripping leaves. Vines strangling their own kin in the everlasting wrestle for sunlight. The breathing of monkeys. A glide of snake belly on branch. A single-file army of ants biting a mammoth tree into uniform grains and hauling it down to the dark for their ravenous queen. And, in reply, a choir of seedlings arching their necks out of rotted tree stumps, sucking life out of death. This forest eats itself and lives forever. (p. 5)

The final sentence goes beyond enumeration; it contains the hierarchical (overarching) idea that all of the previous sentences exemplify. The more typical order is for a broad concept to be stated before specific facts. Kingsolver uses an inductive approach, and the reader is expected to understand the implicit connection between the ideas. You probably did this without being conscious of it, but your students may require instruction and guidance with this discourse level of comprehension.

Often an author uses a more direct approach, such as this pair of sentences from *Brain Surgery for Beginners:* "The human brain is the most amazing bio-computer. It can think, remember, predict, solve, create, invent, control and coordinate" (Parker & West, 1993, p. 12). The list of functions explains and emphasizes the main point. Again, you as a teacher can help your students comprehend text where the author has determined that enumeration is necessary, and you can guide them to connect those lists with other sentences so that the text as a whole is coherent. You might use a think-aloud procedure while reading a passage using this pattern, calling attention to the textual features, such as a colon before a group of examples of a point, a numbered list, bullets, or repeated words or phrases, that alert you to the organization. Note how the following quote by Saunders Redding from a biography of poet Langston Hughes uses strings of words and phrases—in other words, enumeration—to drive home points that involve the compare–contrast pattern:

> There is this difference between racial thought and feeling: what the professors, the ministers, the physicians, the social workers think, the domestics, the porters, the dockhands, the factory girls, and the streetwalkers feel—feel in a great tide that pours over into song and shout, prayer and cursing, laughter and tears. More than any other writer of his race, Langston Hughes has been swept with this tide of feeling. (Meltzer, 1997, p. 221)

A teacher could read this example aloud, using emphasis and pauses to highlight the structure of the sentences. Students can then appreciate the power of the language and the structure the author has used as they ponder the meaning of the passage. They can be guided to pay attention to enumeration cues, such as a colon followed by a string of words or phrases separated by commas, and to use the organization to comprehend the texts they read. They can bring in examples they find in magazines and newspapers. Your goal is that, eventually, your students gain automaticity, so that they recognize and use this pattern along with other organizations of connected ideas without conscious effort.

Enumeration can go beyond the word or phrase level. In the following text, also from Meltzer's biography of the poet Langston Hughes, you can help students respond to the rhythm of the sentences, as well as understand that they work together and are tied together by the final abrupt conclusion. Try reading this out loud:

> Somebody in Washington wants to put Dr. Du Bois in jail. Somebody in France wanted to put Voltaire in jail. Somebody in Franco's Spain sent Lorca, their greatest poet, to death before a firing squad. Somebody in Germany under Hitler burned the books, drove Thomas Mann into exile, and led their leading Jewish scholars to the gas chamber. Somebody in Greece long ago gave Socrates the hemlock to drink. Somebody at Golgotha erected a cross and somebody drove the nails into the hands of Christ. Somebody spat upon his garments. No one remembers their names. (Meltzer, 1997, p. 206)

I hope you can see by these examples that enumeration can be an important pattern of organization that enhances arguments, clarifies and exemplifies assertions, and adds to the force and beauty of narration and exposition. If your students get in the habit of recognizing and paying attention to its use in texts, they will strengthen their discourse knowledge and increase their comprehension abilities. Writing and spoken discourse can improve, also; we deal with these further in Chapters 7 and 8.

COMBINING AND APPLYING PATTERNS OF ORGANIZATION

In reality and in text, the patterns of organization are not discrete, occurring in isolation; nor should they be in our thinking and teaching. That is artificial. The following scenario shows a teacher, Ms. Ramalho, guiding her students before, during, and after their reading of an information book as part of a middle school interdisciplinary unit.

> As you know, you've been learning in all of your subject areas about the topic of disease. As mathematicians, you've looked at the numbers involved in various epidemics and worked with those numbers to ask questions and solve problems. You've flagged our classroom time line across the top of the wall and our world map at points when and where plagues have occurred. You've played the role of scientists as you investigated how certain diseases affect victims and how they spread. Now, we're about to begin a fascinating book called *When Plague Strikes: The Black Death, Smallpox, AIDS* by James Cross Giblin. Most of you are familiar with this author of informational books; many of you have taken out *The Mystery of the Mammoth Bones, The Riddle of the Rosetta Stone,* and *Let There Be Light* from our classroom library.
>
> You also know that I've encouraged you to look for patterns of organization in the texts you read, to use them to help you understand, study, and remember information, and also to use them in your own writing to organize your thinking and help your readers. *When Plague Strikes* uses all of the patterns of organization, and it is a really powerful book that I think you'll find intriguing and thought-provoking. I've created a chart for you to fill in as you go along, or at the end of each section—whichever is the best comprehension strategy for you as a reader. Let's look it over first so you know what you'll be particularly looking for.
>
> Across the top I've put categories that I considered important as I read the book. Giblin deals with each of these topics in each of the three sections of the book. The first category has to do with CAUSES:

How did the epidemics start? The second will involve INFORMATION—fill in the boxes in this column with statistics, facts about the plagues that you found important or interesting. The third has to do with HUMAN NATURE AND THINKING. In every epidemic described in this book, people looked for scapegoats to blame when they couldn't understand the reasons for such magnitude of suffering. We'll be comparing, contrasting, and critiquing people's reactions to crisis. The final column will help you organize what you learn about the EFFECTS of each epidemic. Find out the political, social, and economic impact they had, as well as the advances in science and medicine.

You can write free responses in your dialogue journal as you read. Write whatever you want, in whatever format you want. In addition, as usual, I also want you to monitor your comprehension; be metacognitive. Ask yourself and the author questions, make predictions, note where your hypotheses get confirmed or disconfirmed, note places where you have difficulty understanding what the text is saying. In short, be an active reader. And let me know if you're confused and could use a bit of help. When we finish the book, we'll go over our compare–contrast chart, have a discussion, and see where our reading and thinking will lead us next.

Ms. Ramalho allows some class time for silent reading; during this time, she's available for those with questions or experiencing difficulty. She might have the book on tape for certain students; she may read aloud to a small group, or have partners reading off in corners. Students are allowed to collaborate as they fill in the chart. After the students have read the book, filled out the chart, discussed what they learned from the book, and given their response to and evaluation of the book itself, Ms. Ramalho gives a follow-up project:

You'll all do independent reading having to do with one of the plagues discussed in Giblin's book or a different one. You can use the categories from our chart to help you think about and organize the information you learn. You can choose to read one of the following three books: *Fever: 1793*, by Laurie Halse Anderson, which is a fictional story about a family, as well as a well-researched account of an epidemic in America during its early days; *The Hot Zone*, a popular book by Richard Preston about the Ebola virus; or *Flu: The Story of the Great Influenza Pandemic of 1918 and the Search for the Virus that Caused It*, by Gina Kolata, a recent nonfiction selection that represents the continuing fascination with this historical event. You'll learn science and medicine, statistics, history; you'll ponder ethical questions and look at noble and not so noble exam-

ples of human nature in times of crisis. You'll come away from your book changed.

Some of you may prefer exploring reference materials and the Internet for information about a particular disease that has or is causing havoc among populations, families, and individuals. That's fine. Ms. Bresnahan, our librarian, and I will be here to help you develop questions and search for answers. The chart will probably work for you too; though if it doesn't, we'll come up with new ways to organize your thinking and the information you're finding. All of you will have the opportunity to share what you've learned so that we all learn from each other and our knowledge of the big picture will grow.

Remember, as you read, look for clue words and phrases that alert you to the author's use of sequence or time order, cause–effect, and compare–contrast. They help comprehension.

> *Getting Ready to Teach 6.3* (see page 197)

> *Getting Ready to Teach 6.4* (see page 198)

> *Getting Ready to Teach 6.5* (see page 198)

Part One has encouraged you to provide wide reading experiences and explicit comprehension instruction to your students. Teachers should explain and model strategies, perhaps by thinking aloud as they implement them using authentic texts; monitor the students' practice; scaffold instruction based on students' needs; and reduce feedback and instruction as students become independent. Teachers also should show students how to transfer the use of strategies to various learning contexts and types of text. Pressley (2000), in his review of the research on comprehension instruction, emphasizes, "Teaching to stimulate the development of comprehension skills must be multi-componential and developmental. . . . Comprehension instruction can be enhanced by long-term instruction that fosters development of the skills and knowledge articulated by very good readers as they read" (p. 557). At the same time, we must heed Block's (1999) warning, "No matter how well students engage in comprehension strategies, if they do not have the opportunity to read what they want, they may never fall under the spell of wonderful texts" (p. 100).

PART TWO

Helping Students to Think and Read Critically

I'm sure you've heard the phrase *critical thinking* as a goal for our students and for everyone else, because we're living in times that demand it more than ever. But what is it? How is critical thinking different from just plain thinking? Take a moment to define the term for yourself. Free associate, make a semantic web, jot down examples, anything to help you operationalize the concept and become aware of what you already know about it. Compare your ideas with others'. Then reflect on these two examples of advice from chemist Linus Pauling. As he accepted the Nobel Prize for Chemistry, he said to his audience:

> When an old and distinguished person speaks to you, listen to him carefully and with respect—*but do not believe him.* Never put your trust in anything but your own intellect. Your elder, no matter whether he has gray hair or has lost his hair, no matter whether he is a Nobel laureate, may be wrong. . . . So you must always be skeptical—*always think for yourself.* (Hager, 1995, p. 108)

Another time he exhorted a group of college students:

> You must always search for truth. . . . Truth does not depend upon the point of view. If your neighbor does not see things as you do, then you must search for the truth. If a statement is made in one country and not another, then you must search for the truth. (p. 103)

DEFINING CRITICAL THINKING

Let's examine a few definitions of critical thinking set forth by educators. You'll see some similarities and some differing points of emphasis. Using them together, you should begin to have a richer understanding of the concept.

1. Three characteristics . . . could be likened to a "cognitive engine" that propels the critical thinking process. These three elements . . . include (1) the ability of the learner to draw upon background knowledge, (2) the ability of the learner to obtain or derive meaning from diverse sources of information, and (3) the ability of the learner to recognize or generate objectives that direct attention and regulate thinking. These elements are used interactively, with constant adjustments being made in order to reach a solution to a problem. (Ryder & Graves, 1998, p. 149)

2. Critical thinking encompasses a variety of deliberative processes aimed at making wise decisions about what to believe and do, processes that include more than just evaluation of arguments. The best way to teach critical thinking is to integrate logic, both formal and informal, with a variety of skills and topics useful in making sound decisions about claims, actions and practices—and to make it all palatable by presenting it in real-life contexts. . . . Critical thinking is simply the careful, deliberate determination of whether we should accept, reject or suspend judgment about a claim—and of the degree of confidence with which we accept or reject it. (Moore and Parker, 1995)

3. **Critical Thinking** The thought processes characteristic of creativity, criticism, and logic in literature, the arts, science, and other disciplines; divergent thinking. (NCTE & IRA, 1996, p. 71, Glossary)

4. Critical thinking is reasonable reflective thinking that is focused on deciding what to believe or do. (Ennis, 1996, p. 396)

5. . . . three types of skills—interpretive skills, verification skills, and reasoning skills—constitute what are usually referred to as critical thinking skills. . . . Mastering critical thinking skills is . . . a matter of intellectual self-respect. We all have the capacity to learn how to distinguish good arguments from bad ones and to work out for ourselves what we ought and ought not to believe, and it diminishes us as persons if we let others do our thinking for us. (Hughes, 2000, p. 23)

One way to think about thinking is to categorize the process according to levels. Several decades ago in the *Taxonomy of Education Objectives: The Classification of Educational Goals. Handbook I: Cognitive Domain* (1956), Bloom and Krathwohl proposed six categories of thinking levels: knowledge, comprehension, application, analysis, synthesis, and evaluation. These labels and levels have been applied, argued, criticized and adapted ever since.

For example, Carol Booth Olson, in a book called *Thinking Writing* (1992), describes a major collaborative effort of a group of teachers who modified Bloom and Krathwohl's categories to meet their purposes:

> In our integration of thinking and writing, we have reconceptualized Bloom's taxonomy in light of our own classroom experiences and thirty years of research. We perceive all thinking, whether it be at the knowledge level or evaluation level, to be critical. Generative writing requires that writers tap into all levels of the taxonomy—to recall, to express, to organize, to examine, to create, and to evaluate. However, these acts of cognition do not necessarily occur one at a time or progress in a certain order. . . . We also contend that all thinking levels pose their own difficulty; knowledge is not always a simpler behavior than comprehension. . . . The taxonomy is not simply linear but is, instead, multidimensional. (p. 13)

CAN CRITICAL THINKING BE TAUGHT?

Of course we want our students to become independent thinkers, critical thinkers. And as content area teachers, we are responsible for helping them reach this goal. But how is it reached? Can higher-level thinking actually be *taught*? This question has generated much debate and research, and experts sometimes disagree on how teachers should handle teaching in this area. Csikszentmihalyi (1996) believes, "It is easier to enhance creativity by changing conditions in the environment than by trying to make people think more creatively" (p. 1). The same can be said for critical thinking; Brown (1993) contrasts two dominant approaches to instruction in thinking:

> One aims to teach elements of thinking and problem solving directly, either as subjects in themselves or, more popularly, as dimensions of any subject matter. The other aims to develop a comprehensive literateness, assuming that thoughtfulness will necessarily evolve along the way.
>
> In the first camp, one finds many teachers trying to move their students through the stages of Bloom's taxonomy—synthesis, analysis, interpretation, and evaluation. . . . In the second camp, one finds people whose roots lie more in the humanities than in the sciences, more in progressive educational philosophy, language, sociolinguistics, reading, writing, and literacy studies. For these theorists and educators, a whole-language approach to instruction, or an experience-based, child-centered approach, or a constructivist, hands-on, active-

learning approach, is primary; thinking, problem solving, and creativity are things that naturally happen in an environment designed to encourage the construction and negotiation of meaning. (pp. 238–239)

Johnson (2000) has labeled three types of thinking instruction. The first is the *stand-alone approach*, where teachers teach thinking skills separately from any subject-matter content, and then teach how to transfer those skills to situations and content areas. Second, the *immersion approach* rejects the direct instruction of thinking skills in favor of allowing thinking to develop naturally as a result of being engaged in content-related activities calling for high levels of thinking. Finally, Johnson recommends the *embedded approach*, using the meaningful context of content-area instruction to teach thinking skills that students can immediately apply and that will help them learn the subject matter more deeply. The curriculum is enhanced, and mastery is realized over time with repeated exposure, instruction, and practice.

There will be opportunities every day for you to use such an embedded approach in your subject area, for your content will supply you with authentic examples of problems that call for much thought. Brown exhorts us:

> If you want young people to think, you ask them hard questions and let them wrestle with the answers. If you want them to analyze something or interpret it or evaluate it, you ask them to do so and show them how to do it with increasing skill. If you want them to know how to approach interesting or difficult problems, you give them interesting or difficult problems and help them develop a conscious repertoire of problem-solving strategies. If you want them to think the way scientists and historians and mathematicians do, you show them how scientists and historians and mathematicians think, and you provide opportunities for them to practice and compare those ways of thinking. (p. 232)

I hope that these ideas sound familiar to you at this point because I have tried from the very beginning to have you think critically using real texts. You were required to do some hard thinking about societies, rules, freedom, and pain after reading *The Giver*. In Chapter 3, you had to really think about what teaching might be like in a school that had thrown out the textbooks. The excerpts from literature and primary sources in each chapter are meant to challenge and enhance your thinking about literacy and pedagogy. The rest of this chapter introduces ways that you can enhance the development of critical thinking as your students become literate and knowledgeable in your subject area. Actually, Part One gave you a start; the comprehension strategies introduced there and the critical-thinking strategies coming up are not mutually exclusive; the former often called for higher-level thinking.

STRATEGIES FOR FOSTERING CRITICAL THINKING AND HIGH-LEVEL COMPREHENSION

Research shows that readers must be strategically engaged in the construction of meaning (American Psychological Association Presidential Task Force on Psychology in Education, 1993; Learner-Centered Principles Revision Work Group, 1995). This section presents some strategies you and your students may find useful. But first, I want to emphasize our recurring theme of authenticity. There are many exercises and published instructional materials ready to assist you with the task of teaching critical-thinking skills. Most don't supply any data showing that students ever transfer these skills and apply them to actual situations in their lives. So, seek to become proficient in using the strategies that truly make sense in the context of your subject. Different curricular topics, educational goals, and student needs will help you determine which approaches fit best at any given time.

Learning How Practitioners in the Disciplines Think

Recall that in Chapter 4 you were given suggestions for helping students develop procedural knowledge through learning about practitioners in various academic fields. This is a very broad strategy, a *heuristic*. Before you give students any specific strategies to use for enhancing their own critical thinking, you can give them lots of scenarios showing the real thinking of real people in real contexts. Here's one example. Scientists met in small groups after World War II to discuss what they had learned from the experience of two atom bombs being dropped on cities of Japan. Much of their thinking and discussion involved new scientific knowledge, but they also pondered the future and the ethics of weapons and war. Much critical thinking was occurring as they questioned whether it was immoral to have developed the atomic bomb. Chemist Linus Pauling, recognizing that the bomb meant a changed role for scientists, wrote, "The problem presented to the world by the destructive power of atomic energy overshadows, of course, any other problem. . . . I feel

that, in addition to our professional activities in the nuclear field, we should make our voices known with respect to the political significance of science" (Hager, 1998, p. 80). Pauling acted on this belief; he sent a petition to American scientists asking them to support a ban on all nuclear testing, and received more than 2,000 signatures, including some from Nobel Prize winners. He gathered 9,000 more from the world's scientific community and presented the petition to the United Nations (p. 111).

What a story for our students to think about! All those professionals critically thinking about the situation and coming to a decision, one way or another. How would our science students respond?

We could continue Pauling's story for our math, science, and social studies students; you'll find interdisciplinary connections as you read. In 1951, during the anticommunist repression in the United States, a military review board demanded that Pauling explain his political views:

> Pauling replied with a long statement in which he made a scientific statement for free speech. The way he saw it, American politics could be thought of as a matter of statistics: "The principle upon which a true democratic system operates is that no single man is wise enough to make the correct decisions about the very complex problems that arise, and that the correct decisions are to be made by the process of averaging the opinions of all the citizens in a democracy. These opinions will correspond to a probability distribution curve extending from far on the left to far on the right. If, now, we say that all of the opinions that extend too far to the right . . . are abnormal, and are to be excluded in taking the average, then the average that we obtain will be the wrong one. And an understanding of the laws of probability would accordingly make it evident to the citizen that the operation of the democratic system requires that everyone have the right to express his [sic] opinions about political questions, no matter what that opinion might be."
>
> Pauling was pointing out that no good scientist would lop off just one end of a set of findings, because the resulting average would be thrown off. In America, the attempt to lop off the views of those on the left wing of the political spectrum would have the same skewing effect— and so he concluded that the best system, the most scientific, democratic system, should be to allow free speech for all. (Hager, 1998, p. 105)

Think about how you might use this text with your students. Might it help them to think critically, and to realize that our everyday lives constantly call for critical thinking?

Through books and articles, other scientists can also serve as co-teachers in our classrooms. Richard Feynman, a Nobel prize–winning physicist, describes the thinking processes he used while on a commission investigating the Challenger explosion. He read earlier documents from engineers and seals experts, and found disturbing contradictions and data in some "flight readiness reviews," so he asked an expert to explain the logic within them. He discovered, "The analysis concluded that a little unpredictable leakage here and there could be tolerated, even though it wasn't part of the original design" (Feynman, 1988, p. 138). Feynman gives his evaluation of *this* thinking:

> If *all* the seals had leaked, it would have been obvious even to NASA that the problem was serious. But only a few of the seals leaked on only some of the flights. So NASA had developed a peculiar kind of attitude: if one of the seals leaks a little and the flight is successful, the problem isn't so serious. Try playing Russian roulette that way: you pull the trigger and the gun doesn't go off, so it must be safe to pull the trigger again. (p. 138)

Think of ways you could have your students use this information to stimulate and propel their own thinking. It could lead to some powerful classroom discussion and increased awareness as they follow current events and debates among politicians, business representatives, scientists, religious groups, military leaders, and medical workers.

ACTIVATING PRIOR KNOWLEDGE   6.2

Did your experiences in middle school and high school enable you to think critically about what you were learning and apply your thinking to real situations outside school? Try to think of some examples when that happened. Or, if you have no examples, try to understand what went wrong. Write for a few moments in your learning log.

Now, read what physicist Stephen Hawking (1993) says on this topic:

> What can be done to . . . give the public the scientific background it needs to make informed decisions on subjects like acid rain, the greenhouse effect, nuclear weapons, and genetic engineering? Clearly, the basis must lie in what is taught in schools. But in schools science is often presented in a dry and uninteresting manner. Children learn it by rote to pass examinations, and they don't see its relevance to the world around them. (Hawking, 1993, pp. 28–29)

Do you agree?

You hold a potential solution to the problem that Hawking describes and that you may have personally experienced. By bringing in books, stories, and current newspaper and magazine articles illustrating the thinking processes of real people in your field, and having the students respond to them and join the conversations, you encourage and facilitate critical thinking by your students. This can work for every discipline. For example, students in a history class could listen to tapes of Abraham Lincoln's major speeches throughout his career; it would be fascinating for them to hear him grapple with the issues facing him and the nation, sometimes changing his mind as his wisdom grew. For years, he agonized over the discrepancy between his personal opinion that slavery was immoral and his belief that it was not within his rights to force others to stop the practice in places where the law allowed it. (Recall from Chapter 3 that his contemporary, John Brown, thought very differently about the slavery dilemma.)

Others' thinking, from both the far and recent past, can help our students' thinking about the difficult issue of what to do when personal conviction and the law clash. We can bring in Thoreau's essay on *Civil Disobedience*, Sophocles' play *Antigone*, and texts by and about conscientious objectors during every war America has fought to provide further contexts within which to think critically about the topic.

ACTIVATING PRIOR KNOWLEDGE   6.3

Speaking of civil disobedience, can you think of a time when educators have been, or might find themselves in, a situation where their convictions about what is good, or not good, for children might be opposed to the law or to school policy? In such a case, what action might be called for? Is it ever all right for a teacher to disobey a law? Write in your learning log for a few minutes, and share your examples and opinions with others.

Many teachers are grappling with what they consider to be harmful assessment practices imposed by their states. A 2001 issue of the *Phi Delta Kappan* included articles with telling titles: "Fighting the Tests: A Practical Guide to Rescuing Our Schools" by the well-known critic Alfie Kohn and "News from the Test Resistance Trail" by Susan Ohanian, which included a chart called "The Honor Roll of Resistance," citing teachers who refused to give standardized tests, sometimes at the cost of their jobs, sometimes resulting in arrest. The topic of assessment is explored in Chapter 10. For now, I present this example to show you that, as a professional, you will be faced with any number of opportunities to exercise critical thinking, to try to understand those whose convictions may differ radically from yours, and to act on your convictions.

You can find numerous examples in educational journals showing how teachers engage their students in thinking like members of a disciplinary field. The following descriptions give you a glimpse into a few such classrooms.

Stoskopf (2001) lists historical-thinking skills that can be employed beneficially in classrooms. He recommends using primary source documents and having students examine them for the following:

- Point of view. How does the author's personal background and status influence what is being written?
- Credibility of evidence. How reliable is the source? Where did it originate, and for what purpose was it used at the time?
- Historical context. How does one see the past on its own terms? While this is never totally possible, historians are vigilant about not allowing present-day values to obscure the sensibilities of a past age.
- Causality. How does one avoid seeing past events as caused by just one factor?
- Multiple perspectives. How does one weigh different interpretations of the same event? (p. 469)

Stoskopf has seen that elementary, middle, and secondary teachers can get students engaged in such historical thinking. He provides an example of a fourth-grade classroom studying the era of the Pilgrims, using primary documents and secondary sources. He describes a seventh-grade unit on immigration, where students studied historical data, formed historical hypotheses, and compared these with other accounts of the demographics of Irish immigration. They wrote narratives about families they chose from actual records, and practiced literacy skills—they sometimes had to read information four or five times, with the teacher's assistance, to understand it. Stoskopf concludes:

> No, the students did not become historians after this eight-week unit. But they did develop self-confidence in their ability to stay with something that did not come to them automatically. They learned "facts" about history, but they did not rush through the curriculum simply to cover more and more. They learned how to think in a different and deeper way, and they were better able to remember the details of the period because the information was embedded in a meaningful context. (p. 470)

Discipline-based inquiry can be taught in any and every subject area. Haugen (2001) explains how lessons using leeches taught students to think like scientists. An inquiry-based program involving the steps of engaging, exploring, explaining, evaluating, and extending or elaborating combined the hands-on experiences of laboratory activities with the use of reference books, journal articles, and the Internet that resulted in the students publishing a report on leeches. The students selected a question and then designed an investigation and researched possible answers. They sent their teams' unanswered questions to experts in the field who had agreed to be their online science partners. Haugen noted that the process was really an extended example of Ogle's K-W-L strategy, which you are familiar with from previous chapters.

Through their authentic research and their extensive reading, students learn that real scientists do not follow just one formulaic approach known as the scientific method. Problems differ; personal styles differ; there are many avenues of inquiry.

ACTION RESEARCH   6.D

Find an article about a classroom where the teacher and the students use an inquiry approach or use the kinds of thinking people in the disciplines use. Figure 6.7 lists possible sources, but you'll find many more as you check current educational literature. Or, visit a classroom, in person or via the Internet, that exemplifies disciplinary exploration and thinking about real problems. Write a reflection about what you learn.

BookTalk   6.7

Charles Wilson Peale was a portrait artist who had no formal scientific training, but whose lifelong interest in science, combined with excellent thinking, led him to the solution of *The Mystery of the Mammoth Bones* (1999). Author James Cross Giblin uses Peale's diaries and journals to tell how he went about the quest that resulted in much scientific knowledge about extinct animals and the age of the earth. You'll be inspired as you read this detailed account of a man so passionate about his two fields of study that he even named his children after artists (Rembrandt, Rubens, Raphael) and scientists (Charles Linnaeus and Benjamin Franklin). Readers get inside the mind of a practitioner to see real thinking working on real issues.

FIGURE 6.7 *Selected examples of articles about discipline-based inquiry.*

Foster, S. (1999). Using Historical Empathy to Excite Students About the Study of History: Can You Empathize with Neville Chamberlain? *The Social Studies*, 90(1), 18–34.

Hynd, C. R. (1999). Teaching Students to Think Critically Using Multiple Texts in History. *Journal of Adolescent and Adult Literacy*, 42(6), 428–436.

Kuhlman, W. D. (2001). Fifth-graders' Reactions to Native Americans in *Little House on the Prairie:* Guiding Students' Critical Reading. *The New Advocate*, 14(4), 387–399.

Lederman, N. G., & Niess, M. L. (2000). Problem Solving and Solving Problems: Inquiry About Inquiry. *School Science and Mathematics*, March, 113–116.

Mayer, R. H. (1999). Use the Story of Anne Hutchinson to Teach Historical Thinking. *The Social Studies*, 90(3), 105–109.

Totten, S. (1998). Using Reader Response Theory to Study About the Holocaust with High School Students. *The Social Studies*, 89(1), 30–34.

AN INQUIRY-BASED CLASSROOM

The national English Language Arts learning standards call for students to think critically, to be able to analyze and critically evaluate texts. Many of the strategy examples discussed earlier show how you can help your students think critically about particular texts and topics. But don't count on the strategies working or transferring to future reading assignments if they're used in isolation or at irregular junctures in your curriculum. Critical inquiry must be an actual stance you and your students adopt and live by throughout your course. The following draws a picture of a teacher who provided a framework and ongoing support for investigating language use. It should help you to visualize what an inquiry-based classroom might look like, and stimulate your thinking about applying the principle of discipline-based inquiry in the courses you teach.

Bob Fecho, a high school teacher, begins his chapter "Crossing Boundaries of Race in a Critical Literacy Classroom" (1998) with a scenario from his classroom that led to his own inquiry into language issues and pedagogy. This is followed by a literature review of works and people who have informed his thinking about the cultural and political aspects of standard and nonstandard English use, critical pedagogy, and critical literacy. Confronted by the dilemma of how to celebrate the diversity of language use while giving his students access to standard codes of power, he "stacked my most accepted and trusted theorists before me" (p. 89). Fecho lets the reader in on his metacognitive processing as he makes his instructional decisions. "I write of this as if it were a free-flowing and continuous package exuding from my brain and becoming whole in the classroom. The reality is that I was making it up as I went along.

My head was a jumble of core beliefs and ideological stances trying to concoct a place for each" (p. 89).

Fecho provided his students with an essential question, a skeleton framework—he asked them how learning connects them to their world. He developed three inquiry projects, the first of which focused on raising issues about the nature of language. He used literature, such as William Gibson's *The Miracle Worker* (1957), from which themes emerged that drove the curriculum for the year. The second third of the year consisted of autobiographical inquiry into language. Using movies as models, students wrote four chapters of an autobiography, at least one of which had to deal with how language affected their lives. New themes, including racism, profanity, empowerment, victimization, and popular culture, emerged from the students' writing. Four major concerns, relating to the nature of Standard English, slang and profanity, Black English, and code switching (shifting language based on social expectations and audience), permeated the students' investigations and led to the final stage of the course: individual investigations based on questions the students generated. They collected data through journal keeping, interviews, and other avenues, and then made tentative assertions and analyses.

Fecho concludes with his realization "that a critical-inquiry classroom is one where multiple perspectives can and, indeed, must flourish" (p. 95) and his belief that "adolescents are capable of conducting substantive inquiry and critique into the nature and impact of language in their lives" (p. 95). I encourage you to read the text in its entirety to experience the rich examples and reflection present there.

Dialogical Thinking Strategy

One of the characteristics of real-life problems is that they are complicated, and decisions have both costs and benefits. Patients with life-threatening illnesses often must weigh and then choose between options that involve medical risks, financial considerations, effects on families, and quality-of-life issues. Business and political challenges involve finances, ethics, long- and short-term goals, and obstacles. There are winners and losers in most situations that call for critical thinking. *Dialogical thinking*, going back and forth between opposing opinions, truly trying to see both sides of an argument or understanding multiple perspectives, is a valuable critical-thinking skill. Teachers can promote dialogical thinking by playing devil's advocate (make the students aware that this is what you are doing) during discussions of problematic issues. One approach you can teach your students is to draw up a visual representation of the pros and cons of potential actions to help them think before they draw conclusions. Sometimes, they can contribute ideas to such a chart from their own background knowledge. At other times, they can use information from a text you supply, or they can do research to learn the advantages and disadvantages relative to a topic they're studying. Figure 6.8 shows an example regarding the controversial issue of global warming. Students can discuss this chart and then use it as a model as they explore various viewpoints on other issues. They might use a similar poster as they give an oral presentation on cloning, immigration policies, or technology in schools. Figure 6.9 provides a guide for applying dialogical thinking to the issue of pet cloning.

FIGURE 6.8 *An example of dialogic thinking applied to a current problem.*

PROS AND CONS

Controversy about the likelihood of global warming centers around its possible deleterious effects. The issue has its share of optimists who even predict bene-	ficial effects from global warming. The following are some of the arguments and counterarguments one is likely to encounter:
Optimists: The increase in carbon dioxide will act as a fertilizer, stimulating the growth of plants. These plants will absorb the excess carbon dioxide.	Pessimists: Plant matter (or biomass) cannot absorb these enormous quantities of carbon dioxide—unless you plant trees over an area of three billion acres. In addition, plants and animals produce carbon dioxide in cell respiration. It has also been found that some plants "shut down" their absorbing capacity if they are exposed to high concentrations of carbon dioxide.
Optimists: As the Earth gets warmer, the growing season in high latitudes will be extended, and there will be an increase in the amount of arable land. Global warming will produce an agricultural bonanza. We will be able to grow pineapples in Wisconsin.	Pessimists: Lands in high latitudes, such as northern Canada, do not have the topsoil to sustain intensive cultivation. In addition, the expected speed of global warming will not give natural systems a chance to adapt to change. What we are more likely to see is an environmental mismatch, with unknown consequences.
Optimists: Aerosols will continue to slow the pace of warming.	Pessimists: Aerosols do not remain in the atmosphere as long as carbon dioxide. Carbon dioxide remains for at least one hundred years, while aerosols can wash out in days.

From *Who Gives a Gigabyte?* by G. Stix and M. Lacob. Copyright © 1999 by John Wiley and Sons. Reprinted with permission of John Wiley and Sons, Inc.

FIGURE 6.9   *A reading guide for an economics lesson on finance, budgeting, and ethics.*

DIRECTIONS: Before writing anything down, think of what comes to mind when you hear the word *cloning*. Then take a few minutes to brainstorm about the pros and cons of pet cloning. Fill in the chart provided below. If you need help getting started, here are some things to think about:

- the 55 million pet dogs in America
- the little girl whose cat just got hit by a car
- the numerous animals in shelters waiting to be adopted
- the boy whose favorite dog has become old and feeble
- the high costs of the cloning procedure
- the likelihood (or lack thereof) of successful cloning

PROS

_____

_____

_____

_____

CONS

_____

_____

_____

_____

Meet with a partner to share your lists. If one side is longer than the other, take on the perspective of someone who is in favor of or opposed to pet cloning, and imagine what arguments each would use. Also, try to categorize the specifics you have in the columns. Which are economic arguments? social? ethical? practical?

Now, read the article "CLONING—Copy Cat—The First Cloned Pet Sure Looks Harmless. Would a Cloned Human?" (*Time*, February 25, 2002, pp. 58–59). Add to your chart any new information you have obtained. Then, answer the following questions:

1. How might cloning eventually affect our society?

_____

2. Would you be willing to spend $1,000 for a chance to get your pet cloned?

_____

3. Assuming you or a friend answered yes to Question 2, how might you earn and budget the money for the procedure?

_____

_____

4. Think of other ways that cloning could relate to math. Make a list. You can collaborate with your partner on this.

_____

_____

5. List other procedures or policies where cost is a factor that sometimes affects decisions involving ethical or controversial issues.

_____

_____

—Erika Moshier

BookTalk 6.8

The series *Taking Sides* exemplifies dialogic thinking. Each volume asks questions relating to a broad topic, then provides a "Yes" essay and a "No" essay by experts in the field. For example, *Taking Sides: Clashing Views on Controversial Issues in Race and Ethnicity* (1994), edited by Richard C. Monk, asks, among other things, "Should Bilingual Education Programs Be Stopped?" It provides an affirmative answer in an article by history of education professor Diane Ravitch, followed by an article with an opposing answer by professor of linguistics Donaldo Macedo. Students could analyze and evaluate the strength of the arguments and add their opinions to the debates presented in these books. Other volumes in the series include *Taking Sides: Clashing Views on Controversial Issues in Business Ethics and Society* (1994), edited by Lisa H. Newton and Maureen M. Ford, and *Taking Sides: Clashing Views on Psychological Issues* (1996), edited by Brent Slife.

The REAP Strategy

Read–Encode–Annotate–Ponder (Eanet & Manzo, 1976; Manzo & Manzo, 1997) is a structured approach to critical thinking about a text. It consists of the following steps:

1. R: Read to discern the writer's message.
2. E: Encode the message by translating it into your own words.
3. A: Annotate by cogently writing the message in notes for yourself or in a thought book or on an electronic response system.
4. P: Ponder, or further reflect on, what you have read or written, through discussion and by reviewing others' responses to the same materials and/or your own annotation. (Manzo & Manzo, 1997, p. 170)

As with other strategies, the REAP steps represent what skilled readers often do. As they read, they might jot in a margin a personal reaction (positive or negative), a critique, a connection to a current event or another text, a question about the author's intent or use of a literary device. As you model the strategy, show your students the different types and levels of thinking that can occur during annotation. Manzo and Manzo categorize REAP responses into two categories: *reconstructive responses*, which include summarizing and questioning, and *constructive responses*, which include personal views, critical responses, contrary responses, creative responses, and discovery responses. This last type consists of practical questions that must be answered before the text can be judged for accuracy or merit, thus leading to more reading, research, and rethinking. As students apply and practice the strategy and become increasingly independent, you can help them self-monitor and evaluate how well the strategy is working for them.

ACTION RESEARCH 6.E

The best way for you to make the REAP strategy your own is to try it out. Follow the four steps as you read the text in Figures 6.10 and 6.11. Then, write a reaction synthesizing the two articles, as well as bringing in your own thoughts and information from other sources on the subject of genetic engineering in light of this new discovery of unforeseen consequences. As you ponder, evaluate how well these writers have made their points. Do you disagree with anything either has said? Where would you place yourself regarding this issue, if one end of a continuum said "Halt all production now!" and the other was labeled "Full speed ahead!"? How well did the REAP strategy work for you, and for those with whom you discussed your responses and your thinking?

If you find the REAP strategy beneficial, and if you have students for whom you think it might be helpful, model the strategy, using these articles and your own step-by-step notes. Or you can teach them using texts relevant to the curriculum you teach. You might ask students to bring in newspaper, Internet, or magazine articles to see whether the strategy works for different types of text. Give students guided practice, and encourage them to use the strategy on their own, with texts from their other classes and with self-selected reading. They could keep a REAP section of their learning logs or a REAP file on their laptops.

Directed Reading–Thinking Activity

The *directed reading–thinking activity* (Haggard, 1985; Stauffer, 1980) is a structured yet flexible strategy that can help you guide your students through reading a particular text; eventually, the "directed" part is eliminated as students learn to apply the strategy's steps to enhance and monitor their own comprehension and use their thinking skills as they make predictions. There are pre-reading, during-reading, and post-reading stages.

FIGURE **6.10** *REAP strategy sample text 1.*

Cornell bioengineering study: Canary in the mine shaft

A century ago, coal miners would take a canary down into the shaft with them to test whether the air was breathable. If the bird keeled over, they knew they had better get out fast.

Scientists should be paying the same brand of heed to the monarch butterfly. It may be warning us about impending ecological disaster.

Researchers at Cornell University have concluded that the pollen from a genetically engineered insect-resistant corn may be killing the butterfly's larvae. Until the discovery was revealed last week, the corn had been thought to be safe for "friendly" insects, as well as humans and other mammals. The research raises concerns that bioengineering may lead to unintended consequences for other species.

Development of the hybrid corn has been hailed as a major breakthrough in agriculture. It produces a natural toxin that kills an insect, the European corn borer, responsible for $1.2 billion in crop losses a year. The new product eliminated the need to treat corn with insecticides, which were only marginally effective against the corn borer and are toxic for other species. The bioengineered strain of corn will be planted on about 16 million acres this year.

Pollen from the "Bt" corn is carried by the wind and comes to rest on other plants such as milkweed, the only thing that monarch caterpillars eat. Research conducted before the hybrid corn was approved for commercial use did not study the possible effects of windblown pollen, the Cornell scientists said. Researchers "weren't really thinking about the toxin flying around and how it affects feeding on their own host plants," said Linda S. Rayor, a Cornell entomologist and co-author of the study.

In the laboratory, monarch larvae that ate milkweed that had been dusted with the pollen of Bt corn ate less, grew at a slower rate and died faster than larvae that were fed milkweed that hadn't been dusted. The Cornell scientists plan to study the effect of the pollen on other species of insects.

Predictably, the report was not welcomed by the corn industry, where the bioengineered corn has increased in popularity every year since it was introduced in 1995. Corn growers cited the environmental advantages of bioengineered crops—reduced use of pesticides and herbicides, as well as more abundant food. They called for more research before any conclusions are reached about the safety of the hybrid varieties.

On the other side of the question is the Union of Concerned Scientists, an independent alliance based in Cambridge, Mass. "This should help people understand that genetically engineered crops bring with them risks that have not yet been properly raised or studied," said Jane Rissler, a UCS plant pathologist. She said the UCS plans to ask the federal Environmental Protection Agency to halt approval of all engineered corn varieties.

It would seem prudent to err on the side of safety. The risks of delaying approval of bioengineered crops would seem to hold far less potential for harm than the possibility of a genetic genie being inadvertently released to create biological havoc.

This is not a call to halt bioengineering. The practice holds great promise for feeding an increasingly crowded planet. Nonetheless, genetic research and development must include complete research on its effects on species not targeted by the new strains. The Cornell researchers—and their monarch subjects—may have alerted us to a real peril in time to head it off.

From "Cornell Bioengineering Study," May 24, 1999, The Herald Co., Syracuse, NY ©1998/1999 *Herald-Journal/The Post Standard*. All rights reserved. Reprinted with permission.

Before reading, the teacher assesses the students' schemata relative to the topic and perhaps supplies some relevant background knowledge. She teaches any necessary vocabulary, or encourages students to use the surrounding context to figure out what certain words mean. She also helps the students set a purpose for reading and predict what the text might be about or what points might be raised or covered. They might write down hypotheses and then share them. This can be done with partners or in small groups.

For example, Mr. Yang is a math teacher whose class will be learning about probability. He's chosen to use the chapter "The Mathematics of Kindness: Math Proves the Golden Rule," from the book *The*

Universe and the Teacup: The Mathematics of Truth and Beauty by K. C. Cole (1998). He asks his students to free associate and make a class chart based on the terms *probability* and *game theory*. He also asks whether they know what the Golden Rule is. Most do, and he posts a chart with "Do Unto Others as You Would Have Them Do Unto You" on the wall. After that, Mr. Yang teaches four vocabulary words that he has determined are crucial to his students' understanding of the text: *paradox, dilemma, altruism,* and *symbiosis.* He tells them that they may encounter a few other unfamiliar words, but they should be able to figure them out by the way they are used in the essay's context. Next, he asks them

FIGURE **6.11**   *REAP strategy sample text 2.*

Unintended consequences: Genetic engineering worth some risks

The short story, as I recollect it, was set in a future where time travel had become possible. A fellow signed up to tour the primeval past and, like others, was cautioned to remain on the floating path and to touch nothing, because even the smallest alteration in the past could have huge consequences. He made the trip and marveled at the exotic plants and creatures of an era beyond reckoning. He scrupulously stayed on the path, but returned to his own time to find everything changed grotesquely, and in no way for the better. Puzzled, he sat down, only to discover, from the evidence on his shoe sole, that in the ancient past he had stepped on a butterfly.

The tale came back recently with the news that a study has found that a popular new corn, genetically altered to ward off insect pests but believed harmless to other insects, produces a pollen that kills monarch butterflies.

No one seems to know quite what to make of this, so far. The pollen is quite toxic to monarchs exposed to it in the laboratory, but it is not clear whether many of the butterflies encounter it in the fields.

The real danger may be quite small, or not quite small. No one knows. But everyone does know this: monarch butterflies are lovely, one of those occasions of grace that the same nature which produces droughts and volcanoes and other tumults tosses off casually, as if to make up in small things for its larger lapses.

The science of genetics is beyond me. . . . And I am not among the instinctive naysayers who, like the Luddites, would smash every novelty out of fear it surely will bring more ill than good. The status quo, by definition, won't get us anywhere.

There are risks in any change and we are reaching a point, as I understand it, where our cleverness may offer us huge changes from this still new science and bring them ever faster. Genetic engineering holds the promise, among other benefits, of more food, more safely produced. This corn, for instance, lets farmers forgo pesticides. That's good.

But such is our vanity, forever triumphing over experience, that we believe in our ability to extrapolate all the consequences of our innovations, and to judge each good or not good and weigh the balance soundly.

There are those who would so straiten genetic engineering that it could barely move. Never mind that it might—just might—be the technology that ends illness and hunger and the human strifes, from bellyache to war, that come of those.

The same science that is improving corn harvests has been approved for growing potatoes and cotton, too. I suppose we must now wonder whether there will be side effects we regret. Even the canniest science cannot repeal the law of unintended consequences, but mere alarmism does more to stymie than to guide. We have to try. It is in us to try.

We must be careful, though, not to step on the butterflies.

Tom Teepen is national correspondent for Cox Newspapers. *He is based in Atlanta.*

From "Unintended Consequences: Genetic Engineering Worth Some Risks," by Tom Teepan, 5/26/99. Copyright © 2002, Cox News Service. Reprinted with permission.

what they think they might learn from this text and accepts any predictions as valid.

Mr. Yang directs his students to read silently to a certain place in the text, at which point they discuss which, if any, of the class's predictions were confirmed. He conveys that this is not a contest, that the "right" predictions were not necessarily any more clever than the ones that were disconfirmed. He says, "Think of what you do when you read a mystery; you're making guesses as to who committed a crime, or why, or how; and there will always be a few surprises in a good story."

The students then make further predictions based on the line where the reading begins again— "Axelrod invited experts in game theory to a tournament of repeated games of prisoner's dilemma" (p. 118). What do the students think will be the outcome of this tournament? On the next page, they predict again, at the point in the text when Axelrod holds a follow-up tournament in which not only game theorists, but researchers in biology, physics, and sociology also participate, and they predict yet again when, "In a final round, Axelrod wanted to see what would happen if he pitted all the programs against each other in a kind of Darwinian evolution." (p. 119). Mr. Yang predicts that motivation will be high as students read to have their hunches verified or to find out what happened instead, and why. His prediction is confirmed.

In the post-reading phase of the activity, Mr. Yang guides the students in a debriefing as they discuss whether their purposes for reading have been met and whether they had to revise their predictions and thinking as new information and explanations were given in the text. At this point the students are able to state the main ideas and subordinate details, and ask any remaining or newly generated questions.

In Mr. Yang's role as math teacher, he might ask students to state what they learned from the text about game theory and probability. He'd ask if there were any surprises, and he might get answers such as, "Yeah, I would have thought 'survival of the fittest' meant being competitive instead of cooperative, but now I know that's not always true," or "I can't believe that 14 robots learned to cooperate to retrieve a puck even though they weren't programmed to. Maybe people should learn from them!" He'll encourage conversation, inquisitiveness, student theory-building, and then say, "Now you're ready to begin our textbook chapter on probability. Before opening to page 234, any predictions about what you'll learn?"

Figure 6.12 lists guidelines for implementing a directed reading–thinking activity.

> ### Getting Ready to Teach 6.6 *(see page 198)*

Strategies Involving Questioning

Teacher-Generated Questions

The questions teachers pose to students are highly influential in guiding learning (Alexander, Jetton, Kulikowich, & Woehler, 1994; Schellings & van Hout-Wolters, 1995). Look way back at Literature Circle Guide and worksheet for *The Giver* in the Introduction. Recall that the first set of questions about *The Giver* was very different from the second. I started you thinking back then about the value and importance of questions. Many readers of the novel, of course, do better with *no* questions than with chapter by chap-

ter checks that slow down the reading and make it less enjoyable. Yet, other readers might require teacher direction, and could find questions helpful as they construct meaning from this unusual and sometimes ambiguous dystopian work. As a content area teacher, it's important that you know *when* and *how* to use questions, and how to ask the kinds of questions that evoke the best thinking from your students. Once you know this, you can evaluate the questions in your students' textbooks or on supplementary instructional materials such as worksheets or publisher-provided tests.

One classification of questions divides them into levels. *Literal-level questions* can be answered directly from the text because the information is explicitly stated. *Interpretive* or *inferential-level questions* can be answered by piecing textual information together or by figuring out what is implied by the words of the text. Here readers perceive connections among the ideas presented and conceptualize the ideas created by those connections (Herber, 1978). *Applied* or *evaluative-level* questions require students to go beyond the text and answer from their background knowledge, or to give opinions or bring their feelings into their answer. They may require readers to make critical judgments about the ideas or the reasoning presented in the text. Again, looking at the questions on pages 5 and 7, you can see that all levels are covered in the first set of questions. Yet, the questions in the second set are likely to lead to more interesting and critical thought and discussion. They are more challenging, and they offer students some choice in the direction they want their thinking to go. The novel is rich and complex enough to allow for these avenues and many more. Perhaps students can construct their own questions that are even better for them to pursue.

Because you will be very familiar with the texts you use and with the students you teach, you will

---

FIGURE 6.12   *Guidelines for implementing a directed reading–thinking activity.*

1. Assess the students' prior knowledge about the topic and provide any necessary background information.

2. Teach any necessary vocabulary, and encourage students to use context to figure out other unfamiliar terms.

3. Help students set a purpose for reading and make predictions about the text.

4. Have students read silently, checking periodically to verify their predictions about the text. Use questions such as "What do you think?" "Why do you think that?" "Was your prediction confirmed?" "What evidence shows it was (or was not) confirmed?" and "Does anyone want to change a prediction based on what we've read so far?"

5. As a post-reading activity, guide the students to determine whether their purposes for reading have been met, ask them to summarize what they have learned from the reading, and ask them if they had to revise their predictions based on new information encountered in the text.

   Direct teaching of skills can follow, along with appropriate enrichment activities.

be in a position to determine what kinds of questions you should use. As students answer questions and discuss a text, you can learn to ask probing, clarifying, or follow-up questions to foster higher-level thinking such as analysis, synthesis, and evaluation. Your questions can also encourage creativity and inquisitiveness on the part of your students. You'll find that questions don't always fit neatly into the three categories, and that's all right.

ACTION RESEARCH   6.F

Read the following questions relating to the editorial at the beginning of this chapter, "How Cruel Can Teachers Get?" Classify the questions according to their level: *literal, interpretive,* or *applied.* Decide which of the questions you think readers, or at least particular readers, might find helpful, and add any questions you think might also aid comprehension and further thinking about the topic.

L I A   What is the summer requirement for stu-
○ ○ ○   dents in North Syracuse High School?

L I A   What is the editorial writer's opinion of
○ ○ ○   the requirement?

L I A   What is the writer's opinion of the reac-
○ ○ ○   tion of some of the students?

L I A   Do you think schools should mandate
○ ○ ○   summer reading? Give pros or cons, then
            the rationale for your decision.

L I A   What was your reaction to the editorial?
○ ○ ○   Was it an effective spoof? Evaluate the
            techniques the author used to craft the
            text.

Next, select a text in your content area and create a *three-level guide* (Herber, 1978) using literal, interpretive, and applied level questions that could help students create meaning and think critically about the topic. Figure 6.13 shows an example of a three-level guide created by a preservice math teacher.

Question–Answer Relationships

Becoming familiar with the three question levels described previously and learning about *question–answer relationships* (QARs) may help students to understand the kinds of questions they're asked to answer. Raphael (1984) suggested the following categories for questions:

1. *Right There.* Words used to create the question and words used for the answer are in the same sentence.
2. *Think and Search.* The answer is in the text, but words used to create the question and those used for an appropriate answer would not be in the same sentence.
3. *On My Own.* The answer is not found in the text. (pp. 304–305)

Variations on these terms exist. You may prefer to think of text-based questions as either *right-there* or *putting-it-together,* while questions requiring information from both the text and the reader can be called *author-and-you* QARs. Attending to the type of question and thinking about the reader's role in answering it is a metacognitive process that can help students as they think about ideas in text.

You could look through this textbook for examples of questions that represent each type. For example, think once more about *The Giver.* A question such as, "What color eyes does Jonas have?" is a *right-there* question, for the text supplies the answer. The question, "What, besides eye color, do the characters who have light-colored eyes have in common?" is a *think-and-search* question. By putting together information the text provides in different places about the several characters with light eyes, readers can construct an answer. The question "What might be the significance of the light-colored eyes?" or "Why do you think the author chose to point out the eye color of the characters?" is an *on-my-own* question. No amount of looking through the book will uncover the answer. Thinking, discussing, and relating the text to other stories with color symbolism can lead to plausible answers, though students will not come up with exactly the same conclusions, and that's fine. When you ask questions that go beyond the text, an extended investigation and stimulating project can result. For example, you might ask a class, after they have finished *The Giver,* if they think the story could be prophetic, warning about what our society could become. They could then list ways that our society *has* become either more or less like that of the novel's dystopian society since 1993, when the book was published. Students might look up data about infanticide and euthanasia, debate recent laws (such as those having to do with wearing bike helmets) that might make life safer but take away some freedoms, or interview parents about mandatory preschool. Figure 6.14 provides an example discussion guide that uses *think-and-search* and on-my-own questions.

Getting Ready to Teach 6.7 (see page 198)

FIGURE **6.13** *A three-level guide.*

DIRECTIONS: After reading the book *The History of Counting*, by Denise Schmandt-Besserat and Michael Hays (2000), answer the following questions. For the first part, you can find answers to the questions directly stated in the text. For the second part, you have to think about the question and search the text to support your answer; you have to make inferences and/or connect pieces of information. For the third part, use the knowledge gained from reading this text and your own previous knowledge to answer the questions.

LITERAL LEVEL:

1. In Papua New Guinea, what method of counting did the Paiela people use?

2. The most universal way of counting, the one the majority of people use today, is known as what?

3. What is the term for the largest number known today?

4. To what group of people do we owe the invention of abstract numbers?

INTERPRETIVE LEVEL:

1. Why are the digits of our counting system called Arabic numerals? Use the text to support your answer.

2. What are some of the advantages of using the Arabic numerals?

3. Who is believed to have invented the first counting system, and for what purpose was it invented?

APPLIED LEVEL:

1. Why do you think that numerals were first invented?

2. Which of these systems, Arabic, Roman, Hindu, Egyptian, or Greek, would you prefer to count with? Why?

3. Do you believe that zero has a numerical value, or is it an example of an abstract concept of a number? Explain your answer.

—*Jayson St. Croix*

FIGURE 6.14 *A preservice teacher's guide to discussion using* think-and-search *and* on-my-own *questions.*

DIRECTIONS: We have read *Bridge to Terabithia*, by Katherine Paterson (1977), and *Mick Harte Was Here*, by Barbara Park (1995). We have also read some excerpts from articles and nonfiction books from the school library on the topic of families grieving a child's death. Now, it's time for you to put it all together and talk with each other about what you've learned and how you're feeling. Start by sharing your journal responses and asking each other any questions that are on your mind. Then, use any of the following questions to continue the discussion.

1. How does the type of relationship between the main character and the character who dies in each book affect the main character's relationship with his or her family?

_____

_____

_____

2. How does the way Phoebe's parents cope with Mick's death differ from the way Leslie's parents cope with her death? What do you think might be reasons for the differences?

_____

_____

_____

3. Both Jess and Phoebe go through a period of disbelief after being told of the deaths. What are some examples of their denial? How does this phenomenon connect to what we've learned about what the experts say about the grieving process?

_____

_____

_____

4. Even though the deaths were accidental, both Jess and Phoebe blame themselves for the tragedies. How does each character resolve the feeling of guilt? Do you think they would have acted differently if the deaths were anticipated (if, for example, someone had died of cancer)?

_____

_____

_____

5. Which book did you like better? Why? What will you take away from each story? What would you say to Phoebe or Jess?

_____

_____

_____

_____

Student-Generated Questions

As important as good questioning is as a teaching strategy, you'll also want to foster good questioning from your students at every phase of the reading process. You can teach them to survey a text before they start reading and formulate questions based on titles and subtitles. This strategy helps them focus and read actively.

ACTION RESEARCH ▶▶▶ 6.G

Try this yourself. Imagine that a professor in an education course you're taking has assigned the chapter "The Corruption of Children's Literature and Literary Study" in Sandra Stotsky's (1999) *Losing Our Language: How Multicultural Classroom Instruction Is Undermining Our Children's Ability to Read, Write, and Reason.* Based just on this data (the assignment and the title), what are you wondering? What do you think might be explained? What guesses do you have about the author? What might her agenda be?

Now imagine you skim the assigned chapter and find these subtitles: "Pseudo-Literature and Its Uses," "A Pedagogy of Exploitation: Abusing the Study of Genuine Children's Literature," "A Pedagogy of Manipulation: Grounding Literary Understanding in Feelings," "Origins of a Pedagogy Emphasizing the Student's Personal Life," and "Why Was Devotion to Literary Quality and Literary Study Abandoned So Rapidly?" Formulate further questions that you hope will be answered by the author. Write in your learning log.

A strategic reader continues to question the author during the actual reading of the text. You can teach your students to use a procedure called, appropriately, *Questioning the Author* or QtA (Beck, McKeown, Hamilton, & Jucan, 1997). The process involves the whole class as they read a text for the first time so that they can actively and collaboratively grapple with concepts and construct meaning from the material. The teacher asks queries such as "What is the author trying to say here?" "Did the author explain that clearly?" "Does that make sense when compared with what the author has told us before?" (Beck et al., 1997). As you and your classmates read the Stotsky chapter from Action Research 6.G, queries initiated by the instructor might help you follow the author's reasoning and understand what she contends the educational establishment has done to corrupt the teaching of children's literature. Ideally, after modeling and guided practice, students internalize this kind of active questioning and apply it independently of the teacher.

I hope that after you read and critiqued the chapter by Stotsky you had lots of questions: for the author, for the instructor, for yourself. It is the teacher's responsibility to lead you to sources, people, and texts that could help you answer those questions.

Getting Ready to Teach 6.8 *(see page 198)*

Another way to help students become good questioners is to model and practice the ReQuest strategy (Manzo, 1969) in your classroom. The teacher and students silently read a portion of the text (depending on the difficulty of the text and the ability of the students, this could be as little as a sentence or as much as a few paragraphs). The students then ask the teacher comprehension questions about the passage. Then, the roles are reversed as the teacher asks the students questions. This continues with subsequent sentences or paragraphs until the teacher asks the students to predict what the rest of the material will be about and to set a purpose for reading further. Later, the teacher facilitates a post-reading discussion. The teacher can point out whether the students are asking literal, interpretive, or evaluative questions, and can model and encourage the use of questions calling for higher-level thinking.

BookTalk 6.9

Characters in quality literature for adolescents must face the same kinds of situations as real people do, and must exercise careful thinking when they encounter complex problems. In *Silent to the Bone,* by E. L. Konigsburg (2000), Connor is faced with a double-layered problem. He must prove to the authorities that his best friend did not drop his baby sister, as he has been accused. But in order to do that, he must figure out how to communicate with Branwell, who is in a juvenile detention facility and has not uttered a word since the 911 call was made back when the baby was severely (perhaps critically) injured. You can follow along as Connor analyzes data, tries solutions, forms hypotheses, and grapples with aspects of the dilemma.

FIGURE **6.15** *A teacher's reflection after reading* The Phantom Tollbooth.

Reading Phantom Math

Jennifer St. Onge

I have attempted to teach my students to read their text-books, and I devote several lessons to this each year. However, I am always disappointed with my results; my students seem to read their textbooks as they would a novel, but with much less comprehension. A technical text requires slow, repetitive reading that is frequently interrupted for the sake of self-monitoring. Perhaps, by asking them to immediately jump from the narrative or expository text they are accustomed to, and into tech-nical text, I am asking them to do the impossible. By first starting with a novel that requires slow and careful reading, and later, through activities involving several types of technical genre, possibly my students can grow accustomed and even skilled in the area of technical reading.

The Phantom Tollbooth requires reading strategies similar to those required to read a math textbook. This novel contains so many clever puns, riddles, twists, and turns, that a "quick read" would [enable students to] glean little understanding of the full meaning of the book. For example, as Milo travels through The Lands Beyond, the first character he meets is the Whether man. In response to Milo's question regarding the road to Dic-tionopolis, he replies:

> "Well now, well now, well now, . . . I don't know of any wrong road to Dictionopolis, so if this road goes to Dic-tionopolis, it must be the right road, and if it doesn't it must be the right road to somewhere else, because there are no wrong roads to anywhere. Do you think it will rain?"

Actually, this strange little man has a very good point, but it would probably be lost on a reader who does not stop to reexamine the Whether Man's words.

Not only is *The Phantom Tollbooth* an excellent exer-cise in detailed reading, but hopefully, it imparts to the students the value of math and its unique nature. When Milo questions the importance of numbers and problems, as do many of my students, the Dodecahedron replies:

> "If you had high hopes, how would you know how high they were? And did you know that narrow escapes come in all different widths? Would you travel the whole wide world without knowing how wide it was? And how could you do anything at long last . . . with-out knowing how long the last was? Why, numbers are the most beautiful and valuable things in the world."

In Digitopolis, the reader is challenged to comprehend the concept of averages, infinity, and fractions through physical descriptions and through careful reading.

The realization that there are different modes of reading only struck me in college; I wasted hours before that epiphany, reading things I did not understand. Through guidance, repeated modeling, and practice on increasingly technical texts, students can learn to be effective readers, and to employ appropriate reading strategies to any genre—even to math textbooks. The goal of Milo's journey was to return Rhyme and Reason to the Kingdom of Knowledge. As teachers, it is our job to ensure that these two never depart from the knowl-edge that we try to impart to our students.

A related strategy is *reciprocal teaching* (Palincsar & Brown, 1984), which gets students actively involved in predicting, clarifying, generating ques-tions, and summarizing. After the teacher teaches and models each of these steps, students form dyads or triads and one person at a time plays the role of the teacher and leads a discussion of the text using the steps. The student asks questions that call for thinking beyond the literal level.

CONCLUSION

Please listen in on the reflection shown in Figure 6.15 by a middle school math teacher about a book,

about her own reading, about her students' reading. It represents active reading and critical thinking, and so can serve as a model for you.

This chapter has provided suggestions for help-ing students comprehend texts; recognize text struc-tures and patterns of organization; and think critically about ideas, concepts, and positions in texts, as well as to become intellectually engaged and eager to learn more about topics. It's important to remember that these strategies are not there just for our convenience in planning and teaching. We must model the strategies and provide practice using authentic materials and the real contexts of our dis-ciplines and our classrooms so that students can internalize them. Our goal is also to help our stu-

BookTalk 6.10

There's a picture book about a little girl who goes to bed with her dog. Just a few words on a page; it looks simple, easy, cute. Don't be deceived! The narrator of Michele Lemieux's *Stormy Night* (1999) can't fall asleep because "Too many questions are buzzing through my head" (unpaged). The line drawings add to the mood as the text spells out, on various pages, some things that many of the adolescents we teach also wonder about: "Where does infinity end?" "Where do we come from?" "Who am I?" "Is there only one of me in the world?" "Is there anyone watching over me?" "Will the world come to an end some day?" The narrator gives names to some fears and some hopes. Her imaginative, meandering ponderings, along with the clever art work, have the potential to stimulate much thought and many new questions from readers. Here's evidence from one reader's journal, with a response-within-a-response:

> What a wild book! . . . It took me a while to get through it. But then, I had to go back through it because I found it so amazing. . . . The questions that are posed and the

thoughts that are conveyed are really deep. Kids are deep thinkers. At least my kids are deep thinkers. . . . [later] I'm back. . . . I took the book to my son, Ben. Ben is 13 years old, so I thought he would be a good specimen to try this book out on, and I wasn't disappointed!

Ben took his time looking through the book. When I asked him what he thought, his reply was, "It's all the same questions I have when I go to bed, before I go to sleep. I lay there and all these things go through my head. . . . It's got simple wording with adult concepts. Good questions. It's nothing to joke around about. Wow. Amazing. Why, Why, Why and How? *Stormy Night*. I like it." Then he goes on to say how he always thinks about infinity questions. He says, "If it begins, it would have to have an end. If it has a starting point, but, it can't because infinity goes on and on. But, there has to be a starting point. . . ."

Out of the mouths of babes. . . . It's a good book.

—Elizabeth Richardson

dents to become strategic learners, knowing when to apply the strategies that work best for them. Some students do better with certain strategies than with others. So, encourage self-selection, adaption to personal needs, and self-assessment whenever possible. Recent research has indicated that what makes a difference in students' comprehension has to do not so much with a particular strategy as with the cognitive and metacognitive processes students use as they read, set goals, and proceed appropriately with their reading (Pressley, 1995). Simpson and Nist (2000) remind us that, for strategic learning, "we want students to think about the thinking processes they are using when they read and study, not just the strategies" (p. 535).

Getting Ready to Teach

6.1 Choose a text in your content area that uses sequence as a major pattern. Create a reading guide or time line to help your students comprehend and remember the material.

6.2 Choose two texts that you have read and create a picture or diagram showing any compare–contrast relationships. Or, write a brief analysis showing the relationship. You'll have a model to show your students as you guide them to use compare–contrast to their advantage as they read, write, and study. The following excerpt from an article that compares characters in children's classics can serve as an example for you:

> The structure of *Harriet the Spy* and *A Wrinkle in Time* is very like that of the *Alice* books. Both books confront their heroines with worlds that make no sense to them. Both girls are . . . alienated—alone and unhappy, often among confusing, inadequate, unsympathetic strangers . . . both [stories] are about their heroines' journeys and characters and through places very much like those found in Wonderland or Through the Looking Glass, and each ends, like the *Alice* books, with the heroine's assertion of her own individuality.
>
> Both books include one atypical boy, who in each case is the boyfriend, but who does not rescue the heroine. And, most importantly, both girls learn that love is the solution to their alienation. . . . What's more, they both learn the importance of love on their own without the help of their respective families or boyfriends. Both have as guidance only the advice of wise women, very like the mythological figures, the fairy godmothers or goddesses of folklore, who often assist young initiates through their passage to adulthood. (Wolf, 1988, pp. 135–137)

6.3 You should provide your students with direct instruction and practice recognizing organization patterns in text. The following sentences are ones I've collected for that purpose. I adhered to the criteria that my examples had to be authentic (not made up for the purpose of creating a worksheet) and had to be interesting or thought-provoking. Determine which relationships, time order (TO), cause–effect (CE), compare–contrast (CC), problem–solution (PS), or enumeration (E), are exemplified in each quote. There may be more than one, and you may find some disagreement when you compare answers with your peers. That's ok; listen to each other's reasoning. When you are done, begin a folder or computer file labeled "Patterns of Organization," where you can collect your own content-specific examples and encourage your students to add their discoveries from their wide reading. You might devote a part of your class website to this activity.

1. "Criticizing liberal education within academe is like criticizing motherhood in a maternity ward" (Noddings, 1993, p. 28).

2. "Curing cancer would do to the health care industry what the end of the Cold War did to the defense establishment" (Dreazen, 1998, p. A8).

3. "People ask me what I am going to do next. I feel I can hardly write a sequel to *A Brief History of Time*. What would I call it? *A Longer History of Time? Beyond the End of Time? Son of Time?*" (Hawking, 1993, p. 38).

4. "Chloe thought she would drown in her own sweat . . . Lot's wife was not as sweaty as she. Neither was the Atlantic or the Pacific. Between the sweat and the tears, she was being pickled in her very own brine" (Konigsburg, 1993, p. 27).

5. "I'm sorry to disappoint prospective galactic tourists, but . . . if you jump into a black hole, you will get torn apart and crushed out of existence. However, there is a sense in which the particles that make up your body will carry on into another universe. I don't know if it would be much consolation to someone being made into spaghetti in a black hole to know that his particles might survive" (Hawking, 1993, p. 116).

6. "The name *black hole* was introduced only in 1967 by the American physicist John Wheeler. It was a stroke of genius: The name ensured that black holes entered the mythology of science fiction. It also stimulated scientific research by providing a definite name for something that previously had not had a satisfactory title. The importance in science of a good name should not be underestimated" (Hawking, 1993, p. 116).

7. "[Linus] Pauling was a scientific giant, imaginative, bold, and unafraid of anyone and anything. He leaped over the boundaries of disciplines, from chemistry to physics to biology to medical research. He fizzed with ideas, which seemed to shoot off as fast as sparks from a pinwheel. He tied concepts and information together in ways no one had before and used his persuasive, outgoing personality to convince the world he was right. He was audacious, intuitive, stubborn, charming, irreverent, self reliant, self-promoting—and, as it turned out, almost always correct" (Hager, 1998, p. 9).

8. "Don't try to make life a mathematical problem with yourself in the center and everything coming out equal" (Kingsolver, 1998, p. 309).

9. "Among the themes in [Elie] Weisel's writing are the conflicts between silence and speech, madness and sanity, indifference and empathy, hope and despair" (Bayer, 2000, p. 88).

10. "With ever more refined tools and techniques, the genetic engineer manipulates a DNA molecule that would be almost a meter long if unwound from the nucleus of a human cell, yet is so infinitesimally thin that 5 million strands can fit through the eye of a needle" (Stix & Lacob, 1999, p. 2).

11. "When Albert Schweitzer walked into the jungle, bless his heart, he carried antibacterials and a potent, altogether new conviction that no one should die young. He meant to save every child, thinking Africa would then learn how to have fewer children. But when families have spent a million years making nine in the hope of saving one, they cannot stop making nine. Culture is a slingshot moved by the force of its past" (Kingsolver, 1998, p. 528).

6.4 Choose several pages of a text within your field to examine and analyze in terms of organization and relationships. It can be a story, a document, a section of a textbook chapter, or a newspaper or magazine article. Code it in the margins using the symbols TO (time order), CC (compare–contrast), CE (cause–effect), PS (problem–solution), or E (enumeration), and underline clue words in the text. Determine whether there is an overarching pattern of organization used by the author. Then, decide how you could best help your students cue into the relationships within the text in order to deepen their comprehension. Create a set of directions or a guide to enhance their reading.

6.5 Choose a book you have recently read, and create a poster representing one or more of the main patterns of organization that the author employs.

6.6 Select a text that is appropriate for students in your content area to read. It might be a short story, or a chapter from a biography, or an account of an event. As you read the text, mark spots where you could stop and ask students to make predictions about what will come next. Then, try out the directed reading–thinking activity you've created with a student or a peer.

6.7 Create at least one question at each of the literal, inferential, and evaluative levels for each of the texts on genetic engineering in Figures 6.10 and 6.11. Aim for questions that you think would really help students comprehend the passages, think about the implications of the ideas presented, and form judgments based on the information given. Then, label your six or more questions in terms of what kind of QAR is represented. Compare your questions with others, and discuss which are the most helpful or stimulating questions and why that might be. Or, follow the same procedure for a text you select related to your discipline.

6.8 Go through a newspaper and identify articles that involve or call for critical thinking in some way. Perhaps the *issue* dealt with is controversial, or a *person* mentioned has had to weigh options and make an informed decision. How might you guide students to ask questions of the author that could help them comprehend and evaluate the texts? Create a guide for them to use, or write a narrative explaining how you would facilitate their critical thinking relative to the text.

Writing in the Content Areas

You've no doubt noticed that writing was addressed and activities and strategies incorporated in previous chapters of this book. Many of the Activating Prior Knowledge and Action Research activities and sample reading guides involved writing. It is an integral component of literacy —very much connected to the process of reading; it's not just an add-on. Although we should think of literacy as holistic, sometimes the interrelated components have to be separated in order to discuss and understand them; it's simply impossible to talk about everything simultaneously. Therefore, in this chapter, the focus is on writing in the content areas—but not in total isolation; you'll see that reading, talking, listening, and thinking are still involved.

In Part One, I talk about writing in general, letting you know where the field stands and helping you understand theories and concepts. You will learn much about what composition experts advocate in terms of products and process; you will learn writing theory and have opportunities to write, and to think about the place writing has in your professional and personal life. In Part Two, I discuss content area writing specifically, and explore practical aspects such as activities, strategies, and assignments you can use in your subject area classroom. You will create opportunities for your students to learn through writing, as well as to show what they have learned and how they think through writing. In Part Three, the focus is on helping English language learners write and learn through writing in your content area classes.

"The Scripture rule, 'Unto him [her] that hath shall be given,' is true of composition. The more you have thought and written on a given theme, the more you can still write. Thought breeds thought. It grows under your hands."

THOREAU, 13 FEB 1860

PART ONE

Writing: Who Does It? Why Do It? How to Do It? Let's Try It!

ACTIVATING PRIOR KNOWLEDGE　　**7.1**

Quickly answer the following questions:

1. Would you advise a friend to take guitar lessons from someone who doesn't play the guitar?
2. Would you take skiing lessons from someone who doesn't ski?
3. Would you send your child for writing lessons to someone who doesn't write?

I'm sure the first two questions were simple for you. But the third may have caused you to pause because, in actuality, many students are given writing instruction in classrooms by teachers who do not practice the craft. You *will* be a teacher of writing, as well as a teacher of reading in your content area; it is your responsibility to show your students how to think through writing, as well as how to use writing to demonstrate their knowledge and skills. I hope you'll take this quote by writing expert Donald Graves (1993) to heart:

> Teachers are the most important learners in the classroom. It is the quality of our learning . . . that [is] the source of greatest influence, far transcending any elegant methodologies we may have acquired. We invite children to join us as we explore better ways of writing, to try new investigations in science, to look for other ways to solve a mathematical problem. (p. 361)

WRITING PROCESSES

Perhaps you recall your teachers providing formulas for writing essays or reports. These may have worked very well for you, or you might remember feeling resistant about organizing index cards, handing in an outline before you could start writing, or writing a thesis statement in a certain place in the introductory paragraph. Actually, researchers, teachers, and writers have discovered over the past several decades that there is no one correct way to write—people have unique styles and preferences that work best for them, and individuals follow different procedures depending on their purposes and targeted audiences (Calkins, 1986; Flower & Hayes, 1984; Mof-

fett, 1968; Murray, 1985; Perl, 1979; Scardamalia, Bereiter, & Goelman, 1982). Yet, most people do demonstrate that they go through processes that can be viewed as overlapping stages, which are not usually neat or discrete, or as linear as some textbooks would have you believe. The writing process is *recursive*; that is, writers tend to circle back to earlier stages because of things that happen at later stages. You'll read examples demonstrating this later in the chapter. Now, let's look at some generally accepted categories of writing stages that researchers and authors of all types and ages have observed, including brainstorming and prewriting, drafting and revising, editing, and publishing.

ACTIVATING PRIOR KNOWLEDGE　　**7.2**

Take a moment now to take stock of your present writing. Make a list of the types of writing you do in your daily life. How much of it is academic? Is any of it creative writing (at least loosely defined)? Is any self-sponsored, writing that you *choose* to do as opposed to writing that was assigned? Do you practice the type of writing you expect your students to produce for you and for school or state assessments?

Now, take a few minutes to sketch a brief writing autobiography. When and how did you learn to write? What kinds of writing were required of you as a student? What other types of writing did you participate in, and for what purposes? For what audiences do you write? Did you ever, and do you now, think of yourself as "a writer"? In what ways has your writing changed over time?

Brainstorming and Prewriting

This stage, also known as *rehearsal*, starts as soon as a person gets an idea or assignment or recognizes a need to produce a text of some sort. The wheels start turning, and the writer might experience fear, or dryness, or excitement. Sometimes, the ideas are tumbling around so fast they can't all be captured. This stage can be chaotic, and that's normal. Some writers (not all by any means) organize their ideas and write an outline before they actually begin a draft of the piece. It's a good idea at this stage to think of what the writing's purpose is and who the intended audience is.

Here's an example of a writer at the prewriting stage. In the book *Anastasia Krupnik*, by Lois Lowry (1979), the title character is sitting in a class, having just been told by her teacher that they were going to write poetry to share during Poetry Week:

> Somewhere, off in a place beyond her own thoughts, Anastasia could hear Mrs. Westvessel's voice. She was reading some poems to the class; she was talking about poetry and how it was made. But Anastasia wasn't really listening. She was listening instead to the words that were appearing in her own head, floating there and arranging themselves into groups, into lines, into poems. (pp. 7–8)

The prewriting stage often includes data collection and other forms of research so that the writer has new information to ponder, analyze, synthesize, and write about. Nancie Atwell (1998) compiled an inventory showing the range of writing genres her middle school students have produced, including editorials, book and CD reviews, reports of sports events, letters to a variety of audiences, speeches, oral histories, eulogies, webpages, parodies, computer programs, biographies, advertisements, and children's books. Such a list, along with a cumulative list of topics your own classes create, can help spark students' efforts to write. Atwell calls these "writing territories" (p. 120), a phrase I like because it implies student ownership and control.

Drafting and Revising

The drafting and revising stages involve the actual physical text composition. Though some students at all levels think of a first draft as the final draft, writers usually go through multiple drafts. Drafts can be done on a computer, though some prefer doing early drafts by hand, and some writers dictate their drafts into a tape recorder or to a scribe. Students should understand that it's natural if their first drafts are sloppy or a bit chaotic, because drafts are subject to change. Some revision might happen as the writer is drafting, or a writer can complete a draft before thinking about how she will change it, perhaps allowing some incubating time between drafts. Revising often involves major changes in terms of subject matter, organization, and style. Here's what Betsy Byars, a noted author of children's books, says about this stage:

- I start on the word processor and write as much as I can. Then I print it.

- I take what I've printed, go sit somewhere else—like the porch—read it, say, "This is terrible," and start working on it.

- I go back to the word processor, put in the changes, and print it.

- I take what I've printed, go sit somewhere else, say, "Oh, this is still terrible," and rewrite it.

- I keep doing this until I say, "This is not as terrible as it used to be," then, "This is getting better," and finally (hopefully), "This is not bad at all." (p. 2)

Brockman (1999) also provides authentic examples of this stage, using five students who were writing essays about Lorraine Hansberry's *A Raisin in the Sun* (1959). During the various stages of their writing, the students made significant choices that show the recursive nature of writing. For example:

> Alice planned to compare Walter Lee Younger to her aunt's ex-husband because both men drink too much. As she initially envisioned the document, then, her focus was going to either be alcoholism or alcohol abuse. When she began writing, however, her focus changed. Her drafting pulled her away from alcoholism in the direction of spousal abuse. In the end, she reconceptualized the entire essay to accommodate her new focus. (p. 85)

Writers often revise based on comments from editors or peers they've entrusted with their drafts. Based on this, teachers often require or encourage *conferencing*, either with the teacher or with fellow students. Part Two of this chapter offers suggestions as to how you can utilize conferencing time and teach skills to the students so that they can truly be a help to one another.

Editing

At this point, the writer is proofreading, checking grammar, spelling, and cohesiveness at the sentence and paragraph level. Again, this is not always a discrete stage. Some writers edit as they draft and can't continue pouring out ideas till they back up the cursor and fix that typo. There are also times while editing that we are struck with a new idea that requires us to head back to the drafting board for some major reorganization. Published writers have copy editors to go over their manuscripts at this crucial stage; students often choose proofreading buddies to exchange papers with—it's usually easier for us to see others' mistakes than to catch our own because we're so close to our own work and know what it's *supposed* to say. There's a rough draft of the Declaration of Independence housed in the Library of Congress that shows the messiness of the writing at the revising and editing stages. There are numerous cross-outs and substitutions, most made by Thomas Jefferson, but some contributed by John Adams, Benjamin Franklin, and others—the changes show both political compromise and an attention to word choice.

Publishing

At last, a piece is ready to be read by or presented to an audience. Publication can be informal, such as when a teacher displays student writing in the hallway, on a bulletin board, or on a class website. Some teachers have authors' teas, allowing student writers to read from their works in an atmosphere of celebration. Some have class magazines individually bound for students, with contributions from the members of writing workshop or from student researchers involved in a group inquiry. You can laminate pieces and file them in attractive boxes for the students to peruse, or paper the classroom walls with poems, reports, position papers, drawings, and letters. Encourage your students to give their writing accomplishments as gifts to family and friends. They can let their voices be heard by sending letters to the editor of their local newspaper or creating a student column in the newsletter their school district shares with the community. Put the published letters into a class collection or post them prominently for others in the school, or the public library, to see. Publication can take an oral form too. Students can videotape book and movie reviews, recite their poetry or opinion mini-essays over the loudspeaker during morning announcements, sing or read their work at a podium in your classroom or at a school assembly. Listen to suggestions and ideas from your students regarding original and innovative publication formats and places to post or perform works they've composed.

Seeing one's work go public can be a time of intense and changing emotions, as Barbara Kingsolver attests in her reflection on the publication of her first novel *The Bean Trees* (1988):

> For many, many years I wrote my stories furtively in spiralbound notebooks, for no greater purpose than my own private salvation.... The pages that grew in a stack were somewhat incidental to the process. They contained my highest hopes and keenest pains, and I didn't think anyone but me would ever see them.... Now it was going to be laid smack out for my mother, my postal clerk, my high school English teacher.... To find oneself suddenly published is thrilling—that is a given. But how appalling it also felt I find hard to describe. (Kingsolver, 1995, pp. 36–37)

Is some sort of publication always necessary? Well, no, but it's nice and can be rewarding and motivating. A young girl who lives near me had a journal reflection she wrote during several of her childhood years about her parents' divorce selected by the editors of *Chicken Soup for the Teenage Soul* (Canfield & Hansen, 1993), and was quite excited. Figure 7.1 lists possible avenues to publish student writing. Writer Anne Lamott, in her humorous *Bird by Bird: Some Instructions on Writing and Life* (1994), gives both a warning and a promise of compensation:

> Publication is not all it's cracked up to be. But writing is. Writing has so much to teach, so many surprises. That thing you had to force yourself to do—the actual act of writing—turns out to be the best part. It's like discovering that while you thought you needed the tea ceremony for the caffeine, what you really needed was the tea ceremony. The act of writing turns out to be its own reward. (p. xxvi)

In one school district I visit, it is mandated that yellow cards delineating the steps of *the writing process* be posted in every classroom, elementary through high school. There are arrows, going from left to right, between BRAINSTORM, PREWRITE, DRAFT, CONFERENCE, REVISE, EDIT, and PUBLISH. Although some teachers and students may find these reminders helpful, remember that:

- There are *many* writing processes.
- Not all writers follow the same steps in the same order.
- The steps tend to be recursive rather than linear.
- Not all writing is or was ever meant to be published.
- Even individual writers follow different stages and procedures depending on subject, purpose, audience, time constraints, mood, and so on.

Writing is not magic, nor is it something that only the truly gifted can do well, but neither is it something that can be easily produced by simply plugging in the steps of a formula listed over a chalkboard.

LEARNING FROM THE PROS: THE WRITING PROCESSES OF PROFESSIONAL WRITERS

The preceding caveat does not mean that we as teachers have nothing to offer students. Maxine Hairston (1994) notes that in recent years, writing experts have learned to study the principles that

FIGURE 7.1   *Possible places to send student manuscripts.*

Blue Jean, P.O. Box 90856, Rochester, NY 14609

Merlyn's Pen, P.O. Box 1058, East Greenwich, RI 02818

"My Turn" Essay Competition (Kaplan and *Newsweek*), www.kaptest.com or 1-800-KAP-TEST

Scholastic Art and Writing Awards, Alliance for Young Artists and Writers, Inc., 555 Broadway, New York, NY 10012

Skirball National High School Essay Contest, www.skirballinstitute.org

The Trincoll Journal, e-mail: journal@trincoll.edu

Virtualology, www.virtualology.com/studentsubmission

Voices from the Middle, NCTE, 1111 Kenyon Road, Urbana, IL 61801

working writers use, and teachers have helped students to develop some of the same practices. She has compiled some helpful conclusions, including:

- Most writers don't wait for inspiration. They write whether they feel like it or not.
- Professional writers consistently work in the same places with the same tools—pencil, typewriter, or word processor . . . they take the trouble to create a good writing environment for themselves.
- Successful writers make plans before they start to write, but they keep their plans flexible, subject to revision.
- Successful writers usually have some audience in mind and stay aware of that audience as they write and revise.
- Even successful writers often have trouble getting started; they expect it and don't panic.
- Successful writers stop frequently to reread what they've written and consider such rereading an important part of the writing process.
- Successful writers revise as they write and expect to do two or more drafts of anything they write.
- Like ordinary mortals, successful writers often procrastinate and feel guilty about it; unlike less-experienced writers, however, most of them have a good sense of how long they can procrastinate and still avoid disaster. (pp. 471–472)

No matter what our content area, we can provide a positive atmosphere, good modeling, and constant encouragement to our student writers. We can display inspirational quotes such as the following on our classroom walls and our webpages:

Writing is hard work. A clear sentence is no accident. Very few sentences come out right the first time, or even the third time. Remember this as a consolation in moments of despair. If you find that writing is hard, it's because it *is* hard. It's one of the hardest things that people do. (Zinsser, 1994, p. 488)

BookTalk 7.1

Would you like to give your students a lovely example of a writer going through the stages of the writing craft? Introduce them to Randall Jarrell's *The Bat-Poet* (1996). The flying protagonist's response to nature and life takes a creative form, and his composing processes are detailed, even including an example of writer's block and advice from a "peer consultant":

But it was no use; no matter how much the bat watched, he never got an idea. Finally he went to the chipmunk and said in a perplexed voice, "I can't make up a poem about the cardinal."

The chipmunk said, "Why, just say what he's like, the way you did with the owl and me."

"I would if I could," the bat said, "but I can't. I watch him and he's beautiful, he'd make a beautiful poem; but I can't think of anything." (p. 25)

The Muses have not abandoned the bat forever. Later, he's listening to and thinking about a mockingbird:

And at that instant he had an idea for a poem. . . . He flapped slowly and thoughtfully back to his rafter and began to work on the poem.

When he finally finished it—he'd worked on it on and off for two nights—he flew off to find the chipmunk. (p. 27)

Students will appreciate, after reading this account of the bat's struggles, that finishing a piece of writing requires hard work, inspiration, careful observation, and time. They might be inspired by this little artistic creature to write in response to their environment or to issues raised in your class. They might even take on the voice of a bat or another creature, as Jarrell did in this delightful tale of beauty. This book is ideal for reading aloud to a class and has appeal for a wide age range.

If you are a teacher who believes in having students read far beyond their textbooks, you should build and continually increase your classroom library so that your students can read content-related material in many genres. They'll recognize many authors and will surely have some favorites—use this to your advantage when helping them to write. There are resources available that can let your students, and you, in on the secrets of the trade as described by the published writers themselves. Guide them as they ask questions about authors and then search for answers. The next sections answer questions related to writing process, using some relevant quotes from winners of the Newbery Medal for social studies-related books.

Where Do Writers Get Their Topics and Ideas?

Students sometimes lament that they have nothing to write about; they don't know how to generate ideas. Writers often give tips and stories that can help. Lois Lowry wrote *Number the Stars* (1989) based on information and details a close friend gave her about growing up in Europe during World War II. Mildred Taylor has written family stories her father told her of "great-grandparents and of slavery and of the days following slavery; of those who lived still not free, yet who would not let their spirits be enslaved" (1976, p. vii). One result was *Roll of Thunder, Hear My Cry* (1975). Russell Freedman, whose *Lincoln: A Photobiography* (1987) won the Newbery Medal, says he enjoys writing about "people whose lives have something to tell us, perhaps, about leading our own lives. . . . I was drawn to Eleanor Roosevelt because of the quality of her heart; to Crazy Horse because of his courage and his uncompromising integrity; to Abraham Lincoln because of his spirit of forgiveness" (Freedman, 1988, p. 451).

Karen Hesse, winner of the 1998 Newbery Medal for her historical novel in free verse *Out of the Dust* (1997), says she loves research, dipping into another time and place and asking tough questions. She immersed herself in documents that allowed her to understand life in the heart of the Dust Bowl during the Depression, and saturated herself "with those dusty, dirty desperate times, and what I discovered thrilled me" (Hesse, 1998, pp. 424–425). She based the book partly on articles in the 1934 *Boise News* that told of a mother who accidentally poured kerosene on a lit stove. She explains, "I never make up any of the bad things that happen to my characters. I love my characters too much to hurt them deliberately. . . . It just so happens that in life, there's pain; sorrow lives in the shadow of joy, joy in the shadow of sorrow" (p. 423).

Learning about the authors' excitement while researching may help our students as they explore and gather information for their writing. Elizabeth George Speare, author of *The Witch of Blackbird Pond* (1958), a historical novel set in Puritan times, challenges young people, "Follow my own process. Take some little incident that you read about in a history book. Try to imagine that you are actually there. . . . What would conversations around you be about? What would the place look like? Write about it" (Kovacs & Preller, 1991, p. 131).

Do Writers Really Revise Their Drafts?

The short answer is yes, which might surprise students who see revision as a school-imposed rule or as busywork. Karen Hesse gave the manuscript of *Out of the Dust* first to her daughters and revised it based on their comments; then she gave it to friends, revised it based on their comments, and continued this process, listening very closely to her readers' remaining questions. However, authors don't always act on the advice they are given. For example, Lois Lowry's editor felt she had too many references to the high, shiny boots of the Nazi soldiers in *Number the Stars*. But Lowry had met a woman who, as a toddler, hid under floorboards and watched her Jewish mother being taken away by soldiers. When the woman was asked what she recalled, she answered that she remembered the high, shiny boots. So, Lowry kept all of the references to the boots in her book, deciding, "If any reviewers should call attention to the overuse of that image . . . I would simply tell them that those high shiny boots had trampled on several million childhoods, and I was sorry I hadn't several million more pages on which to mention that" (Lowry, 1990, p. 420). Our students can learn from these mentors that conferences and feedback are good, but they own their writing and are responsible for final decisions.

Other questions students might choose to ask published writers include how they first got published, how much money they make from their writing, what they do when they're not writing, what they like to read, when they first started writing, and what they do when someone doesn't like their work. Teachers can facilitate the process of finding sources that answer these and other student questions. Figures 7.2 and 7.3 list resources that provide students, and you, with a good start.

There are also visiting authors' programs that your school could become involved with—the students can receive answers to their questions first-hand. Students might be motivated to read the

FIGURE 7.2   *Resources for exploring the processes of writers.*

Carter, B., & Abrahamson, R. F. (1990). *Nonfiction for Young Adults: From Delight to Wisdom*. Phoenix, AZ: Oryx Press.

Fletcher, R. (2000). *How Writers Work*. New York: Harper-Trophy.

Keyes, R. (1995). *The Courage to Write: How Writers Transcend Fear*. New York: Henry Holt.

King, S. (2000). *On Writing: A Memoir of the Craft*. New York: Scribner's.

Lamott, A. (1994). *Bird by Bird: Some Instructions on Writing and Life*. New York: Anchor Books.

L'Engle, M. (1972). *A Circle of Quiet*. San Francisco: Harper & Row.

Hedblad, A. (1998). *Major Authors and Illustrators for Children and Young Adults*. Detroit, MI: Gale.

Marcus, L. S. (2000). *Author Talk*. New York: Simon & Schuster.

Murphy, B. T. (1999). *Black Authors and Illustrators of Books for Children: A Biographical Dictionary* (3rd ed.). New York: Garland Publishers.

Paterson, K. (1981). *Gates of Excellence: On Reading and Writing Books for Children*. New York: Elsevier-Dutton.

Paterson, K. (1990). *The Spying Heart: More on Reading and Writing Books for Children*. New York: Dutton Children's Books.

Paterson, K. (2001). *The Invisible Child: On Reading and Writing Books for Children*. New York: Dutton Children's Books.

Welty, E. (1995). *One Writer's Beginnings*. Cambridge, MA: Harvard University Press.

author's works prior to the visit, and funding can be raised through such organizations as a parent–teacher association or a community or business–school partnership. After an author visit, more opportunities for writing may arise as students reflect on what they learned and write follow-up messages, perhaps to the author's website. Refer to the book *Dear Author* (Read Magazine, 1995) for examples of letters readers have written about books that have affected them deeply.

A good way for you and your students to add some authors to your circle of acquaintances is through the Twayne's *Young Adult Author Series*. Separate volumes "present" a wide variety of writers, including M. E. Kerr, Chris Crutcher, Richard Peck, S. E. Hinton, Robert Cormier, Madeleine L'Engle, Cynthia Voigt, Gary Paulsen, Ouida Sebestyen, and Avi. Biographical information is combined with words from the authors about how they write, advice for young readers and writers, and personal anecdotes that help the writers come alive for young readers. Some chapters deal with the interpretation of the authors' major works. The series is a wonderful reference to have as your students explore what it means to be a writer at any level, of any genre.

Another way students can learn from the pros is to read examples of authentic writing in the disciplines. *Galileo's Commandment: An Anthology of Great Science Writing*, edited by Edmund Blair Bolles (1997), is a wonderful place to start. You and your students can read excerpts of pieces by Isaac Asimov, Stephen Jay Gould, Leonardo da Vinci, Charles Darwin, Pavlov, Marie Curie, Carl Sagan, Voltaire, Albert Einstein, Primo Levi, and many more great people who composed expository masterpieces. Students will no longer be able to think of writing as simply an academic exercise. These writings went places! Similarly, *The Art of Science Writing*, by Dale Worsley and Bernadette Meyer (1989), contains fascinating essays that deal with people, ideas, and writing issues.

BookTalk 7.2

If you like gossip, you'll like Kathleen Krull's 1994 *Lives of the Writers: Comedies, Tragedies (and What the Neighbors Thought)*. It includes discussions of the eccentricities, as well as the writing processes, of 20 famous writers, including Mark Twain, Louisa May Alcott, Emily Dickinson, Langston Hughes, Zora Neale Hurston, and Edgar Allen Poe. Your students might know that Charles Dickens wrote *A Christmas Carol, Oliver Twist,* and *Great Expectations,* but they might not have known that at age 12 he was working in a rat-infested factory, that he attended public hangings whenever he could, that *Oliver Twist* was the first book in the English language with a child as its hero, or that the objects on Dickens' desk had to be positioned exactly the same each day before he could write. They'll know thought-provoking facts, as well as much fun trivia, when they finish this book.

FIGURE 7.3 *"How-to" resources on writing in various genres.*

Bentley, N., & Guthrie, D. W. (1995). *The Young Producer's Video Book: How to Write, Direct and Shoot Your Own Video.* Brookfield, CT: Millbrook Press.

Bentley, N., & Guthrie, D. W. (1998). *The Young Journalist's Book: How to Write and Produce Your Own Newspaper.* Brookfield, CT: Millbrook Press.

Day, R. A. (1998). *How to Write and Publish a Scientific Paper.* Phoenix, AZ: Oryx Press.

Dragisic, P. (1998). *How to Write a Letter.* New York: Franklin Watts.

Geffner, A. B. (1995). *How to Write Better Business Letters* (2nd ed.). Hauppauge, NY: Barron's.

Giblin, J. C. (1990). *Writing Books for Young People.* Boston: The Writer.

Goldberg, N. (1986). *Writing Down the Bones.* Boston: Shambahla Press.

Hand, B., Prain, V., Lawrence, C., & Yore, L. D. (1999). A Writing in Science Framework Designed to Enhance Science Literacy. *International Journal of Science Education, 21*(10), 1021–1035.

Hulme, J. N., & Guthrie, D. W. (1996). *How to Write, Recite, and Delight in All Kinds of Poetry.* Brookfield, CT: Millbrook Press.

Janeczko, P. B. (1999). *How to Write Poetry.* New York: Scholastic.

Ledoux, D. (1993). *Turning Memories into Memoirs: A Handbook for Writing Lifestories.* Lisbon Falls, ME: Soleil Press.

Mirriam-Goldberg, C. (1999). *Write Where You Are: How to Use Writing to Make Sense of Your Life: A Guide for Teens.* Minneapolis, MN: Free Spirit Publishing.

Phillips, E. H. (1999). *Shocked, Appalled, and Dismayed!: How to Write Letters of Complaint that Get Results.* New York: Vintage Books.

Sheffield, C. (1999). *Borderlands of Science: How to Think Like a Scientist and Write Science Fiction.* Riverdale, NY: Baen.

Wilson, E. O., & Bilger, B. (2001). *The Best American Science and Nature Writing 2001.* Boston: Houghton Mifflin.

Zinsser, W. (1998). *On Writing Well* (6th ed.). New York: HarperPerennial.

ACTIVATING PRIOR KNOWLEDGE 7.3

I've briefly outlined and explained current thought on the writing process, and you've been given a few quotes and examples showing bits of what some writers have to say about their writing processes. Now, on a sheet of paper, reflect through writing on how *you* write. Can you identify the typical stages in your own work? How do you get your ideas? What do your prewriting and drafting stages look like? How would you describe your revision stage? How much time do you spend at the different stages? Do you ever get "writer's block"? Do you have any rituals you follow as you write, or are there any special tools that you use? (Some writers use a special pencil; I need several flavors of ice cream to keep me going.) Where do you write best? When? Under what circumstances? Are you a solitary writer, or do you involve others, asking for help or feedback?

As you think, you'll probably realize that the answer to each question is "It depends." It depends on the assignment, or the purpose for your writing. It depends on the audience; will it be a teacher who reads the finished product, or a newspaper editor and possibly the subscribers, or your friends and colleagues? Now, think of at least two specific cases in your recent past. Choose one self-initiated piece of writing and one school paper or other assigned topic, and reflect on the stages again. Understanding your own writing, the cognitive, affective, and physical aspects of it, will help you to understand your students' needs as they write in your content area and will help you talk with them about their writing and encourage them to write to learn and to express themselves.

ACTION RESEARCH

We're off on a collaborative writing adventure to give you a feel for going through the writing process stages. It will result in a new text about teaching and learning. You are responsible for a short essay that may become part of a compilation, perhaps in hard copy, perhaps on a class webpage. The book must have a theme relevant to a content area literacy course for teachers, so you have two broad options:

1. Write a memoir of some learning experience you have had.
2. Write a description of a teacher you have known.

As you write, be aware of the recursive stages you go through, and keep a record of the piece in progress; save drafts and journal entries. The following paragraphs will help you reflect on your composing process.

PREWRITING. How do you think of ideas and identify a topic for your essay? You might read several samples to get your thinking started and your memory jogged. One sample, Bailey White's "One-Eared Intellectual," is found in Figure 7.4. Other suggestions are listed in Figure 7.5. Notice the crafting of the essays or sections of the books that relate to describing teachers. Experiment with ways to tell your story.

DRAFTING. Do you write right at the computer? Are you following an outline? Are ideas changing or new ideas coming to you as you write?

PEER REVIEW/CONFERENCING. In class or out of class, meet with two or three people in a writing conference. Each of you should read your piece aloud, and invite the listeners' responses and suggestions. As you listen to others' texts, think of how they affect you. Be as specific as possible in your response to others' drafts. When my students say to their group members, "Oh, that's good. Don't change a thing," the writer hasn't learned much. But if a listener explains what made her laugh, what part wasn't clear, or how the ending might be stronger, or when she gives a specific suggestion, such as "I think a bit of dialogue would make this confrontation between you and the principal come alive," the writer has something new to think about.

REVISION. Consider your peers' reactions and decide where you want to go with future drafts. You might reject some of their ideas; you might surprise yourself with a whole new direction or a different slant or point of view. Play around some more with the crafting of your essay.

EDITING. Proofread your work. Read it out loud so you can hear how the sentences sound. Use a spellcheck and grammar check. Many people do not pick up their own sentence level errors, so giving your text to someone else—a parent, sibling, or buddy editor—to go over is a good idea. Offer to reciprocate.

PUBLISHING. Prepare copies of your text for your classmates. Be sure you have a title, and your name and e-mail address. A few people in my classes always volunteer to work on a cover, creating titles such as *Looking Ahead by First Looking Back* and *Yesterday's Lessons: A Compilation of Memoirs by Tomorrow's Teachers;* they use original artwork or graphics found on the Internet. Collect all of the essays and combine them with your own, or post your essays on a class website. Your final step is to read the book and enjoy! My students are invariably amazed at the variety of topics and styles of writing represented in the finished product. There will be a lot to respond to—that's what the e-mail addresses are for. Send a note to someone whose essay made you understand a particular point of view, or concept about pedagogy, or teacher behavior. Let someone know if you had a similar experience to the one she wrote about, or if you respectfully disagree on some point. In short, let your fellow writers hear from their fans.

FIGURE **7.4** *Example of a description of a teacher: "One-Eared Intellectual."*

In my town there lives a man with an enormous intellect and only one ear. When I was a little girl, I thought that the two things were connected, that giving up one ear was simply the price you had to pay to be that smart. Later I learned that he had lost the ear in an automobile accident and had gotten his education in the usual way at Duke University.

Mr. Harris has a pair of glasses with an artificial ear attached to the temple. It matches his real ear perfectly; and as long as he keeps his glasses on, everything is fine. . . .

Mr. Harris is not stingy with his knowledge. He loves to teach people things. His hobby is substitute teaching. So about once a month he calls me on the phone. "Any teachers sick or pregnant at your school?" he asks.

"No," I say, "We're all fine."

Mr. Harris's dream is that a teacher will take a maternity leave. That would give him six weeks in the classroom, maybe more, if there are complications.

Mr. Harris could teach anything, but he always teaches physics. It doesn't matter if the class is supposed to be English, political science, history, kindergarten, or second grade—Mr. Harris just walks in, sweeps the teacher's lesson plans off the desk, and teaches physics.

Mr. Harris has been teaching physics as a substitute teacher for many years now, and the people in our town are remarkably knowledgeable in the subject. You can walk up to almost anybody on the street and ask, "Do you know any physics?" That person will get a wild look in his eye, gasp, and recite, "Yes, momentum is the product of the mass and the velocity of a particle." Or, "Hard radiation is ionizing radiation with a high degree of penetration." Or, "A watt is the power resulting from the dissipation of one joule of energy in one second."

You see, Mr. Harris is a vigorous teacher. He doesn't just wander around the classroom with a piece of chalk in his hand and mumble. He gets excited about physics. He yells. He bangs on the desk. He scribbles wildly on the chalkboard. And invariably, in his pedagogical heat, he will forget himself for an instant and whip off his glasses. The ear comes off too. It is an unforgettable moment. Whatever Mr. Harris is saying when that ear comes off is seared into memory forever. It's the ultimate audiovisual aid. (White, 1993, pp. 197–199)

From *MAMA MAKES UP HER MIND AND OTHER DANGERS OF SOUTHERN LIVING* by Bailey White. Copyright © 1993 by Bailey White. Reprinted with permission of Perseus Books Publishers, a member of Perseus Books, L.L.C.

ACTION RESEARCH 7.B

This is an alternative to constructing a class book using the two options given in Action Research 7.A. This topic involves a bit of research on your part, but might be appropriate for a content-area literacy course you're taking. Choose a practitioner in your discipline (Figure 7.6 provides examples of practitioners who might be investigated) who has made or is making a major contribution, and find out what that person was like as a middle school or high school student by reading relevant sections of biographies or autobiographies. There may be great value to reading about the passions and personalities of the many gifted teens who will be represented in your class book, because all of you will have some very bright, talented students who might require special attention, encouragement, methods, and materials. You may be surprised at the patterns that you'll discover, such as the number of teachers feeling threatened by gifted students, or not knowing what to do with them, or supporting them in unique ways. So, enjoy the choosing, the research and discovery, the writing about the person's adolescence, and the written reflecting on what you can learn about how gifted individuals learn and how you might best teach them. I'll start you thinking by providing an excerpt from a biography of a brilliant scientist in Figure 7.7.

This is a project you might do with your own students, too. Set up a center with biographies and autobiographies representing various levels of difficulty that explore the lives of practitioners of diverse backgrounds and both genders. The resulting class book is a way of celebrating students' research, thinking about, and writing about important people in the discipline when they were at the ages of the students themselves.

FIGURE 7.5   *Examples of descriptions of teachers or learning experiences.*

Albom, M. (1997). *Tuesdays with Morrie: An Old Man, a Young Man, and Life's Greatest Lesson.* New York: Doubleday.

Ayers, W. (1993). *To Teach: The Journey of a Teacher.* New York: Teachers College Press.

Byars, B. (1991). Miss Harriet's Room, In *The Moon and I.* Englewood Cliffs, NJ: Messner.

Cisneros, S. (1991). Eleven, In *Woman Hollering Creek.* New York: Random House.

Cohen, M. C. (1991). *A Lifetime of Teaching: Portraits of Five Veteran High School Teachers.* New York: Teachers College Press.

Dillard, A. (1987). *An American Childhood.* New York: HarperCollins.

Houston, G., & Lamb, S. C. (1992). *My Great Aunt Arizona.* New York: HarperCollins.

Kidder, T. (1989). *Among Schoolchildren.* Boston: Houghton Mifflin.

Rodriguez, R. (1983). *Hunger of Memory: The Education of Richard Rodriguez, An Autobiography.* New York: Bantam Books.

Schmidt, P. A. (1997). *Beginning in Retrospect: Writing and Reading a Teacher's Life.* New York: Teachers College Press.

FIGURE 7.6   *Examples of practitioners whose teenage years could be researched and written about.*

MATH, SCIENCE, AND TECHNOLOGY

Elizabeth Blackwell, Rachel Carson, George Washington Carver, Jacques Cousteau, Marie Curie, Albert Einstein, Paul Erdös, Dian Fossey, Bill Gates, Jane Goodall, Barbara McClintock, John Forbes Nash, Carl Sagan

FINE AND PERFORMING ARTS

Mary Cassatt, Chuck Close, Martha Graham, Wolfgang Amadeus Mozart, Pablo Picasso, Jackson Pollack, Vincent Van Gogh, Georgia O'Keefe

SOCIAL STUDIES

Jane Addams, Susan B. Anthony, Shirley Chisholm, Mohandas Gandhi, Malcolm X, Nelson Mandela, Harriet Beecher Stowe, Mother Teresa

FIGURE 7.7   *An excerpt about the adolescent years of a scientist.*

Feynman himself thought that his grammar school, Public School 39, had been stultifyingly barren: "an intellectual desert." At first he learned more at home, often from the encyclopedia. Having trained himself in rudimentary algebra, he once concocted a set of four equations and showed it off to his arithmetic teacher, along with his methodical solution. She was impressed but mystified; she had to take it to the principal to find out whether it was correct. . . .

In physics club Feynman and his friends studied the wave motions of light and the odd vortex phenomenon of smoke rings. . . . [On math team] squads of five students from each school met in a classroom, the two teams sitting in a line, and a teacher would present a series of problems. . . . Feynman lived for these competitions. . . . For all the best competitors, the goal was a mental flash, achieved somewhere below consciousness. In these ideal instants one did not strain toward the answer so much as relax toward it. Often enough Feynman would get this unstudied insight while the problem was still being read out, and his opponents, before they could begin to compute, would see him ostentatiously write a single number and draw a circle around it. Then he would let out a loud sigh. (James Gleick, 1992, pp. 30–34)

From *Genius: The Life and Science of Richard Feynman,* by James Gleick. Copyright © 1992 by Voyager.

BookTalk   7.3

We know writers can write memoirs of their lives, which of course would include anecdotes showing learning experiences. Is it possible to write a memoir of the writing process? The title of Stephen King's *On Writing: A Memoir of the Craft* (2000) suggests an affirmative answer. He combines writerly advice, lots of examples from the works of his favorite authors, descriptions of his teachers (imagine having a young Stephen King in your class), and memories of adolescent experiences that he learned from, so it's a perfect book to stimulate your own memoir writing. In addition, after introducing a scenario and suggesting a creative exercise to tackle, King invites readers to drop him a line at www.stephenking.com to let him know how it worked, in other words what the writing process was like. So, if you want a famous audience for your writing, read this book and accept your invitation to join Stephen King's writing community.

LITERARY CHARACTERS WHO WRITE: MODELS AND MOTIVATORS

In previous chapters you learned about using literature involving characters who care about vocabulary and language, and characters who are readers and problem solvers. There are also many books featuring characters who write in a variety of settings and genres. No matter what your subject area, there are literary models you can use to make points in your content lessons and help students reflect on the purposes and processes of writing. There are examples of characters who keep journals, such as Anastasia Krupnik keeping track of her rapidly growing gerbil population using her science notebook (Lowry, 1984). Here's an example of a literary character's correspondence related to history: in Irene Hunt's Newbery Honor Book *Across Five Aprils* (1964), letters from soldiers describing the Civil War are interspersed. When young Jethro Creighton faces a dilemma about hiding a deserter, he writes to the president, who responds with a letter that ends:

> May God bless you for the earnestness with which you have tried to seek out what is right; may he guide both of us in that search during the days ahead of us.
>
> Yours very sincerely and respectfully,
> Abraham Lincoln (p. 147)

Letters from Rifka, by Karen Hesse (1992), consists of a series of letters composed by a 12-year-old Jewish girl as she flees Russia for America in 1919. She uses the blank pages and margins of her poetry book, a gift from her cousin, to write letters telling of the trials that so many immigrants had to endure. She writes her last letter from Ellis Island, before sending her cousin the book, in hopes that its words will offer comfort: "At last I send you my love from America. Shalom" (p. 145). You can see how this book could tap into the affective realm of your students' learning, while building content knowledge and expressing the value of writing.

Some books for adolescents have characters completing writing assignments for school. For example, in Edward Bloor's *Tangerine* (1997), Paul is part of a group working on a science project related to tangerine growing. Readers are let in on aspects of their collaborative exploration. Also, the entire stories of both *The Outsiders* (Hinton, 1967) and *Rats Saw God* (Thomas, 1996) are framed as school assignments.

BookTalk   7.4

Have you ever kept, or do you now keep, a diary? Several series of books written in diary form enable readers to appreciate the genre and get to know the innermost thoughts of the characters. They also get the feel for different places and periods of history and learn particular content, as well as explore larger concepts relating to war, justice, gender roles, emigration and immigration, societal expectations, individual responsibility, courage, and truth. Scholastic's *Dear America* series features strong female characters struggling and growing in various eras and circumstances—from Puritan life to World War II. The parallel *My Name Is America* series features male main characters. In the *Royal Diaries* series, also by Scholastic, prominent young adult authors weave tales based on real royalty and actual historical events. You can enter the courts of well-known queens and princesses such as Elizabeth I, Cleopatra, Marie Antoinette, and Anastasia, or travel to Angola, Africa, in the sixteenth century to get to know Nzingha, Warrior Queen of Matamba, who fought to keep her people from being put on Portuguese ships heading for Brazil and slavery. These diaries—offering personal perspectives, struggles with family, contemplation of right and wrong, romance, and betrayal—emphasize that history is indeed full of wonderful, relevant stories and lessons about our fellow humans.

FIGURE **7.8** *Books featuring characters who write.*

Avi. (1990). *The True Confessions of Charlotte Doyle.* New York: Orchard Books.

Avi. (1991). *Nothing But the Truth.* New York: Orchard Books.

Bantock, N. (1991). *Griffin and Sabine: A Novel Correspondence.* San Francisco: Chronicle Books.

Blos, J. W. (1979). *A Gathering of Days: A New England Girl's Journal 1830–32.* New York: Scribner's.

Cleary, B. (1983). *Dear Mr. Henshaw.* New York: Morrow.

Crutcher, C. (1995). *Ironman.* New York: Greenwillow Books.

Friedman, R. (2000). *How I Survived My Summer Vacation: And Lived to Write the Story.* Chicago: Front Street/Cricket Books.

George, J. C. (1959). *My Side of the Mountain.* New York: Dutton.

Haddix, M. P. (1996). *Don't You Dare Read This, Mrs. Dunphrey.* New York: Simon & Schuster.

Johnston, J. (1994). *Adam and Eve and Pinch Me.* Boston: Little, Brown.

Little, J. (1989). *Hey, World, Here I Am!* New York: HarperCollins.

Myers, W. D. (1999). *Monster.* New York: HarperCollins.

Paterson, K. (1978). *The Great Gilly Hopkins.* New York: Crowell.

Your students should think about and monitor their own composing processes, and literature again provides examples of metacognition. In Madeleine L'Engle's Newbery Honor Book *A Ring of Endless Light* (1980), the narrator writes a sonnet for a dead baby dolphin and concludes, "I had not, as it were, dictated the words, I had simply followed them where they wanted to lead. . . . I felt the good kind of emptiness that comes when I've finished writing something" (p. 172). When a friend asks her where she is when she's in the middle of a poem, she replies, "I'm not sure. I'm more in the poem than I am in me. I'm using my mind, really using it, and yet I'm not directing the poem or telling it where to go. It's telling me" (pp. 162–163). Students can use this passage as a springboard to discuss how they feel when writing; for example, troubled at the beginning, euphoric in the middle, frustrated at the revision stage, or satisfied at the end. For some, this quote will resonate; others will contrast the character's writing process with their own.

Figure 7.8 provides a sample of books containing literary characters who write. There are many more. Some may be appropriate for your classroom library; you might choose others to read aloud or assign as a supplement to other curricular materials.

PART TWO

Teaching Writing in the Disciplines

Imagine being interviewed for your first teaching job and being asked the question, "How will you teach writing to your middle school or high school students?" Your initial reaction might be, "Excuse me, I'm the one here about a math position," or "I'm going to teach chemistry; the English teacher down the hall will handle writing," or "Of course, I'll *use* writing in my history class, but I expect the students to come to me knowing *how* to write." But then you'd remember what you've learned about every teacher being a literacy teacher. In a classic study with subject matter classroom teachers, Langer and Applebee (1987) found that writing activities improve learning in the disciplines in several ways:

- Students can use writing to gain relevant knowledge and experience in preparation for new activities.
- They can consolidate and review what has been learned
- They can extend ideas and experiences.

The researchers concluded, "Our analyses of the students' papers and their self-reports indicated that writing used to reformulate and extend knowledge led to more complex reasoning" (p. 136).

What does it mean for you to be a teacher of writing? Mulcahy-Ernt and Stewart (1994) explain your role well:

> The role of the content-area teacher is not to instruct students explicitly in the writing process, but to create literacy opportunities in the classroom so that the students will use reading and writing for learning. Much of school learning emphasizes academic literacies, the type of reading and writing for learning about the world, for developing an aesthetic taste, or for exploring one's own ideas and feelings. (p. 107)

The rest of this chapter discusses specific ways you can teach your students to develop their writing skills and use writing strategies to learn and explore your content, as well as to demonstrate knowledge and discipline-based thinking.

ACTIVATING PRIOR KNOWLEDGE   7.4

Your own experience as a student can inform your present thinking about where and how writing will fit into your courses. So, follow these steps to tap into your prior knowledge.

STEP 1. Make a chart of the different subjects you took in high school. Think back to the types of writing you did in these subjects. Was writing considered important? Was it used as a tool for learning or only to show what you had learned? Are there memorable products you wrote, papers or projects you were proud of? Were you a confident writer in the various courses you took?

STEP 2. Think of yourself as a teacher of whatever discipline you are pursuing. How will you use writing in your course? What place will it have? What types of writing should your students have ability or proficiency in?

STEP 3. Think again of your preferred discipline, the one you hope to teach and encourage young people to understand and perhaps pursue for a future career. What kinds of writing skills are required of people who actually work in the field? What genres and types of writing are important and useful to them? What are some specific examples of texts you have read that were written by scientists, mathematicians, doctors, historians, musicians, artists, or business or government leaders?

KINDS OF ACADEMIC WRITING

Part One discussed writing processes in general. The past two decades have also seen the flourishing of research, theory, and practice related to the more specific topics of writing in the disciplines and writing across the curriculum. Applebee, Auten, and Lehr (1981) researched the kinds of writing high school students were asked to do in six subject areas. They found that writing activities, though numerous and consuming an average of 44 percent of classroom time, consisted of *mechanical* writing (e.g., worksheets, fill-in-the blank exercises, math calculations) and *informational* writing (e.g., summaries, notetaking, essays). Students were rarely given the opportunity for personal writing or writing for intellectual exploration. Fulwiler (1986) concluded from observational studies that there was little sustained writing in classrooms that was personal. In 1994, Applebee found students spending an average of only two hours a week on writing, and their writing performance showed that many students at each grade level continue to have serious difficulties producing effective persuasive, informative, or narrative writing. Yet, evidence from classrooms (Atwell, 1998; Brown, 1994; Harwayne, 1992; Rief, 1992) indicates that it doesn't have to be this way. Researchers have found many benefits to a variety of writing, including that reading and writing can work together to promote critical thinking (McGinley, 1992; Shanahan & Tierney, 1991; Tierney, Soter, O'Flahavan, & McGinley, 1989), and that writing essays enabled students to gain knowledge, as well as improve their thinking about the actual content (Langer, 1986).

Another way writing can be categorized is to think of it as either *explanatory* or *exploratory* (Hairston, 1994). Both are appropriate to promote in your content area classroom. Explanatory writing tends to be about information, and the writer knows much of what she is going to say or knows where to find the material needed for the work, whether it be a research paper on the aftermath of the Vietnam War, a report on how a school district will pay for and implement new technology, or an essay on saving endangered species. Hairston explains, "The material for such a paper already exists—you're not going to create it or discover it within your subconscious. Your job as a writer is to dig out the material, organize it, and shape it into a clearly written, carefully supported essay" (p. 472). Writers of explanatory material usually plan, and often can follow traditional outlines, methods, and patterns of organization. As content area teachers, you can help your students identify their task, determine audience and purpose, organize informa-

HOW EARLY DOES WRITING ABOUT CONTENT BEGIN?

Children who are at the emergent stage of literacy already have important thoughts that are connected to learning in content areas. Notice the invented spelling in these two war stories written by first graders:

> I was in worldwar 2. I was on the U.S.A team. the other team was British Colambia. I was trying to out run a bomber with an army plane. The other plane was shooting at me but I knocked him out of the sky. Another plane was in the sky but I knocked him out of the sky too. I was captured by the other team but I got out and got away.

> The War Chapter I

> It was the day of the Sevle War. It was South Amareca against North Amarica. North Amar was winning.

> South Amarica had lost five men alredredy. The Tank is here! Chapter 2.

> The solgers came marching ahed of the tank. The soljers shouted with joy. The tank is here! The captain of South Amarica looked afraid. He said to his men we have to hurry or we will lose. In the House Chapter 3. The men ran to the house. They wanted to get thary lunch frist. but when they got to the house it was emtey! Then theye new what happend The war was over nobody had won.

Teachers can celebrate the imagination and willingness to experiment with narrative writing shown by children. And we can encourage continued exploration and invention through composing as they progress through their school careers.

---

tion, draft, revise, and edit. The strategies described throughout the rest of this chapter provide concrete ways to do that.

Exploratory writing is also very useful for your content area students. Writers of this type usually only have a partial idea of what they will say or where the writing will take them. The material doesn't already exist, ready to be found and synthesized; writers have to read, ask people questions, develop new insights or combinations of ideas, find and express a point of view. Because so much is learned along the way, the process is different from what works when writing an explanatory piece, and very likely is messier. Even the main idea may change along the way, and an outline may be written after a draft rather than before, if it is needed at all.

These two types of writing are not mutually exclusive; you can model and encourage students to combine them to make essays stronger and more interesting.

WAYS OF USING WRITING IN CONTENT AREA CLASSES

This section explains a number of ways that students in your content areas can write in order to learn, to better understand material they read, to think critically and reflectively about content, to improve their writing skills, and to show what they have learned.

Writing in Preparation for Reading

If students are asked to reflect in writing and perhaps commit themselves to a stance on an issue before reading a text on a particular topic, their minds will be activated so that they will be motivated to read and actively engage with the information. They will also be cognizant of the background knowledge they can bring to the text, especially if students share and discuss their pre-reading writing. This can be considered one form of an anticipation guide, which you learned about in Chapter 1. Here is an example of an in-class writing assignment that students can be given before reading Peter Dickinson's science fiction novel *Eva* (1988) and related articles on ways scientists are using animals to advance medical treatment for humans:

> Drivers in many states are given the opportunity to sign a donor card at the time they get or renew their drivers' licenses, letting it be known that in case of an accident that takes their life, they wish their organs to be donated for transplant. Imagine that sometime in your driving future you can also indicate one or both of the following:

> ■ In case of impending death, if my body cannot be saved, I wish my mind and memory to be implanted in the body of an animal or another human whose mind has gone.

> ■ In case of impending death, if my mind cannot survive, I wish to donate my body to be the host of someone else's mind.

Write for about 10 minutes on whether you would agree to either of these wishes, or if you would honor similar wishes of a loved one if a doctor left the decision up to you. You can react in terms of practical or ethical considerations. (Based on an anticipation guide by student Erica Lyon.)

Figure 7.9 shows a preservice social studies teacher's use of the "What If?" strategy in a writing guide to activate students' thinking and emotions in preparation for their reading assignment.

BookTalk   7.5

In the event this exercise made you curious about the book, allow me to insert a booktalk. As you know, medical knowledge and technology have advanced to the point where doctors can do things now that raise questions regarding morality and ethics. Readers are confronted with some hard choices in the futuristic novel *Eva* by Peter Dickinson (1988). After an accident, Eva awakes in a hospital to find that her mind has been implanted in the body of a chimpanzee, while her old body is dead. Her parents chose this bold and risky course of action over losing her altogether. Think what science can learn through this great experiment! And think of future possibilities if the experiment succeeds! This book is guaranteed to generate lively discussion among the animal lovers, future sociologists and medical workers, science fiction fans, and imaginative students in your social studies, health, science, or English classes. Its multiple themes make it a good choice for interdisciplinary study.

> *Getting Ready to Teach 7.1* (see page 235)

Writing to Imitate a Writer's Style or Structure

A valuable strategy students can use involves writing their own stories or information pieces based on formats of model books you provide. They can pay attention to published authors' dialogue, techniques, and story development and then experiment themselves. For example, students may be familiar with the McKissacks' *Christmas in the Big House, Christmas in the Quarters* (1994). They could use that same con-

trasting pattern to write about life today in suburbs, urban areas, and rural places.

Introduce your classes to the concept of *intertextuality*, "one writer (or film-maker or artist) elaborating upon or consciously paying homage to the works of another" (Abair & Cross, 1999, p. 85). Intertextuality was at work in Jean Little's poem "After English Class," which you read in Chapter 3. When it is done with humor as a spoof, it's known as parody. (Recall the BookTalk on page 70 on *The New Way Things Work* and *The Way Things REALLY Work*.) Students may be familiar with examples that abound in the television show *The Simpsons*. They might have fun writing poems copying the rhythm of a famous poem but substituting their own topics.

Modeling their writing on published texts serves multiple purposes because the strategy forces students to pay attention to writing styles, structures, tones, and conventions, and it provides an avenue for them to express their own emotions or convey their knowledge of a topic. They might produce classroom books for future classes, or they could "publish" texts for younger students in the school, explaining content area principles. For example, after reading Thomas Locker's *Water Dance* (1997), a picture book with beautiful oil paintings and a poetic text that explains the water cycle, science students could create companion texts illustrating and detailing other aspects of meteorology. Or, after reading *The World in 1492* (Fritz et al., 1992), social studies students could be divided into groups to make other books for a series of books like the prototype, each group choosing a different important date to explore and write about. A good resource to get them started is *The History Puzzle: An Interactive Visual Timeline* by Cherry Denman (1995). This activity can be very enjoyable and can stimulate creativity, originality, and collaboration.

Math students could read *Sir Cumference and the First Round Table: A Math Adventure* by Cindy Neuschwander (1997) and, after learning about the parts and properties of a circle from characters such as Lady Di of Ameter and her son Radius, could create their own stories explaining other mathematical principles. Math teacher Genevieve F. Wahlgren (1997) reports exciting results when her students created mathematical storybooks about topics such as negative exponents after examining examples of professional mathematics writing. They held peer conferences over drafts, and interacted with the school's computer specialist and media specialist as they used word processing and graphics to complete their books.

Content area teachers can combine literature and creative writing to enhance the understanding

FIGURE 7.9   *An anticipation guide involving student writing.*

DIRECTIONS: React in writing to the following "WHAT IF?" prompts.

1. WHAT IF you lived in a climate that was desperately hot and dry, where temperatures can reach 130 degrees F? In this heat, WHAT IF you were forced to dress every day in heavy cloth covering you from head to toe?

    _____

    _____

    _____

2. WHAT IF you were forced into marriage for reasons other than love that you would never have the opportunity to understand? WHAT IF your family forced this marriage? WHAT IF you were still a teenager? (Picture yourself married now.)

    _____

    _____

    _____

3. WHAT IF your happiness depended on the kindness of others? WHAT IF the one to determine whether you shall live, die, smile, or cry was not you? WHAT IF every aspect of your life was under surveillance and out of your control?

    _____

    _____

    _____

4. WHAT IF you were born into a country where the birth of one gender was considered a blessing and the other a curse? WHAT IF you were born of the cursed gender?

    _____

    _____

    _____

5. WHAT IF you lived in a land where polygamy is condoned? WHAT IF your father had several wives?

    _____

    _____

    _____

A certain woman who lived this life didn't need to ask these WHAT IF questions. While reading the book *Princess: A True Story of Life Behind the Veil in Saudi Arabia*, by Jean Sasson (2001), keep these questions and your answers in mind. This is an attempt to further your understanding of the diversity of cultures in this world. What is acceptable in one culture can be punishable in another. Write a brief reaction to the book and reflect on how the WHAT IF questions affected your reading.

Note: This book tells the story of one Saudi princess. You cannot judge the country or the culture just by this book. We will be doing more research, and we'll be talking about whether there is such a thing as universal human rights and how we might react to situations where these rights are violated.

—*Judith Miller*

of curriculum. Kliman and Kleiman (1992) describe an activity called *My Travels with Gulliver* (Education Development Center, 1991) where students used writing as a vehicle to travel with Swift's Gulliver and conduct mathematical investigations, reporting their findings through stories and journal entries. The novel was used as a springboard to get students to learn such skills as making size comparisons and using scale factors to calculate giant sizes.

Freewriting and Responding to Prompts in Journals

Another way to use trade books is to encourage students to respond freely after reading literature purely for pleasure or as part of their course work. I give my students the following suggestions for their journal responses:

> In your dialogue journals, you have the opportunity to respond in any way you like to the books and articles you read. The best way is to let the book speak to you and respond accordingly. Don't decide beforehand what kind of a response you will do.
>
> Aim for depth of understanding, insight, and application to educational and literary theory. Some possible ways of responding include:

- Discuss the emotional impact the story had on you.

- Discuss the writer's craft. Analyze the structure or write some favorite sentences.

- Respond in terms of traditional "English class concepts": character development, symbolism, theme, foreshadowing, setting, irony, and so on.

- Apply it to your teaching situation. How might you "teach" this work of literature? Create some interpretive and applied-level questions to facilitate a class discussion.

- Connect to other books you've read.

- Imagine how a teenager might read this book.

- Write to the author or to a character.

- Write out part of the story from another character's point of view.

- List or discuss the content area knowledge the book provides.

- Apply a type of literary criticism to this work.

- Write a review of the book for a magazine or newspaper.

- Write a letter to a friend, telling her why she absolutely must read this book.

- Play around with ideas for a sequel, or rewrite the ending.

- Create a visual representation of this work—a poster, a graphic organizer or concept map showing relationships, a work of art demonstrating your response.

- Connect the literary work to issues we've discussed in class (censorship, bibliotherapy, writer's craft, defining and judging quality).

- Write a poem.

- Have a character write to a character in another book, or a historical figure, or someone you know.

Journal writing, with or without teacher prompts, can also help students reflect on nonfiction trade books and on textbook selections. A colleague of mine, Dr. Christine Walsh, used the guided writing strategy (explained more fully later in this chapter) before and after her education class read a draft of Chapter 3 of this book. Figure 7.10 shows the questions she handed out prior to giving the students the text, and those she gave out during the next class meeting to guide their post-reading responses.

Notice that the teacher provided a purpose and an audience for the writing she asked the students to do, which is great in terms of authenticity. But her primary goal was to help her students reflect on their reading; she elicited their thoughts and helped them apply the text to their own situations.

In *Using Journals with Reluctant Writers: Building Portfolios for Middle and High School Students*, Abrams (2000) shares journal-related activities he developed for "'alternative education' students, . . . the teenagers who don't fit into traditional settings, such as the chronic non-attenders, students who have trouble with the law, girls who are pregnant, students with learning difficulties, youth who question every authority figure, students who have trouble with drugs, teenagers who are having difficulty growing into adults" (p. 1). He has found that the activities work well with students who are at risk of failure because our educational system has failed to meet their needs. You will at some point have students in your class fitting every one of these descriptions, so learning about these activities and then creating others to fit your curriculum can be helpful. For each of 45 topics, Abrams provides prompts to stimulate students' thinking as they write in their journals, then an essay prompt, an extension activity, and a suggested video to watch and react to. Often, he includes a suggested reading. For example, for the topic "Occupations," he provides prompts for journal writing, including the following:

- Some people believe that you should be paid according to how difficult your job is. What jobs should be paid the most in our society? Why?

FIGURE 7.10 *Structured journal response guide to a textbook excerpt.*

PRE-READING QUESTIONS:

1. In general, how do you feel about reading textbooks? Are they helpful to you? Do you enjoy them? Do you always faithfully read textbook assignments? Would you say you read them more actively or passively?

2. What resources other than textbooks do you learn from? What kinds of texts do you use with your students? List as many as you can.

3. Can picture books be used with secondary students? If so, how?

4. In what ways, if any, do you use poetry in your classroom?

POST-READING RESPONSE GUIDE:

Directions: After reading Chapter 3 of Sharon Kane's textbook in progress, please respond in letter format directly to Sharon. Use examples from the text to illustrate your thoughts. (Don't just tell.) Especially helpful feedback might include, but not be limited to:

- What you liked about the chapter (be specific)
- What ideas you will use from the chapter (mention your grade level/content area and how you already use ideas or want to use them)
- What you didn't like or understand about the chapter (be specific)
- What you think in general about her approach (language, style, audience, voice, etc.)
- What questions you have about something she wrote
- What you think is missing or, if added, would strengthen her chapter
- What about the organization of the chapter? Does it make sense? Is it easy to follow?
- What is the overall value of this text for literacy teachers?
- Other thoughts and reactions

What jobs are the most overpaid in our society? Why do you think so?

■ What characteristics are important to you when you think of a future occupation? Would you rather work inside or outside? Alone or with others? Do physical labor or work with your mind? (p. 76)

Abrams gives the essay prompt, "Complete a resume or write an interest letter to a possible employer," and an extension activity suggests filling out a career assessment to discover possible career interests. He recommends, describes, and gives guiding questions for the video *My Bodyguard* (Devlin & Bill, 1980), and he reviews and provides questions for Karen Cushman's Newbery winner *The Midwife's Apprentice* (1995).

Abrams provides tips for effective teacher–student communication through journals, including jotting personal notes to students, increasing the possibility of dialogue, and using current situations inside or outside the classroom whenever possible. Use Abrams' structure as a model—create journal and essay prompts and recommend related videos, texts, and activities about such curricular topics as stem cell research, environmental engineering issues, peace initiatives, voting reform, art appreciation, use of technology in schools, programs to alleviate poverty, gender equity issues, or economic growth issues.

Writing Book Reviews

We often hear jokes, as well as moans, when the topic of the dreaded *book report* is raised. Most of us remember having to prove we read a book by writing a report, sometimes monthly or weekly, usually following a prescribed formula. Ask your peers about book reports and you'll elicit confessions of copying from book jackets, reporting on imaginary books, and so forth. But think about it—virtually no one outside a classroom has to write a book report! On the other hand, *book reviews* are a wonderful genre, and we can give our students many examples of this evaluative form of writing from real sources as we encourage them to try their hand at crafting reviews of content area-related books they've read.

I keep a "Book Review File," where I collect published reviews, as well as student-written ones. For example, in an issue of the *Journal of Adolescent and Adult Literacy*, there are several reviews of Gary Paulsen's Civil War novel *Soldier's Heart* (Davenport, 1999)—three written by college secondary education students and one by their professor. These are great models to share with my English

and social studies preservice teachers. Literature circle members sometimes decide to write a group review of a selected title. I teach a graduate class called "Teaching with Young Adult Literature," and one day I brought in a review I had found in the newspaper that asked why so many books for young readers emphasize the ghastly and grotesque, and accused even the award winners of being unwholesome and potentially harmful. The reviewer bemoaned, "To find a book worth reading, a youngster must wade through a sludge of sadism, abuse of senior citizens, the passage of bad checks, loveless sexual encounters, incest, unwanted pregnancies, sexual molestation, obscenities, corruption, verbal and physical abuse, illegitimacy and rape" (Koretz, 1999, p. 17). One targeted book was Han Nolan's *Dancing on the Edge* (1997), winner of the 1997 National Book Award and a book that was on my required reading list. My students could react, therefore, not only to the novel but to the reviewer's comments:

> The central character (neither heroine nor anti-heroine, but a psychotic young girl) not only sets herself on fire, but also is confused as to whether or not the conflagration was an accident. The story ends with much psychobabble from a psychiatrist who has the distracting habit of rolling around his office on a chair fitted with wheels. (Koretz, 1999, p. 17)

Most of my students vehemently disagreed with this reviewer (wondering among other things *what was her problem* with a chair on wheels), and countered her opinions with strong positive reviews of the novel. Your students can send their reviews in to journals, or to websites that invite reviews, and they can post reviews around the classroom and respond to those written by others. The opportunities are endless. The following is a letter I received from an eighth grader, Natasha, whom I met just once and subsequently sent a copy of Nolan's book. Here's her unsolicited review:

> Dear Sharon,
>
> I finished *Dancing on the Edge!* Thanks for giving it to me!! Here's my honest opinion . . .
>
> I started out thinking I was going to love it. I thought all the aura and séance stuff was really cool & spiritual. I liked it up until the point where she was sent to the hospital for her burns. I was really inside her mind, but it went downhill from there. I didn't like when she went into therapy at the hospital, and I didn't like the psychiatrist at all. At that point, it started getting away from the spiritual stuff and turning into a "problem novel." I hated all the scenes with the psychiatrist. I thought it was getting whiny but

the low point was when the author portrayed Gigi as a bad phony person. (And the Aunt as a good person changed through psychology.) In the end it turned out happily, all due to the wonders of therapy. Really, I don't like books with therapists solving everything, because that stuff is phony to me. It was well written, though. I just wish it had stuck with the spiritual stuff.

The "problem novel" category is hard to fill with good books, and *Dancing on the Edge* is pretty good. I have two suggestions of "problem novel" books I liked a lot. *The Tulip Touch* + *Speak*. They are both really well written & not whiny at all. Also, both heroines solve their own problems themselves without therapy! That I like. *Speak* is about a girl getting raped, but it's very subtle and not superficial or scary. *Tulip Touch* is about being friends with a troubled girl, and is very powerful.

> *Getting Ready to Teach 7.2* (see page 235)

Writing to Reflect on Thinking Processes

Recall that Chapter 4 dealt extensively with metacognition, especially in terms of students monitoring their reading and thinking processes. In various exercises earlier in this chapter, I asked you to reflect on your writing processes. Although you have participated in these various stages of composing for years, you may not have been consciously aware of the fact that you were prewriting or revising as you were drafting. Now, as a result of completing the exercises' prompts, you have thought about your writing metacognitively. When students write about the thinking process they go through to write a piece or solve a problem, they learn something that may transfer to other situations and might also help us as we guide them. Recall in Chapter 4 when I demonstrated how you could model a "think-aloud" for your class as you read a text. Similarly, your students can benefit by watching you write a piece in front of them:

> Sharing and demonstrating [your] craft with students, metacognitively thinking aloud during different types of text composition. Thus, student writers observe firsthand the realistic joys and frustrations of refining a thesis statement, reorganizing ideas, omitting unnecessary details, deciding on vivid words to describe a setting or characters in a short story, creating imagery in a poem, or engaging in other contextual aspects of writing. (Sanacore, 1998, p. 394)

National and state standards for most of the disciplines require student reflection on process, and some assessments in math now require students not only to solve multistep problems, but also to explain in writing how they arrived at their solution. This is an example of metacognitive thinking, and a good rationale for incorporating writing into math class.

Calculus teachers Joanna O. Masingila and Ewa Prus-Wisniowska (1996) use writing to both develop and assess their students' understanding of concepts. Sometimes, they require writing from carefully constructed prompts, encouraging students to connect new ideas with prior knowledge. One example they give is, "Explain the similarity in, and difference between, using a vertical line to test whether a rule is a function and using a horizontal line to test whether a function is a one-to-one function" (p. 96). The authors found that writing from a prompt

> allows students to express and teachers to see the personal nature of making sense of a new idea. A new idea makes sense for a student if he or she is able to link it with a network of mental representations. Writing from a prompt encourages students to forge new links and think reflectively about the links they have already made. (p. 97)

These same teachers involve their students in writing performance tasks to demonstrate and communicate their understanding. The students first complete a task or conduct a mathematical investigation and then write out the process they went through. Masingila and Prus-Wisniowska found the use of group performance tasks to be especially valuable, as students collaborate and assess and build on one another's ideas. Through writing, their critical thinking is put into words.

Consider having your students write instructions related to some topic in your field, whether that might translate to specifying directions along the Oregon Trail, writing recipes, creating a computer program, or instructing readers how to compose a business letter or get started using instant messaging. Grandgenett, Hill, and Lloyd (1999) set out to help elementary students develop procedural reasoning, which involves breaking a process down into distinct steps, through a writing activity—writing a "how to" manual for building kites. In the construction phase, they led the class discussion and asked science-related questions as students planned the characteristics and dimensions of a product model. Students then made box kites, researching to find answers as challenges arose. Phase 2 asked the students to record the steps they used to build their kites, with other students as their intended audience. After sharing the instructions and consulting with peers, they revised their work based on the feedback received. Finally, they created diagrams to accompany the text, added a title page, and published their manuals. The authors watched their students become "in turn, architects, writers, scientists and artists as they developed their how-to manuals" (p. 146). Reasoning and writing went hand in hand.

The RAFT Strategy

Students' thinking, as well as their writing skills, may be enhanced by understanding and then arguing from a point of view other than their own. The RAFT strategy (Santa & Havens, 1995) provides a way to do that. The acronym RAFT stands for Role, Audience, Format, and Topic—all aspects students must pay attention to as they write. The teacher creates content area-based writing prompts, assigning each of these parts to students based on material they have read and topics they have covered; or students may make their own decisions. For example, in terms of *role*, students could be asked to think as a political leader, a fictional character, a slave at the time the Civil War was imminent, or even a virus or a river. Audiences can vary similarly, as can formats. The students' aim in RAFT writing pieces is to use an authentic voice for a particular purpose, such as explaining or persuading. I'm in favor of giving the students as much control and choice within the guidelines of this activity as possible. That way, you'll enjoy reading the different creative products, and the students, through sharing, will be exposed to a larger number of possible ways of reasoning. As Alvermann and Phelps (1998) remind us, personal motivation is crucial in writing, and "a role or topic that may seem 'creative' to one person may hold little attraction to another. Not every student will be eager to write from the point of view of a rain forest animal, Captain Ahab's second mate, the unknown variable in a two-step equation, or a red blood cell traveling through the circulatory system" (p. 282). Interestingly, since this quote came out, *Ahab's Wife, or The Star Gazer: A Novel* (Naslund, 1999) has become a best seller—a good example of the RAFT strategy because the novelist takes on an unusual point of view—that of Ahab's wife—to spin a story off a classic!

Show examples of published writing that model the RAFT strategy. Letters to the editor in a newspaper often identify the writers' role or identity, address particular people or communities, or explain their reasons for expressing their opinions on a particular topic of concern. Certain novels exemplify characters who come at an issue from varying, sometime opposing, perspectives. *Bull Run*, a novel of the

Civil War by Paul Fleischman (1993), has 16 narrators, equally divided between the South and the North, each telling his or her version of what happened during the war. Diane Siebert has a series of geography-related poems, *Mojave* (1988), *Heartland* (1989), and *Sierra* (1991), with a desert, heartland, and mountain (respectively) narrating about themselves and their characteristics. A social studies, earth science, or English teacher can ask her students to listen as the voice from *Sierra* begins:

> I am the mountain,
> Tall and grand.
> And like a sentinel I stand.
>
> . . . I am the mountain.
> Come and know
> Of how, ten million years ago,
> Great forces, moving plates of earth,
> Brought, to an ancient land rebirth;
> Of how this planet's faulted crust
> Was shifted, lifted, tilted, thrust
> Toward the sky in waves of change
> To form a newborn mountain range. (unpaged)

From *Sierra* by Diane Siebert. Text copyright © 1991 by Diane Siebert. Used by permission of HarperCollins Publishers.

In class, students could do some expressive writing, creating similar poems using the voice of the Mississippi River or a glacier or an ocean. Or they might choose a different format, such as a letter or travel brochure or obituary.

Here's a sample RAFT assignment a science teacher might give after students have read Peter Dickinson's *Eva*, the novel discussed earlier in this chapter. "Choose a character (ROLE) from the novel and write a piece explaining his or her position on one of the TOPICS relevant to the story. Choose a logical AUDIENCE and an appropriate FORMAT and tone."

One student might write an impassioned plea from Eva's mother begging the medical community to halt the procedure of implanting human minds into the bodies of chimpanzees, citing the difficulties she now has relating to her daughter. Another could write a report in the voice of Eva's researcher father arguing the importance of *continuing* the procedure and the subsequent research. A particular student who is a proponent of animal rights might choose to take on the role of the ghost of Kelly, the chimp that was killed so that its body could host Eva's mind. Someone interested in animal cognition could play around with the thoughts that might be going on in the chimpanzees who interact with Eva/Kelly, wondering about her differences as they try to learn the knot-tying skills she teaches them.

The format chosen for this might be a personal reflection with self as audience.

The benefits of the RAFT strategy can be far-reaching because in actuality, almost all writing done in the disciplines, whether research reports, government documents, funding proposals or interoffice memos, requires the writers to identify their role, know their intended audience, adhere to sometimes very narrowly prescribed and rigid formats, and stick to the topic at hand. Tell your students that RAFT can be with them forever as a valuable tool (or even a life-saving device) through their writing lives!

> ### Getting Ready to Teach 7.3 (see page 235)

Quick Writes

Sometimes, you may find you have students who are so used to regurgitating information that that's what they think you mean when you ask them for a response to a lesson or a reading. Or they're so familiar with fill-in-the-blank comprehension exercises that they're reluctant or afraid to write anything at all unless given a strict framework. Encouraging them to think actively about what they're hearing or reading, to be aware of their reactions, and to write succinctly can work wonders. Quick Writes (Ruddell, 1993) are brief, open-ended opportunities for students to reflect on their immediate learning experiences. They can be used to focus a class discussion, emphasize the key points of a lecture, or require students to synthesize information. I know a teacher who asks students in her social studies education class to fill out an "exit slip" every day before they leave, stating a key point they understood from the class and responding to it. Here's what one looks like:

> KEY POINT: I heard you say over and over again today that all of us exhibit some racist characteristics without even realizing it.
>
> MY RESPONSE: Oh, boy, I'm feeling angry and frustrated, and, yes, guilty. You know what? I feel like you tried to MAKE us feel guilty. Well, I haven't done anything wrong. It's not my fault there was slavery, or Jim Crow laws, or riots, or that there are neo-Nazi groups today. I am not a racist! Please stop telling me that I am.

The teacher uses the cards to reflect on the students' understanding of the lesson; she can post the index cards in the room so the students learn from each other, and can use them as a transition to future lessons.

Similarly, teachers can use entrance slips at the beginning of a class to focus attention on the day's topic, or during a lesson to see how well students are understanding it and to help students reflect on ideas and information.

Summary and Essay Writing

A summary is a statement of the main points of a reading without commentary from the student. It is a good way for students to separate main ideas and essential supporting details from less crucial details and to show they comprehend a text. The process of condensing a longer text into a shorter one stimulates students to think actively about and synthesize main ideas, making it a valuable study strategy. Because students use their own words to restate the important points, they will likely understand and remember the information (Hill, 1991). Students can be taught to attend to good topic sentences, combine related ideas, and delete redundant material. Encourage students to summarize reading assignments in their notebooks.

At times, it is appropriate to require students to write short explanatory essays to show what they have learned. They should identify a thesis and organize the information they have in a coherent manner; they may show their analysis of one or more texts or use an organizational pattern such as comparison, cause and effect, general to specific, spatial order, time order, or order of importance. Try to create assignments that actually assist the students in their thinking and organizing for writing. Ask yourself questions such as:

- What exactly do you want your students to do?
- How do you want them to do it?
- Have you provided enough information, preparation, and guidance?
- Who should the audience be?
- How does the assignment fit your objectives and fit into the context of the course or unit?
- How much time will be allowed?
- How will the written pieces be evaluated? (Lindemann, 1987; White, 1999)

Share your answers with your students. It is most helpful to respond to the students in their drafting stages, while their thinking is in progress and they're more receptive to suggestions, rather than wait until they have completed the essay and handed in their final product.

Guided Writing

There are times when providing a structure for student writing is appropriate and beneficial, and there are any number of ways to guide the students. Creating writing guides that help students respond to texts and explain their thinking and learning is one of the most important ways you teach and support them as they strive to grow in content area knowledge. The *Guided Writing Procedure* (Konopak, Martin, & Martin, 1987; Smith & Bean, 1980) provides sequential steps, including:

1. Brainstorming prior knowledge
2. Organizing and labeling the ideas generated in small groups or as a whole class (perhaps creating a semantic web)
3. Writing individually on the topic using the information dealt with thus far
4. Reading an assigned relevant text
5. Revising their first piece of writing based on their comprehension of the text

Some form of assessment completes the procedure. Research has shown that this procedure results in higher-level thinking and better synthesized information on assessments (Konopak, Martin, & Martin, 1990).

Teachers can adapt the Guided Writing Procedure to suit their purposes, or start from scratch to create writing guides that generate the kind of product they want. For example, a science teacher might ask students to create a FAQ sheet on topics relating to weather—students can decide together what might qualify as "Frequently Asked Questions," and then answer them to show they know the information and to share it with others who may not. A tighter structure, maybe even a template, can be offered to students as they write up lab reports.

For example, a seventh-grade health teacher provides the following guidance to his students who are writing reports for his class. He requires each student to choose a disease or disorder, research a number of reference sources, and write an essay (perhaps for inclusion in a class book or webpage) consisting of paragraphs that detail information in the following order: *causes, symptoms,* and *treatments.* Students can learn a lot as they read their classmates' pieces, and the structure provided can help them in terms of comprehending and remembering. The teacher allows individual writers to adapt his guidelines to

fit *their* needs and writing styles. Figure 7.11 is an essay written by a seventh-grade boy in response to this assignment. Notice how he weaves the academic information into his personal narrative.

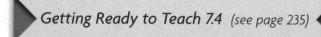

Getting Ready to Teach 7.4 (see page 235)

Writing Letters in the Content Areas

Chapter 3 introduced *Letters of a Nation: A Collection of Extraordinary American Letters,* edited by Andrew Carroll (1997), and explained how real letters can be used to help students analyze and think critically about issues. Now, I'd like you to think about such a source in terms of encouraging your students to write. Students can use the real letters as models for their own writing. They can experiment with taking on the roles of famous people and writing creative letters to each other based on the examples provided in books such as Carroll's or *Famous Letters : Messages and Thoughts that Shaped Our World* edited by Frank McLynn (1993).

Secondary students should also know how to write business letters for various purposes. You might ask them to bring in copies of real business letters their family members have written, either for their jobs or from home. Provide some of your own and keep a file for future reference. You can also help your students write business letters for authentic purposes—to express opinions, complaints, or praise or to request information. One sixth-grade team I visited was planning a class trip to Cape Cod at the end of the school year. For months preceding the expedition, students wrote to chambers of commerce and other offices in places they would be visiting, asking those questions they really wanted answered. The replies they received further validated their teachers' assertions that business letter writing is an authentic task that takes place outside, as well as within, classroom walls.

High school students often have an urgent need to learn how to write a cover letter for employment or for college applications. Writing about their strengths and interests may seem daunting to students, thus providing an authentic opportunity for teaching and learning. You can let students know that such letters have been necessary for centuries, and provide the following example from Leonardo da Vinci's 1482 letter to the Duke of Milan seeking employment as a military engineer:

> I am emboldened . . . to seek an appointment for showing your Excellency certain of my secrets.

FIGURE 7.11 *An essay written for a seventh-grade health class.*

My mother had just gotten off the phone and she was crying.

"What's wrong?" I asked.

"The new baby's gonna have Down Syndrome."

This came as a shock to me. My aunt had already had six perfect kids; why should this one be any different? Also, kids make fun of retarded kids. Was he going to be made fun of?

Three months into her pregnancy, my aunt went to get a test. This was to assure her, since she was 41, that there would be nothing wrong with Mario (his name had already been picked out). One month later, the results came in; Mario Anthony Mazza was going to have Down Syndrome.

For the next five months, my mother kept bringing books home from the library about Down Syndrome. People with the condition have 47 chromosomes instead of the 46 that other people have. It's amazing that one chromosome, one tiny, microscopic chromosome, could mean the difference between a [genetically] normal person and one with Down's. The more I read, the more surprised I was with the disorder. Only one out of every 1,000 babies gets it and it is caused by an abnormality with the genes in one parent. I still can't figure out why it happened to my aunt's seventh baby and not her first.

Down Syndrome was named after a British physician by the name of John Langdon Hayden Down, who first explained the disorder in 1866. The condition was called Mongolism, but that term is not used much today because it's very offensive. . . .

Physical therapy is used to develop the poor muscles that most Down's babies have. (Mario's brothers and sisters have to fly him around like an airplane.) The most serious threat to Mario, however, was possible heart problems. This, along with respiratory disorders, is somewhat common among Down's babies.

As the months went on, we prayed for Mario's case to be mild. Some babies with the disorder are more severely retarded and have to be institutionalized. At these homes the babies do not develop to their full potential. But for some babies, the potential is very high. Christopher Burke, star of the TV show *Life Goes On*, makes more money than most people. Another child with Down Syndrome I read about could do fifth-grade math when only in fourth grade. In these cases, Down Syndrome could easily be called Up Syndrome!

It was October 2, and Mario was a week overdue. Finally, the call came. Mario was born. Tests had been done to see if he had any heart disorders and there were none. He was healthy as could be.

Mario is now three months old and doing great. He smiles all the time and hardly ever cries. Everything about him is beautiful. He has a lot of hair that his mother spikes sometimes. Although he got tons of toys for Christmas, the most important thing he has is our love.

—*Pat Kane*

---

1. I can construct bridges which are very light and strong and portable, with which to pursue and defeat the enemy; and others more solid, which resist fire or assault yet are easily removed and placed in position. . . .

3. I can also make a cannon which is light and easy to transport, with which to hurl small stones like hail, and whose smoke causes great terror to the enemy so that they suffer heavy losses and confusion. . . .

8. In times of peace, I believe that I can give you as complete satisfaction as anyone in the construction of buildings both public and private, and in transporting water from one place to another.

I can further execute sculpture in marble, bronze and clay, also in painting I can do as much as anyone else, whoever he may be. (McLynn, 1993, p. 57)

He got the job.

There are innumerable authentic ways to use letter writing and letter reading in your subject areas. For example, ninth-grade teacher Sharon Morley involved her class in a project based on Jim Burke's *I Hear America Reading: Why We Read What We Read* (1999). She composed a letter that she sent to newspapers around the country, inviting readers to write to her class about how reading has affected their lives. They received dozens of responses to the pilot phase of the project. Her students read and discussed them, found patterns, learned about the geographic areas the respondents lived in from the descriptions in their letters, and used the recommendations in the letters as they selected new books to read for a reading workshop and for pleasure reading at home. The students composed new letters to send to other newspapers.

The students in my education class joined the project; some chose to correspond with some of the people who had written to Sharon Morley's class; others wrote letters to their hometown newspapers or their alma maters, asking teachers and students to tell us about their reading experiences. One newspaper editor posted a college student's invitational letter on the paper's website, soliciting responses electronically.

> **Getting Ready to Teach 7.5** *(see page 236)*

> **Getting Ready to Teach 7.6** *(see page 236)*

Writing Research Papers

Are research papers in high school worth the time and effort on the part of teachers and students? You may recall dreading a research assignment, only to find that you really got into the topic once you started. Or you might have experienced having your initial excitement about exploring a topic squelched when a teacher seemed to care more about the correctness of your footnotes than about your discoveries and analysis of data. Research projects have the potential to enhance content learning, while combining exploratory and explanatory writing. In the early stages and early drafts, students can be writing to learn about their selected topic and about how they think about it and what they wish to say about it. As they revise, they can concern themselves with how they should present their information and write to show what they have learned. Teachers can instruct about such things as proper formatting, use of the Internet, and the use of citations within the context of the students' inquiry and writing processes.

White (1999) notes that the research paper has been slipping out of fashion in recent years, and warns teachers, "The basic problem in teaching the research paper is to reverse students' preconception that research means collecting other people's opinions and patching them together with a bit of rhetorical glue" (p. 20). I think we can help students realize that research is done outside classroom walls all the time by people in various work fields, as well as by consumers. Perhaps the most important step is to formulate an important question or to recognize a need to know about something. Virtually anyone who has had a loved one diagnosed with an illness knows the value of research; we search for books, articles, Internet sites, and people who can give us information about colon cancer, drug addiction, clinical depres-

sion, whatever. Students can brainstorm together to list reasons why product marketers, doctors, English teachers, and other professionals might do research, as well as how they might go about finding answers to their questions.

Let's say you're an American history teacher who will collaborate with an English teacher on a joint research paper assignment for your students. You want your students to formulate a question they really care about investing time on investigating. You might show your class an example of a historian who went through essentially the same process you expect of them. Peter Burchard comes to your aid. In the Introduction to *Lincoln and Slavery* (1999), he tells his readers what prompted his research:

> In my youth, I happily embraced what had become the Lincoln myth. Later, when I learned about his early compromises over slavery, I found excuses for him. When I heard what he said about the possibility of segregation of the races, I was . . . uncomfortable. . . . It saddened me to learn that, until two years or so before his death, he promoted the almost universal belief that black people were inherently inferior to those of other races. . . .
>
> I have always wished that I could talk to Lincoln, ask him questions, listen to him, wished that I could get acquainted with the flawed and complicated man behind the myth.

In a bibliographical essay at the end of the book, Burchard shares his process of seeking answers to his questions about Lincoln and slavery. He used some primary sources, such as *The Black Abolitionist Papers* (Ripley, 1992) and Lincoln's recorded speeches, proclamations, and letters, as well as secondary sources by several well-respected Lincoln biographers. One interesting path he took was to analyze what Lincoln's contemporary, ex-slave Frederick Douglass, had to say about Lincoln's words and actions. The results of Burchard's authentic search to understand the president and the issue are recorded in *Lincoln and Slavery*, a book I would certainly want in my classroom library.

Students today can get just as passionately interested in researching particular topics. Eleventh grader Guillaume was also intrigued with the motivations leading to Lincoln's actions. After some initial research, his thesis statement became: "The outcome of the Civil War was directly affected by the religious beliefs of Lincoln and other renowned theologians as they were able to turn the war between the States into a struggle over righteousness and morality." He pored through books such as Chesebrough's

"God Ordained This War": Sermons on the Sectional Crisis, 1830–1865 (1991), Lincoln and the Preachers (Jones, 1948), and The Almost Chosen People: A Study of the Religion of Abraham Lincoln (Wolf, 1959). Guillaume's research paper was not simply the grudging fulfillment of a school assignment; it represented a young historian's synthesis and interpretation of the data he delved into.

Students as Collaborative Researchers

Elaine Murphy (2001) encouraged her eighth-grade students to use several kinds of writing as they researched a topic that would actually make a difference in their curriculum and other students' lives. The district was asking questions related to what literature should be taught in the twenty-first century, and had formulated a checklist of criteria related to dismantling of stereotypes, providing opportunities for discussion that could foster community relations and respect for diversity, and promoting higher-level critical-thinking skills. Murphy's students read books of their choice and contributed to an annotated bibliography organized by topic. As they read, they kept journals relating the books to the topic question, their personal experiences, and the problems and values of their community. Students shared their journals through the process of serial collaboration:

> Each student read the journal of another student, wrote questions, or offered new perspectives in the space below the writing of the journal's owner and passed the journal to still another student, who repeated the same process. The passing process continued until five students had the opportunity to respond to the journal. In this way students received exposure to five different novels being read by other students, and each journal owner received five new perspectives on the novel he/she was reading and writing about. The last person in the journal-passing chain also selected a single insight . . . for sharing with the large group. . . . I also read each journal, offering my own questions and encouragement and clarifying points of confusion. (p. 112)

These eighth-grade researchers wrote paragraph-length book blurbs or reviews on the books they read (some submitted theirs to the NCTE journal Voices in the Middle for publication consideration). They then conducted library research on topics presented in their books, such as cerebral palsy, restorative justice, obsessive-compulsive disorder, and peer pressure. The next phase of the project involved students reading a variety of real-world persuasive texts, such as a Nike T-shirt advocating volunteerism, a letter to the editor, brochures from other schools, a public service ad, and movie reviews. Students were required to analyze the writing and identify the thesis and intended audience, as well as judge the effectiveness of visual and rhetorical elements. Finally, students submitted their own persuasive pieces, using a variety of formats, aimed at a number of different, real audiences. Students benefited from the reading, writing, thinking, and constructive social action involved in this research project.

Teenagers as Reader Response Researchers

An effective way to combine reading and writing, as well as develop higher-level thinking skills, is to have students analyze their classmates' responses to a text and write a report synthesizing the data and reporting their findings. I model this strategy by passing out index cards to my students and asking them to write a free response to a poem I read. I collect the cards, and the next day read an analysis I've written of the data they gave me. I might say:

> I found that your responses fell into two main categories, which I labeled text-based responses and reader-based responses. Text-based responses included the following: seven people talked about the way the poem sounded, mentioning things such as rhyme, rhythm, and repetition; eight used evaluative terminology in their responses; 17 people referred to the narrator as a boy, while two pictured a girl. Tori and Malik both used the word theme, though each had a slightly different way of stating that theme. Rodney wondered about the title's meaning in relation to the poem. The reader-based responses were also interesting: four people were stimulated to write about their own childhood memories, and one wrote an entire narration of the time her gerbil got lost in her house, never even mentioning the poem she had just heard.

After I read my report of primary research and we discuss how I organized and thought about and interpreted the data, someone invariably asks, "What were you looking for?" The old "What do you want? What's the correct answer?" questions surface. I assure them that I'm interested in whatever happens when a reader comes together with a text. From then on, we begin every class with a student reading a short text she's selected. She can request a free response, or she can ask specific questions of her respondents. She then becomes responsible for writing a paper analyzing the data she collects, drawing tentative conclusions about texts or readers, and discussing the significance of her findings. In short, she must conduct herself as a researcher. I'm always amazed at the range of topics students write about, and the depth of their theorizing based on the data they obtain from classmates.

Model and use this strategy in your content area classes with any number of types of text. For example, social studies teachers could ask students to bring in newspaper and magazine articles on political situations or other current events; science teachers can help students find texts dealing with ethical dimensions of scientific breakthroughs. This "Student Turns Reader Response Researcher" project has multiple benefits. First, it enables the class to function as a community. The rest of the class knows that the reader for the day is depending on them for thoughtful responses so that he'll be able to write a good paper. That gives them a meaningful reason for writing, and they usually do their best. Equally important is the fact that the daily writing activity is enjoyable. Students are eager to listen to the texts their classmates have selected, and often want to pursue a discussion of interpretations after writing their responses. Finally, the research focus and multiple avenues of exploration get the students to go far beyond the traditional questions they associate with texts: "What is the main idea? What do the symbols mean? What is the theme of the work?" Instead, students formulate the questions they want answers to, and go about gathering and analyzing data that either produces knowledge related to their questions or raises further important questions about readers and texts. They share what they create and learn from each other's contributions to the community research.

Creative Writing for Deep Understanding

Writing can help students explore concepts in your content area classes in new and playful ways. We know, though our students might not, that many mathematicians, scientists, journalists, artists, politicians, musicians, architects, economists, environmental engineers, and historians learn and think new thoughts as they scribble, write notes to themselves or to colleagues, draft versions of new ideas they're trying to pin down, or apply new ideas to old contexts. Mathematician and teacher Peggy House considers the most significant outcome of using writing activities to be her students' recognition "that mathematics has a playful dimension, a recreational fascination as well as a serious purpose, creativity as well as precision" (1996, p. 94). She recalls her own use of imagination when, in eighth grade, she received the assignment to write an autobiography of a nickel, and she "played with ideas of multiples and factors, decimals and fractions, shape, and size, and more" (p. 89). Following are two of her students' responses to her request to think about what number they would choose to be:

> My reason for wanting to be Zero is that nothing would be expected of me.
>
> If I was Zero, transportation would never be a problem because I could just roll to my destination. Also . . . I could easily visit my best friend, one, and we could make a perfect ten.
>
> Another advantage of being Zero is that, no matter how many other zeros are around, the crowd never increases. Also, no matter how big a number is, all I have to do to bring it down to my size is to multiply with it. . . . (Mike, p. 90)

> I would be π, because pi is one of the most distinguished numbers around. Not only that, but pi goes on forever. And I would be of untold importance to geometry. . . .
>
> As the number pi, I would have many friends. I would be inseparable from the circles, and, since I would contain many digits who appear in a most unpredictable fashion, I would never become stale or uninteresting. (Don, p. 90)

House's students also create mathematical newspapers with math-based puzzles, cartoons, features, advertisements, and editorials. They show their understanding of topics by constructing limericks and problem stories for peers to solve; they write parodies, sequels, and spin-offs of other literary works with such titles as *The Wizard of Odds*, *Equilaterella*, *Alice in Cartesian Land*, and *Star Tech: The Next Iteration*. Here are two verses of a long song her students composed:

My Favorite Things

Arc sines and cosines, a heavenly vision;
Cubic equations, synthetic division;
Functions with zeroes that make my heart sing:
These are a few of my favorite things. . . .

Inverse relations, continuous functions;
Logical thinking, the rules of disjunctions;
Infinite series with limit and bound:
These are the things that will make my heart pound.
(pp. 93–94)

From "Try a Little of the Right Stuff," by Peggy House. Reprinted with permission from *Communication in Mathematics, K–12 and Beyond: 1996 Yearbook*, copyright © 1996 by the National Council of Teachers of Mathematics. All rights reserved.

You can see that they used specialized vocabulary and complex concepts that show a comfort and familiarity with their subject. These students are not merely having fun; they're learning.

Seventh-grade teacher Leslie Franks, inspired by Leggo and Sakai's (1997) query, "What would happen if science and writing were presented as interrelated ways of knowing the world?" (p. 20), asked her students to write about weather using a variety of genres. For three weeks they recorded information and observations, and responded daily to one of five prompts. Franks added an art component, having students draw pictures of cloud formations and of summer and winter solstice. After writing solstice poems, about 80 percent of the students could explain the reason for the seasons, far more than could do so after being taught the concept in both geography and science classes. Even more were able to articulate a quality definition for winter and summer solstice. Students told their teacher in written reflections that keeping a science journal and painting and drawing "helped them learn more and more about themselves as learners, both in science and in writing" (Franks, 2001, p. 324).

Document-Based Questions and Essays

A prevalent type of writing required in social studies classrooms and on some standardized tests uses *document-based* or *data-based questions* (DBQs). As the name suggests, the questions call for students to comprehend, interpret, and analyze documents or other data the teacher or test provides. Then, the students synthesize information from two or more sources related to a theme, issue, or problem in order to craft an essay noting patterns or contrasting information found in the various data. This type of reading and writing calls for higher-level thinking skills, going beyond literal comprehension. DBQs have been used on advanced placement exams for many years, and provide an authentic form of assessment because, as high school social studies supervisor Alice Grant points out, "They measure not only what students have learned, . . . but also the intellectual habits they've developed in the process and whether they can apply those skills to completely new information they haven't seen before" (Strachan, 2000, p. 24). When answering DBQs, students perform tasks similar to what historians and social scientists actually do with data sources: generalize and think critically, forming conclusions, hypotheses, and opinions.

What kind of data are used for these DBQs? All genres can be represented. Teachers have brought together poetry, excerpts from political documents in archives, quotations from philosophers, eyewitness accounts, letters, memoirs, political cartoons, maps, charts, tables, paintings, diary entries, and official memos. For younger, inexperienced, or struggling readers or writers, you can start teaching and modeling the synthesis that DBQs require using just two sources. Some high school teachers challenge advanced students with as many as eight pieces of data to work with.

I've been encouraging you to keep folders with materials you gather related to various curricular topics. Now, you can consider those folders or files as data banks for DBQs. For example, one of the principal themes running through my high school social studies course is that of freedom. I'm also responsible for teaching students about world religions. Recently, I came across an article called "Religious Freedom in the World: A Global Comparative Survey Sponsored by Freedom House" (*American Educator*, 2001). Within the text of the article, there are several charts listing countries and the percentages of their populations belonging to various religions. There is also a chart called "Religious Freedom by Area" that is color-coded to rate the degree of religious freedom particular countries possess. There are color photographs of Holy Kaaba pilgrims in Mecca, Saudi Arabia; schoolgirls praying at the funeral of a classmate in Java, Indonesia; a Cuban woman kneeling before a shrine; Caodai sect worshippers praying in Vietnam; a pentecostal service in Tanzania; Pope John Paul II visiting Poland; and more. I've got a great start for my data bank. I might look for a letter from a religious leader from one of the countries labeled as "not free," such as China, Iran, or Pakistan. I could find an essay or statement made by a person who had escaped from a country where the practice of religion was not tolerated, and maybe a position statement of an international interreligious organization that promotes freedom of religious expression. I might be able to add oral reports from students who have emigrated from other countries.

By examining and reflecting on these various documents related to the topic of worldwide religious freedom and repression, students gain so much more than they would simply by reading about and learning what religions are practiced in countries around the world. They have the opportunity to take positions on issues, support their conclusions, draw analogies, and see issues from multiple perspectives; they may very well desire to research the topic of religious persecution further.

How can you teach this kind of thinking and writing within the context of your curriculum? Have your students watch, allowing for comments and questions, as you model the process using an overhead projector or computer and LCD projector. A history lesson might begin like this:

> Teacher: We've been studying events leading up to the American Revolution. Let's look at several pieces of data I found in the book *Countdown to Independence: A Revolution of Ideas in England and Her American Colonies: 1760–1776* (Bober, 2001). I'll show them one by one on the overhead:
>
> 1. Here's a quote from the pamphlet "Letters from a Farmer in Pennsylvania, to the Inhabitants of the British Colonies," by John Dickinson, which was influential in arousing opposition to the Townshend Acts, which, you'll recall, allowed arbitrary taxation of the colonists by Parliament:
>
>> *Let these truths be indelibly impressed on our minds—that we cannot be happy without being free—that we cannot be free without being secure in our property—that we cannot be secure in our property if without our consent others may as by right take it away.* (p. 123)
>
> 2. Now here's a picture of the cover of an English publication by the great writer Samuel Johnson. The title is *Taxation No Tyranny; An Answer to the Resolutions and Address of the American Congress.* The caption underneath gives a quote from it, where Johnson wonders how it is "that we hear the loudest yelps for liberty among the drivers of slaves?" (p. 265).
>
> 3. Here's a photograph of an American teapot with a political slogan inside a decorative border: No Stamp Act.
>
> 4. Here we have a map of the 13 colonies.
>
> 5. Now this is a political cartoon created by Benjamin Franklin. It shows a rattlesnake, in pieces, all labeled with the initials of individual colonies. Underneath the picture are the words, "JOIN, or DIE" (p. 36).

The teacher allows a discussion about these data, and clarifies or expands information based on the students' responses and questions. Then, she introduces a question leading to a DBQ essay:

> The last sentences in this great book were written by John Adams to his wife Abigail. The 'accomplishment of [the Revolution] . . . was perhaps a singular example in the history of mankind. . . . Thirteen clocks were made to strike as one' (p. 321). Now, use the data supplied from the book and your knowledge of the decades leading to the American Revolution to write an essay about how the war came about, leading to Adams' reflection.

The teacher facilitates student discussion of how they might organize their ideas, connect the pieces of data, and use the data to support their points. He or a student can outline and draft the essay as the rest watch and take notes. Students can flesh out the essay for homework or follow the modeled process to write a different DBQ essay.

Data-based writing is not limited to the social studies. Think of the various sources I mentioned about teaching the subject of robotics. Articles, books, pictures, cartoons, first-hand accounts by inventors, critiques by fellow scientists, statements by patients who have artificial hearts or other robotic devices implanted, and poems can be sources the students can use to analyze and synthesize information. English teachers can use a combination of works by certain authors, works about those authors, or interpretive studies of the authors' works. Figure 7.12 lists some resources that can help teachers find documents and other data that make curricular

BookTalk 7.6

Want to take students on a literary field trip through American history? One way to do that is by using documents that shaped thinking and led to action. Using *Words That Built a Nation: A Young Person's Collection of Historic American Documents* by Marilyn Miller (1999), your students can focus on the writing and the content of the Declaration of Sentiments presented at the Seneca Falls Convention, or excerpts from Harriet Beecher Stowe's *Uncle Tom's Cabin*, Woodrow Wilson's "Fourteen Points," Martin Luther King's "March on Washington Address," Richard Nixon's letter of resignation, John F. Kennedy's speech at the Berlin Wall, Rachel Carson's *Silent Spring*, Cesar Chavez's speech to striking grape workers, and more. Readers can savor quotes like "The Eagle has landed," "Remember the Ladies," and "December 7, 1941—a date which will live in infamy" in their contexts, and with background information about the authors and responses to the documents, as well as photographs to aid comprehension. Instead of just learning about *Brown v. Board of Education of Topeka*, students can read the Supreme Court's decision that Earl Warren authored. The words and the presentation of the documents in this book are powerful. History is not forgettable when your students experience it through this book.

FIGURE 7.12   *Resources for obtaining documents and data related to curriculum.*

Houghton Mifflin Education Place: www.eduplace.com.

Document Based Question (DBQ) Activities: http://jefferson.village.Virginia.edu/vcdh/fellows/dbg.html

Modern Humanities: www.modernhumanities.org/dbg8197.html

Minding Their DBQs: www.nysut.org

National Geographic Online: www.nationalgeographic.com

CNN News: www.cnn.com

Government Documents: www-sul.stanford.edu/depts/jonsson

Block, H. (2000). *Herblock's History: Political Cartoons from the Crash to the Millennium.* Washington, DC: Library of Congress.

Greenwood, J. T. (2000). *The Gilded Age: A History in Documents.* New York: Oxford University Press.

Holzer, H. (Ed.). (2000). *Abraham Lincoln the Writer: A Treasury of His Greatest Speeches and Letters.* Honesdale, PA: Boyds Mills Press.

Lepore, J. (Ed.). (2000). Encounters in the New World: A History in Documents. New York: Oxford University Press.

Mankoff, R. (Ed.). (2000). *The New Yorker Book of Political Cartoons.* Princeton, NJ: Bloomsburg Press.

Seedman, R. F. (2001). *The Civil War: A History in Documents.* New York: Oxford University Press.

Smith, B. G. (2000). *Imperialism: A History in Documents.* New York: Oxford University Press.

Smith, K. M. (Ed.) & Gross, J. L. (1999). *The Lines Are Drawn: Political Cartoons of the Civil War.* Athens, GA: Hill Street Press.

---

inquiry exciting and fruitful, and can be used as data for the students' writing.

Writers often really do the type of thinking and constructing that DBQs require of students; knowing this may help your students understand the purpose of the exercises you ask them to do to practice the method. In his acceptance speech when he was awarded the Laura Ingalls Wilder Medal by the American Library Association in 2001, Milton Meltzer discussed his research and writing method. For his first book, he decided to write about something he knew little about, but wanted to know a lot about, which was African-American history. He had grown up in Worcester, Massachusetts, which had been a station on the Underground Railroad. He had read the antislavery poets in school, including Walt Whitman, who used the first person to narrate the perspective of a slave; James Russell Lowell, whose "lines hurt, for he indicted whites of his time who failed to protest slavery" (Meltzer, 2001, p. 426); and John Greenleaf Whittier, whose poems and life story proved to Meltzer that words had consequences. Meltzer began his research for his book on black history in the 1950s, discovering that the subject was almost entirely omitted from school books, and that university scholars' published work "served to harden racism and entrench inequality" (p. 427).

Meltzer decided to combine narrative text with paintings, drawings, photographs, and facsimiles of documents, posters, and cartoons, a structure he has used ever since. So, you could use Meltzer's books themselves as sources of multiple pieces of data that students can interpret and synthesize. Figure 7.13 lists some of his works, which have to do with social change: "How it comes about, the forces that advance it, and the forces that resist it, the moral issues that beset men and women seeking to realize their humanity" (p. 427). Students can study his style and the structure of his books, and use them as models when they put together a story based on data they discover through research.

As with other literacy strategies, you can't just give the students the DBQs and the data and expect them to be able to write an essay. You must *teach* them how to analyze, interpret, compare and contrast, apply background knowledge, and synthesize. Scaffold instruction so that they aren't overwhelmed with the task. The think-aloud procedure discussed in Chapter 4 allows you to model your own thinking as you read documents and write about them. Start simply—every day in city newspapers there are political cartoons. Paper your walls with them as the year goes on, and spend just a moment letting the students hear your thoughts as you interpret a cartoon in light of current events, or inviting students to do the same for their classmates. Then, comment on a newspaper article and an editorial on the same topic, working your way up to using multiple data sources addressing an issue from different or opposing viewpoints. Write an essay on chart paper and share your thoughts as

FIGURE 7.13   *A sampling of Milton Meltzer's books containing multiple forms of data.*

Meltzer, M. (1976). *Never to Forget: The Jews of the Holocaust.* New York: HarperCollins.

Meltzer, M. (1980). *The Chinese Americans.* New York: Crowell.

Meltzer, M. (1982). *The Hispanic Americans.* New York: Crowell.

Meltzer, M. (1984). *The Black Americans.* New York: Crowell.

Meltzer, M. (1987). *Mary McLeod Bethune: Voice of Black Hope.* New York: Viking.

Meltzer, M. (1988). *Rescue: The Story of How Gentiles Saved Jews in the Holocaust.* New York: Harper & Row.

Meltzer, M. (1989). *Voices from the Civil War: A Documentary History of the Great American Conflict.* New York: Crowell.

Meltzer, M. (1990). *The Bill of Rights: How We Got It and What It Means.* New York: Crowell.

Meltzer, M. (1990). *Crime in America.* New York: Morrow.

Meltzer, M. (1991). *Brother, Can You Spare a Dime?: The Great Depression, 1929–33.* New York: Facts on File.

Meltzer, M. (1992). *The Amazing Potato: A Story in Which the Incas, Conquistadors, Marie Antoinette, Thomas Jefferson, Wars, Famine,* Immigrants, and French Fries All Play a Part. New York: HarperCollins.

Meltzer, M. (Ed.). (1993). *Lincoln, in His Own Words.* New York: Harcourt Brace.

Meltzer, M. (1994). *Cheap Raw Material.* New York: Viking.

Meltzer, M. (1994). *Theodore Roosevelt and His America.* New York: Franklin Watts.

Meltzer, M. (1996). *Tom Paine: Voice of Revolution.* New York: Franklin Watts.

Meltzer, M. (1997). *Langston Hughes: An Illustrated Edition.* Brookfield, CT: Millbrook Press.

Meltzer, M. (1998). *Witches and Witch Hunts.* New York: Blue Sky Press.

Meltzer, M. (1999). *Carl Sandburg: A Biography.* Brookfield, CT: Twenty-first Century Books.

Meltzer, M. (2000). *Driven from the Land: The Story of the Dust Bowl.* New York: Benchmark Books.

Meltzer, M. (2000). *They Came in Chains: The Story of the Slave Ships.* New York: Benchmark Books.

Meltzer, M. (2001). *There Comes a Time: The Struggle for Civil Rights.* New York: Random House.

Meltzer, M., & Anderson, B. (2002). *Ten Kings: And the Worlds They Ruled.* New York: Orchard Books.

you draw from your available sources; weigh the reliability, validity, and importance of the evidence; analyze conflicting perspectives, cross out lines you decide to change; create a thesis statement, introduction, and conclusion; use supporting evidence in middle paragraphs, and so on.

You can also guide students and give them a process to follow as they tackle a DBQ. For example, you can instruct them to:

- Read the question carefully to determine the required task, underlining key words, names, places, and issues.

- Write down what they already know about the topic and period.

- Identify each document's type, author, time written, point of view.

- Group documents according to relationships (e.g., data that support a position, data that do not).

- Outline their essay.

- Construct an introduction, a thesis statement, body paragraphs, and a concluding paragraph explaining evidence from the data.

Students who have delved into curricular topics, argued and critiqued positions, found primary sources, formed hypotheses, and expressed opinions in your classroom throughout the year should not find these data-based essays foreign or threatening. For those you see struggling, examine their work-in-progress and talk to them to find out where the difficulty lies. Then, decide whether to try easier DBQs (perhaps with fewer data sources or a simpler task), to reteach parts of the process, or to model the procedure again. Encourage students to deal with this as a powerful way to think and write, and help them as they practice the craft. And, of course, have many books in your classroom library that include multiple perspectives and varied data. Chapters 8 and 9 provide many titles of books that contain interviews and visual texts that have potential as stimuli for data-based writing.

BookTalk 7.7

Your students might be surprised at how many scientists are capable of beautiful and accessible prose. *Galileo's Commandment: An Anthology of Great Science Writing*, edited by Edmund Blair Bolles (1997), is full of examples from astronomy, physics, biology, geology, chemistry, and other disciplines. Teens who read Isaac Asimov's science fiction might enjoy his "Death in the Laboratory" in this volume. Galileo Galilei offers his "First Look through a Microscope" in 1610, and Marie Curie writes of "Obtaining Radium" in 1923. Scientists respond to, interpret, and argue with others' work, as in Stephen Jay Gould's "The Misuse of Darwin," Noam Chomsky's "The Case Against B. F. Skinner," and Bertrand Russell's "What Einstein Did." Fans of literature will be intrigued by Edward Harrison's "The Golden Walls of Edgar Allen Poe." There's something for everyone in this collection.

WRITING FOR CRITICAL THINKING AND SOCIAL ACTION

In the last chapter, you were encouraged to learn and construct ways to help your students use higher-level thinking skills in a variety of ways. Writing is one excellent way to promote such thinking. As your students write their thoughts about what is going on around them, current events, controversial issues in your discipline, and literature, they clarify their thinking and discover new ideas and potential solutions. Of course, reading is often an integral part of this process too. For example, I cut out several articles from one Sunday's *Syracuse Herald-American* newspaper that content area teachers might fruitfully use as stimuli for writing and thinking, including: "Global Warming: Can We Change Our Wasteful Ways?" (Clubb, 2001), "Teen Dramas Played Out in Shades of Black and White" (Smokes, 2001), "Should We Leave Okinawa?" (Webb, 2001), and "Left-behind Mines Pose Risk for Animals" (Mydans, 2001). The topics cross disciplinary lines, their relevance and interest level are high, and there is plenty of room for growth and new thinking as students refine their initial responses to the texts after exploring other sources and differing opinions of scholarly experts and caring citizens. The following examples show teachers using writing for the purposes of fostering critical thinking and promoting positive action for social change within the classroom and beyond.

Randy Bomer (2000) attempts to plant the seeds of social action as he teaches his students to use writing to think critically. You might be wondering, how does someone *teach* others this skill? Bomer starts with himself, reflecting:

> I don't know how to assist students in learning to write in a particular way, or how to lead discussions about strategies and lenses, unless I am doing some of the same sort of writing myself.... I have to use my own living, thinking and writing as exemplars. A teacher's own writing not only lends credibility to the teaching: it also provides me with material for minilessons and conferences. (p. 114)

Bomer demonstrates his writing process to his students, then provides structured assistance, often through writing conferences, to students as they apply a critical lens to their writing. He encourages students to question authority, to look at situations through the lens of fairness or identity, to try on the perspectives of others through their writing, and to examine the implicit critique beneath feelings of anger and indignation. Bomer concludes, "It is time for us as teachers to invite students to wake up to their world in their writing and to think" (p. 120).

Similarly, high school teacher Linda M. Christenson (2000) consciously tries to teach writing and reading in a predominantly African American, working-class neighborhood, as "a sustained argument against inequality and injustice" (p. 54). Her senior-level Contemporary Literature and Society course carries both history and English credit, and is centered on the question: "Is language political?" Her students write poetry and critical essays in response to texts about culture and language written from diverse perspectives; they explore their linguistic heritage, and they "write the world." Christenson explains what this means in terms of the teacher's role:

> Creating a critical-literacy classroom still means teaching students to read and write. But instead of only asking students to write essays that demonstrate a close reading of a novel or engaging in a literary evaluation of the text, critical literacy creates spaces for students to tackle larger social issues that have urgent meaning in their lives.... When students are "steeped" in evidence from one of the units, they begin to write. I want them to turn their anger, their hurt, their rage into words that might affect other people. We talk about [potential] audiences and outlets—from parents, to teens, to corporations. (pp. 62–63)

Christenson helps her students write a test using the format of the SATs but the content, culture, and vocabulary of their school. They travel to nearby colleges, where they give their test to preservice teachers and discuss the results and implications. "My students have a real audience whose future teaching practice will hopefully be enlightened by their work. They see that what they learn in school can make a difference in the world, and so can they" (p. 64).

Griselle M. Diaz-Gemmati (2000) uses writing to confront racism inside and outside of her classroom; her article can help you glimpse her teaching methods. After a literature circle argument stemming from the students' reading of Harper Lee's *To Kill a Mockingbird* (1995), the teacher asked the class to help her construct a word cluster on the board, using not the dictionaries and thesauruses they usually employed for the strategy, but rather their honest opinions and beliefs. She wrote the word *stereotype*, and the following ensued:

> The class sat strangely still for a few moments. The members of Nancy's and Shelley's literature group silently stared at the word. Other hands around them shot up.
>
> "A belief about something."
>
> "A notion."
>
> "A judgment."
>
> The chalk in my hand tap-danced as I hurriedly wrote their responses on the blackboard.
>
> "Is a stereotype good or bad?" I prompted.
>
> "Bad!" was their chorused reply.
>
> "Why?" I attempted to look at each of them in turn as I spoke.
>
> "Because," Nancy spoke for the first time that morning, "it's like saying all blondes are dumb." Shelley's head flew up and her icy blue stare bore into Nancy's face. (p. 83)

Diaz-Gemmati asked her students to cluster the word *prejudice* in their literature circles. Issues on the prejudice of age, religion, gender, race, and roles came out in subsequent class reports. The students had written their way to new knowledge and insights, and continued the journey in their personal journals. The teacher added related topics such as affirmative action and civil rights; together the class researched and examined the *Brown v. Board of Education* case, as well as issues of integration and segregation in their school and neighborhood. The students brought up the teacher's minority status as a Puerto Rican teacher, causing her to feel "yanked out of my neutral zone. I now was categorized, labeled, seen differently. I was no longer just the teacher" (p. 93). But she used this to help her teach. "These kids no longer tiptoe around issues of race" (p. 94).

These descriptions were intended to help you visualize some of the many ways teachers model, instruct, and create or seize opportunities for writing to think critically about content and issues. Now, I'd like you to take this opportunity to think through writing. How might you apply these lessons to your own teaching in your content area? What kinds of writing to think could you teach your students to do so that, in Christenson's words, "They see that what they learn in school can make a difference in the world, and so can they" (p. 64)?

> **Getting Ready to Teach 7.7** *(see page 236)*

ADAPTATIONS FOR STUDENTS WITH WRITING DISABILITIES

The writing process will be extremely difficult for some of the students you teach, and accommodations or different forms of instruction will be necessary for them to be successful at completing the writing tasks you require. Students with identified writing disabilities may have IEPs calling for resources such as the use of a scribe or a note taker. These students dictate what they want to say and another person does the handwriting for them. Other students might benefit from being able to use a laptop or word processor at their desks, or might need to speak their reflections into a tape recorder. Talk with your students to determine what difficulties they're having, and seek assistive technology and human resources to support them.

As you instruct students in writing the particular kinds of reports or genres required for your subject, struggling writers might need more examples, more direct instruction and modeling, more opportunities to revise drafts, or more time to complete the writing tasks. Work with the students and other professionals in your school to enhance their writing experiences and growth.

At times, you might give alternative assignments to certain students who have a writing disability. They can give an oral presentation, for example, applying and synthesizing information that the other students are writing about. Instead of taking a paper-and-pencil test, they might demonstrate their learning better on an oral exam.

Some students may come to you already feeling defeated in the area of writing due to repeated failures throughout their years of schooling. If they lack confidence, they may not like to write and may resist or act as though they don't care. So, when you have students who do not complete writing assignments, discover the reason why and work to reverse some of the damage that earlier experiences caused.

HELPING ENGLISH LANGUAGE LEARNERS WRITE IN CONTENT AREAS

Consider this explanation given by a nonnative English speaker about his writing process:

> While choosing Chinese words is second nature to me, extracting the proper English word is much more difficult. In casual communication, my inner thoughts are like free river flowing down directly from my mind to the paper. I can write whatever appears in my mind. When I wrote compositions, I come into trouble. There are many good sources I could get from the Chinese culture while I write in Chinese; such as literary quotations, famous old stories, and ancient word of wisdom. These rich sources definitely influence my paper quality in Chinese. Unfortunately examples like this are very hard to translate into English. Sometimes I try to make a joke, but it loses its impact in translation. (Connor, 1997, p. 198)

As a content area teacher who uses writing as an integral part of the learning process, you must become aware of how you can help English language learners with their writing. Although you are expected to be neither a writing nor an ELL expert, you can encourage ELL students and help them realize that "their writing in English is not bad just because it exhibits some rhetorical features of their first language" (Connor, 1997, p. 208). If you understand that there are differences in the written products of native English speakers and ELL students, and have a great respect for the language they come to you with, even as you help them acquire the language of their new school community, you'll look on these differences not as "errors" that imply deficiencies, but simply as differences. Connor concludes:

> Teachers need to be aware of cultural differences in their students' writing and understand their students' composing and revising behaviors. In addition, they need to be sensitive to differing interactional patterns across cultures and adjust collaborative writing groups and other classroom activities accordingly. (p. 208)

So, learn all you can about the cultures and backgrounds of the students in your classroom. Celebrate all the knowledge about language and writing they bring with them, even though it may be different from what you're used to and from your expectations for native English speakers. Quinn (2001) encourages teachers:

> Finding information on immigrant cultures is as easy as asking pertinent questions and observing children's actions in the school. Talking with students and bringing the literature of all cultures into a classroom will provide the wisdom and food for thought that a teacher needs to teach immigrant children. Creating an environment in which all students are welcome moves marginalized students within the lines of a classroom community and gives them the courage and time to experiment with American ways of life. (p. 49)

How does this advice translate into practice? Educational journals are full of teachers' stories of their own learning in terms of how to teach literacy to students from different cultures. For example, Shafer (2001) shares his own and his students' growth during the two years he taught in a rural, Spanish-speaking community of migrant families outside Miami. He recognized two goals common to teachers working with nonnative speakers of English:

> There is an urgent need to move judiciously, to teach English with a clear understanding of the fealty these students have for their parents and the heritage they personify. At the same time, there is the concomitant desire to introduce them to an English-speaking world that will offer them increased opportunities both economically and socially. (p. 37)

Shafer crafted his writing instruction and assignments around a series of problems that related to his students. He taught them the importance of using Standard American English, for example, as they wrote formal letters to potential employers. "Instead of mechanically adhering to rules from a book simply as a way to complete an exercise, they were applying them to a literacy experience that made sense. Suddenly correctness was seen in an authentic context" (p. 41). Grammar became part of a problem-solving strategy. Shafer showed his respect for the sophisticated use of *code-switching* (the alternating use of two languages for a purpose) when his students were using other genres such as letter writing.

Content area teachers can help ELLs by using reading as preparation for writing and writing as preparation for reading. If students read about a topic from multiple resources representing a range of difficulty levels both before and during writing, they build a sufficient repertoire of vocabulary and concepts (Farnan, Flood, & Lapp, 1994; Krashen, 1981). Students also can organize their thoughts about content topics through writing before reading assigned texts. These strategies may also be appropriate for other students in your classes, including those struggling with literacy for any number of reasons. You can find many resources in books and articles and online that give practical suggestions and share activities that have worked for middle and secondary content area teachers. For example, in *New Ways in Teaching English at the Secondary Level* (Short, 1999), dozens of innovative classroom techniques for ELL and mainstream groups are described, many involving writing in various disciplines. Within that volume, teacher Beti Leone recommends the use of daily math journals, where students answer the questions: "What did I learn about math today?" and "How can I use what I learned outside of math class (e.g., at home, on the job, in recreation, in other classes)?" (p. 187). Other chapters share how teachers can scaffold students' writing about famous artwork, create graphic organizers that include questions about science and social studies topics, create poster adaptations of short stories, and many other strategies for ELL and their non-ELL classmates to write to learn and to improve their writing.

In an aptly named article, "What's a (White) Teacher to Do about Black English?" (2001), Jonsberg shares how she both shows and teaches respect for her bilingual students who speak Black English, or Ebonics. She refuses to accept adjectives such as "corrupt," "broken," or "defective" to describe dialects. She helps her students, Black English speakers included, learn not to talk about "bad English" and "good English," but instead to recognize the rule structures of different dialects and "different forms of a living and continually changing English" (p. 52). She recognizes the obligation of teachers to help students be facile and fluent in Standard American English, to open up the "Language of Wider Communication" (Smitherman, 1997), but is convinced that we and our students can together "find some ways to play with language that will bring all these ideas to the surface without pedantry and prescription, without alienation from either (or any) kind of speaking" (p. 53). A noble goal for all of us.

Hollie (2001), while expressing a philosophy similar to Jonsberg's, laments:

Still, many African American students will walk into classrooms and be discreetly taught in most cases, and explicitly told in others, that the language of their forefathers, their families, and their communities is bad language, street language, the speech of the ignorant and/or uneducated. (p. 54)

Hollie shares instructional strategies that can "facilitate the acquisition of Standard American English in its oral and written forms without devaluing the home language and culture of the students" (p. 54). The author's research-based recommendations include designing instruction around the strengths and learning styles of ELLs and infusing their history and culture into the curriculum. You can apply these principles in ways that make sense in your specific curricular area as you help all your students write well in your discipline. Figure 7.14 provides a summary of recommendations for helping ELLs write in the content areas.

CONCLUSION

There are many ways you can use writing to your students' benefit, inspiring them to grapple with the challenges of your discipline, while reinforcing knowledge and thinking skills. In addition, the sharing of your writing and your enthusiasm, commitment, and encouragement can promote a lifelong love of learning. Sanacore (1998) urges teachers and administrators to foster the writing habit among students by building a positive professional attitude toward writing in school, creating a learning environment that nurtures writing growth, providing extended blocks of time for writing across the curriculum, guiding writers in a variety of experiences (including expository, narrative, poetic, and descriptive), helping writers to go public, supporting a visiting authors program, and inviting parents to be partners in promoting

FIGURE 7.14 *Recommendations for helping ELLs write in the content areas.*

- Show respect for all languages in your classroom.
- Learn about the cultures and backgrounds of your students.
- Bring the literature of different cultures into your classroom.
- Create writing assignments that are meaningful to your students, including ones that ask them to use Standard American English for authentic purposes.
- Use reading as a preparation for writing and writing as a preparation for reading.
- Assign daily or regular journal writing.
- Design instruction around the strengths and learning styles of your students.

the lifetime writing habit. I think he gives very sound advice.

Stephen King concludes his book *On Writing* (2000) not so much with advice as with encouragement, which I'd like to pass along to you and your students now:

> Some of this book—perhaps too much—has been about how I learned to do it. Much of it has been about how you can do it better. The rest of it— and perhaps the best of it—is a permission slip: you can, you should, and if you're brave enough to start, *you will*. Writing is magic, as much the water of life as any other creative art. The water is free. So drink.
>
> Drink and be filled up. (p. 270)

I'd like to end this chapter with two of my favorite sentences from E. B. White. They close *Charlotte's Web* (1952) and deliver one of the best compliments I've ever heard: "It is not often that someone comes along who is a true friend and a good writer. Charlotte was both" (p. 184). May the same be said of you and your students.

CHAPTER SEVEN

Getting Ready to Teach

7.1 Choose a book, article, movie, or other text your students might read or see in your content area class. Design a pre-reading writing assignment to activate their background knowledge, their thinking, and their emotions in a way that prepares them to engage actively with the material. This is a type of anticipation guide, which you are already familiar with, but the focus this time is on having your students *think* through writing.

7.2 Start a book review file of your own. Some educational journals, such as *English Journal, Journal of Adolescent and Adult Literacy*, and *Voices from the Middle*, have regular review columns that you can clip and save. Newspapers and magazines contain reviews, as do bookstores and websites. Some reviews are as well written as the literature itself, so you'll also learn writing strategies for the genre. Enjoy! And, of course, you can write some of your own to include, adding your voice to those of published reviewers. Invite your students to contribute reviews, also. Post them around the room or put them up on a school website.

7.3 Create a RAFT assignment based on a relevant text in your content area. Give students suggestions and guidance for writing. Be sure to take on the role of a student as you try out your own assignment. The following examples might spark some ideas:

1. Take on the role of Thomas Jefferson at the First Continental Congress. Argue your position of wanting to break away from England with your fellow delegates.

2. Write a memo from the point of view of your principal regarding proper behavior in the school hallways and stairways. Do not at this point try to give any other position. Be as convincing and rational as possible.

3. Write a letter to your Board of Education, which is considering changing the name of your school from Mulberry Street School to Elizabeth Blackwell Middle School. Let your voice, whether pro or con, be heard in the debate.

7.4 Choose a text appropriate for middle or secondary students in your subject area. Create a writing assignment based on one or more of the types of academic writing and instructional strategies described in the section "Ways of Using Writing in Content Area Classes" (e.g., imitation, freewriting, quick writes, summaries, etc.). Write clear directions for your students, and reflect on how it might benefit them, what you expect to get from them, and what you might discover from their writing.

7.5 It's time for you to try your hand at writing a letter. Choose from the following options or create one that serves a need or interest of yours:

1. Select a topic currently being debated in the news, and write a letter to the editor of your local paper expressing your opinion. Be sure to send it; don't view it just as an academic exercise. Save it in a "Letters to the Editor" file to share with your own students.

2. Write a letter to a person actually working in the field you are preparing to teach. It might be a local scientist, artist, historian, actor, accountant, or politician; or write to a scholar at a university or research center regarding a study or article you read, giving your opinions or asking any questions the text elicited. Again, send it. You may get a response that you can share with your students.

3. Write a letter using a primary source letter from a noted person in the field you teach as a model for style or formality, or write a letter responding to the position expressed in that letter.

7.6 Design an assignment for students that provides opportunities for them to use letter writing to express their opinions about issues relevant to your course or to seek information from people in your field. Be sure to supply names and addresses for them or sources where they can access these themselves. The Internet is a good source of addresses.

7.7 Design a plan for incorporating writing assignments into your teaching of a particular curricular topic. Think of specific ways you might use a variety of expressive and expository genres to help your students explore information; reflect on their own opinions, biases, and uncertainties; and share their knowledge and ideas. The following types of writing can get you started, but don't limit yourself to these: journal entries, poems, reports, observation logs, folktales, autobiographical writing, short fiction, memoir, essays (using the patterns of organization explained in Chapter 6), how-to manuals, letters, and advertisements.

Speaking and Listening: Vital Components of Literacy

As you know from your own experience and from Chapter 5, language is alive and dynamic, and thus the meanings, or at least the nuances and connotations, of words change over time. The glossary entry for *literacy* in the *Standards for the English Language Arts* (NCTE & IRA, 1996) reflects this:

The standards outlined in this document reflect a contemporary view of literacy that is both broader and more demanding than traditional definitions. Until quite recently, literacy was generally defined, in a very limited way, as the ability to read or write one's own name. A much more ambitious definition of literacy today includes the capacity to accomplish a wide variety of reading, writing, speaking, and other language tasks associated with everyday life. (p. 73)

Although "consensual agreement on a single definition [of literacy] is quite implausible" (Soares, 1992, as cited in Harris & Hodges, 1995), educators recognize the importance of fluency in speaking and listening; in other words, *oral literacy,* or *oracy* (Harris & Hodges, 1995). Manuel (1998) claims, "To be able to understand, critique and learn from spoken information is as necessary as the ability to read and write with precision and clarity" (p. 265). She points out instances where students are, on a daily basis, required to use spoken language:

to negotiate with colleagues; interact with peers; nurture youngsters; empathize; decipher, decode and interpret complex audio-visual messages; speculate about the future and reminisce about the past; greet and converse with familiar people and strangers; and grapple with an array of challenges in their public and private worlds. (p. 266)

"How do we enable students to become more like the members of a jazz quartet, whose interplay good conversation sometimes seems to emulate? Conversation is akin to deliberation, a process that searches for possible answers and explores blind alleys as well as open freeways."

ELLIOT EISNER, 2002, P. 582

The NCTE/IRA *Standards for the English Language Arts* include attention to oral literacy and communication skills. Standard 4 states, "Students adjust their use of spoken, written and visual language (e.g., conventions, style, vocabulary) to communicate effectively with a variety of audiences and for different purposes" (p. 33). But no longer can we consider oral literacy to be the sole responsibility of English teachers, as so many educators have in the past. Integrating oral language activities with other disciplines' curricular material "ensures that students learn the material more thoroughly and practice speaking and listening skills in a focused but varied environment" (Maxwell & Meiser, 1997, p. 117). The National Council for Teachers of Mathematics' Standard 2 addresses "Mathematics as Communication," positing that students should "be able to reflect upon and clarify their thinking about mathematical ideas and relationships, express mathematical ideas orally and in writing, and ask clarifying and extending questions related to mathematics they have read or heard about" (p. 140). National and state standards for other disciplines make similar claims. Helping our students become skilled listeners and speakers is everyone's job. Welcome the challenge enthusiastically, because increased oral literacy can serve to help students reflect on, learn about, and grapple with issues related to all content areas.

Because in this book we're concerned with the construction of meaning in content area classes, the NCTE/IRA's larger, more complete definition of literacy works well; all of the components are meaning-making activities. Although the ideal would be to consider all of the aspects of literacy together because they are interrelated, in this chapter I focus on listening and talking, as I did with writing in Chapter 7. In the examples, however, you'll often see evidence of listening and talking working together with reading and writing as students' literacy and content knowledge grow.

PART ONE

Speaking

ACTIVATING PRIOR KNOWLEDGE   8.1

Think of a time when you talked something (e.g., a problem, an issue, a text, a new idea) through with one or more people. Did new knowledge or understanding result? How did that happen?

Now, recall a class you were a part of at some level (middle school, high school, or college) where you think good discussions occurred. How did that happen? What was the teacher's method? Her role? How was student behavior in that class? What were the discussions about? Was the whole class involved or were students in small groups? Did leaders emerge?

Most of us like to talk. We may not all like to talk in a large group, but we can think of circumstances where talk is enjoyable and fulfilling, and sometimes leads to new insights or plans. We can demonstrate this to students by mentioning the historic July 9, 1848, discussion at the Hunt House near Seneca Falls, New York, where Elizabeth Cady Stanton and four other women expressed dismay over the voteless, propertyless status of women and decided to hold a convention. The Women's Rights Movement was conceived. Ten days later that convention was held, 300 joined the conversation, and the Declaration of Sentiments was adopted. Talk led to action and change. Einstein and friends met regularly for years in a discussion group they called the Olympia Academy. They ate cheese, sausages, fruit, and tea, and they talked in order to learn, sometimes becoming so raucous that neighbors complained. The discussions had a large influence on Einstein's work (Severance, 2001, pp. 35–36).

The same is happening in some classrooms today. I recently visited a sixth-grade class that was holding fund-raising projects in order to send money to children in developing countries so that they would not have to work long hours in factories. The initiative came from the students themselves after they had read about the problem, talked about their thoughts and feelings, and conducted research looking for solutions. Social justice was not just presented as an ideal here; action followed the productive discussion.

It's well documented, and personal experience probably tells you anyway, that most teenagers love to talk—on the phone, on the Internet, in class. Talk has been used as a means of learning since at least the days of Socrates, who used his questioning techniques to elicit talk from his pupils, leading to new knowledge and understanding. Research confirms that discussions help children clarify their thinking and increase their understanding of what they read. Some contemporary students have been fortunate enough to have attended elementary schools, and maybe also middle schools, where talk is valued as a productive way of learning and meaning-making; it is sanctioned and even encouraged. Yet, Bean (1998) notes that, unfortunately, as students move into the upper grades, "academic purposes for reading outpace affective purposes at a time when adolescents respond affectively to their surroundings. Classrooms isolate students from each other at a time when they value conversation" (p. 158). In upper middle grades and in many high schools, talk is discouraged; it may be seen as too hard to control. Quiet and orderliness are valued. Student verbalization during teacher-led reading lessons is often limited to brief, literal-level, text-based responses (Carlsen, 1991; Gambrell, 1987) despite research that demonstrates an increase in inferential, higher-level comprehension when students discuss what they read (Gambrell, Pfeiffer, & Wilson, 1985; Kapinus, Gambrell, & Koskinen, 1991).

Bean (1998) heard from teenagers that there is a notable absence of classroom discussion in their schools, but there are plenty of worksheets to be completed silently and alone. He believes some teachers buy into what he calls a "myth of adolescence—that it is a hiatus or plateau period during which we really should expect very little from students beyond trying to keep them at bay through seatwork" (p. 156). Assumptions such as this too often result in "curriculum planning and delivery that optimizes teacher control and limits students' expression" (p. 156). Wells (1996) studied students in a ninth-grade setting who were not allowed to talk while learning. Students created an underground literacy consisting of elaborate secret notes and letters to each other, providing an authentic audience and context for writing that was missing in the classroom.

Fortunately, many teachers have discovered that talk is healthy and productive in middle school and high school subject area classes and have published accounts of their success and suggestions for others. For example, Nancie Atwell (1998) uses an image to convey the kind of talk that occurred in her classroom when she switched to a reading workshop approach. "My students taught me that the context of books they choose is ripe for rich, dining room table talk about literature" (p. 34). Her students surprised her by reading an average of 35 books per year, but she warns that reading alone is not enough. "Oppor-

tunities for social interaction around literature are another component of a reading workshop. Literary talk with a teacher and peers is crucial to kids' development as readers" (p. 40). Learning does not occur by passive absorption of text or talk (Resnick, 1987); rather, meanings that are constructed and evolve during discussion and interaction become more than a sum of individual meanings; they are actually a new set of meanings (Gambrell & Almasi, 1994; Langer, 1992). Figure 8.1 lists resources that allow you to listen in on some interesting and stimulating classroom and out-of-school conversations and student voices.

All talk is not equal. The following sections deal with a variety of types of school talk and give examples and ideas for you to think about as you prepare to teach your subject. Keep in mind that one type of discussion is not inherently better than another; you should vary your formats and procedures depending on your objectives and the particular students you teach.

WHOLE CLASS DISCUSSION

ACTION RESEARCH   8.A

If possible, have a discussion about discussions with a few other people who are preparing to be teachers. Some of the questions you might consider include:

- What should classroom discussions look like and sound like?
- What is the teacher's role in a classroom discussion?
- What might some ground rules be for discussion? What is the proper balance between too much control and not enough?
- How can a teacher encourage high-level thinking and critique during a discussion about a text or a curricular or current issue?
- How does one evaluate what goes on in a discussion?

As you might expect, I do not provide a "correct" answer to any of the questions in the box above; rather, I advise you to listen carefully to talk in those classes you observe or participate in, and revise and refine your own thoughts according to what you learn. You can also reap the benefits of other observers' findings, interpretations, and reflections by reading books and articles focusing on classroom talk. Following are some examples.

Pace and Townsend (1999) noticed very different conversational styles and results in two classrooms

FIGURE 8.1   *Resources that allow you to listen to young people.*

Allison, A. (1999). *Hear These Voices: Youth at the Edge of the Millennium.* New York: Dutton.

Atkin, S. B. (1993). *Voices from the Field: Children of Migrant Farmworkers Tell Their Stories.* Boston: Little, Brown.

Atkin, S. B. (1996). *Voices from the Street: Young Former Gang Members Tell Their Stories.* Boston: Little, Brown.

Atwell, N. (1998). *In the Middle: New Understandings About Writing, Reading, and Learning.* Portsmouth, NH: Heinemann.

Bolden, T. (2001). *Tell All the Children Our Story: Memories and Mementos of Being Young and Black in America.* New York: Abrams.

Brown, C. (1994). *Connecting with the Past.* Portsmouth, NH: Heinemann.

Franco, B. (Ed.). (2001). *Things I Have to Tell You: Poems and Writing by Teenage Girls.* Cambridge, MA: Candlewick Press.

Franco, B. (Ed.). (2001). *You Hear Me? Poems and Writing by Teenage Boys.* Cambridge, MA: Candlewick Press.

Hynds, S. (1997). *On the Brink: Negotiating Literature and Life with Adolescents.* Newark, DE: International Reading Association and New York: Teachers College Press.

Gambrell, L. B., & Almasi, J. F. (Eds.). (1996). *Lively Discussions!: Fostering Engaged Reading.* Newark, DE: International Reading Association.

Gaskins, P. F. (1999). *What Are You?: Voices of Mixed-race Young People.* New York: Henry Holt.

Krogness, M. M. (1995). *Just Teach Me, Mrs. K.: Talking, Reading, and Writing with Adolescent Learners.* Portsmouth, NH: Heinemann.

Landau, E. (1988). *Teenagers Talk About School . . . and Open Their Hearts About Their Closest Concerns.* Englewood Cliffs, NJ: Messner.

Mahiri, J. (1998). *Shooting for Excellence: African American and Youth Culture in New Century Schools.* Urbana, IL: National Council of Teachers of English.

Okutoro, L. O. (Selector). (1999). *Quiet Storm: Voices of Young Black Poets.* New York: Jump at the Sun/Hyperion.

Ousseimi, M. (1995). *Caught in the Crossfire: Growing Up in a War Zone.* New York: Walker.

Pipher, M. B. (1995). *Reviving Ophelia: Saving the Selves of Adolescent Girls.* New York: Ballantine Books.

Peterson, R., & Eeds, M. A. (1990). *Grand Conversations: Literature Groups in Action.* New York: Scholastic.

Philbrick, R. (2001). Listening to Kids in America. *The ALAN Review, 28*(2), 13–16.

Pollack, W. S., with Schuster, T. (2000). *Real Boys' Voices.* New York: Random House.

Routman, R. (2000). *Conversations.* Portsmouth, NH: Heinemann.

Shandler, S. (1999). *Ophelia Speaks.* New York: HarperPerennial.

Springer, J. (1997). *Listen to Us: The World's Working Children.* Buffalo, NY: Groundwood Books/ Douglas & McIntyre Ltd.

Squires, B. (1995). *Listening to Children: A Moral Journey with Robert Coles.* Social Media Productions in cooperation with the Center for Documentary Studies at Duke University. PBS Video.

Veljkovic, P., & Schwartz, A. J. (Eds.). (2001). *Writing from the Heart: Young People Share Their Wisdom.* Philadelphia: Templeton Foundation Press.

Wilhelm, J. D. (1997). *You Gotta BE the Book: Teaching Engaged and Reflective Reading with Adolescents.* New York: Teachers College Press and Urbana, IL: National Council of Teachers of English.

where *Hamlet* was being read. In the first, discussion was teacher-controlled. The following is the researchers' interpretation of a particular exchange:

> First, the instructor demonstrated that he was searching for a specific answer to his question . . . , a question he finally answered himself. Second, he dismissed the efforts of Roxanne as she consulted the text to answer the question. His reply to Roxanne—stating a line then restating the question—was nonresponsive and empha-

sized his textual knowledge and his desire for a specific answer. Third, he answered the question, which is an interpretive one, as though it had a fixed, correct answer. Finally, he suggested he knew Hamlet's perspective. . . . The instructor's responses and nonresponses suggest he is the sole source of knowledge in this setting. (p. 44)

In contrast, in the second classroom, described by the researchers as a dialogic class, multiple perspectives were examined and considered. After presenting an excerpt from a verbatim transcript of an initial discussion, Pace and Townsend again list several points of interpretation:

> First, though the teacher was the major contributor, she did not initiate this line of exploration or assume that she knew Hamlet's thoughts. Rather she entered a process of discovery with her students. Second, her language was laced with uncertainty markers ("I think," "sort of," I'm not sure") that signaled the pliable nature of her thinking about Hamlet and suggested that she was not looking for "right" answers. Third, she modeled text referencing as a way of investigating literary meaning, thereby demonstrating a strategy that students might use in her absence to construct their own understandings. As is typical in a dialogic classroom, this teacher encouraged students to try out their ideas. She reminded them that "you have to make up your mind as you go along," an instruction that supported the ambiguous nature not only of this play but of the study of literature in general. (pp. 45–46)

These two examples of discussion types can be applied to texts beyond literature. For instance, if you are a science or social studies teacher, you might bring in newspaper articles and editorials about an environmental controversy involving the school neighborhood and encourage the kind of thoughtful discussion evident in the second teacher's methods. No matter what your subject area, you can encourage students to think through talking, to learn through listening to others, and to engage in discussion that could lead to a desire to learn more and to act.

How involved, and how directive, should you be in class discussions? That depends on a number of factors. You might find that some of your classes need little structure or facilitation from you, while others flounder without your direct involvement. At times you might choose to say virtually nothing to avoid influencing the students' grappling with a text. Sometimes, I join my thoughts and responses to others. In some instances, I remind them that I'm just another reader, and my opinion isn't privileged; but in other circumstances, I might hold some knowledge that they don't have that makes my voice more one of authority. Young (1998), after analyzing interactions in several classrooms, concludes:

> I also no longer think that teachers need to strive for a neutral position in class discussions. Teachers can voice their opinions in learning environments that encourage disagreement, debate, and respect for all voices. I no longer think that adolescents are uninterested in the opinions of teachers either. (p. 261)

Teachers must make many decisions as they facilitate discussions. Listen in on a scene from Chris Crutcher's novel *Staying Fat for Sarah Byrnes* (1993). Ms. Lemry is the teacher of a class called Contemporary American Thought, an elective course designed to help students examine their beliefs. Ms. Lemry begins by setting some ground rules and explaining her decisions:

> A number of you have chosen abortion as your topic. . . . Let me warn you, this is a topic that can get out of hand. *Adults* don't handle it well. I'd be surprised if there weren't people in the room who have had experience with abortion, either directly or through friends. So I'm going to keep a tight rein on things. I will feel free to remove you from the discussion, or even the room, if you're disrespectful toward other people's views. (p. 85)

Having a whole class discussion about a curricular topic or current interest is a common activity in classrooms, and it is appropriate for many purposes. However, too often, perhaps especially in math classes, what is called discussion is little more than going over problems and answers. It's perfectly fine for a teacher to ask questions early on in a unit to find out what students know about a topic or how they initially feel about a sensitive current issue in the school, the community, or the world. Or, if a complex topic, such as applications of statistical procedures, is being covered, the teacher may realize it is unwise to send students off in small groups until they are more comfortable and have more to contribute. Conley (1995) points out that during whole group discussions, teachers can guide students through the writing process, teach vocabulary and concepts, play devil's advocate or use some other form of generating controversy to further reasoning skills, provide transitions, generate new ideas, and form conclusions. "Whole class discussion is most appropriate for uncovering misconceptions, demonstrating skills and procedures, and covering some fairly simple facts or concepts in a short amount of time" (p. 317).

Some educators favor teacher-oriented discussion at the beginning of a school year or unit, gradually moving toward student-centered discussions as the students develop their own strategies for understanding text and gain independence (Applebee, 1992; Gambrell & Almasi, 1994). In an effort to combat the appalling statistics showing "that American students spend, on average, three hours of a five-hour school day sitting passively while their *teachers* talk," Krogness (1995, p. 99) laid the groundwork for class discussions and taught her students specific techniques such as asking questions that require more than a yes/no answer and verbalizing problems in terms of what is wrong rather than who is at fault. But she also set rules for herself. "I promised not to explain or defend my point of view during this discussion, but I would keep the conversation moving, act as a monitor, and record each speaker's thoughts on a big, yellow legal pad" (p. 111).

I like to hold a whole group discussion based on a common text early in any given semester. I tell my students that I *could* form smaller groups, and I *will* for future works that we read, but at this point, I can't be everywhere at once eavesdropping, and I can't bear to miss out on a single thing that's said! I want us to have a common bond and a common frame of reference for future lessons. But I also recognize that when I have a large circle we're losing something in terms of opportunities for more people to do more talking.

Unfortunately, the most typical form of classroom discussion is *recitation* (Alvermann, 1986; Alvermann, O'Brien, & Dillon, 1990; Hoetker & Ahlbrand, 1968). I'm sure you recognize the format: the teacher asks a question and calls on a student, the student responds, the teacher gives feedback. Then, the cycle is repeated. Here's what recitation might sound like:

> Teacher: Why did the Giver show Jonas the tape of his father releasing the baby? Moreka?
>
> Moreka: Well, I think he respected Jonas and they sort of had a pact to be truthful. He wanted him to know the truth.
>
> Teacher: Good answer! Any other ideas? Jacob?
>
> Jacob: The Giver knows how whacko the society has gotten. The only way he'll get Jonas to take action with him is to rile him up and make him see the evils that are hidden from everyone else.
>
> Teacher: Ah, and it worked, didn't it. So, what was this plan for action they came up with? Claudia?

If you observe a session like this, which some would not even call a true discussion, you may notice that it is quite likely that some students are not engaged. Also, it may seem like it is more a game of "Guess what's in the teacher's head," or more of a comprehension check than an open sharing of ideas and reactions. You might be surprised at the number of students who agree with the child who concluded, "We have discussions so that kids who go to the bathroom can know what they missed" (Almasi, 1996, p. 3). There are ways to avoid this stilted quality and stifling atmosphere. Bean (1998) asserts, "A constructivist classroom is the antithesis of a place where the teacher controls learning with prepackaged answers to teacher-generated questions" (p. 160). An authentic discussion adds new ideas and insight, not just a recapitulation of what a text or teacher has said. The teacher can encourage students

to ask real questions they want answers to, or to initiate discussion by reading aloud a journal response to a text. Teachers can ask questions that indicate an interest in the students' reactions and that raise more issues and possibilities, questions that actually invite participation instead of preordained answers about the text. In one classroom, the students and teacher brainstormed to come up with a list representing what might or should happen during a discussion, posting the resultant chart that included the verbs "question, clarify, refine, explain, justify, predict, speculate" (Gambrell & Almasi, 1996, p. 75). In my classroom, when a student directs a comment to me, I may say, "Look to your classmates, not to me. Talk to each other." They're not used to doing this, so I must force myself to be the facilitator, modeling for them how to keep the conversation going in productive directions without taking over and acting like the ultimate authority.

That doesn't necessarily mean I can never give an opinion. Once, during a heated discussion on *The Giver* with preservice teachers, a student named Darryl said he didn't think this book should be read by middle school students because of the suicide in it. I looked around and no one seemed willing to take him on, so I said, "Let me join in as another reader, not the teacher. *What* suicide?" He referred to Rosemary's asking to be released and injecting herself. I replied, "I don't see that as suicide any more than Socrates drinking the hemlock, or St. Appolonia throwing herself into the flames her persecutors had prepared for her to spare them the act of killing her." At that point others jumped in, allowing me to sit back and let it go on without me. Rapport had already been established, so Darryl did not think I was attacking him personally just because I offered an alternative to his interpretation. The students knew that I valued different opinions, that I was not looking for the recitation-type talk most of them had experienced when they were secondary school students. It was fine with me if Darryl changed his mind and fine if he stuck by his original theory (which he did).

Another time, several in our whole class literature circle on *The Giver* thought that Lois Lowry would be in favor of euthanasia today, citing as evidence that the old people in the novel were released. I used this as a teaching opportunity, helping them to see the release of the old in the context of the whole story. It takes a lot of skill for a teacher to know *when* to do *what* during a discussion. We don't want to discourage thoughtful answers and tentative hypothesizing, but neither should we accept interpretations that are clearly outside those possible or plausible from the text. Think of other fields (e.g., music, the theatre, woodworking, chem-

FIGURE 8.2   *Recommendations for facilitating classroom discussions.*

- Encourage students to ask questions to which they want answers.
- Ask questions that raise issues and possibilities.
- Brainstorm a list of meaningful ways to participate (e.g., question, clarify, refine, explain, justify, predict, speculate).
- Direct students to speak to each other rather than to you.
- Model ways to keep the discussion productive.
- Give an opinion when appropriate.

istry), where a wiser or more experienced mentor guides beginners. Given the right atmosphere, rapport, and spirit, we can help our students rethink initial responses. And, luckily, the burden of giving or receiving a grade is totally absent during such discussions. Also, accept that if students stick to their original thinking, even if you consider it flawed, the sky will not fall; they will have many more opportunities to read material that will help them think deeply, grow in knowledge, and understand literary concepts and dimensions.

How does one achieve a classroom climate that is conducive to thoughtful, stimulating, and knowledge-building discussion? This is your responsibility as the teacher, whether the class is discussing a work of literature, a textbook selection, a newspaper editorial, a movie review, or a student-initiated, school-related concern. Figure 8.2 provides a summary of recommendations for facilitating classroom discussions, and following are additional points to consider.

Seating Arrangements

There is no one best way to have students arranged for discussion, and you have to work within the constraints of your room and its furniture. Recall when you were in classrooms where the desks were in rows and may have been bolted to the floor. The students all faced the front of the room, so they could look only at the teacher, the faces of people next to them, and the backs of a lot of heads, unless they sat in the front. When everyone faces the front, those students who sit near the back often cannot hear remarks made by those ahead of them. This situation hardly leads to fruitful, enjoyable conversation. You can't think of any group that gathers to talk whose members *choose* to sit that way—such a scenario is preposterous.

Perhaps the most important thing to remember is to arrange the students so that they can make eye contact with each other. Many teachers prefer a horseshoe configuration, which is fine if the teacher must

be separate, perhaps to put notes on the board or project something from a computer onto a screen. Often, I ask students to move their desks or tables into a large circle when we have a whole class discussion. I sit among them, choosing a seat on the side or in the back of the room. (If I remain in the front, I find that the circle doesn't quite close in around me; the gaps tell me they still separate me as the teacher.) As the talk progresses, if students tend to look at me, I gently remind them to look at the person who last talked or to the group in general rather than at me.

Setting Guidelines

If students are allowed to be a part of setting the discussion rules, they are usually quite reasonable. They do understand that it makes sense for one person to talk at a time, for speakers to feel secure about not being unkindly laughed at or put down, for all but the speaker to be listening carefully. They'll also agree that the speakers should make an effort to project their voices in consideration of the listeners, that there should be no side conversations or whispering going on, and that certain individuals or subgroups should not be allowed to dominate the discussion. You and your students may decide together that a person's right to pass on a given issue should be respected. You are responsible for walking that fine line—encouraging the quiet or shy students to participate without making them feel pressured or uncomfortable. Also, you should be aware of gender issues. Research has shown that even teachers who thought boys and girls had an equal voice in their classes are often surprised when they review a taped discussion or a scripted conversation and discover that this is not the case (Sadker & Sadker, 1994). The same holds true in terms of race, social groups, and students with disabilities or special educational needs. At times, you may find it helpful to debrief after a discussion and decide together whether some rules should be adjusted for future talk. Remain flexible.

Realistic Expectations

Don't expect instant success and perfection from the students or from yourself. You will get better at facilitating with practice. You might audiotape or videotape some of your class discussions, and analyze them later to reflect on your comments and decisions, as well as to check on whether the interactions are balanced and fair. Don't be too hard on yourself—we all can think of the "perfect" teacher comment after our class has left the room, when we don't have the pressure of making split-second decisions. In general, if the discussion is animated and shows that thinking, questioning, and new understanding are present, consider it a success. If those things are not occurring, perhaps a colleague or mentor could watch the tape, or come in and observe, and offer suggestions. Remain confident as you continue to learn through talk and listening just as you want your students to.

You can facilitate discussion in a number of ways. The method selected depends on the topic, the particular mix of students involved, the time available, and so on. You might start off with a question that requires reasoning-level skills, perhaps based on a text the class has just read, and call on one student, who then calls on another to continue. After that person gives an opinion or a problem-solving suggestion, she calls on yet another, perhaps from among those with hands raised, to continue the discussion. You might stay fairly quiet until the talk runs out of steam or a response requires correction, clarification, or expansion.

Cangelosi (1996) provides six thoughts to keep in mind as you raise questions calling for student responses.

1. Provide periods of silent thinking between when a question is asked and when an answer is expected to allow each student to ponder and reason.

2. Have all students write out their answers first, allowing you time to preview the responses and decide whom to call on for the most provocative or interesting discussion, and providing the students with confidence as they speak their thoughts.

3. Raise the question *before* calling on a student, encouraging all to listen carefully and engage in thoughtful mental response.

4. Use responses by some students to formulate subsequent questions for others, perhaps asking one student to contrast her answer with one just articulated.

5. Use questions that are specific, not vague, and ones that relate to a central theme or problem, as well as connect to one another.

6. Base questioning sessions on previous learning activities and apply the ideas generated to subsequent learning activities. (pp. 290–291)

Figure 8.3 (pages 246–247) shows a task sheet a math teacher uses as part of a concept lesson on arithmetic sequences, and a discussion he facilitates to encourage reasoning skills in his students.

SMALL GROUP DISCUSSIONS

Think of great discussions you've had, perhaps with your roommate late into the night in your dorm room or with a close friend in a coffee shop after a movie. Sometimes, five or six people can get into an animated discussion that's just as good, though of course different. However, if 25 people are at a party, there is not just one conversation going on, with one person talking while everyone else politely listens and waits for a turn. So, depending on your purposes, you'll find much to be gained from smaller group discussions. Here are a few of the ways I've used small groups when talk is a focus:

■ Groups evaluate different levels of curricular materials from a variety of publishers.

■ Students divide into "discipline groups"—the preservice math teachers sit at a table, the social studies education majors sit together, the artists congregate, and so on. The class reads a text, such as a chapter from Stephen J. Gould's *Full House: The Spread of Excellence from Plato to Darwin* (1996), and the groups discuss it. Later, we compare to learn whether groups had different insights or opinions; everyone's understanding is broadened by listening to other perceptions and reactions.

■ I give booktalks on a number of books, usually connected to a theme such as time, memory, schooling, or coming of age; or to a genre such as nonfiction, poetry, journal article, short story, or young adult problem novel. Students choose the work they want to read, and later join a discussion group with others who have read the same text.

■ I randomly divide students into groups of perhaps four or five. Then, I give case studies describing students who are having difficulty in school for various reasons. The groups brainstorm ideas and solutions that will help those students' learning and lives in school, as well as outside the school walls.

The more real examples you can think of, the more likely you will realize that discussion is valuable and does indeed lead to insight, learning, growth, and action. Lives have been turned around as a result of attending AA meetings. Busy people come together weekly at local bookstores to talk about their reading and writing and hear about what other people are reading and writing. Town meetings are held to discuss environmental, economic, political, or educational controversies. You must point out to your students that discussion in your classroom is not just a time filler, a social break, or a frill; rather, it's an authentic way to help them grapple with the content and concepts of your course, to converse with each other over important documents or literature.

What is your role as the teacher when your students are working in small groups? It depends. At times, if you've set up guidelines and expectations, the best thing you can do is to stay out of their way. Supply resources, serve as a consultant to groups that solicit your help, monitor interactions, observe and take notes on individuals you're learning about as they contribute, struggle, or disengage. If you find that more structure is necessary for the students to be productive, assign roles within groups such as facilitator, reporter, vocabulary builder, and summarizer. Give optional guide questions to be used if conversation lags, or suggestions for products, such as semantic maps, to be completed during the talk.

It takes work to build a discourse community, and teachers face challenges as they teach students to learn through talking and listening. The *Professional Teaching Standards* issued by the National Council of Teachers of Mathematics (1991) identifies aspects of the teacher's role in classroom discourse, including the following:

- posing questions and assignments that challenge and engage students' thinking;
- listening carefully to their ideas;
- deciding which of the things students bring up to pursue in depth;
- monitoring participation and deciding how and when to encourage individuals; and
- deciding when to clarify issues and when to allow students to struggle with difficulties. (p. 35)

Silver and Smith (1996) warn teachers of potential pitfalls along the journey of building discourse communities and advise them not to expect perfection at the beginning. They caution that teachers must take the time necessary to build trust, comfort, confidence, and respect; must set norms such as allowing criticism of ideas but not of people; and "must ensure that the mathematics does not get lost in the talk and that progress is made along the path not only toward a real mathematical discourse community but also toward the increased mathematical proficiency of all students" (p. 24).

At first, students may not know how to talk to each other about literature, research articles, national news pieces in magazines, or other texts; they may be reticent or feel insecure because they are so used to, conditioned by, and dependent on the recitation format described earlier. They may "consider small-group work a waste of time and may even resent the fact that they don't have the opportunity to share their thoughts with the teacher" (Simmons & Deluzain, 1992, p. 159). You might have to model the procedure, perhaps by handpicking a few students to join you in discussing a newspaper editorial and then having the class point out things that worked well and things that impeded further sharing. Bring in volunteers from the community or from among your colleagues to take part in a discussion of an event that your students could analyze and comment on before they go off in their own groups.

Be patient with your students as they develop skills and strategies for discussion groups; don't expect everything to be smooth and perfect. In *Grand Conversations: Literature Groups in Action* (1990), Peterson and Eeds remind us, "Dialogue has its tough moments, when ambiguity prevails and tension mounts. After all, meaning is being examined from different perspectives. It can be, and usually is, a messy process" (p. 22). But it's worth it. Dialogue can be used as pedagogy, to construct meaning. It provides practice in learning to attend to the facts, practice in discriminating between values within a context that naturally provides demonstration, and practice giving and attending to relevant feedback.

In time, you'll find that "students tend to assume a multitude of roles that are traditionally reserved for the teacher, such as inquisitor, facilitator, and evaluator as well as the more familiar role of respondent" (Almasi, 1996, p. 7). Research has shown that in student-led discussions, when students were allowed a participatory role in the interpretation of texts, they engaged in problem solving and higher-level thinking (Gambrell & Almasi, 1996). The benefits of talk within small groups are many and varied.

You'll be amazed at what you can learn about your students and their thinking by listening to them as they talk about issues and problems. In fact, when students work in small groups to solve mathematical problems, their cognitive behavior mirrors that of expert problem solvers (Artzt & Armour-Thomas, 1992; Schoenfeld, 1987). Artzt and Yaloz-Femia (1999) reported surprising discoveries when analyzing the dialogue of fifth graders doing mathematical problem solving in small groups. Students were given a problem showing a number line with a 0 point and a 1 point a few inches apart, with a picture of a cricket jumping from the 1 back toward

FIGURE 8.3 *Task sheet used in a lesson on arithmetic sequences.*

EXAMPLES

3, 3.1, 3.2, 3.3, 3.4, 3.5, 3.6

−13, −2.9, . . ., 130, 141, 152

The amount of money each hour in a radio giveaway jackpot that begins with $100 and increases by $20 every hour until there is a winner.

15, 10, 5, 0, −5, −10, . . .

The amount of money in Betty's jar each Saturday if she starts with $60 and puts in exactly $7.50 each Friday night. (She never removes money or puts any in at any other time.)

22.6, 22.6, 22.6, 22.6, 22.6, 22.6

The number of bricks in the first, second, third, fourth, etc. row, arranged as follows:

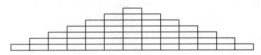

NONEXAMPLES

7, 0.7, 0.07, 0.007, 0.0007, 0.00007

46, 6.78, 2.60, 1.61, . . . 1.02, 1.00, 1.00, 1.00

The monthly savings account balance of a person who puts in $750 the first month and leaves it there, allowing it to collect interest at the rate of 4% compounded monthly.

The ages of all the people in our class, listed in alphabetical order.

. . . 16, 9, 4, 1, 0, 1, 4, 9, 16, . . .

1, 2, 4, 8, 16, . . . , 1,048,576

1, 1, 2, 3, 5, 8, 13, 21, . . .

HOW ARE THE EXAMPLES ALIKE? HOW DO THEY DIFFER FROM THE NONEXAMPLES?

Write your first conjecture here:

_____

_____

_____

Write your second conjecture here:

_____

_____

_____

Write your third conjecture here:

_____

_____

_____

Write your fourth conjecture here:

_____

_____

_____

(continued)

FIGURE 8.3 *Continued.*

Mr. Citerelli: Bill, read your first conjecture.

Bill: The examples are alike because they're all in the same column. The nonexamples are in a different column.

Mr. Citerelli: That surely can't be contradicted. Now, let's hear an idea that might explain what I had in mind when I grouped the examples on the left and the nonexamples on the right. Okay, Mavis, you start: keep it going.

Mavis: The first thing I noticed is that both columns contain sequences. But those on the left have more of a pattern to them. Jeannie.

Jeannie: The ones on the right have patterns also. So, just having a pattern can't be it. Okay, Mark.

Mark: Not all of them. Look at the second one.

Jeannie: Sure it does—

Mr. Citerelli: Excuse me. Let's allow these two to hash this out in a two-way discussion while the rest of us listen.

Jeannie: The numbers on the second one are getting smaller; that's a pattern.

Mark: Not the last two numbers.

Jeannie: They might if we saw more decimal places. I think it has something to do with taking square roots. I played around with roots on my calculator and there's something related to roots of 46 with those numbers.

Mr. Citerelli: Excuse me. Mark, do you agree that at least some of the nonexample sequences have predictable patterns?

Mark: Sure.

Mr. Citerelli: Those that agree, raise your hands. . . . It looks like that's one thing we agree on. Bill, would you please come up to the board and help us keep track of the points on which we all agree?

Mr. Citerelli: Mavis, do you want to modify your conjecture?

Mavis: No, but I'll withdraw it because we agree that some of the nonexamples have patterns also.

Mr. Citerelli: Thank you. Inez, read yours, and then keep it going.

Inez: You get the next number by adding something to the one before. Okay, Chico.

Chico: That's not right because look at the nonexample. You add something to get to the next one. $1+1=2$, $1+2=3$, $2+3=5$, $3+5=8$, and so on. So, if Inez is right, then that one should be on the left side. Okay, Luis.

Luis: Besides, if Inez is right that you just added something, then the numbers should all be going up, but two of 'em do [sic] down and one stays the same!

Mr. Citerelli: Excuse me. Let's hear from Inez because it's her conjecture we're discussing.

Inez: First of all, Luis, if you add negatives, they go down. Also, I'm changing my conjecture so that it's this: You get the next number by adding the *same* amount to each one.

The discussion continues, with more students joining in, using calculators to test hypotheses on examples and nonexamples, formulating more example sequences, reflecting on processes, generalizing from specifics, with hints from Mr. Citerelli. A follow-up discussion the next day involves students verifying and refining their conclusions. (Cangelosi, 1996, pp. 89–90)

From *Teaching Mathematics in Secondary and Middle School, 2/E* by Cangelosi, © 1996. Reprinted by permission of Pearson Education, Inc., Upper Saddle River, NJ.

the 0. The problem stated, "A cricket is on the number line at point '1.' He wants to get to point '0' but he only hop [sic] half the remaining distance each time." Several questions are asked, such as where the cricket would be on the number line after the first hop, second hop, tenth hop, nth hop. The students are asked to explain why the cricket does or does not ever get to the point labeled 0.

One group of students tried a different tactic to figure out a pattern, and again their talk crossed disciplinary lines. They folded a piece of paper over and over, and realized that even after they were physically unable to fold it anymore, theoretically it could continue to be folded in half. Simone explains,

"I can keep folding this until the Messiah comes! . . . What I'm trying to say is that it's always going to have somewhere to jump. Even if it's half of an atom. . . . I can keep on folding this until I get a million paper cuts" (pp. 122–123). Brian concludes, "It will get so tiny. Like an atom. Like a neutron. . . . It is impossible to stop folding that because it will keep on going, it is impossible for the cricket to reach the 0" (p. 123). The researchers found in the student talk evidence of abstract thinking and mathematical problem solving. They recommend that teachers require each student to write a description of the solution and supporting mathematical reasoning after working in small groups.

FIGURE **8.4** *Examples of student-created discussion questions based on* Jacob Have I Loved.

- Behaviors are modified by conditioning. Have you thought about what has reinforced each character's behavior, both before and in response?
  —*Branden Wood*

- What is the significance of the Captain's house being destroyed in the storm? Is there any symbolism attached to it?
  —*Sarah Beckwith*

- I wonder why the Captain decided to give Caroline the money to go to school off the island instead of Louise. Couldn't he tell she was unhappy there? I wonder what would have happened if Louise did get the money instead of Caroline.
  —*Christianna Hamm*

- Does Caroline have any friends? Was every child/person in town so in awe of her because of her talent or so afraid because she was frail that they didn't talk to her?
  —*Kristen Paglia*

- What are the cultural structures that impact the relationships of the women in this story?
  —*Diane Zeller*

- Do you think there was any love in the grandmother's heart for Louise?
  —*Jeremy Lahnum*

Chambers (1996) offers three types of invitations to talk; ask the students questions relating to:

1. What they noticed or especially liked (the sharing of enthusiasms).
2. What parts they were puzzled by or wondered about (the sharing of puzzles).
3. What patterns they recognized or what similarities to other texts or to their own experiences they found (the sharing of connections).

Ensuing discussions can be full of insight and can lead to critical thinking and sharing by peers.

Questions and topics can be crucial to the success of some small groups. Sometimes, I ask students to create good questions to bring with them to discussion groups, or topics they really do wonder about. I ask them not to use any questions they already know the answers to; such questions are not fruitful discussion starters. Figure 8.4 shows examples of questions my students composed to bring to their discussion groups after reading Katherine Paterson's *Jacob Have I Loved* (1980).

ALTERNATIVE DISCUSSION FORMATS

Inside–Outside Circle

One enjoyable way to get your students comfortable talking with each other about issues is to conduct an "inside–outside circle" discussion (Kagan, 1989).

I was introduced to this strategy when I watched a videotape of a Spanish class at a parents' night. Chris Paul arranged her students into two circles, with each person in the inside circle facing someone in the outside circle. She gave a prompt, such as "¿Que hiuste este fin de semana?" ("Talk about what you did over the weekend"), and students began conversing with their partners. There were a dozen conversations in Spanish going on at once, but the students were focused on their own. After a few minutes, a timer went off, and one circle moved clockwise—a new question initiated a discussion with new pairings. The teacher explained that her students would never get the necessary amount of practice speaking and listening to the language if she used a typical seating arrangement and method of questioning one student at a time. The students loved being immersed in the language and being given so many opportunities in a nonthreatening atmosphere to experiment with conversation.

You are limited only by your own imagination once you start modifying this activity to suit your students' needs and relevant curricular topics. Read an editorial from a current newspaper about the environment, global trading, Internet abuses, economic forecasts, or cheating in and outside of schools, and set the circles to talking. Students can suggest issues they want to discuss. It is a good way to activate background knowledge and prime students for a new unit. Figure 8.5 illustrates a lesson using this approach.

FIGURE 8.5 *A literature activity using the inside–outside circle method.*

INSTRUCTIONS: We've all read Katherine Paterson's *Jacob Have I Loved*, and I'm sure we all agree that the protagonist, Louise, is an unhappy, angry adolescent. I'd like you to think about the question, "Who's to blame?" through writing and conversation. So, draw a line across your paper and label it "Culpability Continuum." Label the ends "Least Responsible" and "Most Responsible." Rank order the characters in the novel (including Louise herself) according to how much you think they were the cause of Louise's misery and place the ordered names on the continuum.

When you're done writing, form an inside and an outside circle, with each person on the inside facing a partner on the outside. When I ring my bell, talk to your partner about how you ranked the seven characters in terms of responsibility, and listen to your partner's ranking and explanation. You might change your mind, or convince your partner that your answer is better justified by textual evidence, or you might agree to disagree. When you hear the bell again, the people in the inside circle should remain where they are. Those on the outside should move clockwise past two people and face the next person you meet. Compare answers again, giving your reasons for your judgments.

Getting Ready to Teach 8.1 (see page 266)

Modified Socratic Seminar

A somewhat similar method was used by high school math teacher Leah Casados (Tanner & Casados, 1998), who modified the "Socratic Seminar" approach (Gray, 1989; Overholser, 1992). After a homework assignment, she formed the class into an inner and an outer circle. Inner-circle students carried on a discussion focusing on the math content of the reading selection and a teacher-given question, while outer-circle students took notes on the discussion. Everyone could participate in the debriefing session, during which the teacher monitored and made improvements to the discussion guidelines for the future. As the activity was used more, students began looking at each other rather than at the teacher, began to initiate their own questions to start discussion, and could analyze group dynamics by watching videotapes of their talks. The teacher concluded, "Using the Socratic Discussion method showed me that my students can become insightful, logical mathematical problem-solvers by talking through ideas and taking ownership of them" (p. 349).

Think–Pair–Share

Another strategy that may help you achieve your purposes for a certain text or curricular topic is the cooperative learning activity think–pair–share (Lymon, 1981). Much research has shown the value of providing students with time to think about responses before contributing to a discussion; the quality of talk is enhanced (Gambrell, 1983; Rowe, 1974). Wait-time is built into the think–pair–share strategy. Following a question, perhaps supplied by the teacher:

- All students take time to formulate their own thoughts on the issue.
- They then pair with another to share and listen.
- Then, two pairs come together in a foursome.
- Finally, students share responses in the larger group.

Teachers may use task cards to remind students of which activity segment is in progress. Baumeister (1992) found that students using this method showed increased reading comprehension and a better ability to recall information than did comparison groups.

Think about how this strategy might play out in a specific content area class. A math teacher could present the class with a conceptual problem, such as "Why does a negative number multiplied by another negative number result in a positive number?" Individually, students jot down a justification, tentative ideas, or hypotheses. After a moment, pairs give feedback to each other, expand or eliminate conjectures, then create foursomes where further refining or arguing takes place. As groups report their thinking and theories to the whole class, a deep understanding of the math concept may replace students' earlier unquestioned acceptance of the rule they had been taught regarding multiplication of negative numbers. The teacher can add relevant information and clarify points that seem to cause confusion.

Getting Ready to Teach 8.2 (see page 266)

Discussion Webs

Structuring student talk using a discussion web helps students consider multiple points of view and helps assure that a few strong voices don't dominate a discussion. Alvermann and Phelps (1998) suggest a five-step procedure, summarized here:

1. prepare for reading;
2. introduce a central question and have pairs discuss the points of view and write reasons in two support columns provided on the web outline;
3. combine pairs so that groups of four can discuss their input and reach a group conclusion (or prepare a majority and minority report);
4. give each group three minutes to present conclusions and one reason, then open the discussion to the whole group;
5. have students use their webs and the ideas they heard to write individual answers to the central question that was proposed. (p. 274)

Figure 8.6 shows a discussion web that could be used with a biology or social studies class reading Barbara Kingsolver's (2002) essay "A Forest's Last Stand."

> **Getting Ready to Teach 8.3** (see page 266)

Electronic Discussions

The boundaries between writing and speaking blur when we consider electronic discussions. The very term *chat room* implies talking, though people joining chat rooms compose and type their words. Not all forms of writing can be described as just talk written down, but electronic discussions very often take on an informal tone that closely resembles what would be used in conversation. That's fine—consider that you have the best of both worlds when students "talk" through their computers. Mahiri (1998) used interactive written discourse through the use of linked computers in his classroom. Initially, students loved writing "real-time" class discussions and found it valuable to have a written record of some good class discussions for future reference. Ultimately, though, they expressed a preference for oral discussions in class (p. 74). On the other hand, Mahiri found that e-mail discussions outside the classroom enabled communication that extended teaching and learning connections.

The possibilities for e-mail discussion groups in all content areas are unlimited. For example, a team of middle school teachers could initiate an interdis-

ciplinary action research project related to local environmental issues. In my community, there is a plan to extend a paved path at Onondaga Lake Park so that it loops the lake. Many skaters, bicyclists, and community leaders are thrilled; environmentalists warn of the destruction of habitats for small animals. Class teams could be formed to research the pros and cons of the plan. Members of the teams can e-mail each other and their teachers to respond to editorials they read in the paper, formulate their own positions, and write letters to business and community groups. They can hold electronic group meetings via instant messaging, noting connections to math, science, literature, and social studies as they study budget figures, research the topics of wildlife habitats and construction, read stories about environmental struggles, and exercise their right to be heard as citizens.

My own students say they benefit from belonging to electronic literature discussion groups. Sometimes, several students read the same text, exchange e-mail addresses or create a mailing list, and discuss the text during or after reading. At times, I have required students to respond to a text just once via e-mail, only to find they have voluntarily jumped into the discussion many times. They respond to what others have contributed, either changing their minds about something they have said previously or arguing or joking about a classmate's input. I ask them to copy me on the e-mail exchange, so I get to listen in, and sometimes chime in as another reader. Figure 8.7 provides suggested resources for using discussion in your instruction.

BookTalk   8.1

One topic that could spark discussion about talking is *selective mutism,* a condition that involves people *not* talking. Students can check reference materials and read informational articles about it. There are several fiction books in which characters either cannot or will not talk, often after a traumatic experience. *Silent to the Bone* (2000), by E. L. Konigsburg is one. Another is Laurie Halse Anderson's *Speak* (1999). Melinda, the narrator, tells no one that she has been raped at a party, but tells the reader about getting sicker and sicker and talking less and less as her ninth-grade year progresses, and she suffers exclusion by her former friends. Imagine the challenge to a writer when her narrator chooses silence! For younger students or those requiring easier reading material, Katherine Paterson's *Flip-Flop Girl* (1994) and Audrey Couloumbis's Newbery Honor Book *Getting Near to Baby* (1999) also deal with selective mutism.

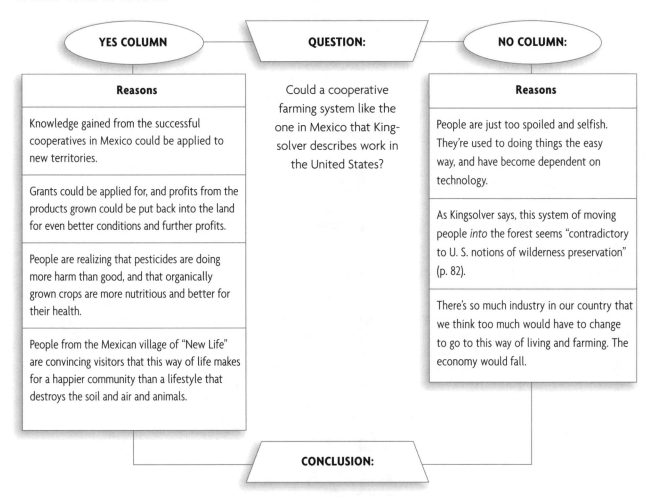

FIGURE **8.6** *An example of a discussion web.*

TEACHER'S INSTRUCTIONS: We have been studying ecosystems and exploring various ways to preserve endangered environments. As you read "A Forest's Last Stand," by Barbara Kingsolver, who is a biologist, a writer, and a social activist, think about this central question: Could a cooperative farming system like the one in Mexico that Kingsolver describes work in the United States? Think about how political, social, scientific, educational, and economic forces would be involved.

YES COLUMN

Reasons

Knowledge gained from the successful cooperatives in Mexico could be applied to new territories.

Grants could be applied for, and profits from the products grown could be put back into the land for even better conditions and further profits.

People are realizing that pesticides are doing more harm than good, and that organically grown crops are more nutritious and better for their health.

People from the Mexican village of "New Life" are convincing visitors that this way of life makes for a happier community than a lifestyle that destroys the soil and air and animals.

QUESTION:

Could a cooperative farming system like the one in Mexico that Kingsolver describes work in the United States?

NO COLUMN:

Reasons

People are just too spoiled and selfish. They're used to doing things the easy way, and have become dependent on technology.

As Kingsolver says, this system of moving people *into* the forest seems "contradictory to U. S. notions of wilderness preservation" (p. 82).

There's so much industry in our country that we think too much would have to change to go to this way of living and farming. The economy would fall.

CONCLUSION:

After serious consideration of the pros and cons, we conclude that, like Kingsolver, we should be optimistic and at least try to convince people that this type of cooperative farming surrounding endangered ecosystems could benefit all. In fact, we'd use her essay as the first step in our persuasive efforts. We will not let nature be destroyed!

FORMAL AND SEMIFORMAL SPEAKING OCCASIONS

Public Speaking

As a content area teacher, it is not likely that you will be responsible for giving public speaking lessons. Yet, your students will be entering a world where it is necessary that they speak with competence and confidence. If all teachers took advantage of the opportunities for relatively formal speaking that fit in with other objectives, more students would get closer to meeting that goal. Some strategies are really simple. A fifth-grade teacher I observed had a podium in the front of his class. A student asked to tell about an experience he had had. He walked up to the podium and stood on it to address the class—the podium was used by speaker and listeners alike as a signal. The boy who was talking was just a bit more formal than usual in his

FIGURE 8.7   *Resources relating to discussion.*

Boyd, F. B. (1997). The Cross-aged Literacy Program: Preparing Struggling Adolescents for Book Club Discussions. In S. I. McMahon & T. E. Raphael (Eds.), *The Book Club Connection: Literacy Learning and Classroom Talk.* New York: Teachers College Press, 162–181.

Chambers, A. (1996). *Tell Me: Children, Reading, and Talk.* York, ME: Stenhouse.

Chandler, K. (1997). The Beach Book Club: Literacy in the "Lazy Days of Summer." *Journal of Adolescent and Adult Literacy, 41*(2), 104–115.

Daniels, H. (1994). *Literature Circles: Voice and Choice in the Student-Centered Classroom.* York, ME: Stenhouse.

Gambrell, L. B., & Almasi, J. F. (Eds.). (1996). *Lively Discussions!* Newark, DE: International Reading Association.

Goatley, V. J. (1997). Talk About Text Among Special Education Students. In S. I. McMahon & T. E. Raphael (Eds.), *The Book Club Connection: Literacy Learning and Classroom Talk.* New York: Teachers College Press, 119–137.

Mowbray, G., & George, J. (1992). *Language Aloud . . . Allowed: In the Middle and High School Years.* Markham, Ontario: Pembroke.

Samway, K. D., & Whang, G. (1995). *Literature Study Circles in a Multicultural Classroom.* York, ME: Stenhouse.

Short, K. G., & Pierce, K. M. (Eds.). (1990). *Talking About Books: Creating Literate Communities.* Portsmouth, NH: Heinemann.

presentation, and his classmates recognized that what he said should be attended to with respect. The teacher told me that virtually all of the students displayed poise and used good volume when standing on the podium. It was used daily, and he credited it with aiding his classroom management. And the students loved it. You could also use an aid such as a microphone (even a nonworking one) for the same purpose.

There may be times in your class when the students are working in small groups and you decide that it might be beneficial for a reporter to tell the whole class what was discovered, produced, or discussed. Using a reporter is not always necessary—if similar things occur or are discussed in the small groups, class time can better be spent moving on to something else. But when you want the groups to learn from each other, encouraging and supporting the students who report to the class is your job.

Even within smaller groups, speaking and presentation skills can come into play. My students create products, such as author centers or themed units, that I want them to share. When we do not have time for every person to come to the front of the room, I sometimes organize a conference-type setting. Two or three people present their work at a time, using the front and back of the classroom and maybe a hallway. The rest of the class chooses which presentation is most beneficial for what they need to learn and play the part of the audience, interacting with the speaker, asking questions and giving feedback and suggestions. We have an agreed-upon rule that no speaker is left without an audience—if students notice that the groups are unbalanced, some move over to the person who needs listeners. Though the groups are small, the presenter is definitely in charge and has the responsibilities of a public speaker; she must be well prepared and must strive to be interesting and use strategies to engage the audience.

There are strategies you can teach your students that can enhance the presentations they give in your content area classes. Encourage them to prepare well, to outline their main ideas and to rehearse what they will say, to use notecards or visual aids when appropriate, to project their voices and speak with expression. Show them how to introduce a subject with an anecdote, a stimulating question or quotation, or a bit of humor. Students generally love to prepare PowerPoint® or other computer-enhanced presentations; much thinking goes into the organization and preparation stages, and the visual format complements the speaker's words, while possibly lessening the anxiety the speaker might feel. No matter what format is being used, presenters should monitor their audience and make adjustments if they see that there is confusion or interest decreases. Of course, each time you present material in class, model strategies for the students—point out techniques as you use them for the students to evaluate and consider for their own use.

You may have to teach the students to make eye contact with the audience, to read or speak with clarity and expression, and to exhibit an air of authority. With practice and modeling and mentoring from you, good progress can be anticipated.

Speaking to Parents and Community

The more authentic you can make the setting and purpose of lessons and experiences involving public speaking, the better results you get. Sharon Morley's ninth graders invite parents and community members to their school each spring for a portfolio celebration. Their written work from throughout the school year is on display, and as adults ask them about particular pieces or about their writing processes, they answer them with a sophistication and seriousness appropriate for the occasion. Similarly, many schools are replacing or supplementing traditional parent–teacher conferences with student-led conferences. A report card might be available, but the student provides a context for the grades by explaining what kinds of work were done and what his self-assessment is at this point in the academic year. In a different example requiring presentation skills, students from Albany County spoke at a press conference in the New York state capital asking for support for a cause, Free the Children, an international network of children helping children that is attempting to end child labor (*The Voice*, 1999). Enhancing speaking skills should not be a goal reserved for those few students who will give graduation speeches and accept scholastic, athletic, or service awards—all of your students must know how to present themselves, their thoughts, and their work well.

Storytelling

Storytelling is a wonderful oral activity for content area classes. I encourage you to become known in your school as a teacher who can make her subject come alive with stories, whether factual or fictional. For example, if you're planning to be a social studies teacher, telling tidbits like the following in the context of your lecture about Henry VIII and his six wives will ensure that none of your students will leave you with the far too common belief that history is boring:

> Henry . . . had Anne [Boleyn] accused of infidelity with five men, one of them her own brother. She and all her supposed lovers were convicted of treason and condemned to death. . . . Anne did not repine at her fate and cheerfully acknowledged the boon that Henry granted her in allow-

ing her to be decapitated by a sword instead of an ax. "The king has been very good to me," she said. "He promoted me from a simple maid to be a marchioness. Then he raised me to be a queen. Now he will raise me to be a martyr." (Fadiman, 1985, p. 69)

You don't have to memorize your content-related stories word for word—develop your own style and flair. At least some students will be inspired to join you—have them prepare relevant stories to share at school functions or with other classes, either at their grade level or perhaps in lower grades. Their confidence and speaking skills will soar with the practice and the reinforcement and appreciation shown by audiences. Some school districts have annual school-wide storytelling competitions or celebrations. Figure 8.8 lists resources you and your students can mine for content-area storytelling purposes.

Reading Aloud

You may be surprised, especially if you are preparing to teach something other than English, at the many ways you can fit various types of drama or public reading into your classes. For example, if you teach biology, you might show students how to read Paul Fleischman's *I Am Phoenix: Poems for Two Voices* (1985), which is all about birds, and *Joyful Noise: Poems for Two Voices* (1988), which contains a wealth of information on various insects. Pair the students and they can entertain each other as they learn while having fun and practicing their oral reading. You might also choose to take the show on the road—to other classrooms or to the local mall. Other texts useful for students reading aloud are stories where multiple voices are represented. For example, *Crossing the Delaware: A History in Many Voices* (1998), by Louise Peacock, helps students understand a variety of perspectives as they read. Students might be assigned various roles, and given time to practice the expressive reading of their parts so that all listeners can understand the historical setting and the complexities of human nature and social interaction involved.

Readers Theatre

Readers theatre is an enjoyable way to help students actively participate in their content learning and to practice speaking and listening skills. Scripts based on other texts can be found or designed to be read by individuals taking on the various roles of historical, scientific, artistic, or literary figures. Readers do not memorize their lines, though reading silently

FIGURE 8.8 *Storytelling resources.*

Bruchac, J. B. (1995). Native Plant Stories. In M. J. Caduto & J. B. Bruchac, *Keepers of Life.* Golden, CO: Fulcrum Publishers.

Bruchac, J. B. (1997). *Tell Me a Tale: A Book About Storytelling.* San Diego, CA: Harcourt Brace.

Creeden, S. (1994). *Fair Is Fair: World Folktales of Justice.* Little Rock, AR: August House Publishers, Inc.

Fadiman, C. (Ed.). (1985). *The Little, Brown Book of Anecdotes.* Boston: Little, Brown.

Gillard, M. (1996). *Story Teller, Story Teacher: Discovering the Power of Storytelling for Teaching and Living.* York, ME: Stenhouse.

Helgesen, M. (1995). *Active Listening: Introducing Skills for Understanding* (Sound Recording). New York: Cambridge University Press.

MacDonald, M. R. (1992). *Peace Tales: World Folktales to Talk About.* Hamden, CT: Linnet Books.

Pellowski, A. (1984). *The Story Vine: A Source Book of Unusual and Easy-to-Tell Stories from Around the World.* New York: Collier Books.

Pellowski, A. (1990). *Hidden Stories in Plants.* New York: Macmillan.

Pellowski, A. (1995). *The Storytelling Handbook.* New York: Simon & Schuster.

Roe, B. D., Alfred, S., & Smith, S. (1998). *Teaching through Stories: Yours, Mine, and Theirs.* Norwood, MA: Christopher-Gordon.

Shannon, G. (1990). *More Stories to Solve: Fifteen Folktales from Around the World.* New York: Greenwillow Books.

Storytelling: Learning and Sharing (Videorecording). (1995). Fallbrook, CA: Coyote Creek Productions.

Trousdale, A. M., Woestehoff, S. A., & Schwartz, M. (1994). *Give a Listen: Stories of Storytelling in School.* Urbana, IL: National Council of Teachers of English.

first is a good idea so that they read smoothly and with good expression. Allow students flexibility in terms of how they perform—where to stand, whether to use simple props, how to deliver certain lines. Figure 8.9 lists resources you can use to introduce and implement readers theatre in your classes.

Readers theatre can make your text, your subject, and your students come alive. Students can create their own scripts, full of dialogue, based on the texts they read and then present dramatic readings to an audience. Any genre, even newspaper articles or textbook passages, can be used as the stimulus text. There's no end to the number of possible creative touches students may include. Recently, a group of my social studies preservice teachers discussed Avi's *Nothing But the Truth* (1991) in a literature circle, and chose to share their experience with the class in a readers theatre presentation. They used information from the book to create a dialogue between two of the many characters locked in controversy. While two group members read their parts, the others stood just outside the classroom door humming "The Star-Spangled Banner," which thematically was very appropriate. An added benefit was that others in the class were convinced to read the book, based on this enthusiastic performance.

Nolan and Patterson (2000) found that skits incorporated into an English as a Foreign Language (EFL) or ESL program were helpful. Because there were fixed sets of lines so that students did not have to create expressions, but could instill their own emotions and creative interpretations, both the form and communicating the message were practiced. Students rehearsed parts in a classroom with the researchers and a teacher who served as monitors and models and emphasized correct pronunciation. The skits were adapted to meet the students' needs, and choruses were added to ensure that all could take a participatory role. During final rehearsals, two surprises were noted. When a student playing a lead role was absent, others were able to step in and take over. Also, students who did not have main roles started prompting those who did, leading the researchers to conclude that many students had learned all the lines of the skit, though they had not been assigned to do so.

Data analysis based on focus group interviews showed that student perceptions concentrated on overcoming the fear of speaking English, the teamwork displayed, and communicative awareness, with statements showing that the students had learned to pay attention to the meaning, not just the words. Students also commented on contextual learning, improved pronunciation, new vocabulary, and nonverbal communication. Nolan and Patterson conclude:

This study implies that teachers could achieve similar effects by rearranging a classroom for a short dramatization and inviting spectators from

Book Talk 8.2

What do you think Galileo sounded like as he talked to friends and foes, trying to convince them that Aristotle was wrong? How might Gregor Mendel have explained his formulation of the theory of heredity? How did conversations about radioactivity go between Marie and Pierre Curie? Storyteller Kendall Haven's *Great Moments in Science: Experiments and Readers Theatre* (1996) provides scripts that students can use to speak as famous scientists and those who learned from them. In each chapter, he gives scientific background on a topic—Benjamin Franklin's discovery of electricity in 1750, Dorothy Hodgkin's discovery of the composition of penicillin in 1943, or Maria Mitchell's discovery of a comet in 1847—then provides a script to help the scenes become real, and to help students take part in the excitement, passion, and controversy that come with breakthroughs in knowledge. The scripts are followed by instruction on conducting related experiments that enable the students to be scientists. Finally, each chapter contains a "Bridges to Books" section that gives keywords, concepts, and questions to begin library exploration, and a "References for Further Reading" list. The chapters help students to see scientists as real people who use procedural knowledge in their jobs and their own learning throughout their lives. The figures in the book may pass along their intellectual curiosity to those portraying them and those watching the skits, which show how the scientists engaged in critical thinking, overcame natural and political problems, and made connections among data and disciplines. Students can participate in the hands-on, voices-on activities provided, then use the model structure to write chapters for class books on other topics, in various disciplines. This book can lead to "great moments" in your courses.

beyond the class grouping, so that students have an audience other than their classmates. When they have to dramatize a skit to an audience that has not seen it previously, the students' performance has to be accurate because it requires real communication. (p. 13)

Consider holding court in your content classroom. Courtroom drama is immensely popular; books, movies, and television shows abound that take advantage of this fact, so why not join them?

Your students can put book characters on trial (especially the villains or the characters they personally don't like!) through scripting and implementing a readers theatre production. They get practice speaking and listening as they take on roles, think through others' presentations and performances, and respond to the unfolding drama. They can put people's (such as Einstein's, Descartes', or Machiavelli's) theories and philosophies, as well as actions, on trial. Combine this creative activity with having them read about real trials relevant to your content areas: those of Clarence Darrow and Galileo in science; Joan of Arc, Benedict Arnold, Nathan Hale, Sacco and Vanzetti, and Nazi war criminals in social studies. If conditions are right, students at all levels show amazing creativity, sensitivity, and insight when they explore topics and create a product to share their findings.

Teachers Reading Aloud

Avi, a well-known author of young adult literature, was asked at a conference what teachers can do to encourage children to read. I expected him to advise teachers to read aloud to their students, which is good, and common, advice. But he surprised me by answering that the best thing teachers could do is to take voice lessons, something he has done. He explained how important it is to read *well* to our students of all ages, and not all teachers come by that skill naturally (Avi, 1999). So, I'll use this

Book Talk 8.3

Have you ever heard of a *documentary novel*? Avi's Newbery Honor book *Nothing But the Truth* (1991) is one. There is no narrator; the multiple points of view of parents, students, the media, teachers, and administrators are represented by newspaper articles, journal entries, letters, memos, faculty room talk, and phone conversations. The story has worked its magic for years. Avi once visited Lawrence, Kansas, where the entire town had been invited to read the book. He remarked that listening to people argue about the student's suspension and the consequences for the teacher as described in the book was like listening to people fighting over something that was actually happening, not a book plot. I highly recommend this book to future teachers because, besides being a great read, it may help you reflect on how to avoid having anyone in your class, including yourself, feel backed into a corner.

opportunity to pass these words of wisdom along to you. Teachers can enhance their own speaking and reading skills in order to make their teaching more interesting, as well as to model techniques for students. It also helps to provide students with a purpose for listening.

Erickson (1996) gives tips for selecting and reading books aloud to reluctant readers. She recommends reading hooking chapters from whole books, though not overdoing it, since students also like to hear shorter sections in their entirety; reading a variety of genres, including nonfiction, magazine articles, factual newspaper accounts involving teenagers, and poetry; allowing students to doodle as they listen; and inviting students to read aloud to their classmates. She lists criteria for selecting texts for read-alouds, such as choosing books that reflect authors from many cultures, and making sure the texts match listeners' social and emotional stages, though stretching students intellectually at times is good. Erickson offers a bibliography of texts meeting the criteria that she has used to entice her students.

> **Getting Ready to Teach 8.4** *(see page 266)*

BookTalk 8.4

Judy Richardson has a book dedicated "To middle and high school teachers who are always seeking effective ways to engage their students." In *Read It Aloud!: Using Literature in the Secondary Content Classroom* (2000), she explains what research and theory indicate about the value of reading aloud, gives principles for selecting and using read-alouds, and offers separate chapters devoted to discussing great texts for read-alouds in science; mathematics and geography; social studies; English and language arts; and music, art, health, and physical education. She also devotes a chapter to read-alouds appropriate for second language learners, and good texts for special populations. You'll find this a great resource; I predict you and your students will end up reading the entire texts of many of the books from which she selects excerpts.

Figure 8.9 lists resources that can help you and your students as you incorporate public reading, speaking, and performing into your curriculum.

FIGURE 8.9 Resources for public reading, speaking, and performing.

Barchers, S. I. (2000). *Multicultural Folktales: Readers Theatre for Elementary Students.* Englewood, CO: Teacher Idea Press.

Boyko, C., & Lolen, K. (Eds.). (2001). *Hold Fast Your Dreams: Twenty Commencement Speeches.* New York: Scholastic.

Cook, J. (1989). *The Elements of Speechwriting and Public Speaking.* New York: Macmillan.

Desberg, P. (1996). *No More Butterflies: Overcoming Stagefright, Shyness, Interview Anxiety and Fear of Public Speaking.* Oakland, CA: New Harbinger Publications.

Donovan, S. (Ed.). (1995). *Great American Women's Speeches* (Sound Recording). New York: Harper Audio.

Fleischman, P. (2000). *Big Talk: Poems for Four Voices.* Cambridge, MA: Candlewick Press.

Frederick, A. D. (1993). *Frantic Frogs and Other Frankly Fractured Folktales for Readers Theatre.* Englewood, CO: Teacher Ideas Press.

Frederick, A. D. (1997). *Tadpole Tales and Other Totally Terrific Treats for Readers Theatre.* Englewood, CO: Teacher Ideas Press.

The Greatest Speeches of All Time (Sound Recording). (1997). Rolling Bay, WI: SoundWorks International, Inc.

Haven, K. F. (1996). *Great Moments in Science: Experiments and Readers Theatre.* Englewood, CO: Teacher Ideas Press.

Kushner, M. L. (1998). *Public Speaking for Dummies.* New York: Harper Audio.

Lamm, K. (1995). *10,000 Ideas for Term Papers, Projects, Reports, and Speeches.* New York: ARCO.

Latrobe, K. H., Casey, C., & Gann, L. A. (1991). *Social Studies Readers Theatre for Young Adults: Scripts and Script Development.* Englewood, CO: Teacher Ideas Press.

Latrobe, K. H., & Laughlin, M. K. (1989). *Readers Theatre for Young Adults: Scripts and Script Development.* Englewood, CO: Teacher Ideas Press.

Mira, T. K. (1995). *Speak Now, or Forever Fall to Pieces.* New York: Random House.

Safire, W. (1997). *Lend Me Your Ears: Great Speeches in History.* New York: W. W. Norton.

Simmons, C. (1996). *Public Speaking Made Simple.* Garden City, NY: Doubleday.

PART TWO

Listening

Everything discussed in Part One on speaking and discussion implied that people were present and listening with interest and comprehension. Neither your presentations nor your students' formal and informal talk will work if listening is not valued and practiced. Listening is absolutely crucial for learning to occur, yet it is all too often assumed that students know how to listen, and that when they are not attending to what is being said, they are at fault or they are choosing to not listen. Actually, listening can be taught and developed; there are ways that you can help improve your own and your students' listening skills. This part discusses aspects of listening and gives you ideas for enhancing the listening that goes on in your classes.

STUDENTS' LISTENING

Part One talked about students and teachers together setting rules for discussion. In conjunction, it makes sense to address listening. Reasonable people agree to listen to those speaking from the standpoint of politeness, but also recognize that listening is what enables them to learn, understand, and form responses (whether they be affirmations, counterarguments, additional examples, or requests for clarification). Listeners can help the person speaking through their nonverbal behavior, such as eye contact, head nodding, leaning forward, smiling or laughing or sighing when appropriate. One of your responsibilities as a teacher is to monitor listening behavior as students discuss in groups, giving hints and strategies when needed and reinforcement when students are listening well.

You can also help your students listen effectively as part of a class group. When your presentations are well prepared and interesting, and when you speak with expression and clarity, it is far easier for students to listen. When they start giving you signals such as looking tired, looking away, or fidgeting, you know it's time to adjust—by changing your speaking strategies, soliciting questions and interaction, or moving on to another phase of the lesson that allows them to move, talk to one another, read, or write.

Guest Speakers and Recordings

It's helpful to give your students a variety of voices and people to listen to. Sharon Morley (1996) invites many people into her classroom to give booktalks. Colleagues, administrators, college professors, community workers, and parents come in to talk about what they like to read and to recommend new best-sellers or old favorites. "Some presenters use 5 or 10 minutes; some use the entire period, spinning the book talk into an encompassing lesson about history, about life, or about what happens when one loves to read" (p. 131). Students come to view these people in a new light after listening to them, and they come to understand that reading is not just a classroom activity, but something people in all walks of life do for entertainment and self-improvement outside school walls. They get practice asking questions of the speakers, now seen as fellow learners, and they get to listen to some of the speakers read passages that are personally meaningful and stimulating.

Students don't always need live speakers to listen to, although the more you can bring in authors and people who work in the fields you teach, the better. You can have many books on tape in your classroom library, representing both nonfiction and fiction related to your subject area. Some students may choose to borrow these because they are auditory learners and prefer comprehending through this format. Others might take them because they spend a lot of time in cars and can listen while traveling. You can also help individuals use their listening skills to learn content and absorb ideas by setting up listening centers in your classroom. These can include books on tape (either professional versions or those made by you and your former and present students) or CDs or software programs that require learning by listening, as well as the machines necessary for listening and recording. Tapes made by students reacting to literature or issues can also be there. Have assignments, project suggestions, writing supplies, blank tapes for student recording, and listening center rules posted at the center. Sometimes, small groups can work at the centers, while other groups are researching in the library, reading or writing silently, and conducting literature circles or collaborative investigations. Figure 8.10 lists books related to various disciplines that are available on tape or CD and are appropriate for a classroom listening center or a classroom lending library. There are many more you will discover.

Hearing or reading aloud the words of actual speeches can make the past come alive for students.

FIGURE **8.10**   *A sampling of audiotaped versions of content-related texts.*

Ackerman, D. (1995). *A Natural History of the Senses.* Los Angeles: The Publishing Mills.

Angelou, M. (1999). *The Maya Angelou Poetry Collection.* New York: Random House Audio.

Douglass, F. (1992). *Narrative of the Life of Frederick Douglass.* Ashland, OR: Blackstone Audiobooks.

Friedman, T. L. (1999). *The Lexus and the Olive Tree: Understanding Globalization.* New York: Simon & Schuster Audio.

Goodall, J., with Berman, P. (1999). *Reason for Hope: A Spiritual Journey.* New York: Time Warner Audiobooks.

In Their Own Voices: A Century of Recorded Poetry. (1996). Los Angeles: Rhino. Word Beat.

Joseph, L., & Vidal, L. (2001). *The Color of My Words.* New York: Listening Library.

McBride, J. (1996). *The Color of Water: A Black Man's Tribute to His White Mother.* Beverly Hills, CA: Dove Audio.

Miller, A. (1995). *The Crucible.* New York: Caedmon.

Rowling, J. K., & Dale, J. (1999). *Harry Potter and the Sorcerer's Stone.* Old Greenwich, CT: Listening Library/Random House.

Sagan, C. (1998). *Life in the Universe: Essays.* Mendocino, CA: Audio Scholar.

Tolkien, J. R. R. (2001). *J. R. R. Tolkien's The Lord of the Rings* (Original Soundtrack Recording). Berkeley, CA: Fantasy Records.

Watson, J. D. (2000). *The Double Helix: The Story Behind the Discovery of DNA.* Novato, CA: Soundelux Audio Publishing.

The Words and Music of World War II. (1991). New York: SONY Music Entertainment/Columbia Records.

Rather than merely reading about the era of McCarthyism in our country, for example, students can listen to their science or history teacher read the words the Nobel prize–winning chemist Linus Pauling spoke to a Senate Internal Affairs Subcommittee in 1960 when he was interrogated about his methods of collecting signatures of scientists throughout the world on an antinuclear petition that was presented to the United Nations. Students getting to know this aspect of Linus Pauling will cheer to find out that three years later he won the Nobel Peace Prize, which he valued even more highly than the Nobel he had previously won for his work in chemistry. They may very well want to hear more from this man.

Interviews

Another way to help students understand the value of listening is to introduce them to the art of interviewing. Figure 8.11 lists titles of books that contain interviews with people in a number of professions or special circumstances. Students may find that they enjoy reading this genre because it allows them to listen in as they read people's actual spoken words in answer to questions. The books also may give them ideas for their own interviewing. Encourage your students to interview each other, you, other teachers and staff members, politicians, community professionals, their own and others' parents and siblings, or people in nursing homes who wish to share their personal histories. Your students will learn a tremendous amount about other people and their reading preferences and ideas at the same time they

BookTalk   8.5

I'm sure you've seen good interviews, and bad, on television. How well an interview turns out is often highly dependent on the skills of the questioner, and the genre is an interesting one for students to investigate. *The Norton Book of Interviews* (1996) is an anthology that allows your students to do just that, while learning content from the words of famous people. They can write out what they would ask Hitler during his years of rising power, then read his words (and his interviewer's description of him) in the 1932 interview with George Sylvester Viereck that appeared in *Liberty.* They can place themselves in Picasso's studio with the interviewer Jerome Seckler in 1945 as the artist talks about what his paintings mean and don't mean. They can be transported to Grand Central Station in 1926 as novelist Willa Cather tells an interviewer from *The Nebraska State Journal* about being in the process of writing a book she's called *Death Comes for the Archbishop.* Conversation becomes the medium for learning in this book of interviews, and who doesn't like to eavesdrop on a good conversation?

are practicing their own communication and literacy abilities. So, find ways whenever you can to fit interviewing into your curriculum.

One of the most talented, versatile, and well-known radio interviewers is Studs Terkel. In *Five Decades of Interviews with Studs Terkel*, consisting of five cassettes, you and your students can listen to the voices of those who might otherwise be merely names in a history book or on the cover of novels. You can hear writer James Baldwin and singer Mahalia Jackson speaking of Civil Rights issues in the 1960s, and ask your students to think about what they might have to say about race relations, humanity, and social justice today. Listen to renowned neurologist Oliver Sacks pondering the mystery of cases like Martin, an institutionalized retarded patient with an extraordinary talent for music appreciation, and learn from economist John Kenneth Galbraith, writer Maya Angelou, actor Woody Allen, playwright Arthur Miller. You can hear the interviewees' laughter, and the skillful probes Terkel uses. The names that the students see in their history and literature books become live people, expressing opinions and explaining how they go about constructing knowledge in their various disciplines.

FIGURE 8.11   *Books containing interviews.*

Bode, J. (1989). *New Kids on the Block: Oral Histories of Immigrant Teens.* New York: Franklin Watts.

Bode, J. (1990). *The Voices of Rape.* New York: Franklin Watts.

Bode, J. (1991). *Truce: Ending the Sibling War.* New York: Franklin Watts.

Bode, J. (1992). *Kids Still Having Kids: People Talk About Teen Pregnancy.* New York: Franklin Watts.

Bode, J. (1993). *Death Is Hard to Live With: Teenagers and How They Cope with Death.* New York: Delacorte Press.

Bode, J. (1995). *Trust and Betrayal: Real Life Stories of Friends and Enemies.* New York: Delacorte Press.

Bode, J. (1996). *Hard Time: A Real Life Look at Juvenile Crime and Violence.* New York: Delacorte Press.

Bode, J. (1997). *Food Fight: A Guide to Eating Disorders for Pre-teens and Their Parents.* New York: Simon & Schuster.

Bode, J. (1999). *The Colors of Freedom: Immigrant Stories.* New York: Franklin Watts.

Bode, J., & Mack, S. (1994). *Heartbreak and Roses: Real Life Stories of Troubled Love.* New York: Delacorte Press.

Bode, J., & Mack, S. (2001). *For Better, for Worse: A Guide to Surviving Divorce for Pre-teens and Their Families.* New York: Simon & Schuster.

Coan, P. M. (1997). *Ellis Island Interviews: In Their Own Words.* New York: Checkmark Books.

Hersch, P. (1999). *A Tribe Apart: A Journey into the Heart of American Adolescence.* New York: Ballantine Books.

Kelley, B. P. (1998). *They Too Wore Pinstripes: Interviews with 20 Glory-days New York Yankees.* Jefferson, NC: McFarland & Co.

Kline, S. (Ed.). (1999). *George Lucas: Interviews. Conversations with Filmmakers Series.* Jackson: University Press of Mississippi.

Landau, E. (1988). *Teenagers Talk About School . . . And Open Their Hearts About Their Closest Concerns.* Englewood Cliffs, NJ: Messner.

Lennon, J. (2001). *All We Are Saying: The Last Major Interview with John Lennon and Yoko Ono Conducted by David Sheff*, B. Golson (Ed.). New York: St. Martin's.

Levi, P. (2001). *The Voice of Memory: Interviews 1961–87/Primo Levi* M. Belpoliti & R. Gordon (Eds.), (R. Gordon, Trans.). New York: New Press.

McGilligan, P. (2000). *Film Crazy: Interviews with Hollywood Legends.* New York: St. Martin's.

Pauling, L. (1995). *Linus Pauling in His Own Words: Selections from His Writings, Speeches, and Interviews*, B. Marinacci (Ed.). New York: Simon & Schuster.

Robertson, J. (1996). *Twentieth Century Artists on Art.* New York: G. K. Hall.

Silvester, C. (Ed.). (1996). *The Norton Book of Interviews: An Anthology from 1859 to the Present Day.* New York: Norton.

Spielberg, S. (2000). *Steven Spielberg: Interviews*, L. D. Freedman & B. Notbohm (Eds.). Jackson: University Press of Mississippi.

Westcott, R. (2000). *Splendor on the Diamond: Interviews with 35 Stars of Baseball's Past.* Gainesville: University Press of Florida.

Zinn, H. (1999). *The Future of History: Interviews with David Barsamian.* Monroe, ME: Common Courage Press.

BookTalk 8.6

What questions would you have for people whose job description includes "adventurer"? What if you could talk with an arachnologist about his fascination with tarantulas? What might you learn from an underwater photographer, an ethologist, a wildlife filmmaker, an archaeologist, a rainforest ecologist, a bioacoustician, a paleontologist? *Talking with Adventurers,* edited by Pat and Linda Cummings (1998), consists of interviews with these people and more. They start with some basic questions, such as "What was the job that got you started in your field?" and "What was the scariest thing that ever happened in your work?" and then let the words of the experts tell their stories, their ambitions, their reflections on problem-solving processes and discoveries. There are terrific photographs, maps, and a glossary. If you enjoy the format of this book, you might also like the Cummings' three volumes of *Talking with Artists.*

Strategies for Improving Students' Listening Skills

There are several structured approaches to helping students be active listeners and aiding listening comprehension. One way is to use an anticipatory guide, just like those shown in Chapter 1 that are used before reading assignments. Such guides activate relevant schema, as well as pique students' interest in the topics and concepts they will hear about. Even more simply, give your students a purpose for listening and tell them what particular information or organizational framework (e.g., cause–effect, compare–contrast) to listen for in a selection. Here is an example from an eleventh-grade New York State Regents English Exam (University of the State of New York, 2001, p. 2) excerpted from the directions given before a listening task, that gives a purpose for listening:

> **Overview:** For this part of the test, you will listen to a speech about writing effective dialogue . . . and write a response based on the situation described below. You will hear the speech twice. You may take notes . . . anytime you wish during the readings.
>
> **The Situation:** As a member of a class on fiction writing, you have been asked by your teacher to prepare an instructional manual for your classmates on the reasons and techniques for using dialogue to improve their writing. In preparation for writing the

manual, listen to a speech by published writer Anne LaMott [sic]. Then use relevant information from the speech to write your instructional manual.

> **Your Task:** Write an instructional manual for your classmates in which you give some reasons and techniques for using dialogue to improve their writing.

An activity called *listen–read–discuss* (LRD) was developed by Alvermann (1987). The teacher lectures on a selected portion of the text. Students then read the material, comparing what is written with what they heard. The final step involves a discussion of the content and what was learned through both routes. For example, an earth science teacher might give a mini-lecture about a trip he took to Mammoth Cave National Park in Kentucky, concentrating on the rock formations he saw, the geological history of the caves, and how it felt to him. Then, students read information from an Internet site about the park or from the book *Mammoth Cave* (Wagoner & Cutliff, 1985). They then discuss what they learned, asking the teacher questions stimulated by their reading.

Getting Ready to Teach 8.5 (see page 266)

TEACHERS LISTENING TO STUDENTS

How early can listening help teaching? Listening to infants and toddlers provides much information about their language and their needs, and informs what should come next in terms of interaction and informal teaching and learning. So, listening helps at any age.

I'll give you an example of a teacher learning from listening to emergent readers in a first-grade classroom. Researcher Pamela Michel (1994) developed what she called *listening questions* (p. 23) to elicit perceptions from children about what reading meant to them. After spending time in their classroom and establishing rapport and a comfortable relationship, she casually asked them, "What is reading?" Listening very carefully to their answers allowed her to ask follow-up questions and probe for fuller explanations. One child astounded her by relating, "I used to think reading was making sense of a story, but now I know it's just letters" (p. 2). Listening to students enabled Michel to conclude how their perceptions were related to the instruction they were receiving and to make recommendations for changes in literacy pedagogy. The children's answers were so insightful and provocative that they formed the basis for Michel's book *The Child's View of Reading: Understandings for Teachers and Parents* (1994).

It's never too early to listen to students, and it's never too late. No matter what the age of your students, by developing your ability to use listening questions, you can use student perceptions and talk to inform your teaching decisions for individuals and for your whole class. Tune in as middle school teacher Jeff Wilhelm (1997) listens to a student explain what the reading process is like for him:

> When you're not into a book yet, it's really obvious [laughs]. It's like you're standing in line on a diving board on a windy day.... It's like you're in pain and you have your arms wrapped around you and the concrete is scratching your feet. The first part of the story is the line and the ladder and the board. When everything comes together and you jump it's like you're in this underwater world like INSTANTLY and then you just stay down there and never come up until someone makes you. (p. 55)

Wilhelm describes how he studied his engaged readers by listening to them, and then asked himself how this could help him teach those less engaged. For example, engaged readers indicated that when they were confused about something they just simply read on, trusting that the author would eventually reveal enough for them to resolve the confusion. The practiced readers could tolerate uncertainty, but the less engaged students often gave up at this point, unable to deal with the ambiguity. Another discovery he made was that

> for less engaged readers, the dimensions of response are order-dependent; I found that the less engaged readers I studied did not respond in connective or reflective ways to their reading unless they first overtly responded on all of the evocative dimensions.... The collected information reveals that we often ask less engaged readers to reflect on something that they have not experienced. This suggests that if we would help them to develop evocative, experiential response to literature, response on other dimensions would be possible for them—and the door to engaging literary worlds would finally be opened. (p. 88)

Wilhelm concludes:

> Through my research, I was helped to see that I needed to be more open and student-centered as a teacher, getting to know each student and what they could do so that I could teach them "where they were," responding to them personally and offering more opportunities for descriptive and artistic response, for free reading and sharing. The research methods themselves helped me to get to know my students as readers. (pp. 85–86)

I encourage you to have a section of your teaching journal devoted to things you hear your students say. Or start a file on your computer for interesting and thought-provoking quotes, questions, and concerns expressed by your students. Some are precious gems you'll smile or laugh over in years to come as the quotes bring back the memories and the faces; others will cause you to reflect, to examine your practices and your ideas of literacy. All will help you know and understand your students better.

ACTION RESEARCH » » » 8.B

Be an observer-researcher at some discussion you are not a part of. It may be a literature circle in a middle school or it may be at a party where a group has informally formed because of a common interest in a topic. Being as unobtrusive as possible, listen and watch carefully to understand the dynamics. The following guide questions may help you focus:

1. Is the talking fairly evenly distributed or is it dominated by one or two people? If the latter is the case, does this seem to be all right with the others? Is a leader emerging?

2. What do the facial expressions and nonverbal communication tell you?

3. Are several divergent opinions being expressed? Is there disagreement? Are people's opinions and thoughts being listened to and valued and accepted?

4. Is any new ground being broken? Is the talk leading to new insights about the topic?

PART THREE

Putting It Together

I hope you've been able to see throughout this chapter how listening and speaking are complementary and work together, often in combination with reading, writing, viewing, and hands-on exploration, toward growth of knowledge and learning. Now, I'd like to share several ideas, strategies, and stories that show many literacy components working together naturally in classroom settings.

COLLABORATIVE SPEAKING AND LISTENING PROJECTS

A business interviewee told a researcher, "We're doing more with groups and teams . . . and we'd like employees who know how to talk and negotiate and synthesize ideas. . . . The bottom line . . . is not standard English—though that is important—but critical thinking, the management of ideas" (Morris & Tchudi, 1996, p. 232). You can help students realize that they are developing skills that will be used throughout their lives at the same time they are learning content and academic skills in your class.

Jigsaw

Here's an example appropriate for a high school biology or English class or for an interdisciplinary activity. All students read at least part of James Watson's *The Double Helix: A Personal Account of the Discovery of the Structure of DNA* (1980), write reactions in their learning logs, and discuss responses in terms of content and literary features. Then, the teacher assigns pairs of students (teams like Watson and Crick, the partners in the discovery) to read commentaries and reviews that followed the book's publication. *The Norton Critical Edition of The Double Helix* (1980) has about 20 of these compiled with the text itself, many with appealing, intriguing names, such as "'Honest Jim' Watson's Big Thriller about DNA," "Notes of a Not-Watson," "Honest Jim and the Tinker Toy Model," "Riding High on a Spiral," "Truth, Truth, What Is Truth (About How the Structure of DNA Was Discovered)?" and "Three Other Perspectives" written by scientists Francis Crick, Linus Pauling, and Aaron Klug. Student partners write a summary and react to this "new" information relative to the class discussion of the book itself. Each pair presents the main points of the new

data or perspective they learned about, and another whole class discussion occurs relative to the book, the man, the subject, and the scientific community that responded to *The Double Helix*. The teacher should make the entire book available for optional reading. She then can give the following booktalk about a second autobiographical account:

> What must it feel like to be the discoverer of something that was previously unknown? What characteristics must a person have to persist in looking for something that has eluded great minds for ages? Students know what it means to collaborate in the classroom, but what does collaboration look like in the scientific world? Francis Crick's memoir, *What Mad Pursuit: A Personal View of Scientific Discovery* (1988), lets readers in on the thoughts and feelings of the co-discoverer of the structure of DNA; it lets the reader inside a brilliant mind. You can learn science concepts as you join Crick and Watson as they unravel a mystery through implementation of the scientific process. You'll also enjoy amusing anecdotes and personal reminiscences and reflections from this author who is a gifted popular science writer. Let yourself in on this "mad pursuit."

Survival!

A project I've used in literature and education classes uses some aspects of the jigsaw model. To prepare students for this "Survival!" unit, I supply the following prompt: "Have you ever been lost? Take a moment to close your eyes and remember the experience. Where were you? How did you feel? What decisions did you make? How did you get back to your loved ones?" I've found that virtually everyone has a story about being lost, whether in a park or shopping mall, long ago at age four or just last month. I give students a chance to recount their adventures and recall the emotions involved, then I follow this oral sharing with a writing prompt: "Imagine that you are stranded and must survive in an isolated area with no human contact. Visualize yourself in one of these settings: a small tropical island in a part of the ocean where planes rarely if ever fly, a vast dark forest, or the frozen north. Spend some time writing to anticipate problems and possible solutions. How will you survive?"

Next, I give booktalks for several novels involving a survival theme. I've used *Hatchet* (1987) by

Gary Paulsen, *Julie of the Wolves* (1972) by Jean Craighead George, *The Iceberg Hermit* (1974) by Arthur Roth, *The Cay* (1991) by Theodore Taylor, *Island of the Blue Dolphins* (1990) by Scott O'Dell, and *My Side of the Mountain* (1988) by Jean Craighead George. You might also include recent nonfiction selections, such as *The Perfect Storm* (1997) by S. Junger, *Into Thin Air* (1998) by J. Krakauer, and *Shipwreck at the Bottom of the World* (1998) by Jennifer Armstrong, all of which contain much science and social studies–related material. The books should represent a range in terms of style and difficulty. Students select one of the books to read, exchange e-mail addresses with classmates who make the same choice, and read and write responses to their group. After a sufficient amount of time, which varies depending on students' literacy skills and other things going on in the curriculum, I allow interest groups to meet and talk—they use the responses they've been sharing via e-mail as a starting point. While they talk, I hang up a chart the length of one wall, either in the classroom or in the hall. Down the left-hand side, I list the titles of the books. Across the top are questions for each group to answer by filling in the appropriate block on the chart. These questions include:

- What is the setting (time and place) of your story?
- How did the protagonist in your story get stranded?
- For how long was your main character in isolation?
- How did your protagonist get food?
- What tools did your protagonist find, make, or use?
- What kinds of shelter did your character use?
- How did your character provide clothing for herself or himself?
- What animals did your character encounter? Were they enemies or friends?
- What other humans did your protagonist encounter before being rescued?
- What struggles within herself or himself did the person deal with?
- How did your protagonist change or grow?
- How was the character rescued or returned to society?
- Did you find the story believable? Give an example to show why or why not.
- How would you describe the emotional reactions your group had to reading this story?
- What content knowledge (e.g., science, social studies) did you gain from this book?

- How would you rate this book? Why should others read it or not read it?

Each cooperative learning group decides how to answer the questions and fill in the chart. If there is not consensus, they decide what to do about that. They may choose, for instance, to put down the majority opinion, or to explain the reason for division within the group. When the chart is completed and all have read and admired it, we hold a compare–contrast discussion. Students who read *Hatchet* and thought that 56 days was a long time for the fictional Brian to be alone in the woods are impressed with the information about Karana of *Island of the Blue Dolphins* (based on a true story) being isolated for 18 years. Sometimes, we stage a television "talk show," hosted by a student volunteer, where students role-play the characters getting together to talk about their harrowing adventures. Often students, after listening to other groups, decide to read several other choices for pleasure. So, talk about literature continues outside the classroom long after my unit has ended.

I also provide a wall map of the world, and each group tacks a sign on the spot where their story takes place. Students can discuss how some of the problems encountered were directly related to geographical locations, climates, and seasons. They talk about what they learned about plants, animals, and the human spirit in the face of adversity. They use reference books and nonfiction trade books to research topics they found fascinating. In addition, some may choose to do an artistic interpretation of their story, responding to it in the form of a painting, diorama, drawing, mobile, or model. Students find that as they synthesize ideas through art, reading, writing, talking, listening, and working cooperatively with their groups, they not only survive the "Survival!" unit, they thrive on the experience.

Social Action and Critical Literacy Projects

Powell, Cantrell, and Adams (2001) recount a project initiated by fourth graders in central Kentucky when they learned in class that Black Mountain, the highest peak in Kentucky, was slated to be strip mined. They were used to inquiry-based learning, and decided they wanted "to learn about the issue so that they might address it from a position of knowledge rather than ignorance" (p. 776). They employed interviewing skills as they sought the perspectives of both the miners whose livelihood depended on the coal industry and the environmentalists who opposed the destruction of the mountain. Once they had done their research, they went into a critical literacy mode—taking action to save Black Mountain:

They wrote to individuals to solicit funds to continue their campaign and subsequently collected thousands of dollars for the project. They alerted local newspapers and television stations and arranged for press conferences to talk about the mountain's future, and they even organized a "Hands Across the Mountain" rally with students from Eastern Kentucky to raise public awareness. (p. 777)

These elementary school children wrote to their governor and state representatives to make their opposition known, and met with mining company officials to hear their perspectives, present their findings, and ask for a response. They submitted a 10-page proposal to the Director of Permits of the Department for Surface Reclamation and Enforcement, making recommendations that reflected their awareness of the complexities of the environmental and economic issues involved.

Later, the students collaborated with eighth graders from Eastern Kentucky to speak to legislators and urge them to develop the mountain for tourism rather than strip mining. Other oral language activities included storytelling sessions, presentations to Harlan County residents, presentations at universities, and talking with families in the mountain region to learn how local activists had fought back. Of course, much reading and writing were done simultaneously. Powell et al. point out that the struggling readers and writers may have benefitted the most because they shared perceptions of changed behavior and literacy motivation during the project, which they recognized as real and important. As the student with special needs whose letter to a professor resulted in raising $500 learned, literacy can make a difference. The authors conclude, "As with the Saving Black Mountain Project, critical literacy often leads to social action as students begin to discover and internalize the problems of society, thereby leading to more transformative uses of written and oral language" (p. 779).

> **Getting Ready to Teach 8.6** (see page 266)

SPEAKING AND LISTENING WITH ENGLISH LANGUAGE LEARNERS

When there is much productive social and academic talking and listening in your classroom, English language learners benefit enormously. Their teachers and peers should combine verbal and nonverbal communication as much as possible. So, when you are giving directions or instruction, use pictures, flow charts, time lines, concrete objects, and maps as often as appropriate. Use gestures, facial expressions, and movements to convey meaning. Repeat words and phrases when necessary, use simulation, and watch closely and ask questions of your ELLs to determine how much scaffolding is necessary and whether the talk in your classroom at various times is within their zone of proximal development.

Group work, where conversation occurs during hands-on activities, is ideal for your second language learners because it provides "important elements for language acquisition—a functional communication situation, comprehensible input, and social interaction around a purposeful task" (Peregoy & Boyle, 1997, p. 52, italics in original). Writing and talking are often going on simultaneously, so can be mutually reinforcing. You might provide your ELLs with a buddy or a home group that remains fairly stable rather than constantly putting them with different people, at least until they feel supported and comfortable.

A good example of the richness of oral language at work can be found in process-oriented science classrooms using an inquiry approach. Perogoy and Boyle explain:

Students work in pairs or groups to define a problem, state a hypothesis, gather data, record observations, draw conclusions relating data to the hypothesis, and explain and summarize findings. . . . Scientific inquiry processes require students to use academic language to convey the thinking involved in observing, classifying, comparing, measuring, inferring, predicting, concluding, synthesizing, and summarizing. (p. 119)

The success of inquiry-based science projects for ELLs is attributable to three major factors: (1) Students investigate real science problems that engage their natural curiosity about the world, such as plant growth, the solar system, electricity, and magnetism; (2) students are actively engaged in investigations involving hands-on activities, actual observations, and lab work rather than solely reading facts and theories in a textbook; and (3) students carry out investigations in groups that promote talking out their thinking and planning. What we see, then, is that inquiry-based science provides many opportunities for higher-level thinking through the use of context-embedded oral language aimed at solving scientific problems, creating ideal opportunities for both language and content learning (pp. 119–120).

Hadaway, Vardell, and Young (2001) advocate scaffolding oral language development for students learning English through the use of content-related poetry. Rather than students focusing on what they don't know about the English language, they are learning about the world and academics *through* powerful language and using language to discover new concepts. They note the example of science teachers in a predominantly ESL setting beginning lessons by chanting poems about scientific topics. "Discussing poems allows students to use the language—both basic communicative and academic—that they are learning to move to higher levels of proficiency" (p. 798). Teachers can highlight new vocabulary, talk about the tone of a poem, and note nonverbal markers such as italics for intonation and emphasis. They can use poetry to encourage students to be problem solvers, rather than mere information receivers, as they guess at meanings and hypothesize, fill in gaps, and approximate meanings—all while enjoying the poetry. Teaching strategies include modeling with poems you enjoy personally, having the whole class read in unison, or having certain groups join in on repeated lines or refrains, groups taking turns reading stanzas with good volume and expression, individuals practicing and reciting solo lines, and innovative alternatives created by the students themselves. Of course, discussion is crucial as students examine the crafts of certain poets, explore possible interpretations and share responses, and think about creating their own content-related poems.

Hadaway et al. recommend that classrooms contain a listening center (Steinbergh, 1994) that highlights poetry and includes some of the plentiful collections of bilingual poetry available today, including *My Mexico—Mexico Mio* by Tony Johnston (1996), *This Tree Is Older than You Are* collected by Naomi Shihab Nye (1998), and *Canto Familiar* by Gary Soto (1995). They recommend exploring more creative teaching ideas at the Potato Hill Poetry website: www.potatohill.com. They conclude:

> All students can enjoy the incredible variety of contemporary and multicultural poetry being written for young people. For English L2 learners, in particular, oral poetry sharing can provide the necessary language practice in a context that is relaxed and pleasurable, where all learners can participate as equals in enjoying the playfulness and power of language through poetry. (p. 804)

CONCLUSION

This chapter provided ideas for profitably harnessing teens' and preteens' natural inclination toward talking, and for using listening skills well. Talk and listening can lead to learning and can connect to other components of literacy. With instruction, modeling, and both guided and independent practice, your students will recognize the importance of oral literacy and will flourish.

Your classroom should be full of productive talk. There will be opportunities for relatively formal speaking, as when students give presentations teaching others what they have learned through reading and research, and many chances for informal talking. Chandler-Olcott (2001), for example, discusses teachers choosing texts with students. The benefits of this include the opportunity to learn about the students' interests, preferences, and needs, and the chance to coach them through strategies they can use later to choose books independently. Chandler-Olcott took students to a local bookstore, where each was to choose two titles to read during a six-week summer program; she found the conversations that took place over the selection were important. If this is beyond the resources you have available, organize a similar field trip to a library. Of course, talking casually to students in your classroom library will yield rich rewards for both you and the adolescents you teach.

Getting Ready to Teach

8.1 Apply the inside–outside circle strategy to a topic in your curriculum that calls for student opinion. You might choose a text that expresses a strong but unusual position, or one that discusses several viewpoints on a controversial issue. Write directions for the students, using Figure 8.5 as a model.

8.2 Select a topic in your subject area that students could talk about in small groups. Find a relevant text to stimulate their thinking and provide a starting point for discussion. Write a plan for a lesson using a small group format. Here are some questions to guide your planning:

1. What will be the best size for the groups?
2. How shall the groups be formed: randomly, self-selected, by ability, by similar interests or goals, girls and boys separated or together?
3. What guide questions or other structure should I provide?
4. What should I be doing while the groups are meeting?
5. How (if at all) will the information obtained or discussion results be shared with the whole group?
6. What potential trouble spots can I anticipate? How might I help students who are confused or seem to be getting off-track?
7. What is the most appropriate follow-up to this lesson? What comes next?
8. How can the lesson be evaluated?

If possible, form small groups to share your plan with others, get their feedback and suggestions, and respond to other plans you hear about. Even better, if you are working with students in a practicum setting, try your lesson out. Or at least talk about it with teenagers and ask them what they think might work and what might have to be changed.

8.3 Using Figure 8.6 as a model, create a plan for a discussion web based on a text you choose or an issue that could be debated in your content area class. If possible, try it out with real students or colleagues; if not, fill the columns in yourself with reasons that could be given for differing perspectives.

8.4 Choose a text that you think would make a good read-aloud in your content area. Read for at least 10 minutes into a tape recorder. Later, listen to yourself, and evaluate the clarity and expressiveness. Would you enjoy listening to a lengthy passage read by this voice? You might listen to some audiotaped books from your public library and analyze the voices you think are particularly effective. Keep practicing, and perhaps start a collection of tapes for a listening center.

8.5 Choose a text in your subject area that you think might prove a bit difficult for students to read independently. Scaffold their learning by preparing a pre-reading lecture based on the listen–read–discuss method. Then, try the strategy by asking a student or colleague to play the role of the listener–reader. Reciprocate if a classmate needs a listener. You'll learn from participating from both perspectives.

8.6 Think about issues, perhaps involving local dilemmas such as the Kentucky children explored, that your students can investigate. Brainstorm various strategies involving talking and listening, as well as reading and writing, that your students might employ. Don't let possible constraints stop you at this point; the Kentucky example shows how youngsters can meet challenges and overcome obstacles through the power of literacy.

CHAPTER NINE

Multiliteracies: Visual, Media, and Digital

ACTIVATING PRIOR KNOWLEDGE 9.1

Recall how your past teachers used various kinds of media in content area courses. List types and examples, then think about how effective its use was. What worked well, and what seemed to be used just for the purpose of consuming time or controlling the class? How did students (you in particular) respond? Was the use of media the best way to learn the material? Did you respond actively to construct knowledge from films, videos, slides, and so forth? Or was your viewing within school contexts more of a passive activity? Finally, did your teachers do anything to prepare you for viewing, evaluating, and learning from the media, or did they let the material stand on its own? Write for a few moments, using specific examples whenever possible.

This chapter continues to broaden the definition and boundaries of the literacy concept. In Part One, I discuss educational issues related to the use of visuals: pictures, graphs, and charts. In Part Two, I deal with media literacy, concentrating on film and television. Part Three examines electronic or digital literacy and discusses the content area teacher's role in helping students construct knowledge using computers, software, and the Internet. Of course, the divisions between these areas are not discrete; artwork can be seen on videos and the Internet, text and pictures are often intertwined, and examples found in one part could also apply to others. As in earlier chapters, I talk about each type of literacy separately, knowing that the boundaries are not distinct. There are opportunities for you to synthesize what you are learning as you proceed.

Visual Literacy

We read many things besides written texts. We read the expressions on people's faces that convey that they are pleased, upset, or anxious. We pay attention to atmospheric conditions and make predictions about the weather; we read political and social atmospheres too. We ponder situations where the verbal messages and nonverbal signals seem to contradict each other. So, your students should be able to understand what you mean when you speak of constructing knowledge from sources other than print. Morris and Tchudi (1996) note the current importance of the ability to comprehend visual texts. "Although at one time they were dismissed as easy to read or only popular, these forms of texts are now deemed critical for reading in contemporary life" (p. 31). Visual displays of information are becoming increasingly important for a number of reasons, and thus the need for what we might call *graphic literacy* is crucial. According to Weaver (1999), "Business leaders complain that new employees lack this skill. This lack of skill is probably highlighted by the increased necessity to read graphics and interpret them in the workplace" (p. vi).

You may have learned in education or psychology courses about the work of Howard Gardner, whose research demonstrates several different types of intelligence. He calls into question the way schools have typically valued linguistic and logical–mathematical ways of thinking more than the other ways, including musical, bodily–kinesthetic, interpersonal, intrapersonal, naturalist, ritualistic, and spatial–visual. According to his theory of *multiple intelligences*, we all have some types of intelligences that are more developed than others, and we all learn differently. As a content area teacher, you should help your students learn using their preferred modes, while helping them to improve the intelligences most connected with your particular subject area (e.g., math, foreign language, physical education, or art). It's good to present concepts and curriculum through a multimodal approach. For a thorough exploration of Gardner's theories and findings, as well as ways to assess your students' strengths in the various intelligences, go to the source. Start with Gardner's groundbreaking *Frames of Mind: The Theory of Multiple Intelligences* (1983), then go on to his application of the theory to education in *The Unschooled Mind: How Children Think and How Schools Should Teach* (1991), and his more recent writings that show his own thinking and development. This chapter focuses on how you can tap into adolescents' spatial–visual intelligence and help them use it to learn and add to their overall literacy capabilities.

We'll start with art, with pictures, and talk about how your students can learn content while reading pictures from both efferent and aesthetic stances. Recall that Rosenblatt (1978) spoke of reading for the purpose of getting information (efferent) and for the purpose of enjoyment, or living and appreciating the experience (aesthetic).

PICTURE BOOKS FOR CONTENT AREA LEARNING

ACTIVATING PRIOR KNOWLEDGE 9.2

Make a list of your favorite picture books, stretching as far back as your memory will take you. What made them so good in your mind? Would you still enjoy them today?

Now, think of picture books that relate to scholastic subjects. Do you know of any picture books that are aimed at adolescents or adults rather than children? Brainstorm a list with others if this is feasible.

BookTalk 9.1

My favorite Howard Gardner book is *Creating Minds* (1993). He exemplifies seven of the multiple intelligences in chapters depicting the lives and thinking of masters in the domains: Freud, Einstein, Picasso, Stravinsky, T. S. Eliot, Gandhi, and Martha Graham. I've read biographies of most of these people before, but Gardner offers a unique lens to look through, and an interesting way to think about talents, intelligence, genius, and creativity.

Chapter 3 introduced the idea of using picture books in the higher grade levels for content area learning. I elaborate here, focusing on the visual aspects and benefits of the texts. The term *picture books* can either refer narrowly to those books that require illustrations in order for the text to be understood, or to those books whose words could stand alone, but whose pictures are integral to the total experience (Brown & Tomlinson, 1993; Miller, 1998). I use the latter, broader meaning here. You might have fond memories of picture books from your early childhood and elementary school days, but think that they are quite inappropriate for the middle and high school students in your math or geography or chemistry classes. Not so! Watson (1998) assures us that in Australia, "the idea of using picture books as teaching aids in classes from Year 7 to Year 12 is now widely accepted. The fear that adolescents would indignantly reject such materials has proved baseless" (p. 182). Many teachers in American high schools have been fortunate to discover the same thing—students appreciate picture books if they are selected judiciously and taught or used in ways the students recognize as relevant. There are plenty of picture books with sophisticated themes and topics that relate to the concepts inherent in your course and may motivate your students as well as help them retain information.

For example, numerous picture books have political messages that can stimulate discussion in a social studies course. Think of *The Butter Battle Book* (Seuss, 1984) that was discussed in Chapter 1. *Faithful Elephants* (Tsuchiya, 1988), *Hiroshima No Pika* (Maruki, 1980), and *My Hiroshima* (Morimoto, 1987) all take place in Japan and give a specific perspective on World War II events. They produce a more visually powerful effect than any social studies textbook could. *Shin's Tricycle* (Kodama, 1995) tells of a young child riding his toy when the atomic bomb fell— they were buried together, but the tricycle was later exhumed and put in the Peace Museum in Hiroshima. Although most of its illustrations are paintings, an actual photograph of the tricycle ends the book. You won't find many students telling you such books are too babyish for them. In fact, you may find the reverse; they may tell you these books should not be in the hands of young children, which could lead to an interesting debate.

The same holds true for picture books with environmental themes, such as *Aardvarks, Disembark!* by Ann Jonas (1990), *The Great Kapok Tree* (1990) and *A River Ran Wild* (1992) by Lynne Cherry, and *The Lorax* by Dr. Seuss (1971); or for those conveying social messages about such topics as homelessness, as in *Fly Away Home* by Eve Bunting (1991) and *We Are All in the Dumps with Jack and Guy* by Maurice Sendak (1993). The latter book was shared with fifth graders, and the children responded favorably, for reasons ranging from "'I like books that need a sharp reader and have hidden messages in the pictures' to 'I loved the significance and the pictures. But the story about being poor is sad'" (Norton, 1999, p. 222). The students were able to dis-

cuss the parts of the illustrations they felt were symbolic, such as the rats, the stars, and the newspaper headlines, and they were able to verbalize what they thought about the themes of the book.

Even alphabet picture books can be controversial, and therefore elicit thoughts, opinions, and discussion in secondary classrooms. Leo Lionni's *The Alphabet Tree* (1968) has letters spelling out "Peace on Earth, Good Will to Men," and when the lead bug is asked where he's taking the message, he responds, "To the President" (unpaged). The book's copyright date gives you a clue as to what was being protested at the time of publication.

I gave my students copies of Eve Bunting's *Smoky Night* (1994), a Caldecott Medal winner about the 1992 Los Angeles riots, which some people think is not an appropriate topic for young children (Dresang, 1999). Here are some of the responses my students wrote:

> I can remember the first day of the LA riots so vividly. My freshman year of high school.
>
> —Brian R. Schultheis

> Awesome book. Most people think the United States is war zone free. But are we really? This book depicts a war of ignorance, one that could be stopped by meeting our neighbors and trying to understand and be tolerant of our neighbors' culture. Many times adults are depicted as educators, but some of the most valuable lessons in life can come from young children, as this book shows. Furthermore, this book can deliver meaning to children, but if adults read with their minds and hearts, and if they try to listen without prejudice, the adults stand to be positively and profoundly affected.
>
> —Lonnie Stallcup

Miller (1998) points out that picture books can be used to increase vocabulary, help students appreciate the diversity of cultures, introduce abstract topics, and provide appealing, quality literature for our students' pleasure reading no matter what the subject area. In addition, picture books often lend themselves to interdisciplinary learning. I love to use *For Everything There Is a Season*, illustrated by Leo and Diane Dillon (1998), in my classes. The text is taken from the book of *Ecclesiastes* in the Hebrew scriptures. It can be taught and discussed in English class as a poem, perhaps along with the song version, "Turn! Turn! Turn!" by Pete Seeger.

Most of the picture books I've mentioned are fictional, though they do deal with topics taught in subject areas. There are also nonfiction picture books, classified as informational books, that can be very helpful and interesting. Norton (1999) gives examples of questions teachers and students can ask when evaluating such books, including

- Are facts and theory clearly distinguished?
- Are differing views on controversial subjects presented?
- Is the information as up to date as possible?
- Are the illustrations accurate?
- Does the book violate basic principles against racism and sexism? (pp. 694–695)

Actually, you might wish to present a book that *is* biased in favor of one side of an issue, and balance it with another that represents the opposing viewpoint. Students can apply their analyzing, comparing and contrasting, evaluating, and persuading skills as they discuss or write about particular texts.

Introduce a third-person account and a first-person account of a particular topic in your curriculum. For example, as you begin to teach about the 1960 court-ordered integration of public schools, share the picture book *The Story of Ruby Bridges* (1995) by psychologist Robert Coles, who met with Ruby during this year, followed by *Through My Eyes* (1999), a memoir written by Bridges herself. The former has watercolor illustrations painted by George Ford—one depicts the day when six-year-old Ruby, rather than walking steadily into the school surrounded by federal marshalls as usual, stopped in the middle of a mob of angry segregationists outside the school in order to pray for them. The latter, an autobiographical account, includes photographs (all in tones of brown) of Ruby, the placard-carrying mobs, the famous Norman Rockwell painting of Ruby in *Look* magazine, Robert Coles and the drawings she did during their sessions, Ku Klux Klan members burning a cross in protest, Eleanor Roosevelt (who wrote to Ruby), and Ruby as an adult. Each book is packed with information and story; together they offer a powerful lesson about our country's history and about the power of love in the face of hate.

You can explore and choose picture books that motivate and extend your students' understanding of academic subjects. They can analyze the perspectives and values represented, as well as the structure of the story and symbolism present in both the illustrations and the text. At the same time, you can teach them to notice the quality of the artwork and ponder the relation between text and pictures. The pictures may stay in the readers' memories and affect their thinking and behavior long after they leave your class. Figure 9.1 lists picture book titles appropriate for various subjects at the middle and high school levels. Figure 9.2 gives titles of biographies that use a picture-book format.

You might still be wondering if your secondary students will resist picture books, insisting that they have outgrown them. I've found that teacher attitude easily solves this potential problem. If *you* respect the picture books that can add information and an aesthetic experience in your courses, students will too. Sometimes, I read Barbara Brenner's *Wagon Wheels* (1978) aloud to my class, and ask them to keep a list of things they learn as they listen to this story of an African American pioneer family moving west. They hear information about dugouts built to survive a Kansas winter, the food and supplies dropped by the Osage Indians that prevented starvation, and the problems encountered (e.g., snakes, prairie fires, sickness). The story tells of three boys, ages 11, 8, and 3, whose mother has died along the way and whose father has gone ahead to look for a place to settle. The boys survive on their own and support each other, then walk 150 miles to find their father. My students cheer at the final sentence, "Looks like the Muldie boys have found their Daddy!" and are delighted when I read them the Afterword, which tells about the real Muldie family the book was based on. Then I show them the book, and they're surprised to discover that they've enjoyed an "I Can Read" book appropriate for very early readers. They trust me from then on; I hear no more talk about "baby books."

Malloy (1999) elicited a similar reaction from the middle school students in her foreign language classes when she introduced picture books written in German. She would read a section, and students would retell what they had understood, showing tolerance and enjoyment with the authentic text. "Their reactions during the event showed they had tenacity for a complex biliteracy task, making meaning with the interesting and useful language of a sophisticated art form" (p. 172). The reader–listeners wanted to repeat the vocabulary of literature and make it their own, and they were moonstruck over the pictures. Malloy's students assured her that they did not consider the exercise babyish. "We're starting to learn German, just like littler German kids, so a book like this is right for us. Can we do another?" (p. 173). The teacher went on to give them captions from the story; students created their own artwork, complete with speech bubbles, signed their German names, and posted their creations in the hall. Malloy's criteria for selection of picture books to use in foreign language classes include that the pictures should be high-quality artwork that reveals the culture of the country and language being studied, and that the language of the text should describe or pertain to what is going on in the accompanying pictures.

FIGURE 9.1   *A sampling of picture books appropriate for middle and high school subject areas.*

MATH

Anno, M. (1983). *Anno's Mysterious Multiplying Jar.* New York: Philomel Books.

Demi. (1997). *One Grain of Rice: A Mathematical Folktale.* New York: Scholastic.

Lobasco, M. L. (1999). *Mental Math Challenges.* New York: Sterling Publishers.

Markle, S. (1997). *Discovering Graph Secrets: Experiments, Puzzles, and Games Exploring Graphs.* New York: Atheneum.

Mori, T., & Anno, M. (1986). *Socrates and the Three Little Pigs.* New York: Philomel Books.

Scieszka, J., & Smith, L. (1995). *Math Curse.* New York: Viking.

Tang, G., & Briggs, H. (2001). *The Grapes of Math: Mind-stretching Math Riddles.* New York: Scholastic.

AMERICAN HISTORY AND GEOGRAPHY

Begay, S. (1995). *Navajo: Visions and Voices Across the Mesa.* New York: Scholastic.

Bartoletti, S. C. (1997). *Growing Up in Coal Country.* Boston: Houghton Mifflin.

Carey, C. W., Jr. (2000). *The Emancipation Proclamation.* Chanhassen, MN: Child's World.

Guthrie, W., & Jacobsen, K. (1998). *This Land Is Your Land.* Boston: Little, Brown.

Lester, J., & Brown, R. (1998). *From Slave Ship to Freedom Road.* New York: Dial Books.

Lourie, P. (1999). *Rio Grande: From the Rocky Mountains to the Gulf of Mexico.* Honesdale, PA: Boyds Mills.

Munro, R. (2001). *The Inside-outside Book of Texas.* New York: Sea Star Books.

Murphy, J. (1995). *The Great Fire.* New York: Scholastic.

Hall, D., & Cooney, B. (1979). *The Ox-cart Man.* New York: Viking.

Krull, K., & DiVito, A. (1999). *A Kids' Guide to America's Bill of Rights: Curfews, Censorship, and the 100-pound Giant.* New York: Avon Books.

St. George, J., & Small, D. (2000). *So You Want to Be President?* New York: Philomel Books.

Summer, L. S. (2001). *The March on Washington.* Chanhassen, MN: Child's World.

ENGLISH

Aliki. (1999). *William Shakespeare and the Globe.* New York: HarperCollins.

Bedard, M., & Cooney, B. (1992). *Emily.* New York: Doubleday.

Gwynne, F. (1976). *A Chocolate Moose for Dinner.* New York: Trumpet Club.

Scieszka, J., & Smith, L. (1989). *The True Story of the Three Little Pigs.* New York: Viking.

Langley, A., & Everett, J. (1999). *Shakespeare's Theatre.* New York: Oxford University Press.

Schnur, S., & Evans, L. (2001). *Summer: An Alphabet Acrostic.* New York: Clarion Books.

Zeman, L. (1992). *Gilgamesh the King.* Plattsburgh, NY: Tundra Books.

WORLD HISTORY, GLOBAL STUDIES, AND CULTURAL STUDIES

Ambrose, S. E. (2001). *The Good Fight: How World War II Was Won.* New York: Atheneum.

Brewster, H. (1996). *Anastasia's Album.* New York: Hyperion/Madison Press.

Cha, D. (1996). *Dia's Story Cloth: The Hmong People's Journey to Freedom.* Stitched by N. & N. T. Cha. New York: Lee & Low/Denver Museum of Natural History.

Demi. (1995). *Buddha.* New York: Henry Holt.

King, E. (1998). *Quinceañera: Celebrating Fifteen.* New York: Dutton.

Major, J. S., & Fieser, S. (1995). *The Silk Route: 7,000 Miles of History.* New York: HarperCollins.

Marx, T. (2000). *One Boy from Kosovo.* Photos by C. Karp. New York: HarperCollins.

Nicolle, D. (1997). *Medieval Knights.* New York: Viking.

Zhang, S. N. (1998). *The Children of China: An Artist's Journey.* Plattsburg, NY: Tundra/McClelland.

ART AND MUSIC

Aaseng, N. (2001). *Wildshots: The World of the Wildlife Photographer.* Brookfield, CT: Millbrook Press.

Aronson, M. (1998). *Art Attack: A Short Cultural History of the Avant-Garde.* New York: Clarion Books.

Brennen, B. (Selector). (2000). *Voices: Poetry and Art from Around the World.* Washington, DC: National Geographic Society.

Davies, A. (2000). *The Encyclopedia of Photography: An A-to-Z Visual Directory, with an Inspirational Gallery of Finished Works.* Philadelphia: Running Press.

Houston, J. (1998). *Fire into Ice: Adventure into Glass Making.* Plattsburg, NY: Tundra. *(continued)*

FIGURE 9.1   *Continued.*

Krull, K., & Hewitt, K. (1993). *Lives of the Musicians: Good Times, Bad Times (and What the Neighbors Thought)*. New York: Harcourt Brace.

Lawler, M. (1999). *Mickey Lawler's Skydyes: A Visual Guide to Fabric Painting*. Lafayette, CA: C & T Publishing.

Macaulay, D. (1997). *Rome Antics*. Boston: Walter Lorraine/Houghton Mifflin.

Miller, C. (1995). *Woodlore*. New York: Ticknor & Fields.

Osborne, M. P. (1998). *The Life of Jesus in the Masterpieces of Art*. New York: Viking.

Rubin, S. G. (2000). *Fireflies in the Dark: The Story of Friedl Dicker-Brandeis and the Children of Terazin*. New York: Holiday House.

PHYSICAL EDUCATION

Forten, F. (2000). *Sports: The Complete Visual Reference*. Buffalo, NY: Firefly Books.

Hoyt-Goldsmith, D. (1998). *Lacrosse: The National Game of the Iroquois*. Photos by L. Migdale. New York: Holiday House.

Macy, S. (1996). *Winning Ways: A Photohistory of Women in Sports*. New York: Henry Holt.

Wilson, S. (2000). *The Hockey Book for Girls*. Toronto, Canada: Kids Can Press.

PHYSICAL SCIENCES

Aulenbach, N. H., & Barton, H. A. (2001). *Exploring Caves: Journeys into the Earth*. Washington, DC: National Geographic Society.

Couper, H., & Henbest, N. (1999). *Space Encyclopedia*. New York: DK Publishing.

Craats, R. (2000). *The Science of Sound*. Milwaukee, WI: Gareth Stevens Publishing.

Gifford, C. (2000). *How the Future Began: Everyday Life*. New York: Kingfisher Publications.

Ride, S., & Okie, S. (1989). *To Space and Back*. New York: Lothrop, Lee & Shepard.

Skurzynski, G. (2000). *On Time: From Seasons to Split Seconds*. Washington, DC: National Geographic Society.

Wagoner, J. J., & Cutliff, L. D. (1985). *Mammoth Cave*. Flagstaff, AZ: Interpretive Publications.

Young, J. (1997). *Beyond Amazing: Six Spectacular Science Pop-ups*. New York: HarperCollins.

NATURAL SCIENCES

Allen, J. (Ed.). (1998). *Anthology for the Earth*. Cambridge, MA: Candlewick.

Anderson, J. (1993). *Earth Keepers*. Photos by G. Ancona. San Diego, CA: Harcourt Brace.

Cerullo, M. M. (1997). *The Octopus: Phantom of the Sea*. Photos by J. L. Rotman. New York: Cobblehill.

Gerstein, M. (1998). *The Wild Boy: Based on a True Story of the Wild Boy of Aveyron*. New York: Farrar, Straus & Giroux.

Jackson, D. M. (1996). *The Bone Detectives: How Forensic Anthropologists Solve Crimes and Uncover Mysteries of the Dead*. Photos by C. Fellenbaum. Boston: Little, Brown.

Ling, M., Atkinson, M., Greenaway, F., & King, D. (2000). *The Snake Book: A Breathtaking Close-up Look at Splendid, Scaly, Slithery Snakes*. New York: DK Publishing.

Mallory, K. (1998). *A Home by the Sea: Protecting Coastal Wildlife*. San Diego, CA: Gulliver/Harcourt Brace.

Montgomery, S. (1999). *The Snake Scientist*. Photos by N. Bishop. Boston: Houghton Mifflin.

Simon, S., & Warnick, E. (1998). *They Swim the Seas: The Mystery of Animal Migration*. San Diego, CA: Harcourt Brace.

Swinburne, S. R. (1998). *In Good Hands: Behind the Scenes at a Center for Orphaned and Injured Birds*. San Francisco: Sierra Club Books for Children.

Tanaka, S., & Barnard, A. (1998). *Graveyards of the Dinosaurs: What It's Like to Discover Prehistoric Creatures*. New York: Hyperion/Madison Press.

Yolen, J., & Lewin, T. (1998). *The Originals: Animals that Time Forgot*. New York: Philomel Books.

TECHNOLOGY

Baker, C. W. (1997). *Let There Be Life: Animating with the Computer*. New York: Walker.

Flynn, M. (2001). *Inside a Web Site*. Danbury, CT: Grolier Educational.

IDG's 3-D Visual Series. (1996). *Teach Yourself Computers and the Internet Visually*. Foster City, CA: IDG Books for MaranGraphics.

Searle, B. (2001). *Inside a Computer*. Danbury, CT: Grolier Educational.

FIGURE 9.2 *Biographies in picture-book format.*

Anderson, W. (Compiler). (1998). *Laura's Album: A Remembrance Scrapbook of Laura Ingalls Wilder.* New York: HarperCollins.

Coburn, B. (2000). *Triumph on Everest: A Photobiography of Sir Edmund Hillary.* Washington, DC: National Geographic Society.

Cooper, F. (1996). *Mandela: From the Life of the South African Statesman.* New York: Philomel Books.

Demi. (1998). *The Dalai Lama: A Biography of the Tibetan Spiritual and Political Leader.* New York: Henry Holt.

Druggleby, J. (1995). *Artist in Overalls: The Life of Grant Wood.* San Francisco: Chronicle.

Fellows, M. (1995). *The Life and Works of Escher.* London: Parragon Book Service.

Greenberg, J., & Jordan, S. (1998). *Chuck Close Up Close.* New York: DK Publishing.

Hanson, J. (1998). *Women of Hope: African Americans Who Made a Difference.* New York: Scholastic.

Harness, C. (2001). *Remember the Ladies: 100 Great American Women.* New York: HarperCollins.

Lyons, M. E. (Ed.). (1998). *Talking with Tebé: Clementine Hunter, Memory Artist.* Boston: Houghton Mifflin.

Lyons, M. E., & Garcia, M. (1999). *Catching the Fire: Philip Simmons, Blacksmith.* Boston: Houghton Mifflin.

Monceaux, M. (1994). *Jazz: My Music, My People.* New York: Borzoi/Knopf.

Myers, W. D., & Lawrence, J. (1996). *Toussaint L'ouverture: The Fight for Haiti's Freedom.* New York: Simon & Schuster.

Myers, W. D., & Jenkins, L. (2000). *Malcolm X: A Fire Burning Brightly.* New York: HarperCollins.

Orgill, R. (2001). *Shout, Sister, Shout: Ten Girl Singers Who Shaped a Century.* New York: M. K. McElderry Books.

Pinckney, A. D. (1998). *Duke Ellington: The Piano Prince and His Orchestra.* New York: Hyperion Books for Children.

Sandler, M. W. (1996). *Inventors.* New York: HarperCollins.

Sis, P. (1996). *Starry Messenger: Galileo Galilei.* New York: Foster/Farrar.

Spivak, D., & Demi. (1997). *Grass Sandals: The Travels of Basho.* New York: Atheneum.

Stanley, D. (1986). *Peter the Great.* New York: Scholastic.

Stanley, D. (1996). *Leonardo da Vinci.* New York: Morrow.

Stanley, D. (1998). *Joan of Arc.* New York: Morrow Junior Books.

Stanley, D. (2000). *Michelangelo.* New York: HarperCollins Children's Books.

Stanley, D., & Vennema, P. (1997). *Cleopatra.* New York: Morrow Junior Books.

Szabo, C. (1997). *Sky Pioneer: A Photobiography of Amelia Earhart.* Washington, DC: National Geographic Society.

Wadsworth, G. (1997). *John Burroughs: The Sage of the Slabsides.* New York: Clarion Books.

BookTalk   9.2

Enhance your classroom library with reference books that lead you and your students to other books in your content area. *Worth a Thousand Words: An Annotated Guide to Picture Books for Older Readers,* by Bette D. Ammon and Gale W. Sherman (1996), begins by giving many reasons for using picture books at higher levels and by giving the criteria they used for the inclusion of a book in this guide, including literary and artistic quality. "The differences between these books and those intended for younger readers center on sophistication, content or subject matter, and length or complexity of art and/or text"

(p. ix). The authors choose books that deal with issues affecting older students in ways that are accessible to varying learning styles. The entries in this work, in addition to the annotations, are coded with symbols indicating teaching ideas, further reading on a topic, writing ideas, research possibilities, read-aloud opportunities, and content area connections.

Other reference books in this category include *Informational Picture Books for Children* by Patricia J. Cianciolo (2000) and *Wordless/Almost Wordless Picture Books* by V. H. Richey and K. E. Puckett (1992).

FIGURE 9.3 *Series books and reference books focusing on visual literacy.*

- Dorling Kindersley. *Eyewitness Books.* There are dozens of beautifully illustrated books that teach about epidemics, energy, the Olympics, impressionism, amphibians, ponds and rivers, force and motion, electronics, mythology, baseball, presidents, pyramids, deserts, crime and detection, sports, crystals and gems, skeletons, Russia, the Renaissance, religion, hurricanes and tornadoes, and so much more. The series is like a library in itself.

- Enslow Publishers. *Decades of the Twentieth Century.* Each decade in this series is presented in a manner accessible to middle grade children. The books are appealing and very informative. The chronological approach is helpful; together, the volumes cause the big picture to become very clear.

- Grolier Educational. *The American Scene: Lives.* This encyclopedia of important Americans includes entries on people from all walks of life, including Houdini, Jesse Owens, Britney Spears, Ruth Bader Ginsburg, and Jackie Robinson.

- Grolier. *Being Human.* There are eight volumes in this series that inform students through pictures and text about various aspects of humanity ranging from personality and behavior to communications and relationships, from the brain and senses to health and wellness.

- Penguin Books. *The See Through History Series.* Books in this collection contain overlays for inside–outside views; their extensive listing includes works on the Industrial Revolution, ancient China, ships and submarines, tombs and treasures, and the Aztecs.

- Kingfisher. *The Visual Factfinder Series.* Each book contains thousands of facts, figures, charts, diagrams, maps, illustrations, and photographs on such topics as science and technology and world history.

- Scholastic. *Voyages of Discovery.* The books are beautifully designed and have overlays, stickers, and cut-away pages that make the books hands-on experiences without appearing the least bit babyish. Topics include bikes, cars, trucks, and trains; water; paint and painting; architecture and construction; and the history of printmaking.

- Scholastic. *The National Audubon Society's First Field Guide Series.* A reader-friendly yet sophisticated set of books packed with illustrations and information about such topics as amphibians, birds, insects, mammals, the night sky, reptiles, rocks and minerals, trees, weather, and wildflowers.

- Chelsea House Publishers. *The Encyclopedia of Musical Instruments.* Volumes in this beautiful set, authored by Robert Dearling, teach readers about percussion and electronic instruments, stringed instruments, woodwind and brass instruments, keyboard instruments and ensembles, and non-Western and obsolete instruments.

- Carolrhoda Books. *Picture the American Past Series.* Volumes invite readers to look and learn about the lives of young people in the times of the orphan trains, the Dust Bowl days, the days of the relocation camps, and the Civil Rights era.

- Heinemann Library. *Picture the Past Series.* Students exploring volumes in this series can be immersed in the lives of people on the Oregon Trail, on a southern plantation, in a Hopi village, on a pioneer homestead. What a literary field trip!

Visual Trade Book Series

Several popular trade book series capitalize on the visual learning modes. For example, *The Usborne Illustrated Encyclopedia: Science and Technology* (Scholastic, 1999) contains over 1,500 illustrations on fewer than 100 pages. Some books advertise even in their titles that their focus is the visual. Figure 9.3 gives an idea of the range of topics covered in such works. Are these books quality literature? Check them out, apply the criteria implicit in Norton's questions on page 270 and decide for yourself.

Wordless Picture Books

If you've been surprised by the number of picture books recommended throughout these chapters as appropriate for secondary content classrooms, you may be amazed at the sophisticated books waiting to be discovered that have *no* words, or almost none. More good news is that there are dozens of profitable ways you can use such resources to help the learners in your courses examine issues and try out creative approaches. Cassady (1998) recommends wordless picture books as no-risk tools for inclusive classrooms. She reminds us:

> Struggling and reluctant readers come in all ages and stages. They usually are caught in the downward spiral of failure that produces dislike and mistrust. This leads to an avoidance practice that leads to a lack of development, to further failure, and so on. In order to end this downward spiral and turn it upward toward success, which leads

to pleasure, trust, and further practice, at least one truly successful activity needs to occur.

Cassady has found that wordless picture books provide that success and enjoyment for struggling readers, and also benefit English language learners. I would add that any students who learn well visually, or who are interested in art, or who enjoy the humor and puzzles and small surprises picture books so often provide, will appreciate the addition of this genre to your classroom library. Here are a few of the many ways you can use wordless books:

1. If you teach a foreign language, your students can tell the story they see in the pictures, using the foreign language vocabulary and structure as much as possible. You'll find them asking you to supply words they really want to know for their stories. Try this with *Tuesday* by David Wiesner (1991). Similarly, students with limited English proficiency can first construct the story in their primary language and then attempt it in English.

2. The books can add to your students' background knowledge and conceptual understanding. For example, *The Story of a Castle* (Goodall, 1986) shows how people of the period lived. The series consisting of *Anno's Journey* (1978), *Anno's U.S.A.* (1983), *Anno's Britain* (1982), and *Anno's Italy* (1980) is rich with cultural symbols and historical icons.

3. Students, perhaps in English class, can use the books as writing prompts. They can add dialogue, imagine the feelings of and relationships between characters depicted, create a story line, or write a review of the book's artwork and overall quality. They can also reflect in writing about how they constructed meaning as they engaged with the pages. Some books, like Graeme Base's *The Eleventh Hour* (1989) can be pored over repeatedly, with new pieces of information discovered each time.

4. After reveling in several examples of wordless picture books, students can try their hand at the genre. They can use a variety of media and styles to create picture books relating to the topics they're learning about. If they feel insecure about their drawing or painting ability, they can experiment with a collage approach, collaborate with others whose skills are complementary, or download graphics from the Internet. They might take a book that is meant for younger students and compose a sequel or a parallel story aimed at older readers. The important thing is that they are reinforcing their own knowledge while creating a product that supplements others' learning and gives the creators a sense of artistic achievement.

Figure 9.4 lists samples of wordless (or almost wordless) picture books that work well in content areas.

FIGURE 9.4   *Wordless picture books for content area learning.*

Anno, M. (1978). *Anno's Journey.* Cleveland, OH: Collins-World.

Anno, M. (1980). *Anno's Italy.* New York: HarperCollins.

Anno, M. (1983). *Anno's U.S.A.* New York: Philomel Books.

Baker, J. (1991). *Window.* New York: Greenwillow Books.

Collington, P. (1987). *The Angel and the Soldier Boy.* New York: Knopf.

de Paola, T. (1979). *Flicks.* San Diego, CA: Harcourt Brace.

Feelings, T. (1995). *The Middle Passage: White Ships, Black Cargo.* New York: Dial Books.

Goodall, J. (1976). *An Edwardian Summer.* New York: Atheneum.

Goodall, J. (1986). *The Story of a Castle.* New York: M. K. McElderry Books.

Goodall, J. (1987). *The Story of a Main Street.* New York: Macmillan.

Goodall, J. (1990). *The Story of the Seashore.* New York: M. K. McElderry Books.

Gurney, J. (1998). *Dinotopia: A Land Apart from Time.* New York: HarperCollins.

Oakley, G. (1980). *Graham Oakley's Magical Changes.* New York: Atheneum.

Rohmann, E. (1995). *Time Flies.* New York: Scholastic.

Spier, P. (1977). *Noah's Ark.* Garden City, NY: Doubleday.

Van Allsburg, C. (1984). *The Mysteries of Harris Burdick.* Boston: Houghton Mifflin.

Vincent, G. (2000). *A Day, a Dog.* New York: Front Street.

Wiesner, D. (1988). *Free Fall.* New York: Lothrop, Lee & Shepard.

Wiesner, D. (1997). *Sector Seven.* New York: Clarion Books.

ACTION RESEARCH   9.A

Find and peruse one or more wordless picture books relevant to your content area, using Figure 9.4 as a starting place. Write a journal response reflecting on what the experience of constructing meaning without text was like for you, or discussing how you might use the book(s) to teach a unit. Speculate about how you might model your reading or introduce the book to a group of students.

Cartoons, Comics, and Graphic Novels

Virtually everyone recognizes the fun that can be derived from cartoon art. The sadness over the retirement and death of Charles Schultz in 2000 was a striking acknowledgment of the impact a comic strip had on generations of readers around the world. Not everyone yet recognizes the additional benefit this visual art form can have on learning. Rothschild (1995) asserts that aficionados know that comics provide a rich array: "Mythology. Intensely honest autobiography. Experimentation. Character studies. Opera. Poetry. Shakespeare. History. In short, the same topics, the same elements, found in mainstream literature" (p. xiii). In this section, I hope to stimulate your thinking about how you can effectively use cartoons in your classroom.

I have a tabbed folder containing cartoons that directly relate to concepts and topics taught in various subject areas. I have "Peanuts" and "Calvin and Hobbes" cartoons about the writing process; "Far Side" cartoons about science, history, and math; "Dilbert" cartoons about technology and business. They can be used as an introduction to a lesson or a motivating tool and can rely on, reinforce, or build background knowledge. I encourage you to start your own file; once you start reading comics in your role as teacher, you'll be amazed at how plentiful the discipline-related cartoons are. The students can join you in your quest for additions to your collection, and can bring in content area-related cartoons they find for classroom wall displays. Cartoons also enhance the students' general and content-specific vocabulary. They have patterns of organization such as cause–effect and compare–contrast, just as other texts do, and many require critical thinking, synthesizing, taking on different perspectives, and making inferences.

A particular type of comic genre is the political cartoon. National and state social studies standards require that students interpret such texts. Political cartoons are found in virtually any daily newspaper—often, they are beside an editorial or letters to the editor, so you and your students can follow current events through a combination of text formats. You can ask guiding questions to help the students figure out what or whose perspective is being represented, what events or other texts are being alluded to, what aspects of the creation make it humorous or effective.

Rothschild (1995) thinks the time has come to recognize *graphic novels*, which are lengthy comic books that contain a single story, as a distinct genre. "Graphic novels use words and pictures in ways that transcend ordinary art and text, and their creators are more than writers and artists. The artist must have a director's eye for shadow, angle, setting, and costume.... In the ideal graphic novel, the text does not distract from the art or vice versa" (p. xiv). Comic books are the home of superheroes (e.g., Spider-man, Batman, Wonder Woman), but "Classics Illustrated" has also made the graphic format the home of such heroes as Jane Eyre, Odysseus, Oliver Twist, Julius Caesar, The Three Musketeers, and Hamlet.

Eliza Dresang (1999) notes the proliferation of comic books as respectable texts as one example of the radical change in literature. "A format that was once thought to signal mindless entertainment may in some instances require greater intellectual engagement than ordinary linear text, because read-

BookTalk   9.3

If you were unaware of the wealth of knowledge that can be gained through comic-book form, investigate the *Beginners Documentary Comic Books* series published by Writers and Readers Publishing. Individual titles include such topics as Black history, Structuralism, Freud, Hemingway, philosophy, biology, computers, Malcolm X, psychiatry, the Black Holocaust, opera, art, the United Nations, rainforests, classical music, and many more. I read *Chomsky for Beginners* by David Cogswell and Paul Gordon (1996) and learned much information about Noam Chomsky's life, predecessors who influenced him (including Plato, Descartes, Rousseau, Karl Marx, and George Orwell), his contributions to the field of linguistics, his thinking about the media, and his views on politics. The book includes an interview with Chomsky, and quotes from this influential linguist are interspersed throughout the text. Your visual learners will love it.

FIGURE 9.5 *Examples of graphic novels and other cartoon titles.*

Avi. (1993). *City of Light, City of Dark: A Comic Book Novel.* Art by B. Floca. New York: Orchard Books.

Briggs, R. (1998). *Ethel & Ernest: A True Story.* New York: Knopf.

Curry, P., & Zarate, O. (1996). *Introducing Machiavelli.* New York: Totem Books.

Eisner, W. (1986). *Will Eisner's New York: The Big City.* Northampton, MA: Kitchen Sink Press.

Factoid Books. (1999). *The Big Book of Grimm, by the Brothers Grimm as Channeled by J. Vankin and Over 50 Top Comic Artists!* New York: Paradox Press.

Giardino, V. (1997). *A Jew in Communist Prague: 1. Loss of Innocence.* New York: NBM Comics Lit.

Giardino, V. (1997). *A Jew in Communist Prague: 2. Adolescence.* New York: NBM Comics Lit.

Giardino, V. (1997). *A Jew in Communist Prague: 3. Rebellion.* New York: NBM Comics Lit.

Gonick, L. (1991). *The Cartoon History of the United States.* New York: HarperPerennial.

Gonick, L., & Huffman, A. (1991). *The Cartoon Guide to Physics.* New York: HarperPerennial.

Gonick, L., & Outwater, A. (1996). *The Cartoon Guide to the Environment.* New York: HarperCollins.

Gonick, L., & Smith, W. (1993). *The Cartoon Guide to Statistics.* New York: HarperPerennial.

Gonick, L., & Wheelis, M. (1991). *The Cartoon Guide to Genetics.* New York: HarperPerennial.

Goulart, R. (2000). *Comic Book Culture: An Illustrated History.* Portland, OR: Collectors Press.

Harris, S. (1989). *Einstein Simplified: Cartoons on Science.* New Brunswick, NJ: Rutgers University Press.

Hirsch, K. D. (1997). *Mind Riot: Coming of Age in Comix.* New York: Aladdin Paperbacks.

Kubert, J. (1996). *Fax from Sarajevo: A Story of Survival.* Milwaukie, OR: Dark Horse Comics.

Mack, S. (1998). *The Story of the Jews: A 4,000-Year Adventure.* New York: Villard.

O'Neil, D. (2001). *The DC Comics Guide to Writing Comics.* New York: Watson-Guptell Publications.

Pustz, M. J. (1999). *Comic Book Culture: Fanboys and True Believers.* Jackson: University Press of Mississippi.

Reynolds, R. (1992). *Superheroes: A Modern Mythology.* Jackson: University Press of Mississippi.

Spiegelman, A. (1991). *Maus II: A Survivor's Tale: And Here My Troubles Began.* New York: Pantheon.

Spiegelman, A. (1997). *Maus: A Survivor's Tale.* New York: Pantheon.

Spiegelman, A., & Mouly, F. (Eds.). (2000). *Little Lit: Folklore and Fairy Tale Funnies.* New York: RAW Junior.

Winick, J. (2000). *Pedro & Me: Friendship, Loss, and What I Learned.* New York: Henry Holt.

ers are called upon to 'read between the frames,' themselves supplying continuity in the blank spaces left by the artist" (p. 23). Rothschild (1995) recognizes that there has been prejudice against the format, but notes that nearly one-third of all material published in Japan is in comic-book form, including technical manuals, textbooks, and histories (p. xvii). Rothschild hopes that educators everywhere will soon appreciate the educational value of the genre. You can decide what place graphic novels will have in your classroom by reading some yourself, paying attention to features that might help you in your teaching and personal learning, and by trying some out with students or peers and listening closely to their reactions. Figure 9.5 lists examples of discipline-related texts in comic-book form.

READERS AND WRITERS LEARNING AND RESPONDING THROUGH ART

So often, students feel that the teacher knows what a text means and their job is to discover what that elusive "right answer" is. Responding to picture books may boost our students' confidence because they may feel more secure about their ability to discuss visual stimuli and may actually teach the teacher something. Several years ago, I asked an 11-year-old artist to read some picture books with an art theme and talk to me about them. Julie's responses were truly instructive:

> Sometimes it's best to let the pen do what it wants to do. Like, a chair can't do anything but be a chair, but a pen can *do* things. . . . I found, in being an artist, and sometimes a writer, you shouldn't be

BookTalk   9.4

We might bemoan the fact that students today tend to shun the classics, and we might feel a bit guilty ourselves for never having made it quite to the end of *Moby Dick* or *Great Expectations*. Try out the library of "Classics Illustrated," and treat yourself to the comic-book style interpretations of Shakespeare's tragedies and such standards as *Huckleberry Finn, Gulliver's Travels,* and *Frankenstein*. These works might very well be the stepping stone to the original works.

You might start by examining *The Complete Guide to Classics Illustrated* by D. Malan (1994) or *Classics Illustrated: A Cultural History, with Illustrations* by W. B. Jones (2002) and going to the "Classics Illustrated" versions of individual classics from there.

bound by restrictions, the laws of physics, you could say. . . . I found that in art there's not a right or wrong way, it's just, it's kind of like, in art, there *is* no right or wrong, there's only *do*.

One day I visited a teacher as she was about to read aloud a chapter from Roald Dahl's *James and the Giant Peach* (1992). She passed out pieces of construction paper and instructed the students to have their markers ready in case they heard something that made them want to draw. I observed that some students drew fast and furiously, using several colors and multiple sheets of paper, while others ignored the paper on their desks, listening in rapt attention with smiles or scared expressions on their faces as the scenes and the teacher's voice changed. From there, I went to another classroom where a teacher scolded a child for drawing when he was supposed to be listening to a story being read. Witnessing the juxtaposition of the two teachers' philosophies in action jarred me into examining my own beliefs about students' drawing. Since then, I have read numerous teachers' accounts of the benefits of encouraging student artwork at every stage of learning.

Nancie Atwell (1998) confesses her distress over a particular eighth-grade student who resisted her structured writing assignments and drew his way through her English class. She even quotes herself as saying regularly, "Jeff, stop drawing and *get to work*" (p. 7). He did the work, but at home, and she was frustrated because he didn't do things her way. Years later, Atwell learned from reading the work of researcher Donald Graves (1975) that it was natural for some writers to plan and rehearse their writing through drawing, and she realized that her well-

intentioned structures had actually served as constraints for Jeff. She learned to learn from her students how best to help them.

Jeffrey D. Wilhelm (1997) experienced a similar "teacher's epiphany" (p. 119) when he interviewed a student about his response to a story and got little beyond, "'Nope, nothing here,' and 'didn't get it'" (p. 119), then saw the student at his seat chuckling over a *Calvin and Hobbes* book. He realized that Walter's comprehension was aided because "he was helped to see and therefore experience the imagined world of the story through the cartoon pictures!" (p. 119). Wilhelm goes on to explain how Walter and his classmates participated in an art project designed to convince reluctant readers that reading involved seeing, a project that "would scaffold and support that sort of 'readerly' visualizing and image-making for the students" (p. 120). His "Symbolic Story Representation," which he adapted from Patricia Enciso's (1990) research using a technique called the "Symbolic Representation Interview," calls for students to create cutouts or find objects that dramatize the texts they have read, as well as how they read them. Students choose to symbolize characters, settings,

BookTalk   9.5

If you're one of the many people who don't get what the big deal is about comic books or don't really enjoy reading the graphic novel format, you can turn to Scott McCloud's *Understanding Comics: The Invisible Art* (1994). Of course, this informational book uses the comic-book form itself, so you get to try out his advice and strategies dealing with the vocabulary of comics, time frames, color, and sequential art. You may or may not be enticed by chapter titles such as "Blood in the Gutter." Another resource is Rothschild's *Graphic Novels: A Bibliographic Guide to Book-Length Comics* (1995), which deals with many subgenres: action/adventure, classics, crime and mystery, horror, mythology and folklore, and nonfiction (including autobiography and biography, history, music, politics, science, sci-fi, and superheroes). It includes a glossary of comic book terminology and slang. Even if *you* aren't won over to the genre, many students will be captivated if you put these books alongside graphic novels in your classroom library.

If the books don't satisfy you, how about a video? Try *The Masters of Comic Book Art* (Viola & Ellison, 1989). Your appreciation for the art form will grow.

themes, or authors and meet with the teacher or classroom reading club to talk through the products they create. Students interview each other, Wilhelm videotapes the presentations, and students talk metacognitively about their reading processes. In a chapter called "Reading Is Seeing," Wilhelm concludes, "The greatest recommendation for including artistic response . . . is that it encouraged very different readers to respond in natural ways, to share that response with each other, and to extend and develop it in unforeseen, socially supported, and personally validating and exciting ways" (p. 138).

Another enthusiastic supporter of combining art and reading is Linda Rief. In *Seeking Diversity* (1992), she details a post-reading project her eighth-grade literature groups completed on the books *Night* (2000) by Elie Wiesel, *Go Ask Alice* (1982) by an anonymous author, and *The Outsiders* (1967) by S. E. Hinton. Student drafts reprinted in the book give an idea of the collaboration and process that took place, and an inserted page of colored photographs of murals shows the powerful end result. Rief and the students discovered rich parallels between the artistic process and the writing process. The teacher was satisfied, concluding, "I want to encourage and celebrate my students' multiliteracies. . . . I need to remember to give my students the opportunities to say things in ways they have 'no

words for'" (pp. 163–164). The young people were satisfied, concluding in a letter to author Elie Wiesel, "Over these months, the painting became less and less of a school project and more a part of our feelings and a challenge to get those feelings out on paper the way we wanted to" (p. 164).

Allowing students to use art as a way to connect with your content curriculum has many benefits. And you might be amazed at what you learn from the adolescent artists in your class. For example, Juliana Bütz is a student who enjoys and learns from drawing. She did both scientific and imaginative drawing in her free time in high school, and did not see them as entirely separate. "I like to draw fantasy stuff, but I want to be believable, have realistic proportions. If you're going to draw a dragon, you want the joints to look as though they would really work" (personal conversation). A teacher discovered Juliana's love of and talent for drawing; he designed an independent study for her so that she could get academic credit for all the work she was doing. She researched her subjects to ensure accuracy in her art, thus learning science and art together, one reinforcing the other. She later commented on her nature drawings, "I didn't copy drawings, or use my imagination for them. I always drew from life." Figure 9.6 shows examples of Juliana's self-initiated scientific illustrations.

FIGURE 9.6 *Sample student drawings done as an independent study.*

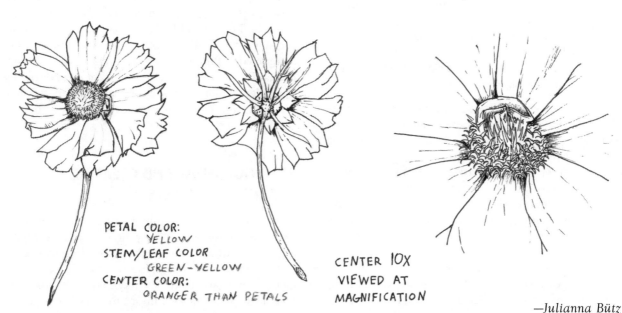

LANCE-LEAVED COREOPSIS TICKSEED   (COREOPSIS LANCEOLATA) FAMILY: ASTERACEAE

PETAL COLOR:
YELLOW
STEM/LEAF COLOR
GREEN-YELLOW
CENTER COLOR:
ORANGER THAN PETALS

CENTER 10X
VIEWED AT
MAGNIFICATION

—*Julianna Bütz*

Bussert-Webb (2001), finding that the young women in a middle school program for pregnant students resisted writing, especially writing that called for anything personal or revealing, asked them to respond to literature through drawing. She found that art helped them to make personal connections to the text, express their values and fears, and relate to one another. Their interpretations of a short story were varied and allowed much discussion about readers' responses. One girl put herself into the picture of the story; another added some fairy tale characteristics; and a third, whose favorite subject was math, focused on math concepts. Bussert-Webb concluded that these previously resistant students could not help but tell their stories when they used art to mediate their understanding of literature. She found that "like reading, drawing is a semiotic process involving the artist, her perception of reality, and her creation. Indeed, drawing an interpretation of a literary work involves a composing process similar to a written response" (p. 516). Think what you might discover when you ask your students (and yourself, as Bussert-Webb did) to respond to a written text, lecture, movie, or other stimulus through a visual representation.

Jessica Whitelaw (Whitelaw & Wolf, 2001) gave her students some instruction in the elements of art in order to hone their visual skills and drew the students' attention to the connection between visual and printed language:

> I tried to provide my sixth-grade students with opportunities to stop and reflect about the meaning of texts and to arrive at a destination they may not have reached without *recognizing* the power of the visual arts. The arts allowed students to see beyond the words on the page, to encompass a larger vision through which they could consider the deeper issues in the text—issues of freedom and control, perfect place/no place, love and lack thereof. (p. 66)

There are many books spanning several genres that have an art focus or theme that you can make available to your students. Some topics may fit directly into your curricular areas, while others might just be in your classroom library, ready to invite students into an artistic realm of thought and into a pleasurable, perhaps new, field of endeavor. They seem to invite response, either emotionally or with art supplies. Figure 9.7 lists sample titles that fit this category.

Your students can use their own drawings or paintings, or artwork found on the Web (including photographs, drawings, diagrams, virtual reality, computer animations, and streaming video) to illustrate texts you've provided or texts they've composed

BookTalk 9.6

Imagine a book that is part historical document, part (almost) wordless picture book, and you'll have an idea of Peter Spier's *We the People: The Constitution of the United States* (1987). The front endpapers show a map of the United States of America in 1787 as executed by Spiers. A four-page introduction gives background on the reasons why the Constitutional Convention was called, and the processes of writing the Constitution and having it ratified. Then comes the main section of the book—the only text consists of the one sentence preamble to the Constitution. For every phrase, beginning with "We, the people," there are pages of small, detailed illustrations depicting scenes from the lives of Americans and the growth of various government agencies and projects throughout the years. Finally, there is the printed version of the Constitution and its amendments, and the closing endpapers showing what the original handwritten version on parchment looks like. Students might wish to use this book as a model to make similar class books based on other famous quotations—perhaps the inscription from the Statue of Liberty, the 1848 "Declaration of Sentiments," or a collection of presidential quotes.

themselves. Bruce (2000), in an article entitled "The Work of Art in the Age of Digital Reproduction," gives suggestions for using art to teach across the curriculum, as well as an annotated listing of sites on the Web that offer art appropriate for content area subjects. Bussert-Webb (2001) gave her students, all pregnant teens, disposable cameras to use as they completed a "Photo Story Project" about their present perceptions and future visions. I have loaned my digital video camera to my preservice teachers for their academic projects. They discover creative abilities they didn't realize they had!

READING, USING, AND CREATING GRAPHS AND CHARTS

As stated at the beginning of Part One, visual literacy is becoming increasingly necessary for everyday types of reading. It's virtually impossible to open a newspaper or news magazine without finding information in chart form or in symbols of some sort. Visual displays are common in magazines, travel guides, signs along highways and in stores, textbooks, manuals, on television, and in software programs.

FIGURE 9.7   Young adult books with a visual arts focus or theme.

Anderson, L. H. (1999). *Speak*. New York: Farrar, Straus & Giroux.

Arnosky, J. (1987). *Drawing from Nature*. Lothrop, Lee & Shepard Books.

Bjork, C. (1999). *Vendela in Venice*. New York: R & S Books.

Bjork, C., & Anderson, L. (1987). *Linnea in Monet's Garden*. New York: R & S Books.

Clemesha, D., & Zimmerman, A. G. (1992). *Rattle Your Bones: Skeleton Drawing Fun*. New York: Scholastic.

Freymann-Weyr, G. (2002). *My Heartbeat*. Boston: Houghton Mifflin.

Holmes, B. W. (2001). *Following Fake Man*. New York: Knopf.

Lowry, L. (1980). *Autumn Street*. Boston: Houghton Mifflin.

Mack, T. (2000). *Drawing Lessons*. New York: Scholastic.

Park, L. S. (2001). *A Single Shard*. New York: Clarion Books.

Rylant, C. (1988). *All I See*. New York: Orchard Books.

Sills, L. (1989). *Inspirations: Stories About Women Artists: Georgia O'Keefe, Frida Kahlo, Alice Neel, Faith Ringgold*. Niles, IL: A. Whitman.

Fortunately, the attention paid to comprehending graphs, charts, and other visual sources of information seems to be increasing in schools today. National standards in mathematics, science, English language arts, and social studies include this area of literacy, and many assessments do also. For instance, the New York State Regents exam in English required

of high school students for graduation always has a major task that involves the analysis of information in graphic form, which must then be synthesized with information from a companion text. The January 2000 exam, for instance, required students to read an article about recycling taken from *Consumer Reports*, along with a chart detailing the pros and cons of recycling. The students then prepared for a debate by writing a persuasive essay, using relevant information from both documents, that agreed or disagreed with the statement that recycling is worth the effort. Similarly, the New York State Global Studies and American History Regents exams have questions involving a number of related pieces of data, including cartoons or graphs or maps, that must be interpreted, synthesized, and written about.

The book *Visual Literacy: How to Read and Use Information in Graphic Form*, by Marcia Weaver (1999), contains explanations and examples showing the wide variety of graphic formats: histograms, bar and column graphs, computer-generated flowcharts, scattergrams, fishbone diagrams, maps, organization charts, blueprints, spreadsheets, and others. It gives step-by-step lessons, suggests questions for readers to ask as they encounter various representations, and gives writing prompts, as well as a pre-test and post-test. The chapter on pie charts has several pictures of these information-filled graphics and explains:

> The unique quality of the pie chart is the fact that it shows you the overall picture of the data as well as a picture of the individual pieces of data. . . . Another characteristic is that the percent of the whole is printed right on the pie segment. There are no measurements to figure out; no hatch marks to read (p. 120).

BookTalk 9.7

Lincoln's Gettysburg Address is powerful by itself, and the historical happenings that give it context, including the story of the consecration of the Soldiers' National Cemetery, are equally capable of evoking readers' emotions. Now, imagine the addition of quality artwork to the lines of the speech. A 1997 publication, *The Gettysburg Address*, is illustrated with black and white scratchboard drawings by Michael McCurdy. One reviewer had this to say:

> Each page provides readers an opportunity to function as participant observers—to view all that went on during this battle from different perspectives: from a panoramic view, then close up, then face-to-face. McCurdy has done a remarkable job of depicting soldiers, statesmen, and onlookers as individuals, each unique as to features, body structure, and age, and each distinctive in his or her emotional responses to the circumstances of this battle and the commemoration service. Historical details, such as the military weaponry and the clothing worn by the soldiers and civilians, are accurately portrayed. (Cianciolo, 2000, p. 162)

FIGURE 9.8 Books and games dealing with visual and spatial skills.

Anno, M. (1997). *Anno's Math Games*. New York: Putnam & Grosset.

Anno, M. (1997). *Anno's Math Games II*. New York: Putnam & Grosset.

Anno, M. (1997). *Anno's Math Games III*. New York: Putnam & Grosset.

Binary Arts Corporation. (1995). *Visual Brain Storms: The Smart Thinking Game*. Alexandria, VA: Binary Arts.

Block, J. R., & Yuker, H. E. (1989). *Can You Believe Your Eyes?* New York: Gardner Press.

DiSpezio, M. A. (1999). *Optical Illusion Magic: Visual Tricks and Amusements*. New York: Sterling.

Gelb, M. (1998). *How to Think Like Leonardo da Vinci: Seven Steps to Genius Every Day*. New York: Delacorte.

Hoffman, D. D. (1998). *Visual Intelligence: How We Create What We See*. New York: Norton.

Levy, J. U., & Levy, N. (1999). *Mechanical Aptitude and Spatial Relations Tests* (4th ed.). New York: Macmillan.

Markle, S. (1997). *Discovering Graph Secrets: Experiments, Puzzles, and Games Exploring Graphs*. New York: Atheneum.

McBride, C. (2000). *Making Magnificent Machines: Fun with Math, Science, and Engineering*. Tucson, AZ: Zephyr Press.

Thorne-Thomsen, K. (1994). *Frank Lloyd Wright for Kids*. Chicago: Chicago Review Press.

Weber, J. A. (2000). *Architecture Everywhere: Exploring the Built Environment of Your Community*. Tucson, AZ: Zephyr Press.

After providing multiple-choice questions, Weaver provides opportunities for application, giving scenarios that call for the construction of pie charts. Similar explanations and projects are found in the other chapters.

When discussing spatial–visual intelligence (one of the separate intelligences identified and made well known by Howard Gardner), Weaver quotes William James, "Whilst part of what we perceive comes through our senses from the object before us, another part (and it may be the larger part) always comes out of our own mind" (p. 191). Can you see how that connects to the theory of reader response and the philosophy of constructivism that has been present throughout this book?

Weaver and Gardner both show that visual intelligence can be increased. Encourage your students to engage in activities and take advantage of opportunities to practice their skills in this area. Fill the walls and your files with authentic materials containing all kinds of symbols and graphic displays brought in by students from newspapers, their parents' workplaces, and magazines. Add charts published by the school to share information with the public about test scores, budgets, demographics, plans for building, and so on. There are also numerous books that provide visual puzzles, conundrums, and challenges, as well as tips for improving one's visual–spatial intelligence and memory. Figure 9.8 lists some of these books.

PART TWO

Media Literacy

By now, you probably can see how blurred the boundaries are between all of these special literacy terms. You might also be wondering if anything lies outside the definition of literacy; it seems to encompass everything. Here is a definition offered by high school English teacher and author Jim Burke (1999), which he culled from many others: "Literacy is the ability to access, analyze, synthesize, evaluate and communicate information and ideas in a variety of forms depending on the purpose of that occasion" (p. 204). Media literacy is a huge topic about which many books have been written. Teachers can teach units on advertising, on the news, on radio, on teen magazines; depending on your content area and the needs and interests of your students, you may explore any number of media types. I concentrate on two in this section: films and television.

LITERACY AND FILM

ACTIVATING PRIOR KNOWLEDGE   9.3

Recall your days as a middle and high school student, as well as college courses if appropriate. What films or film clips do you remember watching in class? How were they introduced by teachers? What was their purpose? What were some follow-up activities? How did they connect to the course content? How valuable did you find them as vehicles of learning? Talk to others to find out if they had similar experiences and reactions.

Too often, teachers who show films in class do not take full advantage of their potential to aid learning. Students tell me that they remember movies as fillers when there was a substitute teacher, or as rewards on Friday for good behavior during the week. I've seen movies being shown in school with no anticipation guide, no purpose-setting, and no follow-up discussion or reflection. In contrast, some teachers select and use films judiciously, leading to far-ranging benefits in their content areas. I hope that the following ideas help you increase your repertoire of ways to take advantage of the fact that adolescents, as well as much of our society, spend time watching movies. Consider viewing as a com-

BookTalk   9.8

We interrupt this chapter for an important announcement. . . . I want to tell you about a multidimensional resource that can bring history to life in your classroom. The book *We Interrupt This Broadcast,* by Joe Garner (1998) and with a foreword by Walter Cronkite, contains photo-essays filled with facts and human interest stories about monumental events of the twentieth century. Two digitally mastered audio CDs add companion narratives, as well as the actual voices of announcers beginning with "We interrupt this broadcast . . ." and continuing with the breaking news of such events as the bombing of Pearl Harbor, the fall of Saigon, Elvis's death, Nixon's resignation, the assassination of President Kennedy, the first person walking on the moon, the Kent State massacre, the killing of John Lennon, the atomic bomb's destruction of Hiroshima. You and your students can listen to, view pictures and artifacts of, read about, reflect on, and discuss 38 important events that seem to come right into your classroom community. *We Interrupt This Broadcast* can be the stimulus for a remarkable literacy event.

ponent of the language arts, right along with listening, speaking, reading, and writing.

The first idea that may come to mind when asked how a teacher can use film in the classroom is to have students compare a book and a movie. Some teachers are afraid, with good reason, that students will substitute watching a movie for reading a book, and so include on summer reading lists only books with no film version (Burke, 1999). But many students really enjoy analyzing both to find similarities and differences and have strong opinions about which version is more powerful, effective, or aesthetically pleasing. Your motivation, guidance, and modeling can help students hone their critical-thinking skills in this area. Books and movies can shape values in a positive way. For example, social studies or English teachers could have students read *Snow Falling on Cedars* (Guterson, 1995), set off the Pacific coast several years after World War II and the internment of Japanese Americans, and then watch the movie. In addition to comparing the two presentation modes and metacognitively reflecting on how they constructed meaning from each, students learn important information in terms of history and geography, and can have meaningful discussions about prejudice, justice, human relations, love, and truth.

Another wise use of film is to supply background knowledge of a difficult topic you will be teaching. If students can visualize some of the concepts and examples they will be reading about, they'll be able to meet the challenge of the text. Better comprehension and retention result. For example, ninth-grade English teacher Sharon Morley has her students watch *Shakespeare in Love* (1999) as they begin studying *Romeo and Juliet*. I know social studies teachers who bring in *Schindler's List* (1993) to help students grapple with the very difficult issues they encounter as they study the Holocaust. The video *The Death of a Star* (1987) might introduce a difficult chapter on supernovas in an astronomy course.

Paul (2000) has used rap, both in video and audio form, with diverse groups of secondary students, as well as with teachers, focusing on rap as a site of critical inquiry. Using guide questions, groups or individuals could react by stating the messages they think the raps or videos convey, agreeing or disagreeing with the messages, and thinking of ways to resist the message if desired. The adolescents Paul worked with found pleasure in studying rap as poetry, and comparing the rap artists' creations to the poetry of Emily Dickinson, Edgar Allen Poe, Gwendolyn Brooks, Langston Hughes, and others. The teachers Paul worked with had some difficulty understanding the rap—which was actually beneficial for thinking about cultural points of reference and the lack of cultural synchronization shared between many teachers and their students, and for metacognitively analyzing where the difficulty in comprehension lay. The teachers discovered different genres of rap, including socially conscious rap and ghetto storytellin' or reality rap. Rap was shown to be a viable site for the practice of critical media literacy because teachers were "exposed to a new way to potentially approach students and culturally synchronize literacy instruction. Additionally, they have had a chance to critically explore significant issues attached to language, culture, and power through texts to which students relate in their everyday lives" (p. 251).

Movies are a natural avenue for helping your students improve their writing skills. If you require or encourage your students to keep journals, they can reflect in writing after seeing movies on their own. They may find that they discover some things about themselves and their thinking that would not have happened without this step. Also, you can start

a collection of published movie reviews, inviting students to bring these obviously authentic pieces of writing to school. You can post them on a wall or have a section of your classroom library devoted to movie reviews. Students can not only discuss whether or not they agree with a reviewer's opinion of a movie, but also can evaluate the review in terms of its style, crafting, and interest level. The next logical step is for students to write their own reviews, experimenting with the various forms they've seen modeled—perhaps sending their reviews to the school or local newspaper, or debating fellow classmates about the worth or theme of a movie and the quality of the actors' performances. The writing possibilities are endless and exciting.

Finders (2000) reminds us that "critical literacy involves understanding both how to *use* and how one is *used by* popular culture" (p. 148). One way you can foster critical viewing is to have students read reviews and critiques of films they might typically watch without consciously making judgments. For example, show a clip from the Disney movie *Mulan*, ask the students what they think about its authenticity in terms of Chinese culture and the values it portrays, then have them read the article "A Mean Wink at Authenticity: Chinese Images in Disney's *Mulan*" (2000) by Weimin Mo and Wenju Shen. The authors give historical details backing their claims that the film is culturally inauthentic, full of distortions and stereotypes, and guilty of using racially coded language. Mo and Shen taught Chinese language and literature in China for 15 years, and with their inside knowledge of both the culture and the original story, claim that "the filmmakers of *Mulan* rob the story of its soul and in its place put jokes, songs and scary effects. Their Disney bulldozer runs over the Chinese culture, imposing mainstream cultural beliefs and values" (p. 137). Your students can look at the movie through a new lens—they can counter the article's position with their own or those of other reviewers if they wish, and apply what they learn to other movies representing various cultures.

Movies can foster critical thinking, as well as reflection on values. Levine (1996) exhorts:

> Teenagers, for the most part, do not need protection from the realities of life. On the contrary, they need as much information and education as possible. *Dead Poets Society* deals with suicide, *Boyz N the Hood* deals with homicide, *Schindler's List* documents genocide. Responsible movies such as these do not hesitate to confront and explore the kinds of difficult topics that interest adolescents. But they provide a historical context, emphasize complexity, explore alternatives,

and show teenagers the consequences of actions that may limit or even destroy future opportunities. They are important movies for teenagers to see. (p. 181)

Create a comprehension guide or discussion questions for a film in the same way you would for printed material. Looking over the instructional strategies in the previous chapters, you'll find that they can be used or adapted for use with films. As with books, the most natural question to get discussion going in a classroom is the one moviegoers say to each other on the way out of the theatre, "Well, what'd ya think?" Focus questions such as the following might also assist your students as they view a film and ponder its significance; they can choose the ones they wish to pursue:

1. What (or whose) point of view is represented in this film? How might the story be told differently using another's point of view?

2. What content information did you learn from this movie? How does it connect with other things you've learned in this class or on your own?

3. What do you see as a pervasive motif, or overall theme, to this movie? Is it well developed? How did the screenwriter or director convey this theme?

4. Reflect on how you made sense of this film. Were there points of confusion for you? Did you combine what you were seeing and hearing with background information you already knew? What surprises did you become aware of as you watched?

5. Which characters are well developed? Which were simple, and which were complex? Did any characters grow or change over the course of the story?

6. What was the importance of the setting? What elements contributed to the successful portrayal of the setting?

7. What symbols did you find? Were they effective for you?

8. Discuss the use of special effects. Evaluate the film in terms of music, artistic quality, and crafting.

9. What values are portrayed in this film? Did you feel it was preachy or manipulative? In what ways? What did you learn about people, human nature, or societies?

10. If you also read the book (assuming there is one), which did you prefer? What differences did you notice? What characteristics were prominent or effective in each mode of presentation?

11. What would you say to a friend who asked you about this movie?

An excellent resource for finding well-done films connected to your subject area is the PBS Video Catalog of Educational Resources (available from PBS Video, 1320 Braddock Place, Alexandria, VA, 22314–1698, or 1-800-344-3337). You can peruse the PBS Video Catalog of Educational Resources to see what is available that matches your curriculum and your students' interests. It's organized according to disciplinary categories and subcategories, and gives informative annotations about the videos included. For example, under the heading "Clash of Cultures," one section is devoted to videos about Native Americans—"Come to Grips with Five Centuries of Conflict: Multiple perspectives let students consider the nations' relationship with its native peoples" (p. 10). Another addresses immigration—"Melting Pot or Mosaic?: Challenge students' perceptions about identity and ethnicity" (p. 11). A third is about African Americans' "Long Road to Equality" (p. 12).

Perusing video rental businesses and talking to the employees might also lead you to treasures. Figure 9.9 lists films and videos appropriate for a variety of disciplines. Many, actually, can be fruitfully used in an interdisciplinary way. You may only show relevant clips from some—appropriate instructional decision making is necessary.

You can invite authors into your classroom via the *Famous Authors* series of video biographies available through www.FilmicArchives.com. The programs include archival documents and portraits as well as relevant social and political background to and commentary on the writers' works. Learn about James Joyce, Virginia Woolf, Mark Twain, Edgar Allen Poe, William Wordsworth, George Eliot, the Bronte sisters, Jane Austen, Walt Whitman, and more!

Getting Ready to Teach 9.1 *(see page 300)*

TELELITERACY

Television's impact on children, as well as the rest of society, is a huge topic that has generated an enormous number of books, so somebody must still be reading! Debate continues among experts and laypeople about the connection between television watching and crime, television watching and literacy, television watching and our general health, values, and behaviors. Statistics are constantly provided about the ever-increasing number of hours children watch television. Neil Postman asks:

FIGURE 9.9 *Samples of films and videos for content area learning.*

ENGLISH

Shakespeare in Love, Romeo and Juliet, Hamlet, Emma, Washington Square, Little Women, To Kill a Mockingbird, Wuthering Heights, A Raisin in the Sun, A Lesson Before Dying, Beowulf, The Rime of the Ancient Mariner, The Glass Menagerie, The Color Purple, Fahrenheit 451, Jacob Have I Loved, Sense and Sensibility, Mark Twain, The Importance of Being Earnest.

FINE AND PERFORMING ARTS

Sister Wendy, Alexander Calder, Moon and Sixpence, Pollack, West Side Story, Tommy, Oliver, Evita, Billy Elliot, Amadeus, Sunday in the Park with George, The Agony and the Ecstacy.

HISTORY AND GEOGRAPHY

The Crucible, Schindler's List, Not for Ourselves Alone, The Grapes of Wrath, Citizen Kane, 12 Angry Men, Secret Daughter, My Brother Sam Is Dead, Midnight Clear, Platoon, Regret to Inform, Saving Private Ryan, Slaughterhouse Five, Animal Farm, Les Miserables, Good Morning, Vietnam.

SCIENCE

Jurassic Park, The Hot Zone, Contact, The Elephant Man, Jane Goodall: Reason for Hope, Outbreak, Dragonheart, Galileo: On the Shoulders of Giants.

MATH

Stand and Deliver, Good Will Hunting, The Phantom Tollbooth, A Beautiful Mind, Infinity, N is a Number, Breaking the Code, Lost World.

PHYSICAL EDUCATION

Chariots of Fire, Hoop Dreams, A League of Their Own, The Field of Dreams, Space Jam, Late Bloomers, The Big Green, Like Mike.

TECHNOLOGY

Star Wars, Star Trek, Close Encounters of the Third Kind, The Dish, October Sky, Toy Story, Independence Day.

Would it not have been possible to foresee in 1947 the negative consequences of television for our politics or our children? . . . Would it not have been possible through social policy, political action, or education, to prepare for them and to reduce their severity? . . . Was it inevitable that by 1995 American children would be watching . . . 19,000 hours [of TV] by high school's end, and by age twenty would have seen 600,000 television commercials? (1999, p. 49)

Others insist that our children actually have a *broader* attention range as a result of actively channel surfing, keeping track of many shows simultaneously, and processing visual information rapidly (Dresang, 1999; Rushkoff, 1996). Dresang depicts children of today as capable and seeking connection through mutually supportive partnerships with other youth and adults, able to handle complexity and speak up for themselves. She sees digital culture as able to provide a nurturing environment for children's capabilities (p. 58).

As educators, we must be knowledgeable about our students' viewing habits and join their conversations with opinions and suggestions. This section represents my attempt to do just that. I raise issues relevant to content area teachers and share ideas about how we can maximize the educational opportunities television provides and enhance our students'

teleliteracy, including critical-viewing skills, thus minimizing television's potentially harmful effects.

Watching Television as a Content Area Teacher

You might be surprised at the number of things on television that are educational. Because this is so, become more aware of the information you learn as you watch, perhaps making notes to share with your students. As much as I love to read, I know that I have increased my knowledge of animals by watching television specials on ants, elephants, polar bears, and beavers. My background in art has always been limited, but Sister Wendy's series *The Story of Painting* (1997) provided an interesting overview and model of how to think about paintings, and motivated me to visit museums and continue my personal art education. I've found history documentaries to be fascinating and thought-provoking, as well as aesthetically and emotionally rewarding. The broader and richer our knowledge, the better teachers we can be. So, watch television consciously wearing your science teacher hat, or whatever other teacher hat you've chosen, as well as your interdisciplinary hat. Then, talk with your students about what you've learned, how you reacted to or critiqued a particular show, how new discoveries or insights connect to your curricu-

FIGURE 9.10   *Sample TV show alert.*

The nineteenth century sounds so far away. Why should you care about what those people of long ago were up to? How can I help make such "ancient" history real for you? Ken Burns' *Not for Ourselves Alone* (1999) focuses on the intimate friendship of Elizabeth Cady Stanton and Susan B. Anthony, based on their passion and lifelong devotion to the struggle to obtain rights for women. The documentary itself is a work of art, full of interesting anecdotes, photographs, quotes, connections to other movements such as abolition, and voices like that of Frederick Douglass. It entertains, uplifts, inspires, and promotes reflection. It's difficult to watch this show and remain apathetic about the right and obligation to vote. A companion site, www.pbs.org/stantonanthony, provides photographs from the documentary, as well as essays and historic documents relating to the women's suffrage movement. The companion book, with the same title (1999), is available as well.

---

lum. Bring up language issues, social justice issues, gender issues. Stimulate debate and critical thinking about the shows and about students themselves as media consumers.

Television critic David Bianculli believes that "educators who fear TV and run from it are heading in the wrong direction; they ought to use it and run with it" (1992, p. 78). I agree. Look through some education publishers' catalogs for resources to enhance your curriculum. Just as you craft and use booktalks, inform your students of upcoming worthwhile shows by giving "TV Show Alerts" (see Figure 9.10 for an example). You can share hints about what they might look for, questions to ask, and suggestions for active engagement with the information. Use reviews published in the newspaper to help you, especially if you haven't seen the show yourself.

Without preaching about how much time kids waste or how they're rotting their brains passively sitting in front of the set, you might raise issues by reading Chris Van Allsburg's picture book *The Wretched Stone* (1991), an allegory depicting sailors uninterested in reality and becoming less than human because they are so addicted to what they're watching on a strange box they've found. You can help them express, and perhaps write about, the benefits they feel they get from watching television, what they learn, how they select what to watch, and what connections they can make to the curricular subjects that are part of their school life.

The same motivational and instructional strategies you have been learning about and developing throughout this book can be applied to television, as well as written texts. The questions you ask and the questioning skills your students learn and develop can help them view shows and critically evaluate the substance and style. Many will welcome the increased ability to become aware of, analyze, and deconstruct purposes, methods used, and conscious and subliminal messages of television advertise-

ments. The patterns of organization found in text, such as cause–effect, compare–contrast, and sequence are equally present in television shows. In "The Simpsons Meet Mark Twain: Analyzing Popular Texts in the Classroom" (1998), Renee Hobbs shows how her students apply the tools of textual analysis to a popular program. In one *Simpsons* episode, they found this list of targets: "the role of government in inspecting the safety of nuclear plants; the use of bribery; the methods for identifying environmental destruction; the emotional pain of lying; lack of respect for elders; Charles Darwin and the theory of natural selection; the worker–boss relationship; women's intellectual freedom in relation to their husbands; and the political campaign process" (p. 50). Quite a lot to think about!

Fisherkeller (2000), based on an analysis of student talk about television, found that the young adolescents, ages 11–13, whom she studied had learned some of the rules of constructing and delivering television shows, and they understood television as a communication system with purposes and values. They noticed the storymaking craft and the plausibility of television, recognized that typical kinds of characters play off one another, and made real-world connections about the roles commercial media systems play in society. Fisherkeller recognizes the overwhelming task teachers have in finding ways to help students be "multiply literate" (p. 604), and recommends that literacy educators, media arts educators, library media specialists, and social studies teachers collaborate. "To accomplish these goals in today's complex media-saturated environment, all of us need to work together, continually and in a critical, reflective manner, to develop our knowledge and competencies as multiply literate members of the world" (p. 605).

Getting Ready to Teach 9.2 (see page 300)

FIGURE 9.11 *Books about television.*

Alexander, A., & Hanson, J. (Eds.). (2001). *Taking Sides: Clashing Views on Controversial Issues in Mass Media and Society.* Guilford, CT: McGraw-Hill/Dushkin.

Baker, W. F., & Dessart, G. (1998). *Down the Tube: An Inside Account of the Failure of American Television.* New York: Basic Books.

Bianculli, D. (1992). *Teleliteracy: Taking Television Seriously.* New York: Continuum.

David, L., & Seinfeld, J. (1998). *The Seinfeld Scripts: The First and Second Seasons.* New York: Harper-Perennial.

DeGaetano, G., & Bander, K. (1996). *Screen Smarts: A Family Guide to Media Literacy.* Boston: Houghton Mifflin.

Leonard, J. (1997). *Smoke and Mirrors: Violence, Television, and Other American Cultures.* New York: The New Press.

Pawlowski, C. (2000). *Glued to the Tube: The Threat of Television Addiction to Today's Family.* Naperville, IL: Sourcebooks.

Postman, N. (1985). *Amusing Ourselves to Death: Public Discourse in the Age of Show Business.* New York: Penguin Books.

Postman, N., & Powers, S. (1992). *How to Watch TV News.* New York: Viking Penguin.

Stay, B. L. (Ed.). (1999). *Mass Media: Opposing Viewpoints.* St. Paul, MN: Greenhaven Press.

Wallace, S., Worsnop, C. M., Tuson, L., & Bean, B. (1998). *The TV Book: Talking Back to Your TV.* Toronto, Canada: Annick Press.

You and the Mass Media (www.FilmicArchives.com).

Because we want our students to read, and they, for the most part, love television, we can have them read *about* this topic. There are good books that can teach them how to watch television well, know what to be suspicious of, and make wise decisions regarding the medium. Figure 9.11 lists examples of informative and provocative books to help students construct knowledge about the medium and their relationship with it. Critical thinking and reading are at work as students critique opinions and point out biases, inaccuracies, fallacies, and valid points made by researchers and authors. These texts may lead to interesting debates, position papers, letters to the editor, and other actions by your students.

It shouldn't be surprising that there are also a number of videos that deal with the topic of television and other media in terms of literacy and learning. These, too, can be helpful to ourselves and our students as we think about the values and drawbacks of television and work on improving our critical thinking in relation to what we see and hear. Figure 9.12 lists examples of media teaching and preaching about media.

Students Creating Television

Most schools and many individual teachers have easy-to-use video cameras that can be put to good academic use, no matter what your subject area. Students can videotape themselves enacting a readers' theatre production or dramatizing different points of view on controversial issues in government, envi-

FIGURE 9.12 *Media on media.*

Big Dream, Small Screen. (1997). Windfall Films, Ltd., PBS Video.

Does TV Kill? (1995). Frontline. Produced by Michael McLeod.

Ericsson, S., & Lewis, J. (2001). *Constructing Public Opinion: How Politicians and the Media Misrepresent the Public.* Northampton, MA: Media Education Foundation.

Halper, A., Fletcher, G. P., Knight, G., et al. (1995). *Trial by Television.* Alexandria, VA: PBS Video.

Knowledge Unlimited. (1997). *The News Media Under Fire.* Madison, WI: Author.

Magee, M. (Director). (1992). *On Television: Teach the Children.* San Francisco: California Newsreel.

Magee, M. (Director). (1996). *Media Literacy: The New Basic?* San Francisco: California Newsreel.

BookTalk 9.9

Looking for a book your students will pore over, talk about, come back to over and over? I've seen it happen with *The Simpsons: A Complete Guide to Our Favorite Family,* created by Matt Groening and edited by Ray Richmond and Antonia Coffman (1997), and the sequel, *The Simpsons Forever! A Complete Guide to Our Favorite Family . . . Continued.* (Groening & Gimple, 1999). Both the graphics and text are extremely detailed. Thousands of tidbits of information from and about the show are supplied, including literary allusions used, quotes and catchphrases that have entered mainstream language, song lyrics, secret jokes, statistics, each episode's blackboard gag, and biographies of major and minor characters. There are instructions on how to read the guide; for instance, a shaded green box in the middle of a page tells of "Movie, TV, literary, musical, or historical moments—this box contains the episode's references to various films, television programs, popular culture, and world history" (p. 13). You could use these books as an introduction to other types of guides readers can take advantage of, or use them just for fun.

ronmental science, or art. They can try out voices, try on the personalities of literary characters they read about, manipulate messages and presentations as they learn about the media and your curricular content. Producing material can help them to think and to be creative.

When my son Patrick was in eleventh grade, his teacher in a course called Scientific Thought divided his class into groups and gave each the task of researching and then teaching the rest of the class certain scientific principles. Patrick's group was responsible for teaching about nuclear fission and fusion. After an initial few minutes of panic over the difficulty of the assignment, they decided that their classmates would learn best by watching a television video. For the next 48 hours, they researched various sources, learned about fission and fusion, discussed how to get the main ideas across to others, and wrote a script involving a spy ring carrying out a mission to construct a nuclear bomb. They scrounged for props, background music, and costumes; made overhead transparencies of diagrams for the lecture taking place within the movie; and filmed their entertaining show, complete with a clip from a movie showing an explosion as the climax.

The lesson was a great success with the fans, and most of the other groups followed suit with their own homemade video lessons on the scientific concepts they were responsible for helping their classmates understand.

You may have similar memories of productions you took part in during your school days, either in courses focusing on the media or within other content area classes. History, science, and English classes can film debates, court cases based on current events, or booktalks for your classroom media library. Sometimes, it's possible to go public beyond school boundaries. For example, the television show *The Incredible Story Studio* encourages students to write stories for television shorts aimed at an audience of their peers. The show has been broadcast in Canada, the United States, Europe, Australia, Israel, parts of Latin America, and South Africa. A 68-page manual instructs student writers about elements such as character development and point of view. So, it certainly is possible to combine television producing and viewing with our curricular goals.

You and your students can make great use of a video camera. I have my students introduce themselves and their favorite book during the first week of class as a student tapes the activity. I bring the tape home to learn my students' names right away, and rapport begins to build because I can connect to them as fellow readers with particular literary interests. Mentor the students and provide instruction as they construct their videos. I certainly am not the technical expert when we film, but I am constantly aware of opportunities for mini-lessons on curricular topics or on effective ways to present ideas and information.

Let's imagine walking together through the corridors of Oswego Middle School in Oswego, New York, which is in a school district that has won an award from the Smithsonian Institute for its instructional use of technology. Here's what we might see on a typical day: In a biology lab, groups of students are using a software program to conduct a virtual dissection of a frog. Students in an English class are using a publishing software program to create a class newspaper that will be distributed in the lunchroom the next day. An art class is designing a webpage, and a French class is watching a screen as their teacher shows a Power-Point® presentation on grammar. Students in a chemistry lab are involved in a videoconference with preservice teachers at Oswego State University—they're explaining the experiment they're conducting and making hypotheses based on the data they have obtained so far. In a math classroom, students are working at computers to solve problems with which they have been challenged. In the television production lab, a daily news show is being produced and taped by students. (The program includes book, television show, and movie reviews.) In the media center, dozens of students from a variety of classes are researching topics on the Internet; some are working independently, others are conferring with teachers or library assistants or working in cooperative learning groups, planning their next steps in the learning process. In the teachers' room, several teachers are at computers typing in homework on a webpage that students and their parents can check every night; others are posting student work or creating new links to sites supporting their curricular topics. The school atmosphere is alive with discovery and enthusiasm. Technology is aiding and enhancing learning.

Dresang (1999) describes the *digital age* as "the societal landscape that has gradually emerged as computers have become more commonplace and as the Internet has become a locale where children can learn and play" (p. 6). She explains that *digital media* are created using bytes made up of bits—they cannot be fixed or frozen in a linear order, but can be endlessly rearranged; such media offer users a high level of interactivity and choice (p. 7). Obviously, the literacy required to comprehend and manipulate digital media is different from a traditional view of literacy.

ACTIVATING PRIOR KNOWLEDGE 9.4

Examine your own digital literacy for a few moments. When and how did you learn to use a computer for various purposes? When you use word processing for written assignments, does that change the way you compose? Does it change the quality of your thinking or your finished product? When you use the Internet to learn about topics in your classes, how does that differ from other kinds of reading and researching you do? Have you used tutorials either in school or at home to learn some subject? What software have you found particularly useful? What electronic games have you, or do you, spend time playing? In general, how has technology enhanced your learning or taken away from it?

Getting Ready to Teach 9.3 (see page 300)

The dichotomies that tend to be set up by advocates and opponents of classroom computer use are rarely helpful and often are misleading. Luckily, you probably won't have to join a pro or con technology camp as you get your first job. The verdict on whether computers and the Internet hold more of a promise or a threat to your future students and to you as a teacher will not be reached easily or soon. After all, television is still viewed as a distraction by some and a fantastic educational tool by others. But real questions *are* constantly being addressed relative to the uses of technology in education because resources are indeed limited and modes of learning and thinking are changing. There is a school district in New York that was mired in debate over whether to require all high school students to own laptops. After listening to strong public opinion, the district made having a laptop optional, at which point a third of the students signed up to buy them. A year later, virtually all students had laptops. Literacy itself is changing rapidly relative to technology, as are teaching and the materials used in our classrooms.

It is impossible for a content area literacy textbook like this to address all facets of technology and learning. I've chosen a few areas to address in this section, and given you suggestions for further exploration of this fascinating, fast-growing field. I introduce a few well-known people who have strong opinions about where technology is leading us and our students in terms of literacy, and then show how some teachers are helping their students use technology to advance literacy, critical-thinking skills, and content area learning. We can apply the compare–contrast pattern discussed in Chapter 6 as we read varying perspectives on the future of literacy and learning in the digital age.

VOICES OF CONCERN

Some predictions are cautious, some downright gloomy; educators are being warned against riding the tide of recent advances in technology and are being asked to recognize potential detrimental effects. Neil Postman, whose views on television you got a glimpse of in the previous section, cautions, "We can adapt ourselves to anything, including talking more to machines than people, but that is not an answer to anything" (1999, p. 42). He recommends that "we be particularly alert when reading books that take a visionary and celebratory stand on technologies of the future" (p. 44). Postman offers questions to help us think critically about technology:

- "What is the problem to which this technology is the solution?" (p. 42)
- "Whose problem is it?" (p. 45)
- "Which people and what institution might be most seriously harmed by a technological solution?" (p. 43)
- "What new problems might be created because we have solved this problem?" (p. 48)

Jane Healy, in *Failure to Connect: How Computers Affect Our Children's Minds—for Better or Worse* (2000), expresses grave concerns about where technology is leading. Connecting children to computers, she asserts, "has yet to demonstrate academic value, and some of the most popular 'educational' software may even be damaging to creativity, attention and motivation" (p. 3). She counts herself among the many educators who have "reluctantly moved from bedazzled advocacy to troubled skepticism" (p. 5) regarding digital technology. Healy worries about the time that computer activity inevitably takes away from other types of learning, how computer use might change developing brains, and the habits being formed as children use computers. She exhorts readers to "think about how to prepare our children for life in an information-loaded but depersonalized landscape. Is it by connecting them to computers, or

by spending comparable time on giving them an early grounding in humanity?" (p. 7). (I wonder how Healy might respond to the example of the children who researched international child labor conditions on the Internet and subsequently raised money for their counterparts in other countries.)

Katherine Paterson, winner of the 1998 Hans Christian Andersen Award for her contribution to children's literature, asks, "Why in a technological society do we care about literature at all?" (2000, p. 2) and follows with, "Is there anything on the World Wide Web that can nourish a child intellectually and spiritually in the sense that the best of books can?" (p. 5). We, as content area teachers, can look for answers to these crucial questions; Paterson begs us to do so: "I want those of us who care about children and their lives in the 21st century to stop long enough to notice and think . . . before we totally surrender our libraries to computer centers and our book budgets to software purchases" (pp. 1–2).

VOICES OF ENTHUSIASM

Many researchers and educators are very optimistic about literacy in the digital age; they do not predict that technology will make reading or books obsolete. But they do see big changes in the recent past and on the horizon that teachers must understand and adapt to. Don Tapscott, in *Growing Up Digital: The Rise of the Net Generation* (1998), offers reassuring words to worriers:

> Everybody relax. The kids are all right. They are learning, developing, and thriving in the digital world. They need better tools, better access, more services, and more freedom to explore, not the opposite. (p. 7)

By his account, only 0.5 percent of online material is violent, racist, or sexual. He sees children using the Internet as an active rather than a passive activity, having control and opportunities to make judgments and decisions.

Tapscott notes that by exploiting digital media, students and teachers can participate in a more powerful and effective learning paradigm. I think the following eight shifts of interactive learning may sound familiar to you at this point, because they are consistent with the kinds of opportunities we've been talking about that reading–writing workshops provide:

1. From linear to hypermedia learning
2. From instruction to construction and discovery
3. From teacher-centered to learner-centered education

4. From absorbing material to learning how to navigate and how to learn

5. From school to lifelong learning

6. From one-size-fits-all to customized learning

7. From learning as torture to learning as fun

8. From the teacher as transmitter to the teacher as facilitator (pp. 142–148)

Eliza Dresang, in *Radical Change: Books for Youth in a Digital Age* (1999), is another who does not fear the changes in literacy that are resulting from technological advances. But she leaves no doubt that Net generation readers are different in the way they learn, think, and construct and deconstruct information. Earlier images, such as "the child-as-innocent-and-in-need-of-protection" (p. 55) and "the child-as-depraved-and-in-need-of-redemption" (p. 56), are giving way to a new ideology of "the child-as-capable-and-seeking-connection" (p. 57). She explains, "Because even very young children have the opportunity to perform demanding tasks when they use technology and because they have the chance to demonstrate understanding of sophisticated topics that they meet in contemporary society, some adults . . . are noticing and acknowledging that children may be more able to handle complexity than was previously recognized" (p. 57). Dresang cites a review of research in the Spring 1997 issue of *Library Trends: Children and the Digital Library* (Jacobson) that indicates "the digital world is fostering involved, learner-directed education with students employing higher-order thinking skills" (Dresang, p. 64).

Earlier in the chapter I alluded to the expanding views of the concept of literacy. Dresang points out that the very definition of the term *reading* has changed because of digital-age materials and digital-age youth.

> "Reading" no longer means interacting with words on a page alone. In an increasingly graphic environment, words and pictures are merging. We see this on computer monitors and television screens, and we are beginning to see it in printed books. . . . The importance of words is not questioned, but the significance of a combined presentation using both words and pictures is heightened in the digital age. (p. 65)

Elizabeth Birr Moje (2000) feels hope for the knowledges and skills students will have in the future, recognizing that they will be different as a result of being shaped by information technologies. But inequality of access to those technologies causes her worry. "The difference between being and not being online may be a deciding factor in the question of who has and who does not in our world of the future" (p. 128).

BookTalk 9.10

What do you know about the microchip? Whatever your answer, you can add to your knowledge about and appreciation for the way microchips are changing the world by savoring *One Digital Day* (Smolen & Erwitt, 1998), from the *Day in the Life* series created by Rick Smolen. One hundred photographers went to 100 locations around the globe on a single day to capture the variety, wonder, and beauty of the microchip at work. It's a marvelous example of an interdisciplinary resource, because your future scientists, business managers, athletes, entertainers, medical workers, environmental engineers, travelers, religious leaders, historians, and clothing designers can all find information and pictures to entice them, fascinate them, and stimulate their own critical thinking and creativity. Teachers might find especially interesting the examples of students with disabilities able to keep pace with their classmates with the help of technology as well as communicate with others who share their experiences, hopes, and concerns via websites.

WHERE AM I ON THE CONTINUUM?

The answer to that question changes every year and fluctuates day by day, depending on whether I've found an exhilarating new virtual tour for my students to take or discovered the cord is missing to the department's LCD projector; whether I'm watching as a team of students proudly delivers a PowerPoint® presentation on education in Japan or looking into a high school media center that has actually placed in storage the books from what was formerly called the library in order to make room for the 185 computers it now houses. I'll tell you a little about my first attempts at using instructional technology.

Ninth-grade teacher Sharon Morley and I were partners on a federal Goals 2000 technology grant. At first, it felt like we had won the lottery. We each had a new laptop, and she acquired an LCD projector, a scanner, and a digital camera. She quickly learned which of her students were familiar with the technology and willing to serve as mentors and assistants. We organized an electronic pen-pal system. But frustration soon set in as problems developed at every stage of our learning and teaching. The "key pals" didn't always get each other's messages and attachments due to different computer systems. Sharon came to campus as a guest speaker, but when she tried to guide my English Methods class through a virtual tour of the Globe Theatre (which had worked perfectly that afternoon in her class-room), she found that when she accessed the site not a single door would open for her! We set up a teleconference between our two classrooms, but the technician who went to her school didn't get the camera in the right places at the right time, voices were muffled, confusion reigned. One of my stu-dents sighed, "They're only a half-mile away. Why don't we just walk there?" We became increasingly uncomfortable with the instructional time that was seemingly being wasted by technological difficulties. It wasn't long before our Goals 2000 colleagues were referring to us as "the conscience of the project" and "Sharon and Sharon Unplugged."

Perhaps not surprisingly, it was literature that rescued me and helped me make sense of our predicament and change my attitude. I read the biog-raphy *Snowflake Bentley* (Martin, 1998), the 1999 Caldecott Medal winner chronicling the years self-taught scientist Bentley painstakingly photographed snowflakes with the recently invented camera. I also read *October Sky* (Hickam, 1999), a memoir telling of a teenager's persistence in the face of repeated failure as he tried to make a working rocket.

I breathed deeply and bought a copy of *Who Gives a Gigabyte?: A Survival Guide for the Technolog-ically Perplexed* (Stix & Lacob, 1999). I was eventual-ly able to help even my resisting and complaining students to realize it was foolish to wait for the tech-nology to be perfected before we tried things. We came to view our trials and errors with instruction-al technology as an analogy for what all aspects of their teaching careers would be: a bumpy road, with

BookTalk 9.12

Eliza Dresang, in *Radical Change: Books for Youth in a Digital Age* (1999), predicts a great future for what she calls handheld books, though these books will be (and already are) radically different because of the effects of technology on both readers and authors. Her handheld book tells of several literary boundaries and barriers that have been broken in chapters such as "Handheld Hyper-text and Digital Design," "Multiple Perspectives," and "Characters, Chaos, and Community." Her book exempli-fies the characteristics of a digital age book; it is full of "bits and bytes," such as marginal annotations, invitations to visit websites along the way, tables and graphs, and illustrations from digital-age children's books. There is a thorough annotated bibliography of recommended books for youth, and many scholarly references for fur-ther exploration of the theories she puts forth. This book radically changed the way I teach my young adult and children's literature courses; it may make a radical differ-ence in how you begin your career as a content area teacher. You can connect to the companion website at http://slis-one.lis.fsu.edu/radicalchange/.

potential for wrong turns and storms, but one lead-ing to a truly exciting destination, and full of stim-ulation and lively learning along the way.

BookTalk 9.11

Have you ever known someone who seemed to relate better to machines than to people? Sara Moone, in Julie Johnston's *Adam and Eve and Pinch-Me* (1994), is a fos-ter child who has been rejected and hurt by so many adults that she prefers talking to her computer. She feels her writing is the one part of her life she has control over and uses the delete key liberally to get rid of thoughts, emotions, events, and people she'd rather forget. But, as life gets more complicated, she realizes she has some questions the machine can't answer. The reader realizes this digital-age youth has reached a turning point when she can't delete the love she's feeling for her foster par-ents, and she has to turn her computer off because her keyboard is getting crusted up. "Tears have a lot of salt in them" (p. 145).

CONTENT AREA TEACHING IN THE DIGITAL AGE

What does all of this mean for you as a content area teacher? You may be focusing on literacy for the first time as you read this book, and now you hear that literacy is radically changing! Will your stu-dents be reading more or less, better or not as well? Will reading be more or less necessary to gaining knowledge and skills in your content area course? Will books be more or less a part of your classroom? How much time should students be spending on computers? Where and how will students get infor-mation and grapple with concepts and issues rele-vant to your course?

You'll figure out answers that satisfy you and positions you're comfortable with as you talk with students, guide their reading and other ways of seek-ing knowledge, and watch them learn using various media. In terms of resources, things have never been better. Tapscott (1998) predicts:

The ultimate interactive learning environment will be the Web and the Net as a whole. It increasingly includes the vast repository of human knowledge, tools to manage this knowledge, access to people, and a growing galaxy of services ranging from sandbox environments for preschoolers to virtual laboratories for medical students studying neural psychiatry. (p. 142)

In Chapter 4, you learned the importance of background knowledge as students learn content. The Internet, including online reference services, can be assumed to have virtually all the background information your students and you might need for any curricular topic, and most students will willingly and actively engage in the search for it. For example, I could ask students to find examples on the Internet of utopias and dystopias before reading Lois Lowry's *The Giver*. Afterward, I might help them find websites with reviews of the book, scholarly essays relating to the book, and information about the author. Students may in turn recommend sites to me about topics they explored for follow-up projects: memory, euthanasia, government control, near-death experiences.

Of course, you can't just *tell* students to do research on the Internet; this, like every other aspect of your job, requires instruction, modeling, mentoring, monitoring, and assessing, as well as creativity and decision making on your part. Bruce (1998) explains that teachers cannot easily separate the use of new technologies in literacy from standard practices; rather, they should combine a variety of old and new tools in innovative ways, thus developing hybrid practices. Similarly, your students are simultaneously developing their technology expertise while gaining content information and strategies that will help them explore the discipline you teach. Technology supplies tools for learning, but the students and you are in a dynamic process that results in that actual learning.

Who can help you answer Bruce's (1999/2000) question, "How can [Web] searching become not only looking up, but truly productive inquiring?" (p. 351). Perhaps you can visit your school cybrarian for assistance! Kapitzke (2001) describes the transition from libraries to cybraries:

The cybrary is an electronic gateway for clients located anywhere to access information located everywhere.... The library was the place students went to acquire a selective tradition of information use and its application to a curricular unit. By contrast, the cybrary must be both a place and a space not only for learning information, but also for learning how to use information. (pp. 451–453)

The specialists in changing libraries can teach you and your students how to utilize the technological treasures of knowledge at your disposal.

As with media texts, students need you to help them be wise consumers and users of technology, and to recognize manipulation and subtle control or enticement. For example, you could instruct your students to explore the Internet site ZapMe!, which provides students, teachers, and parents with many free resources, along with advertising targeted at teen consumers. Students could judge for themselves the worth of the information and entertainment sections, and then read Bettina Fabos' article "ZAPME! Zaps You" (2000). See if they—and you—agree with the author's worry about the limitations and constraints of the offerings, and the cautionary critique of ZAPME!:

It is because of . . . these kinds of calculated attempts to influence pedagogy and the entire educational environment toward a noneducational goal (and then to make educational claims to the contrary)—that educators need to begin questioning the economic and political motives behind the literacy practices related to new technology, and to also help students build these kinds of critical literacy skills. (p. 724)

There are online resources to guide students' site evaluations. One (www.classroom.com/edoasis/evaluation.html) provides online worksheets for educators and students. Another (www.oswego.edu/~hyang2/edu/webevaluation.htm) provides criteria in categories such as accuracy, authority, objectivity, currency, and coverage. Kathy Schrock's Teacher helpers: Critical Evaluation Information (http://school.discovery.com/schrockguide/eval.html) is a comprehensive site that provides other evaluation resources. Gardner, Benham, and Newell (2000) point out that teachers have always had the responsibility of instructing students involved in the research process to check on source quality and credibility. They found that helping students navigate the huge amount of information on the Web is rewarding because their students start applying the same criteria to print sources.

The Internet can help you as you prepare your units and lessons. You'll have stories, interesting trivia, intriguing dilemmas, data, current research results, and visual and auditory aids that make your subject interesting and stimulate your students to question and reflect. You can find resources to help you provide well for those students who are ELLs; for example, the Center for the Study of Books in Spanish for Children and Adolescents' website at www.csusm.edu/campuscenters/csb/. You can find many professional journals online—check out www.gort.ucsd.edu/newjour for a comprehensive list of e-journals and other serial publications. There's a lot to celebrate as you prepare to teach in the digital age.

The tools of technology can also help as you and your students present material and findings to others. Current professional books and journals are full of examples of excitement and enthusiasm related to the use of authoring and presentation programs. Tapscott (1998) remarks:

> Young people are employing everything from photocopiers, video cameras, computers and the Internet to further their media creations.
>
> The best known of these youth media creations is the *zine*—self-published labors of love containing journalistic and creative writing, band profiles, comics, and manifestos, often in the form of parodies.... Increasingly, zines are also distributed over the Net with aficionados offering reviews, descriptions, and buyer contact information on their personal home pages. (p. 82)

Tapscott offers a specific example of a diverse group of high school students with 15 different languages spoken, cooperatively learning about, designing, and presenting webpages. They worked cooperatively in groups, using each other and technology-based resources before going to their teacher for any help. One youngster who spoke almost no English and who would normally not have the courage to present to the class was coaxed by classmates to do so. The result? "'My webpage . . . First time . . . Graphics . . . See link. Thank you.' All the other kids applauded.... Afterward, outside the classroom, he approached [his teacher] and said to him, smiling broadly, 'I am proud'" (p. 155).

Figure 9.13 shows a sample of "The Elizabethan Globe," created by ninth graders in Sharon Morley's class using computer software programs and the Internet.

One of the ways you can increase your knowledge of the instructional uses of technology is to read journal articles and other first-hand accounts from teachers who have used various technologies successfully. For example, Dennis Lawrence (1999) explains the year-long collaborative Internet research his students conduct—they use online tutorials (www.arthes.com/kancrn) to learn the research process and specific strategies, then apply what they learn to their own spinoff research; their results were to be published on a website, the Kansas Collaborative Research Network (http://kancrn.org/).

Content Area Uses of E-Mail

I'm sure I don't have to sell you on the wonders and benefits of e-mail. You've probably communicated this way for years for both social and business purposes. But, you may just be starting to realize how helpful it can be in your classroom as you teach your subject and enhance your students' literacy strategies and study skills. Wolffe (1998) used e-mail journals addressed to him to help reluctant students overcome their fear of math and to expand their mathematical knowledge base. He required students to summarize what had been addressed in the day's class, then talk about an aspect of their learning experience that went well or was problematic. Students asked questions for clarification, expressed frustrations, and wrote reflections on their learning processes that often indicated an improved self-image as math students. Many of my own students tell me they prefer writing to an electronic literature circle to respond to a book read in class instead of writing a response in a journal. They like the idea of an audience who will get their thoughts soon. Here are snippets of an "e-mail circle" discussion among my preservice teachers after reading *Freak the Mighty* by R. Philbrick (1993):

■ I loved how the two characters combined to make a single entity. FREAK THE MIGHTY! Quite the name, eh? I mean this book shows that everyone, no matter how bad they have it, can find a friend, a lesson that I quite frankly find important to everyone from middle school to high school. The reader gains a respect and love for the characters. Our students will gain this respect as well. Maybe they will ask someone they never thought to ask before to hang out. Maybe it will change how students look at the "freaks" in their classes, in their lives. It builds social awareness.

—Jason Gibson

■ I wonder if they would have been willing to trade places. What would have happened if, given the opportunity, they could have swapped bodies? Would Max have willingly sacrificed his health, and ultimately his life, to save Kevin? I think so. But I don't think Kevin would have allowed him to.

What would have happened if technology was advanced enough to give Kevin his "robot body"? Would he have needed Max then? I think the relationship was such a delicate symbiosis, that upsetting the balance of give-and-take (Kevin giving Max his brain, Max giving Kevin his body), that although Kevin's attitude toward Max would probably not change, Max would feel that Kevin didn't need him anymore.

—Sarah Beckwith

■ I thought to respond to this book I would try to relate it to science. I felt that the relationship

FIGURE 9.13 *"The Elizabethan Globe" created by ninth graders.*

June 27, 1640

Volume 4, Issue 68

Only Two Pence

The Elizabethan Globe

"The Newspaper preferred by King Henry VIII"

Inside this issue:

The Queen's Parade	2
New Dessert at Barney's	2
Your Horoscope	3
Today's Weather	3
Shakespeare's Bio	4
New Constable	5
Classified	5

We wish a happy birthday to:

- Prince Arthur of Scotland Turns 12
- Elizabeth Baker, Turns 30
- John Blacksmith Senior Turns 40
- Anne Carpenter, Turns 28
- David Woodcutter Turns 34
- Matt Teacher Turns 20
- The Smith Twins Turned 14

The Joust of the Year

The finals of the "Masters of The Lance" will take place at 6 pm, June 30 at Wembley Castle grounds in Verona. Almost every castle in the eastern half of Europe submitted their best horse, and their best man. During the tournament started off with 100 riders, two riders remain:

After fierce and exciting, battles, Noble Christian, from London, England, and Prince Craig from the Orkney Islands in Scotland.

Here are the basic jousting rules that have been used during the tournament:
1. Only rich families are allowed to play. It is illegal for any commoners to play
2. You need two horsemen,

and two horses.
3. The riders carry a shield and a spear around 10 feet long.
4. The horses run at each other and the object is to knock your opponent off his horse.

Noble Christian has been jousting for 5 years. This is his first time in the "Masters of The Lance" tournament. Christian is the under dog for the final bout. Prince

Craig has been riding for 15 years. He is the 3 time defending champ. "I know this chap might be good, but he is no match for me." said the cocky Prince.

There are rumors that royalty as high as King Henry VIII will watch the bout that could go on for some time, considering they are both undefeated. So if you are interested in the greatest joust of the year, stop by. Tickets are still available.

King Henry the VIII Has a New Favorite Game

King Henry tried out the new game called 'bowls' with Peter of Scotland. At 3 on Wednesday Henry said, "I like that someone of my size could be the best at this game. Considering it doesn't involve running." When the King and Peter played together, King

Henry won 100 - 85.

When we asked Peter, "Do you like this game?"

He replied, "Well I would have liked the game better if I would've won! But I had a great time in the

Kings court ."

Bowl consists of 9 pins, and an 8 inch ball that is rolled to knock the pins down.

between Max and Freak [Kevin] was similar to that of mutualistic relationships in animals. Both characters had some kind of strong point and both had a weak point. They used each other in a way they both found beneficial. Freak was smart and imaginative, which helped compensate for Max's lack of confidence in his own intelligence. Max was big and strong, which helped benefit Freak, who was small and weak. Together, with little Freak on Max's shoulders, they became Freak the Mighty, and they used their combined strong points to go on adventures and quests. This is a perfect mutualistic relationship where both organisms benefit from one another and no harm is done.

—*Jim Knote*

E-mail allows many other voices into your classroom and your lessons. You can invite parents and other community members to serve as "expert friends"—informal consultants in the game of learning. You might have a doctor, a scientist, an accountant, a city council member, a factory worker, a librarian, a machinist, a mother who is home schooling, a systems analyst, a sports commentator, and a secretary on call via e-mail. Your students can ask their parents to volunteer to share hobbies and interests. One student's parent might be a Civil War buff, another a snowmobiler, yet another a gourmet cook. Authentic reading, writing, and learning opportunities are made possible through the medium of e-mail. LISTSERV® software allows groups to grapple with problems, present new ideas, converse about activities that went on in class, and recommend and respond to texts.

E-mail can also stimulate creative writing from your students. Noah Baumbach's article "Van Gogh in AOL" (2000) can be used as a model of someone having fun with the genre. The author's imagination brought Van Gogh into the digital age. In e-mail messages to his brother Theo, we read lines like, "Thank you for the money. With it, I bought a blazing tangerine iMac. . . . Just got an Instant Message from Gauguin, who clearly has me on his buddy list. . . . Visited an Impressionist chat room today. . . . I know you try your hardest to sell my work, but have you considered eBay?. . . . Check out my home page" (pp. 51–52). Students can create e-mail conversations between scientists, political figures, novel characters, and mathematicians they have learned about in your courses. Of course, you can insert some Instant Messages of your own!

We can learn much about adolescents' thoughts, interests, and e-mail writing style by corresponding with them. Here's an unsolicited example I received from a 15-year-old who seems very comfortable composing in her chosen "voice":

> Hey Aunt Sharon, 'tis I, the great and Powerful . . . Alison. Anticlimactic, yes, but impressive to a point. Ok, no it's not. Whatever.
>
> Anyway. So how ye been? I've been pretty good. I just wanted to drop you a line to tell you that come this summer, I'm gonna get me published. IN A BOOK. A real, live . . . oh, wait . . . not live, book. Thought you'd be interested to know that. It's a book o' poetry, *Between Darkness and Light*, and it's being published by The International Library of Poetry.
>
> If you really want to, you can see the poem that's getting published . . . on my website. You can look around if you want (and sign the guestbook), but know that there's an occasional strong word in some of my poems . . .

Developing a Classroom Home Page

Leu and Leu (1999) believe there are four important results to be gained from making a home page for a classroom:

> First, developing a home page helps your students. It provides a location for publishing student work and it allows you to organize safe links to Internet locations . . . you want them to use. Second, . . . as you develop instructional materials and links to information resources, you will find other classrooms visiting your page, benefiting from your instructional ideas. Third, developing a home page enables you to forge a tighter link between home and school. . . . Parents can use your home page to see what is taking place in your classroom and communicate with you. . . . Finally, developing a home page helps the teaching profession. . . . It projects an important image of professionalism to the public—teachers embracing new technologies and using these in powerful ways to guide students' learning. (p. 303)

Leu and Leu give an example showing the steps a certain teacher took to create a classroom webpage and the ways she now uses it. One day, she told her students of a new link that might help them with their Internet research projects, reminded them of an assignment to write to their parents via e-mail or by word processing and printing a hard copy using the classroom computer system, and announced that several messages had been posted by people from other schools who had visited their home page. She encouraged students to read and respond to these communications.

ACTION RESEARCH   9.B

To examine a variety of classroom home pages within a particular school, go to www.oswego.org and explore by clicking on the teachers' names or subject areas. List in your learning log ideas that you think you'd like to include in a home page of your own. If you wish, post a message on the webpage of a class you'd like to know more about.

BookTalk   9.13

There are sites on the Internet that explain how to set up a webpage. There are also software programs designed to lead you through the steps of designing and implementing your own. But, if you prefer to start off by getting cozy and sitting with a nonthreatening book that serves the same purpose, try *Make Your Own Web Page!* by Ted Pedersen and Francis Moss (1998). After introducing several different kinds of sites and ways to make one, it describes and illustrates the basic steps for imagining your personal site, planning it, building it, launching it, and maintaining it. It's easy, illustrated, and full of examples and helpful resources.

BookTalk   9.14

It might surprise you that I want to recommend a book that announces on both the front and back covers, "Read Less, Learn More," but there are more than 300 pages of color illustrations for you to "read" in *Teach Yourself Computers and the Internet Visually* by Ruth Maran (1998). Not even an introductory chapter is written in prose; every chapter consists of pictures with captions and labels. Words are definitely not the focus, and are used sparingly, but effectively, in conjunction with the diagrams and photographs to define terms and explain processes and functions. I found the book a visually satisfying experience that increased my basic knowledge of the subject. I think it's especially helpful for beginners who feel overwhelmed by the technical terminology others seem to be tossing around with such ease.

Getting Ready To Teach 9.4 (see p. 300)

ASSISTIVE TECHNOLOGY FOR STUDENTS WITH SPECIAL NEEDS

Jeff is a seventh grader with a learning disability. Although he's intellectually curious and particularly loves science and social studies, he gets bogged down every night with his homework because he can't decode the multisyllabic words in his textbook. His mother works with him, but she's getting tired of the nightly struggles. Chen is Jeff's classmate. She reads fluently in Chinese, but most of the texts she's responsible for reading are in English, and her vocabulary is much less developed in this second language. Chen's parents do not read English at all, so she must tackle the homework alone. Trying hard is not enough; she simply doesn't know the words.

One day their teacher produces several "Quicktionary Reading Pens" he has recently acquired. Jeff, Chen, and others are allowed to use them in school and sign them out for nights and weekends. Now, when they encounter a word they don't know, they can scan it and see it displayed in large characters on the side of the pen. They can hear the word read aloud from the built-in speaker and press a button to get the definition. They are meeting with success.

The Quicktionary pen is just one example of assistive technology, which, as its name implies, helps people who are struggling with tasks for any reason. Examples of assistive technology range from computerized speech synthesizers, such as physicist Stephen Hawking uses, to screen reading programs for the visually impaired. *Computer and Web Resources for People with Disabilities: A Guide to Exploring Today's Assistive Technologies* (The Alliance for Technology Access, 2000) begins with stories of individuals who have overcome obstacles related to disabilities with the help of computers. Victor, who has cerebral palsy, used a scanning device activated by a switch to communicate; he graduated from a New York State high school with a Regents diploma. John, who also has cerebral palsy, used a computer throughout school and beyond; with a Bachelor of Fine Arts in film and video, he uses a micro-switch on his lip and a pointing device on his head to produce 3-D animation. Dusty has Down Syndrome and has used assistive technology such as screen magnification software in high school and college as she learned keyboarding, word processing, and the use of the Internet. Chase, who became quadriplegic from polio at the age of eight, used multiple forms of assistive technology that could be operated with a mouth stick as he went through high school, college, and law school. He now uses a speech-input program that allows him to bypass the keyboard and dictate to his computer.

This resource guide provides a wealth of Internet addresses to search in order for individuals with disabilities, their families, and educators to find out what technology is available and ways of finding financial support to acquire the assistive technology. It describes how to use various tools such as a touch screen, keyboard additions, electronic pointing devices, trackballs, word prediction programs, reading comprehension programs, writing composition programs, talking and large-print word processors, closed circuit televisions, electronic notetakers, and much more.

Teachers are finding ways to use all sorts of technology, whether labeled assistive or not, in content area classrooms with students who are having trouble succeeding. For example, Brown (2000) presents a model of a study skills program that uses technology both to teach skills and to aid high school students in producing quality work for subject area assignments. The study skills center has 10 multimedia computers, digital and video cameras, a graphic scanner, software programs, and printers; technology is seen not as a subject unto itself, but rather a tool for learning. Structured lessons, skills practice, and independent work all play a part in this program. The software program *Inspiration* aids with planning written papers or presentations and making organizational charts for various core-subject areas. Students are taught how to evaluate websites and cite online sources. They use online references such as www.dictionary.com and www.encyclopedia.com. Student work is published on a classroom website. Some students benefit from a reading software program called *Ultimate Speed Reader*; some use the CD-ROM program *The American Heritage Talking Dictionary*, which provides definitions and synonyms for entered words and speaks the words. Students play computer versions of *Scrabble* and *Hang2000* to aid vocabulary development, *Mindbenders* to improve math strategies, *Grammar Games* to reinforce language skills, *ThinkAnalogies* to enhance recognition of and thinking about relationships, and *Macmastermind* to improve analytical-thinking skills. Brown reports success with the continued integration of new technologies and resources, as they are developed, into study skills programs. Of course, as with other materials, you should check out the electronic learning programs and evaluate them in terms of your students' needs and your philosophy of education. Some programs offer little more than new packaging of the drill exercises offered in standard workbooks. Others are truly innovative, inspirational, challenging, and interactive. Use all programs judiciously, and listen to your students' evaluation of them also.

CONCLUSION

There's no question that schools and modes of learning are changing rapidly along with everything else in the world, and that you must be prepared to teach much differently from the way you were probably taught. Mahiri (2001) promotes literacy practices shaped by "pop culture pedagogy" (p. 382), which uses such modes of transmission as video games, music compact discs, the Internet, television, and movies, with multitextual, multimodal, and often multicultural aspects influencing meaning making and learning. Mahiri laments the slowness of schools thus far to use pop culture as a way to help students overcome the constraints they often perceive on their school learning. He explains:

> If schooling is to survive these pop culture ways of knowing and being, it too must transform. I am not advocating that teachers attempt to significantly incorporate pop culture pedagogy into schools. Pop culture works in young people's lives in context-specific ways that often could not be reproduced in the context of school. Rather I am suggesting that teachers continue to become more aware of the motives and methods of youth engagement in pop culture in terms of why and how such engagement connects to students' personal identifications, their needs to construct meanings, and their pursuit of pleasures and personal power. Teachers should explore how work in schools can make similar connections to students' lives, but the real challenge is to make these connections to and through changing domains of knowledge, critical societal issues, and cognitive and technical skills that educators can justify their students will actually need to master the universe of the new century.

In this chapter, I've tried to give you, the content area teacher, some things to think about in terms of the expanding literacies of today. I hope you'll pursue the topics of media literacy, pop culture, and digital literacy much more thoroughly as you continue growing in your professional career and learning more about how adolescents interact with our rapidly changing technologies and world. The new materials and modes of presentation do not alter the fact that students will always need teachers. They need you to model, instruct, mentor, facilitate, give suggestions, listen, and learn along with them. You can help them be critical consumers of media and information derived and constructed from the media.

Let's end with the question, "Where do books fit in the digital age?" Will technology change literacy to the point of making books and book lovers obsolete? I'll give my prediction by pointing to Negroponte's explanation for publishing *Being Digital* (1995) as "an old-fashioned book" (p. 7):

> Interactive multimedia leaves very little to the imagination. Like a Hollywood film, multimedia narrative includes such specific representations that less and less is left to the mind's eye. By contrast, the written work sparks images and evokes metaphors that get much of their meaning from the reader's imagination and experiences. When you read a novel, much of the color, sound and motion come from you. I think the same kind of personal extension is needed to feel and understand what "being digital" might mean to your life. You are expected to read yourself into this book. (p. 8)

CHAPTER NINE

Getting Ready to Teach

9.1 Begin a file of films, videos, and so forth for the subject you will teach. Search catalogs, bookstores, and libraries. Watch one or more of the resources you find and write a movie review or a "Film Alert" for your students.

9.2 Marnie W. Curry-Tash (1998) asserts, "Many media educators today believe that, just as media constructs a version of world and self, viewers actively 'read' and construct a 'television text' in a way that can be oppositional or subversive" (p. 44). Watch a television show, a documentary, or a video related to a topic you might teach in your content area. Then, create a viewing guide to aid your students' understanding of and critical thinking about the piece. Help them to view actively and attentively and to construct meaning. Tap into their background knowledge. You can connect it to other texts they might have read in your class. You can use the formats that have been used all through this book—graphic organizers, anticipation guides, K-W-L-S, or Venn diagrams.

9.3 Imagine you are being interviewed for a teaching position in your chosen subject area. The department chairperson says, "There is an ongoing dispute among our faculty. Some say computers in classrooms have really made our jobs harder. The kids don't want to do anything but play with the software and surf the Internet; books are becoming obsolete. Other teachers are leading the effort to allocate even more of our limited resources to improve the technology available to teachers and students, insisting that this will result in better literacy and more content knowledge being gained. Where do you stand on the issue?" The chairperson gives no indication of how she, the principal, or the other teachers at the interview feel about the topic.

Spend a few moments writing your response to this challenge. Then, if possible, debate with someone (another candidate for the position, maybe) who has an answer different from yours.

9.4 Begin designing a webpage for your content area courses. If you already have a personal webpage, include parts of it in your new teacher webpage or create a link between the two. Work with other prospective teachers and look at secondary teachers' webpages to get ideas about what to include. You might post some of the things you have written while working through this book, as well as materials you've created for other classes. You might have book reviews and booktalks; sources for researching various topics within your field; pictures, quotes, and cartoons appropriate for the course; annotated bibliographies; and links to other websites. If applicable, scan in action photographs of you and your students, as well as projects they've completed or participated in.

Assessment of Content Area Literacy

When the International Reading Association (IRA) published "Adolescent Literacy: A Position Statement" in 1999, it insisted that the students in our middle and secondary schools deserve, among other things:

Assessment that shows them their strengths as well as their needs and that guides their teachers to design instruction that will best help them grow as readers. . . . Adolescents deserve classroom assessments that bridge the gap between what they know and are able to do and relevant curriculum standards; they deserve assessments that map a path toward continued literacy growth. (p. 103)

Ok, you might be thinking, fine, who can argue with these lofty statements? But what's a content area teacher supposed to do? What does this have to do with me? And how do I learn what I have to in order to get on board and give my students what they deserve in terms of assessment?

Assessment and teaching go hand in hand and must be consistent. It makes no sense to teach according to one philosophy and use assessment tools that reflect a different, perhaps opposing, one. For example, during my early teaching days, I was a seventh-grade reading teacher in a rural middle school, and our district was visited by evaluators from the State Education Department. A man came into my classroom carrying a clipboard and proceeded to go through my files. At one point he asked me, "How many of your students have mastered the skill of making inferences?" I quickly and confidently replied, "None." When he looked up with a surprised expression, I added that *I* hadn't mastered the skill either. We believed in lifelong learning and growth in this school, and I expected that as my students and I grew in experience, knowledge, and wisdom, we would get better and better at making inferences from exceedingly more difficult texts and real-world interactions. The evaluator lived by the philosophy of mastery learning and had an entire page of discrete reading skills he thought my students should have "mastered."

The chapters in this book have espoused a certain kind of teaching—one that is student-centered, one that uses authentic texts such as literature and real-world documents, and one that views learning as constructivist, where students work to make meaning through experience, talking, listening, writing, and reflection. It should come as no surprise, then, that this chapter explains and recommends several types of authentic assessment that will help you know your students' strengths and needs in both their content learning and their literacy. Furthermore, you'll learn how to connect assessment to further instruction that will help you and your students meet the standards and goals set by others and by themselves. Assessment, if properly understood and done well, is one of the best tools at teachers' and learners' disposal.

How to develop good tests related to your subject matter and to find out how well your students are understanding the curriculum and skills you're teaching is a very important topic that is beyond the scope of this book. You might learn how to construct tests in an education class on instructional methods or in a course devoted to assessment and evaluation. What *is* relevant to this book is how those tests and other assessment devices connect to your students' literacy. For example, there might be a student in your class who gets a failing grade on your end-of-unit test. It might look like she did not grasp the concepts you taught, but in reality, it's possible that she could not read some of the words in the questions or misread some of the multiple-choice options. Knowing this is crucial to your decision as to what to do next with this student. Perhaps she needs to have tests read to her. Students with limited English proficiency are often at risk of not doing well on tests they have to read.

Or, perhaps you have a student like Eric in your class. His mother writes:

> Eric's writing ability lagged far behind his reading comprehension and made the successful completion of written assignments almost impossible for him. His struggle with written expression was significant, and it negatively affected his grades in each subject throughout his school years. (Nierstheimer, 2000, p. 36)

What if Eric had the help of a scribe who could record his high-level knowledge about his school subjects? What if he were allowed to use a laptop or to record his thoughts onto a tape? It might take further assessment and some trial and error before the best method of assessing and assisting Eric's learning is found, but Eric, as the IRA's position paper quoted earlier points out, deserves those efforts on our part. So, think about literacy issues when you construct and grade tests and ask your students about how they handled the reading and writing aspects of your evaluations.

This chapter provides you with the knowledge and stimuli necessary to help you learn to use assessment and instruction together to further your students' content literacy. Part One addresses several major issues relating to assessment in general. In Part Two, I explain several literacy assessment strategies you can use in your classroom to inform instruction. Finally, Part Three addresses issues relating to the self-assessment of your instruction and your growth as a content area teacher who is concerned with students' (and your own) literacy development.

PART ONE

General Assessment Issues

ACTIVATING PRIOR KNOWLEDGE 10.1

Reflect on times in your academic life when your knowledge has been assessed. What types of measurement instruments were used? What exactly was being evaluated? For what purposes? And how accurate would you say the assessment results were? What did they tell about you? Write in your log about these or related issues.

Now reflect on your extracurricular activities, such as sports, drama, community service, part-time jobs. How was your performance evaluated in *those* areas? What were the purposes and/or results of the assessment?

I have dealt with assessment issues, at least indirectly, in every one of the previous chapters; it's virtually impossible to discuss instruction and learning without bringing in assessment because they are intertwined. Assessment is inherent in many of the strategies that have been explained and exemplified. Just think about K-W-L-S—the first column asks readers to list what they already know about a topic. That's assessing prior knowledge, which can help you determine what to do next instructionally. In this chapter, the actual focus is on assessment. The text and activities will stimulate and guide your thinking about how you, as a content area teacher, can and should use assessment strategies as you work toward improving and enhancing your students' content knowledge and content literacy. I invite you to jump right in by taking on the teacher/assessor role and react to the student product in Action Research 10.A.

Anastasia, a fourth grader in Lois Lowry's *Anastasia Krupnik* (1979), wrote the science-related poem (see Action Research 10.A, below) for a class assignment, taking eight days and showing a unique process. Finally, after reading and rereading her finished product, she writes this self-assessment at home: "I wrote a wonderful poem" (p. 13). Then, the day came when the class had to read their poems aloud. As you read the following excerpt, notice the different criteria that Anastasia and her teacher use in their evaluation processes:

> Mrs. Westvessel looked puzzled. "Let me see that, Anastasia," she said. Anastasia gave her the poem.
>
> Mrs. Westvessel's ordinary, everyday face had about one hundred wrinkles in it. When she looked at Anastasia's poem, her forehead and nose folded up so that she had two hundred new wrinkles all of a sudden.
>
> "Where are your capital letters, Anastasia?" asked Mrs. Westvessel. Anastasia didn't say anything.
>
> "Where is the rhyme?" asked Mrs. Westvessel. "It doesn't rhyme at *all*." Anastasia didn't say anything.
>
> "What kind of poem is this, Anastasia?" asked Mrs. Westvessel. "Can you explain it, please?"
>
> Anastasia's voice had become very small again, the way voices do, sometimes. "It's a poem of sounds," she said. "It's about little things that live in tidepools, after dark, when they move around. It doesn't have sentences or capital letters because I wanted it to look on the page like small creatures moving in the dark."
>
> "I don't know why it didn't rhyme," she said, miserably. "It didn't seem important."

ACTION RESEARCH 10.A

Imagine that you have been given the following poem (Lowry 1979, pp. 11–12) by one of your students:

hush   hush   the sea-soft night is aswim

    with wrinklesquirm creatures

          listen(!)

to them   move   smooth   in the moistly dark

    here in the   whisperwarm   wet

What is your response to this text? What do you like about it? What suggestions might you have for the writer? What grade would you give it? Is there information that would help you as you assign a grade? Reflect in your log, then discuss your response and possible questions or musings with a group of your peers.

Poem reprinted with permission.

"Anastasia, weren't you listening in class when we talked about writing poems? . . . when we talked about poetry in this class we simply were not talking about worms and snails crawling on a piece of paper. I'm afraid I will have to give you an F. . . . "

At home, that evening, Anastasia got her green notebook out of her desk drawer. Solemnly, . . . she crossed out the word *wonderful* and replaced it with the word *terrible.*

"I wrote a terrible poem," she read sadly. (pp. 12–14)

Excerpt from *ANASTASIA KRUPNIK.* Copyright © 1979 by Lois Lowry. Reprinted by permission of Houghton Mifflin Company. All rights reserved.

How anxious do you think Anastasia will be to write more poetry for this class, this teacher? That little scenario may have elicited a strong reaction from you or maybe a vivid memory of a moment in your school career when your own opinion of your work differed from that of an outside evaluator. Technically, the teacher did nothing wrong. She had established criteria, which Anastasia had not followed, upon which to judge the finished product. Yet, she had choices within the context of her classroom; for example, she could have chosen not to grade this poem, but let Anastasia know that she valued it in its own right, and given her another opportunity to write a poem following the formula outlined for the class. Or she could have decided to be flexible in terms of her criteria, recognizing that this particular student's abilities, needs, and purposes did not match the somewhat arbitrary rules set up in an effort to help fledgling poetry writers. The moment certainly called for teacher decision making in terms of what the next instructional step should be to help Anastasia's growth as a writer. You'll be provided with many such opportunities as you teach and assess your students' work and processes.

ACTION RESEARCH ≫≫≫≫≫≫≫≫≫≫ 10.B

Before moving on, practice responding to two more pieces of student work.

DIRECTIONS: Place a grade on each of the following real samples of student texts, and then write a short note to the writer.

(1) This text was written during a ninth-grade unit on mythology in response to the prompt, "If you could visit the land of the dead, whom would you look for and what would you do?" (You might want to think first about how *you* would answer the question):

> If I could visit the land of the dead, I wouldn't go because I would be too scared. Seeing dead people would make me realize that I won't live forever and I couldn't take it.

(2) The following was written by a tenth-grade student during a poetry unit:

> **The Dark Side**
>
> As devils mock and prey on all who know,
> the secrets that will save the soul of man,
> I dwell in endless thought that burns my eyes.
> The searing pain from which I shall escape,
> engulfs a world that soon will be just dust.
> When sands of time turn into cold black mud
> we all prepare to meet our hopeless end.
> The gallows stand lonely with ghosts of past,
> While screams pierce the silence and winds cry out,
> They look for answers, all they find is pain.

Evaluation isn't easy, is it? In the first example, the ninth-grade English teacher responded, "I understand." The grade? "D." For the second example, which was written by the same student, the grade given by a tenth-grade English teacher was "100," with the comment, "Very good! Nice imagery, perfect blank verse (with a few judicious variations)." Perhaps, you thought that letter or number grades shouldn't be assigned at all. If so, you're not alone. Many experts feel that grades and other outside rewards or negative consequences ultimately hurt students. According to Kohn (1999), "The evidence suggests that, all things being equal, students in a school that uses no letters or numbers to rate them will be more likely to think deeply, love learning, and tackle more challenging tasks" (p. 189).

BookTalk 10.1

Have you, like Anastasia, ever had a piece of work misjudged or not appreciated by others? For all who have ever been rejected and ridiculed, find out what good company you're in by reading *Rotten Reviews & Rejections,* edited by Bill Henderson and André Bernard (1998). You'll smile as you read the critique by *Children's Books* of Lewis Carroll's *Alice in Wonderland:* "We fancy that any real child might be more puzzled than enchanted by this stiff, overwrought story" (Henderson & Bernard, p. 27). An *Atlantic Monthly* reviewer in 1892 summarily dismissed Emily Dickinson: "An eccentric, dreamy, half-educated recluse in an out-of-the-way new England village—or anywhere else—cannot with impunity set at defiance the laws of gravitation and grammar . . . oblivion lingers in the immediate neighborhood" (Henderson & Bernard, p. 33). Read put-downs of T. S. Eliot's *The Wasteland,* F. Scott Fitzgerald's *The Great Gatsby,* J. D. Salinger's *The Catcher in the Rye,* and dozens more works that have been validated by readers over time. These reviews are laughable now, and they should give you courage to risk and endure possible rejection of your work while still valuing your self-assessment.

Every semester, around the middle of the term, I ask my students, "If the president of the college came in right now and announced that we were switching to a Pass/Fail system, how many of you would continue to work as hard as you have been working so far?" A few start to raise their hands, but slowly lower them again, shaking their heads. I am astounded by this. My classes are not random samples of the population; they are all preservice teachers taking a course in their education major, often immediately preceding their student teaching semester. Shouldn't they be working their hardest and learning all they

can in order to become excellent teachers, regardless of what the grading system is? I believe, along with Kohn, that the system they have been raised in is responsible for their over-reliance on grades. Like Anastasia, they must have a teacher's judgment in the form of a letter grade before they can know that they've done a wonderful job.

EVALUATION AND ASSESSMENT: THE SAME OR DIFFERENT?

The terms *assessment* and *evaluation* are very often used interchangeably, and they are close in meaning. However, some experts do differentiate between them, using *evaluation* to imply a judgment of quality, while preferring *assessment* as meaning the gathering and analyzing of data in order to inform instruction or make further decisions. We could consider the grades assigned to the student texts in Action Research 10.B to be evaluations; as far as we know, in each case the assignment is over, and the class is moving on to something else. If the teacher in sample 1 (who wrote, "I understand. D") used the student's paragraph (which probably surprised her) to suggest to the student that he expand his answer, giving specific ways he might do so, or if she modified the prompt so that he could play around with the concept of meeting someone from the past without having to envision being dead himself, *that* would be considered assessment. *The Literacy Dictionary* (Harris & Hodges, 1995) notes that assessment "can form the basis for evaluation, but not the reverse" (p. 76).

STANDARDIZED ASSESSMENTS AND HIGH-STAKES TESTING

The uses and abuses of standardized testing are heavily discussed at every level of society, from parents to politicians, students to songwriters. You have most likely taken a lifetime's worth of tests,

HOW EARLY ARE CHILDREN AWARE OF ASSESSMENT AND EVALUATION?

You've heard about and practiced the use of listening questions (Michel, 1994). Here's a quote from one of the first graders with whom Michel used listening questions: "I love it when I get an 'Excellent.' I like to look at it at my seat. Then I know I'm smart. I try to get one every day. My mom likes them too. It makes her feel happy when I do good" (p. 85). Something about that quote makes me

uneasy. Will this child, or has she already, come to rely on outside reinforcement to judge the worth of her endeavors? I'd want to know how the actual *work* makes her feel, whether the *process* was rewarding. I'd want to make sure her reflection is substantive and that her sense of self-worth is not dependent on staring at an "Excellent" on the back of her hand.

perhaps starting with those measuring your reading ability at the elementary school level, and you may still be facing the GRE to determine your eligibility for certain graduate schools. Now, it's time for you to reflect on literacy assessments using the lens of a content area teacher.

A standardized test is, according to *The Literacy Dictionary*:

> 1. a test with specific tasks and procedures so that comparable measurements may be made by testers working in different geographical areas. 2. a test for which norms on a reference group, ordinarily drawn from many schools or communities, are provided. (p. 242)

The primary purpose of standardized tests is to compare the performance of groups, rather than individuals. Raw scores, representing the actual number of correct answers, are converted to other kinds of scores, such as percentiles, so that comparisons are easier to make. These tests are sometimes used to determine whether a program or a school is effective or successful, but because other factors that the tests don't address may also be at work, it makes sense not to use test scores as the sole criterion for evaluation. It's also important to remember that norm-referenced tests are specifically designed to produce a range of scores, so it's nearly impossible for all students, or all groups, to perform at the "above average" level. But, of course, all participants want their schools or groups to perform well. Unfortunately, this can lead to "teaching to the test"—changing instructional methods or giving up instructional time to practice so students are familiar and comfortable with the test format (Darling-Hammond, Ancess, & Falk, 1995).

Other things to consider when you analyze standardized tests or the scores your students receive include *validity* and *reliability*. In order for a test to be *valid*, it must truly test what it says it is measuring. For example, a reading comprehension test should indeed show how well students understand text. If the students you teach read well in class, but score poorly because the standardized test used passages that required prior knowledge they didn't have, the test was not valid for your group, and the scores should not be viewed as meaningful. This is often a problem for immigrant populations. Diverse students possess different background knowledge from that of majority-culture students.

For a test to be *reliable*, the scores it produces must be dependable, or stable. A group of students should receive about the same score on repeated administrations of an instrument. If your students received very high scores one week and very low scores the next, which scores could you trust? A test must produce consistent results to be considered reliable.

High-stakes tests, which are usually standardized tests, are those where the results determine such things as whether or not a child graduates, passes on to another grade, or is allowed in a certain curricular track, program, course, school, or job. The SAT test, which many of you had to take as you were applying to colleges, is an example of a standardized test, and you may well have considered the stakes high because your scores could heavily influence whether or not you were accepted by the college of your choice.

Be assured also that when you teach in a school, you have to learn about the various standardized tests that are mandated at some level for students taking your course. You must keep abreast of the debate over the uses of various standardized tests, as well as the touted benefits addressed by the proponents and the concerns addressed by the opponents of standardized, high-stakes testing. It is an area conducive to using your critical-thinking skills. For example, once you read the following statement by Peter Johnston, a leading expert in the field, you might react strongly, pursue the matter, and join your voice with others to either refute the claim or work to change the system:

> We can expect high-stakes assessment to continue because the already extreme differences between rich and poor in the United States (and many other countries) continue to escalate. In this context, the combination of a competitive individualism and a meritocracy places tests as the gatekeepers to wealth and opportunity. Tests, particularly literacy tests, are the means of bloodlessly maintaining class differences. (2000, p. 250)

Alfie Kohn (1999) is another reformer who advocates eliminating high-stakes standardized tests because the more teaching comes to imitate the tests, the more teachers are steered away from helping their students learn to think:

> Indeed, the students who ace these tests are often those who are least interested in learning and most superficially engaged in what they are doing. This is not just my opinion: studies of elementary, middle school and high school students have all found *a statistical association between high scores on standardized tests and relatively shallow thinking*. (p. 81)

The International Reading Association has taken a position that "strongly opposes high-stakes testing" (www.ira.org/positions/high_stakes.html). The National Council of Teachers of English formulated resolutions in 2000, including "On Developing a

Test Taker's Bill of Rights" (www.ncte.org/resolutions/testakersrights002000.shtml) and "On Urging Reconsideration of High Stakes Testing" (www.ncte.org/resolutions/highstakes002000.shtml). At professional conferences I've attended recently, there were t-shirts for sale with the message, "High stakes are for tomatoes. End high-stakes tests." They sold out the first day. Some teachers have boycotted the exams—they spend test days on the steps of their state capitols, asking legislators and passers-by to answer questions from past tests in an attempt to show how little the tests have to do with real life and learning and how harmful they can be to students. Parents in some communities have allowed their children to stay home on days of state-imposed tests. As the controversy continues to brew, you, as a professional, are expected to keep current on the benefits and drawbacks of various testing forms, and to offer advice and wisdom to parents, students, peers, and community members. So, determine to keep informed.

Some teachers prefer to work within the system; some join teams of item writers in order to create tests that are as good as possible for their students. There are voices of balance, such as Sheila Valencia's:

> We cannot sit back and watch as the assessment drama unfolds. We must step forward as advocates for assessments that foster better teaching practice, insist on curricular rigor, and value worthwhile student learning and engagement—all the while respecting the public mandate for accountability. (2000, p. 249)

One person who has been able to make peace with her situation is first-grade teacher Jeanne Reardon, who explains that, although she has never found standardized test results to be useful, she recognizes that they are used to judge her students, and so:

> Reading-test reading is a genre that my students must become familiar with to be literate participants in society. When it is . . . taught as a genre along with other genres, students understand this peculiar form and how it works. They become successful comprehension test-takers, and the power of the test is diminished. (1990, p. 30)

She concludes, "I cannot ignore reading tests, nor can I allow them to control my classroom. 'Putting reading tests in their place' is the alternative I use while we search for a form of reading assessment worthy of the classroom literary community" (p. 37).

You may be planning to be a high school science teacher, but you can find similar ways to work within the constraints of the mandated standardized tests your students must eventually take. The teacher's attitude and teaching methods make a huge difference. I know an eleventh-grade Honors student who has come to think of English as nothing more than taking practice tests for Tasks 1, 2, 3, and 4 of the state exam because that's virtually all she has been doing in class for two years—that's the message, intended or unintended, that her teacher conveyed. On the other hand, in the next chapter, there is an example of team teaching by an English teacher and a social studies teacher who prepared numerous wonderful activities with the novel *Things Fall Apart* by C. Achebe (1994). One of the activities was a compare–contrast essay assignment (see pp. 334–335) that was created within the authentic context of the unit. This assignment helped the students think about important issues relative to the literature, while it prepared them for the type of essay they were required to write on the state exam.

AUTHENTIC ASSESSMENT

A major concern about standardized tests is that they are often not authentic; rather, they are artificial. If an assessment score does not really represent what a person understands about a subject or can perform in a real situation, the measurement device is flawed. When physicist Richard Feynman was a visiting lecturer in Brazil, he discovered that his students memorized very well and could pass tests, but they didn't understand the principles and could not apply them to any real situations. *Their* tests did not pass the test of authenticity, so he did not consider them valid measurements. In an address to leading Brazilian professors and government officials later in the year, he startled his audience by saying, "The main purpose of my talk is to demonstrate to you that *no* science is being taught in Brazil" (Feynman, 1985, p. 216). He finished by saying, "I couldn't see how anyone could be educated by this self-propagating system in which people pass exams, and teach others to pass exams, but nobody knows anything" (p. 218). The head of the science education program responded admirably to the criticism: "Mr. Feynman has told us some things that are very hard for us to hear, but . . . I think we should listen to him" (p. 218).

Experts at all levels are working to find ways to assess performance, knowledge, and ability that match real-life tasks. For example:

> In a challenge to the primacy of the standardized tests that millions of Americans have sweated over, the University of Michigan Business School is developing a test of practical intelligence, or common sense, that it hopes will do a better job

of identifying future leaders than the Graduate Management Admission Test, or GMAT, does.

Michigan's new test leads students through an elaborate series of business scenarios that present hypothetical financial statements, press releases, news articles and other information. It then poses a central problem and asks students both open-ended and multiple-choice questions. . . . The test aims to gauge who is able to learn from mistakes, handle changing situations and cope with less-than-perfect information—the same challenges, its designers say, that working people face every day. (Leonhardt, 2000)

Authentic assessment measures student learning by requiring the active construction of responses within the context of performing real tasks. The National Council for the Social Studies states, "To gauge effectively the efforts of students and teachers in social studies programs, evaluators must augment traditional tests with performance evaluations, portfolios of student papers and projects, and essays focused on higher-level thinking" (1994, p. 285).

Sometimes, *authentic assessment* is used synonymously with *performance-based assessment*, but some experts insist they are not identical, though they may overlap so that certain assessments fit both categories. Meyer (1992) gives an example of a direct writing assessment that takes place over four days, requiring students to participate in a standardized series of activities that lead to writing samples. The author then gives a second example of a direct writing assessment that involves a student who, after conferencing with a teacher, selects a paper from her portfolio to submit for assessment. Although both are examples of performance-based assessment— the students perform specific behaviors that are assessed—only the latter is authentic because the context of the former is contrived. In the second case, says Meyer, "performance is assessed in a context more like that encountered in real life; for example, students independently determined how long to spend on the various stages of the writing process, creating as many or as few rough drafts as they saw necessary to complete their final copies" (p. 39).

Authentic assessment and standardized tests are often viewed as mutually exclusive sets, even as enemies, and as the either–or points of a dichotomy. Smith (1994), in a chapter metaphorically entitled "Standardized Testing Versus Authentic Assessment: Godzilla Meets Winnie-the-Pooh," shows through example how standardized tests can yield a great deal of information about students' literacy, including an estimate of overall ability and relative strengths and weaknesses in reading skills and vocabulary knowledge—though certainly not every-

thing a classroom teacher requires to inform instruction. Smith, an admitted writer of standardized tests, thinks the problem is not necessarily with the test themselves:

Pressured to produce good test scores, educators have reversed the proper relationship between tests and teaching. As a result of sustained and direct instruction on only those concepts measured on tests, the instructional process becomes distorted, as does the interpretation of test scores. (p. 216)

He sums up standardized assessment thus:

It began as a fairly reasonable attempt to take an objective look at how well students do in a variety of subject areas, and it has become a monster that dictates curriculum and eats up huge amounts of instructional time. . . . What should we do about it now? Some argue for killing it before it kills us. Others say that it is a genie that simply needs to be put back in the bottle. (p. 222)

The dichotomy of standardized versus performance-based or authentic assessment is beginning to break down. In New York State, for example, test designers are looking for ways to create high school exams that are both standardized *and* authentic, requiring the application of skills and attention to process rather than just the regurgitation of facts and formulas. There are mixed reviews of the new tests—both strong proponents and critics exist, and some teachers are maintaining a wait-and-see attitude or are ambivalent about the tests' worth.

Another ambitious attempt at creating large-scale, performance-based assessments was the New Standards Project (NSP). This national coalition of about 17 states and seven urban school districts attempted to create tests worth taking, tests worth teaching to (Spalding, 2000). Project participants, primarily classroom teachers, came together to create alternatives to the traditional standardized testing of literacy skills that uses multiple-choice formats. They explored performance examinations, projects, and portfolios to be used with students in the fourth, eighth, and tenth grades that appropriately challenged their thinking and elicited rich reading and writing. Spalding (2000) explains that the resulting assessment tasks looked, not surprisingly, like good instruction; however, many of the pilots had to be rejected because the student products, while beautiful, were unscoreable. Other promising tasks were abandoned because the inter-rater reliability did not meet psychometric standards; that is, the degree of inconsistency between the scorers was not acceptable. Spalding reluctantly concludes that the New Standards Project "may not have delivered on its promise to create a national system of tests worth teaching to" (p. 762), but goes on to point out that it was marvelously successful at providing high-quality professional development to the hundreds of teachers involved, thereby most likely benefiting the students, at least indirectly.

We obviously haven't solved the problem of finding a large-scale form of assessment that makes everyone happy and does a good job. So, now let's look at a type of assessment you'll probably find more useful in your quest to help your students become highly interested, literate, and knowledgeable in the discipline you teach.

PART TWO

Classroom-Based Assessments

Let's turn our attention to your classroom. On a regular (actually, daily) basis, you should know how your students are understanding the content and growing in the skills of your discipline. You also should know about their literacy because their strengths and struggles in terms of reading and writing affect how (and maybe even whether) they tackle your assignments and explore your curriculum—their success in your course may be dependent on what you know about their literacy and what strategies you teach them.

Valencia, in an attempt to look into the future of literacy assessment, predicts the strengthening of classroom-based assessment, much of it in the form of performance assessment. "Teachers who understand and focus on content standards, and who make links between instruction and classroom assessment, are more likely to be effective" (2000, p. 248). This part discusses strategies that you, as a classroom content area teacher, can use to learn about your students in terms of their literacies and knowledge. Many teachers recognize that they must work within the constraints of mandated assessments coming from outside the classroom. Within your classroom, however, you have much more control over what and how you assess on a day-to-day basis. You can choose only those strategies that you find valuable and effective in informing your instruction and measuring and enhancing your students' growth. This kind of assessment is never the enemy. It's never meant to be punitive, and it never has the purpose of tricking students.

OBSERVATION

Probably the most important and valuable assessment skill you can develop is observation, which Yetta Goodman (1985) has coined *kidwatching.* You can observe your students at work, individually and in small peer groups, as well as in a whole class setting; during formal and informal activities; while they talk, listen, write, read, or explore information on the Internet. Some teachers carry notebooks or rolls of mailing labels as they circulate and engage the students in conversation; later, they transfer any relevant notes they jotted down in terms of process or difficulties into the student's folder. You can question the students to help them clarify what they're doing and why they're doing it. "Marietta, how did you form your hypothesis? Where will you go to obtain data to test it?" The information you gather can inform your instruction—you may slow or quicken your pace, back up to explain a concept students are having trouble applying, give a mini-lesson on research strategies. As you build rapport with your students, you'll note who is showing signs of fatigue, frustration, or excitement, and you can then proceed or react accordingly.

Zessoules and Gardner (1991) help us imagine observation at work:

> Observe a skilled teacher as she assesses students' work: looking for more than just information possessed, she depends not on discrete instances but entire performances, sampled frequently over time in the classroom. The teacher monitors students' capacities for being thoughtful, creative, curious, and self-directed. She watches for students to make use of the skills they have learned in a variety of contexts—making judgments, drawing connections to their own world and experiences, applying new understandings in thoughtful and meaningful ways. (p. 48)

It's not easy to get to know over 100 students, which is the number many secondary teachers teach each school day. But whenever you can, use what

Jonothan Kozol refers to as a *narrow lens.* "A narrow lens, I think, is often better than a wide one in discerning what a child's life is really like and what distinguishes one child's personality and inner world from those of twenty other children who may live in the same neighborhood and go to the same church or school and, from the vantage point of someone at a university or institute who has to think in terms of categories, might appear to lead the same kind of existence" (2000, p. 15). Your efforts will be worthwhile because your teaching will be aimed at where the students really are; perhaps even more important, your students will realize that you see them as individuals and care about them as learners and people.

Michel (1994) advocates teachers using what she calls *listening questions.* She found that if a young child answered, "I don't know" to a question, either patiently waiting or asking indirect questions often resulted in the child eventually opening up and sharing more thoughts and feelings on the topic. Certainly middle school students are similar; countless times my own children informed me that they did "nothing" in response to the standard question, "What'd you do in school today?" but later, they told stories and reacted to situations if I remained available to listen and nod my head. So, listen carefully as students talk, probing for depth and details when appropriate, being comfortable with pauses, letting the student take the conversation in a chosen direction. You can refer to Figure 2.8 in Chapter 2 for an example of a teacher using listening questions.

BookTalk 10.2

Observation is a kind of reading where the text involved is very complicated and doesn't always say what it means up front. When the text is an adolescent, you have to read between the lines, read what isn't said as well as what is said, and read under the surface for the deep meaning. Miss Harris, the sixth-grade teacher in Katherine Paterson's *The Great Gilly Hopkins* (1978), is a great reader of kids. When Gilly writes a racist message intended to hurt her, Miss Harris reacts not to what has been written but rather to the writer. She sees that Gilly, underneath her tough exterior, is a vulnerable, suffering child. Having read her student correctly, she can turn the tables by responding to Gilly with respect. Miss Harris talks to her about anger, contrasting the anger that is obvious in Gilly with her own anger that she has had to bury. She serves as a role model for teachers who want to comprehend their students' needs and instruct them accordingly.

INFORMAL INTERVIEWS AND CONFERENCING

If you informally interview students often as they work, asking questions about the process they are using to discover information, compose, solve problems, respond to literature, or comprehend reading material, they become comfortable talking about their thinking and working processes. This leads to increased knowledge for you about what and how to teach next, as well as to metacognitive thinking on their part. They may eventually internalize this type of questioning and ask themselves helpful questions about their thinking as they work. You can help even further by modeling and using *think-alouds,* verbalizing your thoughts as you complete a task. Chapter 4 contains an example of a think-aloud using a science text. Here's another example using a math text, with the reader's self-monitoring in italics within brackets:

The Fibonacci series [*Uh-oh*] 1, 2, 3, 5, 8, 13, 21, 34, 55, 89, 144, 233 . . . [*I'm trying to figure out what the next number is, why the progression looks like it does—can't do it right away*] arose in a problem about sexually active bunnies but has since come up again and again in design, both natural and man-made. The seeds in a sunflower, for example, are always positioned along two interweaving spirals, one set turning clockwise, the other counterclockwise. [*I can picture that, but what does that have to do with the numbers in the last sentence?*] The number of spirals in the two sets are not the same; in fact, they are always consecutive Fibonacci numbers. So [*here comes an example—whew*], if there are 144 clockwise spirals, there are always either 89 or 233 counterclockwise spirals. [*I'm supposed to know why this is? Oh, looking back, I see that those 3 numbers are listed in the progression.*] The Fibonacci series has also come up in man-made design because as the series approaches infinity, the ratio between two consecutive terms approaches the "golden ratio" [*I don't know this term*]—the ideal proportions of a rectangle that the Greeks favored in painting and classical architecture (the Parthenon, for example) [*I can picture this—I visited the replica of the Parthenon in Nashville*]. Indeed, Fibonacci numbers have so many connections to other things that an entire journal, the *Fibonacci Quarterly,* is devoted to keeping up with them. [*Even though I still don't really get it, I want to check out this journal to find other examples. Or maybe I'll just search "Fibonacci" on the Internet.*]

(Hoffman, 1998, pp. 208–209)

A teacher could surmise several things about the student who agreed to think-aloud while reading this passage. The reader recognizes when she is confused, but doesn't panic or show too much frustration. She expects that by reading on she'll get examples and be able to make more sense of the concept under discussion. She connects new information with old by looking back at a previous sentence—something skilled readers do. She has not fully comprehended the text, yet is intellectually curious or motivated enough to want to find more examples. And she shows confidence in being able to find information on her own. There is self-assessment going on, and the teacher can use the knowledge gained to make decisions about where to go from here with this student.

During a conference or a lesson, ask a student to retell a story or text he has read. By listening carefully to the retelling, you may be able to assess the following skills or difficulties:

- Picking out main ideas
- Recalling supporting details
- Understanding relationships such as cause–effect
- Recognizing point of view
- Understanding theoretical concepts and technical terms

You can also guide the students to reflect on their study strategies, composing processes, notetaking, skimming and scanning, figuring out the meanings of new words, and other literacy skills. It's amazing how much some students can tell you about their problems and learning processes if you just ask them. Or, you might bring in a book about a topic you know a certain struggling student is crazy about—horses, snowboarding, jazz, whatever. As she looks through the book, talk with her about:

- Her independent reading
- The differences between outside reading and school requirements
- Why she does better in some subjects than others
- How teachers could best help her
- Whether she has sources of help at home
- What kind of academic difficulties frustrate or discourage her

You can also ask questions as students are writing. They can point out areas that are giving them difficulty, ideas they are excited about, what the process of revising has been like for them, and so on. They can ask you questions during these conferences, too. The work-in-progress is in front of you both to refer to as you talk about discovering, learning, and composing.

CONTENT AREA READING INVENTORIES

Although observation is something that good teachers do continually, there are many other measures you can use to get specific information from your students. The Content Area Reading Inventory, or CARI, is a teacher-made tool using the textbook or other materials your students will actually be using. It consists of tasks you expect them to engage in, such as interpreting pictures, graphs, and charts; using a table of contents, glossary, and index; and determining word meanings from morphological analysis and context. You can use the insights gained from the assessment results to plan appropriate instruction and select additional materials to support your lessons, provide practice, and stimulate and challenge your students.

To construct a CARI, plan on several sections. The first part consists of questions that ask the students to interact with the whole textbook to show whether they understand the components and what they are used for. Depending on the textbook, you may have questions relating to the index, preview and review questions, captions, marginal notes, highlighted definitions, or statistical charts. For the second part, you might focus on vocabulary knowledge. Ask for the meaning of specific words from the text and have the students identify whether they already knew the definition; figured it out from context; used their knowledge of prefixes, suffixes, or roots; or remain clueless about the meaning. The next section is an excerpt from the book, perhaps two or three pages long, and questions you create to tap comprehension skills at the literal, inferential, and applied levels. Recall from Chapter 6 that literal-level questions have answers that can be found directly in the text; to answer inferential-level questions, a reader must put together bits of information or grasp something that has been implied; and applied-level questions call for the reader to use background knowledge or make connections to her experience outside the text itself. You can ask students to identify key points or to outline or summarize the selection. Figure 10.1 shows an example of a CARI.

THE CLOZE PROCEDURE

Taylor (1953) first developed the *cloze assessment* that requires students to fill in blanks (while reading) to make sense of a passage by using background knowledge and syntactic and semantic cues from the text. Its purpose is to match readers with appropriate texts. (Recall that the cloze procedure was discussed in Chapter 3 as a way to determine the appropriate-

FIGURE 10.1   *A partial content area reading inventory.*

Dear Fourth Period Students,

Welcome to "Introduction to Statistics." You might be feeling a bit nervous on this first day of class because there are scary stories floating around out there about the difficulty of statistics. Not to worry! It's my favorite subject, and my goal is to make it yours too, or at least to demystify it and make it accessible and interesting to you. I'll do everything I can to help you succeed.

I expect you to do your part as well because we have to work together as a team. Please keep up with the reading, study the excellent examples in this book, work the problems I assign, and let me know if ever understanding breaks down.

For homework tonight, please complete the following questions about yourself and the textbook we'll be using, *Statistics by Example* by Thomas Sincich (1990). Your answers will help me know where to begin as I plan my lessons. This is not a test, and your answers will not be held against you, I promise. So relax, get ready to think, and prepare yourself for a challenging and rewarding experience this year.

PART ONE

1. Why did you sign up for this course?
2. Define *statistics*.
3. Give an example of when you might use statistics or run across them in real life (i.e., outside school).
4. Skim the table of contents in your textbook. What do you notice about the organization of the topics in each chapter?
5. What two types of information will you find in the five appendices?
6. What kinds of information will you find in blue boxes throughout the chapters? (Skim the book until you find the answer.)
7. What things do you find at the end of each chapter?
8. After looking at some examples in the book, what do you see as the difference between a graph and a table?

[Part Two might consist of questions about particular terms and concepts, while Part Three could consist of questions based on the students' reading of a few pages from this statistics textbook.]

ness of the texts you choose.) For example, you can use the cloze procedure to find out which students will have difficulty reading the class textbook, which will require some help, and which will be able to handle it independently or may even need more challenging supplements or a different text. You can construct this type of informal assessment using your own classroom materials. Select a passage of about 300 words, preferably from the beginning of a chapter. Leave the first and last sentences intact. From the remaining text, delete every fifth word and replace it with a blank space, until you have 50 blanks. After modeling the process for the students (who may be unfamiliar with this type of activity) and giving them a short practice exercise with subsequent debriefing, ask them to complete the assessment—try to guess what original words were omitted.

To score the cloze, count the number of exact word replacements. Scoring synonyms reduces the test's reliability (Henk & Selders, 1984) and it takes longer to score. Don't let yourself be troubled by this; everyone is at the same disadvantage. Double the number of correct responses to arrive at the percentage of items the student identified. Bormuth (1968) provides the criteria in Figure 10.2 for determining a student's reading level.

The labels are fairly self-explanatory: *Independent* means the student should be able to handle the material without help, *Instructional* refers to the student who can handle the material with help, and *Frustration* means that the material is simply too hard. For those students at the frustration level, you have to decide whether to offer a more appropriate book, put sections on tape, use a teacher assistant or volunteer who can give significant help, or make other adaptations or accommodations. Too often, struggling readers are double victims—they cannot comprehend the material and then get blamed or penalized for not doing their homework or completing a reading assignment.

FIGURE 10.2 *Cloze assessment reading level.*

CLOZE TEST SCORES	READING LEVEL
Independent	58%–100%
Instructional	44%–57%
Frustration	0%–43%

ACTION RESEARCH   10.C

To see what it's like to complete a cloze assessment, try filling in the blanks of the passage in Figure 10.3. Then, check your answers against those on page 324, which are the words used in the actual text, and figure out the percentage of words you matched. Remember, don't worry if you know your answer makes as much sense and is as appropriate as the one used; there's a reason for not accepting synonyms.

Some teachers prefer to allow synonym replacements because this is more consistent with their philosophy of how people construct meaning. But that takes longer to score, invalidates the scoring system given above, and could lower the reliability of the procedure. So, using the exact replacement criterion is recommended.

It is also possible to construct a modified cloze passage—students are given choices and asked to determine which fits into the blanks best in terms of meaning and syntax. Cloze passages can be used for instruction, as well as assessment, if the passage is reviewed and reasons for correct choices and thinking processes are discussed.

Assure your students that this is not a test—it is just a quick measure to learn how difficult certain subject material is likely to be for them so instruction can be better. Keep in mind that students whose first language is not English may obtain a score that underestimates their comprehension abilities because the procedure is based on a familiarity with English language patterns.

> *Getting Ready to Teach 10.1 (see page 324)*

FIGURE 10.3 *Sample cloze passage.*

Standardized testing is not going to go away. It is part of _____ fabric of our schools _____ our society. It is _____ business for publishers, and _____ are still used to _____ select, and place students _____ —and remove them from— _____ special programs. Still, we _____ can influence how these _____ are given and used.

_____ the school district where _____ teach, pressure from first- _____ second-grade teachers and _____ responses from knowledgeable administrators _____ do away with standardized _____ in those two grades. _____ -grade teachers were vocal _____ conveying what they wanted _____ the superintendent, the director of _____ education, and the board of _____ These teachers were tired _____ crying kids, wasted time, _____ an agenda that did _____ serve students first.

Now, _____ when standardized tests are _____, we treat them as _____ separate form of reading _____ I now call *reading-* _____ *reading.* Because our students are _____ with the format, we _____ it to them through _____ and practice tests. Sure, _____ a waste of time _____ could be better used _____ other ways, but the _____ is students will have _____ take tests throughout their _____ careers, and they need _____ learn how to do _____ successfully. To ignore this _____ is to put them _____ a disadvantage.

One of _____ big objections to standardized _____ is the emphasis on _____ "deficit model." Results are _____ to point up what _____ child can't do. Rather _____ build on the child's _____, standardized tests reinforce weaknesses. _____ to that is the _____ -documented fact that standardized _____ are culturally biased toward white middle-class experiences.

If standardized tests are used in perspective, only as a set of numbers from one given day that has little relation to what we are teaching in school, I can live with them.

Reprinted from *Literacy at the Crossroads: Crucial Talk about Reading, Writing, and Other Teaching Dilemmas* by Regie Routman. Copyright © 1996 by Regie Routman. Published by Heinemann, a division of Reed Elsevier Inc., Portsmouth, NH. Reprinted by permission of the publisher.

PORTFOLIOS

ACTIVATING PRIOR KNOWLEDGE   **10.2**

Have you ever put together a portfolio for an academic class or for some other purpose? What did you include to represent your work and yourself? How did you organize it? Were there ways you showed your processes, as well as the finished products? How did you feel about the portfolio? How and to whom did you present it? Reflect on these questions if applicable. If you have never worked on a portfolio, think about portfolios of others you have seen, or imagine how you might go about creating one that is representative of your work in a certain area, as well as personally valuable to you. What might it look like, especially if you were given complete freedom?

A portfolio is a collection of representative student work that shows progress. As a type of performance-based assessment, portfolios are extremely popular with many content area teachers. They are certainly not a new idea, at least in some arenas—artists, poets, fashion designers, photographers, and others often choose this means of presentation. Writing teachers and their students have found that a portfolio has multiple advantages: It helps students organize and categorize, make evaluative decisions, problem solve, reflect on their processes and their growth over time, and plan future projects. Presenting one's portfolio is an opportunity to point out verbally (or with the use of visuals) one's strengths, talents, and accomplishments, leading to enhanced self-esteem and confidence.

No one set of criteria defines a portfolio. You and your students can determine what to include for your content area, the relative worth of various components, and how it is presented or shared. You can choose a format for presentation that is right for you, whether it be formal or casual, verbal or simply visual, inside your classroom or spread throughout the halls of the school.

For example, in my Content Area Literacy Education class, the students work all semester toward the goal of completing a portfolio that they can share with cooperating teachers while student teaching and with potential employers later on. I insist that particular things they developed during the course be included:

- Sample reading guides showing that they can apply a variety of strategies.
- A literacy autobiography.
- Responses to professional journal articles.
- An analysis of a textbook series.
- An annotated bibliography of literature works they can use in their content area teaching.
- A letter to me reflecting on their practicum experiences.
- A short reflective essay in response to my prompt, "Describe yourself as a teacher of literacy in your content area, or as a teacher–reader."

My students can choose to add other components: a transcribed interview with middle school students, a list of favorite books and authors, a lesson plan or unit they've designed, photos of bulletin boards—anything that represents them as future teachers and exemplifies their emerging personal philosophy.

It's very important that students retain ownership of the project and are allowed to exercise their voice and creativity. The portfolios they bring in on the last day of class look quite different in terms of cover design and organization. Students enjoy talking about their own work and seeing that of their colleagues. We all have a visible sign that much professional growth and learning took place.

Sharon Morley's English classes have a "Portfolio Party" after school hours on a June day. Parents and members of the community are invited to view the products and question the creators. Students are the experts as they interact with the visitors, explaining choices, accepting earned praise, talking of future endeavors, describing how they used technology tools to enhance their products. Their portfolios have a table of contents and examples of their writing in the genres they studied over the year. Their Shakespearian newspapers, which are explained in Chapter 9, are there.

Knight (1992) describes her efforts at using a portfolio approach to assessment in an algebra class. Her students suggested the following items to show their efforts and learning: "daily notes, the Personal Budget long-term project, Lottery Project, scale drawing, their best tests, their worst tests, problems of the week, daily class notes, and homework" (p. 71). She found that students attached significant value to certain assignments she did not consider important. Together, teacher and students negotiated a format and structure for the portfolios. Knight decided to have peers evaluate the completed portfolios and devised a grading matrix. She found several advantages to having students grade each other's work: they received immediate, constructive feedback and they learned more as they read other introductions, reflections, and examples of problem solving. Portfolios proved to be an important tool for self-evaluation, as well as a means to celebrate much learning.

Figure 10.4 lists items that can be included in portfolios. Choose from among these and add others

FIGURE 10.4 *Potential content area portfolio inclusions.*

- lab reports
- drawings and sketches
- scripts of interviews or dialogues
- poems (original or collected)
- interpretations of or responses to literature
- autobiographical essays
- favorite quotes
- pictures selected to accompany texts
- samples of creative writing
- completed math, science, or technology problems with an explanation of the problem-solving process
- reflections on one's writing process
- architectural designs (perhaps for an imaginary building or city)
- compare–contrast essay on people in the discipline

- musical compositions
- outlines and plans for future projects and dreams
- correspondence with pen pals or with business representatives
- letters to the editor (possibly published!)
- book or movie reviews
- samples of collaborative work (could take a variety of forms)
- reflections on personal growth in a subject area
- document-based essays that show synthesis skills
- interpretation of data in graphs or charts
- memoirs
- awards or certificates for achievements
- audio, video, or computer-generated samples of student work

unique to your objectives and goals—tie and weave them together with a theme, reflections, unifying quotes, a purpose. Wilcox (1997) advocates going beyond a *passive* portfolio, which she describes as more of a showcase collection that cannot change and grow. By including a thinking journal and using the portfolio contents to generate new output, the portfolio becomes an *active* one, which is good not only for assessment, but also for valuable ongoing growth.

You might wonder whether there is such a thing as too many portfolios—"portfolio overkill." Or maybe you've experienced the phenomenon as a student yourself, and therefore don't even have to ask. It can become a burden if students have to represent themselves via portfolios in a number of different academic subjects. It makes sense in some situations, especially in a team-taught class, to have students prepare an interdisciplinary portfolio.

Assessing and Scoring Portfolios

Assessment fails unless it leads to positive change in instruction and learning. Teachers in Kentucky learned this when they were required to participate in a yearly, statewide performance-based assessment of each school. Berryman and Russell (2001) describe one school's experience using and scoring portfolios across the curriculum. Two of the required pieces had to be from a content area other than English and had to be "transactive" in nature; that is, they had to write to communicate with a real-world audience. The state's purpose was to assess schools rather than indi-

viduals, but the teachers realized over time that they could learn from scoring the portfolios how to be better teachers of writing and how to help their students be better writers across the curriculum.

The portfolios were scored using a rubric (explained in the next section) with four performance levels: *Novice, Apprentice, Proficient,* and *Distinguished.* Berryman, an English teacher, reports that, during a summer workshop, "I realized for the first time that scoring portfolio pieces could be a way to rethink teaching and learning, define weaknesses, and establish an instructional plan for a department or schoolwide effort" (p. 78). When teachers in content areas other than English were trained to score the portfolios, they were surprised at how much they learned about the students by reading their writing across the disciplines. They also discovered that using writing in their classes had many benefits in terms of both assessment and instruction, without gobbling up precious time:

> The portfolio assessment was specifically designed to encourage professional development, to produce positive "washback" from assessment, rather than the all-too-common negative results of assessment, where teachers teach to the test, and valuable curriculum and teaching are crowded out.... The portfolio assessment was broad enough that it made room for new things in the curricula of various disciplines, instead of crowding things out, as external assessments often do. (p. 80)

Teachers have found that writing in all classes improves students' writing and thinking, and also functions as an informal, time-saving way for teachers to assess ongoing learning. A biochemistry teacher pointed out, "I never give tests, because I don't need to, because I have this daily written interaction with my students. I know where they are, I know what they know. We have a discourse in class all the time" (p. 81).

The use of teacher-assessed portfolios across the curriculum has helped this Kentucky school, these teachers, and these students. The portfolio scores are rising, teachers are collaborating and talking about writing projects and students, and "many teachers work seriously at assigning writing that is purposeful and meaningful in terms of teaching—not just assessing—their content" (p. 3). That's assessment at its authentic best.

USING RUBRICS

Rubrics, used with performance-based activities that demonstrate learning, are scoring devices that help you assess and evaluate student work (Goodrich, 1996/1997). They consist of the following:

- a set of criteria that a score is based on (developed by the teacher alone or together with the student)
- a standard or a method to determine levels of achievement that will translate into scores.

Rubrics can be used at any level with many assessment types. The benefits of well-composed rubrics are many, including helping teachers score students' work fairly and accurately, giving students valuable information about what qualities their work should exhibit, and helping teachers talk together about goals and evaluation. Sometimes, teachers ask students to determine what criteria should be applied to certain assignments, thus guiding their thinking about the components of projects and processes. Figure 10.5 shows a rubric that an undergraduate education student made as part of a unit on Jewish refugees in the United States. A teacher-made rubric appears in the next chapter as part of the unit included there.

USING SHORT QUESTIONS TO ENCOURAGE AND ASSESS UNDERSTANDING

Classroom assessment does not have to be burdensome or time-consuming; ideally, it can be an integral part of your content lessons. Carroll (1999) shows how teachers can use short questions to elicit writing that can be used to develop and assess mathematical reasoning. For example, students can analyze the mistakes in their answers or in the answers of others; Carroll points out that students who are accustomed to making hypotheses, building on prior ideas, and reasoning to move toward a correct answer are not intimidated by errors.

The following problem was used to assess students' mathematical reasoning: "Sheila said, 'I can draw a triangle with two right angles.' Do you agree with Sheila? Explain your reasoning" (Carroll, p. 251). A five-point rubric was designed and refined using the students' examples.

Score

Level 0   off-task response or no response

Level 1   incorrect response with some attempt at reasoning

Level 2   correct response with unclear or incomplete reasoning

Level 3   correct response with good reasoning

Level 4   correct response with exemplary reasoning applying knowledge of triangles and angles

Carroll suggests that classroom teachers can devise even simpler rubrics, such as a three-point scale, to categorize problem-solving responses representing *Little Understanding, Making Progress,* and *Good Understanding.*

Using a rubric like this gives you knowledge of individuals, as well as groups. Carroll reports that this problem was given to 10 classes of fifth and sixth graders who used a curriculum that implemented the NCTM standards, emphasizing reasoning, and 10 classes that used more traditional programs—the results, not surprisingly, showed a contrast. Thirty percent of the fifth graders and 53 percent of the sixth graders using the *standards*-based curriculum scored at Level 3 or 4, while only 4 percent of the fifth graders and 13 percent of the sixth graders from traditional classes reached those levels. Try teaching a lesson or presenting a problem a certain way to your morning classes and a different way to the afternoon classes. Then, compare the students' written responses about their reasoning to assess their understanding and to give you insight as to the kinds of reasoning each method elicits.

STUDENT-LED CONFERENCES

Student-led conferences, or student–teacher–parent conferences, with or without portfolios, are gaining popularity and even replacing traditional parent–teacher conferences in many middle and high schools. They provide an opportunity for students to present and explain their work, as well as reflect on their progress and set new goals—to be an active participant in the assessment process. Such a confer-

FIGURE 10.5 *A student-made rubric.*

Name: _____

SAFE HAVEN: AMERICA'S ONLY HOLOCAUST REFUGEE SHELTER

(1) Presentation is well organized

0 Not all group members participate

2 All participate, but no organization or preparation is evident

4 Some organization apparent, but presentation is unclear

6 Organized, but presentation is not complete

8 Generally well organized with ideas logically arranged, good preparation

10 Excellent organization, all ideas are clearly ordered, well rehearsed

(2) Introduction

0 Ineffective introduction

2 Generic introduction

4 Introduction is entertaining but not relevant

6 Introduction is adequate but fails to make an impact

8 Introduction is informative but does not gain attention

10 Excellent introduction; both informative and attention getting

(3) Presentation is enhanced by visual aids

0 No visuals aids used

2 One ineffective visual aid is used

4 One visual aid is effective

6 Good visuals effectively used

8 Excellent visuals used to effectively reinforce presentation theme

10 Excellent visuals and technology effectively reinforce presentation theme

(4) Background information creates a setting in the audience's mind

0 No background information in discussed

2 Poor, irrelevant background information is discussed

4 Adequate background information, but lacking key elements

6 Adequate and accurate background information is discussed

8 Complete background information is discussed

10 Complete background information, relevant to presentation theme

(5) Presentation utilizes both assigned novels

0 No mention of either novel

2 One novel mentioned ineffectively

4 Both novels mentioned ineffectively

6 Both novels analyzed but without solid examples

8 Both novels analyzed adequately with good examples

10 Both novels incorporated fully to enhance the presentation theme

(6) Describe the living conditions at Fort Ontario

0 No discussion of the living conditions at Fort Ontario

2 Little is mentioned of the living conditions

Presentation Rubric

4 Discusses only the refugees' of government's role

6 Discusses both the refugees' and government's role

8 Complete description of living conditions, but not relating to theme

10 Complete description of living conditions, relevant to presentation theme

(7) Describe the difficulties that the refugees faced in America

0 No mention of any refugee hardships

2 Little is mentioned of refugee difficulties

4 Discusses only internal/external examples

6 Discusses only political/social examples

8 Completely discusses all issues facing refugees

10 Completely discusses all issues, relevant to presentation theme

(8) Describe the relationship between Oswegonians and the refugees

0 No mention of any relationship between the townspeople and the refugees

2 Discusses only negative relationships

4 Discusses only positive relationships

6 Discusses both positive and negative relationships without examples

8 Excellent description of relationships supported by examples

10 Excellent description and examples, relevant to presentation theme

(9) Explanation for closing the Fort Ontario Emergency Refugee Shelter

0 No explanation or discussion of the fort's closure

2 Inadequate discussion of the fort's closure

4 Discussion of fort's closure is incomplete

6 Complete discussion of the events that led to the fort's closure

8 Explains closing and discusses refugees' lives

10 Explains closing, refugees' lives, relevant to presentation theme

(10) What should the federal government do in a similar situation today?

0 No discussion of your feelings

2 Plan is unacceptable

4 Plan is acceptable but lacks complete explanation

6 Good argument, but does not relate to Fort Ontario

8 Solid argument that relates to Fort Ontario

10 Persuasive argument that relates to Fort Ontario

Total Points Earned on Presentation _____

Comments: _____

_____

—*Eric Sullivan*

ence involves a three-way (or more if another parent or invited adult is involved) discussion with the student showing her work, reflecting on her progress, and inviting and answering questions from parents or guardians. Conference preparation requires the student to synthesize ideas and work and to self-assess in terms of skills attained, content understood, desired future explorations and ambitions, and so forth. It's a wonderful chance for the student to practice presentation skills and to listen to input from adults. Together, the team sets goals, talks about ways the student can be supported at home, and celebrates the learner and her accomplishments thus far. Literacy issues (e.g., a student's outside reading habits, anxiety about speaking in front of groups, or favorite writing genres) can be addressed. McLaughlin (2000) suggests giving the parents a reaction form to complete and send to school with their child the next day. This provides an additional opportunity for the parent and child to talk, as well as a structure for getting feedback and additional comments. The form can be added to the student's portfolio.

Your job is to facilitate the conference and ensure that it remains positive—the student, parents, and teacher are all on the same side and all want the best for the student. An honest discussion of the areas in need of improvement, along with suggestions of helpful strategies and materials, need not seem threatening or disheartening. Another of your roles is to provide a comparable experience for those students without parents or whose parents cannot come to a conference. Relatives or neighbors, other teachers, or community members can volunteer to participate in a portfolio celebration or conference.

A student–teacher–parent conference may have ameliorated Eric's situation. He was a strong reader but a struggling student in junior and senior high. Eric's mother describes the numerous impersonal, demeaning, and embarrassing notices of impending failure that were sent home "To the parents of . . ." (Nierstheimer, 2000, p. 34). The reports contained code numbers representing Eric's flaws or misdemeanors—"the progress reports did not communicate with us in any personal or pleasant way and represented to us the lack of power and respect that I believe parents of struggling learners feel" (p. 34). She contrasts this with what might have been:

> As the parent of Eric, I wish that more teachers had taken the time to *know* him . . . to see his strengths, abilities, and interests, not just point out his failures. I wish more teachers had cared more about who he was as a person than how he performed as a student. (p. 35)

Are we listening?

HOW IS TECHNOLOGY CHANGING ASSESSMENT?

In the last chapter, you read some competing opinions relating to technology and literacy—some promising great advances in literacy because of technology, others blaming computers along with other media for the demise of reading and writing skills. So, it shouldn't surprise you that opinions differ as to whether assessment will be helped or hindered as technology advances. Johnston (2000) points out that both assessments and the literacy that will be assessed are in flux:

> Indeed, the literacies we are assessing are constantly changing. Many adolescents who spend their free time (and official school time) surfing the Internet are literate in ways barely imagined by their parents. They filter and simultaneously analyze, respond to, and integrate a wide (almost unlimited) array of images, words, and sounds. This is, and will be, the real-world literacy of information, leisure, and commerce, which schools must help students manage and critically analyze. In other words, technology potentially opens a range of interesting assessment options just as it opens an array of different literacies. (pp. 249–250)

Some schools are having students take tests on a computer, which can track scores, give immediate feedback, and produce printouts to take home to parents. But some of the published materials designed for computers are really very traditional. For example, the Accelerated Reading Program provides multiple-choice tests for students to take after reading those books for which the company has determined difficulty levels. The questions might not be the kind that you encourage your students to ask and answer. If your philosophy calls for rich discussion and using dialogue journals and literature groups, you may find such published electronic tests not to your liking because they tend to include an overabundance of literal-level comprehension questions. So, you can see that teacher decision making is more important than ever.

One option that technology affords is that of collecting and responding to student work via e-mail. As students develop ideas and draft texts, teachers can send feedback and suggestions to the students as fast as they wish. Attending to student work through electronic correspondence can be helpful and reinforcing to students as they are immersed in the process of research, the synthesis of ideas through essays, or creative writing. Students who might be reluctant to call on a teacher in class may actually feel more comfortable discussing problems and learning struggles using the computer. An ongoing assessment before students turn in final papers makes sense. Continue to experiment and find new ways of using computers to assess and instruct—if you find that the two are merging, that's a good sign that your assessment is authentic, meaningful, contextualized, and helpful.

Electronic portfolios are becoming popular with students and teachers. Students can burn personal CDs, scan work in, and design formats for presenting their work. They can learn to incorporate text, video, pictures taken with a digital camera, voices, background music, charts, and graphs. Students are designing their own webpages to show their work and evidence of learning. High school students can invite the admissions staffs of prospective colleges to log on to their websites to get a picture of their academic work and of their lives.

ASSESSMENT OF STUDENTS WITH SPECIAL NEEDS

You can learn a lot about all of your students from the many *formative* (while work or a course is in progress) and *summative* (final) assessment procedures available to you, as well as from attending to the students and their work as you teach. But you may wonder whether you should know or do anything extra for those students with special learning problems. I believe that you should take advantage of any resource at your disposal. If some of your students have had formal evaluations to determine whether they have specific learning disabilities, for example, you may find it valuable to read the evaluation team's records and test reports to better understand those students as learners. You might find that a certain student fails your chapter tests because he has difficulty reading the exam, not because he does-

n't understand the material; another might perform poorly on your essay exams because of a specific writing disability. Once you know this, you can make accommodations in terms of your forms of assessment, as well as your expectations and instruction.

There is also much to learn from talking with the reading specialists and resource teachers who work with your students. You might learn the results of a diagnostic test, such as an informal reading inventory (IRI), given to a student. An IRI consists of a series of passages of increasing difficulty that are used to determine the reader's word identification and comprehension strategies, as well as a reading level. If any assessments (other than the typical ones) were done, it makes sense for you to know about them in order to inform your instruction. For example, if testing revealed that Shannon was a word-by-word reader who focused on reading each word correctly instead of constructing and confirming meaning, the reading specialist might help Shannon realize that generating meaning should be her major consideration. Given this information, a science teacher might encourage Shannon to "self-monitor"—read a few textbook paragraphs and explain out loud what she is thinking and understanding. If Shannon can restate the ideas in her own words, she has comprehended the text.

Also, you might initiate further testing for a student you see struggling. You're not expected to have all of the answers, but you might be the first to suspect that there is a problem that has not yet been diagnosed. Strive to work well with the support people in your district; everyone should want the best for the students and should work together to see that the best happens. Communication, collaboration, and consistency among all teachers working to help a student succeed in literacy and content learning are crucial.

"Everyone" should also include the students' parents or guardians. Families may have to take students for medical testing or other specialized forms of assessment, the results of which bring new information to bear on academic situations. For example, when my son Christopher was in fourth grade, his performance took a dive. Every report card he brought home looked worse in every category, and it appeared as if the problem was due to a lack of effort or laziness—although test grades remained high, his homework completion was inconsistent, his work in school left unfinished. His teacher, Chris, and his parents formed a team to solve the puzzle, but none of us alone or together could figure it out. Chris was a cooperative child who said he thought he was doing the work and didn't mean to cause trouble or get away with anything. We tried checklists, reminders, parent–teacher phone calls, planners—all to no avail. It wasn't until I took Chris to an optometrist the following summer that it was

BookTalk 10.3

At the beginning of summer vacation, Allegra finds out her violin performance has been deemed worthy of allowing her to enter a competition. *The Mozart Season,* by Virginia Euwer Wolff (2000), lets the reader in on a lot of assessment: her teacher's formative assessments and subsequent changes in instruction, Allegra's sometimes painful self-assessments and crucial decisions based on them, and the final, outside evaluation given by the judges at the competition. Read *The Mozart Season* in your teacher role—Allegra and her violin teacher will help you reflect on how you can use assessment and instruction in complementary ways to help your students thrive as learners and people.

BookTalk   10.4

Mrs. Olinski wants to put together a sixth-grade team for a state-sponsored academic competition. Her choices surprise people, but you'll discover as you read *The View from Saturday* (1996), E. L. Konigsburg's second Newbery Medal winner, the wisdom of this first assessment decision and those made throughout the months as she coaches her team to the state finals. The final performance-based evaluation will keep you, a future assessor, on the edge of your seat. You may teach differently after you experience this super example of individual excellence combining with cooperative learning under the direction of a master teacher-assessor.

discovered he had severe perceptual problems that caused an organizational disability. Once we had the assessment, and a pair of glasses, we could work on the real problem rather than the "lack of effort" that was the easiest, but inaccurate, inference based on the data from school. So, please don't give up if you can't figure out exactly what a student's problem is; persistence, creative thinking, flexibility, expert help, and patience may be necessary. And

even if you never identify the cause, don't conclude that the student just wants to fail.

May (2001) debunks "The Laziness Myth," the belief that it's up to the student to learn to read well, regardless of text difficulty or quality, or, in other words, "If he'd just try harder, he'd succeed" (p. 141). He suggests ways that teachers and assistants can help students grapple with texts that are unclear, poorly written, or just plain too hard for their present capabilities. They can teach students to monitor their own reading comprehension through modeling and asking questions about meaning-making; for example, "What is my goal for reading this? How can I picture the events (or steps) the author wants me to follow? What information is missing or confusing that makes me not understand?" (p. 159). Perhaps his strongest suggestion for helping those students who are not succeeding in our classrooms concerns the selection of materials we ask them to read. "With at least 30,000 new school-age trade books being published each decade, there is very little reason for teachers and administrators to have their students stumbling along with no more motivation than to 'get through the textbook assignment'" (p. 158).

Getting Ready to Teach 10.2 (see page 324)

PART THREE

Assessing One's Teaching and Literacy Growth

I hope you can see by now how important and integral a part assessment plays in your teaching. But it's not just students you'll be assessing. Every day, every class period, you should evaluate how your lessons went, how successful they were in terms of student learning, and then make major adjustments or fine-tune accordingly. I've heard teachers say they feel sorry for their first-period classes—each day those students get their teacher's first efforts, but with practice, the lesson gets better throughout the day. (Actually, some schools rotate class schedules, for this and other reasons.)

Figure 10.6 shows questions that might help you evaluate your lessons, especially in terms of the literacy involved. You can adapt them to suit your particular subject, students, and needs.

It's possible that at times your lessons seem to be going fine, but your long-range goals are not being accomplished as expected. Every so often, at the end of a unit, quarterly, or whenever student report cards come out, ask yourself questions similar to those presented in Figure 10.6—focus on your teaching, curriculum, and materials more generally instead of on particular lessons.

ONGOING ASSESSMENT OF YOUR LITERACY AND PROFESSIONAL GROWTH

I've stressed throughout this book my conviction that you must be a reader and a writer in order to help your students develop good literacy skills and

FIGURE 10.6 *Questions that guide self-assessment of lessons in terms of literacy.*

1. Did I open the lesson with an interesting initiating activity—a question, quote, cartoon, scenario? Did the students seem motivated by it?

2. Did I prepare thoroughly in terms of my own reading, researching, and learning about the topic I taught?

3. Were students actively engaged in listening, talking, reading, or writing? How was their thinking challenged?

4. Did I provide further resources so they can independently pursue the topic? Is my classroom library adequate for the unit we're studying? Do I have several genres of relevant materials? Do I have different perspectives represented? Have I given appropriate booktalks to entice them to read? Did I provide relevant website URLs or help them determine keywords to use for an Internet search?

5. In general, how well have I helped the students meet our goals and objectives for this lesson?

habits. No matter your starting point, you should have some way of assessing yourself as your career develops. Think now about starting a record-keeping system to track your literacy accomplishments. I keep a dated journal where I record the titles of books I read and a brief response, often indicating how the book might connect to my teaching and curriculum. You could do the same with articles you read. You might participate, along with your students, in completing a genre wheel by placing a dot in the appropriate category each time you finish a text, and setting goals to branch out to a variety of reading materials as the year goes on.

You can also keep a teaching journal where you record classroom events large and small, reflect on puzzling pedagogical issues (e.g., whether your students' current report card grades adequately reflect their growth and accomplishments), write out possible strategies to improve instruction or your relationships with the students, and record new ideas and materials you've discovered. Teachers who do this are often very glad when they read over the journal after several months and are able to see that they and their students have traveled far from their starting point and have progressed academically and socially. A colleague of mine provided this reflection: "I often feel too busy to write down what's happening in my teaching. But when I do, I love myself because when I find it later, the next time I have to teach it, I feel so thrilled that this is not uncharted territory. I've been here before and I can improve on what happened" (Jean Ann, June 2000).

Figure 10.7 contains a list of biographical or autobiographical accounts of teachers that are fascinating reflections on their own learning and growth, as well as their students'. It also includes books written by researchers who spent time in teachers' classrooms, observing change and eliciting self-assessment from those they studied.

TEACHER PORTFOLIOS

Most schools have a system in place for evaluating teachers, especially new teachers, and providing feedback and suggestions for improvement and growth. Perhaps an administrator, teacher mentor, or peer coach looks over a lesson plan, observes a class, interviews the teacher, and afterwards discusses what she sees and listens to the teacher's perception of the lesson. Use such opportunities to reflect on your teaching and the goals for yourself, as well as your students. Be sure to address literacy issues relating to yourself and your classes as you talk with peers about teaching.

Developing a teaching portfolio is an excellent way to understand yourself as part of the teaching profession. The process, similar to the one described for students, involves selection, reflection, verbalizing your philosophy, making connections to others in the field, and presenting yourself to others. What avenues are you pursuing as a reader and writer? What sorts of support could you use?

Wilcox (1996) encourages prospective teachers to develop what she calls *smart portfolios*, requiring systematic self-assessment and sharing in order to experience the power of reflective thinking. She introduces five essential elements: reading, interacting, demonstrating, writing, and thinking. She has her students choose some kind of container (e.g., a three-ring binder or pocket portfolio) to organize artifacts that show evidence of thoughtfulness and growth in each of these categories. Figure 10.8 shows the examples Wilcox provides of a portfolio's contents.

Wilcox states, "Teachers who know about assessment as instruction will never be satisfied with a portfolio *just* for assessment. The smart portfolio is a powerful tool for professional development and life-long learning" (p. 173). So, don't think of a portfolio in a passive sense, as being just a showcase for past

FIGURE 10.7 *Works by and about teachers.*

Allen, J., Cary, M., & Delgado, L. (1995). *Exploring Blue Highways: Literacy Reform, School Change, and the Creation of Learning Communities.* New York: Teachers College Press.

Ashton-Warner, S. (1963). *Teacher.* New York: Simon & Schuster.

Atwell, N. (1998). *In the Middle: New Understandings About Writing, Reading, and Learning.* Portsmouth, NH: Heinemann.

Brown, C. S. (1994). *Connecting with the Past: History Workshop.* Portsmouth, NH: Heinemann.

Conway, J. K. (1994). *True North.* New York: Knopf.

Hayden, T. (1980). *One Child.* New York: Putnam.

Hynds, S. (1997). *On the Brink: Negotiating Literature and Life with Adolescents.* Newark, DE: International Reading Association, and New York: Teachers College Press.

Johnson, L. (1993). *Dangerous Minds.* New York: St. Martin's.

Mahiri, J. (1998). *Shooting for Excellence: African American and Youth Culture in New Century Schools.* New York: Teachers College Press, and Urbana, IL: National Council of Teachers of English.

Paley, V. (1997). *The Girl with the Brown Crayon.* Cambridge, MA: Harvard University Press.

Perl, S., & Wilson, N. (1986). *Through Teachers' Eyes: Portraits of Writing Teachers at Work.* Portsmouth, NH: Heinemann.

Rief, L. (1992). *Seeking Diversity: Language Arts with Adolescents.* Portsmouth, NH: Heinemann.

Routman, R. (1988). *Transitions: From Literature to Literacy.* Portsmouth, NH: Heinemann.

Tompkins, J. (1996). *A Life in School: What the Teacher Learned.* Reading, MA: Addison-Wesley.

Vinz, R. (1996). *Composing a Teaching Life.* Portsmouth, NH: Boynton-Cook.

Wilhelm, J. D. (1995). *You Gotta BE the Book: Teaching Engaged and Reflective Reading with Adolescents.* New York: Teachers College Press, and Urbana, IL: National Council of Teachers of English.

FIGURE 10.8 *Contents of a smart portfolio.*

READING ARTIFACTS

Book list

Book notes

Summaries

Diagrams

Overviews

Outlines

THINKING (journal) ARTIFACTS

Thinking about our thinking

Responses to prompts

Written dialogues with texts

Mind wanderings and maps

Charts and graphs

Steps in problem solving

Process memos

Reader response

DEMONSTRATING ARTIFACTS

Illustrations

Teacher assessments

Lesson plans

Feedback from others

Video

Checklists

Teacher-made materials

Presentations

INTERACTING ARTIFACTS

Photographs

Journal assessment

Thinking exercises

In-class entries

Group brainstorming charts

Group consensus products

Peer assessments

Problems/solutions

Projects

WRITING ARTIFACTS

Formal papers

Publication piece

Philosophy of teaching and learning

Table of contents

Evaluation of artifacts

Descriptions of effective strategies

Self-evaluations of teaching

Goals

From Bonita L. Wilcox, "Smart Portfolios for Teachers in Training." *Journal of Adolescent & Adult Literacy,* 40(3), pp. 172–179. Reprinted with permission of the author and the International Reading Association.

accomplishments. Wilcox (1997) promises, "An active portfolio which can generate ideas and initiate new ways of thinking offers unlimited possibilities for enhancing teaching and learning" (p. 37). Be sure to share your thinking journal and ongoing portfolio with your students.

> *Getting Ready to Teach 10.3* (see page 324)

OUTSIDE ASSESSMENTS OF TEACHING

How does one distinguish good teaching from bad, excellent teaching from mediocre? As a student, you made judgments of teachers all the time, which may or may not have matched evaluations by administrators, parents, community, or even your peers. The criteria used might have been different, as were the vantage points and purposes. State education departments use certain criteria to certify teachers, often including tests, which are subject to the same concerns expressed over other types of tests. Does a perfect score on a multiple-choice exam about teaching theories and management strategies always correlate with good classroom performance? Campbell (2000) offers this critique of the "general knowledge" portion of the Praxis Series examination, which many states require teachers to pass and which he prepares future teachers to take:

> A typical standardized test. It is mostly a test of recall of information, and I treat it as a test of short-term memory. It is filled with trivia of little significance for effective teaching. This sort of test controls the future for these students. . . . I am going to propose that, if we must have such a written assessment at all, it at least be an authentic test. (p. 405)

In a move consistent with the whole field of assessment, many states have tried to devise measures that are more performance-based and authentic. For example, some teachers are required to submit videos of their teaching for outside evaluation. But is that clip reflective of the teacher's usual style and way of relating to students? Is there a way to objectively score what is seen so that there is inter-rater reliability (the likelihood that different evaluators would arrive at the same or similar scores)? Could bias play a role in such an evaluation? And what about the time involved at both ends—preparing and scoring—and the cost of evaluating videotapes? Similar concerns surround portfolio evaluation and other forms of teacher evaluation, as the search continues for better ways to assess teaching.

A relatively new opportunity for teachers is to become National Board certified; the voluntary certification is currently available in 16 fields. The process of applying is extensive and expensive, but one many feel is very valuable. Teachers are required to compile a portfolio according to standards and criteria set by the National Board, consisting of classroom teaching videotapes, lesson plans, examples of professional accomplishments, samples of student work, and written commentaries in which the teacher reflects on what she is doing and why. The second part consists of a day spent at one of several designated assessment centers, participating in exercises designed around challenging teacher issues. Among other things, teachers evaluate other teachers' practice, answer questions in interviews, demonstrate a knowledge of their disciplinary area, assess student needs and learning, and take exams in their fields. They give interpretive summaries of their accomplishments with families and communities and in the profession. More information can be obtained about National Board Certification at www.nbpts.org.

CONCLUSION

The assessment of literacy in a content area classroom is a major topic, one that requires your continued attention as you gain experience and get to know your students. You've been given information and some ways to think about literacy assessment in general; ways you can assess literacy in your classroom while you instruct for and encourage literacy and growth in understanding of content. I advocated the use of performance-based, authentic assessments that contribute to, rather than detract from, the wise use of the limited instructional time you are given with your precious learners, who are developing at different rates and in different ways. I'd like to emphasize once again that your goals, your teaching, and your ways of assessing must be consistent. Zessoules and Gardner (1991) say it well:

> Rich modes of assessment cannot be activated in a vacuum. Just as standardized tests have produced a testing culture, educators interested in reform must recognize and examine the need for a classroom culture that will sustain the values, merits and practices of more authentic forms of assessment. . . . If one is going to ask students to grasp scientific principles, compose a melody, or write compelling dialogues, then one needs a curriculum that gives students frequent opportunities to investigate, test, and observe nature; to compose and experiment with many melodies; and to craft,

rehearse, and revise many scenes, many times. Just as standardized testing has driven curriculum and instruction in our schools, so too the implementation of new measures must influence and shape the daily life and activities in the classroom. Unless new modes of assessment reach deep into school culture, incorporating pedagogical approaches, expectations and standards of performance, and the education of students' own capacities for self-critical judgment, new forms of testing will be as discontinuous with teaching and learning as they have ever been. (p. 50)

ANSWERS TO ACTION RESEARCH 10.C: the, and, big, results, sort, in, various, teachers, tests, In, I, and, thoughtful, helped, tests, First, in, to, elementary, education, of, and, not, even, required, a, that, test, unfamiliar, teach, demonstrations, it's, that, in, reality, to, school, to, so, reality, at, my, testing, the, used, the, than, strengths, Added, well, tests.

CHAPTER TEN

Getting Ready to Teach

10.1 Try your hand at preparing a cloze passage, and then have a student or a peer complete it so you can practice scoring. I think you're more likely to use this assessment once you experience how simple it is to use and how useful the information can be for helping students.

10.2 Perrone (1991) considers large educational and social purposes as integral to the reconsideration of assessment. Here's what he envisions as a goal:

> [We] want our students to become *active* readers and writers—individuals who read newspapers and magazines, find beauty in a poem or love story, see Romeo and Juliet in their own lives. We want students to develop an optimistic view about the world and their place in it, to take time to really look at the trees or enjoy a sunset or study the stars. We want them to participate in politics and community life, have a vision of themselves as thoughtful mothers and fathers, understand and value work in all its dimensions, and become sensitive to the needs and values of older citizens. We want them to not only be able to locate the Republic of South Africa on a map, but to understand apartheid and feel the pain associated with it. We need to find student assessments that will help us achieve rather than thwart such purposes. (pp. 164–165)

Using this quote as a model, write a paragraph that describes your purposes for your classroom and your courses. What are some specific examples of what you want your students to become and to be able to do? When you have finished, think about the types of student assessments that might help you "achieve rather than thwart such purposes" (p. 165).

10.3 Compose a preliminary introductory page for a teaching portfolio, along with a potential table of contents showing the types of things you would eventually like to include to show the kind of teacher you hope to be. Choose a suitable container to collect your artifacts to begin a smart portfolio that will facilitate your self-assessment and professional growth.

Content Area Literacy: Envisioning Your Future

One of the first things I asked you to do as an active reader of this textbook was to write down words you associate with the word *utopia*. Reading *The Giver* and participating in the related exercises likely enhanced your understanding of the term, the concept, and the genre of utopian/dystopian literature. At one point (Activating Prior Knowledge 1.2), I asked you to imagine a utopian school, your version of educational perfection.

Now, I'd like to return to that theme. Because you've read much more, you've learned and discussed and written about a variety of issues related to literacy in the content areas, you have more to bring to your vision and dreams of what schools and classrooms—especially *your* classroom—should be. You have made yourself part of a long tradition of educational reform and philosophy-building. There have always been critics of schools and educational practices, visionaries who promoted innovative methods, often opening alternative schools in order to teach without the constraints of the status quo. The names John Dewey, Edward Austin Sheldon, Maria Montessori, John Holt, Ivan Illich, Paulo Freire, Frank Smith, and Jonathan Kozol are familiar to many. B. F. Skinner envisioned a utopian school (which some critics consider dystopian) in *Walden Two*. Figure 11.1 lists some books you can explore to get an idea of the variety of the theories and the dedication and passion of the reformers. Be aware that this list includes books that may express diametrically opposed philosophies—I want you to get a variety of perspectives.

"How many a man [woman] has dated a new era in his [her] life from the reading of a book."

THOREAU, *WALDEN*

FIGURE 11.1 *Books by or about educational critics, innovators, and visionaries.*

Bennett, W. (1999). *The Educated Child.* New York: Free Press.

Bickman, M. (Ed.). (1999). *Uncommon Learning: Thoreau on Education.* Boston: Houghton Mifflin.

Bigelow, B., Harvey, B., Karp, S., & Miller, L. (2001). *Rethinking Our Classrooms, Volume 2: Teaching for Equity and Justice.* Milwaukee, WI: Rethinking Schools.

Brown, R. (1993). *Schools of Thought: How the Politics of Literacy Shape Thinking in the Classroom.* San Francisco: Jossey-Bass.

Covington, M. (1992). *Making the Grade: A Self-worth Perspective on Motivation and School Reform.* New York: Cambridge University Press.

Csikszentmihalyi, M., Rathunde, K. R., & Whalen, S. (1993). *Talented Teenagers: The Roots of Success and Failure.* New York: Cambridge University Press.

Daniels, H. (1998). *Best Practice: New Standards for Teaching and Learning in America's Schools.* Portsmouth, NH: Heinemann.

Delpit, L. (1995). *Other People's Children: Cultural Conflict in the Classroom.* New York: New Press.

Eisner, E. (1994). *The Educational Imagination: On the Design and Evaluation of School Programs.* Upper Saddle River, NJ: Prentice Hall.

Finn, P. (1999). *Literacy with an Attitude.* Albany, NY: SUNY Press.

Gallego, M. A., & Hollingsworth, S. (Eds.). (2000). *What Counts as Literacy: Challenging the School Standard.* New York: Teachers College Press.

Hargreaves, A., Earl, L., Moore, S., & Manning, S. (2001). *Learning to Change: Teaching Beyond Subjects and Standards.* San Francisco: Jossey-Bass.

Hirsch, E. D., Jr. (1996). *The Schools We Need: And Why We Don't Have Them.* Garden City, NY: Doubleday.

Holland, H., & Mazzoli, K. (2001). *The Heart of a High School: One Community's Effort to Transform Urban Education.* Westport, CT: Heinemann.

Hurd, P. D. (2000). *Transforming Middle School Science Education.* New York: Teachers College Press.

Kohn, A. (1998). *What to Look for in a Classroom: And Other Essays.* San Francisco: Jossey-Bass.

Kohn, A. (1999). *The Schools Our Children Deserve: Moving Beyond Traditional Classrooms and "Tougher Standards."* Boston: Houghton Mifflin.

Mahiri, J. (1998). *Shooting for Excellence: African American and Youth Culture in New Century Schools.* New York: Teachers College Press, and Urbana, IL: National Council of Teachers of English.

Noddings, N. (1992). *The Challenge to Care in Schools: An Alternative Approach to Education.* New York: Teachers College Press.

Ohanian, S. (1998). *Standards, Plain English, and the Ugly Duckling: Lessons About What Teachers Really Do.* Bloomington, IN: Phi Delta Kappa Educational Foundation, and Burlington, VT: John Dewey Project on Progressive Education.

Sadker, M., & Sadker, D. (1994). *Failing at Fairness: How America's Schools Cheat Girls.* New York: Scribner's.

Schlechty, P. C. (2001). *Shaking Up the Schoolhouse: How to Support and Sustain Educational Innovation.* San Francisco: Jossey-Bass.

Sizer, T. (1996). *Horace's Hope: What Works for the American High School.* Boston: Houghton Mifflin.

Tharp, R. G., Estrada, P., Dalton, S. S., & Yamouchi, L. A. (2000). *Teaching Transformed: Achieving Excellence, Fairness, Inclusion, and Harmony.* Boulder, CO: Westview Press.

In this book, you've already met some of the experts who have spoken out against our present system of schooling and offered their versions of what schools should be. This is a time of rapid change and much talk of the future. An entire issue (January–March 2000) of the scholarly journal *Reading Research Quarterly* was devoted to the theme "Envisioning the Future of Literacy." One article, by Elizabeth Birr Moje, is entitled, "What Will Classrooms and Schools Look Like in the New Millennium?" That's an important question for you as you begin

your career early in that millennium—you have the opportunity to be a voice and a presence that can help determine the answers. Moje expresses hope as she points to more diversity among students, and eventually staff; more parent and community involvement; more access to technology (though she worries about the equality of access). Among her goals for literacy teaching are "teaching youth how to use reading and writing to construct a just and democratic society" (p. 129), and using service learning activities as a way to take students' projects into the community so that students will learn both to navigate multiple discourse communities and to take action in the world outside of school. As more and more students at all achievement levels report feeling disconnected from the world in the confines of a school in which the learning seems contrived, community-based projects will increase motivation and reshape schools of the future. (p. 129)

Many teachers go through a "teaching" pattern. They begin to teach one way, become dissatisfied, find a more rewarding and successful way, and write about their experiences and new approaches. Sometimes, researchers document these changes and new practices. For example, Sondra Perl and Nancy Wilson set out to find out what life was like for six teachers who were making a transition to teaching writing in a writing workshop setting in a particular school district. The authors became participant observers in the classrooms and actually lived with some of the teachers. The result was *Through Teachers' Eyes: Portraits of Writing Teachers at Work* (1986). As a preservice or beginning teacher, you might find the teacher biography and autobiography genre helpful as you imagine both the excitement and pitfalls of teaching literacy in your content area.

We don't have to rely on nonfiction alone for visions of what school is like and what school could be. There are many fictional portrayals of educational settings that are dystopian, utopian, or a combination of both that contain much truth and are very thought-provoking. Read or view the materials listed in Figure 11.2, and imagine yourself in the settings, making tough decisions and having the opportunity to relate to the student characters and to envision how you might open the world of learning for them.

Book Talk 11.1

A murder mystery set in a high school. An English teacher as victim. Potential suspects range from the principal and a guidance counselor to fellow teachers and a myriad of students. Multiple perspectives of the teacher and multiple reactions to the death. Few to no clues; no known motive. Ready to take on the case? Read *Who Killed Mr. Chippendale?: A Mystery in Poems,* by Mel Glenn (1996), and keep your pad and pencil handy to note your suspicions and reflect on the problems and promises of contemporary schools and students.

FIGURE 11.2   *Fictional works and movies about teachers, schools, and learners.*

Anderson, L. H. (1999). *Speak.* New York: Farrar, Straus & Giroux.

Avi. (1994). *Nothing But the Truth.* Thorndike, ME: Thorndike Press.

Cormier, R. (1974). *The Chocolate War.* New York: Pantheon.

Crutcher, C. (1993). *Staying Fat for Sarah Byrnes.* New York: Greenwillow Books.

Crutcher, C. (1995). *Ironman.* New York: Greenwillow Books.

Crutcher, C. (2001). *Whale Talk.* New York: Greenwillow Books.

Duncan, L. (1979). *Killing Mr. Griffin.* New York: Dell.

Glenn, M. (1991). *My Friend's Got This Problem, Mr. Candler: High School Poems.* New York: Clarion Books.

Glenn, M. (1997). *The Taking of Room 114: A Hostage Drama in Poems.* New York: Lodestar Books/ Dutton.

Glenn, M. (2000). *Split Image: A Story in Poems.* New York: HarperCollins.

Hilton, J. (1934). *Good-bye, Mr. Chips.* London: Hodder & Stroughton.

Kaufman, B. (1991). *Up the Down Staircase.* New York: HarperPerennial.

Kerr, M. E. (1975). *Is That You, Miss Blue?* New York: Harper & Row.

Kleinbaum, N. H. (1989). *The Dead Poets Society.* New York: Bantam.

Marshall, C. (2001). *Christy.* Grand Rapids, MI: Chosen Books.

Mr. Holland's Opus. (1996). Hollywood Pictures Home Videos.

October Sky. (1999). Universal City, CA: Universal Studios.

Taylor, M. (1976). *Roll of Thunder, Hear My Cry.* New York: Dial Books.

The Breakfast Club. (1998). Universal City, CA: Universal Home Video.

The Dead Poets Society. (1992). Touchstone Pictures. Boston: DVS Home Video.

Wilson, B. (Ed.). (1992). The Metaphor. In *The Leaving.* New York: Philomel Books.

VISIONS OF WHAT SCHOOLS COULD BE

In "Language Education in the 21st Century: Dreaming a Caring Future" (1998), John S. Mayher tackles the challenge of creating and sharing a utopian vision for schools. He recognizes that some of his ideas will meet with objection, but decides, "Any good prognosticator tries to shape as well as anticipate the future, so I will attend most directly with the schools I would like to see in the next century without being concerned about the feasibility of my dreams" (p. 156). That's the point at which I believe preservice teachers should be, and I hope you are at now. Often, my students say that they love my ideas and methods, but they don't see how they could work in "the real world." They are all too aware of the constraints imposed by national and state standards, state and local curricula, and department guidelines for text selection and assessment. They remind me of my son, whom I called at college to wish a happy birthday. He told me that his day was uneventful, sighing, "I realized that after 21 there are no birthdays to really look forward to." I tell my students that if they are unwilling to dream big, look beyond the boundaries, and be idealists *now*, it's unlikely they'll make much of a difference in the future. So, embrace idealism.

Mayher (1998) begins by chronicling the dystopian influences of present day society, which are "producing a generation of students for whom schooling has been disconnected from learning" (p. 157). Though he proclaims that "no one learns best in the schools we have" (p. 165), he doesn't stay with this grim picture for long: "I am not so naive as to believe that positive thinking alone will solve our problems, but I do know that cynicism and bitterness surely will exacerbate them" (p. 161). Mayher describes a caring learning community á la Nell Noddings, where "the message of commitment to the highest standards would be sent every day" (p. 162). His utopian school has the following characteristics:

- Multigenerational
- Inclusive
- Open almost all the time
- Multipurpose
- Beautiful
- Warm
- Friendly
- Respectful
- Safe
- Democratic
- Explicitly antiracist, antisexist, and anticlassist
- Consistent
- Meaning-based learning environment
- High quality
- Nonhierarchical
- Professional
- Learner and learning centered (pp. 162–164)

He imagines a school environment that "feeds the spirit, the heart, the body, and the mind; where all participants feel welcome and cared for; and where the business of learning and the business of living are not separate but whole" (p. 164). Mayher realizes he is fantasizing but believes the ideal school can be realized. So do I.

Another person who has projected a decade into the future and set down a visionary, though admittedly not utopian, classroom and school setting is Jabari Mahiri, in *Shooting for Excellence: African American and Youth Culture in New Century Schools* (1998). Throughout the book, he cites studies and describes the methods of teachers who exemplify the best characteristics of coaching, "modeling specific skill development, instilling self-discipline in the players, policies for fair and equal participation for all players, and a policy of multiple coaches for each team" (p. 154). His last chapter, "Imagining New Century Schools," invites readers to look through the eyes of a student at a school where literacy is central to the student-centered, exploratory approach espoused by the entire school and community. The school's philosophy is based on the premise that learners

> should leave high school with the fundamental skills to access, analyze, synthesize, and interpret information as a foundation for the continual development of their abilities to make contributions to the knowledge base. These fundamental skills included systematic and analytical thinking skills necessary for solving complex problems. In short, . . . high school should provide an experience in which students learn to learn, and learn to love learning. (p. 149)

In Mahiri's imagined school, teachers and students are very attuned to discourse and language issues. Teachers, characterized implicitly as intellectuals, learn from students and incorporate African American and youth culture in general as they motivate, instruct, and mentor in a *mutable curriculum* that celebrates diversity. One simple sentence in the author's reflection on this possible scenario stays with me: "meaningful change also means changing ourselves" (p. 159). What a challenge he's given us.

Remember the "What if?" strategy you learned in Chapter 6? In the title of his presidential address to an NCTE convention (with the theme "Reimagining the Possibilities"), Jerome Harste asked the question, "What If English/Language Arts Teachers Really Cared?" (Harste & Carey, 1999, p. 1). He didn't find the task of envisioning the future easy, and he recognized that we can't just tinker with the curriculum and call it change because

> it is safe to say that no one can predict what kind of world our grandchildren will find upon graduation. In three generations the world experienced greater change than at any other time in history. The cultural and technological gulf between Socrates and our parents is much less than the gulf between the world our parents knew and the world our grandchildren will enter. (p. 1)

Nevertheless, Harste offers some bold thoughts, such as the following:

> We could even help children understand that they haven't really finished reading until they have taken some form of social action by mentally and physically repositioning themselves in the world. It is not enough, for example, to read about women's rights. You have to act and talk differently, too. (p. 2)

Having come to the end of this textbook and the other texts you've explored along the way, try applying Harste's definition of reading to yourself. How will you "finish reading"? How will you reposition yourself as a content area teacher? How will the adolescents in your care benefit from the changes that have occurred because of your active engagement with the topic of teaching literacy?

Given the dilemma that "what is literacy to us may not be literacy for the parents of the children we teach" (p. 5), Harste still asks the important questions: "How then, do we teach? What are our roles and responsibilities as teachers . . . ? How can multiple discourses, multiple sign systems, and multiple realities inform what we do in the millennium?" (p. 5). He answers by giving examples of teachers from around the country interacting with and encouraging literacy in innovative ways. He tells of teachers having art materials and musical instruments available, as well as a flood of writing materials and books, in their classrooms; others bringing the community into the schools by inviting parents to run discovery clubs that feature gardening, karaoke, karate, and bricklaying; teachers forming study groups; school partnerships with universities. Harste shows by reporting on wonderful ongoing

projects that "what can be imagined can be done" (p. 8). He is not afraid to think utopian thoughts when it comes to schooling: "Wouldn't it be wonderful if we knew how to create spaces so that all voices could be heard in the creation of a more just, a more thoughtful, and a more democratic way of living out the imagination of our elders?" (p. 8).

Nell Noddings (1999) spins out a thought-provoking narrative illustrating the potential a stimulating topic holds for teachers willing to involve students in investigation and inquiry. She takes the question of whether evolution and creationism should both be taught in schools, and suggests that, rather than have school boards debate it and hand down a decision, the students could be encouraged to tackle the question itself. They can learn about the history of evolutionary theory, the great debates relating to it. This might lead to reading biographical information about Bishop Wilberforce, Thomas Henry Huxley, Clarence Darrow, and William Jennings Bryan, leading to other social issues and big questions such as determinism versus free will.

Noddings plays with the variety of subtopics that might arise while discussing evolution, and explains how students with different interests might choose their avenues of exploration. Those interested in animal behavior could tackle the question, "Can human language be shown to be continuous with animal communication, or is it what some scholars have called a 'true emergent'?" (p. 582). She notes that high school girls, who, she says, often require a special intellectual interest, might be thrilled to study the two versions of creation in Genesis, along with how early feminists (e.g., Elizabeth Cady Stanton) and current women's studies scholars interpret and critique the versions. Students could read Native American, Chinese, and African creation stories. They can learn about social Darwinism. Noddings asks us to imagine her vision of what I see as the synthesis of literacy and content learning:

> Imagine how much "cultural literacy" students might gain in a unit of study such as this. Working on their own projects, listening to others, trying to fit whatever direct instruction they receive with the material they are learning on their own, they will come across names, events, and concepts that will add immeasurably to their store of knowledge. (p. 582)

> ▶ *Getting Ready to Teach 11.1* *(see p. 337)* ◀

MY VISION OF AN IDEAL SCHOOL

In this text, I set out a path to and flexible guidelines for the development of a kind of content area classroom different from the ones you most likely attended. My utopian vision is that the preservice teachers reading this book will take the ideas that fit their philosophies and goals, and make them their own as they create intellectually stimulating and literature-rich classrooms and courses. I do not wish any reader to become my clone. Laura Thompson, a preservice teacher, said in response to reading about the wonderful classroom Nancie Atwell describes in *In the Middle* (1998), "I've never yet followed a recipe verbatim, and I don't intend to start now in my new career."

You, future teachers, will implement my dream as you keep reading widely and participating in other literacy activities. Read deeply in your discipline, read the works and discoveries and ideas of prominent people in your field, read professional educational journals for stories about how other teachers are helping students soar in literacy, knowledge, action, and intellectual curiosity. And read for pure enjoyment.

My hope for schools involves you bringing students to the wonders of the world, and those beyond, and bringing those things to them, sometimes through direct experience, sometimes through texts. Consider the case of students in a program in Albany, Georgia, that is designed to encourage youth with physical disabilities or learning disabilities toward careers in technology and science. They asked some "What if?" questions. What if caterpillars, which normally climb upward and use gravity as they build their cocoons downward, were launched into space? Would they become disoriented? Would they adapt? "Aided by area scientists and dedicated teachers" (Wakefield, 2001, p. 32), they hypothesized, and designed an experiment to monitor five caterpillars (the "painted lady" variety) and five cocoons of varying ages that were sent into space.

The phrase "aided by area scientists and dedicated teachers" epitomizes my utopian vision for learners. The Georgia project was made possible by a Texas-based company, SPACEHAB, that brings student projects into space. Its S*T*A*R*S (Space Technology and Research Students) program uses the Internet to "Webcast" nearly real-time images of experiments to students around the world. Want to know the result of the Albany, Georgia, experiment?

> The larvae, floating and turning in the air, slowly spun silky envelopes and slipped inside. And one by one, from the crusted cocoons the students had affixed to the crossbar, emerged three-inch-wide butterflies dappled with pale orange, white, brown and black. Nature had prevailed. (p. 34)

Will your students be able to participate in experiments in outer space? I don't know—maybe. But I'm certain they can go on a literary field trip if you bring the article "The Object at Hand: Painted Ladies in Space" (Wakefield, 2001) from the *Smithsonian* magazine to class. And they can join with other student researchers by visiting the National Air and Space Museum's website. But your students might never learn of these sources if you don't introduce them. You really do possess the power to bring the world to them and launch them into the exciting world of your discipline—through literacy.

There are many innovative and unique learning environments outside the school walls, so pay attention to ideas from the community and business. For example, The Egg Factory is a firm that develops products for companies—it gives aspiring young inventors a chance to be in a creative environment and the support necessary to work on ideas. They encourage thinking outside the box, beyond barriers. Cooperative learning occurs when teams consisting of a business student, a liberal arts student, an engineering student, and a graduating high school senior work on problems. The company pays

BookTalk 11.2

If I could have only one magazine subscription for my class, I might choose the interdisciplinary *Smithsonian*. It offers art, science, history, sports, current events, math, and more in an accessible and attractive format, complete with fascinating photographs. Look at some of the feature article titles in the June 2001 issue that told about students and their painted lady butterflies in space, and think about what subject areas they might be appropriate for:

- "The Leaning Tower Straightens Up" by Richard Covington
- "Mapping Galactic Foam" by Valerie Jablow
- "Sage Grouse Strut Their Stuff" by Scott Weidensaul
- "Women Athletes Put on Their Game Face"
- "Eternal Egypt" by Doug Stewart
- "Across the Russian Wilds" by Fred Strebeigh
- "Cruise to Alaska" by Michael Parfit
- "Dr. Franklin's Plan" by Stephan A. Schwartz

Having the *Smithsonian* in your classroom for those times when students have a few minutes free, or making them available for weekend borrowing, would be a gift, a gift of learning for those minds entrusted to your care.

the interns and shares future profits with them. Now, think of how you could conduct your classroom or a scholastic club after this model.

▶ *Getting Ready to Teach 11.2 (see p. 337)* ◀

PUTTING THE PIECES TOGETHER

Throughout the chapters, I've reminded you that, although it was necessary to discuss the components of literacy separately, they really are inseparable; they're a whole. Similarly, teaching literacy and teaching your content curriculum and disciplinary knowledge will be interwoven. As we bring this textbook experience to a close, I'd like to give you a picture of real teachers and students transacting with text in a high school content area classroom that demonstrates the pieces working together. You'll see motivation and vocabulary issues; background knowledge; metacognition; critical thinking; strategic uses of talking, listening, writing, and drawing. You'll see a picture that can activate your visions of what you want your classroom to be.

The vignette I'm going to summarize and comment on takes place in a high school Math Connections course in an alternative urban high school in Rochester, New York. The teacher, Judi, and two mathematics educators, Margie and Constance, who were there in the role of researchers, chose essays from the text *The Mathematical Experience* (Davis & Hersh, 1981), a book that discusses historical, political, and social dimensions of math. Margie demonstrated, modeled and taught a technique called the "Say Something Strategy" (Harste & Short, 1988) after asking students to read the introductory paragraph. Constance recorded on newsprint the students' immediate responses about the content, the writing, and their understanding or confusion as the discussion unfolded. Margie helped the students value the process by showing them the written ideas that had developed by listening to others and voicing concerns.

> Student partners Char and Jolea selected the essay "Mathematics and War" to read together. They decided to stop after every paragraph to talk, and agreed to let Margie join their conversation. After the first paragraph, Jolea felt stupid, but after a bit of interaction said, "I didn't understand while you were talking but now I understand. I guess a lot of the words I didn't understand" (p. 69). After the second paragraph, the partners discussed the role of astrologers in ancient times and the difference between scientists and

mathematicians. As they continued reading and talking, they mentioned the strategies they were using to comprehend the text, and Char noted that, despite difficult words like *cryptography* and *econometrics*, the text was getting easier for her to read. Jolea, in the midst of reacting to the content of scientists contributing to destruction, metacognitively noted something about her reading process: "I—I got lost up here but when you walked away, I just said well I've got time now, I'll just do it over again. And I got it and I understood it" (p. 73).

> Critical thinking became evident as the girls talked about whether it might be more dangerous for one country to have nuclear weapons than for two; they recognized the complexity of the issue they were reading about. Jolea spontaneously offered a reflection on the process they were using:

>> I don't know if I should say this but—I don't think I'd be able to read from a book [like this] without reading and then talking about it. . . . You know, usually you have to read the whole thing, maybe you do it for homework and then the next day it's not as fresh and you forget the little things that— You remember a couple of things that confused you. But now it's—and you're doing it right away and something's right there. (Borasi & Siegel, 2000, p. 74)

> When asked if she thought she could adapt the strategy to use while doing homework, Jolea answered confidently, "Yeah, I think eventually you can . . . if you do this enough to learn—Just like anything if you do something with someone enough you can usually go solo" (p. 74).

> By the time they finished reading, the partners were grappling with the moral dimensions of mathematics and war and the connections between math and science, based on the text's description of World War I as the chemists' war, World War II as the physicists' war, and World War III "(may it never come)" (p. 75) as the mathematicians' war. The students were engaged in high-level thinking as a result of a thought-provoking text, a strategy that was making the text accessible, and support from a teacher in a comfortable academic environment.

> For homework, students were directed to use the Sketch-to-Stretch strategy (Harste & Short, 1988; Siegel, 1984), making a sketch to show what they had learned from the text. This strategy, too, proved beneficial. Char and Jolea decided to make separate sketches because they had come away from the reading experience with different themes and wanted to draw their interpretations independently. The next day, each girl shared her drawing with the class and explained its meaning. Char's sketch had nine boxes, with one column representing the products of math-

ematicians' thinking at three points in time (a catapult, a bomb, Star Wars), the second representing the mathematicians' moral dilemma as they tried to balance the intellectual challenge of research and the effects on humankind, and the third showing society's positive and negative response to the products. The class compared and contrasted this with Jolea's artistic interpretation. Jolea explained her picture, the feeling underlying it, and the process of reading, discussing, and drawing.

I urge you to read the full account in Borasi and Siegel's *Reading Counts: Expanding the Role of Reading in Mathematics Classrooms* (2000). The authors reflect on what the students gained from this instructional episode involving a generative reading of the "Math and War" essay. Students came to value new connections between math and life and were exposed to information about how math, specifically in its use in warfare, has evolved and grown over time. They discussed the social role of mathematicians, as well as the moral concerns individual mathematicians have had regarding the use of their work for the purpose of war. The authors conclude:

> The extent to which Char and Jolea were able to grasp and elaborate on these themes in their "say something" conversation and their sketches was remarkable. Although these students seem to have thought little about the ethical dimensions of mathematics before reading this essay, their exploration of this issue was quite sophisticated and added new insights and connections to what was presented in the text—an impressive achievement even for adult readers of the same text! And even if some of their classmates had overlooked this issue in their own reading of the text, Char and Jolea's sharing of their sketches gave the whole class an opportunity to appreciate the meaning and importance of ethical issues in mathematics. (pp. 84–85)

The students, through literacy activities, came to a better understanding of mathematics as a discipline and are more likely to remember the information they learned because of their engagement.

Think of what can be accomplished in your courses as you provide rich texts, and opportunities to react to them and apply them to the students' lives—facilitating, modeling, and mentoring as students learn your content and discipline skills. Literacy is the key to your students' success. Strategies alone won't work, but strategies and philosophy together can work wonders. O'Brien et al. (1995) point out that when content literacy strategies are used in conjunction with teaching methods that acknowledge and build on the social construction of knowledge (e.g., discussion and cooperative learning) and when they challenge traditional, technical classroom methods, then "secondary content literacy can be considered radical pedagogy" (p. 446). You're invited to join a revolution.

NEW TEACHERS TEACHING DIFFERENTLY AND MAKING A DIFFERENCE

Out of the blue, I received an e-mail from a former student, Chris Leahey, telling me that he was now using the strategies he had learned in my content area literacy class in his ninth-grade social studies classes and thanking me for providing him with ways to enhance his students' literacy. He also mentioned that he was about to team teach a unit with an English teacher, whom I had also taught. I knew I could learn things from them, so I visited their school, talking with them and observing a class where I interacted with their students. I'd like you to meet these third-year teachers to see how they've applied and adapted some of the principles explained in this book.

Chris's Global Studies curriculum required that he teach colonialism in Africa. He decided he could engage his students in the topic and help them understand its complexity by having them read the novel *Things Fall Apart* by Chinua Achebe (1994). It tells the story of an African village, and of one man in particular, Okonkwo, a leader who encounters conflict both within his tribe and with outside forces of European missionaries and government officials.

Auddie Mastroleo, the English teacher, viewed Okonkwo as a model of a tragic hero and the novel as a model tragedy. Her students had just finished a unit on mythology, full of heroes, some fallen. She had also taken a course on storytelling the year before and had committed one day a week to storytelling in her class; the students, therefore, had explored many African folktales and myths. So, she saw great potential in *Things Fall Apart*. It could help her address the standards *her* curriculum is based on, too. Auddie and Chris eagerly began planning their team teaching, a new endeavor for both.

I visited them in the middle of the unit. They were wildly enthusiastic, surprising even themselves. They had provided some background knowledge, introduced value-laden issues, and discussed perspective by having the students watch *Roots*. They were now listening to students talk about *Things Fall Apart*, as well as reflect on their reading processes. As Auddie and Chris analyzed student work, both were feeling that their goals were being reached and the unit was a great success so far. I asked them to tell me more.

Chris was enamored of the book itself. Because it depicts imperialism from an African perspective, he feels it lends itself to his curriculum and the social studies standards. Beyond that, he said, "I love the book because of its language—'Proverbs are the palm oil in which words fall apart. . . .'" Last year, Chris piloted the book; his students wrote how long each chapter took and the problems they encountered. "They had problems keeping the family relationships straight, so this year we gave the kids a chart to track the family tree, and they made their own family tree. We avoided all worksheet stuff. We told them, 'We're not going to ask you to do anything that won't help you.'" The students drew symbols and animals. Chris was delighted to discover that "the kids saw things about the court case we didn't see—connections—cultural universals—a way of settling disputes." Chris taught a lesson on infant mortality after they read in the book about African babies dying. "I used charts of world mortality rates. We discussed causes of mortality." He noted that his students had written 24 essays so far in his course and were not complaining because of the way he taught. "I give kids problems to solve. The kids become global historians. They must interpret—I don't impart knowledge."

I asked Chris how he answered colleagues who think there's no time to read novels in social studies class. He answered that he didn't use literature as an extra; rather, he taught the required concepts, such as apartheid and imperialism, *through* stories. His students had also read *Sadako and the Thousand Paper Cranes* (Coerr, 1977) and *Hiroshima* (Hersey, 1946) in the context of his lessons on World War II; facts and concepts were taught in the context of the literature. He found time by making teaching through literature a priority. "Besides," Chris quipped, "the curriculum calls for teaching 5,000 years of Chinese history in six weeks. When you have an impossible task anyway. . . ." He summed up the atmosphere in his Global Studies class by saying, "We have an attitude."

Auddie was equally excited about how the team teaching was going and the learning and the changes in the students' attitudes that were occurring. She felt it was the best unit she had taught in her three years as a teacher. Her students had written advice to the characters; she had used supplemental materials like an African drum CD and African photographs; they made book jackets, mobiles, and posters. Students were looking for things online that connect to the book and the issues the book raises. Both teachers had done a lot of informal assessment along the way—Auddie noted that the students with special educational needs were handling the book just fine, with

resources and assistance as needed; no one was being left behind. When I asked what the final evaluation of the unit would be, she laughed and said, "We don't know yet. We work off of what happens each day. You have to be flexible." Months later, she wrote:

> For the final assessment of the unit, we chose to assign separate tasks. In Global Studies, students continued with the unit on Africa and apartheid. They ended the unit with a document-based question in which the students could refer to the team-taught novel. In English, students analyzed and interpreted a poem and wrote a [compare–contrast] essay.

After our interview, I was invited to join Chris's class for the afternoon. He began by showing a transparency of the activity for the day, which involved small groups playing the role of white government officials, and instructed, "As a group, your task is to make a policy for handling different problems that arise in the village." Students picked up folders explaining their various tasks and roles, got in groups, then got right to work on the task. They discussed such issues as intermarriage among races, the consequences of disobeying the colonial policies that had been imposed in the novel, taxation, building schools and churches. Almost every student contributed to the group discussions. This lesson was very organized—the students moved through nine problems quickly and had time to post answers and report on their decisions to the whole group.

Auddie later wrote a paper on the experience, in which she explained:

> My role during data collection was to simply look and listen. I became an observer of my students' behavior, quality of work, and attitude. I also, in a sense, observed myself—metacognition became key. I grew to be aware of my attitude and teaching in this unit. I became an observer, participant, and recorder of data.

As a result of Auddie's careful listening, she learned about students' attitudes:

> Students, before and after class, would often remark about their enjoyment of the activity or the novel itself. Remarks like these were to be heard: "I can't believe he would just kill his own son!" or "How do his wives put up with him?" or "I can't stand the way he is so uptight about not being like his father." Often, on the way out of class, students could be heard talking to each other about the novel. "What part are you on? I just finished reading about the court case." Such comments were the norm and they revealed a deep interest and involvement in the novel and the unit.

Chris and Auddie are both reflective teachers who are very aware of how much they are changing. Chris consciously sets one or two new goals for him-

BookTalk 11.3

A perfect companion to Achebe's *Things Fall Apart* is Barbara Kingsolver's *The Poisonwood Bible* (1998). Told from the perspectives of five female narrators (the wife and daughters of a missionary devoted to "converting the African heathens"), the story starts out in the Congo in 1960 and details the effects of colonialism on the country and society. The interrelationships are complex and often wonderful; the character development is superb; the author's use of language is exquisite. The story is a modern parable, and readers are wiser for having experienced it.

self each year. He mentioned using cooperative learning effectively as one example. "We're continually evolving." Auddie, who is constantly working hard to find ways to make literature more enjoyable for and accessible to her students, has also learned to be patient with herself, stating, "I'm growing into the type of teacher I want to be." Figure 11.3 is part of the packet of reading guides the two content area teachers created to help their students interact with *Things Fall Apart.*

CONCLUSION

Introducing myself to you in the Introduction was much easier than saying good-bye to you is now. What final words to impart? Let's look ahead to your content area classroom. Will it be a good one in terms of literacy?

How does one know, you might wonder, when good literacy is or is not happening in schools? There are experts who would love to be your guides. William J. Bennett, for example, in *The Educated Child* (1999), offers charts with "warning signs" of weak programs in language arts, history and geography, math and science; warning signs of weak testing methods; warning signs of bad teaching. Kohn, in *The Schools Our Children Deserve* (1999), offers a "Visitor's Guide" with "Good Signs" in the left-hand column and "Possible Reasons to Worry" in the other. Reading these books simultaneously emphasized to me how much one's philosophy determines what is judged as good or bad—in many, many cases these authors gave opposing views of what a good classroom looks like, what productive learning looks like, what bad teaching looks like. For example, included in Bennett's list of "Warning Signs of a Weak Language Arts Program" is "students often told 'there are no right or wrong answers'" when analyzing literature" (1999, p. 169). On the other hand, one of Kohn's "Possible Reasons to Worry" is "emphasis on facts and right answers," while a good sign is, "emphasis on thoughtful exploration of complicated issues" (1999, p. 236).

I'd like to add my voice to the conversation. I've not tried to hide my philosophy of teaching as I've given examples and recommendations throughout the chapters, so you can probably guess the kinds of things I consider positive signs of literacy learning or evidence that it's time to be concerned. Here are a few of the questions that I might ask if I visited your content area classroom:

- Is there a classroom library with books and other materials that students can borrow and take home?
- Are current and enticing reading materials on display?
- Do the reading materials in the classroom represent varying levels of difficulty and a variety of genres?
- If I asked the students what some of their teacher's favorite books are, could they tell me?
- If I asked the students what booktalks their teacher has given lately, could they name several titles?
- Are students reading a variety of books beyond the textbook or instead of a textbook? Are they given choices in terms of what they read?
- Are students using writing to explore issues, reflect on their reading, explain ideas, and express themselves? Do they write for real purposes and to real audiences?
- Do students talk and listen to one another about what they've read and heard, about topics being explored, about interesting vocabulary, about the subject matter, about current issues or people working in the discipline? Is it evident from the activity in the room that the teacher understands that learning is social?
- Are visual and media literacy being addressed? Are relevant pictures, graphs, films, and so on explored in thoughtful ways?
- Is the teacher talking with the students while work is in progress to assess in authentic situations and facilitate and support learning?
- Does the teacher assess and provide background knowledge before teaching and providing reading materials?
- Does the teacher motivate the students to explore reading materials and to think critically about the ideas presented in them?

FIGURE 11.3   *Reading guide packet.*

Things Fall Apart

North Syracuse Junior High
Leahey/Mastroleo
Grade 9

Event	Detailed Description of Events	How is this similar to and different from events in our culture?
Ikemefuna's Fate p.		
Engagement p.		
Infant Mortality p.		
Court Case p.		

Task 1: List details from the chapter.

Task 2: Using the details listed, write one word (i.e., descriptor) that captures the overall mood or tone of each chapter.

DESCRIPTOR	DETAILS

PART I PROJECT

Choose **one** of the following assignments to complete for Part I of *Things Fall Apart*.

1. Write a poem about the events or the characters that you have read about in the novel for Part I. You may write more than one poem, but you must have at least 20 lines in all.

2. Create a book jacket for Part I of the novel. You must include an illustration that represents the characters or the events you have read about so far, a brief biography of the author, and a paragraph convincing someone to read this book.

3. Create a book cube for Part I of the novel. Make a 6-sided cube out of a cardboard box and cover it with paper. Illustrate 5 scenes from the novel. On the sixth side write the author's name, the title of the novel, and your name.

4. Write a letter to a character or to the author responding to Part I of the novel. Some things to consider:

    ● Give advice to a character.

    ● Ask questions about the story or about why a character responded in a certain way.

    ● Comment on the book so far.

5. Create a mobile of the characters, scenes, objects, or symbols in the book so far. You must have at least seven ornaments.

Due Date:

FIGURE **11.3**   *Continued.*

Model of a Tragedy	Star Wars	Things Fall Apart
SETTING		
1. Society in Turmoil		
2. Unavoidable code of ethics		
3. Enforcer(s) who oversees the code of ethics		
CHARACTER		
1. *Tragic hero:* man who seems larger than life, not average, and stronger; a special gift with language, and a mysterious birth.		
2. *Tragic flaw:*		
a) physical flaw		
b) character flaw—usually hubris		
PLOT		
1. Hero's flaw causes him to break the code of ethics.		
2. Society is put into turmoil because of the hero's choice.		
3. The enforcer tries to reveal to the hero his mistake.		
4. Hero realizes his mistake and sacrifices himself.		
5. Society is returned to order.		

ESSAY

DIRECTIONS: After reading the novel *Things Fall Apart* by Chinua Achebe and the poem "The Second Coming," by William Butler Yeats, write an essay about a society or an individual in turmoil. Use ideas from both works and the questions from the poem guide to develop your essay. Show how the authors used specific literary elements or techniques to convey ideas.

GUIDELINES:

- Use ideas from both passages to establish the controlling idea about a society or an individual in turmoil.

- Use specific and relevant evidence from both passages to develop your ideas.

- Show how each author uses specific literary elements (conflict, theme, character, point of view, plot) or techniques (symbolism, imagery, irony, descriptive language) to show a society or an individual in turmoil.

- Organize your ideas logically.

- Use language that communicates ideas effectively.

- Follow the conventions of standard written English.

- Line 3a: What "things" could the poem be referring to?

- Line 3b: Visualize this line. What does it look like? What sounds are created?

- Line 4: Anarchy or disorder, violence, and lawlessness appear in the novel. Explain where.

- Lines 5 and 6: With words like "blood-dimmed" and "drowned" predict what the future holds—be descriptive.

  If innocence is "drowned" that means all are guilty. Guilty of what?

- Lines 7 and 8: What happens when the most noble, brave, wise, and respected people lose their strong beliefs, and the most foolish, disrespected cowards are filled with "passionate intensity"?

- Is *Things Fall Apart* an appropriate title for this novel? Explain.

THINGS FALL APART:
A CONCLUSION TO OUR CASE STUDY OF IMPERIALISM

Concept	Examples from TFA
Nationalism (i.e., intense pride in one's country and desire for independence)	
Conflict	
Religious and Cultural Differences	
Desire for Raw Materials and New Markets	
Cultural Diffusion (i.e., the exchange of goods and ideas)	
Technological Advantages	

- Does the teacher provide reading guides and teach strategies to aid comprehension and foster thinking about texts?
- Do the teacher's demeanor and behavior show evidence of intellectual curiosity and an enjoyment of students, learning, and teaching?
- Do all students, including ELLs and struggling readers and writers, feel safe, comfortable, and supported?
- Does the teacher help students make connections between their curriculum and the world outside the classroom walls?
- Is there evidence that home and community literacies and cultures are respected and valued?
- Are there activities that help the students behave like practitioners in the discipline? Have they been introduced through multiple

texts to current practitioners in the field, as well as past contributors?

If the answers to these questions are all YES, I will conclude that yours is a classroom where content area literacy is taken seriously, and I will be happy.

Thoreau helped me begin my book. I'll turn to him again. Here's what he said of his reading a truly good book: "I must lay it down and commence living on its hint. . . . What I began by reading I must finish by acting" (Thoreau, 1999, p. xxxii). He pleads with the reader to be active, to move his words off the page and use them "to solve some of the problems of life, not only theoretically, but practically" (p. xxxiv). I ask you to do the same and wish you well as I join my voice with Thoreau's: "Will you be a reader, a student merely, or a seer? Read your fate, see what is before you, and walk on into futurity" (Thoreau, 1992, p. 105).

CHAPTER ELEVEN

Getting Ready to Teach

11.1 Try your hand at what Noddings has modeled. Pick a question that is being debated in the news, or a topic required in your curriculum, and think of where students investigating it could take it. To which disciplines does it connect? How might one path of research lead to others? How might students with different talents and ways of thinking inquire about it and think about related issues? You might make a graphic organizer to picture the places you and your students could go, given free rein to explore and think.

11.2 Now it's your turn once again to join the community of dreamers. Mahiri (1998) contends that "Metaphors are an intrinsic part of theory building" (p. 23). At the 1999 NCTE conference in Denver, I heard John Noell Moore speak about his class living out the metaphor of the Van Gogh Cafe. I've asked my students to tell me what metaphor, symbol, title, or quote captures the spirit of our class and received such varied answers as "A Field Trip to Uncharted Territory" and "Studio in the Art of Teaching Literacy."

Play with metaphor and language to help yourself envision the spirit of your future classroom. Try

out quotes, titles, and allusions that might represent the community of learners you and your students will be. Or, outline some of the features of your ideal school within which to teach. What will the content area courses you teach be like? How will they be different from the kind of education you had? Where and how will literacy fit in? What books will be in the classroom library of your dreams? What other reading and writing materials will there be? Write a journal entry, or a diagram or other visual representation of your ideal classroom.

References

Abair, J. M., & Cross, A. (1999). Patterns in American literature. *English Journal, 88*(6), 83–87.

Abrams, S. (2000). *Using journals with reluctant writers: Building portfolios for middle and high school students.* Thousand Oaks, CA: Corwin Press.

Acronyms, initialisms & abbreviations dictionary. Detroit: Gale Research Company.

Adams, M. (1990). *Beginning to read: Thinking and learning about print.* Urbana-Champaign, IL: Center for the Study of Reading.

Afflerbach, P., & VanSledright, B. (2001). Hath! Doth! What? Middle graders reading innovative history text. *Journal of Adolescent and Adult Literacy, 44*(8), 696–707.

Alexander, P. A., & Jetton, T. L. (2000). Learning from text: A multidimensional and developmental perspective. In P. D. Pearson, R. Barr, & M. L. Kamil, (Eds.), *Handbook of reading research* (Vol. III, pp. 285–310). Mahwah, NJ: Lawrence Erlbaum Associates.

Alexander, P. A., Graham, S., & Harris, K. R. (1998). A perspective on strategy research: Progress and prospects. *Educational Psychology Review, 10,* 129–154.

Alexander, P. A., Jetton, T. L., Kulikowich, J. M., & Woehler, C. (1994). Contrasting instructional and structural importance: The seductive effect of teacher questions. *Journal of Reading Behavior, 26,* 19–45.

Allen, J. (1999). *Words, words, words: Teaching vocabulary in grades 4–12.* York, ME: Stenhouse Publishers.

Alliance for Technology Access, The. (2000). *Computer and Web resources for people with disabilities: A guide to exploring today's assistive technology.* Alameda, CA: Hunter House.

Allington, R. L. (2001). *What really matters for struggling readers: Designing research-based programs.* New York: Longman.

Almasi, J. F. (1995). The nature of fourth-graders' sociocognitive conflicts in peer-led and teacher-led discussions of literature. *Reading Research Quarterly, 30,* 314–351.

Almasi, J. F. (1996). A new view of discussion. In L. B. Gambrell & J. F. Almasi (Eds.), *Lively discussions! Fostering engaged reading.* Newark, DE: International Reading Association.

Alvermann, D. E. (1986). Discussion vs. recitation in the secondary classroom. In J. A. Niles & R. V. Lalik (Eds.), *Solving problems in literacy: Learners, teachers, and researchers.* Rochester, NY: National Reading Conference.

Alvermann, D. E. (1987). Discussion strategies for content area reading. In D. Alvermann, D. R. Dillon, & D. G. O'Brien (Eds.), *Using discussion to promote reading comprehension* (pp. 34–42). Newark, DE: International Reading Association.

Alvermann, D. E. (1991). The discussion web: A graphic aid for learning across the curriculum. *The Reading Teacher, 45*(2), 92–99.

Alvermann, D. E. (1994). Trade books versus textbooks: making connections across content areas. In L. M. Morrow, J. K. Smith, & L. C. Wilkinson (Eds.), *Integrated language arts: Controversy to consensus* (pp. 51–69). Needham Heights, MA: Allyn & Bacon.

Alvermann, D. E., Hinchman, K. A., Moore, D. E., Phelps, S. F., & Waff, D. R. (Eds.). (1998). *Reconceptualizing the literacies in adolescents' lives.* Mahwah, NJ: Lawrence Erlbaum Associates.

Alvermann, D. E., & Moore, D. W. (1991). Secondary school reading. In R. Barr, M. L. Kamil, P. B. Mosenthal, & P. D. Pearson (Eds.), *Handbook of reading research* (Vol. II, pp. 951–983). New York: Longman.

Alvermann, D. E., O'Brien, D. G., & Dillon, D. R. (1990). What teachers do when they say they're having discussions of content area reading assignments: A qualitative analysis. *Reading Research Quarterly, 25,* 296–322.

Alvermann, D. E., & Phelps, S. F. (1998). *Content reading and literacy: Succeeding in today's classrooms* (2nd ed.). Boston: Allyn & Bacon.

Amabile, T. M. (1983). *Motivation and creativity: Effects of motivational orientation on creative writers.* Paper presented at the 91st annual convention of the American Psychological Association. Anaheim, CA, August, 26–30.

American Educator. (2001). Religious freedom in the world: A global comparative survey sponsored by Freedom House. Author, 25(2), 18–32.

American Psychological Association Presidential Task Force on Psychology in Education. (1993). *Learner-centered psychological principles: Guidelines for school redesign and reform.* Washington, DC: American Psychological Association.

Ammon, B., & Sherman, G. W. (1996). *Worth a thousand words: An annotated guide to picture books for older readers.* Englewood, CO: Libraries Unlimited.

Anderson, R. C., Hiebert, E. H., Scott, J. A., & Wilkinson, I. A. G. (1985). *Becoming a nation of readers: The report of the commission on reading.* Washington, DC: National Institute of Education.

Anderson, R. C., & Nagy, W. E. (Winter 1992). The vocabulary conundrum. *American Educator,* 14–18, 44–47.

Anderson, R. C., & Pearson, P. D. (1984). A schema-theoretic view of basic processes in reading. In P. D. Pearson (Ed.), *Handbook of reading research* (Vol. I, pp. 255–317). New York: Longman.

Anderson, V. (1992). A teacher development project in transactional strategy instruction for teachers of severely reading-disabled adolescents. *Teaching and Teacher Education, 8,* 391–403.

Applebee, A. (1992). Stability and change in the high school canon. *English Journal, 81*(5), 27–32.

Applebee, A. (1994). *NAEP 1992 writing report card.* Washington, DC: Education Information Branch, OERI, U. S. Dept. of Education.

Applebee, A., Auten, A., & Lehr, F. (1981). *Writing in the secondary school: English and the content areas.* Urbana, IL: National Council of Teachers of English.

Armbruster, B. B. (1984). The problem of "inconsiderate text." In G. G. Duffy, L. R. Roehler, & J. Mason (Eds.), *Comprehension instruction: Perspectives and suggestions* (pp. 202–217). New York: Longman.

Armbruster, B. B., Anderson, T. H., Armstrong, J. O., Wise, M. A., Janisch, C., & Meyer, L. A. (1991). Reading and questioning in content area lessons. *Journal of Reading Behavior, 23,* 35–60.

Armbruster, B. B., Anderson, T. H., & Ostertag, J. (1989). Teaching text structure to improve reading and writing. *The Reading Teacher, 43,* 130–137.

Aronson, E., Blaney, N., Stephan, C., Sikes, J., & Snapp, M. (1978). *The jigsaw classroom.* Beverly Hills, CA: Sage.

Artzt, A. F., & Armour-Thomas, E. (1992). Development of a cognitive-metacognitive framework for protocol analysis of mathematical problem solving in small groups. *Cognition and Instruction, 9,* 137–175.

Artzt, A. F., & Yaloz-Femia, S. (1999). Mathematical reasoning during small-group problem solving. In L. V. Stiff (Ed.), *Developing mathematical reasoning in grades K–12: 1999 yearbook.* Reston, VA: National Council of Teachers of Mathematics.

Atwell, N. (1987). *In the middle: Writing, reading, and learning with adolescents.* Portsmouth, NH: Heinemann.

Atwell, N. (Ed.). (1990). *Coming to know: Writing to learn in the intermediate grades.* Portsmouth, NH: Heinemann.

Atwell, N. (1991). *Side by side: Essays on teaching to learn.* Portsmouth, NH: Heinemann.

Atwell, N. (1998). *In the middle: New understandings about writing, reading, and learning.* Portsmouth, NH: Heinemann.

Atwell, N. (1998). *In the middle: Reading and writing with adolescents.* Portsmouth, NH: Heinemann.

Avi. (1999). *If you write about mice and porcupines are you still writing out of your own experience?* Denver: National Council of Teachers of English Convention.

Bailey, T. A., Kennedy, D. M., & Cohen, L. (1998). *The American pageant* (11th ed.). Boston: Houghton Mifflin.

Bakeless, J. (Ed.). (1964). *The journals of Lewis and Clark.* New York: Mentor Books.

Baldwin, R. S., & Leavell, A. G. (1992). When was the last time you read a textbook just for kicks? In E. K. Dishner, T. W. Bean, J. E. Readence, & D. W. Moore (Eds.), *Reading in the content areas: Improving classroom instruction* (3rd ed.). Dubuque, IA: Kendall/Hunt.

Bamford, R. A., & Kristo, J. V. (Eds.). (2000). *Checking out nonfiction literature K–8: Good choices for best learning.* Norwood, MA: Christopher-Gordon.

Barnhart, D. K. (1991). *Neo-words: A dictionary of the newest and most unusual words of our times.* New York: Collier Books/Macmillan.

Baumann, J. F., & Kameenui, E. J. (1991). Research on vocabulary instruction: Ode to Voltaire. In J. Flood, J. M. Jenson, D. Lapp, & J. R. Squire (Eds.), *Handbook of research on teaching the English language arts* (pp. 604–632). New York: Macmillan.

Baumbach, N. (2000). Van Gogh in AOL. *The New Yorker*, March 27, pp. 51–52.

Baumeister. D. (1992). *Think–pair–share: Effects on oral language, reading comprehension, and attitudes.* Dissertation, University of Maryland at College Park.

Bean, T. W. (1998). Teacher literacy histories and adolescent voices: Changing content-area classrooms. In D. E. Alvermann, K. A. Hinchman, D. W. Moore, S. F. Phelps, D. R. Waff (Eds.), *Reconceptualizing the literacies in adolescents' lives* (pp. 149–170). Mahwah, NJ: Lawrence Erlbaum Associates.

Bean, T. W., & Readence, J. E. (1996). Content area reading: The current state of the art. In D. Lapp, J. Flood, & N. Farnan (Eds.), *Content area reading and learning: Instructional strategies* (2nd ed.), (pp. 15–24). Boston: Allyn & Bacon.

Beane, J. (1993). *A middle school curriculum: From rhetoric to reality* (2nd ed.). Columbus, OH: National Middle School Association.

Beck, I. L., McKeown, M. G., & Gromoll, E. W. (1989). Learning from social studies texts. *Cognition and Instruction, 6,* 99–158.

Beck, I. L., McKeown, M. G., Hamilton, R. L., & Jucan, L. (1997). *Questioning the author: An approach for enhancing student engagement with text.* Newark, DE: International Reading Association.

Beck, I. L., McKeown, M. G., & McCaslin, E. (1983). All contexts are not created equal. *Elementary School Journal, 83,* 177–181.

Beck, I. L., McKeown, M. G., Omanson, R. C., & Pople, M. T. (1984). Improving the comprehensibility of stories: The effects of revisions that improve coherence. *Reading Research Quarterly, 19*(3), 263–277.

Bennett, W. (1999). *The educated child.* New York: Free Press.

Berryman, L., & Russell, D. R. (2001). Portfolios across the curriculum: Whole school assessment in Kentucky. *English Journal, 90*(6), 76–83.

Bianculli, D. (1992). *Teleliteracy: Taking television seriously.* New York: Continuum.

Bickman, M. (Ed.). (1999). *Uncommon learning: Thoreau on education.* Boston: Houghton Mifflin.

Bintz, W. P. (1997). Exploring reading nightmares of middle and secondary school teachers. *Journal of Adolescent and Adult Literacy, 41*(1), 12–24.

Blachowicz, C. L. Z. (1986). Making connections: Alternatives to the vocabulary notebook. *Journal of Reading, 29*(7), 643–649.

Blachowicz, C. L. Z., & Fisher, P. (2000). Vocabulary instruction. In P. D. Pearson, R. Barr, & M. L. Kamil (Eds.), *Handbook of reading research* (Vol. III, pp. 503–523). Mahwah, NJ: Lawrence Erlbaum Associates.

Block, C. C. (1999). Comprehension: Crafting understanding. In L. B. Gambrell, L. M. Morrow, S. B. Neuman, & M. Pressley (Eds.), *Best practices in literacy instruction* (pp. 98–118). New York: The Guilford Press.

Bloem, P. L., & Padak, N. D. (1996). Picture books, young adult books, and adult literacy learners. *Journal of Adolescent and Adult Literacy, 40*(1), 48–53.

Bloom, B. S., & Krathwohl, D. R. (1956). *Taxonomy of educational objectives: The classification of educational goals.* New York: McKay.

Bloom, H. (1987). *The closing of the American mind.* New York: Simon & Schuster.

Bloom, H. (Ed.). (1998). *Women writers of children's literature.* Philadelphia: Chelsea House.

Bober, N. S. (2001). *Countdown to independence: A revolution of ideas in England and her American colonies: 1760-1776.* New York: Atheneum Books for Young Readers.

Bomer, R. (2000). Writing to think critically: The seeds of social action. In *Trends & issues in secondary English* (pp. 109–120). Urbana, IL: National Council of Teachers of English.

Borasi, R., & Siegel, M. (2000). *Reading counts: Expanding the role of reading in mathematics classrooms.* New York: Teachers College Press.

Bormuth, J. R. (1968). Cloze test readability criterion reference scores. *Journal of Educational Measurement, 5,* 189–196.

Boyce, L. N. (1996). In the big inning was the word: Word play resources for developing verbal talent. In J. VanTassel, D. T. Johnson, & L. N. Boyce (Eds.), *Developing verbal talent* (pp. 259–272). Boston: Allyn & Bacon.

Boyd, F. B. (1997). The cross-aged literacy program: Preparing struggling adolescents for book club discussions. In S. I. McMahon & T. E. Raphael (Eds.), *The book club connection* (pp. 162–181). New York: Teachers College Press.

Brady, M. (2000). The standards juggernaut. *Phi Delta Kappan, 81*(9), 648–651.

Brel, J. (1968). *If we only have love.* New York: Columbia.

Brock, C. H. (1997). Second-language learners in mainstream classrooms. In S. I. McMahon &

T. E. Raphael (Eds.), *The book club connection* (pp. 141–158). New York: Teachers College Press.

Brockman, E. B. (1999). Revising beyond the sentence level: One adolescent writer and a "pregnant pause." *English Journal, 88*(5), 81–86.

Brown, C. L., & Tomlinson, C. M. (1993). *Essentials of children's literature.* Boston: Allyn & Bacon.

Brown, C. S. (1994). *Connecting with the past: History workshop in middle and high schools.* Portsmouth, NH: Heinemann.

Brown, J. V. (2000). Technology integration in a high school study skills program. *Journal of Adolescent and Adult Literacy, 43*(7), 634–637.

Brown, R. (1993). *Schools of thought: How the politics of literacy shape thinking in the classroom.* San Francisco: Jossey-Bass.

Brozo, W. G., & Simpson, M. L. (1999). *Readers, teachers, learners: Expanding literacy across the content areas.* Upper Saddle River, NJ: Merrill.

Bruce, B. (1998). Mixing old technologies with new. *Journal of Adolescent and Adult Literacy, 42*(2), 136–139.

Bruce, B. (1999/2000). Searching the Web: New domains for inquiry. *Journal of Adolescent and Adult Literacy, 43*(4), 348–354.

Bruce, B. (2000). The work of art in the age of digital reproduction. *Journal of Adolescent and Adult Literacy, 44*(1), 66–71.

Bruns, J. H. (1992). They can but they don't: Helping students overcome work inhibition. *American Educator, 16*(4), 38–47.

Buckley, W. F. (1996). (S. M. Vaughan, Ed.). *The right word.* New York: Random House.

Buikema, J. L., & Graves, M. (1993). Teaching students to use context clues to infer word meanings. *Journal of Reading, 36*(6), 450–457.

Bullock, J. O. (1994). Literacy in the language of mathematics. *American Mathematical Monthly, 101*(8), 735–743.

Burchard, P. (1999). *Lincoln and slavery.* New York: Atheneum Books for Young Readers.

Burke, J. (1999). *The English teacher's companion.* Portsmouth, NH: Heinemann.

Burniske, R. W. (1999). The teacher as a skilled generalist. *Phi Delta Kappan, 81*(2), 121–126.

Burns, M. (1995). *Writing in math class: A resource guide for grades 2–8.* Sausalito, CA: Math Solutions Publications.

Burns, T. R. (1995). A teacher's quest: Our mission isn't entertainment. *New York Teacher,* May 29, 2.

Bussert-Webb, K. (2001). I won't tell you about myself, but I will draw my story. *Language Arts, 78*(6), 511–519.

Caine, R. N., & Caine, G. (1991). *Making connections: Teaching and the human brain.* Alexandria, VA: Association for Supervision and Curriculum Development.

Calkins, L. (1986). *The art of teaching writing.* Portsmouth, NH: Heinemann.

Cambourne, B. (1995). Toward an educationally relevant theory of literacy learning: Twenty years of inquiry. *The Reading Teacher, 49,* 182–192.

Campbell, D. (2000). Authentic assessment and authentic standards. *Phi Delta Kappan, 81*(5), 405–407.

Campbell, J. R., Voelkl, K., & Donohue, P. L. (1997). *Report in brief: NAEP 1996 trends in academic progress.* Washington, DC: National Center for Education Statistics.

Cangelosi, J. S. (1996). *Teaching mathematics in secondary and middle school: An interactive approach* (2nd ed.). Englewood Cliffs, NJ: Merrill.

Carlisle, J. (1995). Morphological awareness and early reading achievement. In L. Feldman (Ed.), *Morphological aspects of language processing* (pp. 189–209). Hillsdale, NJ: Lawrence Erlbaum Associates.

Carlisle, J. F. (1993). Selecting approaches to vocabulary instruction for the reading disabled. *Learning Disabilities Research and Practice, 8*(2), 97–105.

Carlisle, J. F., & Nomanbhoy, D. M. (1993). Phonological and morphological awareness in first graders. *Applied Psycholinguistics, 14*(2), 177–195.

Carlsen, W. S. (1991). Questioning in classrooms: A sociolinguistic perspective. *Review of Educational Research, 61*(2), 157–178.

Carr, E., & Ogle, D. (1987). K–W–L Plus: A strategy for comprehension and summarization. *Journal of Reading, 30,* 626–631.

Carroll, A. (Ed.). (1997). *Letters of a nation: A collection of extraordinary American letters.* New York: Broadway Books.

Carroll, W. M. (1999). Using short questions to develop and assess reasoning. In L. V. Stiff & F. R. Curcio (Eds.), *Developing mathematical reasoning in grades K–12: 1999 yearbook* (pp. 247–255). Reston, VA: National Council of Teachers of Mathematics.

Carter, B., & Abrahamson, R. F. (1990). *Nonfiction for young adults: From delight to wisdom.* Phoenix, AZ: Oryx Press.

Cassady, J. K. (1998). Wordless books: No-risk tools for inclusive middle classrooms. *Journal of Adolescent and Adult Literacy, 41*(6), 428–433.

Cecil, N. L. (1999). *Striking a balance: Positive practices for early literacy.* Scottsdale, AZ: Holcomb Hathaway.

Chall, J. S. (1967). *Learning to read: The great debate.* New York: McGraw-Hill.

Chambers, D. L. (1996). Direct modeling and invented procedures: Building on students' informal strategies. *Teaching Children Mathematics, 3*(2), 92–95.

Chandler, K. (1997). The beach book club: Literacy in the "lazy days of summer." *Journal of Adolescent and Adult Literacy, 41*(2), 104–115.

Chandler-Olcott, K. (2001). Scaffolding love: A framework for choosing books for, with, and by adolescents. *The Language and Literacy Spectrum:* New York State Reading Association, 18–32.

Chen, H. C., & Graves, M. F. (1996). Effects of previewing and providing background knowledge on Taiwanese college students' comprehension of American short stories. *TESOL Quarterly, 29,* 663–686.

Christenbury, L., & Kelly, P. P. (1994). What textbooks can—and cannot—do. *English Journal, 83*(3), 76–80.

Christenson, L. M. (2000). Critical literacy: Teaching reading, writing, and outrage. In *Trends & issues in secondary English* (pp. 53–67). Urbana, IL: National Council of Teachers of English.

Cianciolo, P. J. (2000). *Informational picture books for children.* Chicago: American Library Association.

Cipielewski, J., & Stanovitch, K. E. (1992). Predicting growth in reading ability from children's exposure to print. *Journal of Experimental Child Psychology, 54,* 74–89.

Clark, E. (1993). *The lexicon in acquisition.* Cambridge, UK: Cambridge University Press.

Clubb, O. (2001, March 11). Global warming: Can we change our wasteful ways? *Syracuse Herald-American,* pp. D1, D4.

Colbert, D. (Ed.). (1997). *Eyewitness to America: 500 years of America in the words of those who saw it happen.* New York: Pantheon Books.

Cole, K. C. (1998). *The universe and the teacup: The mathematics of truth and beauty.* New York: Harcourt Brace.

Collins, C. (1991). Reading instruction that increases thinking abilities. *Journal of Reading, 34,* 510–516.

Compton's pictured encyclopedia. (1931). (Vol. 2). Chicago: F. E. Compton & Company.

Conley, M. W. (1995). *Content reading instruction: A communication approach* (2nd ed.). New York: McGraw-Hill.

Connor, U. (1997). Contrastive rhetoric: Implications for teachers of writing in multicultural classrooms. In C. Severino, J. C. Guerra, & J. E. Butler (Eds.), *Writing in multicultural settings* (pp. 198–208). New York: Modern Language Association of America.

Cortez, C. E. (1994). Multiculturation: An educational model for a culturally and linguistically diverse society. In K. Spangenberg-Urbschat & R. Pritchard (Eds.), *Kids come in all languages: Reading instruction for ESL students* (pp. 22–35). Newark, DE: International Reading Association.

Cox, C., & Zarillo, J. (1993). *Teaching reading with children's literature.* New York: Macmillan.

Crafton, L. (1983). Learning from reading: What happens when students generate their own background information. *Journal of Reading, 26,* 586–593.

Cramer, E. H., & Castle, M. (Eds.). (1994). *Fostering the love of reading: The affective domain in reading education.* Newark, DE: International Reading Association.

Crutcher, C. (1993). *Staying fat for Sarah Byrnes.* New York: Greenwillow Books.

Crystal, D. (1995). *The Cambridge encyclopedia of the English language.* New York: Cambridge University Press.

Csikszentmihalyi, M. (1991). Literacy and intrinsic motivation. In S. R. Graubard (Ed.), *Literacy* (pp. 115–140). New York: Noonday.

Csikszentmihalyi, M. (1993). *The evolving self.* New York: HarperCollins.

Csikszentmihalyi, M. (1996). *Creativity: Flow and the psychology of discovery and invention.* New York: HarperCollins.

Cuban, L. (1991). History of teaching in social studies. In J. Shaver (Ed.), *Handbook of research on social studies teaching and learning* (pp. 197–209). New York: Macmillan.

Cummins, J. (1994). The acquisition of English as a second language. In K. Spangenberg-Urbschat & R. Pritchard (Eds.), *Kids come in all languages: Reading instruction for ESL students* (pp. 36–62). Newark, DE: International Reading Association.

Cunningham, A. E., & Stanovitch, K. E. (1998). What reading does for the mind. *American Educator,* Spring/Summer, pp. 8–15.

Curry-Tash, M. W. (1998). The politics of teleliteracy and adbusting in the classroom. *English Journal, 87*(1), 43–48.

Daniels, H. (1994). *Literature circles: Voice and choice in the student-centered classroom.* York, ME: Stenhouse.

Darling-Hammond, L., Ancess, J., & Falk, B. (1995). *Authentic assessment in action.* New York: Teachers College Press.

Davenport, S., with Charbauski, S., Kim, J., & Ramsey, B. (1999). Review of Gary Paulsen's Soldier's heart: Being the story of the enlistment and due service of the boy Charley Goddard in the First Minnesota Volunteers (1998, Delacorte Press). *Journal of Adolescent and Adult Literacy,* 43(2), 204–206.

Davey, B. (1983). Think-aloud. Modeling the cognitive processes of reading comprehension. *Journal of Reading,* 27, 44–47.

Davis, J. (1994). *Why Greenland is an island, Australia is not—and Japan is up for grabs: A simple primer for becoming a geographical know-it-all.* New York: Quill.

Davis, P., & Hersh, R. (1981). *The mathematical experience.* Boston: Houghton Mifflin.

Deedy, C. A. (2000). *The yellow star: The legend of King Christian X of Denmark.* Atlanta, GA: Peachtree.

DeMartino, J. (1998). Honors project (office).

Dial, M., & Baines, L. (1998). The languages of words and numbers. In J. S. Simmons & L. Baines (Eds.), *Language study in middle school, high school and beyond* (pp. 112–124). Newark, DE: International Reading Association.

Diaz-Gemmati, G. M. (2000). "And justice for all": Using writing and literature to confront racism. In *Trends & issues in secondary English* (pp. 76–97). Urbana, IL: National Council of Teachers of English.

DiGisi, L. L., & Willett, J. B. (1995). What high school biology teachers say about their textbook use: A descriptive study. *Journal of Research in Science Teaching,* 32, 123–142.

Dillard, A. (1987). *An American childhood.* New York: Harper & Row.

Dreazen, Y. (1998). What if . . . ?: New issues would arise if a cure for cancer is found. Knight Ridder Newspapers, *Syracuse Herald-Journal,* Tuesday, June 16, p. A8.

Dresang, E. (1999). *Radical change: Books for youth in a digital age.* New York: H. W. Wilson.

Duffy, G. G., & Roehler, L. R. (1989). Why strategy instruction is so difficult and what we need to do about it. In C. B. McCormick, G. Miller, & M. Pressley (Eds.), *Cognitive strategy research: From basic research to educational applications* (pp. 133–154). New York: Springer-Verlag.

Duffy, G., Roehler, L., & Hermann, B. A. (1988). Modeling mental processes helps poor readers become more strategic readers. *The Reading Teacher,* 42, 762–767.

Duffy, J. M., et al. (1989). Models for the design of instructional text. *Reading Research Quarterly,* 24(4), 434–457.

Dunn, M. A. (2000). Closing the book on social studies: Four classroom teachers go beyond the text. *The Social Studies,* May/June, 132–136.

Durkin, D. (1978/79). What classroom observations reveal about reading comprehension instruction. *Reading Research Quarterly,* 14, 481–533.

Dyson, E. (1997). *Release 2.0.* New York: Broadway Books.

Eanet, M. G., & Manzo, A. V. (1976). REAP—A strategy for improving reading/writing/study skills. *Journal of Reading,* 19, 647–652.

Easton, T. A. (1997). *Taking sides: Controversial issues in science, technology, and society* (2nd ed.). Guilford, CT: Dushkin Publishing.

Eisner, E. (2002). The kind of schools we need. *Phi Delta Kappan,* 83(8), 576–583.

Elley, W. B. (1992). *How in the world do students read?* Newark, DE: International Reading Association.

Elster, H. (1999). *The big book of beastly mispronunciations: The complete opinionated guide for the careful speaker.* Boston: Houghton Mifflin.

Emig, J. (1971). *The composing processes of twelfth graders.* NCTE Research Report No. 13. Urbana, IL: National Council of Teachers of English.

Encisco, P. (1990). *The nature of engagement in reading: Profiles of three fifth graders' engagement strategies and stances.* Unpublished doctoral dissertation, Ohio State University, Columbus.

Ennis, R. H. (1996). *Critical Thinking.* Upper Saddle River, NJ: Prentice Hall.

Enriquez, G. (2001). Making meaning of cultural depictions: Using Lois Lowry's The Giver to reconsider what is "multicultural" about literature. *Journal of Children's Literature,* 27(1), 13–22.

Erdsneker, B., Haller, M., & Steinberg, E. (1998). *Civil Service Arithmetic and Vocabulary* (13th ed.). New York: Macmillan.

Erickson, B. (1996). Read-alouds reluctant readers relish. *Journal of Adolescent and Adult Literacy,* 40(3), 212–214.

Estes, T. H., & Vasquez-Levy, D. (2001). Literature as a source of information and values. *Phi Delta Kappan,* 82(7), 507–512.

F. E. Compton & Company. (1931). *Compton's Pictured Encyclopedia.* Chicago: Author.

Fabos, B. (2000). ZAPME! zaps you. *Journal of Adolescent and Adult Literacy,* 43(8), 720–725.

Fadiman, C. (1985). *The Little, Brown book of anecdotes* (C. Fadiman, Ed.). Boston: Little, Brown.

Farnan, N., Flood, J., & Lapp, D. (1994). Comprehending through reading and writing: Six research-based instructional strategies. In K. Spangenberg-Urbschat & R. Pritchard (Eds.), *Kids come in all languages: Reading instruction for ESL students* (pp. 135–157). Newark, DE: International Reading Association.

Fecho, B. (1998). Crossing boundaries of race in a critical literacy classroom. In D. E. Alvermann, K. A. Hinchman, D. W. Moore, S. F. Phelps, & D. R. Waff (Eds.), *Reconceptualizing the literacies in adolescent lives* (pp. 75–101). Mahwah, NJ: Lawrence Erlbaum Associates.

Feynman, R. P. (1985). *"Surely you're joking, Mr. Feynman!": Adventures of a curious character.* New York: Norton.

Feynman, R. P. (1988). *"What do you care what other people think?": Further adventures of a curious character.* New York: Norton.

Finders, M. J. (2000). "Gotta be worse": Negotiating the pleasurable and the popular. *Journal of Adolescent and Adult Literacy, 44*(2), 146–149.

Fink, R. (1995/1996). Successful dyslexics: A constructivist study of passionate interest reading. *Journal of Adolescent and Adult Literacy, 39*(4), 268–280.

Fisherkeller, J. (2000). "The writers are getting kind of desperate": Young adolescents, television, and literacy. *Journal of Adolescent and Adult Literacy, 43*(7), 596–606.

Flavell, J. H. (1976). Metacognitive aspects of problem-solving. In L. B. Resnick (Ed.), *The nature of intelligence* (pp. 231–235). Hillsdale, NJ: Lawrence Erlbaum Associates.

Flesch, R. (1955). *Why Johnny can't read.* New York: Harper.

Flower, L., & Hayes, J. (1984). Problem solving strategies and the writing process. In R. Graves (Ed.), *Rhetoric and composition: A sourcebook for teachers and writers* (2nd ed.), (pp. 269–283). Upper Montclair, NJ: Boynton-Cook.

Foertsch, M. A. (1992). *Reading in and out of school: Achievement of American students in grades 4, 8, and 12 in 1989–90.* Washington, DC: National Center for Educational Statistics. U. S. Government Printing Office.

Franks, L. (2001). Charcoal clouds and weather writing: Inviting science to a middle school language arts classroom. *Language Arts, 78*(4), 319–324.

Freedman, R. (1988). Newbery Medal acceptance. *The Horn Book Magazine, 64*(4), 444–451.

Fried, R. L. (2001). *The passionate learner: How teachers and parents can help children reclaim the joy of discovery.* Boston: Beacon Press.

Fulwiler, T. (1986). The politics of writing across the curriculum. In T. Fulwiler & A. Young (Eds.), *Writing across the disciplines: Research into practice.* Upper Montclair, NJ: Boynton/Cook.

Gallas, K. (2001). "Look, Karen, I'm running like Jell-O": Imagination as a question, a topic, a tool for literacy research and learning. *Research in the Teaching of English, 35*(4), 457–492.

Gambrell, L. B. (1983). The occurrence of think-time during reading comprehension instruction. *Journal of Educational Research, 77*(2), 77–80.

Gambrell, L. B. (1987). Children's oral language during teacher-directed reading instruction. In J. E. Readence & R. S. Baldwin (Eds.), *Research in literacy: Merging perspectives* (pp. 195–200). Rochester, NY: National Reading Conference.

Gambrell, L. B. (1996). Creating classroom cultures that foster reading motivation. *The Reading Teacher, 50,* 14–25.

Gambrell, L. B., & Almasi, J. F. (1994). Fostering comprehension development through discussion. In L. M. Morrow, J. K. Smith, & L. C. Wilkinson (Eds.), *Integrated language arts: Controversy to consensus* (pp. 71–90). Boston: Allyn & Bacon.

Gambrell, L. B., & Almasi, J. F. (1996). *Lively discussions!: Fostering engaged reading.* Newark, DE: International Reading Association.

Gambrell, L. B., Pfeiffer, W. R., & Wilson, R. M. (1985). The effects of retelling upon reading comprehension and recall of text information. *Journal of Educational Research, 78*(4), 216–220.

Gardner, H. (1983). *Frames of mind: The theory of multiple intelligences.* New York: Basic Books.

Gardner, H. (1991). *The unschooled mind: How children think and how schools should teach.* New York: Basic Books.

Gardner, H. (1993). *Creating minds: An anatomy of creativity as seen through the lives of Freud, Einstein, Picasso, Stravinsky, Eliot, Graham, and Gandhi.* New York: Basic Books.

Gardner, S., Benham, H. H., & Newell, B. M. (2000). Oh, what a tangled Web we've woven!: Helping students evaluate sources. In *Trends & issues in secondary English* (pp. 28–39). Urbana, IL: National Council of Teachers of English.

Garner, J. (1998). *We interrupt this broadcast.* Naperville, IL: Sourcebooks.

Garner, R., & Reis, R. (1981). Monitoring and resolving comprehension obstacles: An investigation of spontaneous text lookbacks among upper-grade good and poor comprehenders. *Reading Research Quarterly, 16*(4), 569–581.

Gauch, P. L. (1997). In the belly of the whale. *The Horn Book Magazine*, May/June, 294–299.

Gazzaniga, M. S. (1985). *The social brain: Discovering the networks of the mind.* New York: Basic Books.

Gee, J. (2000). Discourse and sociocultural studies in reading. In P. D. Pearson, R. Barr, & M. L. Kamil (Eds.), *Handbook of reading research* (Vol. III, pp. 195–207). Mahwah, NJ: Lawrence Erlbaum Associates.

Genthe, H. (1998). The incredible sponge. *Smithsonian, 29*(5), 50–58.

Germann, P. J., Haskins, S., & Auls, S. (1996). Analysis of nine high school biology laboratory manuals: Promoting scientific inquiry. *Journal of Research in Science Teaching, 33*(5), 475–499.

Gleick, J. (1992). *Genius: The life and science of Richard Feynman.* Santa Monica, CA: Voyager.

Goatley, V. J. (1997). Talk about text among special education students. In S. I. McMahon & T. E. Raphael (Eds.), *The book club connection* (pp. 119–137). New York: Teachers College Press.

Goldman, S. R., & Rakestraw, J. A., Jr. (2000). Structural aspects of constructing meaning from text. In P. D. Pearson, R. Barr, & M. L. Kamil (Eds.), *Handbook of reading research* (Vol. III, pp. 314–335). Mahwah, NJ: Lawrence Erlbaum Associates.

Goodman, K. S. (1967). Reading: A psycholinguistic guessing game. *Journal of the Reading Specialist, 6,* 126–135.

Goodman, Y. (1985). Kidwatching: Observing children in the classroom. In A. Jaggar & M. T. Smith-Burke (Eds.), *Observing the language learner* (pp. 9–18). Newark, DE: International Reading Association.

Goodrich, H. (1996/1997). Understanding rubrics. *Educational Leadership, 54*(4), 14–17.

Gottfried, S. S., & Kyle, W. C., Jr. (1992). Textbook use and the biology education desired state. *Journal of Research in Science Teaching, 29,* 35–49.

Gough, P. B. (1985). One second of reading. In H. Singer & R. Ruddell (Eds.), *Theoretical models and processes of reading* (3rd ed.), (pp. 661–686). Newark, DE: International Reading Association.

Graesser, A. C., Golding, J. M., & Long, D. L. (1991). Narrative representation and comprehension. In R. Barr, M. L. Kamil, P. B. Mosenthal, & P. D. Pearson (Eds.), *Handbook of reading research* (Vol. II, pp. 171–205). White Plains, NY: Longman.

Graham, A. (1988). Casey's Daughter at the bat. In R. R. Knudson & M. Swenson (Eds.), *American sports poems* (p. 42). New York: Orchard Books.

Grandgenett, N. F., Hill, J. W., & Lloyd, C. V. (1999). Connecting reasoning and writing in student "how to" manuals. In P. A. House & A. F. Coxford (Eds.), *Connecting mathematics across the curriculum* (pp. 142–146). Reston, VA: National Council of Teachers of Mathematics.

Gratz, D. B. (2000). High standards for whom? *Phi Delta Kappan, 81*(9), 681–687.

Graves, D. (1993). *A fresh look at writing.* Portsmouth, NH: Heinemann.

Graves, D. H. (1975). The child, the writing process, and the role of the professional. In W. Petty (Ed.), *The writing processes of students.* New York: State University of New York.

Graves, M. F., Prenn, M., & Cooke, C. (1985). The coming attraction: Previewing short stories. *Journal of Reading, 28,* 594–599.

Gray, D. (1989). Putting minds to work. *American Educator, 13*(3), 15–22.

Green, P. A. (1994). *The Giver,* by Lois Lowry, Teacher Guide. Novel Units.

Green, T. M. (1994). *The Greek and Latin roots of English* (2nd ed.). New York: Ardsley House.

Grolier encyclopedia of knowledge. (1991). Vol. 3. Danbury, CT: Grolier.

Guillen, M. (1995). *Five equations that changed the world: The power and poetry of mathematics.* New York: Hyperion.

Gunderson, L. (2000). Voices of the teenage diasporas. *Journal of Adolescent and Adult Literacy, 43*(8), 692–706.

Gunning, T. G. (1996). *Creating reading instruction for all children* (2nd ed.). Boston: Allyn & Bacon.

Guthrie, J. T., & Wigfield, A. (2000). Engagement and motivation in reading. In P. D. Pearson, R. Barr, & M. L. Kamil (Eds.), *Handbook of reading research* (Vol. III, pp. 403–422). Mahwah, NJ: Lawrence Erlbaum Associates.

Guthrie, J. T., Cox, K., Anderson, E., Harris, K., Mazonni, S., & Rach, L. (1998). Principles of integrated instruction for engagement in reading. *Educational Psychology Review, 10*(2), 177–199.

Hadaway, N. L., Vardell, S. M., & Young, T. A. (2001). Scaffolding oral language development through poetry for students learning English. *The Reading Teacher, 54*(8), 796–806.

Hager, T. (1995). *Force of nature: The life of Linus Pauling.* New York: Simon & Schuster.

Hager, T. (1998). *Linus Pauling and the chemistry of life.* New York: Oxford University Press.

Haggard, M. R. (1985). An interactive strategies approach to content reading. *Journal of Reading, 29*(3), 204–210.

Hairston, M. (1994). What happens when people write? In R. Eschholz & C. Eschholz (Eds.), *Language awareness* (pp. 471–472). New York: St. Martin's.

Hapgood, F. (2001). Living off the land. *Smithsonian, 32*(4), 20–22.

Harmon, J. M. (1998). Vocabulary teaching and learning in a seventh-grade literature-based classroom. *Journal of Adolescent and Adult Literacy, 41*(7), 518–529.

Harmon, J. M. (2000). Assessing and supporting independent word learning strategies of middle school students. *Journal of Adolescent and Adult Literacy, 43*(6), 518–527.

Harris, T. L., & Hodges, R. E. (Eds.). (1981). *A dictionary of reading and related terms.* Newark, DE: International Reading Association.

Harris, T. L., & Hodges, R. E. (Eds.). (1995). *The literacy dictionary: The vocabulary of reading and writing.* Newark, DE: International Reading Association.

Harste, J. C. (1986, December). *What it means to be strategic: Good readers as informants.* Paper presented at the annual meeting of the National Reading Council, Austin TX.

Harste, J. C., & Carey, R. F. (1999). *Curriculum, multiple literacies, and democracy: What if English/Language arts teachers really cared?* Presidential Address, National Council of Teachers of English, Denver, CO.

Harste, J. C., & Short, K. G., with Burke, C. (1988). *Creating classrooms for authors: The reading–writing connection.* Portsmouth, NH: Heinemann.

Harwayne, S. (1992). *Lasting impressions: Weaving literature into the writing workshop.* Portsmouth, NH: Heinemann.

Hatch, E., & Brown, C. (1995). *Vocabulary, semantics, and language education.* Cambridge, England: Cambridge University Press.

Haugen, H. H. (2001). Suckers for science. *Science Teacher, 68*(1), 50–51.

Hawking, S. (1988). *A brief history of time: From the big bang to black holes.* New York: Bantam Books.

Hawking, S. (1993). *Black holes and baby universes.* New York: Bantam Books.

Healy, J. (2000). Failure to connect: How computers affect our children's minds—for better or worse. *Phi Delta Kappan, 81*(5), Supplement, 1–10.

Heath, S. B. (1983). *Ways with words: Language, life, and work in communities and classrooms.* New York: Cambridge University Press.

Henk, W. A., & Selders, M. L. (1984). A test of synonymic scoring of cloze passages. *The Reading Teacher, 38,* 282–287.

Hennings, D. G. (2000). Contextually-relevant word-study: Adolescent vocabulary development across the curriculum. *Journal of Adolescent and Adult Literacy, 44*(3), 268–279.

Herber, H. (1978). *Teaching reading in content areas* (2nd ed.). Upper Saddle River, NJ: Prentice Hall.

Herbst, J. (1993). *Star crossing: How to get around in the universe.* New York: Atheneum.

Hesse, K. (1992). *Letters from Rifka.* New York: Henry Holt.

Hesse, K. (1998). Newbery Medal acceptance. *The Horn Book Magazine, 74*(6), 422–427.

Hill, M. (1991). Writing summaries promotes thinking and learning across the curriculum—but why are they so difficult to write? *Journal of Reading, 34,* 536–539.

Hinchman, K. A., & Zalewski, P. (1996). Reading for success in a tenth-grade global studies class: A qualitative study. *Journal of Literacy Research, 28,* 91–106.

Hirsch, E. D., Jr. (1987). *Cultural literacy: What every American needs to know.* Boston: Houghton Mifflin.

Hirsch, E. D., Jr. (2000). You can always look it up . . . Or can you? *American Educator, 24*(1), 4–9.

Hobbs, R. (1998). The Simpsons meet Mark Twain: Analyzing popular texts in the classroom. *English Journal, 87*(1), 49–51.

Hoetker, J., & Ahlbrand, W. P. (1968). The persistence of recitation: A review of observational studies of teacher questioning behavior. Occasional Paper Series, Number 3.

Hoffman, J. V., McCarthy, S. J., Abbott, J., Christian, C., Corman, L., Curry, C., Dressman, M., Elliot, B., Matherne, D., & Stahle, D. (1994). So what's new in the new basals?: A focus on first grade. *Journal of Reading Behavior, 26*(1), 47–73.

Hoffman, P. (1998). *The man who loved only numbers: The story of Paul Erdos and the search for mathematical truth.* New York: Hyperion.

Hollie, S. (2001). Acknowledging the language of African American students: Instructional strategies. *English Journal, 90*(4), 54–59.

Holmes, B. C. (1983). The effect of prior knowledge on the question answering of good and poor readers. *Journal of Reading Behavior, 15,* 1–18.

Holt, J. C. (1981). *Teach your own: A hopeful path for education.* New York: Delacorte Press/Seymour Lawrence.

Holt, J. C. (1982). *How children fail.* New York: Delacorte Press/Seymour Lawrence.

Holt, J. (1989). *Learning all the time.* Reading, MA: Addison-Wesley.

Hopkins, G., & Bean, T. W. (1998/1999). Vocabulary learning with the verbal–visual word association strategy in a Native American Community. *Journal of Adolescent and Adult Literacy, 42*(4), 274–281.

House, P. A. (1996). Try a little of the write stuff. In P. C. Elliot & M. J. Kenney (Eds.), *Communication in mathematics, K–12 and beyond.* Reston, VA: National Council of Teachers of Mathematics.

Howard, P. J. (2000). *The owner's manual for the brain: Everyday applications from mind-brain research.* Austin, TX: Bard Press.

Hughes, L. (1969). Merry-go-round. In L. Hughes & A. Grifalconi (Eds.), *Don't you turn back* (p. 72). New York: Knopf.

Hughes, W. (2000). *Critical thinking: An introduction to the basic skills.* Peterborough, Ont.: Broadview Press.

Hynd, C. R., McNish, M. E., Guzzetti, B., Lay, K., & Fowler, P. (1994). *What high school students say about their science texts.* Paper presented at the annual meeting of the College Reading Association, New Orleans, LA.

Hynd, S. (1999). Teaching students to think critically using multiple texts in history. *Journal of Adolescent and Adult Literacy, 42*(6), 428–436.

International Reading Association. (1999). *Adolescent literacy: A position statement.* Newark, DE: Author.

Jacobson, F. F. (Ed.). (1997). *Library trends* (Vol. 45). Urbana, IL: University of Illinois Graduate School of Library and Information Science.

Jarrell, R. (1996). *The bat-poet.* New York: HarperCollins.

Johnson, A. P. (2000). *Up and out: Using creative and critical thinking skills to enhance learning.* Boston: Allyn & Bacon.

Johnson, D. D. (2001). *Vocabulary in the elementary and middle school.* Boston: Allyn & Bacon.

Johnson, D. D., & Pearson, P. D. (1984). *Teaching reading vocabulary* (2nd ed.). Fort Worth, TX: Holt, Rinehart & Winston.

Johnson, D. W., & Johnson, R. J. (1999). *Learning together and alone* (5th ed.). Englewood Cliffs, NJ: Prentice Hall.

Johnston, P. (2000). How will literacy be assessed in the next millennium? *Reading Research Quarterly, 35*(2), 249–250.

Jonsberg, S. D. (2001). What's a (white) teacher to do about Black English? *English Journal, 90*(4), 51–53.

Josten, D. (1996). Students rehashing historical decisions—And loving it! *Journal of Adolescent and Adult Literacy, 39*(7), 566–574.

Kagan, S. (1989). *Cooperative learning resources for teachers.* San Juan Capistrano, CA: Resources for Teachers.

Kane, S. (1995). Literary characters who write: Models and motivators for middle school writers. In M. R. Sorenson & B. Lehman (Eds.), *Teaching with children's books* (pp. 49–57). Urbana, IL: National Council of Teachers of English.

Kane, S., & Gentile, C. (1989). A study of diverse responses to an allegorical text. In R. W. Blake (Ed.), *Reading, writing, and interpreting literature* (pp. 218–242). Schenectady, NY: New York State English Council.

Kapinus, B., Gambrell, L. B., & Koskinen, P. S. (1991). The effects of retelling upon the reading comprehension of proficient and less proficient readers. *Journal of Educational Research, 6,* 356–362.

Kapitzke, C. (2001). Information literacy: The changing library. *Journal of Adolescent and Adult Literacy, 44*(5), 450–456.

Kear, D. J., Coffman, G. A., McKenna, M. C., & Ambrosio, A. L. (2000). Measuring attitude toward writing: A new tool for teachers. *The Reading Teacher, 54*(1), 10–23.

Keller, E. F. (1983). *A feeling for the organism: The life and work of Barbara McClintock.* San Francisco: Freeman.

Keller, H. (1976). *The story of my life.* Cutchogue, NY: Buccaneer Books.

Kingsolver, B. (1995). *High tide in Tucson: Essays from now or never.* New York: HarperCollins.

Kingsolver, B. (1998). *The poisonwood bible.* New York: HarperFlamingo.

Kingsolver, B. (2002). A forest's last stand. In *Small wonder: Essays* (pp. 75–87). New York: HarperCollins.

Kliman, M., & Kleinman, G. (1992). Life among the giants: writing, mathematics, and exploring Gulliver's world. *Language Arts, 69* (Feb.), 128–136.

Kneeshaw, S. (1999). Using reader response to improve student writing in history. *OAH Magazine of History, 13*(3), 62–65.

Knight, P. (1992). How I use portfolios in mathematics. *Educational Leadership, 49*(8), 71–72.

Kohn, A. (1998). *What to look for in a classroom . . . And other essays.* San Francisco: Jossey-Bass.

Kohn, A. (1999). *The schools our children deserve: Moving beyond traditional classrooms and "tougher standards."* Boston: Houghton Mifflin.

Kohn, A. (2001). Fighting the tests: A practical guide to rescuing our schools. *Phi Delta Kappan, 82*(5), 348–357.

Konopak, B., Martin, M., & Martin, S. (1987). Reading and writing: Aids to learning in the content areas. *Journal of Reading, 31,* 109–117.

Konopak, B., Martin, S., & Martin, M. (1990). Using a writing strategy to enhance sixth-grade students' comprehension of content material. *Journal of Reading Behavior, 22,* 19–38.

Koretz, M. (1999, June 6). Books for young readers. *Syracuse Herald-American, Stars Magazine,* p. 17.

Koskinen, P., Blum, I., Bisson, S., Phillips, S., Creamer, T., & Baker, T. (2000). Book access, shared reading, and audio models: The effects of supporting the literacy learning of linguistically diverse students in school and at home. *Journal of Educational Psychology, 92,* 23–36.

Kovacs, D., & Preller, J. (1991). *Meet the authors and illustrators.* New York: Scholastic.

Kozol, J. (1991). *Savage inequalities: Children in America's schools.* New York: Crown.

Kozol, J. (2000). *Ordinary resurrections: Children in the years of hope.* New York: Crown.

Krashen, S. (1981). The case for narrow reading. *TESOL Newsletter, 15,* 23.

Krashen, S. (1989). We acquire vocabulary and spelling by reading: Additional evidence for the input hypothesis. *Modern Language Journal, 73,* 440–463.

Krathwohl, D. R., Bloom, B. S., & Masia, B. B. (1964). *Taxonomy of educational objectives, Handbook II: Affective domain.* New York: McKay.

Kroeber, A. L., & Kluckhohn, C. K. M. (1952). *Culture: A critical review of concepts and definitions.* Papers of the Peabody Museum of American Archaeology and Ethnology, Harvard University, v. 47, no. 12, pp. 643–644, 656. Cambridge, MA: The Peabody Museum.

Krogness, M. M. (1995). *Just teach me, Mrs. K: Talking, reading, and writing with resistant adolescent learners.* Portsmouth, NH: Heinemann.

Kuhlman, W. D. (2001). Fifth-grader's reactions to Native Americans in *Little House on the Prairie:* Guiding students critical reading. *New Advocate, 14*(4), 387–399.

Kuhn, T. S. (1996). *The structure of scientific revolutions* (3rd ed.). Chicago: University of Chicago Press.

L'Engle, M. (1972) *A circle of quiet.* New York: Harper & Row.

L'Engle, M. (1980). *A ring of endless light.* New York: Farrar, Straus & Giroux.

L'Engle, M. (1980). *A ring of endless light.* New York: Bantam Doubleday Dell.

L'Engle, M., with C. F. Chase. (1996). *Glimpses of grace.* San Francisco: HarperSanFrancisco.

Lamott, A. (1994). *Bird by bird: Some instructions on writing and life.* New York: Pantheon Books.

Langer, J. (1986). *Children's reading and writing: Structures and strategies.* Norwood, NJ: Ablex.

Langer, J. A. (1992). Rethinking literature instruction. In J. A. Langer (Ed.), *Literature instruction: A focus on student responses* (pp. 35–53). Urbana, IL: National Council of Teachers of English.

Langer, J. A., & Applebee, A. N. (1987). *How writing shapes thinking: A study of teaching and learning.* Urbana, IL: National Council of Teachers of English.

Larkin, J., McDermott, J., Simon, D. P., & Simon, H. A. (1980). Expert and novice performance in solving physics problems. *Science, 208,* 1335–1342.

Lasley, T. J., II, Matczynski, T. J., & Rowley, J. B. (2002). *Instructional models: Strategies for teaching in a diverse society* (2nd ed.). Belmont, CA: Wadsworth/Thomson Learning.

Lawrence, D. (1999). The community as text: Using the community for collaborative Internet research. *English Journal, 89*(1), 56–62.

Learner-Centered Principles Revision Work Group. (1995). *Learner-centered psychological principles: A framework for school redesign and reform.* Unpublished document. Washington, DC: American Psychological Association.

Leggo, C., & Sakai, A. (1997). Knowing from different angles: Language arts and science connections. *Voices from the Middle, 4*(2), 26–30.

Leonhardt, D. (2000, May 28). Spotlight on common sense. *Syracuse Herald-American,* p. D1.

Lester, J. H., & Cheek, E. H., Jr. (1997/1998). The "real" experts address textbook issues. *Journal of Adolescent and Adult Literacy, 41*(4), 282–291.

Leu, D. J., Jr., & Kinzer, C. K. (1999). *Effective literacy instruction, K–8* (4th ed.). Upper Saddle River, NJ: Merrill.

Leu, D. J., Jr., & Leu, D. D. (1999). *Teaching with the Internet: Lessons from the classroom.* Norwood, MA: Christopher-Gordon.

Levine, M. (1996). *Viewing violence: How media affects your child's and adolescent's development.* Garden City, NY: Doubleday.

Lindemann, E. (1987). *A rhetoric for writing teachers.* New York: Oxford University Press.

Lipson, M. Y. (1982). Learning new information from text: The role of prior knowledge and reading ability. *Journal of Reading, 14,* 243–261.

Little, J. (1990). After English Class. In J. Little & S. Truesdell (Eds.), *Hey, world, here I am!* (p. 28). New York: Harper & Row.

Lloyd, C. V. (1998). Engaging students at the top (without leaving the rest behind). *Journal of Adolescent and Adult Literacy, 42*(3), 184–191.

Lobel, A. (1971). *On the day Peter Stuyvesant sailed into town.* New York: Harper & Row.

Loewen, J. W. (1995). *Lies my teacher told me: Everything your American history textbook got wrong.* New York: The New Press.

Lowry, L. (1979). *Anastasia Krupnik.* Boston: Houghton Mifflin.

Lowry, L. (1990). Newbery Medal acceptance. *The Horn Book Magazine,* pp. 412–421.

Lowry, L. (1993). *The giver.* Boston: Houghton Mifflin.

Lowry, L. (1994, July/August) Newbery Medal acceptance. *The Horn Book Magazine,* pp. 414–422.

Lundberg, I., & Lynnakyla, P. (1993). *Teaching reading around the world.* IEA Study of Reading Literacy.

Lymon, F. (1981). The responsive classroom discussion. In A. S. Anderson (Ed.), *Mainstreaming digest.* College Park: University of Maryland, College of Education.

Maggio, R. (1997). *Talking about people: A guide to fair language.* Phoenix, AZ: Oryx Press.

Mahiri, J. (1998). *Shooting for excellence: African American and youth culture in new century schools.* Urbana, IL: National Council of Teachers of English, and New York: Teachers College Press.

Mahiri, J. (2001). Pop culture pedagogy and the end(s) of school. *Journal of Adolescent and Adult Literacy, 44*(4), 382–385.

Maida, P. (1995). Reading and notetaking prior to instruction. *Mathematics Teacher 88*(6), 470–473.

Malloy, M. E. (1999). Ein Riesen-Spafs! (Great fun!): Using authentic picture books to teach a foreign language. *The New Advocate, 12*(2), 169–184.

Manuel, J. (1998). Reviewing talking and listening in the secondary English curriculum. In W. Sawyer, K. Watson, & E. Gold (Eds.), *Reviewing English* (pp. 264–276). Sydney, Australia: St. Clair Press.

Manzo, A. V. (1969). The ReQuest procedure. *Journal of Reading, 11,* 123–126.

Manzo, A. V., & Manzo, U. (1997). *Content area literacy: Interactive teaching for active learning.* Upper Saddle River, NJ: Merrill.

Masingila, J. O., & Prus-Wisniowska, E. (1996). Developing and assessing mathematical understanding in calculus through writing. In P. C. Elliot & M. J. Kenney (Eds.), *Communication in mathematics, K–12 and beyond* (pp. 95–104). Reston, VA: National Council of Teachers of Mathematics.

Maxwell, R. J., & Meiser, M. J. (1997). *Teaching English in middle and secondary schools* (2nd ed.). Upper Saddle River, NJ: Merrill.

May, F. B. (2001). *Unraveling the seven myths of reading: Assessment and intervention practices for counteracting their effects.* Boston: Allyn & Bacon.

Mayher, J. (1998). Language education in the twenty-first century: Dreaming a caring future. In J. S. Simmons & L. Baines (Eds.), *Language study in middle school, high school, and beyond* (pp. 154–166). Newark, DE: International Reading Association.

McCombs, B. L. (1989). Self-regulated learning and academic achievement: A phenomenological view. In B. J. Zimmerman & D. H. Schunk (Eds.), *Self-regulated learning and achievement: Theory, research, and practice* (pp. 51–82). New York: Springer-Verlag.

McCrae, C. D. (1998). *Presenting young adult fantasy fiction.* New York: Twayne Publishers.

McDonald, S. P. (1936). Casey—Twenty years later. In H. Felleman (Ed.). *The best loved poems of the American people* (p. 286). Garden City, NY: Doubleday.

McElvaine, R. S. (2000). *The Depression and the New Deal: A history in documents.* New York: Oxford University Press.

McGinley, W. (1992). The role of reading and writing while composing from sources. *Reading Research Quarterly, 27*(3), 226–248.

McLaughlin, M. (2000). Assessment for the twenty-first century: Performance, portfolios, and profiles. In M. McLaughlin & M. Vogt (Eds.), *Creativity and innovation in content area teaching* (pp. 301–327). Norwood, MA: Christopher-Gordon.

McLynn, F. J. (Ed.). (1993). *Famous letters: Messages and thoughts that shaped the world.* Pleasantville, NY: Reader's Digest Association.

McMahon, S. I. (1996). Book club: The influence of a Vygotskian perspective on a literature-based reading program. In Dixon-Krauss (Ed.), *Vygotsky in the classroom: Mediated literacy instruction and assessment* (pp. 59–76). New York: Longman.

McMahon, S. I., & Raphael, T. (1997). *The book club connection: Literacy learning and classroom talk.* New York: Teachers College Press.

Meltzer, M. (1997). *Langston Hughes: An illustrated edition.* Brookfield, CT: Millbrook Press.

Meltzer, M. (2001). *There comes a time: The struggle for civil rights.* New York: Random House.

Meyer, C. A. (1992). What's the difference between "authentic" and "performance" assessment? *Educational Leadership, 49*(8), 39–40.

Michel, P. (1994). *The child's view of reading: Understandings for teachers and parents.* Boston: Allyn & Bacon.

Middleton, J. L. (1991). Student-generated analogies in biology. *The American Biology Teacher, 53*(1), 42–46.

Miller, L. D. (1993). Making the connection with language. *Arithmetic Teacher, 40*(6), 311–316.

Miller, M. (1999). *Words that built a nation: A young person's collection of historic American documents.* New York: Scholastic.

Miller, T. (1998). The place of picture books in middle-level classrooms. *Journal of Adolescent and Adult Literacy, 41*(5), 376–381.

Miner, A. C., & Reder, L. M. (1996). A new look at the feeling of knowing: Its metacognitive role in regulating question answering. In J. Metcalfe & A. P. Shimamura (Eds.), *Metacognition: Knowing about knowing.* Cambridge, MA: MIT Press.

Mo, W., & Shen, W. (2000). A mean wink at authenticity: Chinese images in Disney's *Mulan. The New Advocate, 13*(2), 129–142.

Moffett, J. (1968). *Teaching the universe of discourse.* Boston: Houghton Mifflin.

Moje, E. B. (1996). I teach students, not subjects: Teacher-student relationships as contexts for secondary literacy. *Reading Research Quarterly, 31,* 172–195.

Moje, E. B. (2000). What will classrooms and schools look like in the new millennium? *Reading Research Quarterly, 35*(1), 128–129.

Monseau, V. (1996). *Responding to young adult literature.* Portsmouth, NH: Boynton/Cook.

Montapert, A. A. (1982). *Inspiration and motivation.* Englewood Cliffs, NJ: Prentice Hall.

Moore, B. N., & Parker, R. (1995). *Critical thinking* (4th ed.). Mountain View, CA: Mayfield.

Moore, D. W. (2000). How will literacy be assessed in the next millennium? *Reading Research Quarterly, 35*(2), 246–247.

Moore, D. W., Bean, T. W., Birdyshaw, D., & Rycik, J. A. (1999). Adolescent literacy: A position statement (for the Commission on Adolescent Literacy of the International Reading Association). *The Journal of Adolescent and Adult Literacy, 43*(1), 97–111.

Moore, D. W., Moore, S. A., Cunningham, P. M., & Cunningham, J. W. (1994). *Developing readers and writers in the content areas K–12* (2nd ed.). White Plains, NY: Longman.

Moore, J. N. (1997). Deconstruction: Unraveling *The Giver.* In J. N. Moore (Ed.), *Interpreting young adult literature: Applying literary criticism in the secondary classroom* (pp. 75–94). Portsmouth, NH: Heinemann.

Moore, J. N. (1999). Imagining the Van Gogh Cafe: Designing instruction for multiple literacies in the English classroom. NCTE Conference, Denver, CO.

Morley, S. (1996). Faculty book talks: Adults sharing books and enthusiasm for reading with students. *Journal of Adolescent and Adult Literacy, 40*(2), 130–132.

Morris, P. J., & Tchudi, S. (1996). *The new literacy: Moving beyond the 3Rs.* Portland, ME: Calendar Island Publishers.

Morrow, L. M. (1992). The impact of a literature-based program on literacy achievement, use of literature, and attitudes of children from minority backgrounds. *Reading Research Quarterly, 27*(3), 250–275.

Morrow, L. M. (1996). Motivating reading and writing in diverse classrooms. (NCTE Research Rep. No. 28). Urbana, Il: National Council of Teachers of English.

Moss, B. (1991). Children's nonfiction trade books: A complement to content area texts. *The Reading Teacher, 45,* 26–32.

Mowder, L. (1992). Domestication of desire: Gender, language, and landscape in the *Little House* books. *Children's Literature Association Quarterly, 17,* 15–19.

Mulcahy-Ernt, P., & Stewart, J. P. (1994). Writing and reading in the integrated language arts. In L. M. Morrow, J. K. Smith, & L. C. Wilkinson (Eds.), *Integrated language arts: Controversy to consensus.* Boston: Allyn & Bacon.

Mundy, J., & Hadaway, N. (1999). Children's informational picture books visit a secondary ESL classroom. *Journal of Adolescent and Adult Literacy, 42*(6), 464–475.

Murphy, E. (2001). In search of literature for the twenty-first century. *English Journal, 90*(3), 111–115.

Murray, D. (1985). *A writer teaches writing* (2nd ed.). Boston: Houghton Mifflin.

Myers, W. D. (1991). *Now is your time!: The African American struggle for freedom.* New York: HarperCollins.

Mydans, S. (2001). Left-behind mines pose risk for animals. New York Times News Service. *Syracuse Herald-American*, March 11, p. A5.

Myhill, D. (2000). Misconceptions and difficulties in the acquisition of metalinguistic knowledge. *Language and Education, 14*(3), 151–163.

Nadis, S. (1994). Fantastic voyage: Traveling the body in microbiotic style. *OMNI Magazine*, Winter, p. 9.

Nagy, W. E. (1989). *Teaching vocabulary to improve reading comprehension*. Newark, DE: International Reading Association.

Nagy, W., & Anderson, R. C. (1984). How many words are there in printed school English? *Reading Research Quarterly, 19*, 304–330.

Nagy, W., Anderson, R., & Herman, P. (1987). Learning word meanings from context during normal reading. *American Educational Research Journal, 24*, 237–270.

Nagy, W., Herman, P., & Anderson, R. (1985). Learning words from context. *Reading Research Quarterly, 20*, 233–253.

Nagy, W. E., & Scott, J. A. (2000). Vocabulary Processes. In P. D. Pearson, R. Barr, & M. L. Kamil (Eds.), *Handbook of reading research* (Vol. III, pp. 269–284). Mahwah, NJ: Lawrence Erlbaum Associates.

Naisbitt, J., with Naisbitt, N., & Philips, D. (1999). *High tech high touch: Technology and our search for meaning*. New York: Broadway Books.

Nasar, S. (1998). *A beautiful mind: A biography of John Forbes Nash, winner of the Nobel Prize in economics*. New York: Simon & Schuster.

Nash, O. (1953). *The moon is shining bright as day*. New York: Lippincott.

National Academy of Sciences. (1996). *National science education standards*. Washington, DC: National Academy Press.

National Council for the Social Studies. (1994). *Expectations of excellence: Curriculum standards for social studies*. Washington, DC: Author.

National Council of Teachers of English, & International Reading Association. (1996). *Standards for the English language arts*. Urbana, IL, and Newark, DE: Authors.

National Council of Teachers of Mathematics. (1990). *Curriculum and evaluation standards for school mathematics*. Reston, VA: Author.

National Council of Teachers of Mathematics. (1991). *The professional teaching standards*. Reston, VA: Author.

National Research Council. (1994). *National science education standards: An enhanced sampler*. Washington, DC: National Academy of Sciences.

Negroponte, N. (1995). *Being digital*. New York: Knopf.

Nell, V. (1988). *Lost in a book: The psychology of reading for pleasure*. New Haven, CT: Yale University Press.

Newkirk, T., & McClure, P. (1992). *Listening in: Children talk about books (and other things)*. Portsmouth, NH: Heinemann.

Nierstheimer, S. L. (2000). "To the parents of. . . . ": A parent's perspective on the schooling of a struggling reader. *Journal of Adolescent and Adult Literacy, 44*(1), 34–36.

Niles, O. S. (1985). Integration of content and skills instruction. In T. L. Harris & E. J. Cooper (Eds.), *Thinking and concept development: Strategies for the classroom* (pp. 177–194). New York: College Entrance Examination Board.

Noddings, N. (1992). *The challenge to care in schools: An alternative approach to education*. New York: Teachers College Press.

Noddings, N. (1999). Renewing democracy in schools. *Phi Delta Kappan, 80*(8), 579–583.

Nolan, H. (1997). *Dancing on the edge*. San Diego, CA: Harcourt Brace.

Nolan, R. E., & Patterson, R. B. (2000). Curtains, lights: Using skits to teach English to Spanish-speaking adolescents and adults. *Journal of Adolescent and Adult Literacy, 44*(1), 6–14.

Nolan, T. E. (1991). Self-questioning and prediction: Combining metacognition strategies. *Journal of Reading, 35*(2), 132–138.

Norton, D. (1999). *Through the eyes of a child: An introduction to children's literature*. Upper Saddle River, NJ: Merrill.

O'Brien, D. G. (1988). Secondary preservice teachers' resistance to content reading instruction: A proposal for a broader rationale. In J. E. Readence & R. S. Baldwin (Eds.), *Dialogues in literacy research* (pp. 237–243). Chicago: National Reading Conference.

O'Brien, D. G., Stewart, R. A., & Moje, E. B. (1995). Why content literacy is difficult to infuse into the secondary school: Complexities of curriculum, pedagogy, and school culture. *Reading Research Quarterly, 30*(3), 442–463.

O'Flaven, J. F. (1989). *An exploration of participant structure upon literacy development in reading group discussion*. Unpublished doctoral dissertation, University of Illinois-Champaign.

Ogle, D. M. (1986). K–W–L: A teaching model that develops active reading of expository text. *The Reading Teacher, 39*(6), 564–570.

Ohanian, S. (2001). News from the test resistance trail. *Phi Delta Kappan, 82*(5), 363–366.

Ohlhausen, M. M., & Jepson, M. (1992). Lessons from Goldilocks: Somebody's been choosing my books but I can make my own choices now. *The New Advocate, 5*(1), 31–46.

Oldfather, P. (1993). What students say about motivating experiences in a whole language classroom. *The Reading Teacher, 46*(8), 672–681.

Oldfather, P., & Dahl, K. (1994). Toward a social constructivist reconceptualization of intrinsic motivation for literacy learning. *Journal of Reading Behavior, 26,* 139–158.

Olson, C. B. (1992). *Thinking writing: Fostering critical thinking through writing.* New York: HarperCollins.

Orr, D. W. (2000/2001). Verbicide. *American Educator,* Winter, 26–29, 48.

Overholser, J. C. (1992). Socrates in the classroom. *Social Studies, 83*(2), 77–82.

Pace, B. G., & Townsend, J. S. (1999). Gender roles: Listening to classroom talk about literary characters. *English Journal, 88*(3), 43–49.

Palincsar, A. S., & Brown, A. L. (1984). Reciprocal teaching of comprehension-fostering and comprehension-monitoring activities. *Cognition and Instruction, 1,* 117–175.

Palmer, R. G., & Stewart, R. A. (1997). Nonfiction trade books in content area instruction: Realities and potential. *Journal of Adolescent and Adult Literacy, 40,* 630–641.

Pardo, L. (1997). Reflective teaching for continuing development of book club. In S. I. McMahon & T. E. Raphael (Eds.), *The book club connection: Literacy learning and classroom talk* (pp. 227–247). New York: Teachers College Press.

Paris, S. G., & Winograd, P. (1989). How metacognition can promote academic learning and instruction. In B. F. Jones & L. Idol (Eds.), *Dimensions of thinking and cognitive instruction* (Vol. 1, pp. 15–52). Hillsdale, NJ: Lawrence Erlbaum Associates.

Paterson, K. (1981). *Gates of excellence: On reading and writing books for children.* New York: Lodestar Books.

Paterson, K. (2000). The future of literature: Asking the question. *New Advocate, 13*(1), 1–15.

Paul, D. G. (2000). Rap and orality: Critical media literacy, pedagogy, and cultural synchronization. *Journal of Adolescent and Adult Literacy, 44*(3), 246–252.

Pauling, L. (1995). *Linus Pauling in his own words: Selections from his writings, speeches and interviews.* (B. Marinacci, Ed.). New York: Simon & Schuster.

Paulos, J. A. (1988). *Innumeracy: Mathematical illiteracy and its consequences.* New York: Farrar, Straus & Giroux.

Paulos, J. A. (1991). *Beyond numeracy: The Ruminations of a numbers man.* New York: Knopf.

Pavonetti, L. (2001). Celebrating diversity through children's literature: An interview with Leo and Diane Dillon. *Journal of Children's Literature, 27*(2), 45–51.

Peck, R. (1994). *Life and death at the mall: Teaching and writing for the literate young.* New York: Delacorte.

Peregoy, S. F., & Boyle, O. F. (1997). *Reading, writing, and learning in ESL: A resource book for K–12 teachers* (2nd ed.). New York: Longman.

Perfetti, C., Britt, M., Rouet, J. F., Georgi, M., & Mason, R. (1994). How students learn and reason about historical uncertainty. In M. Carretero & J. Voss (Eds.), *Cognitive and instructional processes in history and the social sciences* (pp. 257–284). Hillsdale, NJ: Lawrence Erlbaum Associates.

Perl, S. (1979). The composing process of unskilled writers. *Research in Teaching English, 13,* 5–22.

Perl. S., & Wilson, N. (1986). *Through teachers' eyes: Portraits of writing teachers at work.* Portsmouth, NH: Heinemann.

Perrone, V. (1991). Moving toward more powerful assessment. In V. Perrone (Ed.), *Expanding student assessment* (pp. 164–166). Alexandria, VA: Association for Supervision and Curriculum Development.

Peters, C. W. (1996). Reading in social studies: Using skills and strategies in a thoughtful manner. In D. Lapp, J. Flood, & N. Farnan (Eds.), *Content area reading and learning: Instructional strategies* (2nd ed.), (pp. 181–207). Boston: Allyn & Bacon.

Peterson, R., & Eeds, M. (1990). *Grand conversations: Literature groups in action.* New York: Scholastic.

Piaget, J. (1952). *The origins of intelligence in children.* New York: International University Press.

Pikulski, J., & Tobin, A. (1982). The cloze procedure as an informal assessment technique. In J. Pikulski & T. Shanahan (Eds.), *Approaches to the informal evaluation of reading* (pp. 42–62). Newark, DE: International Reading Association.

Posamentier, A. S., & Stepelman, J. (1995). *Teaching secondary school mathematics: techniques and enrichment units.* Englewood Cliffs, NJ: Merrill.

Postman, N. (1995). *The end of education: Redefining the value of schools.* New York: Knopf.

Postman, N. (1999). *Building a bridge to the eighteenth century: How the past can improve our future.* New York: Knopf.

Postman, N., & Powers, S. (1992). *How to watch TV news.* New York: Penguin Books.

Powell, R., Cantrell, S. C., & Adams, S. (2001). Saving Black Mountain: The promise of critical literacy in a multicultural democracy. *The Reading Teacher, 54*(8), 772–781.

Pressley, M. (1995). More about the development of self-regulation: Complex, long-term, and thoroughly social. *Educational Psychologist, 30,* 207–212.

Pressley, M. (2000). What should comprehension instruction be the instruction of? In P. D. Pearson, R. Barr, & M. L. Kamil (Eds.), *Handbook of reading research* (Vol. III, pp. 545–561). Mahwah, NJ: Lawrence Erlbaum Associates.

Pressley, M., & Afflerbach, P. (1995). *Verbal protocols of reading: The nature of constructively responsive reading.* Hillside, NJ: Lawrence Erlbaum Associates.

Pressley, M., El-Dinary, P. B., Gaskins, I., Schuder, T., Bergman, J., Almasi, L., & Brown, R. (1992). Beyond direct explanation: Transactional instruction of reading comprehension strategies. *Elementary School Journal, 92,* 511–554.

Pressley, M., Wharton-McDonald, R., Hampson, J. M., & Echevarria, M. (1998). The nature of literacy instruction in ten grade-4/5 classrooms in upstate New York. *Scientific Studies of Reading, 2,* 159–194.

Pressley, M., Wood, E., Woloshyn, V. E., Martin, V., King, A., & Menke, D. (1992). Encouraging mindful use of prior knowledge: Attempting to construct explanatory answers facilitates learning. *Educational Psychologist, 27,* 91–110.

Quinn, A. E. (2001). Moving marginalized students inside the lines: Cultural differences in classrooms. *English Journal, 90*(4), 44–50.

Raphael, T. E. (1984). Teaching learners about sources of information for answering comprehension questions. *Journal of Reading, 27*(4), 303–311.

Ravitch, D. (1995). *National standards in American education: A citizen's guide.* Washington, DC: The Brookings Institute.

Ravitch, D., & Finn, C. (1987). *What do our 17-year-olds know?: A report on the first national assessment of history and literature.* New York: Harper & Row.

READ Magazine. (1995). *Dear author: Students write about the books that changed their lives.* Berkeley, CA: Conari Press.

Reardon, J. (1990). Putting reading tests in their place. *The New Advocate, 1*(1), 29–37.

Resnick, L. B. (1987). *Education and learning to think.* Washington, DC: National Academy Press.

Richardson, J. (1994). Coordinating teacher read-alouds with content instruction in secondary classrooms. In G. Cramer & M. Castle (Eds.), *Fostering the life-long love of reading: The affective domain in reading education.* Newark, DE: International Reading Association.

Richardson, J. (2000). *Read it aloud! Using literature in the secondary content classroom.* Newark, DE: International Reading Association.

Richey, V. H., & Puckett, K. E. (1992). *Wordless/ Almost wordless picture books.* Englewood, CO: Libraries Unlimited.

Rieck, B. J. (1977). How content teachers telegraph messages against reading. *Journal of Reading, 20*(8), 646–648.

Rief, L. (1992). *Seeking diversity: Language arts with adolescents.* Portsmouth, NH: Heinemann.

Ripley, C. P. (1992). *The black abolitionist papers: 1985–1992.* Chapel Hill: University of North Carolina Press.

Robinson, F. P. (1946). *Effective study.* New York: Harper & Row.

Roller, C. M. (1996). *Variability not disability: Struggling readers in a workshop classroom.* Newark, DE: International Reading Association.

Roller, K. (1990). The interaction of knowledge and structure variables in the processing of expository prose. *Reading Research Quarterly, 25,* 79–89.

Romines, A. (1997). *Constructing the* Little House: *Gender, culture, and Laura Ingalls Wilder.* Amherst, MA: University of Massachusetts Press.

Rosenblatt, L. M. (1938/1995). *Literature as exploration* (5th ed.). New York: Modern Language Association.

Rosenblatt, L. M. (1978). *The reader, the text, the poem: The transactional theory of the literary work.* Carbondale & Edwardsville: Southern Illinois University Press.

Rosenblatt, L. M. (1985). Viewpoints: Transaction versus interaction—A terminological rescue operation. *Research in the Teaching of English, 19*(1), 96–107.

Rosenthal, N. (1995). *Speaking of reading.* Portsmouth, NH: Heinemann.

Rothschild, D. A. (1995). *Graphic novels: A bibliographic guide to book-length comics.* Englewood, CO: Libraries Unlimited.

Routman, R. (1996). *Literacy at the crossroads: Critical talk about reading, writing, and other teaching dilemmas.* Portsmouth, NH: Heinemann.

Routman, R. (2000). *Conversations.* Portsmouth, NH: Heinemann.

Rowe, M. B. (1974a). Reflections on wait-time: Some methodological questions. *Journal of Research in Science Teaching, 11*(3), 263–279.

Rowe, M. B. (1974b). Relation of wait-time and rewards to the development of language, logic, and fate control: Part II—Rewards. *Journal of Research in Science Teaching, 11*(4), 291–308.

Ruddell, M. R. (1993). *Teaching content reading and writing.* Boston: Allyn & Bacon.

Ruddell, R., & Unrau, N. (1994). Reading as a meaning-making construction process: The reader, the text, and the teacher. In R. Ruddell, M. R. Ruddell, & H. Singer (Eds.), *Theoretical models and processes of reading* (pp. 996–1056). Newark, DE: International Reading Association.

Rumelhart, D. (1976). *Toward an interactive model of reading* (Report No. 56). La Jolla: University of California, San Diego, Center for Human Information Processing.

Rumelhart, D. (1981). Schemata: The building blocks of cognition. In J. Guthrie (Ed.), *Comprehension and teaching: Research reviews* (pp. 3–26). Newark, DE: International Reading Association.

Rushkoff, D. (1996). *Playing the future: How kids' culture can teach us to survive in an age of chaos.* New York: HarperCollins.

Ryan, M. (1994). The day they threw out the textbooks. *Parade Magazine,* February 20, pp. 10–11.

Ryder, R. J., & Graves, M. F. (1998). *Reading and learning in content areas* (2nd ed.). Upper Saddle River, NJ: Merrill.

Sadker, M., & Sadker, D. (1994). *Failing at fairness: How America's schools cheat girls.* New York: Scribner's.

Sanacore, J. (1998). Promoting the lifelong love of writing. (Reading Leadership). *Journal of Adolescent and Adult Literacy, 41*(5), 392–396.

Santa, C., & Havens, L. (1995). *Creating independence through student-owned strategies: Project CRISS.* Dubuque, IA: Kendall-Hunt.

Saul, W., Reardon, J., Schmidt, A., Pearce, C., Blackwood, D., & Bird, M. D. (1993). *Science workshop.* Portsmouth, NH: Heinemann.

Savage, J. F. (1994). *Teaching reading using literature.* Iowa: RIE Document CS011590.

Sawyer, W., Watson, K., & Gold, E. (Eds.). (1998). *Reviewing English.* Sydney, Australia: St. Clair Press.

Scardamalia, M., Bereiter, C., & Goelman, H. (1982). What writers know: The language process and structure of written discourse. In M. Nystrand (Ed.), *The role of production factors in writing ability.* New York: Academic Press.

Schallert, D. L., & Roser, N. L. (1996). The role of textbooks and trade books in content area instruction. In D. Lapp, J. Flood, & N. Farnan (Eds.), *Content area reading and learning: Instructional strategies* (2nd ed.), (pp. 27–38). Boston: Allyn & Bacon.

Schatz, E. I., & Baldwin, R. S. (1986). Context clues are unreliable predictors of word meanings. *Reading Research Quarterly, 21,* 439–453.

Schellings, G. L. M., & van Hout-Wolters, B. H. A. M. (1995). Main points in an instructional text, as identified by students and their teachers. *Reading Research Quarterly, 30,* 742–756.

Schlick Noe, K. L., & Johnson, N. J. (1999). *Getting started with literature circles.* Norwood, MA: Christopher-Gordon.

Schoenfeld, A. H. (1987). What's all the fuss about metacognition? In A. H. Schoenfeld (Ed.), *Cognitive science and mathematics education* (pp. 189–215). Hillsdale, NJ: Lawrence Erlbaum Associates.

Schulz, C. (1995). Peanuts. In *Syracuse Herald American,* August 27, 1995, Comics Section, unpaged.

Schumaker, J., & Lenz, K. (1999). *Adapting language arts, social studies, and science materials for the inclusive classroom.* Reston, VA: Council for Exceptional Children.

Schwartz, D. M. (1998). *G is for googol: A math alphabet book.* New York: Scholastic.

Segal, E. (1977). Laura Ingalls Wilder's America: An unflinching assessment. *Children's Literature in Education, 8,* 63–70.

Seife, C. (2000). *Zero: The biography of a dangerous idea.* New York: Viking.

Seuss, Dr. (1984). *The butter battle book.* New York: Random House.

Severance, J. B. (2001). *Einstein: Visionary scientist.* New York: Clarion Books.

Shade, R. (1991). Verbal humor in gifted students and students in the general population: A comparison of spontaneous mirth and comprehension. *Journal for the Education of the Gifted, 14*(2), 134–150.

Shafer, G. (1997). Reader response makes history. *English Journal, 86*(7), 65–68.

Shafer, G. (2001). Standard English and the migrant community. *English Journal, 90*(4), 37–43.

Shanahan, T., & Tierney, R. J. (1990). Reading-writing connections: The relations among three perspectives. In J. Zutell & S. McCormack (Eds.), *Literacy theory and research: Analysis from multiple paradigms* (pp. 13–34). Chicago, IL: National Reading Conference.

Shanahan, T., & Tierney, R. (1991). Research on the reading–writing relationship: Interactions, transactions, and outcomes. In R. Barr, M. L. Kamil, P. Mosenthal, & P. D. Pearson (Eds.), *Handbook of reading research* (Vol. II, pp. 246–280). New York: Longman.

Short, D. (1999). *New ways in teaching English at the secondary level.* Alexandria, VA: Teachers of English to Speakers of Other Languages.

Short, K. G., Harste, J., & Burke, C. (1996). *Creating classrooms for authors and inquirers.* Portsmouth, NH: Heinemann.

Shriver, M. (2000). *Ten things I wish I'd known—Before I went out into the real world.* New York: Warner Books.

Siegel, M. (1984). Reading as signification. *Dissertation Abstracts International, 45,* 2824A. (Indiana University).

Siler, T. (1996). *Think like a genius.* New York: Bantam Books.

Silver, S., & Smith, C. (1996). Building discourse communities in mathematics classrooms: A worthwhile but challenging journey. *Communication in Mathematics, K–12 and Beyond.* National Council of Teachers of Mathematics Yearbook, 20–28.

Simmons, J. S., & Deluzain, H. E. (1992). *Teaching literature in middle and secondary grades.* Boston: Allyn & Bacon.

Simpson, M., & Nist, S. L. (2000). An update on strategic learning: It's more than just textbook strategies. *Journal of Adolescent and Adult Literacy, 43*(6), 528–541.

Sinatra, G. M., Beck, I. L., & McKeown, M. G. (1992). A longitudinal characterization of young student's knowledge of their country's government. *American Educational Research Journal, 29,* 633–662.

Sincich, T. (1990). *Statistics by example* (4th ed.). San Francisco: Dellen.

Sippola, A. E. (1995). K–W–L–S. *The Reading Teacher, 48*(6), 542–543.

Sizer, T. (1992). *Horace's school: Redesigning the American high school.* Boston: Houghton Mifflin.

Sizer, T. (1996). *Horace's hope: What works for the American high school.* Boston: Houghton Mifflin.

Skinner, B. F. (1948). *Walden two.* New York: Macmillan.

Slapin, B., & Seale, D. (1992). *Through Indian eyes: The Native experience in children's books.* Philadelphia: New Society Publishers.

Slavin, R. E. (1986). *Jigsaw II: Using student team learning* (3rd ed.). Baltimore: John Hopkins University, Center for Research on Elementary and Middle Schools.

Smith, C. C., & Bean, T. W. (1980). The guided writing procedure: Integrating content reading and writing improvement. *Reading World, 19,* 290–298.

Smith, F. (1985). *Reading without nonsense* (2nd ed.). New York: Teachers College Press.

Smith, F. (1988). *Joining the literacy club: Further essays into education.* Portsmouth, NH: Heinemann.

Smith, J. K. (1994). Standardized testing versus authentic assessment: Godzilla meets Winnie-the-Pooh. In L. S. Morrow, J. K. Smith, & L. C. Wilkinson (Eds.), *Integrated language arts: Controversy to consensus* (pp. 215–229). Boston: Allyn & Bacon.

Smith, M. (1991). Constructing meaning from text: An analysis of ninth-grade reader responses. *Journal of Educational Research, 84,* 263–271.

Smith, M. W. (1996). Conversations about literature outside classrooms: How adults talk about books in their book clubs. *Journal of Adolescent and Adult Literacy, 40*(3), 180–186.

Smitherman, G. (1997). Moving beyond resistance: Ebonics and African American youth. *Journal of Black Psychology, 23*(3), 227–232.

Smokes, S. (2001, March 11). Teen dramas played out in shades of black and white. *Syracuse Herald-American,* p. D1, D5.

Smolen, R., & Erwitt, J. (Creators). (1998). *One digital day: How the microchip is changing our world.* New York: Times Books/Random House in association with Against All Odds Productions.

Snodgrass, M. E. (1995). *Encyclopedia of utopian literature.* Santa Barbara, CA: ABC-CLIO.

Soares, M. B. (1992). Literacy assessment and its implication for statistical measurement. (Paper prepared for the Division of Statistics, UNESCO, Paris).

Sober, E., & Wilson, D. S. (1998). *Unto others: The evolution and psychology of unselfish behavior.* Cambridge, MA: Harvard University Press.

Soukhanov, A. H. (1995). *Word watch: The stories behind the words of our lives.* New York: Henry Holt.

Spalding, E. (2000). Performance assessments and the new standards project: A story of serendipitous success. *Phi Delta Kappan,* June, pp. 758–764.

Spears, R. A. (1998). *NTC's American English learner's dictionary: The essential vocabulary of American language and culture.* Lincolnwood, IL: National Textbook Company.

Spretnak, C. (1997). *The resurgence of the real.* Reading, MA: Addison-Wesley.

Stahl, S., Hynd, C., Britton, B., McNish, M., & Bosquet, D. (1996). What happens when students read multiple source documents in history? *Reading Research Quarterly, 31,* 430–456.

Stahl, S. A., Hynd, C. R., Glynn, S. M., Carr, M. (1996). Beyond reading to learn: Developing content and disciplinary knowledge through texts. In L. Baker, P. Afflerbach, & D. Reinking (Eds.), *Developing engaged readers in school and home communities.* Mahwah, NJ: Lawrence Erlbaum Associates.

Stanovitch, K. E. (1980). Toward an interactive-compensatory model of individual differences in the development of reading fluency. *Reading Research Quarterly, 16,* 32–71.

Stanovitch, K. E. (1986). Matthew effects in reading: Some consequences of individual differences in the acquisition of literacy. *Reading Research Quarterly, 21,* 360–407.

Stauffer, R. G. (1980). *The language experience approach to the teaching of reading.* New York: Harper & Row.

Steinbergh, J. (1994). *Reading and writing poetry: A guide for teachers.* New York: Scholastic.

Stephens, J. (1998). Visual literacy: Enabling and promoting critical viewing. In W. Sawyer, K. Watson, & E. Gold (Eds.), *Reviewing English* (pp. 164–173). Sydney, Australia: St. Clair Press.

Stephens, J., & Watson, K. (Eds.). (1994). *From picture book to literary theory.* Sydney, Australia. St. Clair Press.

Stevens, R., & Slavin, R. (1995). The cooperative elementary school: Effects on students' achievement, attitudes, and social relations. *American Educational Research Journal, 32*(2), 321–351.

Stille, D. R. (1997). *Extraordinary women of medicine.* New York: Children's Press.

Stix, G., & Lacob, M. (1999). *Who gives a gigabyte?: A survival guide for the technologically perplexed.* New York: Wiley.

Stoskopf, A. (2001). Reviving Clio: Inspired history teaching and learning (Without high-stakes tests). *Phi Delta Kappan, 82*(6), 468(–473.

Stotsky, S. (1999). *Losing our language: How multicultural classroom instruction is undermining our children's ability to read, write, and reason.* New York: The Free Press.

Strachen. (2000). Minding the DBQs. *New York Teacher,* XLI (11), 24.

Straczynski, J. M., & Romita, J., Jr. (2001). *The amazing spiderman,* Vol. 2, No. 36. Marvel Comics.

Swinburne, S. R. (1999). *Once a wolf: How wildlife biologists fought to bring back the gray wolf.* Boston: Houghton Mifflin.

Syracuse Herald-Journal. Canary in the mine shaft: Cornell bioengineering study. (Editorial). Author, May 24, 1999, A6.

Taba, H. (1967). *Teachers' handbook for elementary social studies.* Reading, MA: Addison-Wesley.

Tamplin, R. (Ed.). (1995). *Famous love letters: Messages of intimacy and passion.* Pleasantville, NY: Reader's Digest Association.

Tanner, M. L., & Casados, L. (1998). Promoting and studying discussions in math classes. *Journal of Adolescent and Adult Literacy, 41*(5), 342–350.

Tapscott, D. (1998). *Growing up digital: The rise of the Net generation.* New York: McGraw-Hill.

Taylor, M. (1976). *Roll of thunder, hear my cry.* New York: Viking Penguin.

Taylor, W. L. (1953). Cloze procedure: A new tool for measuring readability. *Journalism Quarterly, 30,* 415–433.

The Norton book of interviews. (1996). New York: Norton.

The Reading Teacher, September, 2000

Thompson, M. C. (1996a). Formal language study for gifted students. In J. VanTassel, D. T. Johnson, & L. N. Boyce (Eds.), *Developing verbal talent* (pp. 149–173). Boston: Allyn & Bacon.

Thompson, M. C. (1996b). Mentors on paper: How classics develop verbal ability. In J. VanTassel, D. T. Johnson, & L. N. Boyce (Eds.), *Developing verbal talent* (pp. 56–74). Boston: Allyn & Bacon.

Thoreau, H. D. (1999). *Uncommon learning: Henry David Thoreau on education* (M. Bickman, Ed.). Boston: Houghton Mifflin.

Tierney, R., Soter, A., O'Flahavan, J., & McGinley, W. (1989). The effects of reading and writing upon thinking critically. *Reading Research Quarterly, 24,* 134–173.

Torrey, B., & Allen, F. H. (1962). *The journal of Henry D. Thoreau.* New York: Dover.

Travers, D., & Hancock, J. (1996). *Teaching viewing.* Campbelltown, SA: Curriculum Resources.

Tuccillo, D. P. (2001). Happily ever after? Teens and fairy tales. *The ALAN Review, 28*(2), 66–68.

Turner, J. C. (1995). The influence of classroom contexts on young children's motivation for literacy. *Reading Research Quarterly, 30,* 410–441.

University of the State of New York. (2001). Regent's High School Examination: Comprehensive Examination in English, Session One, January.

U. S. Department of Education. (1999). *1998 NAEP Reading report card for the nation.* nces.ed.gov/naep

Usnick, V., & McCarthy, J. (1998, March). Turning adolescents onto mathematics through literature. *Middle School Journal,* pp. 50–54.

Vacca, R. T., & Vacca, J. L. (1993). *Content area reading* (4th ed.). New York: HarperCollins.

Valencia, S. W. (2000). How will literacy be assessed in the next millennium? *Reading Research Quarterly, 35*(2), 247–249.

Van de Walle, J. A. (1998). *Elementary and middle school mathematics: Teaching developmentally* (3rd ed.). New York: Longman.

Vermette, P. J. (1998). *Making cooperative learning work.* Upper Saddle River, NJ: Prentice Hall.

Victor, E., & Kellough, R. D. (1997). *Science for the elementary and middle school* (8th ed.). Upper Saddle River, NJ: Merrill.

Vinz, R. (1996). *Composing a teaching life.* Portsmouth, NH: Boynton/Cook.

The Voice. (1999). Kids for kid's sake. Vol. 27(3) Albany, NY: United University Professors, 13.

Vygotsky, L. (1962). *Thought and language.* (E. Hanfmann & G. Vakar, Eds. and Trans.). Cambridge, MA: MIT Press.

Vygotsky, L. (1978). *Mind in society: The development of higher psychological processes.* (M. Cole, V. John-Steiner, S. Scribner, & E. Souberman, Eds.). Cambridge, MA: Harvard University Press.

Wade, S. E., & Moje, E. B. (2000). The role of text in classroom learning. In M. L. Kamil, P. B. Mosenthal, P. D. Pearson, & R. Barr (Eds.), *Handbook of reading research* (Vol. III, pp. 609–627). Mahwah, NJ: Lawrence Erlbaum Associates.

Wahlgren, G. F. (1997). Creating a Mathematical Storybook. *Mathematics Teaching in the Middle School,* pp. 126–127.

Wakefield, J. (2001). The object at hand: Painted ladies in space. *Smithsonian, 33*(3), 30–34.

Walczyk, J. J., & Hall, V. C. (1989). Is the failure to monitor comprehension an instance of cognitive impulsivity? *Journal of Educational Psychology, 81*(3), 294–298.

Watson, K. (1998). Picture books in the secondary classroom. In W. Sawyer, K. Watson, & E. Gold (Eds.), *Reviewing English* (pp. 182–187). Sydney, Australia: St. Clair Press.

Watson, T. (2000). Misconceptions and mistakes. *Education in Science, 189,* 16.

Weaver, C. (1994). *Reading process and practice: From socio-psycholinguistics to whole language* (2nd ed.). Portsmouth, NH: Heinemann.

Weaver, M. (1999). *Visual literacy: How to read and use information in graphic form.* New York: Learning Express.

Webb, J. (2001). Should we leave Okinawa? *Parade Magazine,* March 11, pp. 4–6.

Webster's encyclopedic unabridged dictionary of the English language. (1996). New York: Random House.

Weir, C. (1998). Using embedded questions to jump-start metacognition in middle school remedial readers. *Journal of Adolescent and Adult Literacy, 41*(6), 458–467.

Wells, G. (1992). *The meaning makers: Children learning language and using language to learn.* Portsmouth, NH: Heinemann.

Wells, M. C. (1996). *Literacies lost: When students move from a progressive middle school to a traditional high school.* New York: Teachers College Press.

Wentzel, K. R. (1996). Social and academic motivation in middle school: Concurrent and long-term relations to academic effort. *Journal of Early Adolescence, 16,* 390–406.

Wentzel, K. R. (1997). Student motivation in middle school: The role of perceived pedagogical caring. *Journal of Educational Psychology, 89*(3), 411–419.

White, B. (1993). *Mama makes up her mind: And other dangers of southern living.* Reading, MA: Addison-Wesley.

White, E. B. (1952). *Charlotte's web.* New York: HarperCollins.

White, E. M. (1999). *Assigning, responding, evaluating: A writing teacher's guide* (3rd ed.). New York: St. Martin's.

White, T. H. (1958). *The once and future king.* New York: Putnam.

Whitelaw, J., & Wolf, S. A. (2001). Learning to "see beyond": Sixth-grade students' artistic perceptions of *The Giver. The New Advocate, 14*(1) 57–67.

Whitin, D. J., & Whitin, P. E. (1996). Fostering metaphorical thinking through children's literature. In P. C. Elliot & M. J. Kenney (Eds.), *Communication in mathematics, K–12 and beyond* (pp. 60–65). Reston, VA: National Council of Teachers of Mathematics.

Wilcox, B. L. (1996). Smart portfolios for teachers in training. *Journal of Adolescent and Adult Literacy, 40*(3), 172–179.

Wilcox, B. L. (1997). Writing portfolios: Active vs. passive. *English Journal, 86*(6), 34–37.

Wilhelm, J. D. (1997). *"You gotta BE the book": Teaching engaged and reflective reading with adolescents.* New York: Teachers College Press, and Urbana, IL: National Council of Teachers of English.

Wilhelm, J. D. (2001). *Improving comprehension with think-aloud strategies.* New York: Scholastic.

Wilson, E. O. (1998). *Consilience: The unity of knowledge.* New York: Knopf.

Wilson, E. O. (2002). The power of story. *American Educator, 26,* Spring, 8–11.

Wilson, J. (1960). Casey's revenge. In H. Felleman (Ed.). *The best loved poems of the American people* (p. 286). Garden City, NY: Doubleday.

Wily, J. P. (1998). Coming to terms. *Smithsonian,* December, 28–30.

Winograd, P. N., Wixson, K. K., & Lipson, M. Y. (Eds.). (1989). *Improving basal reading instruction.* New York: Teachers College Press.

Winter, J. (1988). *Follow the drinking gourd.* New York: Trumpet Club.

Wolf, V. L. (1988). A comparison of characters in children's classics. *Children's Literature Association Quarterly 13*(3), 135, 137.

Wolffe, R. (1998). Math learning through electronic journaling. In D. Reiss, D. Selfe, & A. Young (Eds.), *Electronic communication across the curriculum* (pp. 273–281). Urbana, IL: National Council of Teachers of English.

Wood, S. N. (2001). Bringing us the way to know: The novels of Gary Paulsen. *English Journal, 90*(30), 67–72.

World Book Encyclopedia. (2000). Chicago: World Book, Inc.

Worthy, J. (1998). On every page someone gets killed!: Book conversations you don't hear in school. *Journal of Adolescent and Adult Literacy, 41*(7), 508–517.

Wurman, R. S. (1989). *Information anxiety.* New York: Doubleday.

Yager, R. E., & Penick, J. E. (1990). Science teacher education. In W. R. Houston (Ed.), *Handbook on research in teacher education* (pp. 657–673). New York: Macmillan.

Yenika-Agbaw, V. (1997). Taking children's literature seriously: Reading for pleasure and social change. *Language Arts, 74*(6), 446–453.

Young, A., & Fulwiler, T. (Eds.). (1986). *Writing across the disciplines: Research into practice.* Upper Montclair, NJ: Boynton/Cook.

Young, J. P. (1998). Discussion as a practice of carnival. In D. E. Alvermann, K. A. Hinchman, D. W. Moore, S. F. Phelps, & D. R. Waff (Eds.), *Reconceptualizing the literacies in adolescents' lives* (pp. 247–264). Mahwah, NJ: Lawrence Erlbaum Associates.

Young, T. A., & Vardell, S. (1993). Weaving readers theatre and nonfiction into the curriculum. *The Reading Teacher, 46,* 396–406.

Zessoules, R., & Gardner, H. (1991). Authentic assessment: Beyond the buzzword and into the classroom. In V. Perrone (Ed.), *Expanding student assessment* (pp. 47–71). Alexandria, VA: Association for Supervision and Curriculum Development.

Zinsser, W. (1994). Simplicity. In P. Eschholz, A. Rosa, & V. Clark (Eds.), *Language awareness* (pp. 486–489). New York: St. Martin's.

Ziv, A., & Gadish, O. (1990). Humor and giftedness. *Journal for the Education of the Gifted, 13*(4), 332–345.

Trade Books Cited

Abbott, E. (1963). *Flatland: A romance of many dimensions* (5th ed., Rev.). New York: Barnes & Noble.

Achebe, C. (1994). *Things fall apart.* New York: Anchor Books.

Aliki. (1998). *Marianthe's story: Painted words; Spoken memories.* New York: Greenwillow Books.

Ambrose, S. E. (2001). *The good fight: How World War II was won.* New York: Atheneum Books for Young Readers.

Anderson, L. H. (1999). *Speak.* New York: Farrar, Straus & Giroux.

Anderson, L. H. (2000). *Fever: 1793.* New York: Simon & Schuster Books for Young Readers.

Anno, M. (1978). *Anno's journey.* Cleveland, OH: Collins-World.

Anno, M. (1980). *Anno's Italy.* New York: Harper-Collins.

Anno, M. (1982). *Anno's Britain.* New York: Philomel Books.

Anno, M. (1983). *Anno's mysterious multiplying jar.* New York: Philomel Books.

Anno, M. (1983). *Anno's U.S.A..* New York: Philomel Books.

Anonymous. (1982). *Go ask Alice.* New York: Avon Books.

Armour, R. (1969). *On your marks: A package of punctuation.* New York: McGraw-Hill.

Armstrong, J. (1998). *Shipwreck at the bottom of the world.* New York: Crown.

Arnold, N. (1997). *Nasty nature.* New York: Scholastic.

Ash, R. (1999). *The top 10 of everything 1999.* New York: DK Publishing.

Asimov, I. (1966). *The fantastic voyage: A novel.* Boston: Houghton Mifflin.

Atwood, M. (1986). *The handmaid's tale.* Boston: Houghton Mifflin.

Avi. (1991). *Nothing but the truth.* Thorndike, ME: Thorndike Press.

Babbitt, N. (1975). *Tuck everlasting.* New York: Farrar, Straus & Giroux.

Ballard, R. (1988). *Exploring the Titanic: How the greatest ship ever lost was found.* New York: Scholastic.

Banks, R. (1998). *Cloudsplitter.* New York: Harper-Flamingo.

Barnes, P. W., & Barnes, C. S. (1996). *House mouse, Senate mouse.* New York: Scholastic.

Barrett, R., & Beard, H. (1993). *The way things really work (And how they actually happen).* New York: Viking.

Base, G. (1986). *Animalia.* New York: Harry N. Abrams.

Base, G. (1989). *The eleventh hour.* New York: Harry N. Abrams.

Bayer, E. (2000). *Elie Wiesel: Spokesman for remembrance.* New York: Rosen Publishing Group.

Beard, H., & Barrett, R. (1993). *The way things really work.* New York: Viking.

Benet, R., & Benet, S. V. (1961). *A book of Americans.* New York: Henry Holt.

Bloor, E. (1997). *Tangerine.* San Diego, CA: Harcourt Brace.

Bloor, E. (1997). *Tangerine.* New York: Scholastic.

Bober, N. S. (2001). *Countdown to independence: A revolution of ideas in England and her American colonies: 1760–1776.* New York: Atheneum Books for Young Readers.

Bodanis, D. (2001). *E=MC2: A biography of the world's most famous equation.* New York: Berkley Books.

Bolles, E. B. (Ed.). (1997). *Galileo's commandment: An anthology of great science writing.* New York: Freeman.

Brenner, B. (1978). *Wagon wheels.* New York: Harper & Row.

Bridges, R. (1999). *Through my eyes.* New York: Scholastic.

Bronte, C. (1943). *Jane Eyre*. New York: Random House.

Brothers Grimm, The. (1972). *Snow White and the seven dwarfs*. (R. Jarrell, Trans.). New York: Farrar, Straus & Giroux.

Bunting, E. (1991). *Fly away home*. New York: Clarion Books.

Bunting, E. (1994). *Smoky night*. New York: Harcourt Brace.

Bunting, E. (1998). *So far from the sea*. New York: Scholastic.

Burchard, P. (1999). *Lincoln and slavery*. New York: Atheneum Books for Young Children.

Burke, J. (1999). *I hear America reading: Why we read what we read*. Portsmouth, NH: Heinemann.

Byars, B. (1977). *The pinballs*. New York: HarperCollins.

Canfield, J., & Hansen, M. V. (1993). *Chicken soup for the soul: 101 stories to open the heart and rekindle the spirit*. Deerfield Beach, FL: Health Communications.

Canfield, J., Hansen, M. V., & Kirberger, K. (1997). *Chicken soup for the teenage soul: 101 stories of life, love and learning*. Deerfield Beach, FL: Health Communications.

Carlson, L. M. (Ed.). (1995). *Cool salsa: Bilingual poems about growing up Latino in the United States*. New York: Fawcett Jupiter.

Carolrhoda Books. *Picture the American past series*. Minneapolis, MN: Author.

Carroll, A. (Ed.). (1997). *Letters of a nation: A collection of extraordinary American letters*. New York: Broadway Books.

Carroll, L. (1963). *Alice in Wonderland and Through the looking glass*. New York: Macmillan.

Carroll, L., & Zwerger, L. (1999). *Alice in Wonderland*. New York: North-South Books.

Cavendish, M. (Ed.). (1995). *War diary 1939–1945*. Secausus, NJ: Chartwell Books.

Chelsea House. *The encyclopedia of musical instruments series*. Philadelphia: Author.

Cheney, E. D. (1995). *Louisa May Alcott: Life, letters, and journals*. New York: Gramercy Books.

Cherry, L. (1990). *The great kapok tree: A tale of the Amazon rain forest*. San Diego, CA: Harcourt Brace.

Cherry, L. (1992). *A river ran wild*. San Diego, CA: Harcourt Brace.

Chesebrough, D. B. (1991). *"God ordained this war": Sermons on the sectional crisis, 1830–1865*. Columbia: University of South Carolina Press.

Coerr, E., & Himler, R. (1977). *Sadako and the thousand paper cranes*. New York: Putnam.

Coerr, E., & Young, E. (1993). *Sadako*. New York: Putnam.

Cogswell, D., & Gordon, P. (1996). *Chomsky for beginners*. New York: Writers and Readers Publishers.

Cole, J., & Degen, B. *The magic school bus series*. New York: Scholastic.

Cole, K. C. (1998). *The universe and the teacup: The mathematics of truth and beauty*. New York: Harcourt Brace.

Coles, R. (1995). *The story of Ruby Bridges*. New York: Scholastic.

Conroy, P. (1980). *Lords of discipline*. Boston: Houghton Mifflin.

Conroy, P. (1986). *The prince of tides*. Boston: Houghton Mifflin.

Conroy, P. (1987). *The water is wide*. New York: Bantam Books.

Conroy, P. (1996). *Beach music*. London: Black Swan.

Cormier, R. (1977). *I am the cheese*. New York: Pantheon Books.

Cormier, R. (1986). *The chocolate war*. New York: Dell.

Couloumbis, A. (1999). *Getting near to Baby*. New York: Putnam.

Creech, S. (1994). *Walk two moons*. New York: HarperCollins.

Crick, F. (1988). *What mad pursuit: A personal view of scientific discovery*. New York: Basic Books.

Crutcher, C. (1986). *Stotan!*. New York: Greenwillow Books.

Crutcher, C. (1993). *Staying fat for Sarah Byrnes*. New York: Greenwillow Books.

Crutcher, C. (1995). *Ironman*. New York: Greenwillow Books.

Cummings, P., & Cummings, L. (Eds.). (1992). *Talking with artists. Volume 1*. New York: Bradbury Press.

Cummings, P., & Cummings, L. (Eds.). (1995). *Talking with artists. Volume 2*. New York: Simon & Schuster Books for Young Readers.

Cummings, P., & Cummings, L. (Eds.). (1998). *Talking with adventurers*. Washington, DC: National Geographic Society.

Cummings, P., & Cummings, L. (Eds.). (1999). *Talking with artists. Volume 3*. New York: Clarion Books.

Cushman, K. (1995). *The Midwife's apprentice*. New York: HarperTrophy.

Dahl, R. (1988). *Matilda*. New York: Scholastic.

Dahl, R. (1992). *James and the giant peach*. New York: Cornerstone Books.

Dakos, K. (1990). Call the periods call the commas. In K. Dakos (Ed.), *If you're not here, please raise your hand: Poems about school* (p. 46). New York: The Trumpet Club.

Davis, K. C. (1999). *Don't know much about history.* New York: Avon Books.

de Saint Exupéry, A., & Woods, K. (1943). *The little prince.* New York: Harcourt, Brace & World.

Deedy, C. A. (2000). *The yellow star: The legend of King Christian X of Denmark.* Atlanta, GA: Peachtree.

Denman, C. (1995). *The history puzzle: An interactive visual timeline.* Atlanta, GA: Turner.

Dewdney, A. K. (1997). *Yes we have no neutrons: An eye-opening tour through the twists and turns of bad science.* New York: Wiley.

Dickens, C. (1998). *Oliver Twist.* New York: Tor.

Dickens, C. (1999). *Great expectations.* Wickford, RI: North Books.

Dickens. C., & Goodrich, C. (1996). *A Christmas Carol.* New York: Morrow.

Dickinson, P. (1988). *Eva.* New York: Delacorte.

Dillard, A. (1987). *An American childhood.* New York: HarperCollins.

Dillard, A. (2000). *Pilgrim at Tinker Creek.* Thorndike, ME: Thorndike Press.

Dillon, L., & Dillon, D. (1998). *For everything there is a season.* New York: The Blue Sky Press.

Dorling Kindersley Eyewitness Books series. New York: Author.

Dresang, E. (1999). *Radical change: Books for youth in a digital age.* New York: H. W. Wilson.

Duncan, A. F. (1995). *The National Civil Rights Museum celebrates everyday people.* Mahwah, NJ: Bridgewater Books.

Ekeland, I. (1993). *The broken dice: And other mathematical tales of chance.* Chicago: University of Chicago Press.

Elster, C. H. (1999). *The big book of beastly mispronunciations: The complete opinionated guide for the careful speaker.* Boston: Houghton Mifflin.

Elster, C. H., & Elliot, J. (1994). *Tooth and nail: A novel approach to the new SAT.* San Diego, CA: Harcourt Brace.

Enslow Publishers. *Decades of the twentieth century series.* Berkeley Heights, NJ: Author.

Erickson, P. (1998). *Daily life on a southern plantation 1853.* New York: Lodestar Books.

Everett, G. (1993). *John Brown: One man against slavery.* New York: Rizzoli International Publications.

Fine, A. (1997). *The tulip touch.* Boston: Little, Brown.

Fitzhugh, L. (1964). *Harriet the spy.* New York: Harper & Row.

Fleischman, P. (2001). *Seek.* Chicago: Cricket Books.

Fleischman, P., & Beddows, E. (1985). *I am Phoenix: Poems for two voices.* New York: Harper & Row.

Fleischman, P., & Beddows, E. (1988). *Joyful noise: Poems for two voices.* New York: Harper & Row.

Fleischman, P., & Frampton, D. (1993). *Bull Run.* New York: HarperCollins.

Forbes, E. (1999). *Johnny Tremain.* New York: Putnam Doubleday Books for Young Readers.

Fowles, J. (1969). *The French lieutenant's woman.* Boston: Little, Brown.

Frank, A. (1952). *The diary of a young girl.* New York: Modern Library.

Freedman, R. (1987). *Lincoln: A photobiography.* Boston: Houghton Mifflin.

Freedman, R. (2000). *Give me liberty!: The story of the Declaration of Independence.* New York: Holiday House.

Fried, R. L. (2001). *The passionate learner: How teachers and parents can help children reclaim the joy of discovery.* Boston: Beacon Press.

Fried. R. L. (2001). *The passionate teacher: A practical guide.* Boston: Beacon Press.

Fritz, J. (1983). *The double life of Pocahontas.* New York: Putnam.

Fritz, J. (1987). *Shh! We're writing the Constitution!* New York: Putnam.

Fritz, J., Paterson, K., McKissack, P., McKissack, F., Mahy, M., & Highwater, J. (1992). *The world in 1492.* New York: Henry Holt.

Gelb, M. J. (1998). *How to think like Leonardo da Vinci: Seven steps to genius every day.* New York: Delacorte.

George, J. C. (1972). *Julie of the wolves.* New York: Harper & Row.

George, J. C. (1988). *My side of the mountain.* New York: Dutton.

George, J. C. (1991). *Who really killed Cock Robin?: An ecological mystery.* New York: HarperCollins.

George, J. C. (1992). *The missing gator of Gumbo Limbo: An ecological mystery.* New York: HarperCollins.

George, J. C. (1996). *The case of the missing cutthroats: An ecological mystery.* New York: HarperCollins.

Giblin, J. C. (1988). *Let there be light: A book about windows.* New York: Crowell.

Giblin, J. C. (1990). *The riddle of the Rosetta Stone: Key to ancient Egypt.* New York: Crowell.

Giblin, J. C. (1995). *When plague strikes: The Black Death, Smallpox, AIDS.* New York: HarperCollins.

Giblin, J. C. (1999). *The mystery of the mammoth bones: And how it was solved.* New York: HarperCollins.

Giblin, J. C. (Ed.). (2000). *The century that was: Reflections on the last one hundred years.* New York: Atheneum Books for Young Readers.

Gibson, W. (1957). *The miracle worker.* New York: Knopf.

Glenn, M. (1996). *Who killed Mr. Chippendale?: A mystery in poems.* New York: Lodestar Books.

Goodall, J. (1986). *The story of a castle.* New York: M. K. McElderry Books.

Goodall, J., with Berman, P. (1999). *Reason for hope: A spiritual journey.* New York: Warner Books.

Gordon, K. E. (1997). *Torn wings and faux pas: A flashbook of style, A beastly guide through the writer's labyrinth.* New York: Pantheon Books.

Gould, S. J. (1996). *Full house: The spread of excellence from Plato to Darwin.* New York: Three Rivers Press.

Graham, L. (1980). *John Brown: A cry for freedom.* New York: Crowell.

Graves, D. (1998). *How to catch a shark: And other stories about teaching and learning.* Portsmouth, NH: Heinemann.

Greene, B. (2000). *Summer of my German soldier.* New York: Scholastic.

Groening, M., & Gimple, S. M. (1999). *The Simpsons forever!: A complete guide to our favorite family . . . continued.* New York: HarperPerennial.

Groening, M. (Creator), Richmond, R., & Coffman, A. (Eds.). (1997). *The Simpsons: A complete guide to our favorite family.* New York: HarperPerennial.

Grolier Educational. *Being human series.* Danbury, CT: Author.

Guterson, D. (1995). *Snow falling on cedars.* New York: Vintage Books.

Hansberry, L. (1959). *A raisin in the sun: A drama in three acts.* New York: Random House.

Harris, S. (1977). *What's so funny about science?* Los Altos, CA: William Kaufman.

Harris, S. (1982). *What's so funny about computers?* Los Altos, CA: William Kaufman.

Harris, S. (1989). *Einstein simplified: Cartoons on science.* New Brunswick, NJ: Rutgers University Press.

Hawking, S. (1988). *A brief history of time: From the big bang to black holes.* New York: Bantam Books.

Hawking, S. (1993). *Black holes and baby universes.* New York: Bantam Books.

Haven, K. F. (1996). *Great moments in science: Experiments and readers theatre.* Englewood, CO: Teacher Idea Press.

Heinemann Library. *Picture the past series.* Chicago, IL: Author.

Henderson, B., & Bernard, A. (Eds.). (1998). *Rotten reviews & rejections.* Wainscoot, NY: Pushcart Press.

Herbst, J. (1993). *Star crossing: How to get around in the universe.* New York: Atheneum.

Hersey, J. (1946). *Hiroshima.* New York: Knopf.

Hesse, K. (1992). *Letters from Rifka.* New York: Henry Holt.

Hesse, K. (1996). *The music of dolphins.* New York: Scholastic.

Hesse, K. (1997). *Out of the dust.* New York: Scholastic.

Hesse, K. (2001). *Witness.* New York: Scholastic.

Hickam, H. H. (1999). *October sky.* New York: Dell.

Hill, J. B. (2000). *The legacy of Luna: The story of a tree, a woman, and the struggle to save the redwoods.* San Francisco: HarperSanFrancisco.

Hine, A. (Ed.). *This land is mine: An anthology of American verse.* Philadelphia: Lippincott.

Hinton, S. E. (1967). *The outsiders.* New York: Bantam Doubleday Dell.

Hoffman, P. (1998). *The man who loved only numbers: The story of Paul Erdos and the search for mathematical truth.* New York: Hyperion.

Hoose, P. (2001). *We were there, too: Young people in U. S. history.* New York: Farrar, Straus & Giroux.

Hoose, P. (2001). *We were there, too!: Young people in U. S. history.* New York: Melanie Kroupa Books.

Houston, J. W., & Houston, J. D. (1995). *Farewell to Manzanar: A true story of Japanese American experience during and after the World War II internment.* New York: Bantam Books.

Hunt, I. (1964). *Across five Aprils.* Chicago: Follett.

Jackson, L. B. (1997). *I have lived a thousand years: Growing up in the Holocaust.* New York: Simon & Schuster Books for Young Readers.

Jarrell, R. (1996). *The bat-poet.* New York: HarperCollins.

Johnston, J. (1994). *Adam and Eve and pinch-me.* Boston: Little, Brown.

Johnston, T. (1996). *My Mexico—Mexico Mio.* New York: Putnam.

Jonas, A. (1990). *Aardvarks, disembark!* New York: Greenwillow Books.

Jones, C. F. (1991). *Mistakes that worked: 40 familiar inventions and how they came to be.* New York: Delacorte.

Jones, C. F. (1996). *Accidents may happen: Fifty inventions discovered by mistake.* New York: Delacorte.

Jones, E. D. (1948). *Lincoln and the preachers*. New York: Harper.

Jones, W. B. (2002). *Classics illustrated: A cultural history, with illustrations*. Jefferson, NC: McFarland.

Joyce, J. (1992). *Ulysses*. New York: Modern Library.

Junger, S. (1997). *The perfect storm: A true story of men against the sea*. New York: Norton.

Juster, N. (1961). *The phantom tollbooth*. New York: Scholastic.

King, S. (2000). *On writing: A memoir of the craft*. New York: Pocket Books.

Kingfisher. *The visual factfinder series*. New York: Author.

Kingsolver, B. (1988). *The bean trees*. New York: Harper & Row.

Kingsolver, B. (1995). *High tide in Tucson: Essays from now or never*. New York: HarperCollins.

Kingsolver, B. (1998). *The poisonwood bible*. New York: HarperFlamingo.

Knowles, J. (1960). *A separate peace*. New York: Macmillan.

Kodama, T. (1995). *Shin's tricycle*. New York: Walker.

Kolata, G. B. (1999). *Flu: The story of the great influenza pandemic of 1918 and the search for the virus that caused it*. New York: Farrar, Straus & Giroux.

Konigsburg, E. L. (1993). *T-Backs, t-Shirts, COAT, and suit*. New York: Atheneum.

Konigsburg, E. L. (1996). *The view from Saturday*. New York: Atheneum Books for Young Readers.

Konigsburg, E. L. (2000). *Silent to the bone*. New York: Atheneum Books for Young Readers.

Krakauer, J. (1998). *Into thin air*. New York: Anchor Books.

Krull, K. (1993). *Lives of the musicians: Good times, bad times (and what the neighbors thought)*. San Diego, CA: Harcourt Brace.

Krull, K. (1994). *Lives of the writers: Comedies, tragedies (and what the neighbors thought)*. New York: Harcourt Brace.

Krull, K. (1995). *Lives of the artists: Masterpieces, messes (and what the neighbors thought)*. San Diego, CA: Harcourt Brace.

Krull, K. (1997). *Lives of the athletes: Thrills, spills (and what the neighbors thought)*. San Diego, CA: Harcourt Brace.

Krull, K. (1998). *Lives of the presidents: Fame, shame (and what the neighbors thought)*. San Diego, CA: Harcourt Brace.

Krull, K. (2000). *Lives of extraordinary women: Rulers, rebels (and what the neighbors thought)*. San Diego, CA: Harcourt Brace.

L'Engle, M. (1962). *A wrinkle in time*. New York: Farrar, Straus & Giroux.

L'Engle, M. (1973). *A wind in the door*. New York: Bantam Doubleday Dell.

L'Engle, M. (1980). *A ring of endless light*. New York: Bantam Doubleday Dell.

Landau, S. (2001). *Dictionaries: The art and craft of lexicography*. New York: Cambridge University Press.

Lee, H. (1995). *To kill a mockingbird*. New York: HarperCollins.

Lemieux, M. (1999). *Stormy night*. Toronto, Canada: Kids Can Press.

Levine, E. (2000). *Darkness over Denmark: The Danish Resistance and the rescue of the Jews*. New York: Scholastic.

Lincoln, A., & McCurdy M. (1997). *The Gettysburg Address*. Boston: Houghton Mifflin.

Lionni, L. (1968). *The alphabet tree*. New York: Pantheon.

Little, J. (1986). After English class. In J. Little (Ed.), *Hey, world, here I am!* (p. 28). New York: Harper & Row.

Locker, T. (1997). *Water dance*. San Diego, CA: Harcourt Brace.

Loewen, J. W. (1995). *Lies my teacher told me: Everything your American history textbook got wrong*. New York: The New Press.

Loewen, J. W. (2000). *Lies across America: What our historic sites get wrong*. New York: Simon & Schuster.

Lowry, L. (1979). *Anastasia Krupnik*. Boston: Houghton Mifflin.

Lowry, L. (1984). *Anastasia, ask your analyst*. Boston: Houghton Mifflin.

Lowry, L. (1989). *Number the stars*. Boston: Houghton Mifflin.

Lowry, L. (1993). *The giver*. Boston: Houghton Mifflin.

Lutz, W. (1990). *Doublespeak: From revenue enhancement to terminal living: How government, business, advertisers, and others use language to deceive you*. New York: HarperPerennial.

Lutz, W. (1996). *The new doublespeak: Why no one knows what anyone's saying anymore*. New York: HarperPerennial.

Lyons, M. E., & Branch, M. M. (2000). *Dear Ellen Bee: A Civil War scrapbook of two Union spies*. New York: Scholastic.

Macaulay, D. (1973). *Cathedral*. Boston: Houghton Mifflin.

Macaulay, D. (1975). *Pyramid*. Boston: Houghton Mifflin.

Macaulay, D. (1977). *Castle.* Boston: Houghton Mifflin.

Macaulay, D. (1987). *Unbuilding.* Boston: Houghton Mifflin.

Macaulay, D. (1993). *Ship.* Boston: Houghton Mifflin.

Macaulay, D., with Ardley, D. (1998). *The new way things work.* Boston: Houghton Mifflin.

Malan, D. (1994). *The complete guide to Classics Illustrated.* St. Louis, MO: Malan Classical Enterprises.

Maran, R. (1998). *Teach yourself computers and the Internet visually* (2nd ed.). Foster City, CA: IDG Books Worldwide.

Martin, J. B. (1998). *Snowflake Bentley.* Boston: Houghton Mifflin.

Maruki, T. (1980). *Hiroshima no pika.* New York: Lothrop, Lee & Shepard.

Mathis, S. B. (1975). *The hundred penny box.* New York: Viking.

McCloud, S. (1994). *Understanding comics: The invisible art.* New York: HarperPerennial.

McDonald, S. P. (1936). Casey—Twenty years later. In H. Felleman (Ed.), *The best loved poems of the American people* (p. 286). Garden City, NY: Doubleday.

McKissack, P., & McKissack, F. (1994). *Christmas in the big house, Christmas in the quarters.* New York: Scholastic.

McLynn, F. (Ed.). (1993). *Famous letters: Messages and thoughts that shaped our world.* Pleasantville, NY: Reader's Digest Association.

Meltzer, M. (2001). *There comes a time: The struggle for civil rights.* New York: Random House.

Melville, H. (2001). *Moby Dick, or, The whale.* New York: Penguin Books.

Merriam, E., & Smith, L. (1995). *Halloween ABC.* New York: Macmillan.

Miller, M. (1999). *Words that built a nation: A young person's collection of historic American documents.* New York: Scholastic.

Mills, C. (1998). *Standing up to Mr. O.* New York: Scholastic.

Mochizuki, K. (1993). *Baseball saved us.* New York: Lee & Low.

Monk, R. C. (Ed.). (1994). *Taking sides: Clashing views on controversial issues in race and ethnicity.* Guilford, CT: Dushkin.

Morgan, A. H. (1930). *The field book of ponds and streams.* New York: Putnam.

Mori, T., & Anno, M. (1986). *Socrates and the three little pigs.* New York: Philomel Books.

Morimoto, J. (1987). *My Hiroshima.* New York: Viking.

Morpurgo, M. (1990). *Waiting for Anya.* New York: Scholastic.

Morrison, T. (1987). *Beloved.* New York: Knopf.

Murray, K. M. E. (2001). *Caught in the web of words: James A. H. Murray and the Oxford English Dictionary.* New Haven, CT: Yale University Press.

Myers, W. D. (1991). *Now is your time!: The African American struggle for freedom.* New York: HarperCollins.

Myers, W. D. (1999). *Monster.* New York: Scholastic.

Nash, O. (1953). *The moon is shining bright as day.* New York: Lippincott.

Naslund, S. J. (1999). *Ahab's wife, or the star gazer: A novel.* New York: Morrow.

Neuschwander, C., & Geehan, W. (1997). *Sir Cumference and the first round table: A math adventure.* Watertown, MA: Charlesbridge.

Newton, L. H., & Ford, M. M. (Eds.). (1994). *Taking sides: Clashing views on controversial issues in business ethics and society.* Guilford, CT: Dushkin.

Nolan, H. (1997). *Dancing on the edge.* San Diego, CA: Harcourt Brace.

Nye, N. S. (Collector). (1998). *This tree is older than you are: A bilingual gathering of poems and stories from Mexico with paintings by Mexican artists.* New York: Aladdin Paperbacks.

O'Dell, S. (1990). *Island of the blue dolphins.* Boston: Houghton Mifflin.

O'Dell, S. (1997). *Sing down the moon.* New York: Dell.

Oates, S. B. (1984). *To purge this land with blood: A biography of John Brown* (2nd ed.). Amherst: University of Massachusetts Press.

Olds, B. (1995). *Raising holy hell.* New York: Henry Holt.

Paley, V. (1997). *The girl with the brown crayon.* Cambridge, MA: Harvard University Press.

Park, B. (1995). *Mick Harte was here.* New York: Knopf.

Park, R. (2000). *Voodoo science: The road from foolishness to fraud.* New York: Oxford University Press.

Parker, S., & Kelly, J. (1996). *Shocking science: 5,000 years of mishaps and misunderstandings.* Atlanta, GA: Turner.

Parker, S., & West, D. (1993). *Brain surgery for beginners: And other major operations for minors.* New York: Scholastic.

Partridge, E. (2002). *Restless spirit: The life and work of Dorothea Lange.* New York: Scholastic.

Paterson, K. (1977). *Bridge to Terabithia.* New York: Dell.

Paterson, K. (1978). *The great Gilly Hopkins.* New York: HarperCollins.

Paterson, K. (1980). *Jacob have I loved.* New York: Crowell.

Paterson, K. (1994). *Flip-flop girl.* New York: Dutton.

Paulsell, W. O. (1990). *Tough minds, tender hearts: Six prophets of social justice.* New York: Paulist Press.

Paulsen, G. (1987). *Hatchet.* New York: Bradbury Press.

Paulsen, G. (1993). *Nightjohn.* New York: Delacorte.

Paulsen, G. (1998). *Soldier's heart.* New York: Delacorte.

Paulsen, G. (2000). *The beet fields: Memories of a sixteenth summer.* New York: Delacorte.

Paulsen, G. (2001). *Guts: The true stories behind Hatchet and the Brian books.* Thorndike, ME: Thorndike Press.

Peacock, L., & Krudop, W. (1998). *Crossing the Delaware: A history in many voices.* New York: Atheneum Books for Young Readers.

Pederson, T., & Moss, F. (1998). *Make your own web page!: A guide for kids.* New York: Price Stern Sloan.

Penguin Books. *The see through history series.* New York: Author.

Pennac, D. (1994). *Better than life.* Toronto, Canada: Coach House Press.

Perl, L., & Lazan, M. B. (1996). *Four perfect pebbles: A Holocaust story.* New York: Scholastic.

Philbrick, R. (1993). *Freak the mighty.* New York: Blue Sky Press.

Polacco, P. (1994). *Pink and say.* New York: Philomel Books.

Potter, R. R. (1995). *John Brown: Militant abolitionist.* Austin, TX: Steck-Vaughn.

Preston, R. (1994). *The hot zone.* New York: Random House.

Provenson, A. (1997). *The buck stops here: The presidents of the United States.* New York: Harper & Row.

Rapaport, R. (2000). *See how she runs: Marion Jones and the making of a champion.* Chapel Hill, NC: Algonquin Books.

Raskin, J. B. (2000). *We the students: Supreme Court cases for and about students.* Washington, DC: CQ Press.

READ Magazine. (1995). *Dear author: Students write about the books that changed their lives.* Berkeley, CA: Conari Press.

Rees, D. (1997). *Lightning time.* New York: DK Publishing.

Rinaldi, A. (1998). *Mine eyes have seen.* New York: Scholastic.

Rodriguez, R. (1983). *Hunger of memory: The education of Richard Rodriguez: An autobiography.* New York: Bantam Books.

Roth, A. (1974). *The iceberg hermit.* New York: Scholastic.

Sachar, L. (1998). *Holes.* New York: Farrar, Straus & Giroux.

Salinger, J. D. (1951). *Catcher in the rye.* Boston: Little, Brown.

Sanborn, F. B. (1969). *The life and letters of John Brown: Liberator of Kansas, and martyr of Virginia.* New York: Negro University Press.

Santiago, E. (1994). *When I was Puerto Rican.* New York: Vintage Books.

Sasson, J. (2001). *Princess: A true story of life behind the veil in Saudi Arabia.* Van Nuys, CA: Windsor-Brooke Books.

Schmandt-Besserat, D., & Hays, M. (2000). *The history of counting.* New York: Morrow Junior.

Scholastic. *Dear America Series.* New York: Author.

Scholastic. *My name is America series.* New York: Author.

Scholastic. *The National Audubon Society's first field guide series.* New York: Author.

Scholastic. *Royal diaries series.* New York: Author.

Scholastic. (1999). *The Usborne illustrated encyclopedia: Science and technology.* New York: Author.

Schultz, C. (1980). *Charlie Brown, Snoopy and Me, and all the other Peanuts characters.* Garden City, NY: Doubleday.

Schwartz, D. M. (1985). *How much is a million?* New York: Lathrop, Lee & Shepard.

Schwartz, D. M. (1998). *G is for googol: A math alphabet book.* New York: Scholastic.

Schwartz, D. M., & Doner, K. (2001). *Q Is for quark: A science alphabet book.* Berkeley, CA: Tricycle Press.

Scieszka, J., & Smith, L. (1995). *Math curse.* New York: Viking.

Sendak, M. (1963). *Where the wild things are.* New York: Harper & Row.

Sendak, M. (1993). *We are all in the dumps with Jack and Guy.* New York: HarperCollins.

Seuss, Dr. (1971). *The lorax.* New York: Random House.

Seuss, Dr. (1984). *The butter battle book.* New York: Random House.

Shakespeare, W. (2001). *Romeo and Juliet.* New York: Oxford University Press.

Siebert, D., & Minor, W. (1988). *Mojave.* New York: Crowell.

Siebert, D., & Minor, W. (1989). *Heartland.* New York: Crowell.

Siebert, D., & Minor, W. (1991). *Sierra.* New York: HarperCollins.

Simon, S. (1997). *The brain: Our nervous system.* New York: Morrow Junior Books.

Simon, S. (1997). *The heart: Our circulatory system.* New York: Morrow Junior Books.

Simon, S. (1998). *Muscles: Our muscular system.* New York: Morrow Junior Books.

Simon, S. (1998). *Bones: Our skeletal system.* New York: Morrow Junior Books.

Sis, P. (1996). *Starry messenger: A book depicting the life of a famous scientist, mathematician, astronomer, philosopher, physicist, Galileo Galilei.* New York: Farrar, Straus & Giroux.

Skinner, B. F. (1990). *Walden two.* New York: Macmillan.

Slife, B. (Ed.). (1996). *Taking sides: Clashing views on psychological issues.* Guilford, CT: Dushkin.

Sophocles. (1989). *Antigone.* Translated by R. E. Braun. New York: Oxford University Press.

Soto, G. (1995). *Canto Familiar.* San Diego, CA: Harcourt Brace.

Speare, E. (1958). *The witch of Blackbird Pond.* New York: Dell.

Spears, R. A. (1998). *NTC's American English Learners Dictionary: The essential vocabulary of American language and culture.* Lincolnwood, IL: NTC Publishing Group.

Spier, P. (1987). *We the people: The constitution of the United States.* Garden City, NY: Doubleday.

Spinelli, J. (1990). *Maniac Magee.* Boston: Little, Brown.

St. George, J. (1992). *Dear Dr. Bell . . . Your friend, Helen Keller.* New York: Putnam.

Standing Bear, L. (1983). *My people, the Sioux.* Boston: Houghton Mifflin.

Stanley, D. (1996). *Leonardo da Vinci.* New York: Morrow Junior Books.

Stanley, J. (1994). *I am an American: A true story of Japanese internment.* New York: Scholastic.

Stein, R. C. (1999). *John Brown's raid on Harpers Ferry in American history.* Berkeley Heights, NJ: Enslow.

Stewart, I. (2001). *Flatterland: Like flatland only moreso.* Cambridge, MA: Perseus.

Stille, D. R. (1997). *Extraordinary women of medicine.* New York: Children's Press.

Stolley, R. B. (Ed.). (2000). *LIFE: Our century in pictures for young people.* Boston: Little, Brown.

Streissguth, T. (1999). *John Brown.* Minneapolis, MN: CarolRhodaBooks.

Swinburne, S. R. (1999). *Once a wolf: How wildlife biologists fought to bring back the gray wolf.* Boston: Houghton Mifflin.

Tamplin, R. (Ed.). (1995). *Famous love letters: Messages of intimacy and passion.* Pleasantville, NY: Reader's Digest Association.

Tan, A. (1989). *The joy luck club.* New York: Putnam.

Tashjian, J. (2001). *Multiple choice.* New York: Scholastic Signature.

Taylor, M. (1976). *Roll of thunder, hear my cry.* New York: Dial Books.

Taylor, T. (1991). *The cay.* New York: Avon Books.

Ten Boom, C., with Sherrill, J., & Sherrill, E. (1971). *The hiding place.* Washington Depot, CT: Chosen Books.

Terkel, S. (1999). *Voices of our time: Five decades of Studs Terkel interviews.* St. Paul, MN: Highbridge Company (Sound Recording).

Thayer, E. L. (2000). *Casey at the bat.* Illus. C. Bing. New York: Scholastic.

Thomas, R. (1996). *Rats saw God.* New York: Simon & Schuster.

Thoreau, H. D. (1992). *Walden, or life in the woods.* New York: Knopf.

Thoreau, H. D. (1969). *Civil disobedience.* Boston: D. R. Godine.

Tolkien, J. R. R. (1987). *The hobbit, or, there and back again.* London: Unwin Hyman.

Tompkins, J. (1996). *A life in school: What the teacher learned.* Reading, MA: Addison-Wesley.

Tsuchiya, Y. (1988). *Faithful elephants.* Boston: Houghton Mifflin.

Twayne's United States author series: Young adult authors. Boston: Twayne Publishers.

Van Allsburg, C. (1991). *The wretched stone.* Boston: Houghton Mifflin.

Vincent, G. (2000). *A day, a dog.* Asheville, NC: Front Street.

Vinz, R. (1996). *Composing a teaching life.* Portsmouth, NH: Boynton/Cook.

Wagoner, J. J., & Cutliff, L. D. (1985). *Mammoth cave.* Arlington, VA: Interpretive Publications.

Ward, G. C. (1999). *Not for ourselves alone: The story of Elizabeth Cady Stanton and Susan B. Anthony: An illustrated history.* New York: Knopf.

Watson, J. (1980). The Double Helix: A personal account of the discovery of the structure of DNA. In G. S. Stent (Ed.), *Norton critical edition: Text, commentary, reviews, original papers.* New York: Norton.

White, E. B. (1945). *Stuart Little.* New York: Harper & Row.

White, E. B. (1980). *Charlotte's web.* New York: HarperTrophy.

White, T. H. (1958). *The once and future king.* New York: Putnam.

Whitman, W. (1992). *Leaves of grass, the deathbed edition.* New York: Quality Paperback Book Club.

Wiesner, D. (1991). *Tuesday.* New York: Clarion Books.

Wiesel, E. (2000). *Night, and related readings.* New York: Glencoe/McGraw-Hill.

Williams, W. F. (2000). *The encyclopedia of pseudoscience: From alien abductions to zone therapy.* Chicago: Fitzroy Dearborn.

Wilson, E. O. (1998). *Consilience: The unity of knowledge.* New York: Knopf.

Wilson, J. (1936). Casey's revenge. In H. Felleman (Ed.), *The best loved poems of the American people.* Garden City, NY: Doubleday.

Winchester, S. (1998). *The professor and the madman: A tale of murder, insanity, and the making of the Oxford English Dictionary.* New York: HarperCollins.

Winter, J. (1988). *Follow the drinking gourd.* New York: Trumpet Club.

Wolf, W. J. (1959). *The almost chosen people: A study of the religion of Abraham Lincoln.* Garden City, NY: Doubleday.

Wolff, V. E. (1998). *Bat 6.* New York: Scholastic.

Wolff, V. E. (2000). *The Mozart season.* New York: Scholastic Signature.

Worsley, D., & Meyer, B. (1989). *The art of science writing.* New York: Teachers and Writers Collaborative.

Writers and Readers Publishers. *Beginners Documentary Comic Books* (series). New York: Author.

Wurman, R. S. (1989). *Information anxiety.* Garden City, NY: Doubleday.

Yolen, J. (1990). *The devil's arithmetic.* New York: Puffin Books.

Youngson, R. M. (1998). *Scientific blunders: A brief history of how wrong scientists can sometimes be.* New York: Carroll & Graf.

Other Media

Burns, K. (1999). *Not for ourselves alone: The story of Elizabeth Cady Stanton and Susan B. Anthony.* PBS Home Video.

Mulan. (1998). Burbank, CA: Walt Disney Home Video.

My bodyguard. (1980). Beverly Hills, CA: Twentieth Century Fox Home Entertainment/CBS Fox Video.

Outbreak. (1995). Burbank, CA: Warner Home Video.

PBS video catalog. 1320 Braddock Place, Alexandria, VA 22314-1698

Roots. (1977). New York: ABC.

Ruby Bridges. (1998). Buena Vista Home Entertainment.

Snow falling on cedars. Universal City, CA: Universal.

Schindler's list. (1993). Universal Pictures. Universal City, CA: MCA Universal Home Video.

Shakespeare in love. (1999). Miramax Films/Universal Pictures/The Bedford Falls Company. Burbank, CA.

Death of a star. (1987). Boston: WGBH Educational Foundation.

Sister Wendy series. (1997). *The story of painting.* Beverly Hills, CA. CBS/Fox Video; BBC video.

Viola, K., & Ellison, H. (performer). (1989). *The masters of comic book art.* Santa Monica, CA: Rhino Home Video.

Author Index

Subject Index